THE GREAT
CASTLES
OF EUROPE

vmb
PUBLISHERS

Contents

1 The coat of arms of Mary Stuart at Falkland Palace, one of the royal palaces of the Scottish Stuart dynasty.

2-3 Chaumont Castle, the feudal fortress of the Counts of Blois until the 15th century, was later rebuilt with round watchtowers and ornamented with conical roofs and Renaissance influences.

4-5 A marble staircase in the fairy tale castle of Neuschwanstein leads to the gilt apse of the Throne Room, which contains the painting Christ in His Glory and representations of six canonized kings and the Twelve Apostles.

7 The walls of Eilean Donan Castle housed one of the great Scottish heroes, Robert the Bruce. Pursued by the English, the future King of Scotland was given refuge by John MacKenzie, the Lord of Kintail. Once crowned king, as a sign of his gratitude, Robert the Bruce sent a lieutenant to the castle, transforming it into one of the most important royal garrisons.

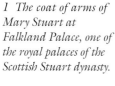

vmb
VMB Publishers®
An imprint of White Star s.p.a., Italy

THE BEST OF CASTLES
© 2007 White Star s.p.a.
Via Candido Sassone, 22/24
13100 Vercelli, Italy
www.whitestar.it

ISBN 978-88-540-0805-2

Reprints:
1 2 3 4 5 6   11 10 09 08 07

Printed in China

Taken from:

CASTLES OF SCOTLAND -
Places and History
© 2001 White Star s.p.a.
ISBN 10: 88-8095-692-2
ISBN 13: 978-88-8095-692-1

CASTLES OF BAVARIA -
Places and History
© 1998 White Star s.p.a.
ISBN 10: 88-8095-467-9
ISBN 13: 978-88-8095-467-5

CASTLES OF THE LOIRE -
Places and History
© 1996 White Star s.p.a.
ISBN 10: 88-8095-878-X
ISBN 13: 978-88-8095-878-9

Preface

by Enrico Lavagno

One evening, at the end of the 15th century, a servant entered a room of Glamis Castle, in Scotland. It was Saturday and five minutes before midnight. The man begged the Lord of Glamis and his guest the Earl of Crawford, for the love of God, to interrupt the card game in progress: it was sacrilegious to play on Sunday. The Earl raised an eyebrow slightly and yelled that the game was not over and that, indeed, if the devil agreed he would continue playing with the devil himself until Judgment Day. The guests laughed, but it would be for the last time, because that game left them chained to the table forever, damned and invisible.

This is only a legend, but one that explains the fascination that castles hold for us. In that spirit, this book is dedicated to famous castles such as Glamis, which are perhaps the most characteristic creations in the history of post-Classical West, offering a guide in images and words of the most notable examples to be found in Europe in this field.

The problem is the variety, so rich and diverse because Europe, as the soul of the Old World, is the place where castles took their shape and name between the 5th and 6th centuries, in the fading light of the sunset of both the Ancient World and the Roman Empire. For this reason the pages that follow limit themselves to the most important centers, to historical regions that were, and in certain respects still are, transmitters of unmistakable messages of dominion and supremacy that the castles spread to neighboring lands.

Scotland, the Loire Valley, Bavaria: in these places, in different times and ways, the most important chapters in the history of the West were written, this same history that spurred the emergence of some of the most famous castles in the world, finding their natural and perfect counterparts there. And just as much, the resplendent walls of Chenonceaux, Amboise and Neuschwanstein, no less than the gloomy ones of Glamis and Holyrood, are not only part of great history and events of continental significance, but are also part of the chronicle of daily life, with the biography of the characters and with the psychology of the individuals. Within the walls of the castle are found not only memories of wars that were planned there, peace treaties signed there, sieges suffered, but also the lives of lords and ladies, of troubadours, of alchemists and artists, of servants, of garrisons in the guardrooms and of farmers who supplied the castles and who took refuge in them in times of danger.

The stones of *castrum* architecture have the characteristic of reflecting different visions of the world, besides different personal and collective lives. Indeed, there is no one model of a castle, but many, each one adapted to its own natural and human panorama. That is why this "walk through the castles" offers flashes of immediate understanding of complex and even dull matters: each nation that built castles has transposed its own character on them. Take Bavaria, for example. The singular absence of any Renaissance characteristics in Bavarian castles has a precise explanation.

9 Neuschwanstein Castle was never completed: the entire second floor, which is not open to the public, consists of empty rooms and bare brick walls.

*10-11 Cheverny
Castle, made of
Bourré stone with
slate roofs, is an
architectural
ensemble with a
classical style that
marks a development
in the evolution of
the Loire châteaux.*

*10 top The large
drawing room, in
Louis XIII style,
contains a wealth of
furnishings, from the
large red carpet at the
foot of the fireplace to
the furniture and
decorations in blue
and pure gold.*

12-13 At the center of the southern façade of the entrance portico is set the white marble coat of arms of Prince Albert, while at the foot of the western side is the foundation stone laid by Queen Victoria on the 28th of September, 1853.

14-15 The Bed Chamber in the Rich Rooms of the Munich Residenz was used as a direct model for the Bed Chamber at Linderhof, which is shown in the picture. Despite their similarities, in particular the bed alcove with its magnificent gold embroidery, there are significant differences, especially in the frescoed ceiling of Linderhof, which does not appear in Cuvilliés' original model.

In terms of economics and human life, the Thirty Years' War cost the nation so dearly that it wiped out the workforce and the circulation of funds necessary to build and develop the kingdom. Conversely, in France, the kings were able to afford and promote national development. In Bavaria, next to large Baroque castles we find Romanesque and Gothic castles among the biggest on the Continent, places in which the knights of long ago still felt at home, reflecting elements of the population and economy entirely devoted to the destructive and often devastating military arts of the Middle Ages.

Scotland, for its part, contributed more than the rest of Europe to creating the special mythology of castles, having some that have maintained their original appearance of sentinels at the edge of the world, rising stone upon stone, stark and forbidding. The idea of Scotland seems inseparable from that of the castle, which in that land has ancient roots, dating back to the Late Neolithic period and the Bronze Age. And yet, even in a land that in many areas is lightly populated and often of poor soil, abundance is seen in the mixture of ideas from very different populations, from the peaceful pre-Celts to the ingenious Celts, from the Roman invaders to the terrible Saxons and Vikings, up to the Normans, who one after other transferred to this land their own conceptions of defense and of human and courtly affairs. One result was the building of brochs, isolated cylindrical towers dating from before the time of Christ; another is the compact buildings that belonged to the hereditary aristocracy of the medieval Highlands, whose primary defensive function is leavened with the beauty of legend and landscape. Many of these earlier structures are not far from lavish Victorian castles, which are more often oversized country residences than defensive facilities.

In contrast to the Bavarian and Scottish situations, the Loire Valley reflects the economic miracle of post-Roman France, which made the country the most stable European power up to modern times. Hence the dark Medieval fortresses that were quickly transformed into the famous castles of the kings of France. They were fabled even in their own time, luminous jewels of refinement in which the absolute monarchs amused themselves by keeping the illustrious minds of their times in gilded prisons amid the sites of sumptuous courts and memorable feasts.

Turning pages of stone to read history has the advantage of immersing the visitor in an odd place in time that is neither legend nor history, but both, and that lives in the creaking of ceiling beams, in the wind on the walls, in the atmosphere of secrets. From one stone to another, from one page to the next, this book lowers drawbridges across time, telling stories of departed men and of events long past. Without this ephemeral transit between fortress and castle we would lose a part of ourselves and forgo the delights of imagination rekindled.

Castles of Scotland

SECTION ONE

16-17 Drummond
Castle, with its
famous garden, is
located in Central
Scotland. It stands on
a rise and the terraces
overlook the

marvellous and
painstakingly
groomed lawns laid in
the form of the cross of
St Andrew. The
sundial in the center
dates from 1630.

18 top Eilean Donan Castle, one of the most spectacular in Northern Scotland, takes its name from the island on which it stands. Part of the castle was built in 1220 by Alexander II as a defensive fortress against the Vikings. Later, Alexander III presented it to Colin Fitzgerald, the son of the Irish Earl of Desmond, the ancestor of the McKenzies.

18-19 *The rock of Dunnottar Castle, overlooking the North Sea, was inhabited from ancient times. Legend has it that St. Ninian founded a Christian settlement here in the 5th century. In 1276*

Bishop Wishart of St. Andrews consecrated a stone building that was destroyed 20 years later. The ruins of the fortress extend over a vast area. The best preserved sections are the gatehouse and the prison.

19 top *Castle Stalker on the West Coast between Oban and Fort William is an austere tower house built in the middle of the 16th century and the home of the Stewarts of Appin. Surrounded by wild landscapes of immense appeal, the castle protected the banks of Loch Linnhe from the attacks of enemy clans.*

19 bottom *Set on the small island of Mousa off South Mainland, the largest of the Shetland Islands, Mousa Broch is perhaps the best preserved of the over two hundred defensive structures dating from the beginning of the Iron Age present in Scotland. When the brochs were no longer needed for defence they were used as the basis for settlements and the agricultural exploitation of the land.*

From the establishment of the kingdom of the Scots under King Kenneth MacAlpine in 843 to the Union with the English Crown in 1707, all of the Scottish castles played a principally defensive role. High, turretted and surrounded by walls and bastions they were apparently impregnable and as well as protecting the local lord, served as his administrative center and the residence of his family, servants and soldiers. The fortified tower, or tower house, was the most common form and was found in both the remote Highlands and the fertile valleys of the Borders, at the confine with England. Composed of three storys linked by spiral staircases in stone or wood, the last of which was overhanging, the tower house was a feature of over 1000 years of Scottish history, from the defensive towers of the Picts and the Scots to the noble palaces of the Victorian era. The form evolved over the centuries with the addition of new elements, but the most fascinating examples are those that have managed to retain the characteristic tower motif. Many have survived such as Threave Castle in Dumfries and Galloway, one of the oldest, and the castles of Craigmillar and Crichton, which were originally two tower houses successively extended. The earliest Scottish fortifications date back to the Iron Age. Between 800 BC and 400 AD there were numerous hill forts, earthworks or stone walls constructed to defend the villages from the neighboring tribes or the incursions of the Romans (AD 71-84). One of the most famous hill forts is located at Dunnadd in Argyll, the ancient capital of the kingdom of Dalriada. Another form of defensive structure were the brochs, tall towers with double walls in stone, cylindrical in form and tapering slightly towards the top. In spite of the Scandinavian origin of their name, the brochs were built long before the arrival of the Norwegians and probably co-existed with the hill forts. They were over thirty-three feet high and were inhabited by the ruling family, but in times of danger they could accommodate up to two hundred persons. Among the best conserved brochs is that of Mousa in the Shetland Islands.

21 top left The isolated ruins of Crichton Castle stand on the bank of the River Tyne, at the foot of Moorfoot Hills in the Lothian region close to Edinburgh. Built in the 14th century and extended during the following two centuries, the castle was the home of Sir William Crichton, the Scottish Chancellor during the reign of James II.

21 bottom right The magnificent gardens of Edzell Castle were created in 1604 by Sir David Lindsay. The Pleasance is a formal garden surrounded by walls in sculpted stone, pots of flowers and niches for birds. The ruined tower house dates from the 15th century. In 1562 Mary Stuart held a council here during the royal army's campaign against the Gordons.

20 top left Caerlaverock Castle has an unusual triangular plan and it conceals an internal façade with symmetrical Renaissance decoration. The principal elements are the semi-circular or triangular windows and the pediment of the doorway sculpted with mythological or heraldic motifs.

20 top right In the 13th century at St. Andrews, on the North coast of the Fife peninsula, a fortified bishop's palace was constructed in which James I and James III were educated. St. Andrews Castle was at the center of the conflict during the religious wars and was almost completely demolished to provide material for the construction of the port's sea-wall.

20-21 and 21 top right The aerial view shows Crathes Castle and its beautiful gardens. Yew hedges separate the Color Garden in which the dominant colors are yellow, red and violet, from the more formal Fountain Garden, based on blue, and the Rose Garden. The most recent creation is the Golden Garden dedicated to the memory of Lady Burnett who was responsible, together with her husband Sir James, for this green oasis.

In 1066 the marriage between Malcom III Canmore and Margaret, who was raised at court in London, brought Norman customs and traditions to the wild Scotland. The first feudal castles date from this period. The earliest examples took the form of mounds dominated by a wooden tower and surrounded by a moat, at the foot of which stood wooden houses within a courtyard surrounded by a palisade. There are no surviving examples of this "motte-and-bailey" castle, but they are clearly depicted in the Bayeux Tapestry. At Hawick in the Borders, however, the earth mound on which the wooden tower once stood can still be seen. Over the course of the following two centuries stone castles almost completely replaced the old wooden structures. In a number of the castles constructed after the mid-fourteenth century there was an evident desire to improve the defensive capabilities that previously relied exclusively on the buildings' massive structure. In the castle of St. Andrews in Fife, for example, the tower is no longer set in the middle of the bailey and the principal entrance to the castle is incorporated within it. At the end of the fifteenth century decorative and ornamental elements began to increase in importance, especially in the royal residences. The richness of these constructions drew heavily on French Renaissance motifs, probably due to the alliances and close ties of kinship between the Stuarts and the French royal family in that period.

Falkland Palace, James V's favorite residence, has nothing in common with the original tower house, embellished as it is with a wealth of towers, turrets, medallions and pilasters. The sculptural decoration of the North Wall of Crichton Castle in the Borders region, completed in 1585, was moving in the same direction, as was Caerlaverock Castle in Dumfries, in which the massive, austere exterior contrasts with the elegance of the internal courtyard.

22 top left Aerial view of Culzean Castle on the West Coast, a few miles from the city of Ayr. Standing on the cliff-top, this is one of the most impressive stately homes in the whole of Scotland, the fruit of the creative genius of Robert Adam who designed it in the 18th century to replace the existing 200-year-old castle.

22 top right Austere and turreted, the Gothic Revival Abbotsford House, the home built by Sir Walter Scott, stands on the River Tweed, a short distance from Melrose. The writer responsible for the

invention of Romantic Scotland and the author of novels set in the Highlands such as Rob Roy, Ivanhoe and The Pirate was so attached to these lands that he built his ideal house here.

22-23 An aerial view of Balloch Castle, the ancient home of the Lennox family. Set in a great park on the shores of Loch Lomond in Western Scotland, the castle was built in 1808 in the Gothic Revival style. Fine

views of the lake and the gardens with the attractive contrast between the Mediterranean plantings and the wild nature of the mountains can be enjoyed from the house.

23 top The library in Mellerstain House is one of Robert Adam's masterpieces. The main feature is the stuccoed ceiling that still retains the delicate pastel colors of pale green, dark green and pink specified by the architect in 1773. A round painting of Minerva by Zucchi decorates the circular medallion. Robert Adam was also responsible for the white and green fireplace and the mirror cupboards between the windows.

23 bottom The sitting room of Dalmeny House, the Gothic Revival house overlooking the Firth of Forth on the outskirts of Edinburgh, is furnished with French furniture that was once part of the collection of the Rothschilds of Mentmore and came to Dalmeny through the marriage of the 5th Earl Archibald, Prime Minister between 1894 and 1895, and Hannah, the daughter of Baron Meyer de Rothschild of Mentmore.

This greater attention to the external appearance of the buildings led to the development of the ornamental potential of the defensive elements. This tendency can be seen in the castles built in the Northeast of Scotland from the late sixteenth century. Castles such as those of Crathes and Fyvie are at the same time both fortresses and elaborate works of art. With the Act of Union of 1707 the Scottish castles' defensive function was made largely redundant. Although for 40 years, up to the massacre of Culloden, the Jacobites maintained their opposition to the Crown, Scotland enjoyed a period of peace. The families of the old nobility, made even richer by the expropriation of terrain from the small landowners, began to build great palaces. They were then flanked by the families of the great merchants and those of the early industrialists who commissioned leading architects to build their homes. The years between the eighteenth and the nineteenth centuries saw the establishment of a successful architectural dynasty, the Adams, sensitive to neo-classical and Italian influences. Among the Adam family's most important creations were the beautiful Charlotte Square in Edinburgh, Hopetoun, Mellerstain and Culzean Castle, characterized by extremely simple, clean external lines contrasting with the opulence of the interiors. In the second half of the last century, thanks to the novels of Sir Walter Scott, Romanticism led to a revival of interest in the Medieval world and the

Scottish traditions. Architecture was not immune to this new trend and the period saw the construction of houses decorated with towers, ogives and dark inlaid wood. Sir Walter Scott's own residence, Abbotsford, and Dalmeny House are good examples, while Balmoral Castle, the royal family's summer residence, remains the best example of the neo-baronial style, the leading exponents of which were the architects David Bryce and Gillespie Graham.

Mellerstain House

Scone Palace

Drum Castle

26-27
Castle Tioram,
the powerful castle
belonging to the
MacDonalds of
Clanranald was
built early in the
14th century on a
remote island in
Loch Moidart.
Accessible by land
only at low tide, it
was frequently
attacked by the rival
Campbell clan and
was burned down
in 1715.

28-29 The impressive
library of Dunrobin
Castle built by Sir
Robert Lorimer,
contains over ten
thousand volumes,
with numerous rare
and precious editions.
Most of the works are
concerned with the
development of the
Highlands and
Scottish law.
There is also a fine
Chippendale desk and
a 19th-century globe.
A portrait of the
Duchess Eileen Butler
who married the
Duke of Sutherland
in 1912 hangs on the
wall. There is a
precious oriental
carpet on the floor.

Thirlestane Castle

Caerlaverock Castle

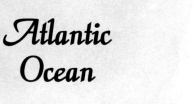

Castle Fraser

Atlantic Ocean

Orkney Islands

Outer Hebrides

North Sea

Thurso

Dunrobin Castle

Oykel

Dunvegan Castle

The Highlands

Brodie Castle

Cawdor Castle

Fyvie Castle

Inverness

Spey

Deveron

Haddo House

Isle of Skye

Loch Ness

Don

Castle Fraser

Drum Castle

Caledonian Canal

Craigievar Castle

Grampian Mountains

Balmoral

Crathes Castle

Aberdeen

Fort William

Braemar

Dunnottar Castle

Loch Linnhe

Castle Stalker

Blair Castle

Tay

Glamis Castle

Mull

Scone Palace

Dundee

Oban

Perth

St. Andrews

Inveraray Castle

Drummond Castle

Falkland Palace

Loch Lomond

Hopetoun House

Atlantic Ocean

Stirling Castle

Linlithgow Palace

Edinburgh

Glasgow

Edinburgh Castle
Holyrood

Thirlestane Castle

Mellerstain House

Brodick Castle

Tweed

Traquair House

Floors Castle

Ayr

Abbotsford House

Teviot

Arran

Culzean Castle

Drumlanrig Castle

Esk

Dee

Dumfries

Northern Ireland

North Channel

Caerlaverock Castle

England

THE CASTLES OF
MARY QUEEN OF SCOTS

*31 top left
After 1633, the year
of Charles I's visit,
no member of the
reigning family
ever returned to
Linlithgow Palace
with the exception of
Bonnie Prince Charlie
who spent a single
night here in 1745.*

*The following year,
during the march
northwards to subdue
definitively the
residual forces of the
Jacobite rebellion,
the troops of the Duke
of Cumberland set
fire to the castle,
reducing it to its
present state.*

*31 top right Detail
of the entrance to the
palace decorated with
four coats of arms,
copies of the originals
that represented the
four knightly orders,
from right to left, The
Garter, The Thistle,
The Golden Fleece
and St. Michael.*

*30 top A portrait of
Mary Stuart, Queen of
Scotland and pretender
to the throne of
Elizabeth I. The sword,
the scepter and the jewels
worn by the Queen are
today conserved in
Edinburgh Castle.*

*30 bottom Mary Stuart
became Queen just after
her birth, because of the
death of her father,
James V. Before Mary
was three years old, the
English king Henry VIII
sent an army to demand
the fulfilment of the
marriage proposal
between his son Edward
and Mary. The episode
is known in history as
the "rough wooing."*

*30-31 Linlithgow
Palace dominates the
town and the small lake.
Although it is now
roofless, this impressive
building is still in a fair
state of preservation.
Of great beauty, its
central courtyard is
a concentration of
centuries of Scottish
history with the
extensions and additions
built at the behest of
diverse monarchs of the
Stuart dynasty. The
Stuarts were
accustomed to spending
long periods in this
palace.*

Mary Queen of Scots, the heir to
the powerful Stuart dynasty
that had long fought against
England and had brought sophisticated architecture and
tastes to the Scottish court, came to
the throne during the tragic years of
the religious struggles between
Catholics and Protestants. The daughter of James V and the French Princess,
Mary of Guise, Mary Stuart had a turbulent life of love and betrayal, intrigue
and assassinations that have made her a
legendary figure. She was born on the
8th of December, 1542, at Linlithgow
Palace, one of the Stuarts' favorite residences on the shores of the Firth of
Forth, mid-way between Edinburgh
and Stirling. With its powerful red
towers reflecting in the water, the castle was built in 1425 by James I on his
return to Scotland after eighteen years
of imprisonment in England. His successors introduced modifications and
refurbishments that transformed the castle into a palace rivalling those of
France, as was confirmed by Queen
Mary of Guise. The diverse styles of
the façades facing the interior courtyard
recount the history of the palace: to the
east is the Great Hall and the original
entrance of James I, to the north the
new wing built by James IV, to the west
the state apartments added by James
III and to the south the English-style
façade built by the sovereign and the
queen Margaret Tudor.
Mary's father, James V, died of a heart
attack just six days after her birth.

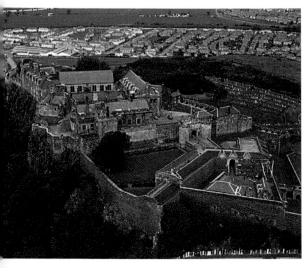

32 center left and right At the center of the struggle for independence, Stirling Castle was retaken by the Scots in 1297 thanks to William Wallace (photo on the right) following the Battle of Stirling Bridge, then a

wooden structure linking the north and south of Scotland. Having been regained by the English and retained for ten years, in 1324 it was again conquered by Robert the Bruce at the Battle of Bannockburn.

32 bottom left Stirling Castle was built in its present form between the end of the 14th and the 16th centuries. James IV ordered the building of the Great Hall and the gatehouse. James V

on the other hand was responsible for the spectacular palace, built with the help of French masons. James VI, at whose behest the Royal Chapel was built, was the last Scottish sovereign to reside in the castle.

32 top left and 33 Following the moat and the first gateway to Stirling Castle, the road climbs to the internal gateway. A ramp on the left leads to the Queen Anne Gardens while a third entrance opens onto Lower Square overlooked by the royal palace

with its decorated façade, a masterpiece in the Renaissance style. Together with the palaces of Falkland and Linlithgow, this is one of the few examples of how the ideas of the European Renaissance found expression in Scotland.

The coronation of the infant Mary took place in the austere castle at Stirling where she lived until she departed for France as the fiancée of the Dauphin at just five years of age.

Set in a strategic position on the principal road linking the north and south of Scotland, Stirling was already fortified in prehistoric times. Through here passed all the Scottish kings, including Alexander I and William the Lion who also died here. Significant battles in Scottish history were fought around the castle, including that of Stirling Bridge in 1297 when the Scots, led by William Wallace, defeated the English army. Attacked on a number of occasions by the English during the wars of independence, Stirling was the last Scottish fortress to surrender in 1304. With the Stuart dynasty the castle became a royal palace, as can still be seen today. James II reinforced the defences, lending the castle its severe, invincible air, but he also constructed the Great Hall to house the Scottish Parliament and State ceremonies. James IV began work on the Renaissance-style royal palace eventually completed by his son James V who was crowned in the chapel of Stirling Castle, as was later the case with his daughter Mary and his grandson James VI in 1566.

Mary spent her childhood and youth in France in order to escape the wars with England. Educated in the luxury of the French court, in 1558 she married the Dauphin who the following year was crowned as King Francis II of France. At sixteen years of age Mary Stuart was the Queen of France and Scotland, as well as the heir to the throne of Anglican England given that her cousin Elizabeth was childless. However, a widow at eighteen, she left her mother-in-law Catherine De Medici in order to return to her homeland, a Catholic Queen in a now Protestant country.

With the exception of the inhabitants of the Highlands, the doctrines of the Protestant preacher John Knox had opened a breach in the spirit of the Scots. Charismatic and sophisticated, the young sovereign found herself at the center of political intrigues and religious power struggles. The Puritans never forgave her joie de vivre, the luxury with which she surrounded herself and her many love affairs.

34 top A view from above of Holyrood Palace and the ruins of the abbey that, legend has it, was founded in 1128 by David I, the son of Malcom III and Margaret. One day, while out hunting, the king was dismounted and wounded by a stag but was saved by his crucifix. He gave thanks by constructing the abbey. The name Holyrood derives from the words Holy and Rood, a synonym of cross.

34-35 Holyrood
Palace was built as a
lodge for the abbey's
guests and from the
16th century was
developed into a
royal residence.
The lodge was made
more comfortable by
James IV. In 1529 the
northwest tower was
built to house the royal
family. This is now
the oldest surviving
part of the palace
and was the scene of
many tumultuous
scenes in the life of
Mary Stuart: Mary
married Lord
Darnley in the abbey
and Bothwell in
what is today the
Picture Gallery.

35 top left The
oldest part of the
castle, the Historical
Apartments, are
closely tied to the
history of Scotland
and Mary Queen of
Scots. On the first
floor of the tower are
the two rooms in
which the queen
lived and which
were the scene of the
brutal assassination
of Davide Rizzio.
The embroidery
work completed by
Mary during her
long imprisonment
in England is
exhibited in a
display case.

35 bottom left
At the center of the
large square that
extends in front of
the entrance to the
palace stands a
fountain, a 19th-
century copy of the
one built at
Linlithgow on the
occasion of the
marriage of James
V and Mary of
Guise, the parents of
Mary Queen of
Scots. On the
occasion of the
wedding wine
rather than water
flowed from the
spouts.

35 right The statue
of the unicorn
stands out on the
pilasters of the
gateway to Holyrood
House.

Mary established her court at Holyrood Palace in Edinburgh. Built in
the twelfth century as an abbey, it was
transformed into a royal residence by
James IV, determined to make Edinburgh the center of his kingdom. The
royal apartments, decorated in the
Renaissance style and richly furnished,
are still today the residence of Queen
Elizabeth II and Prince Philip during
their visits to the city. Thanks to a pa-

pal disposition Mary Stuart married her
cousin Henry Darnley in 1565. The
ceremony was followed by three days
of dancing and banqueting. The royal
couple's chambers can still be seen in
the palace, including the room in
which the queen met her enemy John
Knox and the one in which she spent
the afternoons playing the harp, writing poetry or listening to her secretary,
and perhaps her lover, Davide Rizzio
from Turin. The liaison between Mary
and the Italian came to a tragic end.
One evening, when the Queen was in
the sixth month of her pregnancy, a
group of armed men sent by Darnley
attacked Rizzio, who vainly tried to defend himself by clinging to the Queen.
He was finished off with stab wounds,
but not before having crossed the royal
bedchamber dripping blood.

Holyrood Palace is also the starting point of the Royal Mile, the road that, lined by towering grey façades, climbs the hill to Edinburgh Castle. Mary took this road in the tumultuous days following the assassination of Rizzio in order to seek refuge behind the powerful walls of the castle. The symbol of Scotland is stern and apparently invincible, even though it was actually conquered on a number of occasions by the English. The oldest part of the complex is St. Margaret's Chapel, a stone building probably constructed at the behest of King David I in memory of his mother around 1130. Little remains of the ancient fortifications as they were incorporated into the extensions of the sixteenth and eighteenth centuries. The Royal Palace, the old Parliament Hall and the National War Memorial to those who fell during the Great War all overlook the interior courtyard, Crown Square. From the 16th century onwards the royal family preferred to live in more comfortable accommodation such as the palaces of Holyrood, Linlithgow and Falkland. The castle thus became the seat of government and a general military headquarter. Mary gave birth to the heir to the throne, the future James VI of Scotland, who became also James I of England after the death of Elizabeth I, in a small room on the 19th of June, 1566. She lowered the baby in a basket from a window so as to remove him from the danger of possible plots, the situation had precipitated. A plot in which Mary herself may have been involved, resulted in her second husband, Lord Darnley, being strangled. His remains were found in a building destroyed by an explosion. Three months later, to widespread disapproval, the Queen married the principal suspect of her husband's murder, James Hepburn, the Earl of Bothwell, who in the meantime had been cleared by the judges.

38 top left
The massive ruins of
Hermitage Castle rise
isolated by a torrent on
the remote moors of
Liddesdale, to the
north of Newcastleton.
Founded in the 13th
century, the castle was
rebuilt 200 years later
in an austere and

turreted style. Its
fame is linked with
the story of the Earl of
Bothwell and Mary
Stuart who, in order
to visit her beloved
wounded in a
skirmish on the
nearby border, did
not hesitate to ride 80
miles on horseback.

The marriage, celebrated in 1567 according to the Protestant rite, was the last straw for the Scottish noblemen, who attacked the couple. The queen managed to gather troops loyal to the crown and faced the rebels at Carberry Hill near Edinburgh. After a day of heated exchanges, Mary surrendered. Isolated and rejected as a sovereign, she was imprisoned in the fourteenth-century castle of Loch Leven, today in ruins, which was built on an island in the middle of the loch. The young queen remained a prisoner for almost a year, during which time she lost the twins she was carrying, but succeeded in escaping by boat, dressed as a peasant woman after having seduced Willie Douglas, the son of the Lord of the castle. An army of six thousand men loyal to the Queen engaged in battle with the anti-Catholic faction that supported the year-old King James VI at Laganside near Glasgow. They were defeated and Mary Stuart fled southwards. She spent her last night in Scotland at Dundrennan Abbey before crossing the Solway Firth and seeking the help of her cousin Elizabeth I of England. Rather than receiving support, she was imprisoned for nearly twenty years in the Tower of London before being executed in 1587.

During the seven years of her reign, Mary Stuart visited most of Scotland, staying in castles that are still associated with her name. One of the most celebrated is Hermitage Castle, a massive stone building standing isolated on the moors bordering England, where Earl Bothwell, not yet her third husband, was wounded in a skirmish. From Jedburgh, to where she had gone to superintend the hearings of the Court of Justice, the sovereign rode to her lover's aid. During the return journey she fell from her horse and lay in a coma for some days in a tower house at Jedburgh. Craigmillar Castle, one of the Queen's favorite residences, stands not far from Edinburgh. The assassination of her second husband was apparently ordered in the massive sixteenth-century central tower surrounded by two curtain walls.

38 bottom left Just
a few miles separate
Edinburgh and
Craigmillar Castles,
the latter being a
brick tower with an
impressive curtain
wall raised in the
15th century, with
additions being made
over the following
centuries. This castle
was one of Mary
Stuart's favorites and
the area around it is
still known as Little
France after the
French servants of
Mary's court. It
would appear that it
was within these walls
that the plot against
Lord Darnley, Mary's
second husband, was
hatched.

38 top right
Borthwick Castle,
near Edinburgh, was
built in 1430 by the
1st Lord Borthwick
and is one of the most
powerful fortified
structures in
Scotland. Mary
Stuart visited the
castle in 1567, shortly
after her marriage
to Bothwell.

38-39 Castle Campbell stands on a rocky crag in the heart of the wooded Ochil Hills. Dating from the 15th century, this tower house was the property of Colin Campbell, the 1st Earl of Argyll and chancellor of Scotland during the early years of the reign of James IV. In 1566 the castle was visited by the reformist preacher John Knox, Mary Stuart's great adversary. The Queen herself visited the castle in 1563. In 1645 it was conquered and burned by the Marquis of Montrose. A building in the French Renaissance style is linked to the castle.

39 top Loch Leven Castle stands on an island in a small lake at the southernmost tip of Perthshire. With its massive tower and curtain wall, it was used as an escape-proof prison from the 16th century. Mary Queen of Scots was imprisoned here for almost a year in 1567.

40 top and 40-41 Falkland Palace rises at the foot of the gentle Lomond Hills in the heart of the rich Fife Peninsula. Between 1453 and 1463 James II and Mary of Guiderdal transformed the ancient fortress into a royal palace. The current appearance of the palace dates from the 16th century and was the work of the French and Scottish master masons working for James IV and James V, respectively the grandfather and father of Mary Queen of Scots. The palace is closely associated with the life of the tragic queen. In 1542, in fact, when Mary was just a few days old, her father James V died of a heart attack.

No trace remains, however, of Dunbar Castle to where the queen fled with Lord Darnley following the assassination of Rizzio and to where she returned a few months later on her honeymoon with Bothwell. Razed to the ground by her enemies following the Battle of Carberry Hill, it was definitively destroyed by Cromwell.

Mary spent what were perhaps the happiest days of her tormented life far from the intrigues of Edinburgh in Falkland Palace, the Stuart's favorite house. Originally built as a hunting lodge, the palace was enlarged by James IV who established an elegant court there. In preparation for his marriage to the daughter of the King of France, James V transformed Falkland into a Renaissance palace with the help of master craftsmen summoned from France. The palace is set in extensive grounds that also contain the world's first tennis court.

41 left and top right
The coat of arms of the Stuarts of Bute decorates the façade of the guardhouse that defended the entrance to Falkland Palace. It housed the private apartments of Keeper, the constable and guardian of the royal palace. The 3rd Earl of Bute acquired the palace and the title of Keeper in 1887. Lord Bute undertook a restoration project that was completed in 1900.

41 bottom right
The royal borough of Falkland around the royal castle is composed of a few simple, single story stone houses. The Bruce Fountain in stone with four bright red lions stands in the square at the end of Main Street, in front of the church and the two halls designed by Thomas Barclay and built between 1800 and 1801.

42 top The Keeper's Bedroom on the second floor of the palace, was used by Michael Crichton Stuart and his wife Barbara when, at the end of the 2nd World War, they transformed

Falkland Palace into their home. The bedroom is dominated by a four-poster bed that is said to have belonged to James VI. Superbly figured, it dates from the 17th century.

42 bottom Completely rebuilt by Lord Bute, the Drawing Room is welcoming but simple, in line with the austerity of the post-war period when it was used by Michael Crichton Stuart and his wife Barbara who

was responsible for the draperies. There are portraits of James V and his second wife Mary of Lorraine, James VI, Mary Queen of Scots, Anne of Denmark, Charles II and Catherine of Braganza.

42-43 The Old Library at Falkland Palace has an elaborate ceiling with trompe l'oeil decoration dating from 1895. The room was used as a study by Michael Crichton Stuart. On the walls

are a royal hunting trophy and portraits of the family, including engravings of the 3rd Earl of Bute, Prime Minister George III and the great-grandfather of the 3rd Marquis.

43 top left During the brief years of her reign, Mary Stuart initiated work on the palace and its furnishings. Like her father and her grandfather, the queen loved to escape from the oppressive atmosphere of Edinburgh, made all the more intolerable by the austerity of the Reformation, to the tranquility of Falkland. In 1562, shortly after her return from France, the queen washed the feet of 19 virgins in Falkland Chapel, a number corresponding to the years of her reign.

43 top right The Tapestry Gallery linked the royal apartments with the Chapel and the keeper's apartments. Lord Bute restored the corridor and added the oak ceiling. The gallery is covered with 17th-century Flemish tapestries acquired in Holland, that were exposed when the royal family was living in the palace.

44 top The residence of the Roxburghe family, Floors Castle is surrounded by an agricultural estate extending over 56,000 acres along the banks of the River Tweed. The estate is composed of 50 tenanted farms, two grouse moors, 3900 acres of woodland, a golf course, a thoroughbred stud farm and salmon fishing reserves.

44-45 Built on a cliff dropping sheer to the sea, Tantallon Castle was considered to be impregnable as it was protected from attack by land by a double moat. Direct attacks and even incendiary arrows in fact failed to conquer the castle and it surrendered only in 1661 after 12 days of bombardment by Cromwell's troops under the leadership of General Monk.

SOUTHERN SCOTLAND

Southern Scotland is a region of golden hills, fields bordered by high hedges, stately homes and ruined abbeys, but also of forests and bleak heather-covered hills recalling those of the Highlands. The areas bordering England, to the south of the Scottish capital of Edinburgh, rarely enjoyed long periods of tranquility. From the incursions of the Roman legions until the Act of Union, the valley of the River Tweed and the Pentland and Moorfoot Hills were the theaters of savage and bloody battles. One of the most disastrous was the Battle of Flodden Field of 1513 in which the Scots were routed by the English army and James IV was killed. The Scottish king's year-old son succeeded him as James V, the future father of Mary Queen of Scots. In these turbulent lands, the castles represented the Scots' defensive kingpins. In the city of Harwick, close to the border, are the remains of one of the country's oldest defensive structures: an artificially raised earth mound that was once protected by palisades and on which stood a wooden lookout and defensive tower. At the foot of the tower a palisade protected houses and their inhabitants. No trace of the tower remains, but the Motte, the artificial mound, is still today the focal point of the Common Ridings, the costumed reconstructions that commemorate the site's tumultuous history. The ruins of Tantallon Castle standing above a rocky cliff at the mouth of the Firth of Forth are some of the most evocative in the whole of Scotland.

45 top The present-day appearance of Abbotsford, the home of Sir Walter Scott, dates from 1853 when the West Wing with the chapel, the kitchen and the servants' quarters was added. When Scott was alive he received in this house Maria Edgeworth, Wordsworth, Thomas Moore and Washington Irving. After the writer's death Queen Victoria visited Abbotsford and took tea with the family.

45 bottom The west façade of Hopetoun House overlooks the great park on the shores of the Firth of Forth, criss-crossed by nature trails open to the public. The hand of the architect William Bruce can be seen in the linearity of the façade.

46 top and 46-47 Set close to Edinburgh, Dalmeny House is the Gothic Revival home of the Earls of Rosebery and is filled with French furniture and paintings by Gainsborough, Reynolds and Lawrence. The house stands in extensive grounds that reach the seashore and within which pheasants with beautiful colored plumage wander undisturbed and sheep graze on the roadsides.

47 The home of the Hay family since 1696, Duns Castle stands in the southern part of the Borders region. The current owner has restored the castle to make it more comfortable without altering the characteristics of its rich past. The lake and grounds are particularly fine. The photos show the dining room and a detail of the exterior.

Built in the fourteenth century by the Douglas family in red sandstone, Tantallon was the last Medieval castle with curtain walls and an entrance tower to be constructed in Scotland. The austere and isolated Traquair House standing in the Tweed Valley is even older and its history is linked with that of Mary Queen of Scots and Bonnie Prince Charlie. In spite of its position close to the border and the unwavering devotion of its owners to the Stuarts, the castle has survived to the threshold of the new millennium virtually intact. The estate is still inhabited by the original owners who belong to a branch of the Stuart family. Thirlestane is another castle still inhabited by its owners, although its Medieval core has been extended and rebuilt over the centuries. At the end of the eighteenth century, following the Union with England, the region settled into a period of prosperity. The economic well-being resulting from the nascent industries led to a flourishing of the arts, architecture and literature. The area's most famous figures were no longer the representatives of the old aristocracy, but rather architects such as William and Robert Adam and poets and writers such as Robert Burns and Walter Scott. Edinburgh became a center of the arts and expanded with fine new quarters constructed in the Georgian style. The great Borders and Lothian estates also saw the construction of numerous mansions surrounded by parks and gardens. Among the most important were Hopetoun House on the western edge of Edinburgh and Mellerstain House, set between the River Tweed and the Cheviot Hills. Both were fruit of the Adam family genius. The initial designs by William Adam were subsequently developed by his sons, in particular Robert. William Adam was also responsible for the original design of Floors Castle, located close to the town of Kelso, amplified a century later by the architect Playfair. Floors Castle is today the largest inhabited castle in Scotland and was chosen as a location for the film *Greystoke*, in which it was the home of Tarzan. The revival of the legends of the Highlands influenced the country houses constructed by the great landowners of the Lowlands during the last century such as Dalmeny House, overlooking the Firth of Forth, or Abbotsford House, the beloved home of Sir Walter Scott, the writer and creator of the myth of romantic Scotland.

Surrounded by a large park on the South bank of the Firth of Forth, just a few miles out of Edinburgh, Hopetoun House was originally built by Sir William Bruce, the architect of Holyrood Palace, for the 1st Earl of Hopetoun, Charles Hope. The estate had been acquired in 1678 by his father John Hope, a descendant of a family of traders and judges. Unfortunately, John was never

able to live on the new property as he died in a shipwreck while accompanying the Duke of York, the future James VII of Scotland (James II of England). Work on the house began in 1699 with the construction of a central body that was extended in 1712 by William Adam and, following his death in 1748, by his three sons, John, Robert and James who were responsible for the decoration of the interiors between 1752 and 1767. The result is highly effective even though the hands of the different architects can be detected. The western façade with the classical central body is the work of Bruce. In contrast, the eastern façade, with the curving colonnades linking the wings to the central body is a theatrical stroke of genius by William Adam, undoubtedly one of his masterpieces. Inside the house, the staircases and the wooden paneling with inlaid flowers and fruits are by Bruce, while the salons with their stuccoed and gilded ceilings display the neo-classical touch of the Adams. Paintings by artists of the caliber of Rubens, Titian and Canaletto can be seen throughout the house, acquired by members of the family during the frequent foreign trips customarily taken in the last centuries by young members of the noble families. The opulent house was not inhabited throughout the year, however. The members of the family would spend weeks at the spa in Bath or would stay London while they enjoyed court life when they were not traveling in the direction of Paris or Rome.

48 top The Red Drawing Room is the only room in the house to retain its original function. The gilded stucco work of the ceiling is one of the most magnificent examples of Rococo decoration in Scotland and was the work of John Dawson. The red damask wallpaper dates from 1766. The furniture was made to measure to be set against the walls. In the 18th century, in fact, the room was used for entertaining. Only occasionally were small tables placed in the room. The white marble Italian fireplace features neo-classical decoration. The sofas and armchairs are upholstered in red damask.

48 bottom The staircase is undoubtedly the principal feature of the house designed by Bruce. The pine panels are carved with floral and fruit motifs, the work of Alexander Eizat who had already worked with Bruce at Holyrood Palace. The banister rail is carved from oak. On the walls hang the paintings commissioned to William McLaren in 1967 by the 3rd Marquis of Linlithgow in memory of his wife.

48-49 and 49 top
The western façade of the Georgian house is reflected in the waters of the lake. The grounds offer broad views of the shore of the Firth of Forth and the hills of the Fife peninsula. In early spring the grounds are ablaze with thousands of daffodils followed by primroses, bluebells and, in early summer by rhododendrons and azaleas. The extent of the park can be appreciated in the aerial view (top).

50 top left
Sir William Bruce designed this bedroom for the young 1st Duke. It is composed of a series of three chambers including a dressing room and wardrobe. The wall covering with gilded decorations is the work of James Norrie of Edinburgh.

50 bottom left
The oak panels of this bedroom have led to it becoming known as the Wainscot Bed Chamber. The decoration dates from the early 17th century, with a series of wallpapers from Antwerp datable to the same period.

50 center right
The current Great Library is composed of numerous small, inter-connecting rooms that were originally used as bedrooms or writing rooms. The rebuilding and redesignation of the rooms was the work of Adam in 1720.

The library features books collected by the family with works on archaeology, law, philosophy, religion and European history. The environment is austere but very welcoming with the walls fully lined with wood and perfectly preserved books.

50 top right
The Yellow Drawing Room occupies the original dining room. The stucco-work on the ceiling is by John Dawson and the door and window frames

are by John Paterson, while the furniture in the Rococo style is by James Cullen. The yellow damask silk covering the walls is the original 1850 covering.

John MacKay, in his *Journey Through Scotland* published in 1728, writes, "The attractive palace and gardens are set in a great park, full of deer and surrounded by a stone walls. To the south of the main road there is the vegetable garden and close by the lodge for pheasants. Below the Earl's great terrace there is an oyster farm so that the kitchen can be supplied in great quantities throughout the year." On the 29th of August, 1822, Sir John Hope, the 4th Earl of Hopetoun, welcomed George IV to his home during his visit to Scotland, the first sovereign to set foot in the country after Charles II. The road from South Queensferry was completely repaved for the occasion and the gates of Hopetoun were opened to allow the people to see the king.

The Hope family created a charitable trust in 1974 to ensure the preservation of Hopetoun House, opening the main rooms to the public and reserving a wing of the house for themselves. During the summer months the house provides a magnificent setting for recitals of classical music.

50 bottom right *The service room was created at the same time as the State Dining Room while a large kitchen was fitted out on the floor below. This photo shows*

the system of bells used to call servants from the various rooms. Hot dishes were carried from the kitchen to the dining room in a steam-heated container.

51 The State Dining Room was designed in the 19th century by the architect James Gillespie Graham. It is a sophisticated and thorough example of the late period Regency style with original decor and furnishings such as the gilded stucco work of the frieze, the large

rayed medallion of the chandelier, the fireplace, the gold wall coverings and the elaborate drapes. The great mahogany table dates from 1820. There are numerous paintings on the wall including a portrait of the Countess of Hopetoun by Gainsborough.

THIRLESTANE CASTLE

The ancient royal village of Lauder, to the South of Edinburgh, is famous for hosting one of the oldest Common Ridings, the historical reconstructions of the cavalry skirmishes that took place throughout the Borders region. Thirlestane Castle stands on the bank of the River Leader and has been the home of the Maitland family from the sixteenth century to the present day. The castle boasts the most imposing and diversified façade of any in Scotland, with a host of symmetrical round or square towers and turrets, topped by parapets or pinnacles. The original tower, incorporated into the present building in pinkish stone with grey slate roofs, dates back to 1225. It was transformed into a residence by William, the secretary of Mary Queen of Scots. His brother John, the 1st Duke of Maitland, secretary and Chancellor to James VI, transformed it into a luxurious home with an oblong structure in red stone and a circular tower at each corner. A century later his grandson, the Duke of Lauderdale whose ghost is said to still haunt the castle, worked on the extension of Thirlestane with the royal architect Sir William Bruce, responsible for the rebuilding of Holyrood Palace in Edinburgh. Bruce added two massive square towers to which David Bryce in turn added two wings in dark stone during the last century. The interiors were renewed during the Victorian period, preserving the ceilings decorated with stucco-work from the sixteenth century. The castle also features the attractive old kitchens, and a nursery with a collection of antique toys including model soldiers, puppets, dolls, rocking horses and dolls' houses. The Borders Country Life Museum deals with the domestic life, agriculture and sport of the past centuries.

52 top right In 1840 the castle's kitchen was incorporated into the new South Wing where it continued to operate as we see it today until the end of the Second World War. The center of the room is dominated by the great work table. A laundry was created in the adjacent rooms.

52-53 The complex façade of Thirlestane Castle, the result of successive extensions, appears in all its beauty in the light of the sun that emphasizes the different color of the stone and accentuates the movement of the structure dominated by the tall central tower.

54 *top left The magnificent portrait of Lady Grisell Hume, the wife of George Baillie, by Maria Varelst. Lady Grisell is the most important figure in the history of Mellerstain. When she was a girl of just twelve years of age she carried secret messages written by her father Sir Patrick Hume to his friend Baillie who was imprisoned in the Tolbooth in Edinburgh.*

54 top right and 54-55 The terraced gardens on the south side of the building provide panoramic views of the Cheviot Hills and the lake, the habitat of swans, Canadian geese and other wild birds. The lake was originally designed by George Baillie, after his exile in the Low Countries, on the model of the Dutch canals, and then it was successively extended.

MELLERSTAIN HOUSE

55 top The small drawing room presents an intimate and informal atmosphere, with a Gothic touch in the stucco-work of the ceiling. Above the Robert Adam fireplace hangs a richly decorated mirror.

55 center The Music Room is a fine example of Robert Adam's versatility. The ceiling, decorated with eagles and sphinxes, still features the colors applied in 1773. The mirrors were also designed by Adam. The portrait above the fireplace by William Aikman depicts Patrick Hume, the 1st Duke of Marchmont and father of Grisell Hume. On either side of the fireplace hang portraits by Maria Vareslet depicting Lady Grisell's daughters, Lady Murray and Lady Binning.

55 bottom The Drawing Room features a stuccoed ceiling with the original color scheme specified by Robert Adam in 1778. He also designed the fireplace with the two lateral tables. Above the fireplace hangs a portrait of Isabella d'Este from the School of Parmegianino. The sumptuous Napoleon III-style carpet comes from Aubusson.

This large Georgian house is another of the Scottish masterpieces by the Adam architects, and it can be considered as a symbol of the architectural canons of the era: first and foremost the integration of architecture and natural beauty. The austere lines of the façade thus echo those of the Italianate garden with its terraces that descend towards the lake and the slopes of the Cheviot Hills in the background. The principal entrance overlooks green lawns, shrubs and low trees that grow denser as they approach the edge of the woods. Mellerstain House was constructed in two phases. The first two low wings with the tranquil charm of country cottages were designed by William Adam in 1725. The broad central block was completed forty-five years later, between 1770 and 1778, by his son, the famous architect Robert Adam: austere Gothic lines, yellow stone and battlements as the only concession to decoration. The house was built for the Baillies of Jerviswood, descendants of the rich Edinburgh merchant George Baillie who had bought the estate in 1742 and who had lived until his death in a large old house called Whiteside that stood not far from the present Mellerstain House. Many years were to pass before his grandson, who was also called George, after years of exile in Holland and economic privations, managed to return to his homeland in the retinue of the Prince of Orange, King William III.

56 top Luminous and welcoming, the small library occupies chambers that were originally designed as dressing rooms. The decor is the work of Robert Adam and dates from 1778. Among the pictures hanging on the walls is a portrait of Thomas, 6th Duke of Haddington by Sir Godfrey Kneller.

56-57 The library is full of classical references, beginning with the four long panels placed above the bookshelves with figures in white stucco against a dark green background. The scenes depict classical motifs such as the Nine Muses, the Sacrifice of Iphigenia, the Labors of Hercules and the Pleading of Priam for the Body of Hector.

*57 top The Great
Gallery is a long
room that houses a
small museum with
objects collected by the
family over the last
two centuries. The
ceiling was designed
by Robert Adam, but
never completed.
Among the paintings
on the wall is* The
Burgomaster Le
Blom of Antwerp
*attributed to Van
Dyck.*

*57 bottom The Stone
Hall features a
William Adam
fireplace with
precious Delft
ceramic tiles. The
landscape above the
fireplace depicts the
River Tweed at Kelso
and was painted by
R. Norrie in 1725.
The round table dates
from the Victorian
period. Helmets and
halberds complete the
furnishings.*

The Mellerstain estate was restored to its rightful owner and work began on the construction of a new house built to the designs of William Adam. George Baillie's wife, Lady Grisell Hume, became a legendary figure and her *Household Book* is considered a classic text providing insights into the social life of the era. On her death it was another grandson, George Haddington Baillie, who was responsible for completing the construction as we see it today.

Inspired by the classical architecture he had seen while on the Grand Tour through Greece and Italy he chose Robert Adam as his architect. The hand of the maestro is evident in the decoration of the elegant interiors which still today retain their original pastel colors and the ceilings decorated with stuccowork and medallions. The high point is the library with a play of pastel colors (pale green, pink, a bluish grey and ivory) in which the stucco decorations, the medallions, the bookshelves and the panels with classical figures are inserted. On the second floor is another of Adam's masterpieces, the Great Gallery with its Ionic columns. In this case, however, the ceiling was never finished. It remains a mystery as to what such a vast and sumptuous room in such an isolated part of the house was intended to be used as. It can only be reached via a secondary staircase and through a salon in the Oriental style. Mellerstain House also boasts a fine collection of antique furniture and paintings, among which is a Van Dyck.

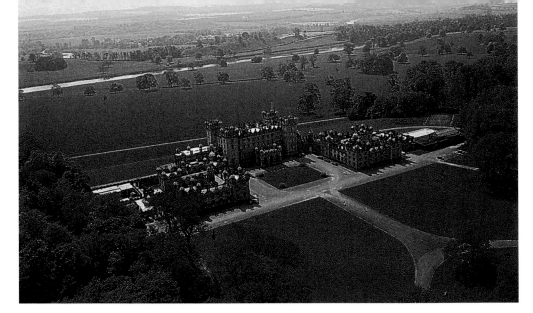

FLOORS CASTLE

58 top Floors Castle is surrounded by gardens and a park designed by William Adam. However, prior to the transformation of the house, the formal gardens were also extended, being transformed into an open park reaching the bank of the River Tweed.

58-59 On the north side can still be seen the original central body designed by William Adam, to which were added the lateral towers and the two wings which repeat to a smaller scale the symmetrical design of the central element.

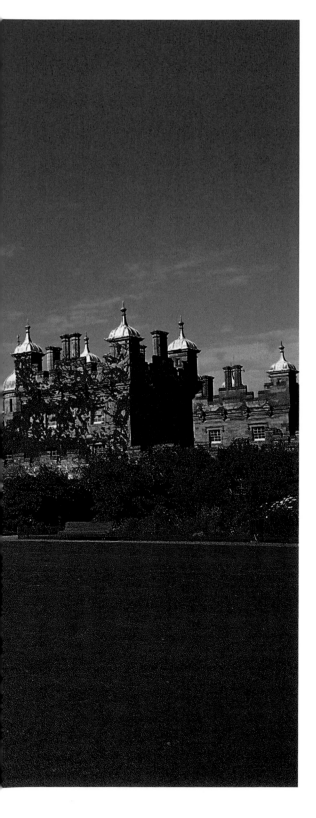

Floors Castle, set on a natural terrace at the foot of the Cheviot Hills, stands at the center of an estate in the Tweed valley, a few miles from the town of Kelso. Work on its construction began in 1721 at the behest of John, the 1st Duke of Roxburghe, an active promoter of the Act of Union, who commissioned William Adam to enlarge the earlier fortified castle and to create a residence in the Georgian style. All that remains of the great architect's design is a painting by William Wilson hanging in the sitting room.

James, the 6th Duke, had Adam's building "embellished" and in 1849 the architect William Playfair gave free reign to his imagination and talent, adding such a quantity of turrets, spires and cupolas as to make the castle resemble, according to a comment by Sir Walter Scott, that of Oberon and Titiana, the king and queen in Shakespeare's *Midsummer Night's Dream*. Early this century, thanks to the marriage of the 8th Duke to a rich American heiress, May Goelets, Floors Castle was endowed with an important art collection.

In the 1930s diverse modifications were made to the interior, in particular to the sitting room and the ballroom which were completely refurbished in order to exhibit the Brussels and Gobelins tapestries.

59 top The entrance hall is dominated by the portrait of the 3rd Duke painted in Rome by Pompeo Batoni in 1761-1762. Above the fireplace there is a large painting by Hendrick Danckerts that shows Charles II strolling with his court in Horse Guards Parade. In the background can be seen Whitehall. At the center of the room stands an oak table with lion's paw feet.

59 bottom This attractive room was refurnished by Duchess May in 1930 to make it less formal. On the walls can be seen a recent portrait of the present Duke by Howard Morgan, and a painting of Floors Castle in the design by William Adam. There is a small water-color of Kelso signed by Turner on the small table alongside the fireplace.

60 The great
ballroom was
designed by Playfair
in 1842 and enjoys a
broad view over the
river. In the 1930s
Duchess May covered
the 19th-century
decorations with oak
panels on which hang
18th-century Gobelins
tapestries depicting
Neptune, Ceres, Venus,
Cupid and Juno.

61 Designed as a
billiards room by the
architect Playfair, this
room was subsequently
converted into a
dining room. It today
houses a rich collection
of silverware,
including the cutlery
created by Paul Stort

in 1819 and the cups
with gilded silver
handles made by
Paul de Lamerie in
1726. Among the
portraits hanging
on the walls is one
of the actress Peg
Woffington
by Hogarth.

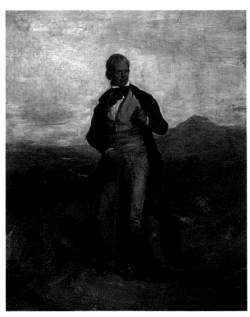

62 top In 1831, at sixty years of age, Sir Walter Scott undertook a journey to the Mediterranean, visiting Malta, Naples and Rome in the hope of regaining his health. He

62 top In 1831, at sixty years of age, Sir Walter Scott undertook a journey to the Mediterranean, visiting Malta, Naples and Rome in the hope of regaining his health. He returned to Abbotsford House the following June but was very ill. He had his bed carried into the dining room where he died gazing out at his beloved river.

The valley of the River Tweed was the area of Scotland beloved of Sir Walter Scott, the writer whose novels contributed to the nineteenth-century fashion for romantic Scotland and to the revival of bagpipes and kilts that had been virtually abandoned following the defeat at Culloden. He had been aware of the beauty of the region ever since his childhood spent on his grandfather's farm at Sandyknowe close to Mellerstain House. When, in 1799, he was appointed Sheriff of Selkirk he was able to settle definitively in the Borders. In 1812 he acquired Cartleyhole Farm where he began work on a series of new novels including *Waverley* and *Rob Roy*. Ten years later he demolished the old farmhouse and began work on Abbotsford House, so named in commemoration of the fact that the land had once belonged to the wealthy Melrose Abbey. The new building with its turrets and battlements was designed by William Atkinson in imitation of a Scottish baronial castle of the previous centuries. Typically, Scott turned the house into a concentration of elements symbolizing Scottish Romanticism, from the sword said to have belonged to the outlaw hero Rob Roy MacGregor to a reproduction of the portal of the nearby abbey. In the library, a large room overlooking the river, the walls are lined with the 9000 volumes collected by the writer, while the ceiling is an exact replica of the one in the chapel at Rosslyn.

62 center and bottom Abbotsford House is a distillation of 19th-century Scottish Romanticism. A lover of the legendary past of Scotland, the writer was in fact proud of his homeland and an enthusiastic expert on the heroes of the Highlands such as Rob Roy or the glorious William Wallace, of whom he collected relics and mementoes.

62-63 Surrounded by greenery, Abbotsford House, seen in this aerial photo, is a triumph of Gothic Revival decoration. It houses the Scott Museum which recounts the life of the novelist and exhibits many of the objects he collected during his lifetime or received as gifts.

63 top In 1812 Sir Walter Scott moved with his family to Cartleyhole and between 1817 and 1821 extended the small farm until it reached the size of the present-day Abbotsford House, of which the façade overlooking the river can be seen here. In 1830, when the writer was declared bankrupt, his creditors allowed him to keep the estate.

64 top The library is the most beautiful room in Abbotsford House, overlooking the River Tweed. The over nine thousand volumes are arranged around the walls. Some of them carry the legend "Clausus Tutus Ero" engraved on the spine, an anagram of Gualterus Scotus. The ceiling was deliberately copied from the one destroyed in the Abbey at Rosslyn.

64-65 The entrance hall at Abbotsford is panelled in oak. Some of the panels are finely carved and came from the Auld Kirk in Dunfermline. Others actually came from Holyrood Palace. In this room one can also admire armor, helmets and other objects collected personally by Sir Walter Scott on the battlefield at Waterloo.

65 top left Between the drawing room and the dining room lies the small armory which in Scott's day was used as a smokers' corridor and now contains a vast collection of pistols and swords, including a Highlands broad sword. Some of the objects are associated with Rob Roy, the legendary Scottish hero and protagonist in one of Scott's novels.

65 top right Sir Walter Scott died on the 21st of September, 1832, in the dining room, which is still used today for family meals. "It was such a quiet day, that the sound he loved most, the gentle murmur of the voice of the Tweed over its pebbles could clearly be heard while we were gathered around his bed," wrote his son-in-law Walter Lockhart.

65 center right Not accessible to the public, the private study is full of memories and relics of the family. The descendants of Sir Walter Scott still live in the 19th-century house although it has now been opened to the public.

65 bottom right Sir Walter Scott's writing desk was made as a copy of the one owned by his friend John Morrit using wood from a ship of the Spanish Armada. In this room the writer, who collected ancient Scottish poems and stories so as to rewrite them in the form of ballads and novels, produced some of his historical novels.

TRAQUAIR HOUSE

Massive and imposing, with small windows and two low wings, Traquair House is the oldest continuously inhabited building in the whole of Scotland. Its origins are lost in the mists of the first millennium, although it is first documented in 1107 when it was used as a lodge by Alexander I when hunting in Ettrick Forest. Alexander was the first of a long line of Scottish kings who stayed at Traquair and it remained a royal residence until the thirteenth century. During the reign of David I, the successor to Alexander, local laws were proclaimed, justice was dispensed and assemblies of the clan chieftains were held at Traquair. Many of the Traquair Charters, such as those signed by King William the Lion which granted the status of city to Glasgow, are still preserved in the castle and are exhibited to the public in rotation in the museum room and the library. On the death of Alexander III in 1286 the oldest dynasty of Scottish kings was extinguished and the period of peace in the Borders was interrupted. During the war for independence Traquair became a strategic element in the defensive system thanks to its position on the riverbank. The course of the Tweed was actually diverted in the mid-seventeenth century by the first Earl of Traquair in order to prevent damp from undermining the foundations of the castle. Occupied by the English during the reigns of Edward I and II, the castle returned to Scottish hands thanks to Robert the Bruce. Then, for 150 years the property passed from one owner to another as the political climate shifted. When James III came to the throne in 1460 he granted Traquair to his favorite Robert Lord Boyd. In 1478 the uncle of the King, the Duke of Buchan, became the owner. It was then inherited by the Duke's brother James Stuart, an ancestor of the current owners. The Stuarts of Traquair supported Mary Queen of Scots and, subsequently, the Jacobite cause.

66 top and 66-67 Traquair House, the oldest inhabited house in Scotland, is surrounded by a luxuriant garden overlooking the River Tweed. During the religious wars a Catholic priest was concealed in the house in a secret room that can still be seen on the third floor, adjacent to the library where religious services were held.

66 bottom A soft rug, two sofas and an armchair in front of the fireplace lend the Lower Drawing Room a warm, welcoming atmosphere. The mirror above the fireplace and the paintings flanking it on the same wall are particularly fine.

67 top The High Drawing Room conserves a simple, tranquil appearance, with white sofas, doors and walls and a collection of portraits of women: Christian Anstruther, the wife of the 6th Earl of Traquair, Lady Isobel and Lady Jean Seton painted by Cornelius Jansen. Gilded panels and decorations are set above the doors and the fireplace. In a corner of the room is a harpsichord by Andreas Ruckers from 1651.

The castle thus became a haven for Catholic priests, as demonstrated by the priest's hole, accessed by a secret flight of steps.

In 1566 Mary Queen of Scots stayed at Traquair with Lord Darnley. A blanket embroidered by Mary and her ladies-in-waiting remains as evidence of her passing. The ceremonial entrance, the Bear Gate, named after the bears decorating the pilasters, has been locked since 1745 when the Earl of the day wished good luck to Bonnie Prince Charlie and swore that it would not be opened until the Stuarts had been returned to the throne.

The present appearance of Traquair House is the result of diverse transformations executed principally during the fifteenth and seventeenth centuries. The defensive tower of the ancient Scottish kings has been incorporated into the mansion house; in the mid-16th century a new wing was added with a rectangular tower protecting the West side, while another wing dates from the end of the seventeenth century.

Inside the house there are collections of ceramics and porcelain, portraits of local noblemen, the beds in which royalty slept during their stays and a beautiful library with a wealth of antique books which are not in the best of condition due to the damp. The chapel is decorated with wooden bas-reliefs from Flanders. The cellars house a collections of tools and the fascinating system of bells used to summon servants.

WESTERN SCOTLAND

70 top
The general symmetry
of Drumlanrig Castle
is also seen in the
details such as the
windows, the chimneys
and the turrets.
The fascinating 17th-
century building in
pink stone is
surrounded by a large
park delimited by the
wild Dumfrieshire
Hills.

70-71 Built in 1270
and extended over
the course of the
centuries,
Caerlaverock Castle
features three corner
towers, one of which
has been completely
destroyed. The
entrance on the north
side gives an
impression of great
solidity but the castle
was nonetheless
conquered by the
English immediately
after construction
had been completed.

Irish monks brought Christianity to the land of the Picts and the Scots by way of this rugged coastline in which the border between lake and sea is uncertain. Tradition has it that they brought with them the Stone of Destiny which has ever since symbolized the power of the Crown and upon which the kings and queens of Great Britain are still crowned in Westminster Abbey. From the fifth century onwards the Celts joined forces with the local peoples to create the small kingdom of Dalriada. The royal capital was a fortress perched on the hill of Dunadd and surrounded by water and marshes. Today, on the crag that overlooks the wilderness of Crinan Moss, all that remains are ruined walls, a hollowed stone and a panel with inscriptions in *ogham*, the oldest form of Celtic writing, all symbols of the coronation ceremony. Tradition has it that in 574, St. Columba crowned King Aidan, perhaps the first Christian ceremony to be held in the British Isles. The raids of the Vikings and their settlement on the coast that so closely resembled their native fjords, slowly eroded the power of the tiny kingdom. The capital was moved to Dunstaffnage, to the North of Oban, where in 850 Kenneth MacAlpine took steps to fuse his kingdom with that of the Picts, transferring the court and the Stone of Destiny to Scone in Central Scotland. In 1060 with Malcom Canmore, the region became part of the Kingdom of Scotland albeit retaining a degree of independence thanks to the power of the local nobles. During the twelfth century a chieftain from Morven, Somerled, married the daughter of a Norwegian king thus obtaining vastly increased power and giving rise through his three descendants to the diverse branches of the MacDonald clan. Towards the end of the century the head of the Campbell clan was Cailen Mor of Loch Awe whose descendants became the dukes, earls and marquises of Argyll. The relative autonomy of the region with respects to the Crown continued until 1455 when James II took Threave Castle, the home of the Douglas clan, the Lords of Galloway. This five-story tower house was built on an island in the River Dee by the 3rd Earl of Douglas between 1369 and 1390. Dating from the late thirteenth century is Caerlaverock Castle, a fortress with an unusual triangular plan surrounded by a moat, austere on the outside but with an internal courtyard elegantly decorated with Renaissance motifs. Following the wars for independence there was a long period of internal conflict as the various clans struggled for power and land, at times supporting, at others rebelling against the Scottish Crown. The most tragically famous episode was that of the massacre of the MacDonalds by the Lords of Argyll, the Campbells. The government in England had set a date, the 31st of December, 1691, for the definitive submission of the clans to the Crown.

The MacDonalds of Glen Coe reached Fort William late and were unable to find the magistrate authorized to hear their oath of allegiance. They thus journeyed to Inveraray to swear the oath. The paperwork arrived in Edinburgh just a few days late but this was sufficient to provoke extremely severe punishment: on the 13th of February 1692 at Glen Coe over 200 persons were massacred including women, old people and children. The castle of the Dukes of Ar-

gyll, the leaders of the Campbell clan, is located at Inveraray and in its present form with turrets and false battlements dates from the eighteenth century. Culzean Castle, an elegant neo-classical mansion by Robert Adam overlooking the sea, dates from the same era and is surrounded by a large park. Another great Scottish ar-

chitect, Sir William Bruce, was responsible for the design of Drumlanrig Castle, in the heart of Dumfries and Galloway, a region in the Southwest of Scotland. Brodick Castle on the island of Arran is the result of repeated and successive extensions, the last of which dates from the mid-Victorian period.

72 top Dunstaffnage Castle stands on a rocky promontory dominating Loch Etive. The current building dates from the 13th century and presents a powerful curtain wall and three defensive towers. In the mid-18th century it became the prison of Flora MacDonald, the woman from Skye who aided the escape of the unfortunate Bonnie Prince Charlie, the last of the Stuart dynasty to lay claim to the Scottish throne.

72 bottom Romantic
and imposing, in spite
of being partially
ruined, Threave
Castle is reached by
boat across the River
Dee. Following the

battle of Flodden
Field a defensive ring
with walls and towers
was added. Only the
bare walls remained
after the Covenanters'
siege of 1640.

72-73 Bothwell
Castle in Strathclyde
was fought over at
length during the
wars of
independence. Part
of the original

circular tower still
exists today, although
the majority of the
castle is the result of
additions made
during the 14th and
15th centuries.

INVERARAY CASTLE

75 right Halberds from the 16th and 17th centuries, Brown Bess muskets from 1740, axes from 1847 and 18th-century Scottish broadswords are exhibited in the armory. All of the arms are carefully displayed in a circular arrangement echoing the arches of the room. The display cases contain collections of Scottish daggers, powder flasks and the belt and dagger of Rob Roy.

74-75 In this aerial view Inveraray Castle appears in all its glory, made all the more romantic by the symmetry of the gardens and by the wild natural surroundings. The Gothic towers, the pinnacles and the eclecticism of the external decoration make it a true fairy-tale castle.

75 top left The tapestry gallery was furnished between 1780 and 1790 according to the sophisticated French taste with a rich collection of Beauvais tapestries made to measure for the castle. The richness of the room is enhanced by the stucco-work and the painted decoration by the artist Girard. The coat of arms of the 7th Duke and his third wife Anne Colquohon Cunningham is inlaid in the marble top of the small round table.

75 bottom left The Victorian bed chamber contains the maple wood writing desk presented by Queen Victoria to her daughter Louise on the occasion of her marriage to the future Duke of Argyll. Between the two windows can be seen a depiction of the wedding ceremony in the chapel at Windsor painted by Sydney Hall.

Inveraray is a village built during the eighteenth century on the shores of Loch Fyne, close to the mouth of the River Aray from which it takes its name. Developed on a cross-shaped plan, the castle is a perfect example of neo-classical architecture. It was commissioned by Archibald, the 3rd Duke of Argyll, who established an ambitious plan to replace the crumbling Medieval castle built in 1457 by his ancestor Colin. In order to create the new stately home and the grounds that were to surround it, the old village was demolished and completely rebuilt a short distance away. The work was completed between 1770 and 1780 in the face of myriad difficulties given that at that

time there were no viable roads within forty miles. The new residence of the Campbells, the Dukes of Argyll, one of Scotland's most powerful families who led the Covenanters during the religious wars of the mid-seventeenth century, was designed by the architect Roger Morris of the Palladian school. The symmetrical appearance of the building was, however, modified during the last century when, following a fire, the corner towers were capped and garrets were added, topped with minuscule tympanums in an incredible medley of styles. The resulting building features turrets like those of fairy-tale castles and magnificently decorated halls. The best of these is the great dining hall with colored ornamental motifs painted in 1784 by the French painters Girard and Gruinard.

76 One of a pair of geese from the Chinese Chi'en Lung dynasty (1736-1795) exhibited in the dining room. This goose is holding a fish in its beak, while its pair has an eel. The two ceramic sculptures were used as soup tureens. Along with the miniature cannon in embossed silver and gold they are among the rarest pieces in the castle.

S et between the peninsula of Kintyre and the West Coast, the small island of Arran is dominated by the peak of Goat Fell. At its foot, overlooking Brodick Bay, stands a romantic Victorian-looking ivy-covered castle built in red stone. Surrounded by luxuriant grounds, up until 1957 the castle was the home of the Dukes of Hamilton in which they studied, gardened and received guests in a very informal atmosphere. On the death of the last owner, Duchess Mary Louise of Montrose, the castle passed to the state and thence to the National Trust for Scotland. The castle was built in the thirteenth century on the ruins of an earlier Viking fortress. However, only parts of the base of this Medieval tower, once of strategic importance in the defence of the Clyde estuary, have survived.

76-77 and 77 top In the photo appears the avenue leading to Brodick Castle, an elegant Victorian manor house with ancient Medieval origins. Around the castle extends a large formal garden with flower beds and rhododendrons planted by the last Duchess of Montrose. In 1980 the woods of Brodick Castle became the first natural park in the Scottish islands managed by the Countryside Commission for Scotland. The woods are inhabited by squirrels, peregrine falcons and even the golden eagle.

On the death of William, the 2nd Duke of Hamilton, at the Battle of Worcester, Cromwell's troops occupied the castle in 1652 and a new wing was added. In spite of the successive interventions, the castle was not inhabited by the family until the end of the last century when, on the crest of the wave of interest in the Highlands and attracted by the wealth of game, the Hamiltons decided not to develop the estate which actually represented a minor part of their patrimony centering on Hamilton Palace in Lanarkshire. In 1843 Alexander, the 10th Duke, commissioned an extension to the castle on the occasion of the marriage of his son William, the future 11th Duke, and the German princess Mary of Baden, a cousin of Napoleon. The design of the new wing, to the west of the old tower, was entrusted to

James Gillespie Graham, one of the architects of Edinburgh's New Town. The result is a castle of baronial appearance in which the new elements fuse perfectly with the old and the linear design of the fenestration contrasts harmoniously with the battlements and the gargoyles of the roof. Gillespie was responsible for the entrance hall, dark and imposing, with arms and hunting trophies along with an oak fireplace inlaid with the family's coat of arms. The castle houses a rich collection of silver, porcelain and paintings, including works by Watteau and Turner, part of the remarkable collection of William Beckford, father-in-law of the 10th Duke. There is also an attractive library with equestrian prints on the walls, and a kitchen with an exceptional battery of copper pans. In the castle grounds, the walled garden dates from 1710, but the true masterpiece is the rhododendron garden established by the Countess of Montrose and considered to be one of the most beautiful anywhere in Great Britain with dozens and dozens of diverse varieties. There is also an interesting ice room that was packed with snow gathered from the mountains or imported from Canada during the winter to provide a year-round supply for the conservation of food before the introduction of refrigerators. In 1980, the woodlands on the estate were declared a Country Park with 10 miles of marked footpaths along the Hamilton and Montrose families' favorite walks.

79 top right
A portrait of the
Duke of Alençon
by François Clouet
hanging in the
drawing room. The
work once belonged to
Charles I as testified
by the symbol on the
back.

CULZEAN CASTLE

The windows look out onto the grey sea of the Firth of Clyde and the narrow strip of land called the Mull of Kintyre that ventures out into the ocean. Inside there is stucco-work, pastel colors and crystal chandeliers. It is in the salon of Culzean Castle on the Southwest Coast, a few miles from the celebrated Turnberry golf course, that the barren, romantic scenery of the region contrasts most magnificently with the elegance of the Georgian architecture and decoration of Robert Adam. The castle stands at the top of a cliff that drops sheer to the sea and is surrounded by the large estate inherited in 1744 by Sir Thomas Kennedy, the 9th Earl of Cassillis. The existing Medieval castle was composed of a round tower with a room on each floor, a purely defensive structure lacking any form of creature comfort. The Duke therefore decided in 1760 to add a long wing overlooking the sea. However, the new construction reflected his pragmatic spirit that was more interested in the modernization of the estate than in the elegance of his home. This situation changed seventeen years later when the Earl's brother David, the 10th Earl of Cassillis, called upon the most celebrated architect of the era, Robert Adam, to rebuild Culzean Castle and make it more suitable to the worldly lifestyle of the period.

80 top and center
The traditional home of the Kennedy family; Culzean Castle, inherited by the 9th Earl of Cassillis in 1744, immediately took the place of Dunure, the family's ancient castle. Robert Adam's design has a classical linearity that, however, does not disdain Medieval touches such as the slits and crenellated turrets.

80 bottom Culzean Castle is surrounded by extensive grounds transformed into a Country Park, and a large walled garden, the lake of swans and various buildings such as Camellia House. A group of naturalist guides is at the service of visitors to provide guided botanical tours. The park headquarters was opened in 1970 in the Robert Adam-designed Home Farm.

80-81 and 81 top Set in a spectacular position at the top of a cliff dropping sheer to the Firth of Clyde, Culzean Castle dominates the whole of the West Coast. The imposing but severe exterior is softened by the large green lawns, the flower beds and the terraces on which even tropical trees flourish.

The old building was demolished and replaced with a round tower that accentuated the romantic aura of the complex as a whole. Inside, on the first floor, Adam designed the stunning Saloon, a symbol of the elegance of the century, and dealt personally with every last detail of the furnishing. The interiors in fact constitute one of the last and most successful works of the architect and his team of artists and craftsmen who had already proven their talents at the houses of Hopetoun and Mellerstain near Edinburgh. The circular ceiling panels were painted by the Italian artist Antonio Zucchi, the marble fireplaces were the work of Peter Henderson of Edinburgh while the great round carpet was woven not far from Culzean to a specific design. Adam's masterpiece, though, is the oval staircase located in what was once a dark, cramped interior courtyard behind the tower. Sober and elegant, the staircase rises between two stories of Corinthian columns while the play of curved lines creates an impression of movement. When David Kennedy died in 1792 without heirs, Culzean Castle passed to his cousin, Captain Archibald Kennedy of New York whose home address was No. 1 Broadway. During the last century the symmetry of Adam's original design was lost with the construction of a new wing. In 1945, Charles Kennedy, the 14th Earl of Cassillis, presented the castle to the National Trust for Scotland on the condition that the upper floor was made available to General Eisenhower as a sign of the Scottish people's gratitude for his feats during the war. A great park extends around the castle in which woodland alternates with avenues of rhododendron and Italian gardens overlooking the sea. Artificial corridors link the fountain of the Court Garden to the large walled garden where the typically British art of contrasting flowers of various heights and colors is seen to best effect.

83 top left The dining room occupies what were originally the library and the master dressing room. Vast and imposing, it is dominated by a long 18th-century table and Chippendale-style chairs. The painting above the mantelpiece by Ben Marshall dates from 1800 and depicts the 12th Duke of Cassillis, subsequently nominated Marquis of Aisla.

83 top, right The oval staircase is one of Adam's masterpieces and one of the principal features of Culzean Castle. It has a double row of Corinthian columns on the first floor and Ionic on the second to accentuate the perspective. The stairs, together with the banister and the red carpet, create a contrast of colors and curving lines.

DRUMLANRIG CASTLE

84 center left
The beautiful drawing room, richly decorated with wooden inlays, contains pieces of great value such as the two 17th-century French cabinets from Versailles, the magnificent portraits and the fine mirrors.

84 bottom left
Originally this attractive wood-paneled room was the entrance hall. Transformed into a dining room it has a stuccoed ceiling dating from the 19th century. Family pictures hang on the wall.

Drumlanrig Castle was originally built in the fourteenth century as a Douglas stronghold, but little trace of the early structure remains. The present castle with four corner towers was built by William Douglas, the 1st Duke of Queensberry in the decade between 1679 and 1691. It is the work of different architects, also Sir William Bruce is known to have worked on the plans, and the final result is a unique example of late seventeenth century Renaissance architecture in pink sandstone. When the castle was completed the Duke was so shocked by how much it had cost that he felt uneasy to live there. From an architectural point of view Drumlanrig constitutes the link between the fortresses built prior to the Act of Union and the "mock" castles constructed by the nobility as country houses. Drumlanrig has nothing of the Romantic fortified castles of other parts of Scotland. Its monumental appearance confers an air of great severity, unusual for a private home in the heart of the countryside. However, as soon as one enters the interior courtyard this austerity is mitigated. The entrance has a vaulted arch with Renaissance decoration and a Gothic structure supporting a terrace.

84 top left
The entrance hall is an attractive room lit by arched windows. Above the fireplace is exhibited a piece of embroidery said to have been done by Mary Stuart during her long imprisonment.

The large carpet on the floor with the coat of arms of the Douglas Heart family was woven in 1985. The hall's finest piece is the Rape of the Sabine Women *attributed to Giovanni da Bologna (1524-1608).*

84 right The oak staircase and balustrade were among the first of their kind Scotland. That which in all the other Scottish castles is a simple passageway, at Drumlanrig takes on the role of a veritable art gallery with paintings of international importance from the Madonna with Yarnwinder by Leonardo to the Old Woman Reading by Rembrandt along with other works by Hans Holbein, Murillo, Joost Van Cleef and a Madonna from the School of Correggio.

84-85 and 85 top Drumlanrig Castle, a pink sandstone construction, stands on a hill (Drum) and the end of a long (lang) ridge (rig). Surrounded by woods, this castle is one of the first examples in Scotland of the Renaissance style applied to civic architecture. Among the guests to have stayed at Drumlanrig were James VI, Bonnie Prince Charlie, Queen Elizabeth II and Prince Philip and also Neil Armstrong, the first man to have set foot on the moon.

86 top At Kirkwall, the capital of the Orkney Islands, off the North coast of Scotland, stand the beautiful ruins of Earl Patrick's castle, begun in 1607 by Earl Patrick Stuart, the brother of Mary Stuart and the illegitimate son of James V.

THE HIGHLANDS

*I*nhabited ever since ancient times, as testified to by over 500 brochs, the defensive towers having been built 2000 years ago, the Highlands has not always been an immense pasture for millions of sheep. Once upon a time the northernmost region of Scotland, this harsh, beautiful land, was covered with forests and the cultivated fields of the Highlanders, peoples of Celtic origin who lived in agricultural communities, the clans, ever ready to go to war at the behest of their chieftains. One of the most powerful of these clans was that of the McLeods; descendants of the Vikings of the Isle of Man. Their castle was at Dunvengan, on the Isle of Skye. The Scandinavian blood was mixed with that of the Celts of the Kingdom of Alba and reinforced the powerful clan communities which frequently engaged in struggles amongst themselves. The chieftains lived in defensive towers such as those of Eilean Donan Castle, the home of the MacKenzies, or Cawdor Castle, the residence of the Thanes of Cawdor. At the end of the Stuart dynasty the Highlands witnessed repeated revolts against the ruling house of Hanover. The region's castles such as Blair or Braemar changed ownership on a number of occasions and in some cases were transformed into barracks for troops. In 1715 there was an unsuccessful revolt led by the Duke of Mar who intended to bring James Edward, the younger son of James I, to the throne. The Highlanders were defeated at Sheriffmuir and the British army constructed new roads from Crieff to Fort William in order to keep the region under military control. Bonnie Prince Charlie returned from exile in France in 1745, landing in the Hebrides. He gathered all the clans faithful to the Stuarts at Glenfinnan and the following month entered Edinburgh, installing himself at Holyrood Palace. The rebel troops scored a victory at Prestonpans and advanced through the English Midlands as far as Derby. However, they were defeated at Culloden near Inverness in the April of 1746. Bonnie Prince Charlie had to flee and the repression of the Jacobites was ruthless. The survivors were forbidden to wear their kilts, to bear arms, to speak Gaelic and to play the bagpipes. The lands of the clan chieftains who had supported the Jacobites were confiscated and the clan system was dismantled. This marked the Highlanders' ruin. Accustomed for centuries to paying rent to the clan chieftain for their land in the form of military service, they were unable to find the money demanded by the new landowners. The English lords faithful to the Crown found it more convenient to transform their holdings into pasture or hunting estates. With the Highlands Clearances, the Highlanders were expelled from their lands, their houses were burned to prevent rebellions and any attempt at resistance was repressed. Many people emigrated and by 1860 the Highlands had been emptied. In the meantime, however, English society had developed a love of this wild and remote Scotland, so much so that Queen Victoria ordered the construction of Balmoral Castle, the royal family's current summer residence.

DUNROBIN CASTLE

88 top The elegant
dining room was
redesigned by Sir Robert
Lorimer following the
fire of 1915. The walls
are fully paneled in
wood and are topped
with a classical frieze,
probably of Italian
origin. The room
features a number of
important family
portraits. Above the
fireplace Thomas
Phillips has
immortalized the sons

of the 1st Duke; to the
right is a portrait of
Granville, the 1st
Marquis of Stafford by
George Romney and
on the side wall, the
Duchess Harriet, the
wife of the 2nd Duke,
with her eldest
daughter, Elizabeth.

88 bottom This big
silver cup occupies a
first floor niche in one
of the two turrets of
Dunrobin Castle.

F or centuries Dunrobin Castle has been the home of the Dukes of Sutherland, descendants of Freskin of Moravia who arrived in Scotland at the time of William the Lion. They immediately adopted the customs and culture of their new homeland, to the extent that they transformed themselves into Celtic chieftains and were invested in 1235 with the title of Earl of Sutherland. Their symbol, a Great Cat, led to the name Caithness, the northeastern region of the Highlands. Built on a terrace overlooking the sea, this castle with its turrets and pinnacles has no less than 187 rooms and is the largest home in northern Scotland. Dunrobin, whose name means the "Castle of Robin," is documented for the first time in 1401 as the fortress of the 6th Earl. However, there was also an older part, a Medieval tower dating from 1275, the remains of which can be seen in the windowed corridor. In the seventeenth century two wings were built to the south and the west to form an L-shaped plan. A wide tower with a circular plan united them to the Medieval fortress. In 1785 Elizabeth, the Countess of Sutherland, married Viscount Trentham, the Marquis of Stafford, an English nobleman and one of Europe's richest men thanks in part to the profits of the industrial revolution. A philanthropist with liberal ideas, he established large-scale programs for the improvement of the living conditions, the roads and the economy of the region.

88-89 Overlooking the sea and surrounded by formal gardens of Franco-Scottish inspiration, Dunrobin Castle dates from the 13th century but was extended on more than one occasion from the 17th century onwards. The interiors feature furniture and paintings of great value as well as objects that recount the history of the family and Scotland itself.

89 top Seen from the terrace, the gardens of Dunrobin reveal the intricate design inspired by Versailles and the geometric pattern that develops around the fountain.

90 top The library has taken the place of a bedroom and related dressing room. Entirely lined with bookshelves, it is dominated by the fine portrait of Duchess Eileen, the wife of the

5th Duke, painted by Philip Lazlo. Apart from the ten thousand volumes, some of which are very rare, the library also contains a huge globe by W. & A. K. Johnstone.

90 bottom The nursery contains toys used by the young Sutherlands over the centuries. In the foreground stands a wooden rocking horse while in the background there is a Victorian dolls' house.

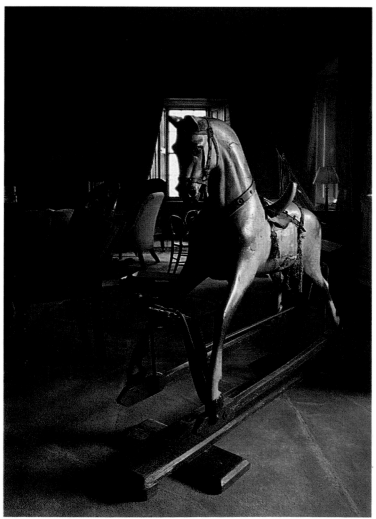

On the coast he had workers' houses constructed that he offered to the tenant farmers who unwillingly left their thatched cottages isolated in the Highland valleys. In reality he contributed to the depopulation of the Highlands. Over 5000 families were evicted from the homes of their ancestors. Their place was taken by the sheep that are still today a constant feature of the region's landscape. During the last century almost the whole of the county of Sutherland in the Northwestern Highlands, that is to say, 1,300,000 acres of land, were owned by the Duchy, making it one of the greatest landowners of Western Europe. The current French-style castle owes its appearance to the 2nd Duke who in circa 1850 summoned Charles Barry, the architect of the House of Parliament in Westminster, in order to transform Dunrobin from a Scottish castle into a stately home. His wife, the Duchess Harriet, was a lady-in-waiting to Queen Victoria. The 3rd Duke constructed at his own expense the Highlands railway and the Victorian-style station that can still be seen not far from the castle. The castle itself features a library with a gigantic globe and hunting trophies and a Sicilian-style bedroom suite acquired by the Duke during a cruise through the Mediterranean. The castle is surrounded by a large park and an Italian garden with borders of roses and shrubs.

90-91 and 91
The new design for the drawing room, which was rebuilt after the fire of 1915, combined two smaller rooms so as to create a large airy salon with a beautiful view over the garden surrounding the great fountain. The ceilings, designed by Robert Lorimer, were created by Sam Wheeler in 1919. The furniture is from the Louis XV period, while the walls are covered with 18th-century tapestries depicting the life of the Greek philosopher Diogenes. The finest works are, however, the masterpieces by Canaletto hanging over the fireplaces.

91 top left The original billiards room designed by Lorimer is today used for the exposition of family heirlooms and ceremonial costumes. The billiards table has been placed in the Gallery, where hunting trophies can be seen behind the arches.

Set in a 70-hectare park a few miles to the east of Nairn, for over eight centuries Brodie Castle was the home of the Brodie family. The castle dates from the fifteenth century with additions and extensions from the sixteenth, but it is thought that the original nucleus was first inhabited by the Brodies in 1160. All of the documentation relating to the origins of the castle and its rebuilding around 1560 was lost in the fire of 1645 when Lord Lewis Gordon, representing the Duke of Montrose, torched the castle during the civil war against the Covenanters. The castle was rebuilt and took on its present appearance in the seventeenth and eighteenth centuries. It features a Z-shaped plan with overhanging turrets and battlements. The extensions to the east, north and northeast made in 1824 are in the neo-Tudor style and were designed by William Burn. The oldest part of the building is the semi-basement kitchen in the North Wing. In 1982 ownership of the castle passed to the National Trust for Scotland.

92-93 Famous for the flowering of many varieties of daffodils in early spring, Brodie Castle is a tower house built on a Z-shaped plan that has developed over the centuries. It is surrounded by a park with nature trails that reach the marsh where wild birds can be observed.

93 top left At the center of the dining room, a large table is surrounded by sixteen chairs dating from around 1840. The table is laid with porcelain plates bearing the coat of arms and motto of the family. Hanging on the walls are portraits recounting centuries of family history.

93 top right The family coat of arms is composed of a shield and the motto "unite" and is seen here in one of the castle's windows. Historians believe the Brodie family descends from a Celtic tribe rewarded with land by Malcom III. The original surname was Brothie and was modified to Brodie early in the 16th century.

CAWDOR CASTLE

Just a few miles from Inverness and the Moray Firth, the Castle of Cawdor is associated with the Shakespearean tragedy, *Macbeth*. The tower with its entrance raised as a defensive measure, was built in 1380 by William Thane of Cawdor, a friend of King James II. Legend has it that a dream prompted him to allow a mule loaded with gold to roam freely and to build a castle at the very place where the animal stopped to sleep. The mule lay down beneath a hawthorn tree around which the original tower was constructed, arranged on four storys linked by a spiral staircase. In 1638 work began on the north wing and the old sitting room was linked by a stone staircase.

94 top left and 94-95 The gardens surrounding Cawdor Castle have a very intimate atmosphere. They are at their best from spring to late summer. The recently restored walled garden offers attractive combinations of colors.

94 bottom left and 95 top The severe, massive Cawdor Castle was built on a slight rise as the private fortress of the Thanes of Cawdor. In spite of the additions made over the centuries, it still has the appearance of a tower house with corner turrets and battlements.

94 right The family coat of arms is set into the walls of the castle that William Shakespeare used as the setting for the tragedy Macbeth with the assassination of Duncan.

96 top In spite of its bleak external appearance, Cawdor Castle has a surprisingly comfortable internal atmosphere. This is not so surprising when you consider that the castle is still the family home. Not all of the rooms are open to the public; the private areas include the intimate and welcoming dining and drawing rooms seen here.

96-97 The drawing room occupies what was once the old hall. The last major rebuilding work dates from the 16th century when a fireplace with the coat of arms of the Calders, the old form of Cawdor was added. Portraits of members of the family such as Pryse Campbell, the 18th Thane of Cawdor, dressed in an assortment of tartans, hang on the walls.

During the civil war the castle escaped lightly with only a few haylofts being torched by the royalist troops led by Lord Montrose. During Cromwell's bloody campaigns Cawdor Castle was allowed not to have to house soldiers and officers, thus safeguarding its rich interior furnishings. In 1684 the castle was transformed into a comfortable home by Sir Hugh Campbell, the 15th Thane. The windows were enlarged, carved fireplaces were installed and two new wings to house the Thane's nine children and numerous servants were built. Further improvements were made around 1720 and the middle of the nineteenth century, but without leading to significant modifications.

97 top The dining room features a late-Victorian style decorated ceiling and tapestries with scenes from the life of Don Quixote on the walls.

97 bottom The stairs are covered with a carpet that features the colors of the Campbell of Cawdor tartan. Antique firearms are arranged on the walls.

98 top left The upper valley of the River Dee is one of the most beautiful and gentlest areas of the Scottish Highlands. The salmon-rich river flows between fertile pastures at the foot of bare hills.

98 top right The attractive drawing room has an informal atmosphere. It features pink walls and 19th-century Persian carpets on the floor. Among the paintings is a portrait of Mrs. Farquharson of Invercauld, the grandmother of the current Lord.

98-99 In contrast with the lavish decoration of other castles in their area, Braemar Castle appears stark, with few windows and no ornamental features. Only the movement of the turrets and battlements enlivens the architecture. The interiors are also simple, almost austere, and testify to the style of life in a Highlands castle.

99 top Adjacent to the dining room, the Morning Room is simple and free of fripperies. Hanging on the walls are portraits of John, the Earl of Mar who built the castle, and one of his descendant, also called John, who led the revolt of 1715.

99 bottom On the first floor of the castle, the dining room has a simple fireplace and a large central table. Note the two globes, one terrestrial and the other depicting the heavens, dating from 1818. A piece of the plaid worn by the Young Pretender, Bonnie Prince Charlie, together with other relics testifying to the family's Jacobite sympathies, are exhibited in this room.

BRAEMAR CASTLE

Braemar is a small village in the upper valley of the River Dee, famous throughout the world for the Royal Highlands Gathering, the traditional Highland games held each summer in the presence of the royal family.

Standing against the magnificent backdrop of the peaks of the Cairngorms the castle has a severe aspect, animated only by the play of turrets and battlements. It was built in 1628 by John Erskine, the Earl of Mar and the treasurer to King James VI. The fortress served as a lodge during hunting trips organized in the Grampian mountains, but also as a bulwark against the increasing power of the Farquharsons. In 1689, during the brief Jacobite rebellion, the castle was conquered and burned by the "Black Colonel," John Farquharson of Inverary, and for sixty years remained a ruined shell. The 39th Earl of Mar inspired the Jacobite rebellion of 1715, on the 6th of September of that year brought together the rebel troops at Braemar, where today stands the Invercauld Arms Hotel. At that time the castle was but a blackened skeleton and was requisitioned by the loyalist troops following the defeat of Mar and the Jacobites at Sheriffmuir. The castle was restored in 1748 and transformed into a garrison for the troops of the Hanoverian government. The very young Adam brothers, John and Robert, had a hand in the reconstruction and went on, of course, to become extremely famous architects. The crenellated curtain wall dates from this period and was based on a star-shaped plan in accordance with Renaissance theories on fortifications.

At the end of the century the castle was converted back into a residence and housed Queen Victoria when she came to attend the Highland Games prior to the acquisition of Balmoral.

BLAIR CASTLE

Set in the heart of the wild Grampian mountains, Blair Castle has always controlled the main road between Edinburgh and Inverness. Its history is closely linked to that of Scotland itself and the struggles between the Highland clans.

The residence of the Dukes of Atholl ever since the time of the Celts, the castle was actually built in 1269 by John Cumming of Badenoch who

took advantage of the absence of the Earl, David, who was involved in the crusades. Hidden amidst the turrets and battlements there is the original tower, still known today as the Cumming Tower.

Over the centuries the castle was subjected to diverse modifications and additions. It also changed hands on a number of occasions due to a lack of heirs or political maneuvering. In 1457 the deeds to the estate were given by James I to his blood brother Sir John Stewart of Balvenie, the founder of the current dynasty and whose motto, conferred by King James III together with the order to put down the insurrection of the MacDonalds in the islands, was "Furth Fortune and fill the Fetters."

The male line was extinguished in 1625 and the title to the castle passed to John Murray, Lord of Tullibardine and a descendant on the maternal side. After his death, Blair Castle was occupied by the Duke of Montrose and in 1652 by Cromwell's troops. Claverhouse, the leader of the Jacobite rebellion, occupied the castle in 1689 and on the 27th of July of that year recorded a famous victory over the government troops in the narrow gorge of the River Garry near Killiecrankie.

The extension and rebuilding of the castle undertaken by the 2nd Duke was interrupted by the Jacobite revolt of 1745 when the pretender to the throne, Bonnie Prince Charlie, marched south with his army of Highlanders, staying for some days at Blair Castle.

100 top The tapestry room on the second floor of Cumming Tower owes its name to the sumptuous tapestries woven in Brussels for Charles I.

100 bottom On the staircase, below a richly stuccoed ceiling, hang portraits of members of the family: the 1st Duke, John, immortalized by Thomas Murray, the 1st Marquis of Atholl, John, depicted by Jacob De Witt in the guise of Julius Caesar, and his wife, Lady Amelia Stanley.

100-101 When Queen Victoria visited Blair Castle in 1844 she described it as a "broad and simple white building." Twenty-five years later the 7th Duke commissioned John and David Bryce to rebuild the castle in the Scottish Baronial style we see today.

101 top The white structure of Blair Castle with its crenellated towers and conical roofs stands out against the green mountains of the central Highlands. Around the castle extends a large estate with sheep pastures, woods, gardens and cultivated land.

102 top The drawing room is the most beautiful room in Blair Castle, with walls covered with crimson damask silk and a ceiling decorated with elaborate stucco-work. Above the white marble fireplace hangs a family portrait by Johann Zoffany depicting the 3rd Duke, his wife and their seven children.

102-103 The Ballroom was built between 1876 and 1877 by the 7th Duke. Beneath a wooden ceiling with exposed beams, this room was used for balls, concerts, receptions and the world bagpipe championships. The partially paneled walls are decorated with various family portraits and hunting trophies.

103 top
The Tea Room boasts a rich collection of dinner and tea services. One of the rarest is the 18th-century oriental service with the coat of arms of the Dukes of Atholl.

103 bottom
The wood-paneled entrance hall was built by the 7th Duke. In pride of place at the center is the portrait of Iain, the last Duke, executed by the painter Carlos Sancha in 1982, on

the occasion of the 25th anniversary of the Duke's accession to the title. A rich collection of arms (guns, pistols, swords, bows and crossbows) are arranged in decorative patterns on the walls.

After being occupied by the troops of the reigning Hanoverian dynasty, in 1746 the castle was besieged by Lord George Murray, the 2nd Duke, at the head of his Atholl Highlanders. This was the last castle in Great Britain ever to be besieged and ironically enough it was by the owner himself. Once the situation had been resolved the 2nd Duke revived his modernization work, following the dominant Georgian style. In 1756 the portrait staircase on the walls of which the Lords of Atholl are immortalized was added. The last intervention dates from the late nineteenth century when between 1869 and 1904, the castle was restored in a Romantic vein. Today it is a white turreted manor house surrounded by an immense forest and pastures with hundreds of sheep.

The last Duke of Atholl, the 10th, who died in 1996 was also the only man in the entire United Kingdom with the right to maintain a private army, the Atholl Highlanders. On his death, the castle and the 70,000-acre estate was inherited by a charitable institute. The title on the other hand went to a distant South African cousin.

BALMORAL CASTLE

104 top left A vast estate extends around Balmoral and ranges from the fertile lands of the valley to the heather-covered hills of the Lochnagar range dominating the area.

104 bottom left The tower stands out from the western façade, rising from the main body of the building, and at the top, below the arrow slits, can be seen a large clock.

Balmoral Castle, the summer residence of the royal family, stands in the upper Dee valley, not far from Braemar. Set at the foot of wooded hills, the castle is surrounded by a vast estate acquired in 1848 by Prince Albert and Queen Victoria, who had both fallen in love with the Highlands. When the royal couple visited Balmoral for the first time Queen Victoria described it in her diary as "a pretty little castle in the Scottish style, surrounded by wooded hills that recall Turingia, the birthplace of Prince Albert." The castle was actually two hundred years old but had been rebuilt a few years earlier by the previous owner, Sir Robert Gordon. The building was not large enough for the needs of the royal family, for their numerous servants and for their state obligations.

In 1852 work thus began on the construction of a new castle in the Gothic Revival style to the designs of the architect William Smith. The new residence in white granite was completed over the following years, while the royal family spent the summers in the old castle. Balmoral is composed of a massive square tower, embellished with four lateral towers and a long three-story wing with large panoramic windows that led Queen Victoria to write, "Not only is the house attractive and comfortable but it has a beautiful view, that the old castle did not."

104 top right The west wing of the palace overlooks the magnificent and painstakingly groomed Rose Garden with the statue of a chamois and the fountain. The luxuriant gardens are at their best when the royal family is in residence at Balmoral during the summer.

104 bottom right A family portrait with Queen Victoria at Windsor Castle in 1890 and views of the Balmoral and Sandringham. The images were reproduced in the volume published on the occasion of the sovereign's jubilee.

105 This aerial view reveals the layout of Balmoral Castle as a whole. The present-day structure is the fruit of numerous modifications made over the years to adapt the summer residence to the needs of the royal family.

*106 The Ballroom,
the walls of which
feature a bas-relief
by John Thomas,
overlooks the granite
steps built in 1857
that lead to the fertile
banks of the River
Dee.*

*107 The Ballroom is
the only room of the
castle open to the
public. Family
portraits and objects
of royal provenance
are exhibited in the
great room
illuminated by tall
windows.*

108 top Dunvegan Castle is the only stately home in the Western Isles and is the house inhabited the longest by a single family in the whole of Scotland. Among the visitors to the castle were James V and Sir Walter Scott.

108-109 and 109 top All around Dunvegan Castle extends a large park crossed by footpaths that lead to two spectacular waterfalls. The benign influence of the Gulf Stream allows plants typical of lower latitudes such as rhododendrons and azaleas to flourish. A short distance away, on the sea shore, colonies of seals bask in the warmth of the sun.

DUNVEGAN CASTLE

*O*verlooking Loch Dunvegan on the northwest side of the Isle of Skye, this castle has always been the home of the MacLeods, the lords of the isles. Tradition has it that Leod was the youngest son of the last Viking king of the Isle of Man and the Hebrides. When King Alexander II defeated the Vikings in 1263 at Lairg, Leod possessed at least half of the Hebrides.

The land of the MacLeods is still extensive but is today restricted to part of the Isle of Skye, Dunvegan Castle and its surroundings up to the Cuillins which rise barren and steep 3260 feet above sea level.

In the thirteenth century, during the period of the first clan chieftain, the castle was no more than a defensive wall protecting a low building with a thatched roof. Around 1340, Malcom, the third MacLeod chieftain, added a massive square tower at the northeast corner of the house.

At the southeast corner there is an elegant fairy-tale tower built at the behest of Alasdair, the 8th chieftain, in around 1500. The tower's four floors are linked by a spiral staircase.

The present Romantic appearance dates from the Victorian era when the castle was extended between 1840 and 1850 by the 25th clan chieftain, to the designs of the architect Robert Brown of Edinburgh. The work cost the notable sum of 11,250 $.

*109 bottom
For seven centuries
the castle has belonged
to the MacLeods and is
associated with the
legend of The Fairy
Flag, a mysterious
and extremely old silk
banner of Middle
Eastern origin which
is said to have the
magical ability to
rescue the clan from
peril. It is said to
have been presented to
a member of the
MacLeod clan by
an enamored fairy.*

The spectacular
ruins of the
Marischals'
impregnable fortress,
Dunnottar Castle,
stand on a cliff
falling sheer to the
North Sea near
Aberdeen. The castle
put up stubborn
resistance to
Cromwell's besieging
troops.

CENTRAL AND EASTERN SCOTLAND

110-111 Over 400 years of history are enclosed within the powerful walls of Castle Fraser. Built in 1575 near Aberdeen by Michael Fraser, the 6th Lord, the two low wings help to emphasize the attractive central tower, making it one of the most beautiful castles in Scotland.

111 Built in sandstone, Kellie Castle in Fife dates from the 14th century. In 1573 a second tower was added to the east and the castle was completed between 1573 and 1605. The southeast tower, with the entrance portal, is a minor masterpiece with overhangs and corner turrets. The gardens are extremely attractive.

Undulating countryside that gives way to wooded hills, bucolic valleys that gradually transform in heather-covered moors: that central and eastern Scotland is a rich and fertile region is demonstrated by the dozens of castles constructed along the course of the River Dee or on Tayside, with a concentration greater than in any other part of the country, with the possible exception of the area around Edinburgh. This is the region of the royal castles of Stirling and Falkland and those of the manors tied to the crown such as Drummond and Glamis. But above all, it is the area in which the Scottish Baronial style of architecture with its towers, battlements and overhangs on a generally simple and linear base can be seen to best effect in buildings such as Craigievar Castle, Castle Fraser and Fyvie Castle.

Numerous stone circles show that these hospitable lands have been inhabited since prehistoric times. The earliest settlers were the Picts who lived here long before the Celts reached Scotland. The Roman legions arrived between the 1st and the 2nd centuries, established their base near Mons Grapius close to the present-day Stonehaven and there defeated the Scottish tribes. They did not remain for long, however, preferring to withdraw south of the wall constructed by Antoninus between the Clyde and the Firth of Forth.

In the 9th century Kenneth MacAlpine united the kingdom of Dalriada with that of the Picts, thus gaining control of much of Scotland. The capital of the new kingdom stood not far from Scone Palace, built with the stones of the ancient abbey. The thirteenth century saw power pass into the hands of the Comyns, the Counts of Buchan, following the marriage between a Comyn and the daughter of a local chieftain. Robert the Bruce's fight against the English was also a struggle against the Comyns, their allies. Then came the turn of the Gordons who exercised almost regal control over the northeast until 1562. This was the century in which the simple Medieval tower houses began to be transformed into vertical palaces. A typical example is Crathes Castle in the Dee valley, built towards the end of the sixteenth century. From the same period, and at a short distance away, is Castle Fraser which features decorative elements of French origin. Haddo House, designed by William Adam for one of the branches of the powerful Gordon family, was built in the Neoclassical and Georgian styles.

FYVIE CASTLE

112 top left and 113 top Fyvie Castle is surrounded by a great English-style park with ponds and lakes. The walled garden which features informal combinations of flowers of all colors is of immense appeal. The park is embellished with sculptures such as the statue of the dwarf of Queen Henrietta Maria, or the 16th-century urn sculpted from Venetian marble.

Fyvie is a village set amidst the woods on the banks of the River Ythan, once famous for its freshwater pearls. Surrounded by a great park with a small lake, the castle is one of the best examples of Scottish Baronial architecture, with five towers commemorating the five great families to have owned the estate through the ages, the Prestons, the Meldrums, the Setons, the Gordons and the Forbes-Leiths.

Originally Fyvie was a royal fortress, surrounded by a hunting forest, as indicated by the Gaelic place name which means Hill of Deer. The castle occupied a strategic position: to the east it was protected by a great marsh and to the north and the west by the meanders of the river. The only line of attack was from the south where the single, well defended entrance led into an internal courtyard.

The oldest castle on the site was probably built in wood, with external defences in beaten earth. William the Lion visited Fyvie in 1211 (or 1214) and Alexander III conceded its statute to him. On the 31st of July, 1296, the English King Edward occupied Fyvie during his punitive campaign in Scotland. Some years later Robert the Bruce administered justice in the an open-air court in the castle's beech forests.

In the fourteenth century the castle took the form of a massive stone keep protected by a high curtain wall reinforced with corner turrets.

112 bottom left and 112-113 A jewel of Scottish architecture, Fyvie Castle emerges from the green countryside with towers and spires that are decoratively topped with statues of musicians. The castle is the fruit of repeated and successive modifications that fortunately have not compromised its harmonious architecture.

112 top right The coat of arms of the Forbes-Leith family, the last owners of the castle. In 1889, Alexander Leith, an American steel magnate, acquired the castle and embellished it with works of art.

The principal entrance through the south wall was defended by further towers, in all likelihood constructed during the period of Edward I's occupation.

The castle remained the property of the Crown until 1370 when it was presented by Robert II to his eldest son John, the future Robert III who in his turn presented it to his cousin, Sir James Lindsay, Lord of Crawford and Buchan. In 1390-91 Fyvie was reassigned to Sir Henry Preston, a cousin of Sir James, who took possession only in 1402. Having become the property of the Medurn family through marriage, Fyvie was sold in 1596 to Alexander Seton, the Chancellor of Scotland, who undertook major extension works and the creation of the triumphant ornamentation of the top floor and the roof that made of this castle a fairy-tale composition of overhanging turrets, decorated pediments, sculpted garrets and pinnacles in the form of hunters or musicians.

Support for the Jacobite cause led to the requisitioning of the Fyvie estate and, in 1694, Seton's grandson died penniless in a Parisian attic where he had fled after having backed the unsuccessful revolution of the Stuarts.

In 1733 Fyvie Castle was acquired by the 2nd Duke of Aberdeen for his third marriage and it was subsequently inherited by the first-born son of this union, William Gordon of Fyvie.

114-115 The entrance hall, furnished by William Gordon, replaced the old fortified entrance on the south side of the castle. The ceilings are richly decorated and the walls are covered with hunting trophies, arms and armor collected by Lord Leith. The armor came from Germany and dates back to the 16th-17th

century. One can also admire a marble bust of Caesar Augustus and the perfectly preserved tusk of an elephant. The most impressive element of the furnishings is the fireplace, surmounted by a relief panel illustrating the Battle of Otterburn of 1388 in which Sir Henry Preston captured Ralph de Percy.

115 top left The dining room was furnished by William Gordon in 1790 and subsequently modified by Lord Leith. The red wall covering, the dark draperies and the stucco-work on the ceiling confer an austere and ceremonial atmosphere upon the room. There are numerous portraits hanging on the wall:

above the fireplace, in a carved wood frame, is the wife of Lord Leith, Marie Louise January; on the door to the servant's quarters hangs a portrait of Lord Leith himself while portraits of Sir William Maxwell of Calderwood and Sir John Stirling of Kippendarie with his daughter hang on the other walls.

115 bottom left A portrait of Ethel Louise Forbes-Leith painted by Luke Fildes in 1906 dominates the Back Morning Room. The sole heir of Alexander Leith, on the death of her father in 1925 she inherited the title that was eventually passed on to her son Andrew, born in 1929.

115 top right and bottom The Billiards Room is located at the base of the Gordon Tower, in what were until 1890 the kitchens. This room was the favorite of the male members of the family for games, smoking and drinking. The billiards table was made by Cox and Yeman of London. Various paintings with Scottish subjects hang on the walls: the most spectacular is The Sound of Many Waters *painted by Sir John Millais. Another depicts the Scots Greys at Waterloo, painted by Colonel F.S. Seccombe in 1891. Hunting trophies and arms are displayed above the fireplace. The castle also boasts an unusual room for bowling.*

At the end of the eighteenth century the new owner drained the marsh on the east side, created a lake, landscaped the park and added the Gordon Tower to the north of the West Wing. In 1885 his descendant, Sir Maurice Duff Gordon was obliged to sell the family estate to resolve his financial difficulties.

Four years later Fyvie Castle and its lands were acquired for 246,130 $

by Alexander Leith, a Scotsman born at Blackford, a few miles from the castle, who had made a fortune in America, becoming one of the magnates of the steel industry. During his lifetime he embellished the castle with suits of armor, tapestries and paintings of the English and Scottish Schools. In 1890 he added the Leith Tower to the west of the Gordon Tower. In 1983, Sir Andrew Forbes-Leith put the property up for sale and after long negotiations it was sold to the National Trust for Scotland.

116 top left The portrait of William Gordon of Fyvie by the Italian Pompeo Batoni is one of the most interesting works of the 18th century. Painted in 1766, it differs from other portraits by the artist who generally lent a gentle air to his aristocratic sitters. Sir William instead wanted to be portrayed as a proud Scotsman in the family tartan, standing in front of the Coliseum as a reference to the heroes of the Roman empire. This portrait is one of the most valuable works preserved at Fyvie Castle.

116 top right and 116-117 The atmosphere of the Music Room which leads off the drawing rooms is typical of the Edwardian style of many British homes of the early 20th century; a blend of antique and modern. The walls are covered with 17th-century tapestries from Brussels woven to the original designs of Peter Paul Rubens. The French Renaissance is well represented by the marble fireplace dating from 1521 featuring extremely colorful tiles with oriental motifs that can clearly be seen in the detail. The organ and the tiffany lamp complete the precious furnishings of this room.

117 top This drawing room on the second floor of the Gordon Tower was built in 1790 as the Morning Room by General William Gordon and was subsequently modified. On the ceiling the stucco-work represents the family coat of arms. With its dark red draperies, the room reflects the tastes of the 18th century. The imposing portrait of General William Gordon painted by Pompeo Batoni is from this era. Above the mantlepiece hangs a portrait of Susanna Archer, the Countess of Oxford, by Sir Thomas Lawrence. Other valuable paintings bear the signatures of Gainsborough, Reynolds and Romney. The furnishing is prevalently Victorian or Edwardian, while the cabinets are in the Louis XV style.

117 bottom The small library contains a rich collection of books dealing with Scottish history and literature and topographical maps. This room was used by Lord Leith as a study. On his desk two electric bells kept him in contact with his assistants. Nautical decoration on the ceiling recalls Lord Leith's own naval career and his father's past as an admiral. Above the door hangs a copy of the portrait of William Elphinstone.

*118 top left
This portrait of Lord
Haddo was painted
by Pompeo Batoni,
an Italian exponent
of the early neo-
classical style.*

*118 top right
Haddo House was
designed in 1731
by William Adam
for the 2nd Earl of
Aberdeen. Many of
the splendid interiors
date from the end of
19th century.*

HADDO HOUSE

118-119 The library occupies the old stable block and is paneled in cedar wood inlaid with ebony. The rare books reflect the 4th Earl's interest in Greek and Latin texts and travel writing. All of the furnishings and the decor date back to the 19th century.

119 left The Morning Room occupies what in Adam's original design were three bedrooms. Transformed into a library by the 4th Earl, the space was eventually transformed into an informal sitting room. The fireplace, the mirror and the stucco-work date from the end of the 19th century. Note, between the two windows, the Irish satinwood cabinet given to the 7th Earl by his wife to commemorate his mandate in Ireland.

When Haddo house was built in the eighteenth century by William Gordon, the 2nd Earl of Aberdeen, to the designs of William Adam, the most famous Scottish architect of the day, it astonished the local nobility accustomed to living in romantic but hardly comfortable turreted castles. The great Palladian house with its two circular corridors linking the lateral wings contrasted with the barren surroundings of eastern Scotland. The construction of Haddo House was extremely expensive, partly because the finest materials were used. These included Norwegian timber for the roof which was completed in 1734 while the second wing was finished a year later. The ambitious Earl was not short of money, however, and he was known as a hard, inflexible land owner who exploited his tenants to the full. The 2nd Earl of Aberdeen died in 1745 and left the house to his son George, the 3rd Earl, a son from his first marriage (the heirs from the 3rd marriage instead received Fyvie Castle), but his amorous relations and worldly lifestyle left him with little time to devote to

property. It was George's grandson George Gordon, the 4th Earl, orphaned at 12 years of age and educated at Cambridge, who took Haddo House in hand. His interest in the Italian Renaissance led him to Italy, Greece, Turkey, Albania, Austria and Germany and resulted in him becoming known as the Athenian of Aberdeen. George Gordon took up a political career and between 1828 and 1830 was the Secretary of State for Foreign Affairs and between 1834 and 1835 the Secretary of State for the colonies. In 1852 he was entrusted by Queen Victoria with the task of forming a new government. Early in this century the 4th Earl commissioned the architect Archibald Simpson to extend Haddo House. William Adam's circular corridors were demolished and the lateral wings were extended: the North Wing contained the stables while the South Wing was reserved for the kitchens and the servants' quarters. Gordon summoned James Giles, a painter and garden designer, for the landscaping of the grounds. The last extension of Haddo House was made at the behest of the 7th Earl who, in 1877, revised the lateral elements in order to create new chambers for the family. In 1880 the architects Wardrop and Reid of Edinburgh definitively transformed the house to make it more suitable to the changing demands of the family. The new arrangement of the entrance and the staircase robbed the western façade of the purity of William Adam's neo-classical design.

119 top right The dining room has been preserved with its 1880 furnishings intact. Portraits of the family and of the Stuarts hang on the walls. The attractive table is laid with silver, crystal and porcelain.

119 bottom right Redecorated at the end of the 19th century, the drawing room at Haddo House is dominated by the painting of David and Goliath by Domenichino that hangs above the fireplace. Among the other pictures exhibited are a Head of St. Peter by Van Dyck and a portrait of Sir Walter Scott and his daughter by Sir William Allan.

CRAIGIEVAR CASTLE

Set in a secluded position in the picturesque Grampian Hills, Craigievar Castle is universally recognized as the best example of a tower house built in Scotland, a happy marriage of local tradition and exotic influences of French origin. Three storys rise on an L-shaped plan, with four in the central tower. In reality the castle is a house built vertically rather than horizontally, with spiral staircases taking the place of corridors. While the lower section is simple and austere, the upper floors are a play of projections, turrets, parapets and spires.

The first reference to Craigievar is found in a statute of 1457 conserved in the castle itself, which indicates the owners of the castle as the Mortimer family. The Mortimers began the construction of the castle, but late in the sixteenth century they suffered financial problems and were obliged to stop work and sell the property. The new lord of Craigievar Castle was William Forbes, the brother of the Archbishop of Aberdeen and a merchant who had made a fortune trading with the Baltic ports, earning himself the nickname Danzig Willie. The profits from his commercial enterprises refinanced the construction of the castle, leaving great expressive freedom to the master mason. Since then the descendants of the merchant have lived for centuries in the castle. In 1963 the property was donated to the National Trust for Scotland, a body that manages dozens of places of historical interest.

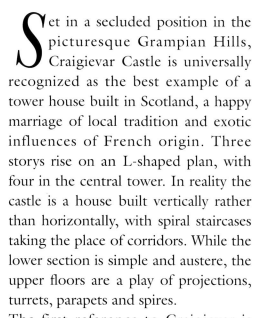

122 top left The Long Gallery takes up the whole length of one wing of the castle and is famous for its vaulted ceiling decorated with oak panels, one of the few in Scotland, with the exception of those of the royal palaces. In this century it was transformed into a library.

122 top right The name "Muse's Room" derives from the decoration of the ceiling depicting the Nine Muses and Seven Virtues. The female figures have led to a suggestion that the room was originally a ladies' drawing room. There is a particularly attractive tapestry designed by William Morris.

CRATHES CASTLE

122-123 and 123 right The gardens at Crathes Castle are divided into eight thematic zones, set on two different levels and separated by yew hedges. They have been designed so that plants are flowering all year round. The layout can be clearly seen in this aerial photograph.

123 left A gardener intent on transforming a yew shrub into a sculpture. The gardens are tended by four gardeners supervised by a head gardener. Much of the current layout was designed by Sir James Burnett and his wife, Lady Sybil, both green-thumbed enthusiasts.

Along with Craigievar, Crathes Castle is one of the best examples of Scottish architecture. Begun in 1553 by Alexander Burnett, it took over forty years to complete the fortress with its L-shaped plan, and it was finished thanks to his great-grandson. In 1656 it was inhabited by Burnett's grandson, the 12th Lord. The history of the building is commemorated in two shields on the eastern façade. The first contains the coat of arms of Alexander Burnett and Janet Hamilton with the date on which work began, the second contains those of Alexander Burnett (the great-grandson) and Katherine Gordon and the date it was completed.

Like all the castles in the Scottish baronial style, Crathes develops vertically. The upper part is a triumph of turrets, overhangs, pinnacles and false battlements while the lower section is more austere, in spite of the opening of Victorian-style windows on the first floor. During the last century an incongruous late-Victorian wing overlooking the upper garden was added. Destroyed in a fire in 1966, it is today restored, but the Victorian additions were not rebuilt. The magnificent eighteenth century grounds feature one of the richest collections of trees in the whole of Great Britain.

GLAMIS CASTLE

Glamis Castle, the home of the 18th Earl of Strathmore and Kinghorne, is one of the most famous castles in Scotland and the birthplace of Princess Margaret. A grandiose avenue leads to a fortified manor house in pink sandstone, all turrets and pinnacles, the result of the romantic additions of the nineteenth century.

Originally the castle was one of the many hunting lodges of the kings of Scotland, although the site had already been inhabited in earlier times. Around the eighth century St. Fergus had built a church there of which a sacred wall remains.

In 1372 Sir John Lyon received the Glamis estate as a gift from King Robert II and four years later he married the King's daughter Joanna. The castle of the epoch is incorporated in the present building, the ramified structure of which is the result of successive extensions. Originally the castle took the form of a tall, slim tower that was easily defended but provided inconvenient living accommodation. The ground floor was occupied by storerooms while the principal hall was located on the first floor and was reached via an external staircase.

In spite of the Lyon family's ties of kinship and centuries of fidelity to the Crown, in the sixteenth century it was deprived of royal support. The cause of the family's disgrace was the marriage between John, sixteenth Lord of Glamis, and a Douglas, the sister of the Earl of Angus, who was suspected of treason.

124 top and 125 top right On the lawn in front of the entrance to the castle stands a baroque sundial with diverse faces, decorated with rampant lions. Together with the turrets and the statues of James VI and his son Charles I, they are all that remain of the walls that once surrounded the castle.

124 bottom The detail shot of a roof shows the sculptural decoration at the summit of Glamis.

124-125 This aerial view of the castle highlights the intricate design of the upper section, a feature of all the Scottish Baronial castles: the conical roofs of the towers and turrets, the battlements and the chimneys.

125 top left This plaque on the façade depicts the coat of arms of the Earl of Strathmore and Kinghorne: a lion and a horse rampant support a shield surmounted by a cross and closed with the motto "In te domine speravi."

Following the death of her husband, Lady Glamis was accused of witchcraft, imprisoned until she became blind and then burned alive in the square in front of Edinburgh Castle. Her young son was also imprisoned and the family property was requisitioned by the Crown. Thus between 1537 and 1542, James V, the future father of Mary Stuart, held court at Glamis with many royal edicts emanating from the castle. On the sovereign's death, John, the 7th Lord of Glamis, was liberated and, thanks to an Act of Parliament, regained his property. The furniture and silver had, however, disappeared following the passage to the royal court. John, the 8th Lord and the Chancellor of Scotland, restored the castle to its former glories. According to one of his guests, an English ambassador, the staff consisted of a butler, two manservants, a musician, a chief cook, a cellar master, a master mason, a head porter with his assistants, a bailiff and an officer. The lady of the house was attended by two ladies in waiting, a seamstress, a personal chambermaid and two further servants.

John's son Patrick was made Earl of Kinghorne by James VI whom he followed to London when, on the death of Elizabeth, the king of Scotland also became James I King of England. Patrick began to make a series of improvements to the castle which resulted in its present appearance, but misfortune was once again to strike at the doors of Glamis.

John ran up huge debts in his support of the cause of the Covenanters who fought against the Church and the episcopacy. His successor Patrick, the 3rd Earl, thus found himself saddled with the astronomical debt of $56,260. In 1670 he arrived at Glamis with his wife and began working to redress the situation. As soon as his financial circumstances began to improve he began work on the castle and was responsible for the transformation of the Great Hall into

the Drawing Room with elegant stucco-work on the vaulted ceiling and the decoration of the Chapel with painted wooden panels featuring biblical scenes. Tradition has it that in the left-hand corner at the back sits the ghost of the Lady in Grey, an unfortunate woman who died as the result of a tragic love story.

128-129 The crypt has conserved its Medieval appearance. The walls are so thick as to be able to house a secret chamber. The furnishings in heavy oak combine well with the hunting trophies, arms and armor.

129 top left A copy of the beautiful portrait of the Queen Mother painted by De Lazlo when she was the Duchess of York hangs in her room. The names of the 14th Earl, his wife and his children are embroidered on the inside of the canopy.

129 right The chapel is the most beautiful room in the whole of the castle, with its walls and ceiling fully paneled in painted wood with sacred scenes, from the Last Supper to the Flight from Egypt, by the Dutch artist Jacob de Wet.

The Lady in Grey is not, however the only ghost to haunt the castle, being accompanied by the enormous and bearded figure of Earl Beardie who played cards with the devil and lost.

The opulent interiors belong to diverse periods from the fourteenth through to the nineteenth century, and contain collections of furniture, porcelain, paintings and historical objects.

The royal apartments are crammed with objects including photographs that document the relationships and the lives of the members of the family. The village of Glamis itself is composed of houses built in 1793 by the Earl of Strathmore for his estate workers.

These long, single-story constructions contain a schoolroom, a kitchen and a room for spinning and weaving wool.

SCONE PALACE

Although the massive stone palace on the banks of the Tay outside Perth dates from the first half of the nineteenth century, Scone is one of the oldest and most sacred sites in the whole of Scotland. Within the estate, in fact, rises Moot Hill, a place name deriving from the Gaelic *Tom-a-mhoid*, meaning "a place where justice is administered." It was here in 846 that Kenneth MacAlpine founded Celtic Abertha, the capital of the unified kingdom of the Scots and Picts. From that date onwards the Scottish kings were crowned on the consecrated Stone of Destiny, brought by MacAlpine from Dunstaffnage. Even when Edward I of England carried the stone to Westminster Abbey in London, where it was incorporated into the Coronation Throne, the Scottish kings continued to be crowned at Scone. On the same site around 1120, King Alexander I founded the first Augustinian monastery in Scotland. The abbey and the abbot's palace were also used as a residence by the royal family. The monastery complex enjoyed great prosperity during the reign of Robert III and the rising city of Edinburgh was annexed to the abbey so that it could benefit from its great wealth. In 1210 William the Lion founded a royal settlement a short distance away, on the site of what is today the city of Perth. On the 27th of June, 1559, the monastery was sacked by the fanatical followers of John Knox, inflamed by one of his sermons held at St. John Street in Perth.

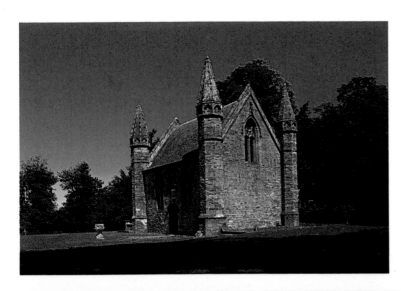

132 top The Ambassador's Room is dominated by the purple four-poster bed carrying the coat of arms of King George III and the royal monogram. The bed was presented to Lord Stormont when he was the ambassador to the French court. On the walls hang a portrait of him by Allan Ramsay and another of Lady Elizabeth, the ambassador's daughter, with Dido the daughter of the chambermaid the Duke had freed from slavery.

132-133 The Long Gallery is in fact around 142 feet long, an unusual size for a Scottish house which were generally developed vertically.

The feet of many sovereigns have trodden the wooden floors inlaid with blackened peat bog oak. In 1580 the ceiling was frescoed with hunting scenes featuring James VI and his court, but was covered over at the beginning of the 19th century with a more sober Gothic-style ceiling.

133 top left The dining room is very airy and filled with one of the richest collections of ivory in Europe. The long table, covered with a damask cloth bearing the coat of arms of the Mansfields, is laid with a Chamberlain of Worcester tea service decorated with a profusion of fruit and flowers within a blue rim. The chairs are in the Chippendale style. Above the fireplace hangs The Philosopher by Salomon Koninck and, on the right, a portrait of the 1st Earl of Mansfield.

133 bottom left Overlooking green pastures, the old library now contains few books. They have in fact been replaced by examples of Meissen, Sèvres, Ludwigsburg, Chelsea, Derby and Worcester porcelain. These were pieces collected by the 1st and 2nd Earls for everyday use. Above the fireplace hangs the portrait of William Murray, the 1st Earl of Mansfield, by Martin.

133 right This spacious, North-facing drawing room has two fireplaces dating from the 17th century. Above them are two paintings by David Tenirs, one depicting a group of dromedaries, the other a group of monkeys. There is also an impressive seven-feet tall brown bear killed by Sir Lancelot Carnegie when he was the British ambassador to Russia.

The ruins of the royal town and the monastery, and the great estate surrounding them, became the property of the Earls of Gowrie who in the sixteenth century constructed Gowrie Palace using the stones of the old abbey. Following the obscure Gowrie Conspiracy in which James IV would have been killed had he not been rescued by Sir David Murray, the property of the Gowries reverted to the Crown. As a reward the estate was presented to the Murray family, of noble Flemish ancestry and future Earls of Mansfield. Early in the eigteenth century, the 5th Viscount David opposed the Act of Union and during the revolt of 1715 gave hospitality to James III, the Old Pretender, at Scone Palace. His son the 6th Viscount, in his turn opened the doors of the palace to Bonnie Prince Charlie during the revolt of 1745. The viscount's brother William Murray became one of the greatest legal experts of the era and was invested as Earl of Mansfield. However, he lived in Bloomsbury, London, and was too busy to visit Scone. The 2nd Earl found the palace too damp and absolutely unsuitable for living in. It was not until the middle of the last century that the 3rd Earl commissioned the architect William Atkinson to construct a palace in the Neo-Gothic style, the building that can be admired today. Its massive external appearance with numerous lateral towers belies the wealth of the collections of French furniture, clock, tapestries, ceramics and ivory conserved inside.

DRUMMOND CASTLE

Drummond Castle stands on a rocky outcrop, two miles out of Crieff in the heart of Perthshire. Around 1490, Sir John Drummond of Stobhall was given permission by James IV to construct a fortress on land that he had acquired in the Strahearn Hills. James IV, a frequent visitor to Drummond Castle, fell in love with Sir John's daughter, Margaret, but the Scottish noblemen were determined that their sovereign should marry the sister of the English king, Henry VIII and therefore poisoned the young Margaret.

In 1605, on the orders of James VI, the 4th Lord Drummond traveled to Spain with the delegation entrusted with the task of negotiating a peace treaty between the two nations. This enterprise earned him the title of Earl of Perth. The new earl had a wing added to the original tower on the north side. His brother John, the 2nd Earl of Perth, a privy counselor to James VI and Charles I, transformed the castle by adding a low Renaissance-style element between 1630 and 1636, as recorded in the dates incised together with the family coat of arms. The architect of the extension was John Mylne who was also responsible for the sundial obelisk standing in the center of the garden. During the period of suppression by the English army under the leadership of Cromwell, the castle was badly damaged. In 1715 it became a garrison for the troops faithful to the crown and after 1745 the lands of the

Earls of Perth, including Drummond Castle, were confiscated as punishment for their support of the Jacobite cause. Formal gardens in the Renaissance style are laid out at the foot of the castle and are considered to be the most beautiful in Scotland. Box hedges and examples of topiary create a play of light and shadow on the emerald lawns and gravel paths, while the rose garden and the flower beds lend splashes of color to the composition.

134 left and 135
In spite of the modifications made during the last century, Drummond Castle still retains all the features of a 17th-century Scottish Renaissance castle. It is located on a rise with terraces dropping away towards the gardens.

134 right
The garden's design changed throughout the centuries. One of the artificers of the Renaissance transformation of the castle and the garden was John Drummond, the 2nd Earl of Perth who lived between 1584 and 1662.

136 top Italian influences can be seen in the gardens at Drummond in the form of the statues, the fountains and the urns adorning the balustrades. It is thought that many statues were bought in Italy by Charles Barry around 1830.

136 bottom
In September 1842 Queen Victoria stayed at Drummond Castle for three days and recorded in her diary: "Sunday, 11th September... We walked in the garden and it is really very fine with terraces, like an old French garden." The following day, while Prince Albert was hunting in the forest of Glen Artney, the queen strolled amidst the flowers accompanied by the Duchess of Norfolk.

*136-137 and 137 top
From the upper terrace the garden appears in all its glory with the avenues and shrubs tracing the cross of St. Andrew with the 17th-century sundial at the center. Around the base, a mosaic of black and white pebbles forms the Drummond coat of arms.*

Castles of Bavaria

SECTION TWO

Bavaria's unconventional *status* within the Federal Republic of Germany is confirmed by the title that this *Land*, the largest and oldest of the sixteen *Länder* of Germany, uses when it proclaims its boundaries in official documents and signs: *Freistaat Bayern* (the Free State of Bavaria). In all of Germany, no one is as proud of their own uniqueness and independence as the Bavarians, a romantic and combative people that forged the history of Europe for centuries. Bavarians often express their loyalty in descending order: "First Bavaria, then Europe, and then Germany," and in fact they have every right to be proud of their land. Essentially, the only thing missing in its endless list of natural beauties is the sea. The great love that Bavarians have always had for their land can be seen in the respect they have traditionally accorded the countryside. All works by human hands, from the great art cities to rural villages, from imposing fortresses to opulent residences, and from little country churches to the magnificent monasteries, are harmoniously inserted, like jewels in a precious setting, into the multifaceted natural frame created by imposing mountain ranges dotted with emerald lakes, deep forests broken by meandering rivers, and gentle hills interrupted by large, crystal-clear lakes. Located in the heart of Europe, Bavaria's long history can be traced in the architecture of its monuments, echoing the influence of other peoples, wars and glories. The Celts, Romans, French and Austrians have all had their turn at dominating this territory, which takes its name from the Baiuvarii, the Germanic tribe that first settled here. Every culture left its mark on the countryside, in the culture and in the cuisine of Bavaria, but throughout its long, intricate history, the events which probably most affected its modern-day appearance were two major conflicts: the Thirty Years' War and the Second World War. The bigotry and persecution practiced by Catholics and Protestants during the Reformation finally erupted into one of the most devastating conflicts (both in terms of human life and artistic treasures) that Europe had ever known – the Thirty Years' War, which sucked France, Spain, Denmark and Sweden into its vortex of senseless violence.

140 top From the baroque gardens, the horseshoe-shaped staircase leads to the terrace where Linderhof Castle, Ludwig II's pleasant refuge in the valley of Graswang, stands.

140 bottom "Atlas Upholding the World" dominates the tympanum of Linderhof's main façade. The Kingdom of Bavaria's coat of arms, upheld by two winged spirits, appears in the tympanum.

140-141 Ludwig II began construction of Neuschwanstein Castle in 1848 in one of the most beautiful areas of Bavarian Allgäu-Swabia, with the idea of creating the castle of the Knights of the Holy Grail.

141 top In the park at Herrenchiemsee, fountains, geometrical hedges and statues depicting hunting scenes and mythological deities recreate the atmosphere of court gardens during the era of Louis XIV, the Sun King.

After the war, it took Germany forty years to recover from the resulting social and economic collapse (almost a third of the population had been killed). The Wittelsbach family, however, whose name runs like a thread throughout the history of Bavaria, embarked on the great task of rebuilding their land.

As the result of the long war, trading and communication difficulties and an even longer period of recovery, the whole country thus made the transition from the Gothic period directly to the Baroque, almost entirely skipping the Renaissance, which left only rare traces throughout most of Germany. In effect, the new style coming from Italy, so exuberant, rich and sensual, was the perfect antidote to sober Protestantism and all the ugliness of the preceding conflicts.

Newly regained economic well-being made it possible to invest in the best artists of the period, and cities, castles and churches were rebuilt and restored in the new style, adapted to local taste, thus creating the Bavarian baroque.

Unfortunately, in the heat of the moment almost everything that had survived the past catastrophes was made baroque, and even though many Romanesque and Gothic buildings have survived to the present, it is extremely rare to find interiors which were not modified in accordance with the taste of the times.

Unfortunately, World War II left an indelible scar, as Bavaria was one of the areas in Germany with the greatest wealth of artistic treasures. Yet it can still astound us with the uniqueness and variety of its natural beauties and historic monuments.

In this book we have chosen to show Bavaria through the history and images of its fortresses and castles, which function as both a point of departure and a point of arrival in the history of a particular area, town or city. World-renowned for the castles of Ludwig II, Bavaria truly is a land of castles.

There are hundreds of ruins, with fortresses, fortifications, and royal residences that emerge everywhere out of the idyllic countryside as witnesses to the long history of Bavaria, its desire for independence and freedom and its pride in and awareness of its accomplishments. It was difficult to select only a few of these castles, because they all have an individual charm and a unique architecture, interior or position that make them worthy of being added to the most representative groups. We thus decided to divide them into three chapters unrelated to itineraries (although the castles are described in geographical order from south to north), and connect them by historical and architectural groups instead.

The castles of Ludwig II have their own chapter, because they are really not part of the history and architecture of their period, but rather from some sort of dreamtime. The other two chapters are dedicated to fortified castles and residential castles.

142-143 *A true fortified citadel that for many centuries was an impregnable buttress guarding the borders of Lower Bavaria, Burghausen fortress, over 0.6 miles (1 km) long, is the longest fortified castle in Germany.*

143 top *The fortress of Nuremberg played an important role in the history of both Bavaria and Germany, and historically and architecturally is one of the most important fortresses in Europe.*

Neuschwanstein Castle.

Aschaffenburg

Miltenberg

Würzburg

Main

Bamberg

Main

Pottenstein

Bayreuth

Rother Main

Ansbach

Nuremberg

Riedenburg

Regen

Eichstätt

Prunn

Harburg

Danube

Danube

Augsburg

Isar

Landshut

Passau

Rott

Amper

Schleissheim

Isar

Munich

Burghausen

Herrenchiemsee

Inn

Kempten

Starnberger See

Chiemsee

Hohenschwangau

Neuschwanstein

Landshut

Herrenchiemsee Castle.

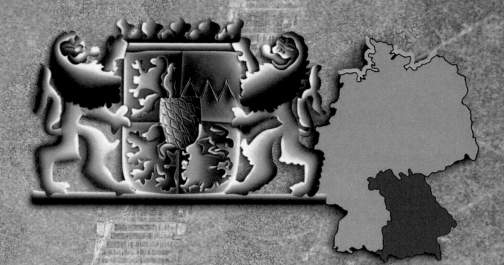

Schleissheim Castle.

Nymphenburg Castle.

146-147 Kaiserburg, one of the most beautiful and imposing fortresses in Germany, has undergone many changes over the centuries. Its massive Sinwell Tower can be seen for miles.

Harburg Castle.

Prunn Castle.

THE DREAM OF LUDWIG II, "THE FAIRY TALE KING"

Some of the most sumptuous and well-known castles in the world are certainly those of that symbol of Bavaria, Ludwig II, whose ministers consistently attempted to block their construction. These amazingly eccentric works were a product of the imagination and dreams of a monarch who was affectionately known as "The Fairy Tale King" by his subjects, but was considered the "Mad King" by his ministers. To understand his castles, one must look at the life of Ludwig II. He was very young when he inherited the heavy burden of a throne which had previously been occupied by two great political figures: his grandfather, Ludwig I, and his father, Maximilian II, who had succeeded in making Munich the European capital of art and culture. Born on August 25, 1845 in the royal palace of Nymphenburg in Munich, he passed a lonely adolescence in the manor of Hohenschwangau. His mother, queen Marie, notes in her diary that the child appreciated art, built churches and castles with his wooden blocks, liked to dress up and was very generous with his toys. This natural character and the type of education he received made him a dreamer. Fantastic images of the historical past, German sagas and a love of the exotic steadily distanced him from reality. As he grew up, he became enamored of the figure of the Sun King and the splendors of Versailles. His father's ideal of a constitutional monarchy was totally contrary to the vision of abso-

lute power and the passion for the Bourbons that had rooted in him. Another passion that caused no end of problems with his ministers was his love for Richard Wagner's music, which at that time was considered a hodgepodge of deafening sounds, discordant and even dangerous. As soon as he came to the throne, Ludwig II began to search for his hero, who had gone into hiding to avoid debts and had left his works incomplete. Thanks to the king's support and enormous monetary contributions, Wagner was able to complete his works, and his music gained international recognition. The veneration and love that the young Wittelsbach felt for the *maestro* were boundless, but unlike his grandfather, who preferred the love of Lola Montez to his reign, Ludwig did not have the necessary strength of character to oppose the orders of his Cabinet, which, worried about the "unbalancing" effect of Wagner's music and personality on the king, banished the artist from the court. The bond of affection between the brilliant composer and the restless monarch is evidenced in the letters the two exchanged, which in their exuberance and passion are not only some of the most revealing documents of the era, but are also a portrait of two unique, creative personalities. The great disappointment that this forced separation caused, besides continued opposition to his rare political decisions, caused him to distance himself even farther from politics and to lose himself in his world of dreams.

*148 top left
This portrait by Franz von Lenbach shows an elderly Richard Wagner. The painting hangs in Herrenchiemsee Castle, although the temple that Ludwig dedicated to the composer is actually Neuschwanstein Castle.*

*148 bottom left
Young King Ludwig II of Bavaria looked like an ideal monarch to his people. Tall, slim and quite attractive, with a very elegant style and demeanor, his amiable nature won over any subjects who were fortunate enough to meet him.*

*148 right
Maximilian II rebuilt Hohenschwangau Castle in Romantic style. This summer residence stimulated the historical romanticism that spurred Ludwig II to build his fanciful castles.*

149 Ludwig II of Bavaria, surrounded by the Wittelsbach dynasty, is shown in this Franz X. Thallmaier painting hanging in Herrenchiemsee Castle.

149

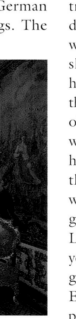

As he could not restore a rule of absolute power, he at least wanted to build a monument to himself. The resulting castles, which he himself designed and conceived, are the product of an unbridled imagination and a taste for the excessive and spectacular that only a king from times past could afford, combined with the period taste for mixing styles of past eras and the king's personal passion for German mythology and exotic settings. The king was not so much a madman as he was an eccentric dreamer, with the power, position and money to satisfy his whims and make his imaginary realm a reality. He loved to dress in the costumes of his legendary heroes, and would depart on nighttime runs on his gilded sleigh, accompanied by his faithful mounted escort. His bizarre behavior accelerated along with his strange deeds, which became increasingly frenzied. All this fed the imagination of the people, who loved his truly kingly excesses and adored him when, tall and handsome, he would come out of nowhere to share his lunch with a woodcutter, or knowledgeably discuss livestock with a shepherd. He was nevertheless quite shy and reserved and hated court occasions. He had very few friends, and the only woman in his life was his cousin Elizabeth, the empress of Austria, known as "Sisi." There was a deep platonic love between the two, who understood each other and shared confidences. Elizabeth was herself a strange character, and like the king was a great aesthete who was obsessed with her beauty. While Ludwig always carried his helmet under his arm so as not to crush his curls, the Austrian empress was obsessed with her weight and constantly engaged in physical activity and diets. Ludwig became engaged to Sisi's younger sister Sophie, perhaps to stop gossip about his relationship with Elizabeth, who was already the empress of Austria, or to put an end to more serious rumors about his homosexuality, but he broke off the engagement only 15 days before the wedding, when the sumptuous coach for the marriage had already been prepared. It is now on display at the Nymphenburg Museum, along with Ludwig's numerous other coaches. But it was neither scandals nor the king's eccentric behavior that finally prompted his ministers to place the king under judicial interdict, but rather his castles.

150-151 Like a magician's spell, the white pinnacles of Neuschwanstein Castle rise out of the early morning mist.

151 top Linderhof Castle, with its pale color and rounded façade, fountains and baroque garden covered with a blanket of snow, almost seems a natural part of the winter landscape.

152 and 153 Schachen Castle, built in the Alps near Garmisch-Partenkirchen, is actually a rustic mountain retreat which Ludwig II wanted for a hunting lodge. It nevertheless deserves to be called a castle because of its interior, which with the king's usual taste for opulence stands in sharp contrast to the simplicity of the exterior and is full of gilt and flourishing touches. Still, to maintain a little of the intimate and cozy atmosphere of a mountain refuge, the monarch furnished several rooms, such as the study (top right), the dining room (center right) and the bedroom (bottom right) in a more simple and sober style.

In order to build and decorate them, Ludwig had gone into debt and had taken out loans of millions of marks from the Bank of Bavaria, and Linderhof and Herrenchiemsee had almost been repossessed by creditors. Yet it was impossible to dissuade the king from what he considered his mission. Citing the pretext that there was a strain of madness on his mother's side of the family (whose brother Otto was epileptic), the Cabinet had the king declared mentally infirm by a team of psychiatrists, whose judgment was then certified by an eminent luminary of the time who never examined the patient personally. Ludwig II was placed under house arrest at the castle of Berg on Starnberg Lake. On July 13, 1886, at the age of 40, overweight and suffering from the effects of tranquilizers and alcohol, he and his physician were found drowned on the banks of the lake that had been the scene of his few happy moments with his beloved cousin.

There are many theories on his death – some say it was a suicide (but why would his doctor have committed suicide too?), or that he tried to flee and was drowned (but he was an excellent swimmer), or that he was murdered because he had become too inconvenient. Whatever the explanation, his death was tragic and senseless. The empress Elizabeth, who was perhaps the only one who understood his soul, made this comment upon Ludwig's death: "The king was not mad; he was only an eccentric who lived in a world

of dreams. They should have treated him more gently..."; Paul Verlaine called him "the only true king of our century." The fruit of his romantic delirium, the castles of Neuschwanstein, Herrenchiemsee and Linderhof, spelled his disaster and his downfall but enriched the future of Bavaria with what are now the greatest tourist attractions not only in Bavaria, but in all of Germany.

NEUSCHWANSTEIN CASTLE

Neuschwanstein was the first of three castles begun in 1869, but was the last to be completed in 1886. Ludwig II did not enjoy it for long. In June of that same year he was deposed and left this castle for his last "escorted" trip to Berg, where he met his end.

This fairy tale castle, which certainly inspired Walt Disney for his cartoons, was based on a childhood dream of the king that prompted him to create a utopian dwelling that would be both a medieval knights' castle and a temple to Wagner.

In his dream, the Swan Knight Lohengrin (in German *Schwan* means swan, which is why this creature recurs as a symbol and name) and the heroes of the Holy Grail spoke to him from the walls of Hohenschwangau Castle, while he eagerly gazed at the hill before it, hoping to capture the fleeting image of a true knight within the crumbling walls of the old medieval castle of Hinterschwangau. Wagner's music deeply touched Ludwig's mind and heart, but part of his attachment to the *maestro* was surely related to their mutual passion-obsession for German mythology. The period's romantic taste for restoring buildings in medieval style merged with his vision of the castle of the Swan Knight Lohengrin as he had seen him on the walls of his father's castle and heard him through the notes of Wagner's music. The astounding result of this dream was a castle so elaborate and perfect that it seems impossible to have been built by human beings using earthly materials, and more likely that divine hands placed it there overnight. Gleaming with a whiteness that stands out even from a distance, it seems to be resting on the treetops. Its five floors are interrupted by a myriad of towers, pinnacled turrets and columns that remind one of the sand castles children build by dribbling wet sand through their fingers.

154 top This photo shows a view from the west side of the castle, with its high octagonal tower and balcony inspired by that of Wartburg Castle.

154 bottom Neuschwanstein's brick entry is a contrast to the white winter world.

155 Neuschwanstein Castle emerges from the mists and clouds like a page in the legend of the Holy Grail.

While the exterior is enchanting, the interior is hypnotic: silks, brocades, lapis lazuli, gilt, bronze majolica, porcelains, marbles, and inlaid and engraved wood are used for all the architectural styles of the past – Gothic, Romanesque and Byzantine – but the sensation is never one of a hodge-podge, but rather the creation of yet another style, recognizable in all his Bavarian castles, which perhaps should be referred to as "Ludwigesque." Neuschwanstein Castle is perhaps the greatest example of 19th-century historicism, when Art Nouveau became the common thread joining the past eras that so greatly influenced the romantic spirit of the times.

What is more, all the king's projects made use of state-of-the-art techniques, with running water and complicated heating and special effects systems. Some stupendous examples include the grotto at Linderhof, the dinner table at Herrenchiemsee that can be raised and lowered through the floor to permit Ludwig to eat in solitude, and the kitchen at Neuschwanstein, ultra-modern for its time. While Maximilian II and Ludwig I built primarily for the public, the castles of Ludwig II were for himself alone.

They were his very life, places where dream and reality merged and history came to life. As he wrote in a letter to Wagner, "in an ideal, monarchic and poetic solitude," he had tried to create an art in harmony with his personal ideal of the universe.

156 The white and blue colors of Bavaria stand out on one of the coats of arms that decorate the windows of the corridor.

156-157 Upon suggestion by Wagner, Ludwig II went to visit Wartburg Castle near Eisenach, the historical setting for the singing contest in Tannhäuser. *The king was so impressed by the castle that he wanted to recreate many of its moods in Neuschwanstein.*

157 top The most beautiful view of the fairy-tale castle is from the Maria Bridge. In the background is the village of Füssen.

*158 left This photo
shows the details of
one of the fanciful
painted friezes that
cover the walls of the
Singers' Room.*

*158-159 and 159 top
Two different angles
of the Singers' Room
show the beauty of the
caisson ceiling,
painted with*

*ornamental motifs
and the signs of the
zodiac, and the string
of brass candelabras
and candle holders
for over 600 candles.*

159 center
The Singers' Room
ends with arcades
of marble columns
that frame
a representation
of the sorcerer
Klingsor's wood.
Above the arcades

are paintings of other
characters in the
Legend of Parsifal,
to whom the room
is dedicated.

159 bottom
Paintings which
portray moments in

the life of the young
Parsifal line the wall
that runs along the
corridor; this one
recounts the episode
in which the young
hero meets and kills
the Red Knight with
his boy's sword.

160 top The saga of Gudrun, Sigurd's widow, who would marry Attila and then assassinate him, is portrayed on the walls of the Waiting Room of the Singers' Room.

160 bottom The central floor of the Throne Room is entirely in mosaic and includes ornamental forms and figures of plants and animals.

161 The two-level Throne Room is in the sumptuous style of a Byzantine church and is modeled after the All Saints' Church in Munich.

162 left top A painting depicting the meeting between Tannhäuser and Venus is shown on the walls of the King's Study.

162 bottom left The symbol of the castle, a white swan, stands on the delicate majolica stove. The word Schwan *is in fact German for swan. The painting above depicts the arrival of Lohengrin.*

162 top right A gilt bronze centrepiece depicting the battle between Siegfried and the Dragon stands on the richly inlaid table in the Dining Hall.

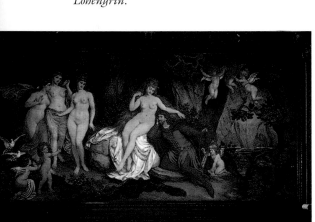

162 bottom right The Living Room is dedicated to the saga of Lohengrin, the Swan Knight, whose deeds charmed the young Ludwig and inspired the creation of the Neuschwanstein Castle. The mural above the sofa recounts the miracle of the Grail.

162-163 The Study is on the third floor, where the king's apartments are located; it is oak-paneled and filled with precious oak furniture. The ceiling is of inlaid wood and the saga of Tannhäuser is painted on the walls.

164 top These canvas paintings depict scenes described in the poetry of Walther van der Vogelweide and Hans Sachs.

164 center As in all his other castles, Ludwig wanted his bed chamber to be especially sumptuous. In contrast with the other rooms in Romanesque style, this room is in late Gothic style. The silver swan ewer over the wash basin is noteworthy. The painting on the walls are dedicated to the poem of Tristan and Isolde.

164 bottom The windows of the Royal Dressing Room look out over the upper courtyard. The violet silk curtains are embroidered with peacocks, a beloved and recurring symbol in Ludwig II's castles.

165 The King's Oratorium is paneled in oak with neo-Gothic ornamentation. The paintings on the walls, the windows and the central triptych represent Saint Louis, Ludwig II's patron saint.

166 top left Murals in the Waiting Room of the royal apartments on the third floor recount the legend of Sigurd, whose saga corresponds to the medieval saga of Siegfried; the version recounted in the Edda is the most ancient collection of Germanic legends in existence. This painting shows Regin as he forges the famous sword Gram for young Sigurd.

166 bottom left The old wise man Gripy foretells young Sigurd's destiny.

166 right Using a sword forged by the dwarf Regin, Sigurd kills Fafnir, who in the guise of a dragon guards the treasure taken from the Nibelungen.

167 This painting in the series painted by W. Hauschild in the Waiting Room of the Singers' Room, portrays King Attila courting Gudrun, Sigurd's widow.

LINDERHOF CASTLE

168 top left
The majolica vases that adorn the eastern flowerbeds are of Nymphenburg make, copied from the originals from Choisy-le-Roi.

168 bottom left
The photo shows one of the two wrought iron nymphs pouring water into the little fountain at the foot of the first terrace on the main parterre in front of the palace.

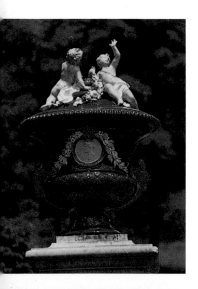

The lovely Graswang Valley where Linderhof stands was a familiar place to the young Crown Prince. His father had already built a hunting lodge there, and when Ludwig II decided to build his Versailles, he originally planned it to be located near his castle at Linderhof. The original 1870 plan underwent many changes, and in the end Ludwig selected Lake Chiemsee for his Versailles project, building Herrenchiemsee Castle on an island in the lake. Linderhof, on the other hand, was designed to be a royal villa, while still keeping the look of Versailles. While it has been compared to the Petit Trianon and is decorated in eighteenth-century style, the castle's construction style is actually the only thing that resembles Versailles. It is the smallest of the three castles, with a more private, if not comfortable, touch. It is the only one of the three which the king saw to its conclusion in 1878, and where he lived most often and for the longest periods of time. The baroque and rococo interior is showy and ostentatious, full of gold and the brilliant blue which was the monarch's favourite color. Swans and peacocks, Ludwig's two favorite animals, are one of its recurrent themes, as at his other castles, but only here does the royal coat of arms of Bavaria appear, both on the façade and in the interior. Despite its majesty and splendor, it was not intended as a state building, but rather as a retreat. While Herrenchiemsee was an ode to Louis XIV and

168 top right Karl von Effner, the director of the Royal Court Gardens, created the artistic design for the gardens in the north and south portions of Linderhof, following the models of the Italian Renaissance. Before the castle, the water from the fountain with its gilt zinc "Flora and Putti," spurts up to 30 m high.

168 bottom right Right behind the palace, a little panoramic temple overlooks a flight of thirty marble steps. At its feet is the wrought-iron fountain of Neptune and a large flowerbed in the form of a Bourbon lily.

169 Linderhof Castle is a small, splendid structure in rococo style that is one of Ludwig II's most elegant creations.

Neuschwanstein a celebration of Wagner and his muses, Linderhof was where the king most clearly expressed his desire to retreat into his fantasy world, where he alone could be the actor and the audience. On the rises of the valley, around the central portion of the royal villa, the king built small structures that became his microscopic fantasy world. The Moorish pavilion and the Moroccan house exude the exotic atmosphere of *The Thousand and One Nights*; in the hunting lodge he could stretch out on animal skins and drink mead to become one of the deities of the Nibelungen; and the Venus Grotto became his Blue Grotto, where he sailed on a gilded, shell-shaped boat. The gardens provide a natural link between the rococo castle and the rugged majesty of the Alpine landscape. Following the example of the Italian Renaissance, he took advantage of the natural features of the terrain to build terraces and waterfalls that allowed the flowerbeds and English gardens to blend into the natural mountain setting.

170 top left
The eastern parterre includes four semirectangular flowerbeds that surround a quatrefoil pond. In the centre is a gilt group of statues entitled "Fame", at the back of the garden is the "Cupid with Dolphins," the central group of another small fountain. A terra-cotta bust of Louis XIV, whom Ludwig II considered an ideal absolute monarch, can be seen in the pavilion that closes off the garden.

170 bottom left
The photo shows one of the innumerable limestone statues that adorn the gardens.

170 top right
The golden statue entitled "Fame" rises above the four-leaf clover-shaped fountain in the western parterre.

170-171 The gilt zinc cupid in the fountain in the eastern parterre seems to be shooting one of his arrows toward Linderhof's east façade.

172 top left
The Moorish pavilion was built by the Berlin architect Karl von Diebitsch for the international Paris Exposition in 1867. Ludwig II bought it for Linderhof's park and had it rebuilt and refurnished, making changes that satisfied his taste for opulence.

172 bottom left
As described for the set in the first act of The Valkyrie, *here is the Hunting Hut, where the king could sink into the mythological world of his heroes in* The Ring of the Nibelungen.

172 right
The magically illuminated area of Venus' Grotto is a reproduction of the inside of Hörselberg, the scene of the first act of Wagner's Tannhäuser, *but the pool illuminated from below draws its inspiration from the Blue Grotto at Capri.*

173 The king of Bavaria's passion for the exotic was completely gratified in the "Thousand and One Nights" atmosphere of the Peacock Room in the Moorish Pavilion. The tails of the enamelled wrought-iron peacocks are studded with hundreds of Bohemian glass stones.

174-175 *A product of the cooperation between the architect Georg Dollmann and the set painter Joseph de la Paix, the model for the Room of Mirrors at Linderhof was the Mirror Room in the Rich Rooms of the Munich Residence.*

175 top *The theme of the Music Room is "The Courtly Festivals," as shown in the large canvas paintings by H. von Pechmann, which depict pastoral and social scenes. The group of stucco putti above the doors are signed by Schmidt.*

175 bottom *Like Herrenchiemsee, Linderhof Castle is richly furnished. The passion for exquisitely made objects and furniture made Ludwig II a true patron of his time for artists and craftsmen from both Germany and abroad. The clock in the photo is Swiss, and the vases are of Meissen porcelain.*

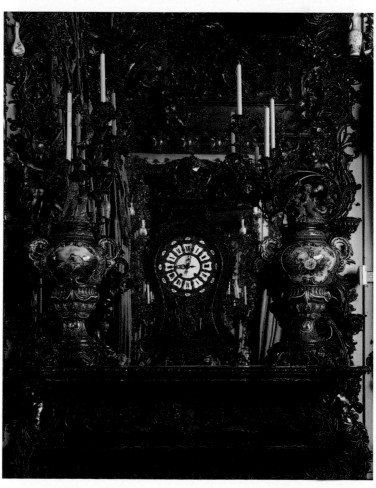

176 Despite the intimate, cozy nature that Ludwig desired for Linderhof, he was unable to resist adding the central halls for court ceremonies, because he thought they were visual proof of an absolute monarchy. In the Audience Room there are in fact clear references to the kingdom of Bavaria in the stucco lunettes and above the throne's baldachin.

176-177 The painting on the left back wall of the Music Room is entitled "Pair of Shepherds at the Fountain," while that on the right is "Shepherd Girls with Bagpipe Player." The musical instrument is an aeolodion, *a combination of a piano and a harmonium. In the centre is a life-size painted Sèvres porcelain peacock.*

177 top The paintings in the East Tapestry Room, like those in the Music Room, were done on rough canvas to give a tapestry effect. The dark door frames are not ebony, but a special black marble from Belgium.

*177 bottom A two-
winged staircase,
a smaller version
of the Ambassadors'
Stairway at
Versailles, leads to the
upper floor. In the
center is a Sèvres vase
which Emperor
Napoleon III is said
to have given to
Ludwig II.*

*178-179
A triumph
of luxury,
Herrenchiemsee
Castle rises out
of a dense wood
on Herreninsel,
the largest island
on Lake Chiemsee.*

*178 top The façade
of the castle can be
seen among the sprays
of water from the
fountains. The castle
is even more
sumptuously
furnished than its
model in France.*

HERRENCHIEMSEE CASTLE

udwig's last great and most ambitious plan was to build a palace that was a replica of Versailles. His dream was to build the royal palace on the site of a modest hunting lodge built by his father near Linderhof, and over a period of five years the architect Georg Dollmann submitted thirteen designs for this "Meicost Ettal" (an anagram for "L'état c'est moi," the motto of Louis XIV). In 1873, based on the last design, which exceeded the original Versailles in size, Ludwig decided to build the palace on the island of Herrenchiemsee on Lake Chiemsee, just a few miles north of Munich. He did not simply copy the French royal palace, but used it as a model for the most typical portions of the structure: the façade, the Ambassadors' Stairway and the king's state apartment. While Versailles is a conglomerate of structures from different periods, Herrenchiemsee was immediately conceived as a unitary system. Based on antique engravings, the Ambassadors' Stairway, which had been demolished in France in 1752, was reconstructed in Ludwig's palace and inserted symmetrically in its two wings.

The façade is larger than that of Versailles, and the Hall of Mirrors and rooms are also larger than the original. The sumptuous baroque bed chamber is different from the original, as is the so-called Small Apartment, a series of rooms not part of the original Versailles.

179 top The Fountain of Latona is a copy of the original at Versailles. The Statue of Latona overlooks the steps, where there are peasants transformed into frogs, with cast lead turtles and amphibians farther down.

179 bottom The great Fountain of Fame, a copy of a fountain in San Idelfonso in Spain, overlooks the north pond. There are

numerous mythological and allegorical figures in cast lead both on the rock and on the edge of the pond.

180 top The oval windows in the frieze area have given the second antechamber its name, the so-called Oeil de Boeuf Room, which is similar to that at Versailles. There is a small bronze statue of Louis XIV in the middle of the room. The paintings on the walls are also dedicated to the Sun King.

180 bottom The great hanging lamp with 108 candles, the centerpiece, the vases and the clocks of the Dining Hall are all in Meissen porcelain. As at Linderhof, due to the king's excessive sense of privacy, the table was lowered down through the floor and sent back up after it was set and prepared.

181 In the Vestibule, divided by columns and pillars, on an extraordinary floor of colored marble, stands a monumental vase of Italian marble, with a pair of peacocks in bronze and translucent enamel. Along with the swan, the peacock was Ludwig II's emblem.

182-183 The Hall of Mirrors, based on a design by Georg Dollmann, is 98 m long, even longer than the one at Versailles. Ludwig II tried to bring the Galerie des Glaçes back to its full splendor by reconstructing furnishings that had been lost for centuries.

These rooms were designed in Louis XV style, in an intentional contrast with the other rooms. The difference in style of the rooms is also due to the fact that the architect changed; Dollmann finished the state rooms and staircase in 1881, and in 1884 Julius Hofman took over to complete the king's rooms. Another significant difference is that at Versailles the rooms have no furniture, as it was destroyed and stolen during the revolution, while Herrenchiemsee is fully furnished.

As he had no models to imitate, all the furniture, porcelain, curtains, bronzes and clocks are original creations of the architects (whose designs the king himself often corrected and

completed), who could indulge in their creative fancies through the skilled artisans of Munich. Seven years of work were necessary on the parade chamber bed alone. Herrenchiemsee Castle should not be considered incomplete; even its original 1870 plan did not provide for any rooms within it other than those which are complete today. In order to celebrate his "absolute monarchy," all Ludwig needed or wanted were the rooms of Versailles. Herrenchiemsee is not a residence, but a monument, a stage for the works of a king who was born too late and could play his role only in fantasy, on an island that could be reached only by boat, far from the banalities of life.

*184 center left
A detail of the
"Astronomy and
History" panel shows
a putto holding up
a medallion with a
portrait of Ludwig
II. This is the only
such panel in the
whole castle, because
the doors were not
completed until after
the king's death.*

*184 top and 184-185
The fireplace in the
Porcelain Room is
of Tunisian marble.
The mirror, the
hanging lamp, the
candelabras, the
vases, the clocks and
the splendid console
tables with delicately
painted putti are all
in precious Meissen
porcelain.*

*184 bottom This
photo shows the
Porcelain Room. The
ceiling is stuccoed,
with a fresco
representing the Spirit
of Art. The precious
desk is made of
rosewood, with
painted Meissen
porcelain surfaces.*

*184 center right
This is another
detail of the room,
showing one of the
paintings with a
mythological theme
that duplicate the
originals hanging in
a room at
Fontainebleau
Palace.*

186 center left
In this painting by Ludwig Behringer (1864), the king is shown on horseback surrounded by his officials.

186 bottom
The halberds of the king's bodyguard are displayed amid the marble busts of the Sun King's marshals. The Bodyguard Room is modeled after the Salle des Gardes, *and along with two other antechambers, the Bed Chamber, the Council Room and the Hall of Mirrors, it is one of the state rooms which were not part of the king's residence.*

186 top The walls in the Hall of Peace are of marbleized colored stucco. A portrait of Louis XIV can be seen above the green Spanish marble fireplace. One of Herrenchiemsee's peculiarities is the oak floors with ornamental rosewood marquetry.

186 center right
The monumental staircase is modeled after the Ambassadors' Stairway at Versailles, which was demolished in 1752. The colored marble and marbleized stucco walls are a faithful duplication of the original, while the stairway at Versailles did not have the glass ceiling. The stucco figures in the niches were to have been of Vipiteno marble. Every time Ludwig came to the castle, the stairway was transformed into a carpet of flowers.

187 The Small Gallery ends the series of rooms that make up the royal apartments. The rooms are based on the Small Gallery at Versailles, which no longer exists. There are allegorical stucco figures in the niches and above the main cornice.

188 center Louis XIV was known for using his bed chamber for the first and last audiences of the day. The sumptuous State Room, which Ludwig II never used, is Herrenchiemsee at its most opulent.

188 bottom The overflowing Blue Room is totally covered with relief decorations of gilt birds in iridescent colours. Mirrors are inserted into the panels so that the room seems to repeat itself endlessly.

188-189 Ludwig II's favourite color, blue, is used for the baldachin, the curtains and the silk and velvet coverings inlaid with gold in the King's Bed Chamber. The headboard of the sumptuous inlaid wood bed depicts the sun that symbolized Louis XIV. A blue ball used to illuminate the room at night stands on a gilt stand with beautiful inlay work.

188 top Luxury abounds in the King's Study as well, which is furnished with rare and priceless objects which are masterpieces of artistic craftsmanship. The great roll-top desk is a copy of the famous Bureau du Roi on display at the Louvre. The spectacular silver and gilt bronze Elephant Clock stands on one console table along with two other elaborate astronomical clocks.

SUMPTUOUS RESIDENCES FOR BAVARIAN NOBLES

190 top The photo shows the Orangerie of the Kempten Residence in this capital of the Bavarian Allgaü. The Residence complex is one of the earliest examples of baroque architecture. The old residence of the abbot princes was designed by Beer in 1651. Its interior clearly shows the transition from baroque decoration to rococo style.

190 bottom The Cathedral and the church tower of St. Lorenz, the largest baroque church in Germany, overlook the artistic gardens in the complex of ecclesiastical buildings that includes the Kempten Residence. The church was built between 1652 and 1666 by M. Beer and J. Serro.

190-191 Neuburg Castle is a Renaissance work which overlooks this city on the Danube. During the 16th century, the Palatine Count Ottheinrich ordered the building of a three-winged structure in decorative Renaissance style on the site of a residential dwelling of the previous century.

As the dark years of the Middle Ages drew to a close, albeit much more slowly than in southern Europe, the scent of the Renaissance managed to permeate even Germany. Bavaria, with a spirit more akin to southern Europe than to the rest of the country, absorbed it quickly. Its cramped fortresses made it impossible to live comfortably, and the need for comfortable quarters suitable for entertaining had grown so rapidly that princes and nobles found it impossible to live in those damp old fortifications, which by now had become useless as a means of defense against more modern techniques of war. The Thirty Years' War interrupted the construction of residences more in line with aristocratic needs, but the 17th century marked the advent of residential castles and dwellings. The rivalry among the various nobles families, among the families of bishop princes, and between bishops and the nobility exploded in a race to see who could build the most sumptuous, ostentatious dwelling. The architectural style in fashion in Italy – opulent, theatrical and fanciful – was the perfect response to the ferment that was enlivening the souls of Bavarian nobles. Counts, dukes and bishop princes began to build airy palaces (in total contrast to the dark, cramped rooms of defensive fortresses) in or near the cities, with entire suites of rooms and richly furnished salons surrounded by fairy-tale parks with enchanting additional structures, such as *orangeries*, pavilions and little temples. Baroque taste spread in all new buildings (and in most of the old ones too), followed by a lighter, more airy and even more whimsical rococo. Thus, residential castles appeared at the dawn of the modern era, united by their style of magnificent showiness, but each with the personal imprint of those who wanted to leave a permanent mark of their power and fame.

191 top Located among the forests and vineyards of Steigerwald, the splendid baroque palace of Pommersfelden is entirely decorated with elaborate frescoes. Its elegant architecture is still almost completely intact. The palace was built around the same time as the Würzburg Residence and the Neue Residence (New Residence) of Bamberg.

THE MUNICH RESIDENCE

The superb Residence stands on the central Max Josef Platz, where it was built on order of Maximilian I and his son Ludwig I. Once the family home of the Wittelsbach family, it is now one of the most splendid museums of the world. When the Swedes conquered Munich during the Thirty Years' War, King Gustav Adolf, admiring the Residence, is said to have murmured, "If only it had wheels!" The Swedes not only did not carry it off, but their king's admiration for the splendid royal palace saved it from serious damage. Today, the Residence is considered one of the most beautiful Renaissance palaces in Europe, although the buildings that crowd around the seven inner courtyards date from the 16th to 19th centuries and are a mixture of all the different styles that alternated during those centuries: Renaissance, baroque, rococo and neoclassical. After the bombardments of the Second World War, the complex had to be almost entirely rebuilt, but most of its sumptuous furnishings were saved and have now been returned to their original positions in the rooms. The sections open to the public constitute the *Residenzmuseum*. The *Alte Residenz*, with its entrance on Residenzstrasse, contains the main court sectors, including the splendid *Altes Residenztheater*, the rococo jewel of architect François de Cuvilliés. The *Königsbau*, with its Renaissance façade built in imitation of the Palazzo Pitti, was commissioned by Ludwig I and now serves as the entry to the Residenzmuseum.

192 top The Residenz, the Wittelsbach family's residential palace, is considered one of the most beautiful Renaissance palaces in Europe, even though the buildings that stand around seven inner courtyards are a combination of Renaissance, rococo and neoclassical styles. The façade on Max Joseph Platz was built between 1826 and 1833 by Leo von Kleuze, using the Palazzo Pitti and the Palazzo Rucellai as models.

192 center Between 1581 and 1586, Duke Wilhelm V ordered the building of the Grottenhof, a structure with four wings and a richly decorated inner garden. Despite changes made, this "garden of secret delights" still exudes the joyous spirit of the Renaissance gardens of southern Europe.

192 bottom The Cave Room, covered in volcanic lava studded with shells, crystals and coloured rocks, opens onto the Grottenhof.

192-193 The Brunnenhof, or Court of Fountains, is a long octagon which was created between 1612 and 1616 by joining new buildings to already existing sections. The Wittelsbach Fountain, which stands in the center, honors the first duke of the dynasty, Count Otto von Wittelsbach, whose bronze statue is upheld by the four elements and the four river deities.

193 top This photo shows the south façade of the Residence, with the statue of Max Joseph Denkmal in the foreground. Unfortunately, what we see of the Residenz today is mostly a faithful reconstruction: the bombardments of 1945 destroyed this masterpiece of five centuries of Bavarian history in just a few hours.

193

The more recent north wing – built between 1837 and 1842 and known as the *Festsaalbau* – contains the *Herculessaal*, now a concert hall. The *Hofgarten*, a magnificent courtyard garden, was embellished during the reign of Maximilian I with porticoes and a little round temple with an interesting frescoed cupola.

The oldest portions of the palace are the *Grottenhof*, built under Wilhelm V in 1585 as a "garden of secret pleasures," and the *Antiquarium* (ordered by Albrecht V in 1568 to hold the Wittelsbach collection of antiquities), the work of Jacopo Strada and the most important Renaissance period secular construction north of the Alps. The most spectacular and extravagant rooms of the royal palace are on the upper floor. The *Reiches Zimmer* represent another splendid piece of German rococo by François de Cuvilliés, decorated with stucco work by Johann Baptist Zimmermann. They lead to the Secret Chapel, a niche gleaming with gilt and lapis lazuli decorations, with floors and walls covered with mosaics of marble and colored stone.

196-197 The most important and, at 66 m long, the largest secular Renaissance room north of the Alps, the Antiquarium was created by Jacopo Strada and Simon Zwitzel under Duke Albrecht V between 1568 and 1571 for the dukes' collection of antiquities.

SCHLEISSHEIM CASTLE

199 The scagliola decorations and marbleized stucco work give the New Castle's chapel an embroidered effect. The gilt stucco work on the ceiling frames the opening to an upper level.

Schleissheim Castle is located in Oberschleissheim, about 20 miles from central Munich. This splendid baroque complex consists of two palaces built one in front of the other. The first, known as the Old Castle, was begun in 1597 as a modest residence for Duke Wilhelm V, based on a design by Heinrich Schön. In 1616 his son, Duke Maximilian I, took it over, and the "refuge" grew into an Italian Renaissance-style palace. Unfortunately, today's structure is only a pale shadow of what it was before the bombardments of World War II destroyed it. Only the outside has been reconstructed, but inside you can still admire an interesting exhibit of "domestic" religious objects like Nativity cradles, representations of the Passion and Easter eggs from eastern Europe.

The Old Castle is obscured by the grandiose New Castle. As early as 1693, the Elector Maximilian II Emanuel decided to expand the existing residence. The work was first directed by Enrico Zuccalli. The War of Spanish Succession put a stop to work until 1719, and Joseph Effner (a Bavarian architect who had studied in France) was commissioned to continue with the project following new plans. Effner hired great names in the architecture of the time, including François de Cuvillés, Johann Baptist Zimmermann and Cosmas Damian Asam, who became involved in a frenetic whirl of creativity. The New Castle was completed between 1847 and 1848, but the connection to the Old Castle which was to have completed the whole structure was never finished. Without counting the galleries and side pavilions, the main building's façade alone measures fully 1082ft (330 m) in length and is covered with precious late baroque ornamentation.

From the opulent ground floor, completely decorated in stucco work and frescoes and dotted with red marble columns, a magnificent staircase leads to the first floor where the *Barockgalerie* contains the most important collection of baroque paintings in Germany.

Even surrounded by all this magnificent baroque art, the *Grosser Saal* still takes the breath away, with a dazzling splendour only slightly dimmed by the superb paintings of Jacopo Amigoni that cover the ceiling with scenes from the history of the Wittelsbach family. The wonderful summer concerts of Schleissheim take place in this hall.

The elegant, French-style gardens, which are absolutely idyllic and a perfect setting for the buildings, are adorned by arabesques of a variety of flowers and colored rocks, geometrical hedges and canals with waterfalls. They were embellished by Joseph Effner and Dominique Girard in 1715. Within them rises *Gartenschloss* Lustheim (the Garden Palace), a lovely little castle built as a wedding gift for Maria Antonia, the wife of the prince. It was designed by Zuccalli as well. Its light, delicately decorated rooms contain one of the most beautiful collections of porcelain in Europe, the Meissner-Porzellansammlung, which blends in superbly with the baroque interior.

200 The large
Tapestry Room is
covered with precious
silk tapestries
depicting battle
scenes. The wooden
furniture is carved
and gilded, and the
porcelain objects
are of Nymphenburg
make.

201 Following the Sun
King's custom of
holding his first and
last audiences of the
day in the bed
chamber, a State Bed
Chamber was also
prepared at
Schleissheim, with an
alcove covered in silk
and velvet interwoven
with gold thread.

202-203 The elegant profile of the New Castle stands out against the clear sky of Bavaria. Rich furnishings and the Art Gallery, with works from the 16th to 18th centuries, give an idea of 18th-century court life.

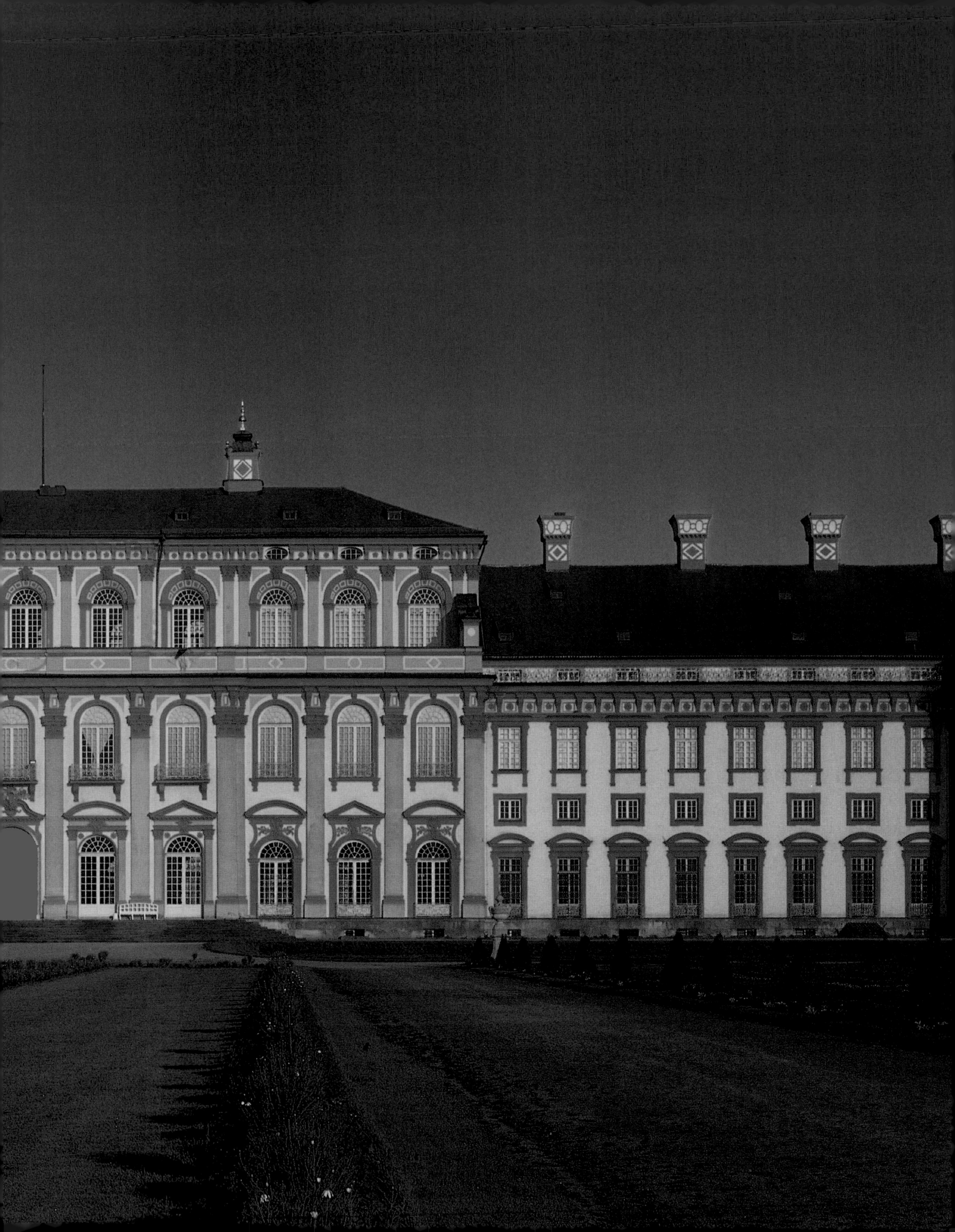

NYMPHENBURG CASTLE

Magnificent Nymphenburg Castle at the gates of Munich was the summer residence of Bavarian royalty until 1918. The spacious complex, whose most noteworthy feature is the large group of separate buildings connected by an absolute symmetry of line, is the result of various phases of work. Its development over the centuries is the result of the creativity of four generations of Wittelsbachs. The oldest part of the palace, the five-story central pavilion, was built in 1662 by Prince Ferdinand Maria, when his wife, Adelaide of Savoy, gave birth to his heir after 10 years of hopes in vain. The sumptuous edifice was designed by the Italian architect Agostino Barelli. Subsequently, the central portion of the palace and the magnificent double stairway at the entrance were designed by Enrico Zuccalli. Adelaide's son Max Emanuel inherited the castle, and in 1704, with the aid of Joseph Effner, he added the final touches that give the palace its present-day appearance: two Italian-style side villas, joined to the two wings of the main building, the court stables, the waterfall in the park, and the *Badenburg*, *Pagodenburg* and *Magdalenenklause* pavilions. During the reign of Karl Albrecht VII, the little villas for court nobles were built around the artificial lake in the courtyard facing the palace; since 1747 they have housed the famous Nymphenburg Porcelain Factory. In the park is the stupendous *Amalienburg*, a hunting lodge the Emperor ordered in honor of his wife Amalia.

204 top This photo shows a detail of the façade of the central pavilion at Nymphenburg, remodeled by the Elector Max Emanuel using late French baroque ornamental motifs.

204 bottom The photo is a view of the Rondell Bauten. Effner's design enlarged the palace by adding a vast semicircular cour d'honneur *in front of the main building. It was designed to include the Elector's stables and apartments for officials. Cuvilliés was responsible for executing the design, working under Karl Albrecht.*

204-205 The oldest part of Nymphenburg Castle is the central pavilion with its five floors. The old summer home had been built in 1664 by Adelaide of Savoy, the wife of the Elector Ferdinand Maria. The romantic princess dedicated the palace to the goddess Flora as "a place for recreation and pastoral pleasures."

205 top *The* Magdalenenklause *pavilion consists of false ruins with feigned poverty meant to imitate the cells of hermits. Built in the middle of the park, it represents a desire to take refuge in solitude and escape formal court life.*

François de Cuvilliés, with the help of stucco work by Johann Baptist Zimmermann and wood decorations by Joachim Dietrich, ensured that even the splendor of the castle's Hall of Mirrors would pale in comparison with the interior of *Amalienburg*.

Maximilian Joseph III further embellished the palace, changing and redecorating many rooms. He also made use of the genius of Zimmermann and the elderly Cuvilliés, and gave the *Steinerner Saal* (Marble Hall) that sumptuous atmosphere that still enchants the spectators who come to summer concerts at Nymphenburg.

Another fascinating room is the extraordinary Gallery of Beauties, a collection of thirty-six portraits of the most beau-

tiful women of the period, painted by Joseph Stieler on commission by Ludwig I. Like his son and grandson, Ludwig I had great aesthetic taste, and like his grandson, his love of beauty caused him to lose his realm.

While Ludwig II's battles with his Cabinet were due to his castles, Ludwig I's problems in governing were due to the beauties of his gallery. Lola Montez, an adventuress of common origins, may not have been the most beautiful of the women in the portraits, but she was certainly the most intelligent. She had great political and personal influence over the king, whose government forced him to exile her. Thereafter, Ludwig I fell into a deep depression and abdicated in 1848.

208 top During his renovation work on the park near Badenburg in 1769, the landscape architect Friedrich Ludwig von Sckell created the Badenburgsee, a little lake with a small Greek-style temple.

208 center Badenburg, unique among its kind, was built by Effner as a small bathing pavilion for Max Emanuel. The photo shows the Banquet Room, with decorations inspired mostly by

agriculture and water. The frescoes are by Jacopo Amigoni, the only ones in Nymphenburg by this Italian artist, who was employed primarily for the frescoes on the ceiling of Schleissheim Castle.

208 bottom Badenburg consists of three large rooms: the Banquet Room, the Bed Chamber and the Bathing Room, which is actually a small but sumptuous swimming pool on two levels of the structure.

208-209 Created as a little hunting lodge for the Elector Amalia between 1734 and 1739, elegant Amalienburg is another splendid project by Cuvilliés. Built in the landscaped garden like the other pavilions, its interior decoration is important due to the artistic effect created by the suite of rooms and the profuse ornamentation.

209 top left The Mirror Room at Amalienburg is the culmination of the interior decoration within Nymphenburg. Zimmermann did the stucco work, which has a silvery hue that gives a rare lightness to such elaborate and dense ornamentation. The exquisite scheme of silver and blue repeats itself endlessly in the refined play of mirrors.

209 top right The kitchen at Amalienburg, is artistically decorated as well: the walls are all entirely covered with white and blue or brightly colored Dutch tiles which form magnificent vases of flowers or depict scenes of daily life in China.

210-211 The park of the Castle was significantly expanded in the 18th century following the fashion of French-style gardens. During the next century, the park was again remodeled according to the tenets of the English-style.

210 and 211 top left The Marstallmuseum building, where a superb collection of gala coaches from the Wittelsbach family is housed, is located south of the Nymphenburg complex. Some of its most precious pieces include the coaches and sleighs of Ludwig II, with the spectacular coach the king had built for his marriage to Sophie, Sisi's sister; the marriage was called off and the coach was never used.

211 top right In the restful atmosphere of the Pagodenburg Living Room, the white and blue color scheme of the Dutch tiles that cover the walls is repeated on the floor, in the paintings on the ceiling and in the furniture.

211 center right The pavilions of the princely summer residence were intended to provide a place of seclusion from incessant court activities, as well as exotic atmospheres that would give the impression of being in distant lands. On the outside, the Pagodenburg is simple, almost austere, but its interior is richly furnished for exclusive parties and exudes an atmosphere of the far-off Orient.

211 bottom right The three rooms on the upper floor of the Pagodenburg are decorated with Oriental motifs. This is one of the Chinese Rooms, with black lacquered panels and painted silk and rice paper.

ANSBACH CASTLE

Ansbach, a pearl of baroque and rococo style, is the capital of Rangau, the central region of Franconia, on the border of the Land of Baden-Württemberg. The city grew up within the Benedictine monastery founded by St. Gumbert in 748. In 1381, the city was taken over by the Burgraves of Nuremberg, the Hohenzollern family, who used it to extend the dominion of Ansbach-Bayreuth. A little later, it was chosen as the residence of one of the dynastic branches, and a splendid fortress on

water was built there as the residence of the Von Brandeburg-Ansbach Margraves. The palace then underwent many renovations, until it was decided to build an entirely new residence.

In 1705 the architect Gabriel de Gabrieli (a native of Rovereto, Italy) was hired, but ten years later he left the job, which was continued by Leopoldo Retti of Como. The Margrave died, and the task of completing the ambitious work passed on to his widow. She expanded the original plan and created the park, the *Hofgarten* (Court Garden), where in memory of her husband she planted two rows of linden trees in the form of a cross. The magnificent Orangerie is located at the entrance to the gardens; today it is used as a concert hall. It was built in 1726 based on the model of two French architectural masterpieces: the side facing the gardens was inspired by the Grand Trianon at Versailles, while the other side was based on the Louvre. The gardens were also the scene of a dark and strange story, with a small stone marker showing the spot where, in 1883, Kaspar Hauser, a mysterious foundling inexplicably adopted by a rich English lord, was beaten to death for no apparent reason. The interior is in early rococo style, with delicate forms and colors. The *Festsaal* is extremely beautiful, embellished with stucco work and frescoes by Diego and Carlo Carlone, as are the brilliant *Spiegelkabinett* (Hall of Mirrors) and the priceless *Gekachelter Saal*, covered with 2800 ceramic tiles from Ansbach.

212 top The elegant façade of the Ansbach Residence, crowned by a balustrade with statues and gracefully dotted with pillars, is the work of Gabriel de Gabrieli and Leopoldo Retti.

212 bottom Every important noble residence of the period had to have an opulent Hall of Mirrors. The Spiegelkabinett of the Ansbach Residence was designed by J.C. Wezler in 1739, and in accordance with the baroque taste of the time is full of gilt and porcelain.

212-213 The Court Gardens lie to the southwest of the Residen. At the entrance is the great Orangerie, based on the Grand Trianon of Versailles. The building, more than 100 m long, is now used as a concert hall.

213 top One of the most noteworthy rooms in the Residence is the Party Room, designed in 1737 by Leopold Retti. Its refined stucco work was done by one of the most important stucco artists of the time, Diego Carlone.

The 820-ft (250-m) ceiling of the two-story room features an allegorical fresco by Carlo Carlone adulating the Margrave Carl Wilhelm Friederich, in the "good government" style thematized throughout art history.

214 top In the center of the large square, dominating the main entrance to the Residence, is the Franconia Fountain, with statues of great men of the region, including the sculptor Tilman Riemenschneider (right) and Matthias Grünewald, a painter, architect and hydraulic engineer (left).

THE WÜRZBURG RESIDENCE

214-215
The magnificent
Residence complex
consists of a central
structure and two
side wings. A
masterpiece
of German Baroque,
the lordly residence
was built between
1719 and 1744 based
on a design by
Balthasar Neumann,
with the assistance of
Lukas von
Hildebrandt from
Vienna and M. V.
Welsch from Mainz.

Würzburg is a lovely city located in a splendid position on the Main River, surrounded by hills covered with vineyards that reach the city center. Its elegant eighteenth-century appearance survived the destruction of the Second World War, and its pearl is the Residence, the most beautiful baroque castle in all of Germany, located in the eastern portion of the city. In 1720 the new bishop prince, Johann Philipp von Schönborn, decided that it was time to build a palace which was larger and more modern than the massive fortress of Marienberg, perched on the hill. By this time, it was no longer necessary to live in a fortified castle, and after the Thirty Years' War the city was experiencing a period of economic growth and had a great desire to rebuild and renovate. The Schönborns were a rich and influential family which had produced at least twelve bishops, all with a passion for building and the gift of good taste. Johann Philipp demonstrated incredible far-sightedness in selecting Balthasar Neumann as his chief architect. This young man who built cannon and bells and until then had designed only his own home, became one of the greatest German architects of his time, and thanks to his genius, the bishop prince realized his dream of building a "castle to excel all other castles," a grandiose sandstone building soaring up splendidly from its own square. A half a century later, Napoleon called it the most beautiful residence in Europe.

215 top This
portrait of Balthasar
Neumann hangs
in the Main and
Franconia Museum
in the Marienberg
fortress. In the
background one can
see his masterpiece,
the Residence. The
Bohemian architect
is shown in armor,
resting on a cannon,
as he was a gunner
in the Episcopal
artillery: architecture
was only a hobby.

215 bottom
The insignia
of the prince-bishop,
surrounded by
allegorical sandstone
statues, can be seen
above the main
entrance.

216 top June concerts have been held in the palace and park behind it since 1922 as part of the annual Festival dedicated to Mozart.

216-217 The garden side of one of the wings of the Residence is shown here. As Johann Philipp von Schönborn wanted to move from the uncomfortable, cold Marienberg as soon as possible, work on the new castle proceeded with all due haste: more than 100 workers labored continuously in the main building yards.

217 Like every princely residence of the period, the court gardens were extremely important. Inspired by French baroque gardens, they surround the palace with colorful flowerbeds dotted with oddly-shaped bushes. Statues of chubby putti and mythological figures created by the court sculptor Peter Wagner are scattered throughout the park.

218-219 The self-supporting vault, which is revealed only as one climbs the three flights of stairs, is totally decorated with world-famous frescoes by Tiepolo. The solidity of this masterpiece of static architecture was definitively tested during the bombardment of 1945, when most of the Residence was destroyed.

Two of Neumann's creations are visible as you enter the vestibule: the staircase and the ceiling, true miracles of static engineering. The ceiling 18 by 32 m, covers the entire area of the grand staircase without the support of a single pillar. Everyone was sure it would collapse before completion, and one of Neumann's rival architects declared that he would hang himself from the ceiling if it held up. Irritated, Neumann asked the bishop prince to test the structure by firing cannon salvoes under it. No test was ever performed, but during the bombardment of 1945, when most of the Residence was destroyed, the staircase and the ceiling survived. The ceiling is also famous for being the largest existing fresco in the world. It is the work of a genius of Italian painting, Gian Battista Tiepolo, who like many other Italian artists of the period was paid handsomely to bring the fashionable style of Italy to Germany. The artist, assisted by his two sons, took three years to complete the ceiling and the other frescoes in the Residence.

Another Italian artist, Antonio Bossi, is responsible for the incredible stucco work in the *Weisser Hall* (the White Hall). Already at the edge of madness, Bossi unleashed his imagination in original, unique forms before succumbing permanently to his psychosis. The whiteness of this hall provides a rest for the eyes before entering the explosion of colours and gilt in the Imperial Hall. Here Bossi's stucco details provide a framework for the strange optical effects that Tiepolo created in his frescoes. Neumann's triumphs continue in the Court Chapel as well, a burst of spiral-shaped columns, curving balconies and intersecting arches, also embellished by Tiepolo's paintings. The Residence's treasures do not lie only in its halls, but in its immense cellars as well, where some of the finest wines of Franconia are produced and aged.

The splendid Baroque Gardens, with the Residence providing the background, are a yearly summer setting for a series of concerts dedicated to Mozart, as well as a lively Wine Festival featuring wine produced in its cellars.

220 left The photo shows the Audience Room with its great tapestries. An extremely elegant majolica stove can be seen in the corner.

220 top right The Hall of Mirrors was totally destroyed during the Second World War, but thanks to the painstaking work of highly specialized artists, it was totally restored.

220 bottom right The Green Room is entirely covered in exquisite lacquered rococo panels.

221 Antonio Bossi did the stucco work for the Residence Chapel, a burst of columns, arches and gilt. The paintings on the altar of this small, opulent baroque church are by Tiepolo.

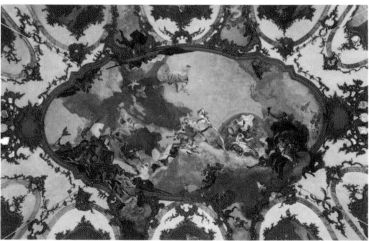

222 and 222-223
The artistic partnership between Bossi and Tiepolo created an unusual freedom of expression in the Emperor's Room. The stucco artist has allowed frescoes to appear from behind the folds of a curtain, as if on a stage. On the edges, a leg, a head, or a cloud peeps out from the frame, blurring the distinction between two- and three-dimensionality. The frescoes on the sides of the walls and on the ceiling show various scenes, including (bottom left) the marriage of Frederick Barbarossa to Beatrice of Burgundy, and (in the picture at right) the bishop of Würzburg and the duke of Franconia discussing "good government."

GIO. BTTA. TIEPO

223 top
The Antechamber
of the Emperor's
Room, decorated
with bizarre
ornamentation and
sinuous rococo motifs
in white stucco, was
Antonio Bossi's last
work before he totally
succumbed to madness.
The room was
prepared just
in time for a visit
by Empress Maria
Theresa in 1745.

224-225 *The Garden Room, which opens out on ground level, was a "buffer zone" used for serving refreshments or as a place for musicians. Bossi hid mirrors within his stucco work that shine with a magical, mysterious light in the glow of the candles. The frescoes by Johann Zick show the contrast between rigid court formality and utopian rustic abandon. The main painting (bottom left) shows the "Banquet of the Gods."*

THE NEUE RESIDENCE OF BAMBERG

*L*ike Rome, Bamberg bears the architectural mark of the secular power of the Church. On the hill that dominates the city center, the same square holds two opposing examples of religious power: the cathedral, the house of God, with its solid and austere Gothic appearance and its four spires that seem to pierce the sky, represents the Church's power of guidance and salvation, while on the opposite side of the square, between the cathedral and the city, stands the sumptuous Residence, the home of the bishop, symbol of the vanity and temporal power of the clergy. The Renaissance-style west wing was completed between 1605 and 1611 by the city of Nuremberg's architect, Jakob Wolff the Elder, by order of the bishop prince Johann Philipp von Gebsattel. The two baroque wings facing the cathedral were commissioned by the man described as "one of the most gifted and impulsive princes who ever occupied the episcopal seat of Bamberg," the elector of Mainz, Lothar Franz von Schönborn (1693-1729). During the early years of his election, he had to restrain his mania for expanding and enriching his residence to meet the fashion of the time, because the cathedral Chapter had imposed a condition that formally forbade him from squandering finances in opulent buildings or improvements on already existing residences. When his insistent pressure finally resulted in a pontifical decree freeing him from this constraint, he immediately commissioned his architect, Leonhard Dientzenhofer, to design a new Residence, which in six years became the building we can admire today. Inside the Neue Residenz is the State Library, with an exceptional collection of 4500 manuscripts dating as far back as the 5th century, 3400 incunabula and 70,000 drawings. The guided visit leads through the Grand Halls, full of magnificent furniture, porcelains and carpets, and the Imperial Hall, a large room which in reality has a rather low ceiling, but which uses perspective frescoes with optical illusions – by the court painter Melchior Steidl – to give an impression of openness and space. Enclosed within the wings of the Residence is the *Rosegarten* (the Rose Garden), graced by the fragrance of a thousand varieties of roses, with bold statues by Ferdinand Tietz eternally overlooking the old roofs of the city below.

*227 top right Finely
painted Oriental-style
decorations adorn the
wooden panels in the
Chinese Room in the
Neue Residence.*

*227 bottom right
The Imperial Hall
is the center of the
Grand Halls; it is
a large, rather low
room in which the
court painter Melchior
Steidl used perspective
frescoes to make the
ceiling appear higher.*

THE BAYREUTH HERMITAGE

228 left One of the great attractions of the Hermitage is the garden, considered one of the most beautiful English gardens in Germany. The paths and colorful parterres are interrupted by extravagant fountains. There is also an artificial grotto and fake ruins, once used as a theater.

Bayreuth is a city with medieval roots, although the architecture of the Margravine Wilhelmine left its elegant baroque imprint. The city is world famous for its astounding *Markgräfliches Opernhaus* (the margravine's most beautiful gift to the city) and the Wagner Festival, and is scattered with splendid palaces and works of art, which make it one of the most attractive cities in northern Bavaria. The city center has two castles: the Renaissance-style *Altes Schloss* (16th-17th century) and the sumptuous *Neues Schloss*, which is also touched by the creative hand of the margravine's, but the most representative and romantic castle is located outside the city gates, among wheat fields and woodlands.

The Hermitage was built around the middle of the 18th century by the margravine Georg Wilhelm, as an ascetic refuge from his luxurious court, and was given to Wilhelmine by her husband Friederich, the successor to the throne of Bayreuth.

The Prussian princess was an emancipated, intelligent and energetic woman who was a talented painter, musician and writer. The daughter of Friederich Wilhelm I and favorite sister of Fredrick the Great, she could have become the future queen of England, but a mistaken political move by her father took her to Bayreuth, a provincial and colorless city in Franconia. Nevertheless, the young Wilhelmine was not to be outdone, and decided to transform Bayreuth into a brilliant center for the arts, using the best artists and artisans of the time. The spartan Hermitage was transformed into a splendid summer residence, in which the margravine took refuge with her artist friends and penned her memories in emotional writings that became a brilliant piece of literature. The rococo palace became the background for the gardens on which the Margrave focused her creative attention. The gardens of the Hermitage were already famous in Bavaria for their design, which was *avant-garde* for the time.

Inspired by the theatrical effect produced by the position of the gardens, Wilhelmine made changes that satisfied her taste for the *mise-en-scène*. She brought in many statues and artificial ruins, among the most spectacular of which were the ruins of the theater. Wilhelmine herself and her friend Voltaire appeared on the stage in *Bajazet*, a tragedy by the French playwright Racine.

The *Neues Schloss* confirms the sensation that the buildings are almost a theatrical backdrop for the gardens.

In the center of the two curved side wings is the isolated *Sonnentempel* (the Sun Temple). Its extravagant covering of fragments of colored glass and blue and green rocks is absolutely unique. Complementing the dazzling effect are the golden Apollo statues on the cupola of the temple, with a team of four horses pulling the sun coach, symbol of absolute power in the style of Louis XIV of France

228 right The Sun Temple is on the Hermitage's formal side, from which the Orangerie extends in two semicircular wings. The outside walls of the complex are covered with fragments of pebbles and colored rocks, an unusual technique rarely used for exteriors.

228-229 The Hermitage's Old Castle was built by the Margrave Georg Wilhelm. The four-winged structure was then presented to the Margrave Wilhelmine, who added two side wings and transformed the interior.

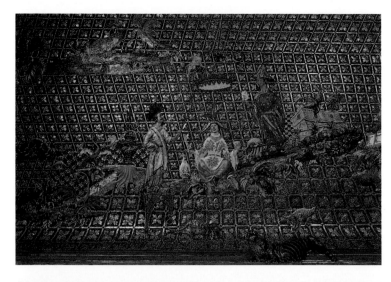

229 top The sumptuous yet intimate Japanese Room at the Hermitage has enamel relief work, some of which, the gift of Friederick the Great, comes from the Far East. Other enamel work was based on ideas by the Margravine Wilhelmine and completed with her assistance. This photo shows a detail of the ceiling with its unusual Oriental motifs.

230 top left The original furnishings still stand in the Gothic-style chapel. The altar by Junker, is one of the most precious pictorial works of the period.

230 top right The Bed Chamber is in true neoclassical style, decorated with panelling and a pink silk canopy embroidered with pure gold thread.

JOHANNISBURG CASTLE IN ASCHAFFENBURG

The city of Aschaffenburg stands on the Main River in Spessart, the far western corner of Bavaria.

In contrast to the gentle natural landscape, the city is a row of massive stone façades along the river, the most imposing of which is Schloss Johannisburg, a legacy of the immense secular power wielded by the prince-bishops of Mainz, who reigned from the 10th to the early 19th centuries. Before being appointed arch prince-bishops and elector of Mainz, Johann Schweikhard von Kronberg had to swear to restore the ruins of the castle of Aschaffenburg, which had been destroyed by the Margrave of Kulmbach. The Renaissance palace, the archbishop's second residence, was built between 1604 and 1614 on a design by Georg Riedinger. A child of his time, the elector yearned for a *grandeur* that would befit his position as an elector of the Holy Roman Empire.

He thus created an imposing red sandstone palace, consisting of four wings with a massive tower at each corner, spending the equivalent of forty-five million marks.

The Johannisburg is one of the most important works of the German Renaissance, as well as one of the largest castles in Germany built at one time based on a single design, and is a grandiose introduction to the architecture of state castles typical of the modern era.

230-231 A witness to the immense secular power of the prince-bishops of Mainz, who ruled here from the 10th to the 19th centuries, Johannisburg Castle's imposing façade is reflected in the Main River.

231 top Titus' Arch is depicted in one of the pieces in the collection of little cork models on display at Johannisburg Castle.

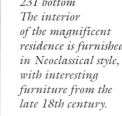

231 bottom The interior of the magnificent residence is furnished in Neoclassical style, with interesting furniture from the late 18th century.

SCHLOSS *EHRENBURG*

232 top left
The picture is a view of one of the two side pavilions, with the façade adorned by architectural balconies.

232 top right The main entrance to Ehrenburg opens to form the Court of Honour on the broad square. The three segments that make it up date back to

the late 17th-century baroque structure, but the façade was redone in neo-Gothic English style in the early 19th century.

232-233
The marvelous Party Room, which dates back to the time of Duke Albrecht, is almost entirely covered with extraordinary stucco

decorations by Carlo Domenico and Bartolomeo Lucchese. It is known as the Hall of Giants due to the twenty-eight massive male caryatid figures who appear to hold up the ceiling. Each one holds a candelabra in an outstretched arm, with the other arm bent above his head to support the ceiling.

Coburg is the capital of Coburgerland, located among the hills of upper Franconia and the last remnants of the Thuringian Forest. Its beautiful historic downtown area still exudes that aristocratic elegance that characterized it until the last century. On the broad Schlossplatz, where fine summer concerts are held among the splendid flowerbeds, is Schloss Ehrenburg, the ducal palace and residence of the Saxe-Coburg-Gotha family until 1920. The powerful family was allied with royal families all over Europe. Albert, the beloved prince consort of Queen Victoria of England, whose descendants still hold the British throne, was descended from this family. Queen Victoria herself, who was a frequent guest at Ehrenburg, was responsible for introducing something which was at the time an absolute luxury and novelty, and which now, among the astonishing riches of the residence, is one of the most popular curiosities for visitors: Germany's first flush toilet, a convenience to which the queen had become accustomed in England and which she was absolutely unwilling to do without during her long stays at Coburg.

Ehrenburg has a neo-Gothic appearance, primarily due to the final retouches of 1811, but the original edifice was built in 1543 by order of Duke Johann Ernst, on the site of a thirteenth-century convent. At that time he was one of the first rulers north of the Alps to abandon a safer but undeniably more austere fortified dwelling on a hill for a more comfortable, stately residence in the center of the city. After the Thirty Years' War, during which Coburg was invaded by enemy troops, the castle was abandoned for nearly a half a century. Duke Albrecht occupied it in 1680 and restored and remodeled it according to the baroque tastes of the times. He is responsible for the opulent Hall of Giants, which owes its artistic importance to its masterpiece of stucco decoration. Neoclassicism left a clear mark on Ehrenburg; many rooms were remodeled under Duke Ernst I (1806-1844), and most of the rococo and baroque furniture was replaced by furnishings, bronzes and clocks bought especially in Paris.

The furnishings in the rooms have been left almost completely as they were, including the family photographs of Queen Victoria on the tables, and this is one of the castle's major attractions. In its less stately and more residential rooms, the place almost seems still inhabited, offering a rare glimpse into a usually inaccessible world.

233 The portraits of Coburg nobles in the Family Room include a portrait of Prince Albert, who married his cousin Victoria, the British monarch. Devastated by the death of her beloved husband at only 42 years old, the queen (who ruled for 54 years) mourned him until her death.

FORTIFIED CASTLES, MEDIEVAL SPLENDORS

234 top In 1277 Pottenstein Castle, located on a steep cliff of dolomitic rock, provided refuge for Saint Elizabeth, who had fled Thuringia after the death of her husband. By the 18th century the castle had fallen into ruins: a Nuremberg pharmacist finally put a halt to its destruction in 1878 when he rebuilt several parts of the castle.

Bavaria's position in the heart of Europe has made it a territory of transit, sometimes for purposes of trade, but more often for conquest.

Ever since ancient times, primitive fortresses of wood and earth were erected to defend the population. When the Romans conquered the ancient territory of Bavaria, they often built their rock fortresses on the ruins of primitive fortifications which they themselves had vanquished.

As the centuries passed, the realm of Bavaria expanded and became richer and more enticing to the peoples on its borders. The Bavarians themselves felt an increasing sense of independence and a desire for conquest.

All over Europe trade was beginning to flourish, and important trading routes, such as the Salt Road and the Iron Road, were opening up and traversing its borders. Numerous fortresses sprang up to protect cities, rivers and valleys and defend these merchant routes. This type of defensive architecture reached its zenith during the medieval Age of Chivalry. In mountainous areas, the fortresses are perched on rocky heights in impossible positions, and almost seem sculpted in the rock.

Their position alone was sufficient to dissuade the most hardened assailant. Fortified castles in hilly areas are true fortified citadels, often with various circular fortifications, and from a distance look like giant transatlantic liners floating in a green see.

234 bottom A visit to the medieval castle of Rosenburg, near Riedenburg on eastern Bavaria's border with Franconia, is a true trip back into the past. In its courtyard, trainers in period costumes and their birds of prey provide visitors with an extraordinary demonstration of hunting with these majestic birds, taking observers back into the past as they watch these raptors gliding over the beautiful Altmühl Valley.

On the plains, in addition to massive walls, the only other defense possible was to surround the castle with water, using the natural attributes of the countryside. Thus, many of the towers and bastions that we still find so romantic today are reflected in lakes, rivers, ponds and wide moats. Wherever they are built, and however diverse their appearances, their structures, all designed for defense, have much in common, including walls, turrets and slit windows to protect their defenders, massive gates with drawbridges, watchtowers, guard towers with alarm bells, wells and granaries to resist sieges, and the residential portion for the noble and his court, a bit more comfortable than the other wings but still very austere and cramped.

The lack of space was another common denominator for these fortresses, which during times of war became refuges for a majority of the population. By the end of the Middle Ages, changing techniques of war made these structures obsolete, and in pursuit of a new-found taste for comfort and luxury, the nobles abandoned them. Many fell into ruin, but many were recovered and restored: the largest have been converted into museums with art galleries open to the public, and the smaller ones were purchased by private parties who restored them not only as residences, but also as lovely inns, comfortable restaurants or small private museums.

234-235 The tall, slender tower of Veldenstein fortress is the emblem of Neuhaus an der Pegnitz, an ancient village with red-tiled roofs and typical lattice-work houses. In 1007 this important commercial city on the southern edge of the dense Veldenstein forest was conquered by Henry II for his new Bamberg diocese.

235 top The Niederhaus fortress is connected to the Oberhaus fortress above by a long rounds walk which has a splendid view of the city, with the colorful confluence of the three rivers that surround it: the pale Danube, the muddy Inn and the deep green Ilz.

236-237 The town of Füssen has an imposing castle with turreted walls and portals known as Hohes Schloss, which dates back to a 4th-century Roman fort. The fortress was built in 1219 and underwent many changes over the centuries, but the transformation into a castle did not alter its defensive character.

238-239 The village of Burghausen with its elegant architecture characteristic of the Inn-Salzach region stands on the banks of the Salzach River under the protective gaze of its massive fortress, which guarded the city's profitable salt trade for over 300 years.

238 top In order to strengthen the defensive power of the fortress, the six courtyards were independent and fortified, separated by deep moats that permitted troops and inhabitants to resist assaults and sieges for long periods of time.

THE BURGHAUSEN FORTRESS

"There is the underground city!" cried Napoleon as he crossed the Salzach River with his troops. It was an appropriate comment, reflecting the defensive position of the city in its role as an important military post along the Austrian-Bavarian border. Featuring the colorful architecture typical of the Inn-Salzach area, this lovely city unwinds along the Salzach River, its main street in the shadow of the longest fortress in Europe, a true citadel of 1030 m.

There are no longer any traces of the old castle from the year 1090, but the foundation walls, the cellars of Duke Henry XII and the inner chapel dating from the 13th century can still be admired in the main courtyard.

In the late fifteenth century, the continuous threat of the Turks prompted an expansion of the fortress that went on for more than ten years; today, most of its structures date from 1480 to 1490. In medieval times, each of the six courtyards that comprise it were separated by a moat, a drawbridge and a gate. To the north, the tuff rise on which the fortress was built expands to 100 m wide, becoming a low terrace. This was the most vulnerable part of the fortress, and indeed, its largest edifice, which enclosed the sixth courtyard to the north and was used as a granary and barracks, was demolished by Napoleon so that it could never again be used as a defense against him. Shortly thereafter, most of the structures which stood around what is now a large green square, were sold to private parties. This was the fate of almost all the buildings, which are still occupied by private owners. Although the current owners do not permit their homes to be visited, as you pass from courtyard to courtyard among the still-inhabited buildings within the castle walls, there is an evocative impression that the fortress is still alive, as it was in the past, when the buildings that now are home to the tranquil citizens of Burghausen served as quarters for soldiers, servants, court officials and their families. In the sixth courtyard the names of the buildings still echo the functions of the people that inhabited them: to the west, built in the 14th century, are the guest quarters and those of the chancellor and the beneficiaries. The round towers to the east and that of the income registrar, carpenters and chimney sweeps, date back to the 15th century, when the buildings, the craftsmen's workshops and a stable completed the courtyard. Crossing a bridge, which is no longer the original, you come to the fifth courtyard. To the east is the building that housed the tax office, and behind it is the courtyard's main point of interest, the outer chapel. This Gothic gem was built by the royal couple that is still commemorated every four years at Landshut, in a famous historical reconstruction of their wedding – Georg the Rich, the Duke of Landshut, and Jadwiga, the daughter of the king of Poland.

239 top The chapel is the point of attraction in the fifth courtyard. A jewel of Gothic style with its pointed bell tower, it was donated to the castle by Duke George the Rich and Jadwiga, the daughter of the King of Poland.

239 bottom The early 16th century clock tower with its added kiosk stands in the center of the broad green open space in the sixth courtyard.

The fifth courtyard is surrounded by a long edifice which was built as a prison in 1715. The structure in front of it was the women's prison. One enters the fourth courtyard through the gate, still in good condition, and inside, to the left, is the torture tower, connected by a passageway to the Witches' Tower, which was used as a prison. In the courtyard, the present-day youth hostel is located in a building that was built in the 19th century on the site of the great granary. To the west is a house with a beautiful Gothic stairway, and before it, somewhat hidden behind the granary, is the former home of the granary custodian, one of the most interesting and unique houses of the fortress. The third courtyard was the arsenal, the ground floor of which was used as a granary. The walls that surround it have swallowtail battlements, in the Middle Ages known as "sermon fingers."

The perfectly preserved Georg Gate is the barrier that protects the two main courtyards, the heart of the fortress. In the second courtyard is the well, the oven, a stable for one hundred horses and the servants' and grooms' quarters. Access to the first courtyard is over a moat 8 m deep and 28 m wide and two gates. The various parts of the residential castle, which now holds the State Museum and the Municipal Museum, open up around the courtyard, but for centuries the walls served as a defense and sometimes as a prison for the lords of the time. Even the unfortunate Jadwiga, principal of the famous "Landshut Marriage", pageant that commemorates her wedding, ended her days there after many years of confinement. The official reason for her imprisonment was that she had borne her husband no male heirs, but the reports of the time maintained that she, ignored by an increasingly absent and unfaithful husband, was caught seeking solace with the fortress' cook.

240-241 This photo shows a view of the complex's oldest buildings, which date back to the Gothic period. In the 1st century BC there was a Celtic fortress on the southernmost point of the ridge (the current position of the residential palace). The fortress took on its present form over the centuries, but the inner chapel and the castle cellars from 1200 can still be admired in their original form.

241 bottom
The stairway on the left wing of the first courtyard, Dürnitz, leads to a Renaissance Gothic room with round arches, which served as a meeting and ball room. The ballroom for servants and domestics was on the first floor.

HARBURG CASTLE

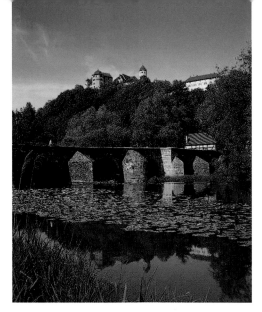

242 top left and 243 top One enters the main courtyard through a series of medieval defensive structures. The courtyard is surrounded by a group of interesting functional buildings, including the Kastenhaus, *which was once a granary, and the* Burgvogtei, *a 16th-century castle.* The Diebsturm, *a 12th-century tower which is the oldest part of the complex, connects to the courtyard.*

242 bottom left Seven centuries of history have been written within these walls. The austerely furnished rooms with their antique furniture are adorned with beautiful caisson ceilings.

242 top right Immersed within the calm countryside, the residential fortress of the counts of Oettingen has gazed down on the tranquil flow of the Wörnitz River for centuries.

242-243 The pale walls of the fortress, with towers and turrets overlooking the forest, stand out against the green landscape.

Near the famous Romantic Road in the northwestern part of Bavarian Allgäu-Swabia, this castle, which seems to come from a fable of dragons and knights, dominates the lovely town with its lattice-work houses. Its towers and turrets rising out of the green woods that surround it make it easy to imagine that its impregnable walls are protecting the long slumber of Sleeping Beauty. First mentioned in an official document in 1093, this fortress was built to defend the imperial road from Nördlingen to Donauwörth. In 1295 the castle was given to the faithful Counts – later Princes – of Oettingen, a privilege which became hereditary in 1407 (their descendants still own it). Today the castle, an architectural hodgepodge that spans seven centuries, is one of the best preserved complexes of its type in southern Germany. The main courtyard can be reached through a series of medieval defensive structures and is surrounded by several interesting functional structures, such as the *Kastenhaus*, the old granary and the *Burgtvogtei*, the 16th-century manor house, now transformed into a small, picturesque hotel-restaurant. The oldest part still standing, the *Diebsturm*, or Thieves' Tower, dates back to the 12th century. The *Fürstenbau*, a 16th-century structure, houses the priceless collection of art that the lords of the castle collected over the centuries, including some masterpieces in wood by the inimitable Tilman Riemenschneider.

WILLIBALDSBURG FORTRESS

244 The fortress holds the Jura Museum. This splendid Jurassic museum gives an evocative picture of prehistoric life in this part of Bavaria. It has a large collection of fossils found nearby, including enormous fish (top), and a rare, intact example of Archaeopteryx (bottom), the link between reptiles and birds.

244-245 The defensive and war-like aspects of the Willibaldsburg fortress made it an impregnable bulwark protecting the baroque city of Eichstätt below and the important Altmühl River and commercial route. At its peak, the fortress was one of the most sumptuous castles in Germany.

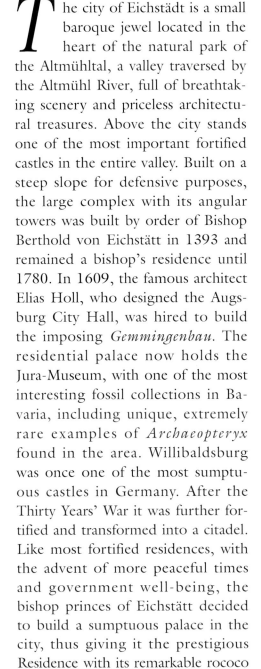

The city of Eichstädt is a small baroque jewel located in the heart of the natural park of the Altmühltal, a valley traversed by the Altmühl River, full of breathtaking scenery and priceless architectural treasures. Above the city stands one of the most important fortified castles in the entire valley. Built on a steep slope for defensive purposes, the large complex with its angular towers was built by order of Bishop Berthold von Eichstätt in 1393 and remained a bishop's residence until 1780. In 1609, the famous architect Elias Holl, who designed the Augsburg City Hall, was hired to build the imposing *Gemmingenbau*. The residential palace now holds the Jura-Museum, with one of the most interesting fossil collections in Bavaria, including unique, extremely rare examples of *Archaeopteryx* found in the area. Willibaldsburg was once one of the most sumptuous castles in Germany. After the Thirty Years' War it was further fortified and transformed into a citadel. Like most fortified residences, with the advent of more peaceful times and government well-being, the bishop princes of Eichstätt decided to build a sumptuous palace in the city, thus giving it the prestigious Residence with its remarkable rococo and neoclassical rooms.

245 top Magnificent Willibaldsburg emerges in the distance against the placid landscape of the Altmühl Valley. The English missionary monk Willibald founded Eichstätt in 745 and became its first bishop.

PRUNN CASTLE

246 top left The simple little chapel is embellished by stucco work on the ceiling and a graceful wooden altar.

246 top right The interior of the fortress is quite bare, due in part to the fact that one of its last uses

was as a Franciscan monastery but the decorations around the doors are worthy of interest and the windows offer a bird's-eye view of the valley and the river.

246-247 Looking like a continuation of the rock on which

they were built, the walls of the Prunn fortress hid the first manuscript of the Legend of the Nibelungen for two centuries. The manuscript was discovered accidentally during remodeling work in 1575.

The castle can be seen in the distance from the valley.

In seeming defiance of human reason, it was constructed on a rock 70 m high overlooking the Altmühl River, and appears to be practically suspended from it.

It is impossible not to marvel at how, almost a thousand years ago, such solid and beautiful buildings capable of resisting wartime attacks and the ravages of time could be built in such seemingly impossible positions. While its view from the bottom of the valley is certainly beautiful, the panorama visible from the castle's rooms and walls is truly breathtaking, with a bird's eye view of the Altmühl valley. It runs uninterrupted for miles and miles, following the tranquil course of the river, which curls through the deep green pine woods, the golden yellow rape fields and the white villages dotted with red. Period documents show that the castle was already in existence in 1037. Its long history has seen many lords, including the von Prunn family, who gave it its name, the Dukes of Bavaria, the brotherhood of the Jesuits of Ingolstadt, and finally, in 1803, the State of Bavaria. The castle is famous for its *Prunn Codex*, an antique manuscript from around 1300, which was accidentally found during a Renaissance restoration of its interior.

The manuscript recounts the first "Song of the Nibelungen," which inspired Wagner to write his Ring cycle.

247 top Since 1037, when the fortress on the promontory was first mentioned, many lords have contended for its possession, including the von Prunn nobles, who gave it its name.

247 bottom The beautiful fortified structure stands precariously on a 230-ft (70-m) cliff. In ancient times it was the most formidable fortress in the Altmühl Valley.

THE FORTRESS OF NUREMBERG

248 High over the roofs of the city, this impressive structure is visible for kilometres. The historic importance of Nuremberg inspired Hitler to choose it as the seat of his new government, for which the city paid dearly when 90 percent of its historic center, considered one of the most beautiful in Germany, was destroyed in a single bombardment on January 2, 1945.

Nuremberg is the second largest city in Bavaria and the capital of one of its regions, Franconia. Because of its key position on many important trading routes, the city reached its economic apex in the Middle Ages, and in 1356, in an edict known as the "Golden Bull," the Emperor Charles IV ruled that each newly elected German king had to hold his first Diet at Nuremberg. With the discovery of America, the economic power of the city declined, but in the 17th century Nuremberg was equally famous for its paintings and its sculptures. Its nearly legendary status in the eyes of many Germans continued over time, so that even Hitler chose it as the seat of his government and the future capital of his empire. After the war, the Allies also recognized its symbolic importance and chose it as the seat for the famous Nuremberg trials of surviving Nazi leaders.

The *Burg* (fortress), perched on a rock at the edge of the old city, gives Nuremberg its unmistakable profile. The odd-looking group of buildings that make it up has grown over the centuries and actually consists of two castles joined together. On the eastern tip of the rocky spur is *Burggrafenburg* (the Count's Fortress), which came into the possession of the Zoller family in the 12th century. This powerful family was at variance with the Imperial City of Nuremberg, which held Kaiserburg, the other fortress on the rock. The conflict went on interminably, and the harshest affront to Count Zoller occurred when the citizens built a new fortified tower right in front of his fortress. The tower, completed in only five months while the Count was away travelling, was used to spy on Burggrafenburg. In 1427 the Zoller family lost interest in the old ruin and sold it to the city.

Kaiserburg (the Imperial Fortress), located on the western tip of the promontory, is the most impressive part of the complex. The first fortress was built in 1050 by King Henry III; around the middle of the 12th century Emperor Conrad III built *Kaiserburg*, which was then expanded and transformed into an imperial residence by

248-249 The city of Nuremberg is first mentioned as "Nuremberc" in an imperial document of 1050. In 1219 it was granted the status of a free imperial city, which it maintained until 1806. Many Imperial Diets were held here, and it was also the seat of the Imperial Court.

249 top A 1492 illustration shows the city surrounded by walls (almost all of which still remain) and dominated by the fortress. The tall towers of the churches of St. Sebald and St. Lawrence can be seen below it; even today they are important artistic monuments in the city.

*250 The double
Romanesque chapel
from the 12th
century is
architecturally the
most important part
of the fortress.
The large sandstone
columns of the lower
chapel stand in sharp
contrast to the
slender columns in
the Emperor's
Chapel, with vaults
which almost seem
weightless.*

Frederick I Barbarossa around 1200. The German empire had no capital, and its emperors and their entourages moved from one residence to another. It is easy to imagine the importance of the fortress of Nuremberg if you consider that from 1050 to 1571 all emperors stayed there, although none of them for long periods of time. This explains the fact that inside the fortress everything appears quite bare and stripped of furnishings. This is not due to the fires and wars the fortress suffered, but was how it looked when the Emperor and his court were not there. Indeed, the shrewd, thrifty citizens of Nuremberg loaned their finest furniture and furnishings to the fortress when the Emperor announced a visit. After he left, the owners took everything back home.

The inner courtyard of *Kaiserburg* is enclosed within a long Gothic-style *Palas* with the residential and state rooms of the emperor and his court. Inside is a lovely two-story chapel, with the upper floor reserved to the nobility and the lower to the servants. In the center of the courtyard outside *Kaiserburg*, dominated by the massive Sinwell Tower, is the house that contains the *Tiefer Brunnen* (Deep Well), fully 50 m deep, which provided water to the fortress as early as the 12th century.

In 1427 the western tip of the promontory was also taken by the city and incorporated into its defenses, but it remained the property of the Holy Roman Empire.

The oldest part of the fortress is the *Fünfeckturm* (Pentagonal Tower), the only remaining part of the original fortress, which shares the eastern part of the promontory with the massive Luginslandturm. After the Zoller family was driven out, the citizens connected the two towers with the Gothic *Kaiserstallung* (the Imperial Stables), which was then used as a granary and now serves as a youth hostel.

250-251 This is a view of the Tiergärtnertor Platz at the foot of the Kaiserburg Residential Palace. The home of Albrecht Dürer, now a museum, stands on the square.

251 top The photo shows Kaiserburg's outer court with the Well House in the center. The Deep Well was dug into the rock to a depth of 50 m. Two truss structures from the 15th and 16th centuries stand in the southwest corner. The lower part of imposing Sinwell Tower dates back to the 12th century, while the upper portion is from 1560.

THE MARIENBERG
FORTRESS

The fortress stands on a hill that dominates the city of Würzburg and the Main River, on the same site where the Celts built their fortifications around 1000 BC. The *Marienkirche* (which can be seen within the fortress), one of the oldest churches in Germany, was built in the 8th century, and in the 13th century the construction and fortification of the Marienberg citadel began. From 1253 to 1720 it served as the residence of the prince-bishops. The castle was transformed into a citadel through various important construction works, which were completed by bishop Rudolf von Scherenberg (1466-1495). Its present-day appearance is the work of Bishop Julius Echter von Mespelbrunn (1573-1617). The Mainfrankisches Museum, Franconia's art museum, is located in the Arsenal. It holds a superb collection of wooden sculptures by one of Germany's greatest sculptors of wood, Tilman Riemenschneider. Riemenschneider lived in Würzburg from 1483 to 1531, when he was killed in a bloody battle during the Peasants' Revolt. At the entrance to the museum is an interesting portrait gallery with portraits of the electors of Würzburg, including the man responsible for building the Residence, Johann Philipp von Schönborn.

*252 top
The surrounding moat has been transformed into pleasant gardens where summer shows are held. In the background, one can glimpse the baroque, onion-shaped cupola of the Kiliani Tower, built when the castle was being fortified in the 13th century.*

252 centre The Main and Franconia Museum located in the former arsenal and bastion of Echter offers a representative look at 2000 years of regional history. Its works are significant and varied, including items such as swords and weapons from this arsenal, famous paintings by local artists and forest rangers, sculptures by Tilman Riemenschneider, handicrafts and everyday objects and old folk costumes.

252 bottom The great winepresses in the arsenal's old section tell the story of wine-growing in the area.

252-253 Resting on a hill covered with vineyards, the Marienberg fortress, an important work of defensive architecture, dominates the city of Würzburg and the Main River.

253 top
The Romanesque
Marienkirche *is the*
oldest monument
in Marienberg.
It was built on the
hill in the 7th
century as a sign
of devotion to the
Virgin Mary, and
the fortress was later
built around it.

254 top left
This photo clearly shows the defensive power of the fortress. One of the two circles of walls with its massive guard towers can be seen below the Veste Coburg's high, sheer walls.

254 top right
The Veste Coburg is one of the largest fortresses in Germany. Its imposing 200x80 m oval form gave it the name of Fränkische Krone, the Crown of Franconia.

VESTE COBURG

254-255 *One enters from the east side over an 18th-century bridge through a baroque portal from 1671. The door to the back, which leads to the first circle of walls, is surmounted by a tower built in 1911 by the czar Ferdinand of Bulgaria, from the house of Coburg-Gotha.*

255 top
The Fürstenbau, *the princely palace built in the 16th century, faces the inner courtyard. Today's façade is the result of remodelling in the lattice-work style of Franconia.*

255 bottom *The thick barrier of the second wall is the last defensive bastion and completely surrounds the inner courtyards, where there are various residential and utility buildings.*

One of the most beautiful fortresses in Europe, Veste Coburg stands on the top of a hill occupied by the Ehrenburg, the city palace park, which reaches the outermost of its three circular fortifications.

From a distance, the numerous watchtowers and the gabled roofs rise from the bands of walls like the points of a crown, giving this fortress its Bavarian name of *Fränkische Krone,* or the Crown of Franconia. The city of Coburg, located in the far north of Franconia, was under the jurisdiction of the Dukes of Saxe-Coburg-Gotha until 1920, when the citizens voted to join Upper Franconia, thus becoming Bavarian. The fortress boasts 750 years of history. In 1353 it belonged to the Wettin family, the rulers of Saxony and Thuringia, and in the 16th century it became one of their main residences.

The descendants of the Wettin family, the Dukes of Coburg, used it as a residence until 1918. The Gothic-style oldest portion was built between the 14th and 16th centuries, when the first circle of fortifications was constructed.

During the 16th century the fortress was transformed into a citadel, and Lucas Cranach the Elder, who stayed there often, helped transform it into a princely residence.

The outer bastions were added during the following two centuries.

The *Steinerne Kemenate,* which

holds a rich collection of art, with works by Cranach, Dürer, Schongauer and Rembrandt, is located to the left of the beautiful courtyard.

In the Hunting Room, the 1632 wall covering, with rare inlay work and carvings, is one of the most beautiful works of its kind.

In 1530 Martin Luther took refuge within its walls, where he paced the silent gardens and rooms as the Diet of Augsburg deliberated its verdict in his heresy trial. The great reformer's room in the fortress can still be visited today.

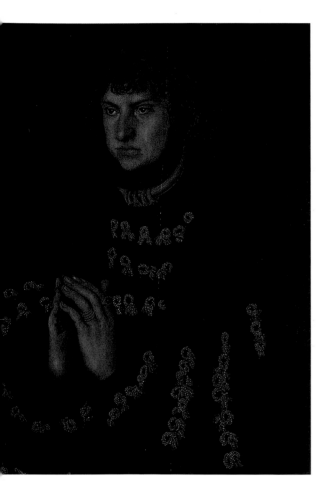

256 This photo shows one of his paintings at the Veste Coburg, a portrait of Johann der Beständige, the bishop prince of Saxony.

256-257 The interior of the Prince's Palace is richly furnished with Renaissance and baroque furniture.

257 top One of the most important rooms in the fortress is the Luther Room, named after Martin Luther, who stayed at the Veste Coburg in 1530. A famous portrait of the reformer by Lucas Cranach the Elder hangs on one of the walls.

257 center A collection of coaches and sleds is on display on the ground floor of the Herzoginbau. Of special note are the wedding coaches from the 16th century and the tournament sleds from the 17th to the 18th centuries.

257 bottom A lavish collection of weapons and war apparatus can be seen in the Guard Room.

Castles of the Loire

SECTION THREE

INTRODUCTION

From Giens to Angers, by the calm waters of what has been called the loveliest river in France and along its major tributaries, hundreds of fortresses and castles appear as if by magic from the woods. But why should there be so many princely residences in this area?

One tragic night 600 years ago, the Burgundians put Paris to fire and sword. Tanguy du Châtel, a faithful servant of King Charles VI, hastened to the palace and, with a group of horsemen, escorted the 15-year-old dauphin of France to safety at Chinon Castle. Thus, on the night of May 28, 1418, began the history of the castles of the Loire. For a century the court of the kings of France, with their

260 top The walls of Chaumont Castle, shrouded in the morning mist, conceal a multitude of secrets and mysteries.

260-261 Chambord Castle, so grandiose as to seem almost unreal, looms up in the distance like a mirage.

261 Shooting parties take place every year in the huge grounds of Cheverny Castle, and the pack of dogs are exercised along the paths of the park under the guidance of a trainer every day.

retinue of noblemen and dignitaries, moved to the banks of the river. The dauphin (who ascended to the throne as Charles VII) and his successors found the Loire Valley to be the ideal refuge from the threats of a turbulent, unsafe capital. Great castles were built, ancient city walls restored and patrician residences erected, housing a wealth of splendors, intrigues, vendettas, courtly pageants and decadent love affairs.

262-263 *Chambord Castle ends the saga of the Loire Valley. Bristling with pinnacles and turrets, containing endless halls and* *chambers, the castle, built on the banks of the magical river, was a king's last dream, intended by Francis I to evoke an entire age.*

263 top *Starting from the northwestern side, the Chapel Tower is followed by the west wing of the galleries (top right), the Dieudonné Tower, the Francis I Tower, the east wing of the galleries and the Robert de Parme Tower.*

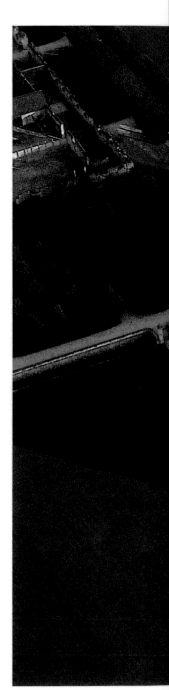

But in a letter written on his return from Madrid on March 15, 1528, Francis I manifested the desire to return "to sojourn in the good city of Paris." The Loire had lost the privilege of being the Valley of Kings. When the court left, the noblemen who had built princely residences, no less magnificent than the royal castles, left too. Thus the lights went out on that enchanted world that, centuries later, still evokes a dreamlike fascination. Princes and kings, courtiers and minstrels, queens and dukes still seem to tread that great stage. An invisible hand holds the strings of their memories. From the time of Louis XI to the present day, it has been said, the centuries have never obscured the fame of this garden, where François Rabelais plucked the roses of life. A million tourists visit it every year not only because of the castles, but also for the countryside, the cuisine, and the secrets held by a region that always has something to say. The villages, with their quiet squares basking in the sun, encircle the larger towns, where the living heart of the Loire beats. Through its markets, riverside restaurants and souvenir shops, to the backdrops of its better known castles, the history of the Loire is recounted in "sound and light." Every stone tells a story, every garden bears witness to the idle pleasures of a king, and every drawing room rings with the echoes of a bygone world. But the Loire Valley is only the main artery of a much larger green heart, also studded with castles steeped in history; the whole region is just waiting to be discovered, by traveling from castle to castle like a courtly minstrel. There are the more famous ones, perched on its banks or nestled in the woods: Chambord, Chenonceau, Blois, Amboise, Azay-le-Rideau, Langeais, Chinon, and so on. To the south, in the ancient land of Berry, there are the more defensive castles designed as military outposts, like the fortress of Culan, Meillant Castle, shrouded in the green mantle of the forest of the same name, and the castle of Ainay-le-Vieil. And there are the lesser known castles to the north, behind the Loire, such as Châteaudun, perched on a steep crag, Montigny-le-Gannelon, with its magnificent furnishings, Maintenon, still as it was when Louis XIV's secret wife lived there and, just outside Paris, Anet Castle, the little kingdom of Diane de Poitiers, mistress of King Henry II, which brings to an end the romantic and dissolute history of the Loire Valley castles.

266-267 *The village of Chenonceaux, about 19 miles from Tours, is famous for the castle of almost the same name (Chenonceau without the "x"), built in the early 16th century for Thomas Bohier, tax collector under Charles VIII, Louis XII and Francis I.*

268-269 *The castle of Sully-sur-Loire, which has the tallest slate roof in the Loire Valley, stands like an island of pale stone suspended over the water.*

The castle of Sully-sur-Loire

Chambord Castle

Valençay Castle

Ussé Castle

Azay-le-Rideau Castle

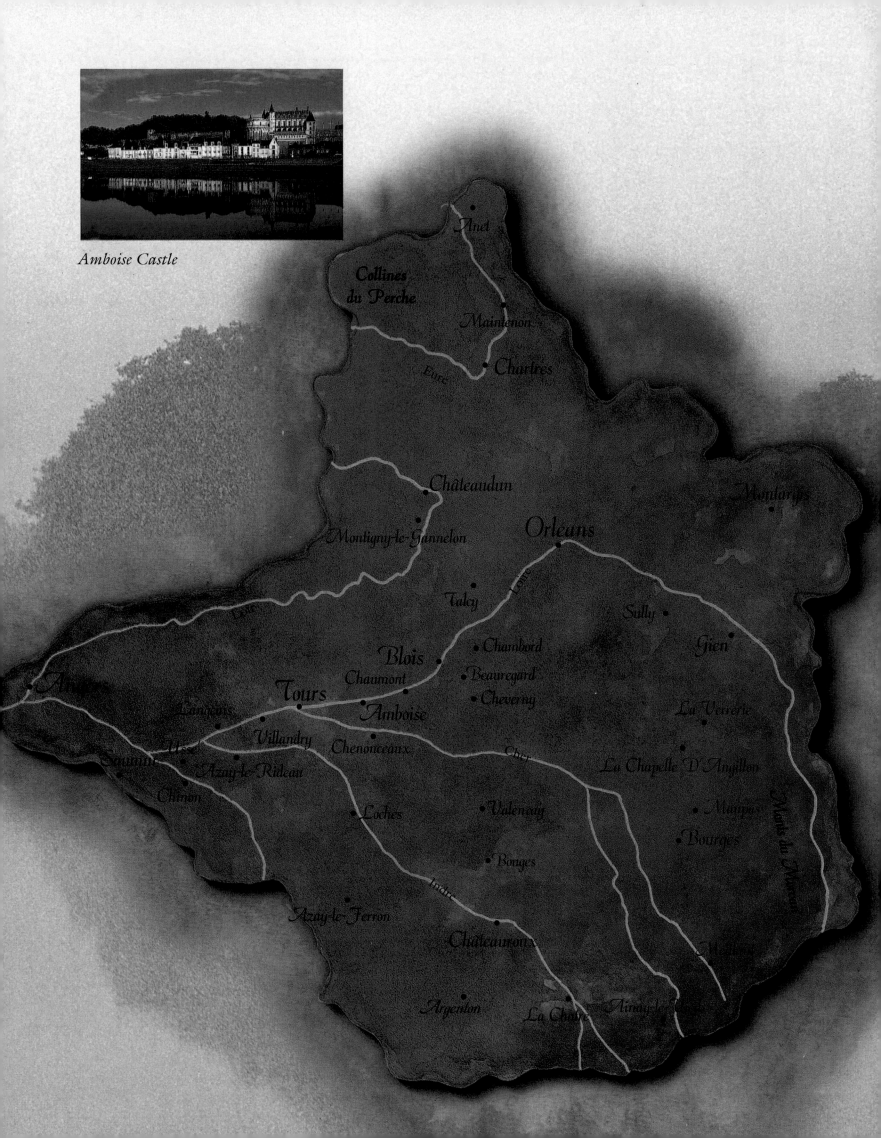

Amboise Castle

Anet

**Collines
du Perche**

Maintenon

Eure

Chartres

Châteaudun

Montigny-le-Gannelon

Orleans

Montargis

Talcy

Loire

Sully

Gien

Loire

Chambord

Blois

Chaumont

Beauregard

Tours

Amboise

Cheverny

La Verrerie

Langeais

Villandry

Chenonceaux

Cher

La Chapelle D'Angillon

Ussé

Azay-le-Rideau

Saumur

Chinon

Loches

Valençay

Maupa

Bouges

Bourges

Indre

Azay-le-Ferron

Châteauroux

Argenton

La Châtre

Ainay-le

Monts du Morvan

THE GENTLE SOUTHERN COUNTRYSIDE

270 top left The fortress of Culan, standing high on a crag, overlooks the Arnon River.

270 center left The perfect French-style garden of Bouges Castle, a linear square of pale Touraine stone with a classical beauty; the castle has no pinnacles or Renaissance influences.

At the southernmost border of the central Val de Loire region, before the architectural grandeur of the famous valley begins, the department of Cher has constructed the historical Jacques Coeur route, which leads to villages and castles. These castles were the theater of war centuries ago, when the area, which forms part of the ancient region once called Berry, divided the possessions of the king of France from those of the king of England. Visitors can still admire these outposts of bygone deeds, long roads and unusual itineraries entwining with the great river, until reaching Bouges Castle – with its precious furnishings – and Valençay Castle – residence of statesman Talleyrand – bring them back to the charm of castles that have never known war. In Culan, the 12th-century stronghold standing high on a spur of rock has the austere features of one who has known the hardships of sieges. It is an awe-inspiring fortress, with mighty round towers overlooking the Arnon. The great 15th-century fireplaces, two precious paintings attributed to Caravaggio, the original windows and precious historical relics testify to its past splendors. Its grandeur was due to the feats of Louis de Culan, admiral of France, who fought all over the world and was Joan of Arc's comrade in arms at Patay and Orléans. Famous personalities and leading statesmen have stayed at the grandiose castle, last but not least being General de Gaulle in November 1951. Indre, which borders on Cher, is another department whose treasures are worth a visit. The most romantic is the magnificent country home of George Sand at Nohant, an aristocratic mansion with many rooms and a peaceful garden on the outskirts of La Châtre village, which inspired the scenario often described in her novels. George Sand, born in Paris in the early 19th century, came to live at her grandmother's house as a child. From Chateauroux it's just a short trip to La Brenne, a little-known region that few tourists visit, except for the elite band of nature lovers who travel with sleeping bags and sleep under the stars. There are no trees, just scrub, moors, meadows, great silences and 400 ponds in this nook where unspoiled nature has an austere, melancholic charm. Every so often, scattered over the wide open spaces, there's a cottage, a castle, like the splendid castle of Azay-le-Ferron, or a secluded village. To the north of La Brenne are Bouges Castle and Valençay Castle, still in the gentle Berry countryside. Fields and forests lead to the discreet elegance of Bouges Castle, a severe square of pale Touraine stone with a classic beauty, devoid of pinnacles, in perfect Louis XV style. It recalls the Trianon at Versailles, partly because of the antique furnishings, collected in a lifetime's research by the last owners, M. and Mme. Viguier, who bought it in 1917.

270 bottom left The mansion of George Sand, in the Berry countryside, where the author lived as a child and later took refuge for long periods of her life.

270 right George Sand's intense look in a portrait at her Nohant mansion.

271 Meillant Castle, shrouded in the green cloak of the forest of the same name, was more defensive than romantic. A flamboyant Gothic polygonal tower can be seen on the inner side of the castle.

GRACE AND STRENGTH: AINAY-LE-VIEIL CASTLE

Ainay-le-Vieil is the southern-most castle in the Loire Valley. The thick octagonal walls of this intact medieval fortress surround the Renaissance grace of the central building, added centuries later, next to the 16th-century Renaissance tower. It is still inhabited by the descendants of Charles de Chevenon de Bigny, the noble knight who bought the property from the Lord of Culan in 1467. It houses historical relics associated with Colbert, Marie Antoinette and, still longer ago, Louis XII and Anne of Brittany. The parapets pass from tower to tower, surrounding the castle with a continuous circle of walls that has won the impressive building the nickname of "Petit Carcassonne." In the great hall is a huge fireplace, meticulously carved with symbols and the royal initials L and A against a blue background of gilded fleurs-de-lys. When spring comes, a thousand varieties of old roses bloom in the castle garden, while in summer the historic castle presents thematic exhibitions and some very popular events.

272-273
Ainay-le-Vieil, the southernmost castle in the Loire Valley, on the borders of Berry, is an extraordinary medieval fortress dating from the 14th century. Massive

towers intersect the polygonal design of the outer walls, which enclose the attractive inner courtyard of the castle, with its Renaissance tower and beautifully furnished interior.

The castle has belonged for five centuries to the descendants of Charles de Chevenon de Bigny, the noble knight who bought the property from the Lord of Culan in 1467.

THE RESIDENCE OF BEAUTIFUL DUCHESS: VALENÇAY CASTLE

274 top and 274-275 Standing at the end of an avenue of plane trees, beyond a monumental gateway, Valençay Castle features classical lines intersected by the great central Renaissance-style keep. Much altered over the centuries, it was transformed by Talleyrand de Périgord into a magnificent gentleman's residence.

A few miles away, Valençay Castle bears witness to the splendors of the First Empire. "Lord of Talleyrand, it is my wish that you purchase a beautiful residence where you can receive the diplomatic corps and foreigners accredited to Paris," said Napoleon to his prime minister in 1803. Talleyrand did not need to be asked twice. At Valençay he found a ruined 16th-century castle, built by Jacques d'Estampes, with an east wing added in the 17th century. He transformed it into that perfection of style and furnishing that can still be admired today by moving from room to room along the grandiose first-floor gallery and looking out over the park, where deer graze. Napoleon paid most of the price so that he could use Valençay Castle himself. In fact, he used it for six years to accommodate the Spanish king Ferdinand VII, who lost his throne through the emperor's fault. On regaining possession of the castle in 1814, Talleyrand refurbished the interior, and after the Congress of Vienna went to live there permanently with his niece by marriage, Dorothée, duchess of Dino. The grandiose palace, which has remained intact since the early 19th century, witnessed 20 years of balls, receptions, literary salons and meetings of the leading contemporary figures in politics and art.

274 bottom The halls of Valençay Castle contain antique furniture and original paintings, like the splendid oval frame containing the portrait of Princess Bénévent of Vigée-Lebrun.

275 top *The
magnificent collection
of paintings at
Valençay includes a
portrait of the famous
minister Talleyrand
(left), and one of
Victoire Alexandrine
Eléonore de Damas,
countess of Talleyrand-
Périgord, who lived in
the late 18th century
(center) and was the
mother of Charles
Maurice Talleyrand,
portrayed by Prud'hon
(right).*

276 and 277
Talleyrand de Périgord
had to give up his lovely
residence at Valençay
between 1808 and
1814 to Ferdinand
VII, King of Spain,
who was exiled there
after being deposed by
Napoleon. Visitors
can see his chamber
(large photo), in First
Empire style, then
proceed along the
large gallery on the
first floor to other
magnificently
furnished rooms
like the Blue Room
(bottom left) and the
cabinet de toilette
(top right).

278 and 279
Napoleon's prime
minister, Talleyrand
de Périgord, regained
possession of his castle
in 1814 and partly
renovated the interior
decoration. Some of
the most interesting
rooms are the ground-
floor hall containing
the table around
which the signatories
of the Congress of
Vienna sat (left-hand
page), the Great Hall
(top left), the Portrait
Gallery (top right),
and the Prince's
Chamber (bottom).

280 and 281 The
Renaissance tower by
Michelangelo's pupil,
Fra Giocondo, and a
window in flamboyant
Gothic style stand out
on the south façade of
Meillant Castle. The
defensive structure of
the castle, which is
still inhabited, can be
clearly seen from the
entrance moat. The
building contains a
wealth of furnishings,
halls and chambers
with painted coffered
ceilings.

FRA GIOCONDO'S LOVELY TOWER: MEILLANT CASTLE

Meillant Castle, enveloped in the green mantle of the forest and the scent of lime trees in spring, reveals its pretty Gothic style with a lawn of strutting peacocks, glistening ponds and the "Lion" tower – a Renaissance construction by Michelangelo's pupil Fra Giocondo – that stands at the center of the façade. Remember this tower when viewing the more famous one at Blois Castle; the Italian Renaissance touch left the first trace of its brilliant harmony here. In fact, it was Charles II d'Amboise, lord of Chaumont and governor of Milan, who introduced into Meillant Castle discreet but perceptible signs of the art he had seen flourishing across the Alps. In the inner rooms, 17th-century Dutch furniture; a great banqueting hall with minstrel's gallery and tapestries made to a design by Raphael; and a spectacular dining room with a Renaissance fireplace, a gilded coffered ceiling (partly painted in bright colors) and Cordova leather wall hangings all bring to life the age of the duke of Charost, owner of the castle during the Revolution, who had a philanthropic bent. The epitaph on his tomb in the castle chapel states, "Everywhere and at all times he did nought but good."

282 top The impressive statue of Jacques-Coeur (left) stands in the heart of Bourges opposite the famous merchant adventurer's mansion (right); the Jacques-Coeur route, which takes in the major castles of the southern Loire region, is named after him.

282-283 In the austere rooms of La Chapelle d'Angillon Castle, author Alain-Fournier found his inspiration for the characters of his famous novels, including Le Grand Meaulnes.

THE LAND
OF JACQUES-COEUR

283 top and center
The castle of La
Chapelle d'Angillon
is one of the few
mansions built in the
Sologne area. Its
severe look is
inherited from the
imposing original
structure dating
from the 11th
century, while the
central section was
inspired by
Renaissance
architecture.

The echoes of war give way to an ancient, bucolic landscape, while the Jacques-Coeur route continues north. After the calm sight of Apremont, the prettiest flowery village in France, comes Bourges, and the impressive statue in the town center of Jacques-Coeur, who gave the capital of Cher its most precious castle. Tall, handsome, and a lover of the sea and great ocean routes, he founded a shipping company whose sailing ships traveled far and wide to supply the king's court with spices, silks, silver, carpets and majolica. He financed Charles VII's military campaigns and was his private and most trusted banker until he fell into disgrace, it is said, because of the pretty Agnès Sorel, the king's mistress, and was thrown into prison. He escaped, embarked on a ship of the papal fleet that attacked the Turks, and died in 1456. His statue, which stands on a stone pedestal opposite the entrance, swathed in marble drapery, seems to admire his castle for eternity. In the heart of Henrichemont Forest, studded with pastures and clearings, castles are still the main leitmotiv. Maupas Castle is famous for its collection of 887 china plates from the oldest and most famous French pottery works, many of which hang on the walls alongside the wooden staircase, and for a silk tapestry of Italian manufacture given by the count of Chambord to the marquis of Maupas in the 19th century. Literary memories and the personalities invented by Alain-Fournier give a special appeal to the castle of La Chapelle D'Angillon. "I have returned to my land, the land that can only be seen by moving branches aside. I have never seen it so fresh, so concealed," wrote Alain-Fournier, when he was already beginning to imagine the adventures of *Le Grand Meaulnes* (published in English as *The Lost Domain*).

Cher, the department that, together with Indre, partly includes the ancient Berry, was a source of inspiration and peace for the author. He learned to read and write at the Epineuil-le-Fleuriel village school, enjoyed staying with his uncle in Nançay, a village comprising a few houses built around a single square, and daydreamed as a child in the great castle of La Chapelle D'Angillon. The dramatic destiny of the Princess of Clèves and the adventures of Le Grand Meaulnes, a young man lost in the memory of a mysterious kingdom where the enchanting Yvonne de Galais lived, accompany the visitor through the austere rooms of this castle. Alain-Fournier, the author of some famous novels, was born in 1886 in the village not far from the castle, but it was the great halls of the historic building that set light to his imagination. Two of them house relics of the writer's fantasy world, while others feature impressive fireplaces, beautiful paintings; a Luca della Robbia sculpture stands in the chapel, and a curious gallery is designed for *jeu de paume*, a fashionable game that was the forerunner of tennis.

283 bottom Maupas
Castle is famous for
its collection of 887
china plates from the
oldest and most
famous French
potteries, which
adorn part of the
wooden staircase and
some of the rooms in
this lovely residence.

SMALL WORLDS, SPECIAL ATMOSPHERES

The land veined by the Cher River still encloses small worlds and an atmosphere of stillness: sleepy villages, roads that disappear into the countryside, abbeys, castles and landscapes untouched by the passage of time. The gentle countryside of Berry leads to the castle of La Verrerie. The Scots were at home here, because Charles VII gave this solitary castle to James Stuart in 1422. They kept it until 1683, when Louis XIV donated it to Countess Louise de Keroualle, Duchess of Portsmouth, and Charles II's mistress. In 1843 a descendent gave it to an ancestor of the present owners, the De Vogüé family. Nested in the greenery of Ivoy Forest is the classic castle with turrets, Renaissance porticoes, richly decorated halls, secret archives, huge, silent grounds, and a stream to provide silvery highlights. Visitors can admire the Gothic chapel, the reception rooms, the billiard room and the library. Some rooms are set aside for paying guests who wish to spend a night as a king amid velvets and canopies, ancestral portraits, tapestries and antique furniture. The world of fishing also appears on a royal frame. A few miles from Gien stands the lonely gray castle of La Buissière, already a fortress in the 12th century. Since 1962 the castle has housed the Fishing Museum, which contains exhibits of all kinds: fossil fish, silver fish, stuffed fish, sculpted fish, drawings of fish.

284 and 285
The gentle Berry countryside and the thick Ivoy Forest surround La Verrerie Castle, with its Renaissance portico in the inner courtyard, and rooms furnished *with antique furniture and damask fabrics. Some of the rooms are reserved for paying guests who would like to spend a night in the magical atmosphere of a great château.*

ANNE DE BEAUJEU'S RESIDENCE: GIEN CASTLE

The history of this small town, which stretches along the banks of the Loire, is closely linked to that of its castle, the first of those overlooking the Loire if the route of the famous river is followed towards the sea. The castle, standing high above the river at a point where the view is limitless, has offered hospitality to Joan of Arc among others. Before attending the coronation of Charles VII, the famous heroine spent a night praying in the wing of the castle now named after her, the only surviving part of the original feudal building.

The castle, overlooking Gien and the Loire, was built of brick and stone for Louis XI's daughter Anne de Beaujeu, Countess of Gien, in 1484. Francis I, Henri II, Charles IX and Henri III all stayed here. It survived unscathed the bombing of the Second World War, which razed the red-roofed town to the ground.

Since 1952 the castle has housed the Hunting Museum, which contains 15 rooms full of weapons of all ages, costumes, rare collections of buttons inspired by the hunt, works of art associated with the subject, tapestries, majolica, watercolors, lithographs, paintings by François Desportes, the famous animal painter to Louis XIV and Louis XV, and the Claude Hettier de Boislambert Collection of 500 hunting trophies. As well as the castle and its museum, Gien also offers another interesting attraction: the ceramic works founded in 1821 by Englishman Thomas Hulm, known as Hall, who wished to introduce the manufacture of fine English china into France. He found the right kind of clay for the purpose near Gien, while wood from the great forest of Orléans stoked the kilns that produced Gien blue, a color that remains inimitable today.

286 top Gien Castle, the first of the castles overlooking the Loire as the course of the famous river is followed, was built on the foundations of a hunting lodge erected for Charlemagne. Its involvement with hunting thus has ancient origins, and still continues today. The castle houses the magnificent Hunting Museum, which includes some lovely tapestries like the one woven following a cartoon by Laurent Guyot (right).

286 and 287 The large hall featuring paintings by François Desportes (1661–1743), with its mighty woodwork, contains numerous works by this famous animal painter who worked at the court of Louis XIV and Louis XV.

SULLY,
A ROMANTIC CASTLE

Sully Castle, a good example of defensive architecture on the border between Berry and Sologne, rises from the water like a romantic vision on the left bank of the Loire and its tributary, the Sange. The great hunting parties of yesteryear took place here, in the huge wooded Sologne Forest. The square tower at the entrance, the round tower on the southeastern side and the keep date back to the 15th century. From the knoll visitors can admire the castle, the park and the moats. Amid the greenery stands the marble statue of the duke of Sully, with a laurel wreath and the marshal of France baton. The Guard Room, with its coffered Vosges wood ceilings, leads to the Great Hall where Voltaire, exiled here after libeling the Prince Regent, Philippe d'Orléans, staged some of his plays between 1716 and 1719. Near the Great Hall, separated by a solid iron door, is the oratory, followed by the King's Chamber, with tapestries, a four-poster bed with blue canopy and wood-paneled walls. Finally, 40 steps lead up to the top floor, where visitors can see the framework of the roof: a brilliantly engineered wooden skeleton. This very tall pitched roof, which dates from the late 14th century, has undergone catapult attacks, but has always withstood them and is still there, like a great upside-down ship's hull, waiting to be admired for its latticework of beams and the unusual design of its roof.

288 and 289 The romantic sight of Sully Castle, a good example of defensive architecture, rises from the water on the border between Berry and Sologne. Among its attractions are the Guard Room, with its ceiling painted in pure gold, the King's Chamber – with tapestries portraying scenes from classical mythology and a blue damask canopy to match the walls – and the extraordinary roof frame, with its upturned-hull shape.

A WORLD
PRESERVED
IN STONE

Tourists who travel through the Loire Valley or merely hear stories about its magnificent residences wonder why so many castles and princely residences were built there. Why by the Loire, and not the Seine, for example, or other no less famous rivers? Because the Loire Valley, with its warm, dry climate, has always been the garden of France; because along the riverbanks there were already fortresses and castles able to accommodate royal guests; and because in the 15th century the king's political survival depended on the resistance offered along the Loire border by the dukes of Berry and Orléans in the south against the English and in the north against the Burgundians. Even after his accession to the throne, Charles VII remained fascinated by the climate and landscape of the gentle Loire Valley. After the Treaty of Troyes (1420), which stripped him of his kingdom, he lived at Chinon, Loches and Amboise with the sole title of Roi de Bourges. Following the legendary liberation by Joan of Arc of Orléans, besieged by the English, in May 1429, Charles VII began to win back his kingdom, but when he was finally able to return to liberated Paris on November 12, 1437, he only stayed a few days. Homesick, he took the court back to Chinon, preferring to pass his life in the gentle Touraine, where he had been bewitched by the beautiful Agnès Sorel. His son, Louis XI, who grew up at Loches Castle, though a restless wanderer by nature, nearly always lived in the castles of Amboise and Plessis-lez-Tours. Charles VIII, who was fond of Amboise, also had no desire to transfer the court to Paris.

After his marriage he spent a year at Langeais Castle; then, on his return from the Italian campaign in 1495, he decided to live at Amboise and convert the castle into a modern residence, for which purpose he summoned skilled craftsmen and artists from Italy. His successor, Louis XII, also chose the Loire, as did Francis I who lived at Blois Castle in the early years of his reign. Three years after his coronation began the construction of his own castle, Chambord. Today, in the summer, many castles stage historical reenactments; sound-and-light shows, pageants and plays to familiarize the public with the history of the best-known castles. The Francis I route follows the ancient road traveled by the king on his way to Italy, while the Vallée des Rois route leads to royal residences and sleepy old-world villages. Even without following a set route, the castles follow one after another. The castle of Chenonceau, the best known and most visited, recounts tales of love and the revenge of betrayed mistresses, while Villandry's charm focuses on its gardens. Cheverny is still inhabited, and the pack of dogs used for fox hunting in the autumn can be seen in its avenues in the afternoons.

Then there's Azay-le-Rideau; Langeais with its tapestries; Ussé, so unreal that it inspired the fairy tale of Sleeping Beauty; Blois, where French history was made and the duke of Guise was assassinated; Chinon, which featured in the destiny of Joan of Arc; Amboise, linked with Italy because of its association with Leonardo da Vinci; and Chambord, which, with its huge size, its 380 chimneys and 406 rooms, exemplifies and concludes the saga of the Loire castles.

290 top left Feudal towers and outer walls give Chaumont Castle, which stands on a hill overlooking the Loire, the appearance of an impregnable fortress. The castle has an air of mystery, the legacy of its association, at the height of its splendor, with a court astronomer who was more of a magician and fortune-teller than a scientist.

290 top right Villandry Castle is a magnificent residence, but its fame is not so much due to the interior as to its magnificent flower and vegetable gardens, whose colors change with the seasons and the crops. These gardens were inspired by ancient documents written by medieval monks.

290-291 Little Azay-le-Rideau Castle, framed by a romantic natural setting of rare beauty, overlooks the Indre River amid lush vegetation with plane trees, lime trees and tall oaks.

292 top *The Salle des Gardes at Langeais Castle, with its classical layout and furnishings: great brass chandeliers, a pale stone fireplace, paneled walls and exposed beams on the ceiling.*

THE INFLUENCE
OF ITALIAN ART

The Loire Valley is an immense setting that, in a way, belongs to the marvelous period of the Italian Renaissance. In the stone friezes, spiral staircases, windows lighting the halls, and castle porticoes – almost everywhere, in fact – Italian influence has left the unmistakable imprint of its grandeur. The façade of Valençay Castle has the same scenic perfection as the 15th century palazzi of Florence, the staircase of Blois Castle repeats the floral motifs of many Tuscan portals, and the names of many famous personalities are linked with the Loire Valley. One such personality was Catherine de Médicis who, when she married Henri II, brought to France the art of good living, the gaiety of the *volta* (a rather daring dance that delighted the court), and the elegance and taste of the great balls and banquets held in Florence under the Médicis.

Another was Leonardo da Vinci, who ended his days at the castle of Clos-Lucé in Amboise, given to him by Francis I. He arrived from Florence, his mules loaded with the canvases of the Mona Lisa, St. Anne and John the Baptist. He warmed himself by the fire in the Great Hall, and in the peace of that retreat organized magnificent parties for his French king, creating flying machines and robots that, when struck on the chest, released pure white lilies and perfumed roses onto the guests.

After his death and the return of Francis I from the Battle of Pavia (1528), the time was ripe for the king to return to the capital. The destiny of the Loire as the headquarters of the court was over. Chambord Castle was finished, and from then on was only used for holidays and hunting parties. However, distant sounds still seem to issue from that kingdom of keeps, pinnacles and parapets: the rustle of silk, the clank of armor, dance steps and the gentle notes of lutes and rebecs.

292-293 Standing alone at the end of a huge park, Chambord Castle incarnates the megalomaniac dream of a king who wished to conclude the age of the splendors and legends of the Loire Valley with the most magnificent castle ever built on the riverbanks.

293 right Blois Castle stands in the heart of the town of the same name on the right bank of the Loire, about 37 miles from Orléans. In the 15th century it was the favorite royal residence of Louis XII, who ordered large-scale extension work.

IN THE FOOTSTEPS OF JOAN OF ARC: CHINON CASTLE

Orléans commemorates Joan of Arc every May 8, when 1000 banners fly from Fort des Tourelles to Place St. Croix. The famous Maid of Orléans, played by a young girl, walks at the head of a great procession. This pageant commemorates the day in 1429 when Joan arrived to liberate the city from the English siege. Her "crusade" had set out from Chinon Castle, where Charles VII had taken refuge after escaping from Paris. Joan arrived there on March 9, 1429, escorted by six men, asking to be brought before the king. It was a dramatic time for France. Henry IV was king of England and king of Paris; Charles VII was only king of Bourges. The states general of the central and southern provinces, which had remained loyal to him, had decided to finance the war against the English, but the dauphin hesitated. Joan waited for two days, praying, until she was eventually received in the Throne Room (sadly now partly demolished; only the monumental fireplace remains, together with what, according to legend, is the footprint of the famous heroine). King Charles VII, who had exchanged clothes with a courtier, was concealed among 300 costumed nobles. But Joan was not to be deceived. She walked straight up to the king, embraced his knees and said, "My name is Joan, and I am sent by the king of Heaven to tell you that you will be crowned true king of the French at Rheims Cathedral." The king doubted her word and sent the girl to Poitiers for medical examinations, to establish whether she was a witch or an envoy of God. Eleven days later, convinced by the results, Charles VII permitted Joan of Arc to march at the head of his army against the English. Until 1450 Chinon Castle on the Vienne, a tributary of the Loire, was the headquarters of the court, which later moved to Amboise and Blois. The castle was used once more by Louis XII in 1498 to receive Cesare Borgia, sent by the Pope to deliver the papal bull annulling his marriage with Joan of France so that he could wed Anne of Brittany, thus uniting Brittany and France. The chronicles tell of a grandiose entrance of 68 mules bearing trunks, crates and chairs covered with gold brocade, accompanied by pages, minstrels and drummer-boys. Men and animals draped in brocades and crimson velvets preceded Duke Cesare, who rode a horse decked out with precious stones and pearls. The duke's costume was so precious and studded with gems and diamonds that it "shone like a lighthouse." The duke, son of the Pope, was received with full honors, although it was already known that as cardinal he had been his sister's lover and his brother's murderer. Little now remains of Chinon Castle apart from the grandiose foundations and some towers, including the Tour de l'Horloge with the bell, Marie Javelle, which has struck the hours since 1399, and the Tour d'Argenton, built towards the end of the 15th century, in the location where Louis XI is said to have held his prisoners.

The king's mistress, Agnès Sorel, lived in the adjacent Coudray Castle, which the sovereign reached via secret underground passages. Joan of Arc was held prisoner in the tower of the same building, as were the Templars, whose heartrending messages can still be read on the walls, centuries later. The countryside around Tours is characterized by precious vineyards that produce the red Chinon, Bourgeuil and Saint Nicolas and the white MontLouis and Vouvray wines that accompany the gastronomic delights of the Loire Valley.

294-295 Seen from the Vienne River, Chinon Castle reveals the defensive and military features of what was one of the most famous fortresses of the 15th century. Here the dauphin of France took refuge when he left Paris during a night of terror; Joan of Arc came to the castle too, to implore the king to grant her the honor of marching at the head of his troops against the English army besieging Orléans.

295 top Chinon, with its slate roofs and the web of narrow lanes at the foot of the castle, offers some major tourist attractions, such as a famous wine and a costume fair that, every August, takes the small town four centuries back in time.

295 right Built on a crag where the Romans had already established a castrum (camp) because of its strategic position on the river, Chinon Castle still has some towers that demonstrate that a veritable citadel, not just a castle, once stood at the summit of the village.

295 bottom Partly destroyed over the centuries, Chinon Castle is more famous for its magnificent architectural design than for its wealth of interior decorations, which include some magnificent Aubusson tapestries.

296-297 and 296 top *Ussé Castle still breathes the enchanted atmosphere of* Sleeping Beauty, *the fairy tale by Charles Perrault that made it famous. Its towers, with their gray conical roofs, and the thick forest all around have helped preserve the magic of this spot over the centuries.*

297 bottom *The world-famous Ussé Castle is now a favorite destination of couples looking for a romantic setting for their wedding.*

USSÉ: SLEEPING BEAUTY'S CASTLE

*U*ssé Castle, an enchanting mixture of pinnacles and pointed turrets, is known as Sleeping Beauty's castle. It was an ancient fortress when it belonged to Jean de Bueil, who married a daughter of Charles VII and Agnès Sorel. Work later began on converting it into a less severe home, bristling with towers and pinnacles. It was such an enchanted castle that it inspired Charles Perrault to write his famous fairy tale; so magical that it has caught the imagination of the Japanese, who travel halfway across the world to get married in this romantic setting. The castle is quadrangular in shape, bounded at the corners by keeps and pinnacles. However, like nearly all those in the Loire Valley, the appearance of the building and the original architectural plans, which date back to the 15th and early 16th centuries, were changed by the various owners. The interior of Ussé Castle is richly decorated, and its rooms, with their 18th-century tapestries and 17th- and 18th-century furniture, constitute veritable museums. Some tapestries also hang on the walls of the long gallery, with its black-and-white tiled floor. Paintings of famous schools line the main staircase and the Salle Royale. A rare piece of Renaissance furniture inlaid with ivory occupies almost an entire wall of the *cabinet florentin*. The chapel, which has a nave with no aisles, was built between 1523 and 1535. It contains 16th-century wooden choir-stalls and an enameled majolica Virgin attributed to Luca della Robbia.

297 top Two ancient cedars (legend has it that they were planted by Chateaubriand) protect the 16th-century chapel. The interior, which has a nave but no aisles, is decorated with wooden choir-stalls dating from the period when the chapel was built. However, the most valuable item is an enameled terra-cotta Madonna made by Luca della Robbia around the mid-15th century.

298 and 299 The
wealth of the interior
of Ussé Castle
matches the charm of
the exterior. The
furnishings, especially
the tapestries and
furniture, enhance
the magnificence of
the 18th-century
galleries and halls.
The Aubusson
tapestries and those
by Flemish craftsmen
depicting rural scenes
are particularly
exquisite. Ancient
weapons and
paintings of a good
artistic level
alternate with
Italian furniture,
like the rare ivory-
inlaid specimen in
the cabinet florentin.

MORE TALES OF LOVE AND WAR: LOCHES CASTLE

Between one military campaign and the next, the sovereigns who lived by the Loire devoted a great deal of time to feasting, jousting and love affairs. They had mistresses whose names have gone down in history and who, in exchange for their loyalty, were rewarded with castles and riches. Charles VII and Agnès Sorel were bound by a true passion, and a castle was the reward for every child she bore (four in all). Loches Castle, the largest, had existed since the 6th century with the name of Castellum. In 840 Charles the Bald gave it to a loyal knight, who passed it on to a niece who married Foulques the Black of the House of Anjou. The castle has an exceptional defensive system of walls and towers. It underwent lengthy sieges in the 13th century in the battle fought for possession of Touraine between the Plantagenet King Henry II of England and his sons Richard the Lionheart and John Lackland against Philip Augustus. In the 15th century it became the favorite residence of Charles VII and Agnès Sorel. She died in 1450, and her body lies in an alabaster sarcophagus in the tower that bears her name. A portrait of the king's mistress in another room (a copy of the original, which is in a private collection) shows the delicate grace of her body and a naked breast escaping provocatively from the laces of a corset. From Loches it is just a short walk to Montrésor, one of the prettiest villages in France. The most famous lord of the manor was Imbert de Bastarnay, who bought the existing fortress in 1493 and converted it into the pretty castle that now belongs to the descendants of Count Branicki, the Polish nobleman who bought the property in the 19th century. A friend of Napoleon III, he was a leading financier and a collector of valuable works of art, now on display: paintings by Raphael, Caravaggio and Veronese, silverware belonging to the ancient kings of Poland, hunting trophies, jewelry and furniture from the Italian Renaissance period.

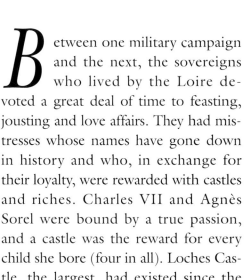

300-301 and 301 top
The warm light of
sunset mellows the
austere design of
Loches Castle. More
of a defensive
bulwark than a
romantic castle, it
has survived intact
over the centuries,
with its famous tower,
the royal gate, and
the chancellery built
by the Counts of
Anjou. The Counts,
who were among the
first owners of the
castle, also ruled over
the town, with its
narrow medieval
lanes huddled at the
foot of the crag.

302 top left Huge fireplaces, shining armor and splendid windows give the interior of the castle a unique, fascinating atmosphere.

302-303 The beautiful Agnès Sorel had a long love affair with Charles VII. Her tomb, watched over by an angel, lies in a tower of the castle.

302 bottom right It was in this room that Joan of Arc delivered her famous speech to King Charles VII in June 1429, urging him to go to Rheims to be crowned king of the French.

303 bottom Pages of history have been written at Loches Castle, from the long love affair between Charles VII and the lovely Agnès Sorel to the imprisonment of Cardinal La Balue, counselor to Louis XI, who betrayed the king to Charles the Bold. He was imprisoned in the Martelet, the gloomy prison with three tiers of cells (cachots) constructed in the Tour Neuve, where Ludovico il Moro, duke of Milan, was also held prisoner by Louis XII.

304-305 and 304 top Saumur Castle, a quadrangle bounded by polygonal towers with conical slate roofs, stands on a rocky promontory that seems to watch over the last stretch of the Loire as it flows towards the sea.

THE CASTLES OF ANJOU

Here the Loire enters Anjou, and before reaching the sea passes by two more famous castles, those of Saumur and Angers. The castle of Saumur, the town that contains the leading French riding school, stands on a rocky promontory. The castle, a quadrilateral with polygonal corner towers, conical roofs of bluish slate and Renaissance-Gothic decorations on a visibly medieval structure, is reached by walking up narrow, steep streets, until the effort is rewarded by a superb view and a visit to the richly decorated rooms. The castle dates from the late 14th century, although its appearance reveals some later additions.

It was the Italian Bartolomeo who built the outer fortifications, which herald the form of the typical Vauban ramparts. A Huguenot stronghold in the 17th century, then a barracks and a penitentiary, it was restructured at the turn of this century and houses three museums: the Decorative Arts

Museum, Toy Soldier Museum and Equestrian Museum, which displays harnesses, trappings and uniforms. Although it has the resources and dynamism of a big city, Angers, with its close-knit network of squares and pedestrian precincts and its clusters of houses over 500 years old, looks like a large village. At the center is its symbol: the squat pentagonal fortress erected by Blanche of Castille, mother of St. Louis, in the early 13th century as a bulwark against the restless Breton populations. Later, at the end of the 13th century, residential buildings, hanging gardens and a chapel for the ducal family of Anjou were added. What was once the residence of the poet-prince René contains the famous *Apocalypse*, about 118 yards of allegorical scenes made with the tapestry technique by 14th-century artists. It has six sections, each divided into 14 episodes, featuring red-blue shades, dragons with huge heads, quadrupeds ridden by Death, sea creatures with macabre features and crude representations of the human face. This is the best visiting card for the itinerary that starts from the castle and continues as far as the *"promenade du bout du monde,"* leading the visitor to the attractive historic buildings in the town center.

305 left and top right Saumur Castle dates from the late 14th century, but like all those in the famous valley it was altered over the centuries and also served various purposes: it was a Huguenot stronghold in the 17th century, then a barracks, and then a penitentiary. It now houses three museums: the Decorative Arts Museum, the Toy Soldier Museum and the Equestrian Museum.

305 bottom right The mighty Angers Castle, a squat pentagonal fortress, was built by Blanche of Castille, mother of Saint Louis, in the early 13th century, to protect the area, which was threatened by the restless Breton populations.

A LADY'S ROMANTIC DREAM: AZAY-LE-RIDEAU

306 and 307 The greenery of the park contrasts with the silvery veil of the Indre River as it flows past Azay-le-Rideau Castle, creating a romantic atmosphere. An enchanting blend of pinnacles and sharp turrets, the castle houses valuable works of art such as a 16th-century portrait by an unknown artist of a young woman reading, a portrait of Louis XIV standing, and a 16th-century portrait of the duke of Guise, nicknamed le Balafré (Scarface).

*I*n the spot where the road from Tours to Chinon crosses the Indre, a left-hand tributary of the Loire, once stood the watchtower of Azay-le-Rideau. This was a medieval fortification surrounded by a deep moat and manned by a garrison of Burgundian soldiers. For 100 years it was no more than a pile of rubble, after Charles VII set fire to the entire village and the fortified tower in 1418, also killing the soldiers of the garrison, to take revenge for the insults he had received. In 1518 the court financier, Gilles Berthelot, treasurer to Francis I, bought the property and commissioned architect Étienne Rousseau to erect a castle in Renaissance style in a pretty spot where the Indre formed a small lake. The work lasted 10 years, until 1529, and was directed by the financier's wife, Philippa Lesbahy. The result was a residence designed for the pure pleasure of living in it, with no defensive purposes. It was built partly on the water, its romantic white image reflected in the lake, with conical towers, slate roofs and pretty ornaments outside and the great right-angled staircase inside. It was Philippa Lesbahy who gave the residence the elegant furnishings it still retains: drawing rooms full of paintings, a collection of blue majolica plates, and walls hung with Gobelin tapestries. That is why the castle is one of the most beautiful in the Loire Valley and was liked so much by Francis I who, taking advantage of a

conspiracy, had no hesitation in confiscating it and exiling the owner, Berthelot. In the King's Chamber, where Francis I almost certainly stayed, is a great fireplace with the initials F and C (standing for queen Claude). It is followed by the Green Room, named after the huge green damask four-poster bed dating from the 17th century, the Red Room, where crimson damask still prevails in the furnishings, and the Banqueting Hall, with its huge fireplace and valuable Brussels tapestries.

308 and 309 Great
tapestries hang from
the walls of the
magnificent
Renaissance-style
rooms of Azay-le-
Rideau Castle,
featuring great
fireplaces, light,
vaulted kitchens and
a simple but elegant
main staircase
leading to the upper
floors. It was Mme
Philippa Lesbahy in
the 16th century who
gave the castle the
gentle, cozy air it still
retains today.
Designed as a
medieval fortification,
it was reduced to a
pile of ruins in 1418,
and finally converted
to a nobleman's
residence in 1529.

310 *More beautiful rooms in Azay-le-Rideau castle bear witness to the famous personalities who stayed there: the Salle à Manger, decorated in Henri II style (top right), the chamber of Francis I with the royal emblem of the salamander engraved on the fireplace (left), and the Blue Room (bottom right), which belonged to Maréchal de la Barre, who was killed in the siege of Nice in 1705.*

311 *A plain four-poster bed, an original marble table, wall hangings and golden yellow curtains with the most popular flower patterns, and a monumental fireplace are the few concessions to luxury in the simple, cozy bedroom of Francis I.*

A CASTLE OF WEAPONRY AND LOVE: LANGEAIS

312 The marriage of Charles VIII to Anne of Brittany was celebrated in Langeais Castle in 1491. The hall where the wedding took place, with its great tapestries and beamed ceiling, remains intact (bottom right). The royal bedchamber, with its four-poster bed (bottom left), exemplifies the furnishings typical of great 15th-century mansions. In Langeais Castle, 13 chambers are hung with 15th- and 16th-century Flemish tapestries. The chapel (top left) has the typical inverted-hull-shaped ceiling.

*I*n the numerous castles that follow the Loire Valley from Gien to Saumur, the desire for beauty replaced the need for defensive security in the century of the Renaissance. Langeais Castle, situated to the west of Tours by the riverside, is the only medieval fortress that has remained intact and has never been changed over the centuries by rebuilding work. After passing through the main door visitors enter the inner courtyard, where they see the ruins of a high wall, part of the ancient fortress built in 994 by Foulques the Red, founder of the Anjou Dynasty, a farsighted politician and strategist, but also a treacherous, cynical feudal brigand.

Langeais Castle and the entire province of Touraine passed to the Counts of Anjou in the 11th century, then to the Plantagenets. During the Hundred Years' War it was occupied by the English on various occasions. The present castle was built by Louis XI. Charles VIII and Anne of Brittany were married there in 1491. The chronicles tell of the magnificent procession that escorted the future bride, clad in a gold and velvet robe decorated with 160 sables, into the king's presence, and of the magnificent banquet with flocks of doves, meat pies, patties containing warblers, quails and turtle doves, and boiled capons covered with fine gold. After the wedding the severe feudal castle must have seemed gloomy to the 15-year-

old bride, who only a year later preferred to move with the court to Amboise Castle. Since then, Langeais Castle has never reappeared in the history books, but the austere style of its walls, the rooms hung with 16th-century tapestries and the valuable antique furniture beautifully recreate the atmosphere of its legendary past.

313 Proud and solemn in its feudal armor, Langeais Castle has survived the ravages of time and war unharmed. The castle, whose features are typical of late 15th-century defensive architecture, overlooks the Loire and the roofs of the village below.

314

GREAT HISTORICAL EVENTS: AMBOISE

314 and 315 Medieval and Renaissance styles are blended in the majestic Amboise Castle, with its stone friezes, spiral staircases and windows casting light on halls and porticoes. Standing high above the Loire, the castle still seems to control its strategic position as a defensive bulwark by the ford. For centuries that was its function, with the result that its walls have witnessed a great deal of history.

Amboise Castle is one of the most important castles in the Loire Valley because of the historical events that took place there and the role it played in introducing Italian art into France. Its origins date from the Gallo-Roman period. In 500 Clovis, king of the Franks, met Alaric, king of the Visigoths, there. They challenged one another to a chivalrous duel, and Alaric was killed. Later, the importance of Amboise grew with the construction of the bridge over the Loire, because there were only seven bridges between Gien and Angers, and anyone who controlled them, thus enabling

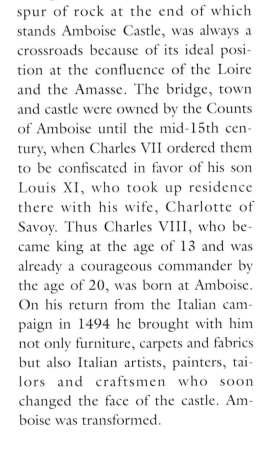

troops to cross the river, would control the entire region.

The promontory of Chatelliers, a spur of rock at the end of which stands Amboise Castle, was always a crossroads because of its ideal position at the confluence of the Loire and the Amasse. The bridge, town and castle were owned by the Counts of Amboise until the mid-15th century, when Charles VII ordered them to be confiscated in favor of his son Louis XI, who took up residence there with his wife, Charlotte of Savoy. Thus Charles VIII, who became king at the age of 13 and was already a courageous commander by the age of 20, was born at Amboise. On his return from the Italian campaign in 1494 he brought with him not only furniture, carpets and fabrics but also Italian artists, painters, tailors and craftsmen who soon changed the face of the castle. Amboise was transformed.

Landscape gardener Pacello Mercogliano created the first Italianate garden; brilliant architects and sculptors embellished the residence in accordance with Renaissance style; and hundreds of Turkish carpets and tapestries from Flanders and Damascus adorned the magnificent rooms.

A solemn tournament was held to celebrate its renovation. On April 7, 1498, Easter Eve, Charles VIII, accompanied by his wife, Anne of Brittany, went to the Hacquelebac Gallery on the way to the tournament field. Charles forgot to bend his head, and though he was by no means tall, he accidentally hit his forehead against the entrance architrave. He still watched the tournament, but then fell into a coma and died at 9 o'clock the same evening. He was succeeded by his cousin Louis d'Orléans, who became King Louis XII, married Charles' widow, Anne of Brittany, and gave Amboise to Louise of Savoy, mother of Francis I of Angoulême, who was heir to the throne. When he became king in 1515, Francis I demonstrated a particular fondness for the castle where he had spent his childhood. He completed the wing begun by Louis XII and summoned Leonardo da Vinci from Italy.

318-319 Magnificent furnishings and original paintings decorate the rooms of Amboise Castle, like the room in Louis Philippe style dominated by crimson fabrics and upholstery.

319 The hall is dominated by the great portraits hanging on the walls, including those of the duke of Orléans (top left) and Maria Amelia of Bourbon (top right).

320 top The elegant Salle aux Poutres, designed and decorated between the 15th and 16th centuries, contains exquisite tapestries, beamed ceilings and priceless antique furniture.

320 left and 321 top and bottom The classic, severe style of the Renaissance period dominates these rooms of Amboise Castle; a good example is provided by the chamber of Henri II, with the large tapestries on the walls, great fireplaces, and four-poster beds.

320-321 The classical style of furnishing characteristic of all the Loire chateaux can be seen in the Salle des Gardes, with its Gothic ceilings, and the rooms adjacent to it.

322 and 323 Amboise Castle not only provided the venue for some major historical events; above all, it provided the base from which Renaissance art was introduced into France because the great Leonardo da Vinci (shown here in a marble bust at top left) moved from Milan to spend the rest of his life there. His tomb is in St. Hubert's Chapel, constructed in flamboyant Gothic style with large windows and a richly decorated portal.

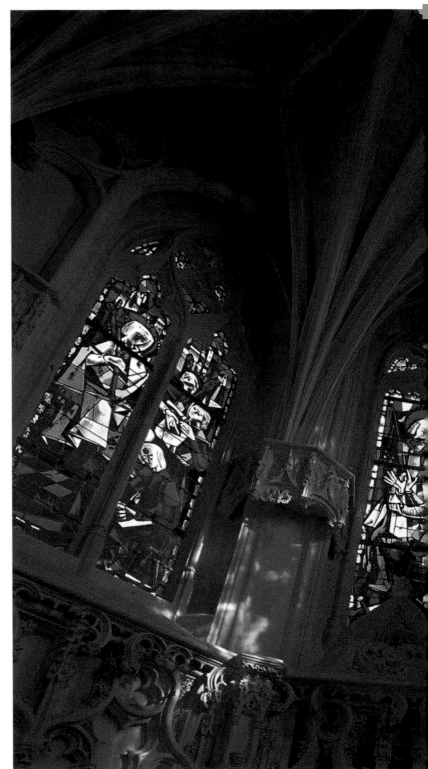

324 and 325 After loading some precious canvases, including the Mona Lisa, onto mules, Leonardo da Vinci left Florence for Amboise at the age of 64. Here Francis I is shown awaiting the great artist, to whom he donated Clos-Lucé Castle, where he spent the rest of his life.

His spirit can be felt in every room, such as the bedroom with the four-poster bed and large stone fireplace where he died, and in the collection on the basement of scale models of brilliant machines that he designed and about which he left detailed notes.

AN ARTIST'S JOURNEY AND A KING'S FRIENDSHIP LEONARDO DA VINCI AND FRANCIS I: FROM AMBOISE TO CLOS-LUCÉ

Leonardo, at the age of 64, loaded the canvases of the Mona Lisa, St. Anne and John the Baptist onto mules, left Florence, and set off for Amboise with his faithful disciple, Francesco Melzi, and his servant, Battista di Villanis. Francis I received the Italian genius at Amboise, and gave him Cloux Castle (now Clos-Lucé) and an annuity of 700 gold scudos. All he required in exchange was the pleasure of conversation with him. From 1516, Leonardo spent the last years of his life in the Loire Valley, masterminding splendid parties, masked balls and artists' conferences, and continuing his studies of engineering and anatomy. He lies in St. Hubert's Chapel in Amboise Castle. On the death of Francis I in 1547, the decline of Amboise began. In the 17th century Louis XIII visited the castle to hunt in the nearby forest, but under Louis XIV the mighty walls became grim state prisons. Amboise castle regained its past glory under Louis XV, who gave it to the duke of Choiseul, and later under Napoleon, who confiscated the castle and gave it to a member of the Directory, Roger Ducos. The latter had insufficient funds to maintain the great building and demolished part of it, but despite this mutilation, the castle still presents a faithful picture of what court life must have been like 400 years ago. There were two mighty towers, about 22 yards tall, with spiral staircases, in which a horse could be ridden right to the top; the king's apartments, the guardroom, and a wonderful view from the large terrace over the Loire and its tributary, the Amasse, complete the picture of one of the most spectacular castles in the valley. A long walk from Amboise is the magic of Clos-Lucé Castle, the residence of Leonardo da Vinci. The king and the "painter-cum-engineer" got along extraordinarily well; both of them enthusiastically cherished fantastic dreams. Leonardo was planning to build prefabricated wooden houses for the populace, to connect all the Loire castles with a series of canals, to make flying machines with wings. His designs and intuitions were ahead of their time in a century of humanists not given to flights of fancy. The time was not yet ripe for the scientific innovations that continually issued from the mind of the great genius, and everything remained on paper. At Clos-Lucé, in the very rooms that witnessed this outpouring of ideas and the long talks between the Italian artist and his royal patron, the astonished visitor can view the collection of manuscripts and the models of machines reconstructed in accordance with Leonardo's detailed instructions.

*326-327 and 326 top
Magic and mystery
inhabit Chaumont
Castle, with its pale
stone and sloping
slate roofs, situated
just a few miles from
Amboise and Blois,
which were so
powerful in the
Middle Ages.*

A QUEEN'S DARK SECRETS: CHAUMONT

The memory of Catherine de Médicis pervades the halls of Chaumont Castle. In 1560, as widow of Henri II, she bought the castle to take her revenge for her husband's adultery and force his mistress, Diane de Poitiers, to exchange it for Chenonceau Castle, which Henri had given her in 1547, when he ascended to the throne. The beautiful Diane could hardly refuse, but did not stay long at Chaumont, preferring exile at Anet Castle, where she died seven years later, far from the gossip of the Loire Valley.

The memory of the great Catherine is still very much alive at Chaumont. Her adviser on the occult arts, the sorcerer Ruggieri, is said to have stayed there, and the existence of a room connected to a tower by a steep staircase has led to rumors of a secret hideaway where the queen and her adviser retired to conduct magic rites and interrogate the stars about the future. Catherine is said to have discovered the tragic destiny awaiting her three children and the imminent advent of the Bourbons at Chaumont. The castle stands on a hill overlooking the left bank of the river. Until the 15th century it was the feudal fortress of the Counts of Blois; it was later rebuilt with round guard towers and softened by the addition of conical roofs and Renaissance influences. It passed through the hands of various owners, including the chatelain who demolished the north wing in the 18th century to obtain a better view of the Loire, and one Le Ray who, also in the 18th century, arranged for the famous Italian pottery maker Battista Nini to stay there. The latter set up his workshop in the stables, and his great kiln in an old dovecote. He made an important contribution to the history of art by reproducing numerous copies of ceramic medallions of the most famous personalities of the period, some of which are on display in the rooms of the castle leading to the chambers of Diane, Catherine and the astrologer Ruggieri.

328 The air of
mystery with which
Chaumont Castle
was rife soon became
a legend; the main
centers from which
this fascination still
radiates are the
chamber of Queen
Catherine de Médicis
(bottom right) in her
favorite green, that of
the sorcerer Ruggieri
(top right), and the
chapel, with its
pointed stained-glass
windows (top left).

329 The narrow
Gothic-style staircase
that runs through the
heart of the castle
perhaps led to the
mysterious laboratory
of the occult arts
presided over by
Ruggieri, the
powerful court
astrologer who
predicted the death of
Henri III, which put
an end to the reign of
the Valois dynasty.

330 and 331 Though it boasts three main buildings, a keep and a court of honor, Villandry Castle does not tell the stories of kings and queens. Spanish magnate Carvallo came to Villandry after the Second World War with the intention of buying the ancient castle to create a special garden. The rooms, with the original marble checkerboard floor (bottom right), can be visited, and the architectural design of the mighty building admired, but then the visitor will inevitably be drawn to the flower gardens, the avenues lined with lime trees and the unusual vegetable garden (top left).

IN BALZAC'S LOVELY COUNTRYSIDE: VILLANDRY

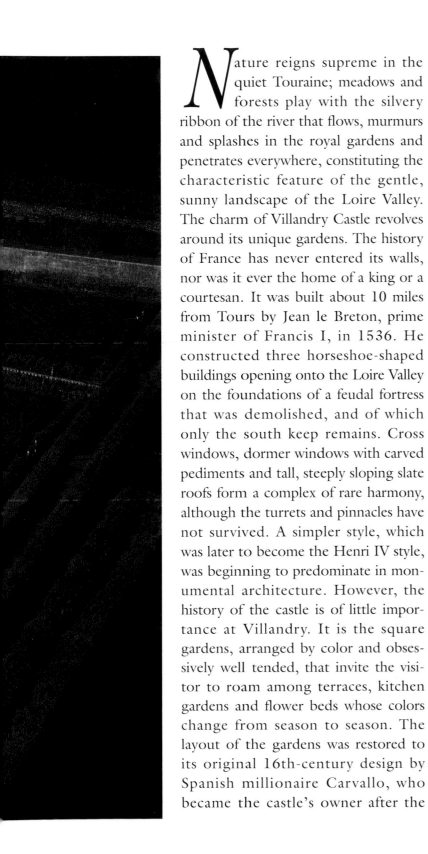

Nature reigns supreme in the quiet Touraine; meadows and forests play with the silvery ribbon of the river that flows, murmurs and splashes in the royal gardens and penetrates everywhere, constituting the characteristic feature of the gentle, sunny landscape of the Loire Valley. The charm of Villandry Castle revolves around its unique gardens. The history of France has never entered its walls, nor was it ever the home of a king or a courtesan. It was built about 10 miles from Tours by Jean le Breton, prime minister of Francis I, in 1536. He constructed three horseshoe-shaped buildings opening onto the Loire Valley on the foundations of a feudal fortress that was demolished, and of which only the south keep remains. Cross windows, dormer windows with carved pediments and tall, steeply sloping slate roofs form a complex of rare harmony, although the turrets and pinnacles have not survived. A simpler style, which was later to become the Henri IV style, was beginning to predominate in monumental architecture. However, the history of the castle is of little importance at Villandry. It is the square gardens, arranged by color and obsessively well tended, that invite the visitor to roam among terraces, kitchen gardens and flower beds whose colors change from season to season. The layout of the gardens was restored to its original 16th-century design by Spanish millionaire Carvallo, who became the castle's owner after the Second World War. After discovering the original designs by Androuet du Cerceau, the architect who created the gardens, Carvallo recreated the original structure, with three terraces built on different levels, avenues shaded by lime trees, straight paths along which flowers blossom, box hedges clipped by topiarists and the curious herbariums of the medieval monks; visitors can stroll through the garden of love and the garden of music, amid mallow and chervil, beets, cabbage seedlings and pumpkins.

333 The ornamental gardens dedicated to love are clearly seen from the panoramic terrace. The designer intended the arrangement of the hedges to reflect the symbols of various types of love: hearts and flames represented tender love, deformed hearts delirious love, swords and daggers tragic love, and fans and letters of the alphabet elusive love.

332 Androuet du Cerceau designed the gardens of Villandry, magnificent green spaces that still retain their original appearance, with three terraces built at different levels. The layout of the gardens not only reflects the taste of the period, but also aims to recreate a philosophical symbolism in the arrangement of hedges and floral decorations. Some very rare species, often from distant regions, were cultivated here in the 16th century.

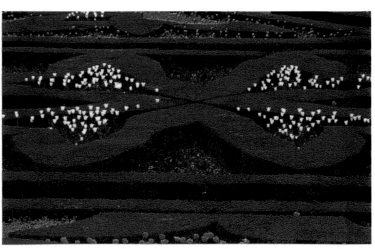

334 *Chenonceau was built for Catherine Briçonnet, given to Diane de Poitiers (portrayed as Diana the Huntress by Primaticcio, bottom left) by her lover Henri II (shown in a contemporary portrait, bottom left), reclaimed by Catherine de Médicis, and passed on to Louise of Lorraine, widow of Henri III, who spent 12 years mourning there.*

THE CASTLE OF QUEENS: CHENONCEAU

Just a stone's throw from the flourishing, idyllic rural town of Montrichard stands the most frequently visited and most romantic castle in the Loire Valley: Chenonceau, known as "the castle of six ladies" because of the role played by six chatelaines in its 400-year history. This *caprice des femmes* is famous for its five-span bridge and the two-storey gallery over the Cher, as well as the 15th-century circular keep, the gardens dedicated to Catherine and Diane, the two women who shared the king's favors, and the interior, including Diane de Poitiers' room, Catherine de Médicis' green study, and the queen's chamber, decorated with Gobelin tapestries. At different times the castle was inhabited by Mme. Catherine Briconnet, who built it with her husband, Thomas Bohier, Diane de Poitiers, who was given it by her lover Henri II, Catherine de Médicis, who reclaimed it on her husband's death, and Louise of Lorraine, widow of Henri III, who mourned her husband's death there, dressed in white according to royal protocol; she is said to have murmured nothing but prayers for 12 years.

After Louise of Lorraine, Chenonceau fell into a period of decline until Mme Dupin became its owner in the 18th century, and one of the most famous literary salons of the age developed

around her and Jean-Jacques Rousseau, her son's tutor. In 1864 the castle was bought by Mme Pelouze, who meticulously restored its original design and then sold it to the present owners, the Menier family.

The grace of its design, the airy beauty of the gallery built by Catherine de Médicis and the tidy grounds once provided the romantic setting for the lives of queens and courtesans, which are recreated every summer evening in a sound-and-light show.

335 So ethereal that it seems to glide through the blue waters of the Cher like a stone galleon, so rich in history that every corner of the expansive grounds and halls evoke the ghosts of the ladies who lived, suffered, rejoiced and intrigued between the walls there, Chenonceau is one of the most famous castles in France.

336 The rooms of the castle are richly decorated, as they must have been at the height of its glory: some good examples are the large kitchen (bottom right), the Gothic gallery with its ogival vaults (left) and the chamber of Gabrielle d'Estrée, King Henri IV's mistress (top right).

336-337 Pure gold and crimson tapestries decorate Louis XIII's chamber, with its magnificent fireplace and the portrait of Louis XIV attributed to Rigaud and set off by a magnificently carved and gilded frame. On the right can be seen the great fireplace with the symbols of the ermine and the salamander, belonging to Francis I and his bride, Claude de France.

337 top The gallery, illuminated by 18 windows ordered by Catherine de Médicis for court banquets, was used as a hospital during the First World War.

*338 top
The Chambre des
Reines is a delightful
blend of style and
luxury; the room is
dominated by Diane
de Poitiers' bed,
which, according to
legend, had an
"extraordinary"
effect on those who
reclined in it.*

*338 left Italian
furniture appeared
in French palaces as
early as the 16th
century. The item
shown in this photo,
decorated with ivory
and mother-of-pearl,
is the work of 15th-
century Florentine
craftsmen.*

339 Diane de Poitiers' bedroom, known as the Chambre des Reines, contains two impressive Flemish tapestries of rare beauty (the one in the picture above portrays scenes from court life) and a massive fireplace decorated with the royal symbols in pure gold (right photo).

338-339 The chamber of César de Vendôme, son of Henri IV and Gabrielle d'Estrée, who owned the castle in the 17th century, contains a wealth of gold and tapestries.

CRIME, INTRIGUE AND COURTLY LOVE: BLOIS

340 and 341 Much of the history of France has passed through this castle, built by the Counts of Blois in the 14th century as a bridgehead on the Loire. However, only a few relics survive of the ancient feudal building, onto which the restorations and alterations commissioned by Charles d'Orléans, Louis XII and Francis I were grafted.

"Great souls," wrote Victor Hugo, "have left faint traces of their memory at Blois Castle." Its complex history has given the grandiose construction various styles, from the flowery Gothic of the façade to the Renaissance style of the famous staircase and the classical look of the Gaston d'Orléans wing. In the 14th century this medieval building, designed as a bridgehead on the Loire, belonged to the Counts of Châtillon, the last of whom sold it in 1391 to Duke Louis d'Orléans,

brother of Charles VI. When the duke was killed in Paris by the Burgundian John the Fearless, the castle passed into the hands of Charles d'Orléans, the family poet. Taken prisoner at the battle of Azincourt, Charles was incarcerated for 25 years, comforted by poetry and great literature. When he was released at the end of the Hundred Years' War, Charles d'Orléans thought no more of battle. At the age of 50 he fell in love with the 14-year-old Marie de Clèves, married her and went back to live at Blois Castle, surrounded by writers, artists and an army of architects who demolished the old fortress and erected a stone and brick building.

The complex, with its magnificent Renaissance staircase, was embellished by Francis I, who ascended to the throne in 1515, married Claude de France, by whom he had seven children, and built the famous staircase and the splendid fireplaces. Catherine de Médicis gave an aura of mystery to the royal apartments; behind secret

*342 bottom
The Renaissance tower
and Louis XII wing
also overlook the inner
courtyard, producing
a monumental
ensemble of rare beauty.
The effect is enhanced
by niches like the one*

*shown here. Appearing
on the main castle
door is this Gothic-
style equestrian statue
of Louis XII,
decorated by the classic
Capetian fleurs-de-lys
and a frieze depicting
a porcupine.*

*342-343 Blois reached
the height of its power
in the 12th and 13th
centuries, and
continued to play an
important role in
French political life
until the 17th century.
In the 18th century,*

*before the Revolution,
the town and castle
attracted the interest
of many French artists.
This watercolor, by
Henri Joseph Van
Blarenberghe, dates
from the late 18th
century.*

doors in her study she concealed precious documents, her famous pearl necklace and, so it was rumored, bottles of poison. Catherine de Médicis' hideaway, which has remained almost intact, still features 237 carved wooden panels that conceal cupboards that can only be opened by pressing a pedal concealed in a plinth. Francis II, Charles IX and Henri III reigned at Blois between 1547 and 1574, directed by their able mother, Catherine de Médicis. The history of the castle recommenced under Henri III. The States General were convened in the huge hall on the ground floor in 1576 to demand the suppression of the Huguenot religion. The States General were again convened in 1588 by Duke Henri de Guise who, supported by the king of Spain, attempted to depose the king. But before going down to the hall where he was expected, Henri III arranged for his rival to be led into a trap and stabbed. The king watched the murder from his chamber. Eight months later, he was to meet the same fate by the hand of Jacques Clément. Until 1617, when Louis XIII sent his mother, Maria de Médicis, into exile there, Blois played no part in history. However, Maria did not stay long. One night, after two years of boredom, she, despite her bulk, climbed down a rope ladder from the window; her son had no choice but to reconcile with his mother after her adventurous escape. However, by then Louis XIII had discovered that Blois, which was quite

a long way from Paris, made an excellent gilded prison. In 1626 he sent his brother Gaston d'Orléans there, promising him sufficient funds to build a residence worthy of his rank. Gaston, forgetting his love of political conspiracy, had the architect Mansart draw up plans for a castle, which required the demolition of the existing wings. For three years, work on a new wing opposite the main door in the courtyard proceeded apace. Then, after the birth of Louis XIV, the danger that Gaston might inherit the throne of France receded; Cardinal Richelieu cut off the funds and the work came to a halt. Gaston, dissatisfied with the new section he had built, went to live in the Francis I wing, and devoted his time to collecting rare plants.

343 top left
The influence exerted in France by the discovery of the Italian Renaissance is due to Francis I, who conducted a military campaign in Italy; this influence is particularly evident in the staircase of the Francis I wing in the inner courtyard of Blois Castle.

343 top right
The Gaston d'Orléans wing (the magnificent staircase of which can be seen in this photo) overlooks the inner courtyard. Work on this wing began in 1635 and lasted for three years, until Cardinal Richelieu cut off the funds required.

344 top Visitors can once again follow in the footsteps of Catherine de Médicis at Blois Castle. Her chamber is rich in gold work and luxurious "trifles," such as the four-poster bed and the unusual floor with its gilded tiles framed with the ever-present fleur-de-lys.

344-345 From
Catherine's bedroom,
access is obtained to
her private hideaway,
its walls covered with
fake panels made of
wood and pure gold
that conceal secret
hiding places.

345 top left and
bottom As at
Chenonceau, the most
luxurious furniture at
Blois came from Italy.
Tuscan craftsmen, in
particular, were very
popular in the 15th
and 16th centuries.

345 right Scenes
from court life were
immortalized by
artists of the period,
as in this tondo by
Ulysse Besnard, which
shows Catherine de
Médicis receiving
some ambassadors.

346 top left and bottom The salamander motif, emblem of Francis I, appears in the friezes on the fireplaces and in the furniture made specially for the king.

346 top right
This portrait shows Marguerite of Navarre, known as Queen Margot, the sister of King Henri III of France.

346-347 More halls, chambers and galleries of the grandiose Blois Castle, with fireplaces bearing the initials and symbols of Francis I and Claude de France, Renaissance furniture and portraits; the wall decorations, however, are typical of the late 19th and early 20th centuries.

347 top Another 39 historical portraits from the French royal court, as well as Margot's, crowd the gallery in the Louis XII wing.

347 bottom The busts of Henri II, Henri III, Henri IV and Charles IX have been placed in the Galerie des Loges, among magnificent pieces of ivory-inlaid Italian furniture and tapestries of the Flemish school.

348 top The portrait of Louis XIV attributed to Hyacinthe Rigaud pays homage to one of the most powerful French monarchs in history; however, Louis XIV never spent even a day at Blois Castle.

348-349 Blois Castle presents the set patterns of what was once the classic style of castle furnishing: the King's Room, with its four-poster bed, the great fireplaces in every room, coffered ceilings and tapestries hanging from the walls.

349 top This picture shows a detail of the beautiful tapestry hanging in the bedroom of Henri III; the three fleurs-de-lys, the king's initial and the royal crown are recognizable.

349 bottom The windows of the Salle des États bear symbols of the Capetian dynasty's power; on the left is the ermine, the emblem of Anne of Brittany, and on the right the porcupine, emblem of Louis XII.

350 and 351 Blois Castle witnessed the ruthless murder of Henri de Guise, treacherously killed by order of King Henri III.

The King's Chamber evokes that tragic December 23, 1588, also immortalized in two famous 19th-century canvases.

352 top left The small Beauregard Castle contains a gallery of 327 portraits, unique in the history of the Loire châteaux. The portraits in the long Galerie des Illustres include that of Henry IV on horseback.

352-353 Beauregard Castle, nestled in Russy Forest, is cradled by the calm Beuvron Valley.

THE CHARM OF GREAT MANSIONS: BEAUREGARD AND CHEVERNY

*L*uxuriant, restful countryside leads from Blois to nearby Beauregard Castle, situated at the end of a long drive that cuts through Russy Forest. This small, secluded private castle, its dimensions still as perfect as when it was commissioned in the 16th century by Jean du Thier, secretary of state to Henri II, is worth a visit for its rooms, the large kitchen decorated as in ancient times, and the gallery containing 327 portraits of famous personalities, which is unique in the history of the Loire castles. This Galerie des Illustres was installed by Paul Ardier in the large first-floor gallery that once contained an attractive 16th-century white marble fireplace. The personalities portrayed are prelates, kings, queens, professors and military commanders spanning two centuries. Some pretty delft tiles in the characteristic blue and white colors, laid along the walls in 1628, decorate the austere row of characters hanging side by side, who recount the history of France. At nearby Cheverny Castle, dating from the 17th century, it is the charm of a great mansion, inhabited for 300 years by the family of the marquises of Vibraye and their successor, viscount of Sigelas, that enchants visitors, who can view its magnificent library, painted halls, grandiose weapons room and a collection of 2,000 hunting trophies. The pack of fox-hunting dogs barking excitably from the kennels on one side of the castle recall the great hunting tradition of the castle's owners.

353 top left The 16th-century Cabinet des Grelots is entirely covered with magnificent wood paneling and paintings depicting such subjects as hunting, music and games.

353 top right The great castle kitchen, with its hanging copper pans, is fascinating.

353 bottom right Joan of Arc is portrayed in the Galerie des Illustres.

354 and 355
The family of the
marquises de Vilbraye
lived in Cheverny
Castle for 300 years.
They retained intact
the majestic
proportions of the
rooms, the
magnificent
furnishings of the
king's chamber, as
well as the castle's
Gobelin tapestries
and paintings and
valuable prints.

A KING'S DREAM: CHAMBORD

*F*inally, we come to Chambord, a mirage from afar and a labyrinth to visit. Visitors should climb the Renaissance staircase, visit the rooms, go out onto the terraces, look down on the huge grounds and come as close as possible to the forest of pinnacles and turrets. This is how the megalomaniac dream of Francis I appears, in all its splendor. That ambitious king, with his ardent temperament and craving for novelty, glory and splendor, concluded his architectural dreams here. Numbers are not everything, but they give some idea of the scale of this magnificent site: 440 rooms, 80 staircases and 365 fireplaces surrounded by about 13,750 acres of perfectly rectangular grounds (about 3,750 of which are open to the public) crowded with deer and wild boar and surrounded by boundary walls about 20 miles long. Chambord is without doubt the most extravagant, exaggerated and majestic castle in the entire Loire Valley. Plundered during the Revolution, belonged then to Marshal Berthier and to the dukes of Bordeaux, then taken over by the government in 1930, Chambord Castle is the unrivaled star of the Loire Valley. Above all it is a hymn to grandeur; with its tufa and slate roof resembling a hanging garden and a thousand pillars, pinnacles, chimney pots and skylights, it would come as no surprise to see fairies or impudent gnomes gamboling there.

356 and 357
The impressive Chambord Castle is the largest in Sologne; it stands not far from Blois, and is surrounded by a huge, ancient park. Its construction was started by order of Francis I, and completed during the

reign of Louis XIV, the Sun King. Not all the rooms in Chambord Castle are furnished, but some of them contain a series of late 16th-century Paris tapestries portraying scenes of the king's hunt, woven following cartoons by Laurent Guyot.

357 top This detail of one of the decorations that frame the tapestries of Chambord recalls motifs with a clearly neoclassical inspiration.

358-359 The twin circular staircase, about 9 yards wide, is the heart of the great castle; two people can go up or down it without meeting. The staircase, with its Renaissance design, terminates at the top with a coffered vault engraved with a salamander, the emblem of Francis I.

359 top left The rectangular chapel on the first floor, situated in a round tower, is the largest room in the castle. It was begun by Francis I and finished under Louis XIV by architect Harduin-Mansart.

359 top right The furnishings of Chambord Castle are luxurious, and great attention is paid to every detail, as demonstrated by this radiator covered with blue and white majolica in the best Flemish tradition.

360 and 361 The Queen's Room, the King's Room and the rooms of the Count of Chambord in Chambord Castle are furnished with valuable furniture, Amiens tapestries, four-poster beds and exquisite carpets.

The luxury exuded by these noble chambers is not reflected in all of the more than 400 rooms in the castle; Francis I's somewhat megalomanic dream of creating the most spectacular, majestic, regal castle in France was brought to an

end by the revolution of 1789, during which Chambord was stripped of much of its finery. However, what remains clearly shows how magnificent it must have been at the height of its glory.

362 Among the most famous portraits at Chambord are those of the castle's founder, Francis I (top left), Henri IV (top right), Louis XIV (bottom left), and Stanislaw Leczinski, king of Poland and duke of Bar and Lorraine (bottom right).

362-363 The Salle de Compagnie at Chambord Castle contains a magnificent collection of portraits of outstanding personalities from the reigning French monarchy and illustrious foreign guests.

363 bottom
This young face with an enigmatic smile belongs to Mlle de Blois, one of the most courted and powerful French women of the time.

364 top Montigny-le-Gannelon Castle, with its alternating brick and stone decoration and tall slate roofs, dates from the late 14th century, when the defensive structure was beginning to be replaced by the castle residence, still grandiose but more worldly than military.

364-365 High above the Loir River (not to be confused with the Loire), Châteaudun Castle, with its feudal bulk and slate roofs, overlooks the small town below. A stronghold demolished by the Norman Rollon in 911 already existed on the site in the 5th century.

CASTLES AND THE REMEMBRANCE OF THINGS PAST

T o the north of the Loire River, in the romantic heart of France, the great castles become few and far between. Here, the landscape has the fragrance of harvest time, the charm of deserted horizons and, to the west, already heralds the Normandy countryside, with its boundless greenery and pastures. This area contrasts sharply with the grandiose Loire Valley and its magnificent castles, but here, unspoiled nature and wide-open spaces still lead to lesser known castles, that are no less rich in memories and links with the history of the Loire Valley. The castle of Châteaudun is impressive for the steep crag on which it perches, and the castle of Montigny-le-Gannelon for its magnificent furnishings. Another king's mistress, Mme de Maintenon, leads the tour through the splendors of the castle named after her, while Diane de Poitiers lies in Anet Castle, and the dream of grandeur cherished by the marquis de Laborde sleeps at La Ferté-Vidame. Memories of Proust fill the country footpaths and lanes of Illiers-Combray against the distant background of Chartres and its huge cathedral, reaching for the sky.

365 At the end of a narrow street in the village of Illiers-Combray stands the small 19th-century middle-class home of Proust's aunt and uncle, where the famous author spent his Easter holidays as a boy. Everything has remained as it was recounted in À la Recherche du Temps Perdu – the inner garden with its rosebushes and hydrangeas and the author's bedroom are still there.

366-367 Montigny-le-Gannelon Castle, like nearly all those in the Loire Valley, stands on the remains of an ancient stronghold, this one dating from the 12th century and overlooking the Loir River. The prettier style of the building erected in the 14th century by Jacques de Renty, and frequently altered over the centuries, can be seen from the large entrance park. In 1831 the castle was bought by Prince Montmorency-Laval, who restored the side overlooking the grounds. His son-in-law, the duke of Lévis-Mirepoix, altered the façade overlooking the Loir River in neo-Gothic style and erected a separate building in Baltard style that contains a collection of ancient agricultural machinery.

MORE HALLS, STAIRCASES AND FORTIFIED WALLS: MONTIGNY-LE-GANNELON AND CHÂTEAUDUN

High above the Loir (not to be mistaken with the Loire), the castle of Montigny-le-Gannelon, already a fortress in the time of Charlemagne, acquired its present name in the year 1000 and its Renaissance style in the 16th century, under Louis XII, when Jacques de Renty demolished the ancient fortress to build a new residence in the contemporary style. All that remains of that project is the Ladies' Tower and the Clock Tower, which were later connected at the base by a Gothic gallery. The property passed through the hands of various owners, statesmen and princes, such as Adrien, lord of Montmorency, duke of Laval and Louis XVIII's ambassador to Rome, Madrid, London and Vienna, who is often mentioned during the visit. This visit is particularly interesting because it is conducted by a member of the present-day family of the viscounts of Talhouët Boisorhand, who live in the castle and know the history and legends of the area. The building was altered on various occasions; the last and most visible alteration was ordered by Count Sigismond de Lévis, who completely rebuilt the east façade overlooking the Loir in 1886.

366 top and 367 right The rooms in the castle, decorated in red, blue and gold, are full of priceless antique furniture and portraits of illustrious members of the family. The castle now belongs to the descendants of the family of viscount of Talhouët, who personally guide visitors through the castle, recounting its history and mysterious legends.

368 left The Gothic-
Renaissance staircase
leads to the large
rooms on the second
floor, hung with
magnificent
tapestries.

368 top right
The dungeon, dating
from the 12th
century, has retained
the amazing inner
framework of exposed
beams.

369 Châteaudun
Castle belonged to the
d'Orléans family,
which extended,
decorated, fortified and
defended it against
enemy attack for four
centuries (from the
14th to 18th centuries).
It was above all Jean
d'Orléans (known
as "the Bastard"
because he was the
illegitimate son of
Louis I d'Orléans)
who undertook the
building of the castle
as it survives now,
incorporating the
tall keep.

368 bottom right
Three different
periods – feudal,
Gothic and
Renaissance – have
given the castle its
grandeur. The 12th-
century keep is built
onto the Sainte-
Chapelle, part of the
Dunois wing, dating
from the 15th
century, which is
illuminated by large
Gothic windows.

The 15 wooden
statues in the chapel
portray members of
the d'Orléans
family, carved in the
images of saints and
beatified
personalities, like
the tiny Saint Agnes
and the Saint
Francis, who are
none other than
Agnès of Savoy
and François de
Longueville.

Around 6 miles from Montigny-le-Gannelon, the towering bulk of another castle is reflected in the river: this is Châteaudun. The unusual design of the castle, which overlooks the main road to Alençon, is very impressive. However, for visitors arriving from the Chartres direction, the gray walls lose their severe look and acquire the harmony of a Renaissance mansion, with the staircase carved like lace, the great fireplaces, the chapel decorated with magnificent wooden statues, and the tapestries hanging in the reception room.

It was Jean le Dunois who first decided to give his home two faces, representing a compromise between the feudal past and the desire for a more modern residence. The Norman architect Colin du Val, who hailed from Longueville, built the decidedly Renaissance north wing (called the Dunois wing) between the 12th-century tower and the buttress overlooking the Loir. There is a magnificent view from the towers, and as the visit proceeds from room to room the guide tells the stories of Thibault the Trickster, who built the feudal castle (of which nothing now remains), and Jean le Dunois, loyal general of Charles VII and comrade in arms of Joan of Arc at the siege of Orléans, who was the guiding force behind Châteaudun.

370 top In Aunt Léonie's famous room (left) at Illiers-Combray, Proust (portrait on right) was overwhelmed by the memories evoked by a little madeleine dipped into the lime tea served by his aunt.

THE VILLAGE OF THE SWEET MADELEINE

370-371 One side of Maintenon Castle, with its red brick towers and rectangular courtyard, is next to the small town of the same name, while the other opens onto the grounds, designed by famous landscape gardener Le-Nôtre. Part of the grounds is occupied by the Maintenon Golf Club, one of the most exclusive golf clubs in France.

371 top Mme de Maintenon lived in beautiful rooms hung with velvets and damasks on the first floor of the castle, which also houses a magnificent portrait gallery where the court balls were held and a well-stocked library.

371 center and bottom Chartres Cathedral, which is part of the landscape seen (just as in Proust's time) from the castle area, is just over eight centuries old, and is a masterpiece of French Gothic art.

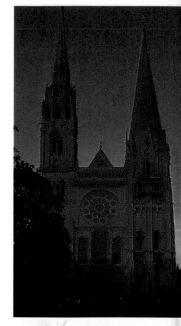

*I*n the huge plain of Beauce, a bell tower pierces the sky like a sharp pencil. "It was the first thing to appear when the train was pulling in to Combray," wrote Proust in *À la Recherche du Temps Perdu*. The pages of his novel seem to turn at every step one takes in the village of Illiers-Combray, which has added the name invented by the author to its own. Here, Proust arrived to spend the Easter holidays at the small house at the bottom of the garden at 4, Rue Docteur-Proust, where many remembrances still remain along with the memory of the sweet, unforgettable madeleine.

Nothing has changed, and on the first floor, Aunt Léonie's room still evokes the atmosphere of that famous page where the author, from the flavor of the morsel of madeleine dipped into the lime tea, recalls past memories. From far off can be seen Chartres Cathedral, which celebrated its 800th anniversary in 1994. At sunset, in the twilit nave, the light sets fire to the reds and blues of the famous 13th-century windows illustrating the lives of the saints, the ancient trades of France, and many Bible stories. The small dark Virgin is venerated at the end of the left-hand aisle. The great statues covering the façade return in the bas-reliefs surrounding the high altar inside, commemorating the art of Jehan de Beauce, who carved the exceptional row of people at prayer in 1514. The still medieval part of the town clusters around the two asymmetrical bell towers in a network of narrow alleys. In the motionless peace of the countryside sleeps Senoches, capital of Perche, the region of good cider. From the small town romantic walks branch off into the nearby forest, around the pond of Lille and La Ferté-Vidame. Nestled in Thymerais Forest, this grandiose patrician residence, now in ruins, still evokes the splendors of the court of the marquis de Laborde, who built his palace in the 18th century on the foundations of the previous castle, where Duke Saint-Simon (author of *Les Mémoires*) lived. The castle was partly destroyed and plundered during the Revolution, and so it has remained until the present day. Fields and meadows protect the abandoned building, which was too large and too magnificent for its bygone splendor to be adequately restored. Maintenon Castle, with its 12th-century keep, the grace of the Renaissance wing and the neoclassical proportions of the side built by Louis XIV, still maintains its royal air. Surrounded by huge grounds, part of which have been sold to the most exclusive golf club in France, the castle was given by Louis XVI to his mistress, Mme de Maintenon, who later became his secret wife. Its drawing rooms and great halls, curtains, velvets, damasks and antique furniture all remain just as they were at the time when the famous lady of the court withdrew with her king to the calm countryside of Eure.

ANET CASTLE: THE TOMB OF BEAUTIFUL DIANE

372 left At the end of the last century the castle was restructured and decorated, and restoration work was carried out on the garden chapel, with its lovely Renaissance dome illuminating an inlaid marble floor that seems to reflect the ornamental motifs of the dome.

From Maintenon it is only a short distance to Anet Castle, the last piece in the huge mosaic of residences associated with the history of the Loire. It was built in 1550 by order of King Henri II, who gave it to his mistress, Diane de Poitiers, as their love nest. The message of this residence is apparent right from the entrance portal, a triumphal arch in honor of "Diana the Huntress," with the naked nymph sculpted by Benvenuto Cellini in the lunette; it was a refuge of pleasure, not a theater of war like many other châteaux of the Loire. The most enlightened minds of the time gathered at Anet, and the king and his mistress went hunting or walked in nearby Dreux Forest. The castle, like many others, was damaged and plundered during the Revolution. It was sold, the furniture was scattered, and part of the castle was demolished by unscrupulous purchasers. In 1820 it was bought by the duchess of Orléans and restored for the first time. However, it was to take years, until nearly the end of the century, before M. Moreau and his descendants restored the home so that it was worthy of the history it recounts. Now preciously decorated, each room evokes the memory of the king's lovely mistress. Four tapestries woven especially for her in 1552 decorate the Salle des

Gardes; other Flemish tapestries drape the walls of the room containing a fireplace decorated with an alabaster medallion by Jean Goujon; the four-poster bed with its canopy bears her initials and sentimental souvenirs belonging to Diane are displayed in the Red Room. In the courtyard is the entrance to Saint Thomas' Chapel. Diane's tomb is in the garden, behind the chapel. After the king's death, she took lonely refuge in this castle, where she lived until her death in 1566. Her last residence closes the romantic and dissolute history of the Loire Valley castles.

372 top and 372-373 Anet Castle was King Henri II's gift to his lovely mistress, Diane de Poitiers. Here the king and Diane retreated for short periods, far from the splendors and court intrigue characteristic of the castles closest to the Loire. The residence, situated on the edge of Dreux Forest, is a gem of secluded Renaissance beauty.

372 bottom right Diane de Poitiers (portrayed here as Diana the Huntress) retired to Anet after the death of King Henri II, when Catherine de Médicis took revenge by confiscating Chenonceau Castle.

373 The spirit of the beautiful Diane can be felt in every corner of the castle, from the splendid main staircase (top left) to the bedroom, with its decorations, tapestries, paintings and four-poster bed (top right), to the Salle des Gardes (center right), decorated with huge Fontainebleau tapestries, to the exquisite wood-paneled Red Room (bottom right).

GENERAL INDEX

PHOTO CREDITS

384 As a palace within a park, Nymphenburg is quite different from other compact palaces like Versailles.
The entire façade is designed to provide access to the park: the galleries that connect the two side wings open onto the gardens, and even the old central portion on the ground floor has wide passageways through which coaches once passed.

Technical Writing, Presentation Skills, and Online Communication:

Professional Tools and Insights

Raymond Greenlaw
United States Naval Academy, USA

Information Science
REFERENCE

Managing Director:	Lindsay Johnston
Senior Editorial Director:	Heather A. Probst
Book Production Manager:	Sean Woznicki
Development Manager:	Joel Gamon
Development Editor:	Myla Harty
Acquisitions Editor:	Erika Gallagher
Typesetter:	Adrienne Freeland
Cover Design:	Nick Newcomer, Lisandro Gonzalez

Published in the United States of America by
Information Science Reference (an imprint of IGI Global)
701 E. Chocolate Avenue
Hershey PA 17033
Tel: 717-533-8845
Fax: 717-533-8661
E-mail: cust@igi-global.com
Web site: http://www.igi-global.com

Library of Congress Cataloging-in-Publication Data

Greenlaw, Raymond.
  Technical writing, presentational skills, and online communication: professional tools and insights / by Raymond Greenlaw.
    p. cm.
  Includes bibliographical references and index.
  Summary: "This book is a collection of work to assist any professional who needs to deal with ethical issues, write up a technical project, give or develop a presentation, or write material for an online audience"--Provided by publisher.
  ISBN 978-1-4666-0237-3 (hardcover) -- ISBN 978-1-4666-0238-0 (ebook) -- ISBN 978-1-4666-0239-7 (print & perpetual access) 1. Technical writing. 2. Communication of technical information. 3. Business writing. 4. Business presentations. I. Title.
  T11.G683 2012
  808.06'6--dc23
                              2011044975

British Cataloguing in Publication Data
A Cataloguing in Publication record for this book is available from the British Library.

All work contributed to this book is new, previously-unpublished material. The views expressed in this book are those of the authors, but not necessarily of the publisher.

This book is dedicated to the four individuals who helped me improve my writing most. My mother, Rox-Ellene Greenlaw, always took a great interest in my writing and always shared her time and energy with me. Whenever I asked her to proofread a manuscript or to make suggestions, she did and her comments always taught me something new and worthwhile. My mom possessed a remarkable command of the English language and an amazing eye for details. Then there is my good friend Dr. Adrian Plante my high-school English teacher. Adrian too took a great interest in my writing, and I was lucky to have him as a mentor during my formative years of study. We read over 50 classics together, and he always provided deep insights during our one-on-one discussions of these works. And, Hugh Willoughby who copyedited several of my books gave me perspective on many topics relating to language. I am sure several grammatical errors remain in this work that Hugh would cringe at, and I apologize to him for not being a better student. Dr. Larry Ruzzo my thesis advisor helped me tremendous with my technical writing via example. He never criticized me but simply showed me how to improve my work. These four individuals inspired me to push forward and complete this manuscript. Whatever is valuable and worthy in this work, I dedicate to them.

Table of Contents

Detailed Table of Contents

Chapter 1

There are four main topics addressed in this book: professional ethics, technical writing, presentation skills, and online writing. These topics and the intended audience of Information Technology (IT) professionals and others working in technical disciplines define the scope of the book. In this chapter, the author motivates each of these subjects by providing a section on who should read this book and a section that summarizes the contents of this book.

Chapter 2

This chapter focuses on ethics for the IT professional. The learning objectives for this chapter are to understand basic ethical principles relating to IT, to develop a framework that supports making informed decisions regarding ethical problems, to apply an ethical code in typical situations, and to understand future trends relating to IT ethics. The author includes material on each of these topics and also sections with conclusions and references. After having mastered the material in this chapter, a reader will have a much-better understanding of ethical principles relating to the IT profession. But, more importantly, a reader will be able to make practical use of that knowledge by applying it in the workplace to solve ethical dilemmas.

Chapter 3

This chapter takes a close look at online-communication forums. IT professionals often have to prepare information for an online forum. Writing for an online audience (what the author calls online writing) is a vastly different activity than writing for an offline audience (called offline writing here), and being good at one form of writing does not ensure that one will be effective at the other form. Thus it is worth carefully exploring the differences in these two styles. The chapter begins by making a comparison between online and offline writing.

The previous chapter covered a wide range of online-communication forums. This chapter focuses on another extremely-popular online forum, namely, the blog. A blog is essentially an online listing and description of related items, and for some individuals it the equivalent to maintaining an online personal journal or activity log. From blogging's origins in late 1997 until now, there has been a tremendous explosion in the number of blogs. The discussion begins here by presenting a history of blogs. The chapter presents a classification scheme for blogs and a number of examples of interesting blogs. It next provides a review of popular blogging software. This software has made setting up, adding content to, and maintaining a blog very simple; this software has help to fuel the popularity of blogging. Tim O'Reilly and others proposed a Blogging Code of Conduct, and the chapter includes a section where the author discusses that code. This material is followed by cautions about blogging. The chapter also reviews a number of IT-related blogs, and wraps up with conclusions and references.

According to one study of the fastest growing areas of employment, desktop publishing was going to experience a 67% increase in the number of employees from the year 2000 to the year 2010, adding about 25,000 new workers (Bear, 2010). And, in an update of that study, it was noted that job growth in this field has slowed some in part because many employers expect all employees to possess good writing skills. There is a great demand for good writers and specifically technical writers. Among other things, professional writers inform people about new products, produce documentation for software, edit manuals, write books, and develop grant proposals. Nearly all people who work in a science-related field or with computers write a great deal. Since writing is a large facet of many jobs, it is important to write well and efficiently. This chapter will help to improve one's writing skills and writing habits.

This chapter provides basic information about the structure of a technical paper. Some of the comments made here can be applied to non-technical papers as well. The chapter begins with a section that discusses the opening of a paper, then discusses the items that appear in the first part of a paper: in particular, the title, authors and affiliations, the abstract, and keywords are discussed. Next, the chapter discusses the role the introduction plays in a paper and the information one typically finds in the introductory section of a paper. The author includes a general section with guidelines about the content of a paper, followed by one about the closing portions of a paper. There, he talks about conclusions, acknowledgments, references, and biographies, and then he describes issues relating to paper submission and how to follow-up with a submission. He includes some other key issues that occur during the submission and acceptance phase of a paper's life cycle. The author includes a few other valuable points in the miscellaneous section, where he discusses submitting to online publications, effective collaboration among coauthors, and reusing one's own work. There is also a brief section with conclusions.

In this chapter, many ethical considerations are discussed when it comes to technical writing. One of the things that discussed is the moral and social responsibilities of scientists. That section describes the moral responsibilities of being honest in research and why it is a grave ethical violation to forge results.

Regarding social responsibility, the chapter examines the issue of speaking out when one believes an ethical violation has been committed, such as when results reported are untrue or dangerous. The author included a section on the responsibility of authors to their coauthors. While working together, authors must have a way to communicate effectively and express their ideas. Once a project is agreed to and commitments are made, coauthors have a moral and ethical responsibility to follow through on such commitments.

Chapter 8

In this chapter, the author covers a number of forms of professional communication. Although this coverage is not comprehensive, there is a discussion of a wide variety of communication mechanisms, and the techniques provided should be extensible to other forms of communication. The chapter starts by discussing four simple rules of communication. If one is able to apply these four basic rules, one will be able to become a much-more effective communicator. Following the four rules of communication, the chapter presents remarks about a wide number of types of communication mechanisms, including email, texting, and telephone calls. It also discusses communication in a group setting. This material is followed by thoughts on taking a message, memorandums, and status reports. The chapter concludes with future trends, conclusions, and references.

Chapter 9

In this chapter the author describes a number of key issues in documenting an event. He covers issues related to details, accuracy, timing, note taking, and audience. He also describes the types of events that typically need documenting. The chapter includes detailed discussions about three types of events that IT professionals are commonly required to document: a computer-bug report, a trip report, and a lab experiment. In each of the corresponding sections, the author describes the specifics of these events. The information provided for these specific events can be generalized and applied to other common events. In this way, the author hopes to prepare readers to be competent to document any type of event that may be required. The chapter ends with conclusions.

Chapter 10

In this chapter, the author considers general topics relating to presentations. The idea is to provide the reader with knowledge that can be put into practical use. It is impossible to cover all the important aspects of presentations in this book, but it is hoped that the reader will find useful items in this chapter. The next chapter covers delivering the presentation and the basic use of PowerPoint. Before launching into the material contained here, here is a roadmap. First discussed are key points relating to topic selection. This section is followed by one on the setting of the presentation. Next discussed are tips for preparing for a presentation, including comments about multimedia. Given the variety of equipment that one might find at a given setting, included are notes about equipment. Many speakers provide handouts to audience members, so a discussion about these items is included too. Of course, if a presentation is not properly advertised, the audience maybe smaller than anticipated. Therefore there is a section on talk advertising. The chapter wraps up with conclusions and references.

In the last chapter, the author described many of the fundamentals of presentations, including items such as the setting of the presentation, multimedia, topic selection, advertising, and equipment. This chapter continues the discussion of presentations with a focus on the delivery, begining with a section on presentation style, discussing things such as inclusion of audio, animations, pictures, tables, and so on. This material is followed by a section on presentation genres. Next, the chapter talks about articles, surveys, and interview talks. PowerPoint is the topic of the next section, and the chapter provides helpful hints about this presentation software. A section on key slides that appear in most presentations, as well as how to craft them, follows. Then the chapter provides a section on how to cope with common-trouble spots. The main content of the chapter wraps up with a section on miscellaneous tips, where a number of useful practical tips are provided regarding presentations. Conclusions and references close out the chapter.

The book now turns its attention to writing a résumé and the equivalent document in academic fields, the curriculum vitæ (CV). These documents represent essentially all that an individual has done in a professional career. In the absence of a face-to-face meeting, these documents represent a person and are used to evaluate a person. Another document called the biographical sketch (or bio sketch for short), used for example with the submission of a talk abstract, is usually much less formal than the résumé or CV. If someone has a résumé, it should be fairly easy to draft a bio sketch, but going in the other direction will require the person to fill in a considerable number of details. Nearly all job openings require the applicant to submit a résumé before the applicant will be considered for the position. A well-formatted résumé could dramatically improve an individual's chances of successfully obtaining a desirable job. Thus the subject of this chapter bears serious consideration.

Professionals and students in scientific fields need to write technical manuscripts such as white papers, technical reports, journal articles, conference papers, dissertations, and theses. LATEX (pronounced "lay-tech," "lay-TEX," or "lah-tech") is a state-of-the-art typesetting system that is ideal for preparing such documents (Lamport, 1994). Note that LATEX is usually typeset with special positioning of the letters "A" and "E," but throughout this work we write it as LATEX because in the fonts used in this book writing all capital letters looks better than trying to write LATEX the way that it is supposed to be written, and similarly, for TEX which is usually written with a special positioning of the letter "E."

Foreword

It is my great pleasure to write the foreword for Dr. Raymond Greenlaw's *Technical Writing, Presentation Skills, and Online Communications: Professional Tools and Insights*. I have known Dr. Greenlaw for over 20 years. In his career in the computing field, which has spanned more than 30 years, Dr. Greenlaw has authored 20 books and over 100 publications in total. Dr. Greenlaw has vast academic experience, currently serving as the Leighton Distinguished Professor of Information Technology at the United States Naval Academy, and previously having worked as a Department Chair and Dean at Armstrong Atlantic State University. Dr. Greenlaw has been the Principal Investigator on many grants and worked as an industry consultant. He played a major role in ABET (Accreditation Board for Engineering and Technology), and he served on the Executive Committee for the Computing Accreditation Commission. I can think of no better person to write a book on technical communications for the Information Technology professional than Dr. Greenlaw.

Based on my personal experience in the computing industry, my own and my colleagues' ability (or lack thereof) to communicate technical concepts effectively has been one of the most-significant determinants of success. Many a talented engineer's career advancement is stymied at an early stage because he or she fails to master these basic and essential skills. In this book, Dr. Greenlaw presents a practical approach to acquiring these skills. He covers many practical aspects of ethics, technical writing, oral presentations, and online writing. I believe that many IT professionals can benefit from reading this book, and they will find new material that they can immediately apply in the workplace or in school. Due to the different levels at which the material is presented, both the relative newcomer to technical writing as well as the seasoned professional will benefit from the wide variety of communication topics that are covered. I highly recommend this book to anyone working in the IT field and to all students of technical communications.

Paul Goransson
Elbrys Networks, Inc.
April 23, 2011

Paul Goransson *is a passionate entrepreneur who has led two boot-strap start-up companies through successful acquisitions by industry giants - Qosnetics by Hewlett Packard (1999) and Meetinghouse by Cisco (2006). Paul held senior management positions with HP's Advanced Networks Division and Cisco's Wireless Networking Business Unit. As Founder and Chairperson of the Elbrys Networks Board of Directors, Paul currently leads corporate strategy and directs Elbrys' Intellectual Property portfolio. Paul received a B.A. in Psychology from Brandeis University in 1975, an M.S. in Computer Engineering from Boston University in 1981, and a Ph.D. in Computer Science from the University of New Hampshire in 1995. Paul is an avid marathoner, mountaineer, triathlete, scuba diver, and outdoor enthusiast. He has completed 6 Ironman triathlons, numerous ultramarathons, and is a NAUI divemaster. He has lived, studied, and worked for extensive periods in France, Algeria, Venezuela, Mexico, and Sweden. Paul co-authored the book "Roaming Securely in 802.11 Networks" as well as numerous articles in technical journals related to computer networking. He is often an invited speaker at technical conferences. Paul owns and manages a 130-acre beef and hay farm in southern Maine in his spare time.*

Preface

INTRODUCTION

This book is about professional communications for the Information Technology (IT) professional. According to one anonymous reviewer, "This manuscript covers the basic topics that are considered essential by most senior faculty members of technical-writing programs." At the broad-brush stroke level, the book addresses four main topics: professional ethics, technical writing, presentation skills, and online writing. These topics are woven throughout the book and some of them are the main subjects of one or more chapters. This preface provides some commentary about each of these four key areas, describe the audience for the book, and follows this description with a more detailed look at the organization of the book. A short discussion about teaching from this book is included. This material is followed by sections on Suggestions and Corrections, an Author's Note, and the Author's Contact Information.

The overarching theme of this book is to provide well-tested, best-practice techniques and strategies in the four main topic areas while focusing on information that can be immediately applied to help the IT professional improve a particular skill. The author describes the generally accepted way of doing something and then illustrates that technique. The approach may seem a bit prescriptive to some readers, but this book is for IT professionals, not creative writers. If the author has succeeded in producing the book that was envisioned, then an individual will be able to turn to almost any page in the book, and find at least one tidbit of information that can be applied directly in the individual's work. Also presented is the big picture relating to the chosen topics, so if a person reads the entire book, the person will have an excellent framework and foundation in the areas of professional ethics, technical writing, presentation skills, and online writing. In short, the learning outcomes of reading and understanding this book are as follows:

The reader will be able to

- Evaluate and come up with a good solution to an ethical problem
- Discuss and explain ethical issues with colleagues and others
- Develop an informed opinion about an ethical dilemma
- Use and apply many basic rules of technical writing
- Possess the writing skills to develop a technical paper
- Develop a well-thought out presentation
- Deliver a good presentation
- Understand the various forms of online communication

- Communicate effectively in a variety of online forums
- Conduct online research

This preface now continues by presenting some thoughts about the four main topics of the book. These topics define the scope of the book.

PROFESSIONAL ETHICS

Regarding ethics, IT professionals encounter many challenging ethical situations and without a proper framework for confronting, evaluating, and resolving ethical situations, the probability of obtaining the best or even a successful outcome is not high. One cannot merely rely on intuition for resolving ethical conflicts. A framework is needed so that ethical principles can be applied uniformly and consistently. Similar violations require similar consequences. Many IT professionals are not currently equipped to handle ethical conflicts. And, rather than merely attempting to deal with issues on an as needed basis when problems arise, one should be prepared in advance. Often ethical decisions must be made on the spot, and there is little time for the unprepared individual to research a situation that requires immediate attention. The book's primary goal regarding ethics is to examine a well-developed ethical code and to work through a few scenarios applying this code of ethics. In other words, a practical hands-on approach to ethics is taken, also focusing on ethical issues relating to writing.

TECHNICAL WRITING

Another major topic is technical writing. If one talks to any employer, teacher, or scientist, one will likely hear complaints about the quality of their employees', students', and assistants' writing, respectively. Even smart people with good language skills struggle with technical writing. This book presents components of a writing toolkit and provides examples of good writing. Also provided is material on manuscript preparation, as well as a wealth of tricks-of-the-trade-type material. Some of these items are strategies and methods that writers having years of experience take for granted, but those writers with less experience have difficulty acquiring and mastering. Learning these tricks and techniques can be made more efficient by gathering them together in one place. In addition to learning how to write particular snippets well, there is a chapter on writing an entire technical paper. And, since many IT professionals have difficulty in thoroughly documenting an event, there is a chapter on that topic. There are also insights into writing various professional communications, including a wealth of material on résumé writing, status reports, telephone messages, and the like. Many IT professionals claim that they suffer from writer's block. The material on writing is of a practical nature and helps one to get started writing. Once this material is learned, IT professionals can immediately use this knowledge to improve their writing. For example, not all IT professionals know that it is considered poor style to begin a sentence with a symbol, such as "x is a real number," rather than writing "The value x is a real number." And, by the way, when should a punctuation symbol be pushed under closing double quotes … In addition, introduction to the LATEX-typesetting system is provided, the typesetting-system of choice for highly technical writing, as is done in computer science, Information Technology, and mathematics.

PRESENTATION SKILLS

Nearly all IT professionals must make presentations from time-to-time. If a person attends any conference on IT, the person will see that many presenters have room for significant improvement. Simply making a presentation once or twice a year is not sufficient practice for becoming an effective presenter. Usually presenters receive little critical feedback on their presentations, so improvements come quite slowly. People truly do not know how they come across or what they are doing wrong. Unlike traditional manuscripts, oral presentations allow a direct interaction with the audience. When delivered properly, they can be powerful and informative. An effective presentation can help secure a job or seal a deal with a client. On the other hand, a poorly executed presentation can keep an individual in the job-search market or lose the person a potential client. The book covers many important aspects of presentations, including analyzing an audience, using PowerPoint effectively, and handling questions. The book also provides information about making presentations effective and convincing. As in other parts of the book, the focus is on a practical approach. For example, "When preparing a survey talk, it is okay to omit things in order to save time or to narrow the focus of the talk." Having developed a great presentation is merely the first hurdle though; one must be able to deliver the presentation effectively. This skill is also learned and needs to be developed, so there is a chapter on the delivery of a good IT presentation. Many of the ideas on presentations are common-sense suggestions, but if a person looks around, the person will find that many IT professionals do not follow these basic rules.

ONLINE WRITING

IT professionals often have to prepare information for an online forum. Writing for an online audience is a vastly different activity than writing for an offline audience, and being good at one form of writing, does not ensure that an individual will be effective at the other form. This book provides material about various online communication forums and presents a classification scheme for them. The popularity of blogging is tremendous and still growing. Therefore, the book contains a discussion and practical tips for bloggers. It describes how to outline, design, and manage a Web presentation. Prior to about 1995, few people conducted research online, but now, nearly everyone does; thus, a chapter about conducting online research is included. The book provides cautions about reliability of information and hints on how to follow-up online research with offline research, as well as information about how to cite online research. As throughout this book, the goal is to provide material that is of a practical ready-to-use nature.

WHO SHOULD READ THIS BOOK?

Anyone with an interest in professional ethics, technical writing, presentation skills, or online writing and possessing some background in one of the following fields can benefit from the use of the book:

- Biology
- Chemistry
- Computer engineering
- Computer science

- Engineering
- Information systems
- Information technology
- Mathematics
- Physics
- Other science-related fields
- Software engineering

This book will be useful for anyone who needs to deal with ethical issues, write up a technical project, give or develop a presentation, or write material for an online audience. The book focuses on practical information and process. The goal is to improve the reader's ability and knowledge in each of these four areas.

ORGANIZATION OF THIS BOOK

Many of the chapters in this book are independent of the others and as a result, one does not need to read them in a linear fashion—one can pick and chose to focus on the particular topic of interest. In the next section of the preface we have more to say about the dependencies of the chapters when we describe how the book can be used for teaching a course. The book contains the following individual chapters, and below is a brief description of each of them:

- INTRODUCTION: This chapter sets the tone for the book and goes into more details about what we intend to cover. There are general sections on professional ethics, technical writing, presentation skills, and online writing.
- ETHICS FOR THE IT PROFESSIONAL: This chapter begins with a discussion of a standard code of ethics. The chapter then explores a number of ethical scenarios and applications of the code of ethics.
- PROFESSIONAL COMMUNICATIONS: Communication is a key part of most jobs. In this chapter we cover material about email, telephone, status reports, and so on. The chapter describes communication in a group setting and how to keep others informed. The chapter wraps up with notes on future trends and conclusions.
- ONLINE COMMUNICATION FORUMS: Here the author compares and contrasts 'online' versus 'offline' writing. The chapter provides a classification scheme for online writing. It provides general information about developing and maintaining a website.
- BLOGGING: The chapter begins with a review of the history of blogs and contains a list of interesting facts about blogs. The author provides a review of some popular free blogging software. Another section provides a few words of caution about blogs and a couple interesting blogging cases. This section is followed by one containing a listing of useful blogs for IT professionals.
- COMMENTS ON MANUSCRIPTION PREPARATION: This chapter provides material on how to prepare for a writing project, how to begin writing, and how to stay productive. This information is followed by more-technical aspects of writing, including tips for writing prose, style issues, and grammatical tips. Other technical writing tidbits are covered throughout the chapter.

- STRUCTURE OF A TECHNICAL PAPER: The author describes the process of writing a technical paper and goes over the basic sections that a typical paper contains. He presents material on the writing process and editing. In addition, the chapter includes thoughts about paper submission and follow-up. The chapter contains miscellaneous points and concluding remarks.
- ETHICAL ISSUES IN WRITING: The author presents material about the moral and social responsibilities of scientists. Given that most research involves collaborators, there is a section about obligations to coauthors. The chapter also describes issues relating to citing the work of others. The chapter contains information on copyright. The author discusses permission issues for figures and tables.
- DOCUMENTING AN EVENT: There are times when one must document an event, and this chapter focuses on how to do that appropriately. It also discusses writing up experiments, bug reports, and trip reports.
- FUNDAMENTALS AND DEVELOPMENT OF A PRESENTATION: This chapter covers many essential topics relating to presentations. From selecting a topic, to the setting for a presentation, to preparing the presentation, to presentation equipment, to supplemental materials, to talk advertisements, the reader will find many valuable presentation tips in this chapter.
- DELIVERING A (POWERPOINT) PRESENTATION AND MORE: This chapter focuses on issues relating to the effective delivery of a presentation. The author focuses on PowerPoint presentations. The chapter covers style issues, presentation genres, key slides to include, trouble spots, the effective handling of questions, how to avoid disasters, and methods for coping with nerves. Many useful tips are included.
- RÉSUMÉS: The author discusses many important topics relating to résumé development in this chapter. He provides insights into résumé writing and covers all the basic sections of a résumé. He also describes how to write a curriculum vitæ. The chapter provides a final checklist for developing a résumé and include material on how to submit a résumé or vitæ.
- INTRODUCTION TO LATEX: Many scientists consider LATEX to be the standard of typesetting systems. This chapter provides a thorough introduction to the LATEX-typesetting system. After reading this chapter, one will have the ability to typeset many different types of documents in LATEX. From installing LATEX on a computer, to creating a LATEX document, to creating one's own environments in LATEX, this chapter covers most of the key introductory elements of LATEX.

Each chapter ends with a conclusions section that summarizes the information contained in the chapter, and when appropriate, it discusses future trends as well. References in this book are included at the end of each chapter. The book includes a comprehensive index for conveniently looking up terms or concepts.

In the next section, a number of ways that the book can be divided up and approached when used as a teaching tool are discussed. However, these reorganization and suggested divisions can also be used by individual readers depending on how they would like to approach the material based on their own experience and knowledge.

TEACHING FROM THIS BOOK

Although this book is intended to be used for self-study, it is entirely suitable to use in a college communications course, a technical writing course, or a course that has a significant component addressing one or more of the following topics: ethics, technical writing, presentations, or online writing. The book could also be used for an advanced high-school course that focuses on one of these topics. The teacher may want to supplement such a course with exercises that ask the student to practice and utilize the material being taught. Such exercises will be easy to generate, but not necessarily easy to grade.

This book is suitable for a course in technical communications. The instructor could cover the majority of topics contained in the book in a semester-long course, omitting topics of less interest depending on the time constraints. Most of the chapters are independent. However, it is best to cover chapter 1 first. Chapter 2 is best covered before chapter 8, and chapter 10 before chapter 11, but otherwise, the chapters can pretty much be covered in the desired order.

This book could be used for a course in ethics. The material in chapters 1, 2, 3, 4, 5, and 8 would be suitable. Chapter 1 contains a discussion of an approach to ethics. Chapter 2 covers ethics for the IT professional, including a discussion of a standard ethical code, ethical scenarios, and case studies of how to apply the ethics code. The focus of chapter 3 is professional communications, and sprinkled throughout that chapter, ethical remarks have been incorporated. Chapter 4 presents online-communication forums, and there are often ethical issues that arise in such groups. The material presented there on developing and maintaining a website could be skipped. Blogging is the subject of chapter 5, and the sections on the history of blogs and cautions about blogging would be appropriate for an ethics course. Chapter 8 contains a discussion on ethical issues in writing. The references provide a wealth of additional topics that could be used to supplement the text.

In a one-semester undergraduate or graduate course in technical writing, the majority of material in the book could be covered. If the course has little emphasis on ethics, chapter 2 could be omitted. If there is little emphasis with online writing, chapters 4 and 5 could be omitted. Chapter 12 on résumé writing could be omitted if time does not permit. A course that focuses heavily on presentations should include chapters 10 and 11, but one that does not can omit these or just cover a portion of them. The amount of material that an instructor can cover will be related to the depth with which the topics are covered. If regular lengthy writing assignments are given, perhaps it will be impossible to cover all the material in the book. On the other hand, if the assignments are kept shorter, more reading from both the text and references can be assigned.

Another approach would be to divide the material by topic. In this case one could divide the material into four or five parts: technical writing, ethics, presentations, going online, and miscellaneous. These could be covered in any desired order subject to the constraints already given. The technical writing part would consist of chapters 3, 6, 7, and 9; the ethics parts would consist of chapters 2 and 8; the presentations part would consist of chapters 10 and 11; the going online part would consist of chapters 4, 5, and 9; and the miscellaneous part would consist of the remaining chapters.

This book can be used to supplement the text or instructor's notes for any course that has an ethical, writing, or presentation component.

AUTHOR'S NOTE

It is my sincere hope that an individual will experience the power of technical communications in the person's chosen field and can use this book to help improve personal communications. Good luck, and above all, enjoy!

Raymond Greenlaw
July 2011

AUTHOR'S CONTACT INFORMATION

Raymond Greenlaw
Distinguished Professor of Information Technology
Department of Computer Science
United States Naval Academy
572M Holloway Road, Stop 9F
Annapolis, Maryland 21402
United States of America
Email address:
greenlaw@usna.edu
World Wide Web personal page:
www.raymondgreenlaw.com

Acknowledgment

As with most of my writing projects, this one is the result of the contributions and inspirations from many different individuals.

I would like to thank the IGI Global staff who I had the pleasure to work with on this project. Emily Golesh and Erika Carter helped with formulating the book so that it would be appropriate for members of the professional IT community. Myla Harty provided timely guidance during the development of the manuscript. Jan Travers helped with some technical details relating to the book.

I would also like to thank the reviewers of the manuscript whose valuable suggestions helped to improve this work. I tried to incorporate as many of their suggestions as possible although not all suggestions were feasible.

I give a very special thanks to Nonglak Treethummakul for her unwavering support and for being there with me while I was working on this manuscript. Her encouragement kept me going forward with this project.

I would like to thank Mirna Morrison and Jonnie Chandler who worked with me at Armstrong Atlantic State University while I was writing the preliminary version of this work. They always made coming into work more fun. A warm thanks to my colleagues at Armstrong Atlantic who provided a supportive environment. Thanks also to my colleagues at the United States Naval Academy and in particular, to Provost Andy Phillips, for helping to create a supportive and flexible work environment.

I give many thanks to Tamara Burton for comments and work on an early draft of this book.

Thanks to the faculty members and the Department of Computer Science at Chiang Mai University who provided a supportive environment for me to work on this book, especially during the spring semester of 2011 and the five summers preceding that. I give warm thanks to Sanpawat Kantabutra for his friendship and support, and for always helping to make me feel at home in Thailand.

Thanks to Pattama "Tui" Longani and Wiriya Techaploog for helping me with editing the manuscript and for helping to convert my original LATEX files into WORD. Special thanks to Tui for her timeliness on this project and also for capturing many screenshots.

This book is partially derived from CSCI 6100, a graduate technical writing course that I introduced and first taught at Armstrong Atlantic State University during the fall of 2002. The following students served as note-takers in that course:

- Roger Beall: Conference paper submission and Cascading Style Sheets
- Andrew Eason: Refereeing and submitting a paper, grant proposals, and web presentations
- Jane Eason: Grammar, LATEX formatting tips, and personal communication
- Fitz Hiltzheimer: Manuscript preparation and Web presentations
- Ruslan Hristov: Introduction, presentations, and writing definitions
- Frank Malinowski: Biographical sketch, typesetting code, and overhead presentations
- Chris McCarthy: LATEX, oral presentations, and SLITEX
- William McVay: Writing conference papers, presentation abstracts, and SLITEX
- Ben Page: HyperText Markup Language and HTML tools
- Dan Riddell: Creating documents, writing techniques, and book publishing
- Janice Stanford: Résumé writing and writing for the web
- DeOnté Tift: Presentations, PowerPoint, and indexing
- Bart Westgeest: Writing conference papers and oral presentations
- Chris Williams: Documentation, email, and presentations
- Stefan Wirtz: LATEX, refereeing, and miscellaneous writing tips

Although not all of these topics made it into the final version of the book, these students deserve an acknowledgment and a great deal of thanks for their hard work.

In the spring of 2009 Ray taught another section of CSCI 6100. The following students did some work on individual chapters of the book, as part of their course. Their contributions are much appreciated, and I warmly thank them for their help.

- Jamie Blondin: Extensible Hypertext Markup Language
- James LaPlante: documenting an event
- Marcel Manning: LATEX
- Les Sears: résumés and CVs
- Russell Smith: email
- Ivan Sopin: writing a research paper

Raymond Greenlaw
United States Naval Academy, USA

Chapter 1
Introduction

ABSTRACT

There are four main topics addressed in this book: professional ethics, technical writing, presentation skills, and online writing. These topics and the intended audience of Information Technology (IT) professionals and others working in technical disciplines define the scope of the book. Although there are at least a couple of chapters devoted to each of these topics, the material about these topics is woven throughout the book, because there is overlap among them. In the next four sections of this introductory chapter, the author provides an overview of approach to professional ethics, technical writing, presentation skills, and online writing. The goal throughout this book is to provide the IT professional with practical techniques, suggestions, and advice that can be immediately applied to improve skills in these four fundamental areas. For example, after reading the chapter on ethics, one will have a foundation and a framework on which to base ethical decisions, and one will have worked through a number of ethical scenarios. In this chapter, the author motivates each of these subjects by providing a section on who should read this book and a section that summarizes the contents of this book.

APPROACH TO PROFESSIONAL ETHICS

IT professionals face many challenging ethical situations and without a proper framework for confronting, evaluating, and successfully resolving ethical situations, the probability of obtaining the best outcome is not high. One cannot merely rely on intuition for resolving ethical conflicts. Many IT professionals are not currently equipped to handle ethical conflicts. And, rather than simply attempting to deal with issues on an as needed basis as problems arise, one should be prepared in advance. Our primary goal regarding ethics is to examine a well-developed ethical code and then to work through a few scenarios applying

DOI: 10.4018/978-1-4666-0237-3.ch001

this code of ethics. In other words, we take a practical hands-on approach to ethics. Although ethical situations crop up in a wide variety of unpredictable settings, the reader will be in a good position to handle most ethical dilemmas by using the techniques described in this book.

We also focus on ethical issues relating to writing. And, after finishing that material the reader will be competent to handle many ethical scenarios regarding writing. We discuss the moral and social responsibilities of scientists. Given that most works in information technology and the sciences are co-authored, we include material on responsibilities to co-authors. Research is rarely done in a vacuum but instead builds on the work of others. Thus we discuss how to cite the literature. We also include material about copyright issues. Sometimes one wants to include a figure or a table from another researcher's previous work. So we present material about obtaining permissions to include such items in one's work.

As the reader can see, we cover many different topics in the ethics domain. It is important to update and expand one's ethical knowledge throughout one's career. Once the material in this book has been mastered, the reader will have an excellent starting point from which to evolve one's ethical base. The reader will also have an excellent understanding of the types of issues relating to IT that fall under the ethics umbrella.

APPROACH TO TECHNICAL WRITING

What is *technical writing*? In the context of this book we define technical writing as written communication in the fields of science or technology that is performed by subject matter experts. Such writing includes computer-system documentation, a research paper, instructions, a manual, or a user specification. We also include many other types of documents that present information in a techni-

cal manner. The writing style in technical writing is more prescriptive than in creative writing. In technical writing we are not so much concerned about entertaining the audience as we are about conveying specific information to our readers in a concise and precise manner. Such writing needs to flow in a logical manner. Although the goal is to convey information, we do not want to bore the reader. Thus the writing needs to be tasteful and suitable for one's audience. Technical writing requires specific knowledge about a field such as biology, chemistry, computer science, engineering, information technology, mathematics, physics, and so on, that is, it requires a subject matter expert.

The origins of technical writing are not clear. When people needed to communicate difficult concepts about technical issues, a new writing style emerged. The first computer algorithm ever written down was by a Persian mathematician named al-Khwārizmī, and one can see the origins of the word 'algorithm' in his name (Wikipedia, 2011). Surely, al-Khwārizmī's algorithm from the 800s must be considered as technical writing. Throughout the second millennium, mathematicians and scientists were regularly making new discoveries and describing their experiments and results in their writings. Their writing was technical writing. As advances in science, mathematics, and computing continued and became more complex in the 1900s, technical writing developed in order to keep pace. "In 1953, two organizations concerned with improving the practice of technical communication were founded in the United States of America: the Society of Technical Writers, and the Association of Technical Writers and Editors" (Wikipedia 2, 2011). At that time technical writing emerged as a discipline. Now technical writing is taught as a class at many institutions throughout the world.

Technical writing has many different facets and genres—book, conference paper, curriculum vit, directions, documentation, instructions, letters, journal paper, and recommendation, among others. Why are skills in good technical writing useful? For example, a well-written letter to an editor explaining one's position with respect to a referee's criticism can help result in a publication. A polished set of documentation can result in users not needing to call a help line and result in a large cost savings for a company. On the other hand, a poorly-written letter of recommendation or a sloppy cover letter might cost someone a job. Obviously, one's best interests are served by a well-written document, as opposed to something that is sloppy and poorly written.

The techniques that we describe in this book can be applied to most types of writing. Becoming a good writer takes much practice, but the benefits are great. Good writers are able to communicate their thoughts clearly on paper. Good writers have a handful of favorite tools available to help them with their writing—a good dictionary (Oxford, 2011; Webster, 2011), a good thesaurus (Roget's, 2011), and a good comprehensive general reference (Chicago, 2011). Another good reference with many helpful suggestions is *A Handbook for Scholars* (Van Leunen, 1992). It is also helpful if one can see examples of good technical writing, and for this we recommend *Selected Papers on Computer Science* (Knuth, 1996). When one sees good examples of technical writing, one can try to incorporate the style used in them into one's own writing. As one develops as a writer, the writing process will take less time and the work produced will be of a better quality.

In this book we provide the writer with many tips and techniques that can be immediately applied to one's writing. The reader should try to write often and apply the items in this book. In using the strategies discussed here the reader can continue to evolve as a writer. We hope that this book will help a reader develop the skills to be able to assess and evaluate one's own work and then improve one's own writing. In addition to developing a good writing style we want the reader to become an efficient writer. Since most IT professionals face hard deadlines, one needs

to be able to write accurately and steadily. After having completed this book and practiced the methods described here, the reader should be a competent technical writer.

APPROACH TO PRESENTATION SKILLS

It is important to communicate clearly whether that communication is written or oral. One can imagine standing in front of a group of venture capitalists requesting funds for a new IT project. How can one persuade them that the project is worth their money? One's approach, style, and delivery are all keys in obtaining their support. When the stakes are so high, one must be thoroughly prepared, be capable of presenting material clearly, and be able to cope with nervousness. In the material in this book on presentations we cover all of these issues and much more. We present material that is appropriate for those new to public speaking, but experts should also be able to obtain a few tips as well. The material is presented so that one can immediately employ the techniques in one's own work.

The standard presentation software in the IT field is Microsoft's PowerPoint. We provide some basic material describing PowerPoint. We emphasize techniques that create clear and well-organized presentations. From selecting a topic to setting up for a presentation to preparing a presentation to delivering a presentation, we cover all bases. We discuss presentation equipment, the setting for a presentation, and supplemental materials. An important issue is how to advertise a talk, and we provide notes about developing advertisements. We cover the development of key slides in a presentation. Many miscellaneous hints are included, and we give advice on how to overcome common trouble spots.

Once a reader has read and practiced the material in this book about presentations, the reader will be well equipped to deliver a quality presentation and also deal with many typical situations that arise during a talk. One will have the confidence necessary to deliver a talk in front of a large audience; one will have the skill to handle difficult audience members and answer questions effectively. And, one will have the tools to continue evolving one's presentation skills. Delivering a quality presentation is a challenging task and for many people a nerve-racking endeavor, but with the assistance of the material provided in this book, the reader can become an excellent public speaker. As throughout this book, we provide practical information that one can apply directly in one's work.

APPROACH TO ONLINE WRITING

Writing 'online' is different than writing 'offline.' Some distinguishing features of writing for the web are *multimedia* and *hypertext*. The web is not restricted to text, figures, and tables. And, text does not need to flow in a sequential fashion. Video and audio segments can be incorporated into multimedia environments. Through hypertext, one can jump around various parts of a web page in a manner that suits one's own interests. Online writing can involve programming and that may require an author to learn new tools, for example, one might want to learn Hypertext Markup Language (HTML) or an HTML editor for creating web pages. Online documents need maintenance and frequent updating; such documents are usually more dynamic in nature than their offline counterparts. We compare and contrast online and offline writing styles. And, we present a classification scheme for the various types of online writing.

Although we do not get into programming in this text, we do discuss developing and maintaining a website. Most IT professionals can easily learn the tools to develop materials for the web on their own. Our focus is on planning and setting goals for one's website. We present techniques for outlining

a website, and this material will help one to work more efficiently and have a more-cohesive design for one's website. We discuss adding content to a website and also website maintenance. The practical nature of the material that we include will help a reader to see the key issues involved in writing for the web.

We include a chapter on blogging. The word 'blog' is short for web log. A blog usually contains commentary on a topic, opinions about issues, or descriptions of events. Items are usually listed in reverse-chronological order. In the chapter on blogging we provide an overview of blogs and their history. There are many sites that offer free blogging software, and we provide a list and brief review of some of the more-popular sites. If one does decide to blog, there are some rules that a professional should follow. And, we discuss some things that one should be aware of when posting information to a blog. We also provide a list of useful blogs for the IT professional. These sites can help the reader stay up to date on important topics of interest in the IT field. As usual, we try to provide practical information that a reader can readily apply in one's daily life.

WHO SHOULD READ THIS BOOK?

Anyone with an interest in professional ethics, technical writing, presentation skills, or online writing and possessing some background in one of the following fields can benefit from the use of the book:

- Biology
- Chemistry
- Computer engineering
- Computer science
- Engineering
- Information systems
- Information technology
- Mathematics
- Physics

- Software engineering
- Other science-related fields

These fields are the primary fields that require technical writing, but to some degree other fields such as the medical and legal fields also require technical writing. This book will be useful for anyone who needs to deal with ethical issues, write up a technical project, give or develop a presentation, or write material for an online audience. The book focuses on practical information and process. The goal is to improve the reader's ability and knowledge in each of these four areas.

The workforce and work habits of the new millennia continue to evolve, and we see more companies allowing, or in some cases even requiring, employees to telecommute. The skills discussed in this book can often be used to perform independent work or individual projects. For example, one might need to develop a website or a blog. Such projects are often well defined in scope. Thus individuals, who want the possibility of working at home or on the road, rather than say at an office, can also benefit from this book. Possessing the skills described in this book may in some cases give more professional freedom.

CONTENTS OF THIS BOOK

In this chapter we outline the contents of this book. Many of the chapters in this book are independent of the others, and as a result, one does not need to read them in a linear fashion—one can pick and chose to focus on a particular topic of interest; one can also use the book as a reference. In what follows we present a roadmap by describing the individual chapters of the book, including a brief description of each of them.

- **Introduction:** This chapter sets the tone for the book and goes into more details about what we intend to cover. There are general sections on professional ethics, technical writing, presentation skills, and online writing.

- **Ethics for the IT Professional:** This chapter begins with a discussion of a standard code of ethics. We then explore a number of ethical scenarios and applications of the code of ethics.

- **Professional Communications:** Communication is a key part of most jobs. In this chapter we cover material about email, telephone, status reports, and so on. We describe communication in a group setting and how to keep others informed. The chapter wraps up with notes on future trends and conclusions.

- **Online Communication Forums:** Here we compare and contrast 'online' versus 'offline' writing. We provide a classification scheme for online writing. We provide general information about developing and maintaining a website.

- **Blogging:** The chapter begins with a review of the history of blogs and contains a list of interesting facts about blogs. We provide a review of some popular free blogging software. Another section provides a few words of caution about blogs and a couple interesting blogging cases. This section is followed by one containing a listing of useful blogs for IT professionals.

- **Comments on Manuscript Preparation:** We provide material on how to prepare for a writing project, how to begin writing, and how to stay productive. This information is followed by more-technical aspects of writing, including tips for writing prose, style issues, and grammatical tips. Other technical writing tidbits are covered throughout the chapter.

- **Structure of a Technical Paper:** We describe the process of writing a technical paper and go over the basic sections that a typical paper contains. We present material on the writing process and editing. In addition, we include thoughts about paper submission and follow-up. The chapter contains miscellaneous points and concluding remarks.

- **Ethical Issues in Writing:** We present material about the moral and social responsibilities of scientists. Given that most research involves collaborators, we provide a section about obligations to co-authors. We also describe issues relating to citing the work of others. The chapter contains information on copyright. We discuss permission issues for figures and tables.

- **Documenting an Event:** There are times when one must document an event, and this chapter focuses on how to do that appropriately. We also discuss writing up experiments, bug reports, and trip reports.

- **Fundamentals and Development of a Presentation:** This chapter covers many essential topics relating to presentations. From selecting a topic, to the setting for a presentation, to preparing the presentation, to presentation equipment, to supplemental materials, to talk advertisements, the reader will find many valuable presentation tips in this chapter.

- **Delivering a (Powerpoint) Presentation and More:** This chapter focuses on issues relating to the effective delivery of a presentation. We focus on PowerPoint presentations. We cover style issues, presentation genres, key slides to include, trouble spots, the effective handling of questions, how to avoid disasters, and methods for coping with nerves. Many useful tips are included.

- **Résumés:** We discuss many important topics relating to résumé development in this chapter. We provide insights into résumé writing and cover all the basic sections of a résumé. We also describe how to write a curriculum vitæ. We provide a final checklist for developing a résumé and include material on how to submit a résumé or vitæ.

- **Introduction to LATEX:** Many scientists consider LATEX to be the standard of typesetting systems. This chapter provides a thorough introduction to the LATEX-typesetting system. After reading this chapter, one will have the ability to typeset many different types of documents in LATEX. From installing LATEX on a computer, to creating a LATEX document, to creating one's own environments in LATEX, this chapter covers most of the key introductory elements of LATEX.

Each chapter ends with a conclusions section that summarizes the information contained in the chapter, and when appropriate, it discusses future trends as well. References are provided in each chapter of the book. The book also has a handy index that is useful for looking up specific topics, relocating material in the book, or for using the book as a reference.

REFERENCES

Knuth, D. E. (1996). *Selected papers on computer science*. Center for the Study of Language and Information. Co-published with Cambridge University Press.

Knuth, D. E., Larrabee, T., & Roberts, P. M. (1989). *Mathematical writing*. The Mathematical Association of America.

Merriam-Webster's Dictionary. (2011). Retrieved on March 20, 2011, from http://www.merriam-webster.com/

Oxford's English Dictionary. (2011). Retrieved on March 20, 2011, from http://www.oed.com/

Roget's Thesaurus. (2011). Retrieved on March 29, 2011, from http://thesaurus.com/Roget-Alpha-Index.html

(2011). *The Chicago Manual of Style* (16th ed.). University of Chicago Press.

Van Leunen, M. (1992). *A handbook for scholars* (*Revised edition*). Oxford University Press.

Wikipedia. (2011). *Muhammad ibn Mūsā al-Khwārizmī*. Retrieved on July 14, 2011, from http://en.wikipedia.org/wiki/Al-Khw%C4%81rizm%C4%AB

Wikipedia. (2011). *Technical writing*. Retrieved on July 15, 2011, from http://en.wikipedia.org/wiki/Technical_writing

Chapter 2
Ethics for the IT Professional

ABSTRACT

This chapter focuses on ethics for the IT professional. The learning objectives for this chapter are to understand basic ethical principles relating to IT, to develop a framework that supports making informed decisions regarding ethical problems, to apply an ethical code in typical situations, and to understand future trends relating to IT ethics. The author includes material on each of these topics and also sections with conclusions and references. After having mastered the material in this chapter, a reader will have a much-better understanding of ethical principles relating to the IT profession. But, more importantly, a reader will be able to make practical use of that knowledge by applying it in the workplace to solve ethical dilemmas.

INTRODUCTION

The field of IT ethics is complex, and as technology continues to evolve at an alarmingly-fast pace, the ethical situations that arise are becoming so complicated that it is no longer sufficient to simply be a good moral person to resolve ethical issues. One needs a framework for solving such complex problems—a code or set of conduct developed by experts, agreed to be used by a given community, and applied in a standard and consistent manner.

When such a code is in place and applied in a fair manner, then any 'reasonable' person would agree that justice has been carried out. Here by 'reasonable person' we mean a typical IT professional who has good morals and meets society's norms. In fact, this latter point is worth elaborating on further, and we do that next.

Most of us instinctively know the difference between what is right and what is wrong. And, since this book is not a philosophy text, we take a common-sense approach in the discussion here.

DOI: 10.4018/978-1-4666-0237-3.ch002

We all agree that it is a bad and unacceptable to steal another person's laptop. In fact, such an act is criminal and punishable by law. However, not all situations are as clear cut, and there are gray areas. That is to say there are ethical situations where two reasonable people might draw different conclusions. Once an ethical problem is discovered, the process of resolving it can be very challenging and sometimes painful. Ethics vary from place to place and country to country. In some parts of the world using pirated software or selling fake Rolexes is not considered a crime by many people, and if it is against the law, the law is certainly not enforced. Let us begin by presenting a code of ethics in the next section. This code will give us a basis for deciding when an ethical violation has occurred.

CODE OF ETHICS

Introduction

Our goal in this section is to describe the well-known *Association for Computing Machinery's (ACM) Code of Ethics and Professional Conduct* (ACM, 1992). We call this document the "Code" for short. This Code is widely accepted in the IT community and has been developed, refined, and applied over many years. Other ethical codes contain similar directives, so in understanding the Code one will have a good handle on understanding other ethical codes. The Code is divided into four parts. It consists of eight ethical standards, a set of nine principles that all computing professionals are to follow, a group of six statements pertaining to those in leadership roles, and two statements about expected compliance with the Code. In the next four sections we go over these four parts of the code. Our main focus will be on sections 1, 2, and 4 of the Code. We start with the ethical standards from the Code.

Ethical Standards from the ACM Code

Figure 1 shows an abridged version of the *ACM Code of Ethics and Professional Conduct*. In this section we focus on the ethical standards. The interested reader should consult the full Code (ACM, 1992). The ethical standards in the Code are as follows:

1.1 "Contribute to society and human well-being.
1.2 Avoid harm to others.
1.3 Be honest and trustworthy.
1.4 Be fair and take action not to discriminate.
1.5 Honor property rights including copyrights and patent.
1.6 Give proper credit for intellectual property.
1.7 Respect the privacy of others.
1.8 Honor confidentiality" (ACM Flier, 2011).

We use the same numbering as given in the original Code so that a reader can easily refer back to the original Code. The basic idea behind each of these eight statements is self evident. However we elaborate a bit on each statement in the domain of computing. We should point out that the Code itself elaborates substantially on each point in the Code. The reader should refer to the full Code for any statement that one feels is not completely clear.

We start with statement 1.1 which says "Contribute to society and human well-being" (ACM, 1992). This piece of the Code is where diversity is addressed. In contributing to human well-being we must respect all cultures and all people regardless of their race, religion, color, national origin, sex, age, marital status, physical handicap, political beliefs or affiliations, and sexual preference. The Code elaborates further: "An essential aim of computing professionals is to minimize negative consequences of computing systems, including threats to health and safety. When designing or implementing systems, computing professionals

Figure 1. An abridged version of the ACM Code of Ethics and Professional Conduct. (© 2011 Association for Computing Machinery. Used with permission.) The full version of the Code is available from http://www.acm.org/about/code-of-ethics

ACM Code of Ethics and Professional Conduct

THE CODE **represents ACM's commitment to promoting the highest professional and ethical standards, and makes it incumbent on all** ACM Members **to:**

- Contribute to society and human well-being.
- Avoid harm to others.
- Be honest and trustworthy.
- Be fair and take action not to discriminate.

- Honor property rights including copyrights and patent.
- Give proper credit for intellectual property.
- Respect the privacy of others.
- Honor confidentiality.

And as computing professionals, **every** ACM Member **is also expected to:**

- Strive to achieve the highest quality, effectiveness and dignity in both the process and products of professional work.
- Acquire and maintain professional competence.
- Know and respect existing laws pertaining to professional work.
- Accept and provide appropriate professional review.

- Give comprehensive and thorough evaluations of computer systems and their impacts, including analysis of possible risks.
- Honor contracts, agreements, and assigned responsibilities.
- Improve public understanding of computing and its consequences.
- Access computing and communication resources only when authorized to do so.

This flyer shows an abridged version of the ACM Code of Ethics. The complete version can be viewed at: www.acm.org/constitution/code

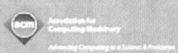

must attempt to ensure that the products of their efforts will be used in socially responsible ways, will meet social needs, and will avoid harmful effects to health and welfare" (ACM, 1992). Given the important of the computing profession to society and the manner in which it is interwoven throughout the critical infrastructure, people working in computing have an obligation to society to "design and implement systems in socially responsible ways" (ACM, 1992).

Statement 1.2 says "Avoid harm to others" (ACM, 1992). This statement is obvious in the sense that it is wrong to cause injury to others. However in the context of computing the statement means we should not do anything that would result in a person, for example, losing computer data, system time, or money due to the intentional destruction or tampering with of computer systems. Consider the case where one releases a virus which infects and damages a number of computers. This act clearly is causing harm to others in that they will need to spend time and money in order to recover from the problem, and they will lose productive time as a result of having their attention shifted to deal with the virus problem. One can imagine a situation where a program still has known bugs, but where engineers are pressured to release the program because the company is badly behind an already announced released date. If the buggy program is a medical program that distributes dosage information for drugs to remote sensors, the potential for harm to its users could be substantial. A programmer involved in the project would face a serious ethical dilemma about whether or not to make others, perhaps people outside of the company, aware of the situation. "If one's superiors do not act to curtail or mitigate such dangers, it may be necessary to 'blow the whistle' to help correct the problem or reduce the risk. However, capricious or misguided reporting of violations can, itself, be harmful. Before reporting violations, all relevant aspects of the incident must be thoroughly assessed" (ACM, 1992). And, in this case, as in many ethical situations, there

may not be a completely clear answer about the course of action that one should take.

Statement 1.3 says "Be honest and trustworthy" (ACM, 1992). Again, we have a self-evidence ethical statement, but in the context of computing the statement means that one should not lie, for example, about the capabilities of a system. One would, for example, violate this statement by making security claims about a system which one knew was not truly secure. Obviously, customers and consumers depend on IT professionals to provide accurate and honest information about the capabilities of computers, software, and related systems.

Statement 1.4 says "Be fair and take action not to discriminate" (ACM, 1992). In addition to the usual implications of such a statement, in the context of computing the statement means that no one should be denied authorized access to computing resources based on "race, sex, religion, age, disability, national origin, or other such similar factors" (ACM, 1992).

Statement 1.5 says "Honor property rights including copyrights and patent" (ACM, 1992). In addition to the usual implications of such a statement, in the context here this statement is primarily referring to respecting copyrights and patents of software and other computer-related material. "Unauthorized duplication of materials must not be condoned" (ACM, 1992). IT professionals should take a leadership role in respecting the work of others.

Statement 1.6 says "Give proper credit for intellectual property" (ACM, 1992). This statement means that IT professionals must protect intellectual property. Proper credit must be given for someone's ideas "even in cases where the work has not been explicitly protected by copyright, patent, and so on" (ACM, 1992).

Statement 1.7 says "Respect the privacy of others" (ACM, 1992). In a computing environment one might have access to a wide range of personal information and data. Such personal information and data should remain private and only be monitored in accordance with the published policies associated with the systems in question. This information should be deleted at the appropriate times, as should old backup materials that are no longer needed for official purposes. "User data observed during the normal duties of system operation and maintenance must be treated with strictest confidentiality, except in cases where it is evidence for the violation of law, organizational regulations, or this Code. In these cases, the nature or contents of that information must be disclosed only to proper authorities" (ACM, 1992).

Statement 1.8 says "Honor confidentiality" (ACM, 1992). "The ethical concern is to respect all obligations of confidentiality to employers, clients, and users unless discharged from such obligations by requirements of the law or other principles of this Code" (ACM, 1992).

We suspect that a reader who has not read through an ethical code before learned an enormous amount by going through these eight ethical standards. There are many important ethical issues that the Code addresses, which one probably would not normally consider, until a problem arises. It is better to be equipped with knowledge of the Code before such problems arise. The Code gives IT professionals a framework from which to make appropriate ethical decisions. One can see from a careful reading of the Code that as IT professionals we have many important ethical obligations to colleagues, our employers, and society.

Principles that Apply to All Computing Professionals

In this section we cover the second part of the Code. Although this Code applies to the computing field, many of the statements in it also apply directly to non-computing fields as well. Let us begin by listing the items in the Code that apply to all computing professionals.

2.1 "Strive to achieve the highest quality, effectiveness and dignity in both the process and products of professional work.

2.2 Acquire and maintain professional competence.

2.3 Know and respect existing laws pertaining to professional work.

2.4 Accept and provide appropriate professional review.

2.5 Give comprehensive and thorough evaluations of computer systems and their impacts, including analysis of possible risks.

2.6 Honor contracts, agreements, and assigned responsibilities.

2.7 Improve public understanding of computing and its consequences.

2.8 Access computing and communication resources only when authorized to do so" (ACM Flier, 2011).

This section of the Code is fairly straightforward. It stresses excellence, integrity, and the responsibilities of an IT professional. Let us take a look at just one statement in detail; a reader should carefully go through the other statements and reflect about their meanings in the context of computing. Statement 2.7 "Improve public understanding of computing and its consequences" (ACM, 1992) indicates that as society's most-knowledgeable people about computing, IT professionals must aim to educate others and help them understand hard-to-grasp computing issues. When we say "hard-to-grasp," we mean hard to grasp for the intended audience, not the IT professional. For example, we have a responsibility to dispelling any computing myths that may be plaguing the public. We need to help inform the public about privacy and security issues relating to computing and the threat level for any given scenario. For example, this effort might involve explaining the concept of firewalls to a user to help illustrate to such a user how one can better secure a computer that will be connected to the Internet.

One should try to abide by these eight principles, and from time-to-time one might find it helpful to review them.

Leadership Imperatives from the ACM Ethics Code

In this section we briefly describe the leadership imperatives that are contained in the Code. Let us begin by listing those items using the same numbering scheme as in the Code. The statements pertaining to leadership are as follows:

3.1 "Articulate social responsibilities of members of an organizational unit and encourage full acceptance of those responsibilities.
3.2 Manage personnel and resources to design and build information systems that enhance the quality of working life.
3.3 Acknowledge and support proper and authorized uses of an organization's computing and communication resources.
3.4 Ensure that users and those who will be affected by a system have their needs clearly articulated during the assessment and design of requirements; later the system must be validated to meet requirements.
3.5 Articulate and support policies that protect the dignity of users and others affected by a computing system.
3.6 Create opportunities for members of the organization to learn the principles and limitations of computer systems" (ACM, 1992).

The meanings of the leadership imperatives are quite clear. For those readers who are in leadership positions it is a good idea to follow these statements and review them periodically.

Expected Compliance with the ACM Code

In this section we describe the two rules pertaining to expected compliance with the Code. They are as follows:

4.1 "Uphold and promote the principles of this Code.
4.2 Treat violations of this code as inconsistent with membership in the ACM" (ACM, 1992).

The meanings and purposes of these two statements are clear and require no further elaboration.

Summary

The *ACM Code of Ethics and Professional Conduct* provides an individual with an ethical framework in the computing field. The Code was developed over a number of years and has withstood the test of time. All professionals in computing fields should know this Code and use it in their work. The Code's framework can be used a basis for resolving ethical conflicts. In the next section we exam a couple of scenarios and apply the Code to them.

ETHICAL SCENARIOS

Introduction

Now that we have a framework to use for solving ethical problems we take a look at a couple of scenarios and apply the ACM Code of Ethics to resolve them. As we walk through these examples, one can think of ethical situations that one has encountered in the past and about how one might have been able to use this framework and the techniques described here to resolve those situations more effectively. Once one has seen a wide range of such cases, one can use these cases to help in resolving new ethical dilemmas. Other researchers have advocated a similar strategy to resolving ethical situations through case analysis (Quinn, 2006).

Pill-Dispenser Software

In this section we look at a hypothetical ethical case involving software that calculates medicine dosages in the form of the number of pills that a patient must take each day.

Scenario

Suppose that one is working for an organization which is developing the pill-dispensing software. With the great advances in medicine the daily dosage is actually calculated based on the person's blood analysis of the day, the person's weight on a given day, the person's level of physical activity, and parameters that a doctor inputs remotely to the patient's record on a regular basis. The development team is several months behind on coding up the software, and the boss (Sally) is asking that the product be released immediately. One programmer (Louis) has been telling Sally about an error in the code which over calculates dosages in a few rare cases. In these instances this over calculation results in a patient being told to consume at most one or two 'unnecessary' pills per day. The bug in the system cannot be tracked down but seems to be due to weird rounding errors in one of the many complex formulas that are included in the program. Sally decides that the product should be released.

We apply the Code to this scenario and then examine what actions Louis might consider. If the software is released, it is clear that the product does not contribute to the well-being of all people (section 1.1 of the Code). In particular, there are medicines which when taken in larger than necessary dosages could be fatal or result in

undesirable side effects. The cost of the medication could also be a factor, as some medications are expensive. Releasing software that has the potential to injury some users is not in the spirit of "avoiding harm to others" (section 1.2 of the Code). If the software gets released, the company is not being "honest and trustworthy" (section 1.3 of the Code) with consumers and perhaps other constituencies as well.

We move on and apply to the second section of the Code to this scenario. In releasing a product that is buggy and harmful one is not "striving to achieve the highest quality, effectiveness, and dignity in both the process and products of professional work" (section 2.1 of Code). One does not "respect existing laws pertaining to professional work" (section 2.3 of the Code) by releasing a product that endangers lives. One does not "give comprehensive and thorough evaluations of computer systems and their impacts, including analysis of possible risks" (section 2.5 of the Code) by releasing software with known bugs and hiding information from consumers about these bugs.

In this case we see that there are at least half a dozen places where the Code has been violated. In this scenario we noted that Louis had already informed Sally about the problem, but that she insisted on releasing the product. What should Louis do? Louis can approach Sally again and show her the ethical violations that will be committed if they release the software. If that fails, Louis can perhaps consult with a colleague at the company or perhaps with Sally's supervisor, of course, going over Sally's head could create problems. Louis could document the problem and its history in a report and distribute it to other company employees. Note that Louis' employment could be in jeopardy depending on Sally's take on the situation. If Louis absolutely thought that more-drastic measures were required, he could possibly take the case to the media. Louis' best options will depend on how-much evidence he can provide which documents the bugs in the system.

Clearly, this situation is a difficult one to handle, especially if Sally never comes around. Finding the right steps to take and achieving the desired outcome may not be possible for Louis without suffering undesirable consequences.

Spying Using Monitoring Software

In this section we consider a case where a systems administrator installs monitoring software on another employee's computer in order to spy on that person.

Scenario

The systems administrator (Leroy) and his girlfriend (Jill) work together at a medium-size university in the South. Jill has convinced Leroy to install monitoring software on her boss' (Tammy) computer. Jill plans to find out if Tammy is really planning to fire her, as has been rumored. One night when Leroy is working late to install operating-system patches he installs software on Tammy's machine which allows both him and Jill to watch Tammy's actions while on her computer and also to read her email. The president of the university (Greg) has become aware of the situation and has been presented with irrefutable evident that Leroy installed monitoring software on Tammy's computer, and that both Leroy and Jill have been reading Tammy's email.

We apply the Code to this scenario and then consider what actions Greg might consider. There are earlier parts of the Code that one could argue Leroy and Jill violated such as "be honest and trustworthy" (section 1.3 of the Code), but let us go to the more-obvious violation of "respect the privacy of others" (section 1.7 of the Code). Clearly, the installation of secret-monitoring software, reading a person's email, and monitoring a person's actions online are all gross violations of privacy. In monitoring another person's email and online actions one is certainly not "honoring confidentiality" (section 1.8 of the Code).

We move on and apply the second section of the Code. In installing spying software Leroy is not "striving to achieve the highest quality, effectiveness and dignity in both the process and products of professional work" (section 2.1 of the Code) for there is no dignity in spying on another employee. In all likelihood the university's policy prohibits installation of spy software so that doing so does not "respect existing laws pertaining to professional work" (section 2.3 of the Code). Leroy did not "honor assigned responsibilities" (section 2.6 of the Code); he violated them by using his position to install monitoring software. Leroy did not "access computing and communication resources only when authorized to do so" (section 2.8 of the Code), but rather Leroy accessed a system that he was trusted to safe guard to suit his own unethical needs. Jill also violated section 2.8 of the code.

In the spying using monitoring software incident we have more than a handful of Code violations. Most universities have a policy for dealing with such computer violations. Greg must make sure that the appropriate hearing is given for Leroy and Jill, and that they have an opportunity to respond to the allegations. However in our scenario the two were guilty of installing and using monitoring software. The university should fire both Leroy and Jill after conversations with the university's legal counsel. Individuals in positions of power, such as system administrators, should not commit (gross) ethical violations. There is little hope that individuals such as Leroy and Jill could ever be trusted again; and furthermore, it is not a good idea to have individuals as unethical as Leroy and Jill around young people.

The two scenarios examined in this section both involved major ethical violations. It may not be possible to diagnose all cases so easily. In the pill-dispensing software scenario determining the right course of action for Louis was extremely challenging. In the spying using monitoring software scenario it was clear what action the university need to take. In the next section we synthesize the ideas presented here and provide a set of steps that one can follow in order to apply the Code. This process should help one be able to resolve challenging ethical situations.

APPLYING THE CODE OF ETHICS

Before being confronted with an ethical dilemma it is important to have an ethical foundation for successfully resolving the situation. The *ACM Code of Ethics and Professional Conduct* gives us that foundation. In general, there are several items that we can rely on for dealing with ethical dilemmas. They are as follows:

- Our own ethical foundation and background
- Our own experience relating to ethical situations
- Our own specialized training or educational experiences in ethics
- Available case analyses
- The input from other members of one's community

IT professionals as a group have a wide range of ethical backgrounds and foundations and experiences. For a moment we ask the reader to pause and consider one's own ethical background and experiences.

- Is it strong?
- Is it weak?
- Where do the beliefs come from?
- What ethical situations have been encountered?
- What emotions were involved?
- Were the situations resolved in a satisfactory way?
- What areas need to be strengthened?
- What specifically can be done for one to become more compliant with the Code?

If one has little educational background regarding ethics or little experience one will need to rely on the Code and perhaps other community members more heavily. In consulting with another community member one needs to make sure to preserve the confidentiality of a situation. And, in some cases, it may not be appropriate to consult with anyone.

Having assessed one's own background, having taken any necessary steps to strengthen one's foundation, and having developed an ethical framework; one is well poised to handle ethical situations. When a situation arises that does not feel right, one should take the time to think through situation. If there appears to have been an ethical violation, one can go back to the Code and try to map the situation to one of the statements in the Code, as we did in the last section. In other words one needs to understand the violation and be able to categorize it in some way. If one is writing down notes about such a violation, one needs to take precautions to make sure that such information remains inaccessible to others and remains confidential. If appropriate, one may be able to consult with a colleague or supervisor. Again, one needs to be aware of and respect confidentiality issues. Depending on one's role in an organization, one may need to take correct measures or one may need to report a situation. The latter steps should be performed with great care. To the extent that a situation permits, one should not rush through any of the aforementioned steps, but instead, one needs to carry out the steps with the utmost care. We summarize the steps in figure 2.

Note that many ethical situations are unique and will require a unique and delicate solution. For example, one may suspect that a long-term colleague has broken into another employee's email Inbox. The first tact to resolving this dilemma might be to have a frank discussion with that colleague. Other violations may require immediate action or reporting to one's supervisor.

Figure 2. High-level steps for approaching and resolving an ethical dilemma. In each step careful thought must be applied, and the consequences regarding any actions taken should be thoroughly considered

1. If something feels wrong, one needs to investigate the situation.
2. One must determine if an ethical violation was committed, and in this step one can try to map the situation to a particular part of the Code, a previous case that one is knowledgeable about, or conduct research to attempt to locate a similar case.
3. If confidentiality will not be violated, one might decide to discuss the situation with a colleague or supervisor.
4. If a violation was committed, one needs to identify succinctly what the violation was and determine one's role in 'resolving' the situation.
5. Depending on one's role in an organization, one may need to take an action such as confronting the party involved or reporting the party involved to a supervisor.
6. After resolving an ethical dilemma, one can take peace of mind in knowing that the right course of action was followed.

For example, suppose that one has found that a colleague is selling classified information to an enemy state. Clearly, such a situation must be handled immediately.

If one is troubled about an ethical situation, one must take peace of mind in knowing that one tried to follow the right course of action. In particular, we may be put in awkward situations by the dishonest acts of others. In resolving such dilemmas we must keep in mind that a wrongdoer placed us in a difficult situation to begin with by inappropriate behavior. We were put in a situation where we were forced to confront a problem. After resolving such a problem, it is natural for some people to have swirling and uncomfortable emotions, but we must move on and try not to be troubled. Again, by acting fairly, justly, and methodically, one can take comfort in knowing that a situation was resolved to the best of one's abilities.

Those in leadership roles have even greater ethical responsibilities, and they might have to resolve ethical situations completely on their own. For leaders section 3 of the Code serves as a useful set of guidelines for helping to educate other group members about ethical rules and other important items.

CONCLUSION

As of this writing, the *ACM Code of Ethics and Professional Conduct* has been around for about 20 years. The Code is still relevant and provides an excellent framework for resolving ethical dilemmas. In fact, for some infractions, it would be worth pointing to a particular section, which a guilty party has violated, as a means of educating that person. The material in this chapter gives a reader the necessary practical tools to address many ethical situations. Some situations can be difficult to handle and can be troubling to resolve. When confidentiality issues will not be violated, one can consult with a colleague or supervisor. Having such a sounding board can be useful. As technologies, laws, and work environments continue to emerge and evolve, new ethical dilemmas will arise. The methods described here can be applied to those situations. We should point out that there are a number of good books devoted to ethics in the IT domain: *A Gift of Fire: Social, Legal, of Ethical Issues for Computing and the Internet* (Baase, 2008); *Ethics for the Information Age* (Quinn, 2011); and *Case Studies in Information Technology* (Spinello, 2002). And, for those in supervisor roles we note that it is always worth reviewing an organization's ethical policies with staff members on periodic bases. Of course, new staff members should be taught about an organization's ethical policies during an initial-orientation session.

REFERENCES

ACM. (1992). *ACM code of ethics and professional conduct*. Retrieved December 1, 2010, from http://www.acm.org/constitution/code

Baase, S. (2008). *A gift of fire: Social, legal, and ethical issues for computing and the Internet* (3rd ed.). Prentice Hall.

Flier, A. C. M. (2011). *ACM code of ethics and professional conduct flier*. Retrieved on April 5, 2011, from http://plone.acm.org/membership/COE_Flyer.pdf

Quinn, M. J. (2006). Case-based analysis: A practical tool for teaching computer ethics. *Proceedings of the Special Interest Group on Computer Science Education*, (pp. 520–524).

Quinn, M. J. (2011). *Ethics for the information age* (4th ed.). Addison-Wesley.

Spinello, R. (2002). *Case studies in Information Technology ethics* (2nd ed.). Prentice Hall.

Chapter 3
Online–Communication Forums

ABSTRACT

This chapter takes a close look at online-communication forums. IT professionals often have to prepare information for an online forum. Writing for an online audience (what the author calls online writing) is a vastly different activity than writing for an offline audience (called offline writing here), and being good at one form of writing does not ensure that one will be effective at the other form. Thus it is worth carefully exploring the differences in these two styles. The chapter begins by making a comparison between online and offline writing.

ONLINE VERSUS OFFLINE WRITING

Prior to the year 2000 most people did more offline writing than online writing, but, around that time there was a dramatic shift and more people began developing online content. In fact, somewhere along the way, many people who did no writing at all began developing materials such as web pages, blogs, and social-networking profiles. New writing styles emerged during this time. After our discussion of online versus offline writing, we include a section that covers various online-communication forums that are particu-

larly relevant to the IT professional. Given the importance of websites to the IT professional, we describe how to develop a plan for creating a website, how to outline a website, how to add content to a website, and how to maintain a website. We focus on a high-level discussion in that section rather than going into a lot of programming details. The chapter concludes with sections on future trends, conclusions, and references.

In this section we explore the similarities and differences between online and offline writing. And, of course, certain pieces of writing will appear in both forms. We should first point out that

DOI: 10.4018/978-1-4666-0237-3.ch003

the chapter on blogging contains a great deal of information about that genre, and the chapters on manuscript preparation and technical papers contain a lot of information which is primarily directed at offline writing. Also, in the next section we cover the various online-writing forums in more detail. Let us begin with general comments about online writing.

Essentially anyone with a computer and an Internet connection can be published. And, in fact, authors can even publish things anonymously. Our focus here is on technical material that is related to information technology and that is published with one's name associated with it. Widely and freely available desktop-publishing software makes it easy for anyone to make a document look professional, but that certainly does not mean the writing itself is of good quality. With online writing there is often no review process involved. So an author is individually responsible for ensuring the accuracy of one's writing. That is, there are no referees who might be able to catch typos or more-significant errors. *Author reputation* is a key concept. An author can spend years developing a good reputation as a credible writer and as a professional. However a reputation can be badly damaged or destroyed by one instance of poor judgment. Thus it is important to make sure that all online material is carefully edited before being published. There tends to be more of a rush to publish online materials, as compared to offline materials, and one should be aware of this fact. One should not get caught up in the rush to publish material rapidly at the expense of the quality of one's work. For a good discussion of the publishing process and print industry we refer the reader *to The Chicago Manual of Style* (Chicago, 2011).

An average piece of online writing may not be archived for as long a period of time as an average piece of offline writing. However one should keep in mind that anything that one ever publishes online *may* be available at anytime in the future. In 2009 Google demonstrated this fact when they brought back web pages from their archives to celebrate ten years of business. Google has also archived more than 20 years of Usenet postings (Google, 2011). We do not think that anyone probably imagined that all Usenet posts would be available forever. Other forms of electronic writing may be around much longer than people anticipated as well. One also should keep in mind that online writing is searchable. Thus someone who is interested in finding online-writing materials usually has a slightly-easier time of identifying everything that an author ever wrote. Given that much-offline material is now appearing online, the gap between online and offline writing is narrowing. As offline material is put online, it too becomes easily searchable.

Online writing usually makes a much-greater use of multimedia. That is, in online writing we may see more than just text, figures, and tables. We may see animations and video too. We may also hear sounds. In online writing the presentation typically includes a greater use of color. The text is often not sequential. Hyperlinks allow a reader to jump around to what the reader deems as the most-interesting parts of a work. Thus with online writing not everything will be read; readers will bounce around via searches and navigational aids. In offline writing readers typically do read continuously through a document in the order in which it is presented. Readers tend to read each word in offline writing. With web pages a reader may only read hyperlinks and not the intervening text. Whereas a typical reader might spend about two minutes on a given page of a book, a person on the web may only spend ten seconds on a web page. And, the person online may be watching a video, listening to music, surfing other sites, and be social-networking all at the same time. We present additional comments about books in the Future Trends section.

ONLINE-WRITING FORUMS

Introduction

This section contains a discussion of online-writing forums. Specifically, we consider electronic journals, mailing lists and discussion groups, homepages, company websites, crowdsourced sites, and social-networking sites. We talk about blogs in a subsequent chapter. Although our list of online forums is not comprehensive, our discussion can be extended to other domains as well, such as content for games, online manuals and guides (also see the next main section on Developing and Maintaining a Website), and commercials. In addition, the material will likely apply to emerging domains. Let us begin with thoughts about electronic journals.

Electronic Journals

Electronic journals are the digital counterpart to printed journals. These scholarly journals are sometimes referred to as *ejournals*. As of this writing, such journals are usually published using Hypertext Markup Language (HTML) or Portable Document Format (PDF). There are also some ejournals that are published using WORD. Richard Zander's *Flora Online* was the first ejournal to receive an International Standard Serial Number (ISSN) (Arlinghaus & Zander, 2008). "*Flora Online* was established by Richard H. Zander, January 12, 1987, to address a perceived need for publication of electronically searchable botanical text and Microsoft Disk Operating System executable programs" (Arlinghaus & Zander, 2008). His coauthor on the article just referenced is Sarah Arlinghaus who founded another of the first ejournals *Solstice: An Electronic Journal of Geography and Mathematics* (Solstice, 2011) in 1990 (Arlinghaus & Zander, 2008). That journal was originally typeset using TEX and emailed to subscribers; *Solstice* is now available via the web and is published in HTML (Solstice, 2011).

Arlinghaus and Zander in their 1993 article about ejournals stated that "Ejournals provide an opportunity to share computerized information with others in an orderly and responsible fashion, within the context of current technology." Many ejournals have sprung up over the years and in practically all fields. Ejournals have evolved with the changing technology. They have the potential to be less expense and can offer a rapid-dissemination model. Many traditional journals offer online versions, and the subscription to the online site is usually 'free' if a subscriber subscribes to the offline version. The great advantages of online journals for researchers is the ability to search, to have access to more than just plaintext, (potential) reduced costs, access to all volumes, and 24−7 accessibility.

In some fields the quality of worked published in ejournals was initially questioned. However since many well-known and top-notch researchers have published in ejournals, they are now generally accepted as being of high quality. Pricing models for e-subscriptions for journals that are not free continue to evolve, as does the manner in which content is presented. The Electronic Colloquium on Computational Complexity (ECCC) publishes papers, short notes, and surveys and also provides news, links, and other valuable information to its intended research community (ECCC, 2011). We mention a few electronic journals on information technology that may be of interest to an IT reader: the *Journal of Information, Information Technology, and Organizations* (JIITO, 2011), the *Journal of Information Technology* (JIT, 2011), and the *Journal of Information Technology Research* (JITR, 2011). Note that institutional subscription rates for electronic journals can be quite high, but in theory, they will be lower than those of printed journals. Individual subscription rates are far lower than institutional rates, and, of course, some online journals are free. There are many ejournals available and new journals are regularly being introduced. Some journals are focused on publishing high-quality research while others are more focused on turning a profit. One should exercise caution when selecting an ejournal in which to publish.

Mailing Lists and Discussion Groups

Introduction

As of this writing, *mailing lists* and *discussion groups* have been around for about 30 years. These were two mechanisms by which early uses of the Internet could communicate with each other. Mailing lists and discussion groups predate the web by about ten years. The ideas to create these communication mechanisms were very innovative at the time. The original interfaces to both of these communication mechanisms would be considered primitive by current standards. But, over the years they have been upgraded to have web interfaces, handle multimedia, and have friendly graphical-user interfaces. In this section we begin by discussing mailing lists in more detail and follow this material with an overview of discussion groups.

Mailing Lists

A mailing list is a list of user email addresses of users who have a similar interest in a given topic. The individuals whose email addresses are contained in the list are called *subscribers*. There are *moderated* and *unmoderated* lists. When someone posts a message to an unmoderated list, all subscribers receive the post. When someone posts a message to a moderated list, the moderator reviews the message, and if appropriate to the list, the moderator sends the message along to all subscribers. Otherwise, the moderator discards the message. The moderator in this case could actually be a team of people rather than an individual, and they may do things such as spam filtering, block messages that are not relevant, and delete foul-language messages. Mailing lists target specific-interest groups, for example, scuba

diving, traveling, or cooking. And, lists can get very specific, for example, scuba diving in Palau. There are various software packages that allow for the management of mailing lists, including additions and deletions of subscribers, archiving of old posts, handling of special addresses, and so on. Lists can be further broken down by other types of attributes as well, such as *digest* or *non-digest*. In a digest posts are typically collated, perhaps edited, and sent out with a table of contents. In non-digest form messages are simply passed along to the list in accordance with whether the list is moderated or not.

When subscribing to a mailing list, one may find that one's inbox fills up quickly depending on the activity level of the list(s) that one subscribes to. Some lists contain little material of value, so it is wise to keep information about how to unsubscribe from a list handy. Most mailing lists seem to follow the 80-20 rule. That is, about 80% of the posts are done by 20% of the subscribers. People who never post to a list but follow along are called *lurkers*. It is usually a good idea to lurk for a while to get the flavor of a given list before posting. And, it is probably a good idea to read through or search the archives before posting questions to a list. If one's question was answered last week, there is no sense in posting it again. One must respect other members of the list and also other Internet users.

Note that not all mailing lists are available at all installations. If at one's work, one needs access to a particular mailing list, one might have to discuss that with the local system administrators. One can also create a new mailing list. Of course, before undertaking this task, one needs to do some research to confirm that the 'new' list does not already exist. One also needs to think through the time commitment required to maintain a mailing list. The website L-Soft maintains the official list of *LISTSERVs*™, and as of this writing, there are 50,241 public lists (L-Soft, 2011). Note that LISTSERV™ is the name of the original mailing-list management software. There are a number of mailing lists related to information technology, and one can search the L-Soft site to find a relevant list in terms of topic and location.

Discussion Groups

Discussion groups have been around since the early 1980s. Originally, discussion groups were an Internet forum that allowed users to communicate about a given topic of mutual interest. As in the case of mailing lists, discussion groups cover a wide range of topics. Another form of discussion group was called a *newsgroup*. Special software is required to interact through a discussion group, and in the case of a newsgroup that software is called a *newsreader*. Generally, someone will post a message to a discussion group. Active users will view these *posts*. Interesting posts might generate comments from other users, and in turn these comments might generate more discussion. The collection of comments related to a given post is called a *thread*. Followers of a given discussion group will read threads which interest them.

Unlike mailing lists which direct email to one's inbox, a user of a discussion group may simply 'look in' on the discussion group at regular intervals. The discussion-group software will manage entries in a discussion group, for example, if a user reads an article, it will be marked as read. Discussion groups also seem to follow the 80-20 rule, and sometimes one person can become dominant in a group. Discussion groups in their original instantiation have faded, and now most discussion groups are used through a web browser. The user interface to discussion groups is now much-more friendly and intuitive. The old newsreaders had cryptic commands and were pretty much only available to tech-savvy users. We should point out that the distinction between mailing lists and discussion groups has blurred a bit. One of the largest collections of groups on the Internet is Google Groups which, as of this writing, reports a total of over 700,000,000 messages archived (Google, 2011).

As in the case of mailing lists, it may be appropriate for an employee to create a discussion group at work. The group can be private and only for employees, or it could be public in nature. Relevant job topics could be the focus of discussions. Such a discussion group can be useful for collaboration, distributing information to a group of users, and for sharing expertise. With the explosion of the Internet and the development of crowdsourcing (discussed later on in this section), there is so much information available at a global level that a local discussion group may only make sense for a very specific topic or for the purpose of developing more collaboration among local team members.

Homepages

In this section we focus on an individual's *homepage*. We define a homepage as a personal web page about an individual. There are other uses of the word "homepage." For example, a homepage can refer to that page that is first loaded when one brings up a web browser, or it can refer to a company's front page. In the next section we discuss company websites. We also distinguish a homepage from a user profile on a social-networking site. Later on in this section we discuss social-networking sites.

A homepage can serve a number of purposes for a person. One's homepage may reside on a company's server in which case one must be sure to follow all company rules, or one's homepage may reside on a non-company server. In the later case one may have more flexibility about what one can display on the web page. A homepage generally serves as a source of biographical information about a person. Professional information such as one's education and areas of expertise can go on such a page. The page can also be a repository of materials, for example, it can contain copies of one's papers, talks, teaching materials, and so on. As a repository, this material is not only useful for others, but also to its originator. For example, while traveling, one can have access to one's papers, talks, teaching materials, and so on. If giving a presentation at another venue which has Internet access, it is helpful to have the presentation linked into one's homepage for backup access.

The level of personal information that one displays on a homepage will depend on one's job, employer considerations, and the types of activities in which one is involved. At some universities, for example, it may be appropriate for a professor to list one's hobbies on a website. Such a listing could foster greater interaction with the students. At other types of institutions a listing of hobbies might not be desirable. It is almost always forbidden to advertise a product for sale on one's homepage if the page is hosted at a place of employment. Such advertising is best done on a separate business website and that is the topic of the next section.

Company Websites

In this section we discuss company websites. A company website typically serves a number of purposes for a company. In this section we focus just on the external face of the company. The company may very well have an Intranet, and certain of its web pages may only be seen from within the company. The comments that we make here can also apply to internal websites. Generally, a company wants to communicate the following information on its website:

- Products and services
- How to get more information
- Details about its leadership team
- General company information
- News and announcements
- Contact information
- Privacy policy
- Terms of service
- Copyright information

And, this information is often displayed in a top-down manner on a web page, as we have listed it here. That is, "products and services" are typically listed near the top of the page, while "copyright information" is usually listed at the bottom of a page.

In Figure 1 we display the home screen for Elbrys Networks, Inc.—an information-technology company based in Portsmouth, NH that specializes in secure personal-sensor platforms (Elbrys, 2011). The first thing to notice about the page is that it is visually appealing. There is a good blend of images and text. The name "Elbrys" derives from Mount Elbrys located in Russia, and an image of the mountain's twin peaks is shown in the Elbrys logo. Prominently displayed on the screen is the company's specialty area: secure personal-sensor platforms. The navigation shown "Home, Products, Solutions, Services, Resources, Support, and Company" is easy to see and to navigate by. Each of these items leads to a pull-down menu of further choices. The company displays announcements and upcoming events on the right-hand side of the page. Beneath the image of many athletes in motion are three other prominent graphics. These clickable graphics lead to information about the company's vision, customer information, and a repository of the company's research that is available to the public (listed under "Whitepapers"). From left-to-right at the bottom of the page are a copyright notice, privacy policy, and terms of service. At the very bottom in the right-hard corner of the page are some additional navigational links.

If one mouses over the "Company" navigational button, one can select the "Executive Team" link. We show the results of this selection in Figure 2. This page clearly and concisely presents information about the company's three top executives. A professional head shot of each team member is provided along with a brief biography; the biographies are personal. They contain professional background material, educational material, and hobbies that are relevant to the company.

Figure 1. Elbrys Network, Inc.'s "home" web page (© 2011 Elbrys Networks, Inc. Used with permission)

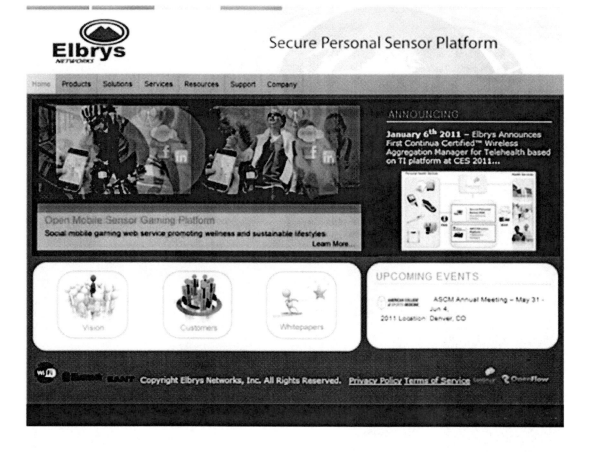

Links are provided to other sites where additional information about the executive team can be obtained. After reading the information on the page, one is convinced that Elbrys Networks, Inc. has a strong, capable, and experienced executive-management team. Two other things to notice about the page are as follows:

1. The other navigational choices from the pull-down menu under "Company" are displayed in the left pane of the screen making for easy navigation.
2. There is effective use of whitespace. Enough blank space is left on the page so that it does not have a cluttered feel. A reader is able to digest the information on the page in nuggets without getting lost.

In Figure 3 we show the results of selecting the "Secure Personal Sensor SDK" from the pull-down menu for "Products." The page contains two bulleted lists which are headed "Key Capabilities" and "Key Benefits." Each of these lists contains three concise descriptive bullets. There is also a link to a "Whitepaper" and a convenient link to contact Elbrys. On the right-hand side of the screen is an appealing graphic showing the Secure Personal-Sensor SDK framework. Other pages throughout the website use a similar style.

We have viewed three pages from the Elbrys' website. In reviewing each of these pages we made some specific comments. General comments are now in order. First, when visiting any pages in the collection of pages at the Elbrys website, one is always clear that one is still at the Elbrys

Figure 2. Elbrys Network, Inc.'s "executive team" web page (© 2011Elbrys Networks, Inc. Used with permission)

Figure 3. Elbrys Network, Inc.'s "products" web page (© 2011 Elbrys Networks, Inc. Used with permission)

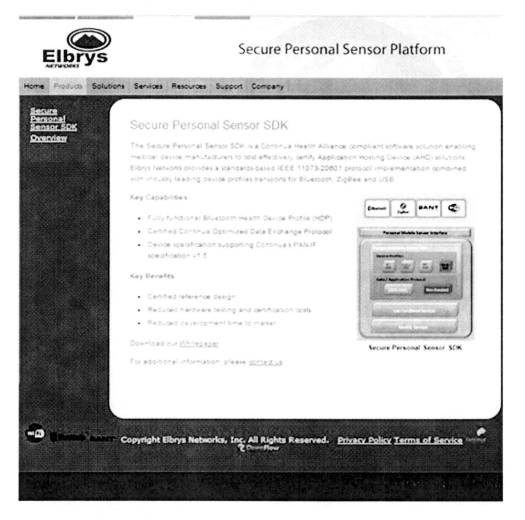

website. The pages are tied together via a common-color scheme and layout. The graphics have a similar flavor. Navigation is done consistently on the pages. And, finally, the pages are bound together using the same footer. This company is a serious IT company developing technical solutions to problems in the personal-sensor space. Its web pages convey this fact. The pages are not too flashy, which might bring into question the company's seriousness, yet they are appealing enough to keep a reader's interest. The pages fit together well and do a good job of communicating all the relevant information in a pleasant way. The balance required to provide just the right amount of information has been achieved—not too little and not too much.

The comments made about the Elbrys website apply to the websites of many other information-technology companies too, and, in fact, to companies in many other domains as well. That is, one will want to tie together pages at a website in a similar fashion as Elbrys has done, including a consistent color scheme, footers, navigation, graphics, and so on. When we discuss developing and maintaining a website later in this chapter, we encourage the reader to look back at the Elbrys web pages for reference.

Crowdsourced Sites

The word *crowdsourcing* is used to describe a system where many individuals make contributions to the overall final result (Howe, 2009). Crowdsourcing is a term that is applied to a collaborative effort.

In technology applications the users involved in such an effort may be distributed all over the world. Perhaps the best-known example of a crowdsourced system is the web encyclopedia called Wikipedia (Wikipedia, 2010). The volume of information that is contained at this site demonstrates the power of the crowd; there are millions and millions of articles written in many different languages. Of course, there are issues about information quality at such sites and techniques are still evolving to address these issues. Another well-known example of crowdsourcing is the social-news website called Digg (Digg, 2010), where users submit news articles, blog posts, or hyperlinks to items, and the crowd (other Internet users) rate the submissions. The top-rated submissions will rise to the front of Digg's homepage. Another well-known example is Flickr (Flickr, 2010), a photo-sharing website, where users share photos, comment on other people's photos, rate photos, and so on. In his book Howe describes many examples of the power of the crowd and how if carefully leveraged, the crowd can provide very-useful information.

Readers who work in the information-technology field, a scientific field, or who are particularly knowledgeable about a given topic should consider participating in a crowdsourced effort. Upon completion of the material in this book, readers will be well-versed in editing and writing, and will be poised to make good contributions to crowdsourced sites. Whether those contributions are editing existing pages, writing snippets, or developing entirely new materials, quality contributions by capable authors are always welcome at crowdsourced sites. We encourage readers to

find a site where they can make a contribution, and then utilize and practice the skills that they have been developing in the course of reading this book there. Extremely-ambitious readers may decide to develop their own crowdsourced site, and for this endeavor we suggest beginning by researching the crowdsourcing-software tools that are freely available for download over the Internet, for example, see (Ushahidi, 2010).

Social-Networking Sites

A *social network* refers to a structure consisting of nodes, which represent individuals, and links, which representation relationships among individuals. The allowable links or the type of links that can be setup will determine the type of social network. For example, a 'friends' social network consists of individuals as nodes with allowable links between any two individuals who are friends. *Facebook* is the best-known social-networking site in the United States (Facebook, 2011). As of this writing, there are over 500,000,000 Facebook users interacting with over 900,000,000 objects and spending over 700,000,000,000 minutes per month on Facebook (Facebook Stats, 2011). Facebook continues to grow. There are many other large social-networking sites in use throughout the world. Social networks have become a key form of communication since they first emerged around 2005. As a means of staying connected with a vast number of friends, social networks have become a dominant online-communication forum.

Numerous businesses have setup platforms that operate through Facebook, and users need to login to Facebook in order to access such businesses. Many entities have Facebook pages now, and someone skilled in IT might be asked to assist in setting up an organization's Facebook page. Most institutions have a policy regarding computer usage while one is at work, for example, restricting sites or types of activities. We caution readers to follow their employer's usage policy and to monitor their usage of social-networking sites. Social networks consume many people's time and some people's time completely.

DEVELOPING AND MAINTAINING A WEBSITE

Introduction

In this section our focus is on guidelines and principles for developing a website. In the previous sections we discussed homepages and company websites, as well as crowdsourced and social-networking sites. The comments provided here apply pretty well to all types of websites. And, by *website*, we mean a collection of web pages that are closely tied together by a theme and a common style. The three figures shown in this chapter from the Elbrys Networks, Inc.'s website depict a common theme and style. Generally, a website resides under one domain and is maintained by an individual or a team of people working together. A couple of well-known websites in information technology are Microsoft's http://www.msn.com and Apple's http://www.apple.com. People working in the field of information technology are often asked to help develop websites, have an inclination to develop their own websites, or are required to develop websites as part of their jobs. Even people who do not specialize in information technology find themselves wanting to put material on the web. And, the comments provided in this section will help guide those efforts.

Readers can find a huge amount of information online about specific software tools for developing websites, as well as locating tutorials regarding nearly every aspect of website development. From AJAX methods to cascading-style sheets to flash to HTML to JavaScript to php to syntax checkers to XML, online one can easily research and find a wealth of material about any given topic of interest. Our goal here is not to describe any particular piece of software or specific techniques

for website development, but rather the high-level process of putting together a website. Let us begin by discussing planning and goal setting.

Planning Ahead and Setting Goals

As with most writing or development projects, initial planning and goal setting are critical steps. The planning phrase consists of at least the following items:

- Analyzing one's audience
- Assessing the scope of a project
- Determining the duration of a project
- Knowing the budget for a project
- Developing a work plan
- Attempting to build in redundancy
- Putting in place recovery steps in the event that something goes wrong
- Knowing the consequences of missing the target deadline

Whether one is developing a site for one's own personal use, for an employer, or as a consultant, one would be wise to consider carefully all of the items in this list. Going hand-in-hand with the planning phase is the goal-setting phase. And, we discuss goal setting next.

In the goal-setting phase for a website one should attempt to write down specific goals that one would like the website to achieve. We list some sample goals in the following:

- Increase the visibility of our company
- Provide educational materials
- Become a well-known repository for information about topic X
- Describe to the world who we are
- Increase online sales
- Provide contact information
- Inform about products and services
- Reach a broader audience

The specific goals that one has for a given website will vary. Our list can help one in honing in one's fixed goals, perhaps stimulating new ideas for goals.

The planning and the goals phases must be coordinated. And, a key item linking these phases together is a *work plan*. A work plan will provide details of items to be completed, completion dates, deliverables, personnel responsible for completing a given task, budget information, and other relevant information. Ideally, one can break down the development of a website into smaller tasks which can then be put into the work plan. The level of detail in a work plan and its size will depend on the scope of the website being developed. We suggest following the two laws of planning and goal setting provided next.

Planning and Goal Setting Quantity Law

The amount of time dedicated to planning and goal setting for a given task needs to increase more than linearly as a function of the total time that a project requires.

Planning and Goal Setting Time Savings Law

The amount of time saved by proper planning and goal setting in the completion of a task increases more than linearly as a function of the complexity of a task.

The first of the planning and goal settings laws states that much-more time needs to be devoted to more-complex projects. For example, if 10 hours of time is adequate for planning and goal setting for a project that will take 200 hours, then 20 hours of planning and goal setting for a project that requires 400 hours will not be sufficient. In the later case one may require 30 hours of planning. The second law of planning and goal setting states that the time savings generated from proper planning will be repaid more handsomely

in more-complex projects. For example, if one saves 50 hours by planning properly for a task that requires 200 hours, then properly planning for a task requiring 400 hours may save 150 hours of time. The two laws combined serve as reminders and guidelines regarding the importance of proper planning and goal setting. Once these tasks have been completed for a website, one can begin to outline the site. And, outlining a website is the topic of the next section.

Outlining a Website

Our focus in this section is on outlining a website. During the planning and goal setting phase, one has already begun this process. We have always found that outlining is best done in the framework of the medium being used. For example, if one is going to code up a web page in HTML, one should use HTML to design the outline. In this manner one can literally see an outline taking shape and progressing. This progress serves as 'encouragement' to an author. Writers often get discouraged by slow progress or lack of productivity, and thus it is important for one to be able to visualize one's advances. For the sake of this discussion suppose that one needs to develop a web-based tutorial for HTML. We consider how one can go about outlining such a website. The comments given here can be generalized to other types of projects as well.

If one is not familiar with the given topic that needs to be outlined, clearly the first step is to research the topic. Once one has a command of the topic, the outlining process can begin in earnest. And, let us suppose that we have finished our research phase on HTML. In this case let us assume that our audience will be beginning HTML users. We can brainstorm about the outline for days on end, but at some point, and probably sooner rather than later, we need to commit some thoughts down on a web page, or the medium of choice for producing the outline. The thoughts should be organized as best as possible at this stage. We want to achieve a balance between generating useful thoughts and having them somewhat organized. That is, we do not simply want random thoughts put down in a random order.

In jotting down the first parts of the outline we will need to recall our planning and goal-setting phase. The outline should be consistent with those activities. After some thought, say we decide to put the following items into a web page or simply down on paper:

- Creating a "hello world" web page
- Basics
- Tag syntax
- Hyperlinks
- Images
- Lists
- Tables
- Advanced items

Notice the first item is simply to get a user creating a single web page. This accomplishment entails a number of hurdles such as access to a web server, being able to enter information into a system, possibly setting file permissions, and so on. Next the outline describes basics and perhaps gives a user additional simple information, while trying to build the user's confidence. This step is followed by a section on tag syntax. Since HTML is a tag-based programming language, early on it is worth going over the general syntax of HTML. This material is followed by a section on hyperlinks. Hyperlinks are certainly one of the most-important and distinguishing features of HTML. A user will want to know how to code up hyperlinks right away. Next we cover in order of perceived importance to a user the topics of images, lists, and tables. These are followed by advanced items. This completes the first draft of the outline.

The proposed outline for the HTML tutorial was organized both in terms of the topics selected as well as the order of the topics. Naturally, there are many details to fill in such as coding up colors and fonts, as well as more-complex items such as cascading-style sheets. However our outline serves as a starting point. It can be expanded, reordered, or tweaked as one sees fit. Once a solid outline is achieved, one can begin adding content. Adding content to a site is the subject of the next section. As one adds content, the outline, which is rather like a table of contents, may need to evolve as well. In addition, design decisions about how many pages to have, what type of navigation to employ, the style of headers and footers, and other issues will need to be decided upon. Sometimes these decisions come more easily when one sees the amount of content that each part of the outline requires.

Adding Content to a Website

The content is material—text, images, sound bites, and so on— that one either already has or plans on producing. For example, one may have some images that can be used on the site, but for other images one may still need to develop them. Carrying forward with the HTML-tutorial theme, one might decide that the website will consist of a central page with links off of it to each of the topics contained in the outline. A template of a page can be created with the desired headers and footers. Pages can be created for each of the topics, and links to and from the central page can be added. At this point one has a shell of the overall site and can see how the navigation is working. Once one has a shell, it is relatively easy to fill in the content. One actually sees the places where the content belongs. It is much easier to fill something out if one has a concrete idea of its scope and location rather than just a vague sense of what needs to be done. For example, if we say to someone put down all of your contact information on this sheet of paper and hand over a blank sheet of paper, this exercise might be more difficult for the person to complete than if we simply handed the person a form with various fields already specified: name, email address, home-phone number, cell-phone number, work-phone number, fax, URL, Facebook name, and so on.

When adding content to a website, one should try to add the content in its final form. By this we mean one should try to produce content that will actually be used in the final product as one enters it. In order words try to produce high-quality material the first time around so that it does not ever need to be modified. This goal is easier said than done but with careful thought while working, and with a great deal of practice, one will become more successful at achieving this goal. If during the content adding phase, one is constantly being distracted because one needs to research a given item, one may decide to pause the content-adding phase and concentrate more on background research. Usually, one can be more efficient at entering content, if one is already a master of the content. Going back and forth from contenting adding to research mode is probably not too efficient. Once the content has been added, one will have a good sense of whether the original design is effective or needs to be modified. During the content-adding phase, one should also monitor the work plan in order to remain on schedule.

Maintenance of a Website

When one designs a website, one must design it with the issue of ongoing maintenance in mind. There are many websites that are out-of-date or have a perennial under-construction sign displayed. Maintenance almost always requires more time than one anticipates. Going back to the HTML tutorial, suppose another item appearing on the outline were "New features." In order to maintain the HTML-tutorial website properly one would need to be monitoring the ongoing developments in the HTML language. As new features were added to the language or old features were depreciated,

one would accordingly need to modify the "New features" portion of the website. Similarly, if one wants to include a link for comments, one must process those comments on an ongoing basis. One could design an FAQ section in order to save time by anticipating user's questions. Of course, larger websites typically require more maintenance. During the design phase, one should give careful consideration to maintenance issues. One should never under estimate the amount of time that it will take to maintain a website in a professional manner.

Summary

In this section we focused on a number of key issues relating to developing and maintaining a website. Key take-away points are as follows:

- The importance of planning and goal setting, and the two laws associated with these activities
- The need to produce a well-ordered and well-thought-through outline
- The importance of creating placeholders where one can actually see where content should be inserted
- The need to think about a website in terms of its maintenance issues even before developing the site

There are many other-important issues relating to website development that we have not covered here, for example, things such as conducting a review of all of the content, verifying that all of the hyperlinks work properly, testing the code on various browser platforms, and so on. As a user gains more experience, one can delve into the details of these and other aspects of website development further. An interested reader can pursue the references provided in this chapter or locate additional references online.

FUTURE TRENDS

As the cost of printing continues to escalate, we may see the gap between offline writing and online writing close even future. Electronic-book readers such as the Kindle (Kindle, 2011), iPad (iPad, 2011), and Nook (Nook, 2011) are getting so sophisticated that even those who held out for a novel that they could curl up with are switching over to these devices. If the migration of materials to electronic forums continues at this pace, we may reach a tipping point where offline publishing almost disappears. The quality of the best online writing now matches the quality of the best offline writing. And, the volume of material being produced through crowdsourced-efforts online simply cannot be matched via offline mechanisms. We see more collaboration among greater numbers of authors, perhaps authors who have never even met one another. With continued advances in technology and software we see authors being able to produce more material and produce it more accurately. Given the vast quantities of material being produced on a daily basis for the web, we do not see the web disappearing at anytime in the future. New technologies will emerge, but people will figure out a way to bring existing content to new platforms. The investments that have been made in web technologies are simply too great to throw away at this point. Thus the general material presented on developing a website will serve readers well for many years to come.

CONCLUSION

In this chapter we covered a wide spectrum of online-communication forums. As of this writing, the level of communication that is possible among people all over the world is the greatest that the world has ever seen. The level of communication may even be reaching a plateau. We are essentially able to communicate with anyone in the world on a moment's notice; we cannot do much better

than that. All types of information can be accessed instantly, even while we are on mobile. Technology will continue to evolve rapidly, and our reliance and dependence on online-communication will continue to grow rapidly. As a result, the consequences of a failure or a successful attack on our critical infrastructure become even greater. Although we will likely continue to use online-communication forums such as email, ejournals, mailing lists, discussion groups, blogs, websites, and social-networking sites, we must evolve our skills to use new communication mechanisms and technologies as they arise, and we must continue to safeguard such technologies carefully as our daily lives depend so heavily on these technologies.

REFERENCES

Arlinghaus, S. L., & Zander, R. H. (1993). Electronic journals: Observations based on actual trials, 1987–present. *Solstice, 19*(2). Retrieved April 4, 2011, from http://www-personal.umich.edu/~copyrght/image/monog17/fulltext.pdf

Arlinghaus, S. L., & Zander, R. H. (2008). Electronic journals: Then and now… A fifteen year retrospective. *Solstice,* 19(2). Retrieved April 4, 2011, from http://www.mobot.org/plantscience/resbot/Repr/Arling-Zand-ElecJour-Solstice08c31.pdf

Christakis, N. A., & Fowler, J. H. (2009). *Connected: The surprising power of our social networks and how they shape our lives.* Little, Brown and Company.

Digg. (2010). *Social news site.* Retrieved December 5, 2010, from http://www.digg.com

ECCC. (2011). *Electronic colloquium on computational complexity.* Retrieved April 4, 2011, from http://www.eccc.uni-trier.de/

Elbrys. (2011). *Secure personal sensor platform.* Elbrys Networks, Inc. Retrieved April 5, 2011, from http://elbrys.com

Facebook. (2011). *Facebook*. Retrieved April 5, 2011, from http://www.facebook.com

Facebook Stats. (2011). *Facebook statistics*. Retrieved April 5, 2011, from http://www.facebook.com/press/info.php?statistics

Flickr. (2010). *Share your photos. Watch the world*. Retrieved December 5, 2010, from http://www.flickr.com

Google. (2011). *20 year Usenet timeline*. Google Groups. Retrieved April 4, 2011, from http://www.google.com/googlegroups/archive_announce_20.html

Greenlaw, R., & Hepp, E. (2001). *Inline/online: Fundamentals of the Internet and World Wide Web*. McGraw Hill.

Howe, J. (2009). *Crowdsourcing: Why the power of the crowd is driving the future of business*. Three Rivers Press. iPad. (2011). *iPad 2*. Apple. Retrieved April 3, 2011, from http://www.apple.com/ipad/

JIITO. (2011). *Journal of Information, Information Technology, and Organizations*. Retrieved April 12, 2011, from http://jiito.org/

JIT. (2011). *Journal of Information Technology*. Palgrave Macmillan. Retrieved April 4, 2011, from http://www.palgrave-journals.com/jit/index.html

JITR. (2011). *Journal of Information Technology Research*. Hershey, PA: IGI Global. Retrieved April 4, 2011, from http://www.igi-global.com/bookstore/titledetails.aspx?TitleId=1100

Kindle. (2011). *Kindle wireless reading device, Wi-Fi, Graphite, 6" display with new e ink pearl technology*. Amazon. Retrieved from http://www.amazon.com/dp/B002Y27P3M/?tag=gocous-20&hvadid=5729884517&ref=pd_sl_992dhxljd6_b

L-Soft. (2011). *CataList: The official list of LIST-SERV lists*. Retrieved April 4, 2011, from http://www.lsoft.com/lists/listref.html

Nook. (2011). *Nook e-reader*. Barnes & Noble. Reference retrieved on April 3, 2011, from http://www.barnesandnoble.com/nook/index.asp

Solstice. (2011). *Solstice: An Electronic Journal of Geography and Mathematics*. Retrieved April 4, 2011, from http://www-personal.umich.edu/~copyrght/image/solstice.html

(2011). *The Chicago Manual of Style* (16th ed.). University of Chicago Press.

Ushahidi. (2010). Open source crowdsourcing tools. Retrieved on December 4, 2010, from http://www.ushahidi.com

Wikipedia. (2010). *The free encyclopedia*. Retrieved December 4, 2010, from http://www.wikipedia.org

Chapter 4
Blogging

ABSTRACT

The previous chapter covered a wide range of online-communication forums. This chapter focuses on another extremely-popular online forum, namely, the blog. A blog is essentially an online listing and description of related items, and for some individuals it the equivalent to maintaining an online personal journal or activity log. From blogging's origins in late 1997 until now, there has been a tremendous explosion in the number of blogs. The discussion begins here by presenting a history of blogs. The chapter presents a classification scheme for blogs and a number of examples of interesting blogs. It next provides a review of popular blogging software. This software has made setting up, adding content to, and maintaining a blog very simple; this software has help to fuel the popularity of blogging. Tim O'Reilly and others proposed a Blogging Code of Conduct, and the chapter includes a section where the author discusses that code. This material is followed by cautions about blogging. The chapter also reviews a number of IT-related blogs, and wraps up with conclusions and references.

INTERESTING FACTS ABOUT BLOGS

This section describes blogs and their history. The word "blog" derives from the words "web" and "log." Jorn Barger is credited with coming up with the term "weblog" (Barger, 2011), and Peter Merholz is credited with shortening it to "blog"

(Blog, 2011). A *blog* is an online grouping of related items that are posted in chronological order and regularly updated. Most blogs are maintained by individuals, but some are maintained by a group of people or by a business. The items in a blog are typically listed in reverse-chronological order, that is, the most-recent items appear at the top of the blog. These items are called *blog entries* or *entries,* for short. An early discussion of blogs is

DOI: 10.4018/978-1-4666-0237-3.ch004

contained in (Greenlaw & Hepp, 2001). A sample blog entry is shown in Figure 1.

There are several things to notice about the blog entry shown in Figure 1. The first point to notice is that the blog entry is text only. The information is easy to read but is not particularly visually appealing. The heading material is centered, and the learning objectives are organized in a bulleted list. Thus the information on the blog is easy to read. The name of the blog in this case is "USNA Cyber-Security Class," and it is shown at the top of the entry. The author of the blog is provided: "Raymond Greenlaw," and this information is followed by the date of the post. In some blogs other users are able to add comments and in this case the "3" in parenthesis means that there have been three comments added to this post. These posts form a *thread*. A thread is simply a collection of related posts. A reader of the blog can read the threads. Most blogs are public, and the people who author blogs, *bloggers*, desire the widest-possible audience or at least a large audience. Other blogs are private, as in the case of this one. The audience for this one is captive in the sense that the blog accompanies a specific class at the United States Naval Academy. Students are required to read the material on the blog. The purpose of this blog is to convey information, not to attract a larger readership. Thus no real effort is made to dress the blog up with nice graphics or multimedia. The effort instead has been devoted entirely to the content.

Many blogs make use of multimedia and include images, hyperlinks, videos, sound bites, and so on. Figure 2 shows a sample entry from the engadget blog; the entry makes use of multimedia. The engadget blog itself uses lots of color, images, and hyperlinks. Note that in the blog entry shown in Figure 2 the name of the author of the entry and date of the posting are displayed. Each blog post on the page has a distinctive eye-catching graphic. Each blog post uses it own style and colors. These styles make it easy to distinguish the various entries. Note that at the bottom of the entry on Eee Pad Transformer source code, one can see the number of tweets (441) and the number of posts (88) made about the entry. Usually, high values for these items mean that readers found the item

Figure 1. A sample blog entry from a class on cyber security at the United States Naval Academy

USNA Cyber-Security Class
By Raymond Greenlaw
Posted 4/11/2011
Comments: (3)

Today's learning objectives are as follows:
- Understand the basic principles of computer forensics
- Be able to explain key points about how to investigate a computer crime or policy violation (incident-response cycle)
- Be able to identify standards for, types of, and rules for evidence
- Understand how to collect evidence
- Learn how to preserve evidence
- Understand the terms *free space* and *slack space* as places in memory where one may be able to recover additional data
- Know the steps involved in a cleanup after a possible attack

'interesting' and therefore took the time to comment on it. Of course, in some cases people may be writing to correct an error or to pick a bone.

Some blogs are more than just a listing of items; they have an interactive feel to them. Perhaps there is a marquee with news items scrolling or perhaps certain popular entries are highlighted and being rotated through cyclically. On some blogs it may be possible to rate items, and this rating can serve as a measure of the popularity of an entry, as can the number of entries in the thread relating to the initial post. The number of tweets made about an entry could also be factored into such a rating.

Before getting too far ahead of ourselves, let us mention common terminology that is used in the *blogsphere*. Blogsphere is a term that is used to define the worldwide collection of blogs and their

Figure 2. A sample blog entry from the engadget blog demonstrating the use of multimedia in a blog post. http://www.engadget.com (© 2011AOL, Inc. Used with permission)

ASUS releases Eee Pad Transformer source code, physical bits to come later

By *Tim Stevens* posted Apr 8th 2011 at 7:24AM

We're still sitting here playing with our Decepticon and Autobot toys, Jetfire and Starscream continuing their battle for airborne supremacy. It's how we entertain ourselves whilst waiting for ASUS to release its Transformer tablet on the world, but now we can at least get our hands on what makes it tick. The source code for that 10.1-inch tablet with its IPS screen and Honeycomb flavor has just been lobbed up onto the company's site and, with just a few clicks, you can continue its trajectory right onto your storage device of choice -- though you'll need to run it through an unzipper before it can really have any impact. What you do with it after that is up to you, but you're going to have to wait a bit longer before you'll have anywhere to deploy the results of the included makefile.

VIA *Android Community*
SOURCE *ASUS*

Tweet 441   DISCUSS 88

associated-user communities. The act of writing or developing a blog is called *blogging*. Later in this chapter we will discuss useful software for blogging. According to BlogPulse™, as of this writing, there were 159,297,624 blogs (BlogPulse, 2011). And, on April 8, 2011 alone, there were 68,825 new blogs added to the blogsphere. The rate of blog creation has almost reached the level of one new blog being born per second. If each new blog added just a single page of content, it would probably take the average reader about ten years to read a day's worth of postings and that is only for these new blogs. The amount of 'information' being added to blogs in just a single day is truly astonishing. We are pretty sure that most of our readers have many friends who maintain blogs. As one can imagine, with almost 160 million blogs available, it can be difficult to zero in on the right blog. BlogPulse™ is a search tool that gathers useful information about blogs and allows one to search the blogsphere. The interested reader should visit BlogPulse™ (http://www.blogpulse. com) or other similar tools to help one explore the blogsphere.

In what follows we describe BlogPulse ™'s opening page. The page makes good use of multimedia. The pages include an attractive graphic at the top, dynamic charts, hyperlinks, a search feature, highlights, live statistics, and so on. The page is quite long. The page is broken down into a number of table-like structures that display the top-five items in each of the table's categories. The page has categories Top Links, Key People, Top Videos, Top Blog Posts, Top Blogs, Key Phrases, Top News Stories, and Top News Sources. The content on BlogPulse™'s page is visually appealing and informative. The navigation on the page is user friendly. This page is an excellent resource for learning more about the blogsphere and popular blogs.

TYPES OF BLOGS

Introduction

In this section we discuss a classification scheme for the blogsphere. Blogs can be broken down into the following four primary categories:

- **Personal:** consisting of diaries or ongoing personal commentaries
- **Business Related:** for disseminating information about or promoting a business; a business; business news
- **Topical:** devoted to the discussion of a particular subject
- **Miscellaneous:** not fitting into one of the previous categories

Of course, one could have a finer partitioning of the blogsphere by splitting out other large categories from the miscellaneous piece or by subdividing one of the other three categories. BlogPulse™'s main screen includes a graphic that displays the number of posts per topic in the blogsphere (BlogPulse, 2011). As of this writing, the graphic displays the following categories: Diary, Memes, MoviesTV, Politics, and Sports. More information about this display can be obtained at the BlogPulse website (BlogPulse, 2011).

We present sample blogs from the personal, business-related, and topical categories of our classification scheme in what follows. Note that the blogs listed in the examples in what follows all meet our definition of blog. Since the early days of blogging, we should note that the term has expanded to include more than just personal diaries.

Personal Blog

In the personal-blog category we include Bruce Schneier's blog (Schneier, 2011). Schneier is an internationally-known expert on computer security. In Schneier's blog he discusses a wide range of topics about computer security. From his blog one can get access to his monthly newsletter, books, essays on security, and access to blog posts. In Figure 3 we depict Schneier's blog. Recent posts to the blog include "Get Your Terrorist Alerts on Facebook and Twitter," "Pinpointing a Computer to within 690 Meters," "Detecting Cheaters," and "Optical Stun Ray" (Schneier, 2011).

In looking at Figure 3 one sees a clean and easy-to-use layout. On the left-hand side of the page is a list of navigational links. These begin with Blog, Crypto-Gram Newsletter, Books, and Essays and Op eds. Via these links one can access a wealth of information on important computer-security issues. The blog posts are listed in the center of the screen. The title of each post is display in a large easy-to-read font. Each post is one to several paragraphs long and is formatted using a block-quote style. At the bottom of each post is a timestamp indicating when the material was posted. There is also a link to comments, and the total number of comments about each entry is shown. If one follows the comments link, one is brought to a listing that provides the comment, the name of the person posting the comments, and a timestamp. Each comment is separated from other comments by a horizontal line.

On the right-hand side of Schneier's blog is his headshot, a search feature, a link to the blog's home, a link to the latest 100 comments, and a set of links leading to the blog's archives. This blog

Figure 3. Bruce Schneier's personal blog on computer security. http://www.schneier.com (© 2011 Bruce Schneier. Used with permission)

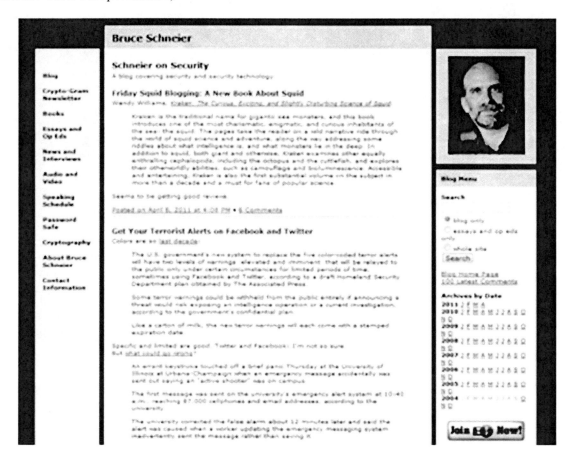

contains serious information about a serious topic. Its layout conveys all the necessary information in a user-friendly format. For a reader with an interest in computer security, we strongly recommend visiting Schneier's blog.

Business-Related Blog

In the business-blog category we include *The Wall Street Journal*. This journal is well-known and highly respected for its business news, world news, and financial information. Many viewers visit the journal's blog to obtain the latest information about stock markets, current world events, and other hot topics. We show an image of the home screen for *The Wall Street Journal Asia* in Figure 6. Recent headlines from the blog include "Fed Takes Foot of the Gas" and "Army Tests Smartphones for Combat" (Wall Street, 2011).

When looking at Figure 4, the first thing one observes about the *Wall Street Journal's* blog is its use of multimedia to create a colorful and dynamic feel. The blog contains an enormous amount of information in a compact space. One sees immediately that great care has been taking in laying out the material for the ease of user access. In the top left of the screen are the time and date, links to various-language editions, and the name of the journal. In the top right of the screen is a convenient search field. Figure 4 shows the

Figure 4. The Wall Street Journal's business blog. http://asia.wsj.com/home-page (© 2011 Dow Jones & Company, Inc. Used with permission)

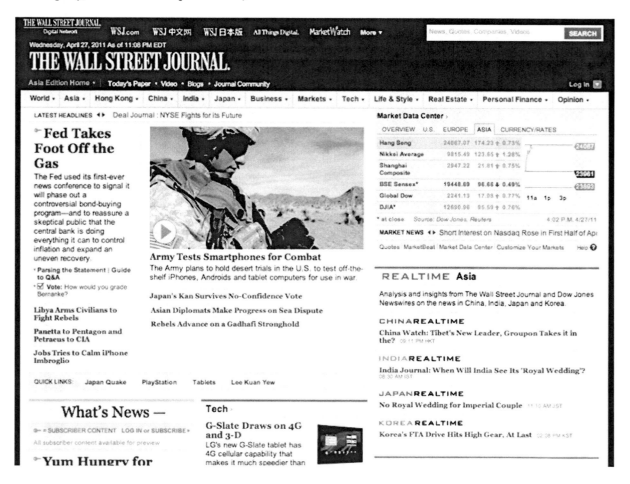

Asia Edition of the journal, and near the top of the screen we see links to prominent players in Asia: Hong Kong, China, India, and Japan. Alongside these are displayed links to Business, Markets, Tech, Life & Style, Real Estate, Personal Finance, and Opinion. Note that just above the Opinion link is a place for subscribers to sign in.

The *Wall Street Journal* is known throughout the world for its quality reporting, and on the left-hand side of the figure moving down, we see a number of current news stories. On the right-hand side of the screen is a market-data overview. As one moves down the page, one cannot help but be amazed by the amount of information contained there. All of the information is laid out carefully in a user-friendly format. We encourage

readers to visit this page to further explore the *Wall Street Journal's* blog (Wall Street, 2011).

Topical Blog

In the topical-blog category we present the United States Government's Whitehouse Blog (Whitehouse, 2011). We show a picture of the Whitehouse Blog in Figure 5. The blog makes good use of multimedia, including graphics, videos, and links. The upper part of the screen contains links to various parts of the government. The main body of the screen is dedicated to recent posts. These posts are in the form of news stories. Each post lists the reporter's name and the time of the post. (Note that throughout this work we often use a

Figure 5. The White House Blog on the topic of United States Government. http://www.whitehouse.gov/blog/

singular form of words such as reporter, scientist, author, or writer, but since writing and research projects are usually conducted by a team rather than an individual, a reader should interpret such usage as either being that of an individual or a team.) Recent posts include "Details on the Bipartisan Budget Deal," "Weekly Address: President Obama on the Budget Compromise to Avoid a Government Shutdown," and "Weekly Wrap Up: America's Energy Future" (Whitehouse, 2011).

On the right-hand side of the screen shown in Figure 5 is a listing of other Whitehouse blogs and beneath that is a listing of links to categories that would be of interest to a typical US citizen. Further down the page is a set of links to archived material. One thing that we should point out about this blog is the absence of a copyright notice. Note that there is a link to copyright information. If one pursues that link, one will find out that according to the rules of the federal government, the information contained in this blog is not copyrighted. Later in this book in the chapter titled "Ethical Issues in Writing," we explore copyright issues in detail.

Summary of Types of Blogs

In this section we presented and described three prominent, well-known, and authoritative blogs. Common themes regarding the blogs were effective use of multimedia, quality layouts, ease of use, important topics, quality of posts, and timeliness. In developing one's own blog, one can keep these three model blogs in mind. One can learn from the styles contained in these blogs about how to create an effective and user-friendly blog. And, as always, one must carefully consider one's audience and what style and method of writing will best suit readers' needs. In the next two chapters, which are on writing, we include a great deal of information on writing styles and audience.

BLOGS FOR THE IT PROFESSIONAL

In this section we describe two blogs that are of specific interest to IT professionals. First, we should note that there are many blogs relating to IT topics, and if one has a specific IT interest, there is likely a blog available which contains a discussion of that topic. So, for specific topics, a reader can simply use a search tool to find an appropriate blog. Here we discuss the following two blogs:

- The Information Technology Blog— Galido.net: Computer tips, tricks, solutions, links and relevant information to IT-related topics blog (Galido, 2011).
- The DownloadSquad blog (DownloadSquad, 2011).

The first blog mentioned provides a user "with information and links to computer tips, tricks, solutions, news and relevant information to IT-related topics" (Galido, 2011). This site "also features a collection of blogs containing links to IT-related software, hardware, news, cool sites, news on gadgets, where to get them, search engine optimization, and more" (Galido, 2011). The blog contains a lot of information about a grab bag of IT topics. Recent posts discuss security tokens, creating and sending videos to phones, sending large email files, and SharePoint. A post from The Information Technology Blog from Galido Network's about a browser compatibility check is shown in Figure 6.

The second IT-related blog that we discuss here is DownloadSquad Switched: The Latest App News is from AOL, Inc. This blog contains a great deal of information about various IT topics. The blog's "mission is to seek out the best in tools, utilities and applications, browser add-ons, distractions, time-wasters and other facets of your digital lifestyle" (DownloadSquad, 2011). Recent posts involve comments and news about Google Hotpot, SeaMonkey, Angry Birds Rio, and Google

Latitude (DownloadSquad, 2011). In Figure 7 we show the blog's main screen.

Given the wealth of information about IT contained in blogs, the reader will have little trouble finding relevant information for any given IT topic. More likely the problem will be wading through the vast amounts of information available. Some readers will no doubt want to share their thoughts and create their own blogs. So in the next section we take a look at a couple of free blogging-software packages which are expressly designed to make blogging easy.

INTRODUCTION TO FREE BLOGGING SOFTWARE

In this section we provide an introduction to two popular free-software packages for creating blogs: Blogger (http://www.blogger.com) and WordPress (http://wordpress.com). These systems are both easy-to-use and free. Let us begin with Blogger.

In Figure 8 we show an image of Blogger's main screen. In order to create a blog using Blogger one needs to have a gmail account. Once a user has a gmail account, the process of creating

Figure 6. The Information Technology blog—Galido.net: Computer tips, tricks, solutions, links and relevant information to IT-related topics blog. http://galido.net/blog/index.php/ITOnlyBlog/ (© 2011Galido Networks. Used with permission)

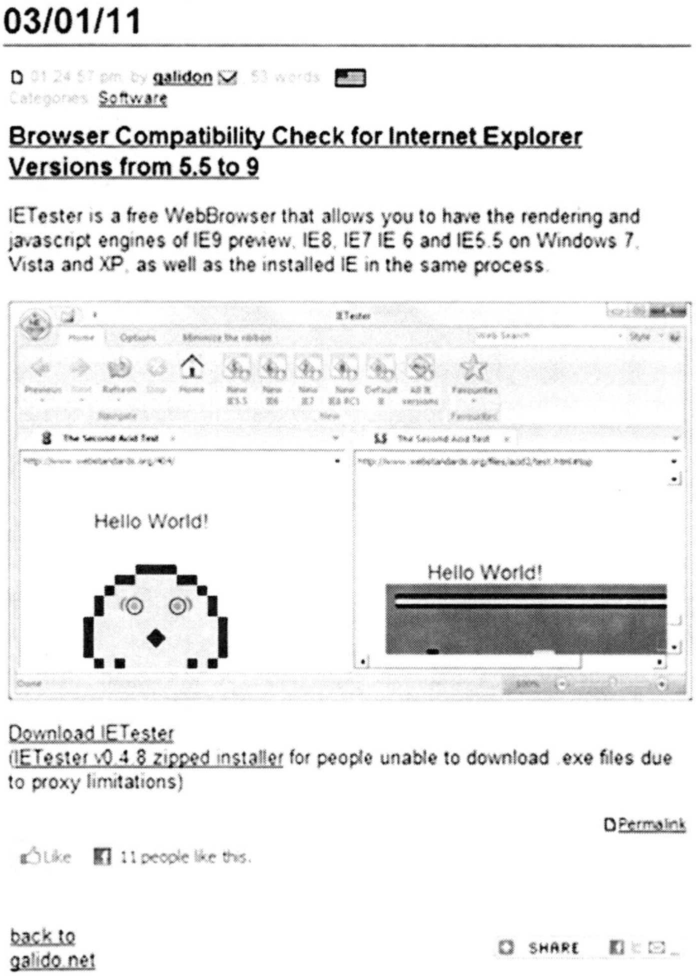

Figure 7. The DownloadSquad blog. http://downloadsquard.switched.com/ (© 2011AOL, Inc. Used with permission)

a blog is simple. There is a "Get Started" button on Blogger's page, and after clicking on that button a user is walked through the steps of blog creation. Google provides a tour and video tutorial about how to use Blogger. The system is very user friendly. Once a user creates a blog, there are many blog templates available to select from in order to choose one's blog style. There is a handy editor for inputting and formatting blog posts. Uploading photos is easy. Once one has created a blog post, the post can be saved, previewed, or published. The program includes a number of design features that make it almost trivial to customize one's blog. There are also features for managing the blog itself.

In Figure 9 we show the home screen for WordPress. In order to create a blog using WordPress one needs to walk through a few simple steps for account creation, provide an email, and then respond by clicking on a link which is sent to the email address that one specified. Once logged into the WordPress site, the process of creating blog posts is straightforward. The system also provides a ten-step tutorial containing many useful points about using the WordPress blogging software, as well as general comments about blog design and styles. The system features a dashboard from where one can control all aspects of the blog. Using the WordPress editor, one can quickly create a post. Posts can be saved, previewed, or published, as was the case with Blogger. The

Figure 8. Blogger's opening screen. http://www.blogger.com (© 2011 Google, Inc.)

program includes many features and suggestions that make the process of developing an interesting blog simple. There are also features for managing the blog itself.

Now that we have the ability to create blogs it is worth considering a blogging code of conduct. Such a code of conduct is the topic of the next section, and there we look at suggestions for online behavior with respect to blogging.

BLOGGING CODE OF CONDUCT

Thus far in this chapter we have looked at many helpful and professional blogs. However blogs are not always a friendly environment to work in, especially for the faint of heart. Many discussions can get heated and can involve foul language, nasty comments, flames, anger, strong opinions, and so on. In view of this fact a number of people have suggested the development of a blogging code of conduct to make the blogsphere more civil and less threatening to users. To this end Tim O'Reilly posted his version of a code of conduct at the O'Reilly Radar blog. We reproduce the initial Draft Blogger's Code of Conduct in what follows:

1. "We take responsibility for our own words and for the comments we allow on our blog.
2. We won't say anything online that we wouldn't say in person.
3. We connect privately before we respond publicly.
4. When we believe someone is unfairly attacking another, we take action.
5. We do not allow anonymous comments.
6. We ignore the trolls" (O'Reilly Draft, 2007).

Most aspects of O'Reilly's proposed code are fairly self-evident; many of the items are clearly intended to make the blogsphere a more-friendly environment. His initial posting generated many interesting responses both supportive and critical of the code (O'Reilly Lessons, 2007). We suggest that readers interested in a Blogging Code of Conduct pursue the previously-mentioned reference for a good discussion about pros and cons of such a code of conduct. There are many informed opinions that are shared in the responses. As members of the IT community, we should certainly follow professional-conduct online. In the next section we provide a few cautions about blogging.

CAUTIONS ABOUT BLOGGING

Introduction

As with many types of online activity, it is wise to take a few precautions. In this section we describe common-sense precautions that one should consider while blogging. The cautions fall into a number of categorizes: personal safety, work related, legal issues, and miscellaneous. We discuss each of these in turn.

Figure 9. The WordPress free blogging-software site. http://wordpress.com/ (© 2011WordPress. Used with permission)

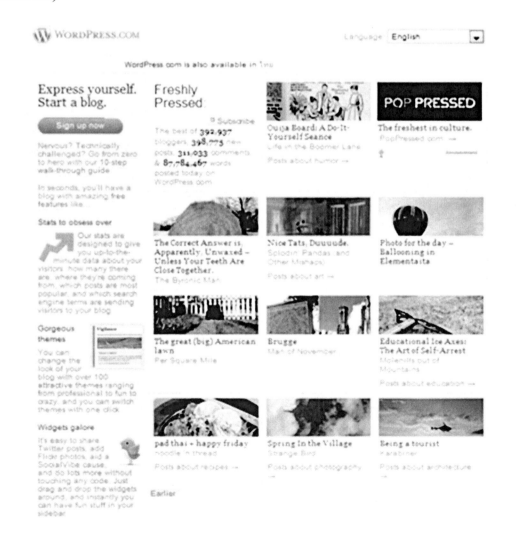

Personal Safety

In the personal-safety category of blogging one should follow the usual online-security precautions that one takes. For example, one must make sure to safeguard private information. And, for this reason there are some bloggers who blog anonymously. Let us consider a case where a blogger is not anonymous. Suppose a person is maintaining a personal blog that is publically available. If a criminal sees that the person lives in a wealthy neighborhood and is going on vacation for a month, it is possible that the blogger's home could become a target for a break-in. One must personally evaluate the risks of putting private-information online. Parents have a responsibility to monitor their children's blogging activity. People do feel real anger online, and there are cases where people have threatened bloggers (BBC, 2007). In general, few bloggers experience real problems; however, one should be aware that the potential for a problem exists.

Work Related

Unless specifically authorized to do so, one should not be updating blogs at work. And, one should not be reading blogs at work either, unless it is part of one's job. Some employers might take offense at an employee maintaining a blog, especially if the blog mentions the workplace or indicates that the blogger is an employee at the given company. If a blog discusses a person's place of employment in a negative light, it is pretty clear that the employer will not be happy with the blog. Each case is unique and the law is not completely clear, but people have been fired from their jobs because of the content contained in their blogs. For those who want to be safe it is probably best to separate personal-blogging activities from any non-authorized work-related activities. If one does decide to stir the pot, one should be prepared for the possibility of disciplinary action, perhaps be-

ing fired, and even a potential lawsuit. In the next section we discuss legal issues.

Legal Issues

Blog-related legal issues will depend on where the blogger is located. If a person writes derogatory remarks about a company or another person, the author could be the subject of a defamation lawsuit. If a person presents false information, the person could be sued for liable. In general, the same types of legal issues that could arise with printed matter can arise with the material on a blog. Later in this book we discuss issues of permissions and describe when it is necessary to request permission of a copyright holder to include copyrighted material in one's own work. But here, we can say that one cannot include items in a blog, unless one is the holder of the copyright of those objects or the objects fall under the Fair Use Laws. For example, it would be illegal to post long passages from the Harry Potter books at one's blog or post short quotes without the proper citations. One must respect the laws of whatever country one is governed by, or else one must be prepared to deal with the legal consequences.

Miscellaneous

In general, it is difficult to remain truly anonymous online. One should realize that one's identity might become available to the public even if one is blogging anonymously. Thus one should only makes posts that one is comfortable having one's name associated with. If one is blogging, one should exercise the same standard cautions that one traditionally exercises while online. One also needs to be aware that in some countries penalties can be severe for posting anti-governmental, anti-religious, or anti-political comments, among others. In Myanmar, for example, a blogger was sentenced to twenty years in prison for mocking a Burmese military leader (BBC Myanmar, 2008).

Summary of Cautions about Blogging

In this section we have included a few cautions about blogging. When blogging, one needs to exercise the usual precautions that one exercises while online. One should be familiar with the laws in the domain where one is working. If one follows the *ACM Code of Ethics and Professional Conduct* (ACM, 1992), which we covered in chapter 2, it is unlikely that one will have any issues. If one decides to push the envelope and move into the more-gray areas of blogging, one should be aware of the potential negative consequences and be willing to take full responsibility for one's actions.

CONCLUSION

Although blogs have only been around for a short period of time, about 15 years as of this writing, they have been extremely influential. In the beginning, blogs started out as what may have seemed like a fad to many, but since that time, they have taken on a life of their own. With nearly 160 million blogs and counting, it is clear that the blogsphere will be around for many years to come. There is a tremendous amount of useful information contained in the blogsphere, and the tools for searching the blogsphere are rapidly developing and improving. Creating a blog is a simple task, but maintaining a blog and keeping it up-to-date requires a considerable and regular effort. As with all online activities, one must take safety precautions, and as an informed member of the online community, one should respect other members of the community. In doing so, the blogsphere will continue to grow in a healthy manner and become an even more-valuable resource in the future.

REFERENCES

ACM. (1992). *ACM code of ethics and professional conduct.* Retrieved from http://www.acm.org/constitution/code

Barger, J. (2011). *Jorn Barger.* Retrieved from http://en.wikipedia.org/wiki/Jorn_Barger

BBC. (2007). *Blog death threats spark debate.* BBC News. Retrieved from http://news.bbc.co.uk/2/hi/technology/6499095.stm

BBC. (2008). *Burma blogger jailed for 20 years.* BBC News. Retrieved from http://news.bbc.co.uk/2/hi/asia-pacific/7721271.stm

Blog. (2011). *Blog.* Retrieved from http://en.wikipedia.org/wiki/Blog

Blogger. (2011). *Blogger: Create a blog, it's free.* Google, Inc. Retrieved from http://www.blogger.com

BlogPluse. (2011). *BlogPulse.* The Nielsen Company. Retrieved from http://www.blogpulse.com/

BlogPluse Live. (2011). *BlogPulse Live.* The Nielsen Company. Retrieved from http://www.blogpulse.com/bplive_full.html

DownloadSquad. (2011). *DownloadSquad: The latest app news.* AOL, Inc. Retrieved from http://downloadsquad.switched.com/

Engadget. (2011). *Engadget.* AOL, Inc. Retrieved from http://www.engadget.com/

Galido. (2011). *Information Technology blog—Galido.net: Computer tips, tricks, solutions, links and relevant information to IT related topics.* Galido Networks. Reference retrieved on 4/8/2011 from http://galido.net/blog/index.php/ITOnlyBlog/

Greenlaw, R., & Hepp, E. (2001). *Inline/online: Fundamentals of the Internet and World Wide Web*. McGraw Hill.

O'Reilly, T. (2007). *Draft blogger's code of conduct*. O'Reilly Radar. Retrieved from http://radar. oreilly.com/archives/2007/04/draft-bloggers-1. html

O'Reilly, T. (2007). *Code of conduct: Lessons learned so far*. O'Reilly Radar. Retrieved from http://radar.oreilly.com/archives/2007/04/code-of-conduct.html

Schneier, B. (2011). *Schneier on security*. Retrieved from http://www.schneier.com/

Wall Street. (2011). *The Wall Street Journal Asia*. Dow Jones & Company, Inc. Retrieved from http://asia.wsj.com/home-page

Whitehouse. (2011). *The Whitehouse blog*. Retrieved from http://www.whitehouse.gov/blog/

WordPress. (2011). *WordPress: Free blogging software*. Retrieved from http://wordpress.com/

Chapter 5
Comments on Manuscript Preparation

ABSTRACT

According to one study of the fastest growing areas of employment, desktop publishing was going to experience a 67% increase in the number of employees from the year 2000 to the year 2010, adding about 25,000 new workers (Bear, 2010). And, in an update of that study, it was noted that job growth in this field has slowed some in part because many employers expect all employees to possess good writing skills. There is a great demand for good writers and specifically technical writers. Among other things, professional writers inform people about new products, produce documentation for software, edit manuals, write books, and develop grant proposals. Nearly all people who work in a science-related field or with computers write a great deal. Since writing is a large facet of many jobs, it is important to write well and efficiently. This chapter will help to improve one's writing skills and writing habits.

GETTING STARTED AND STAYING PRODUCTIVE

In this chapter we describe how to get started writing and stay productive on a manuscript. One frequently hears that a student is suffering from writer's block. With discipline and technique one can remain productive. We present the Laws of Writing and how to develop an effective outline. We discuss a wide variety of writing issues relating to prose. As throughout the book, we try to present practical techniques that one can employ immediately to improve one's writing. Next we present material covering a wide range of style issues, including symbols, notation, and typesetting computer code. Sometimes in trying to get across difficult concepts to an audience, it is important to include figures and tables. Thus

DOI: 10.4018/978-1-4666-0237-3.ch005

we include a section covering these items, plus make general remarks about preparing captions for figures and tables. Rather than trying to produce a comprehensive guide on grammar, we stress key problem areas such as articles, comma usage, hyphens and dashes, plural nouns, pronouns, Roman numerals, accents and special characters, ellipses, and quotations. We also include a section on miscellaneous writing details. There we discuss many topics including acronyms, double negatives, parallelism, and constructs to avoid in formal writing, among others. Let us begin with the section on getting started on and staying productive during a writing project.

Introduction

Spending time on the preparation stage of technical writing has great value. The initial quality of a document may limit its potential for success in its final form. Suppose we jump into a writing project without first knowing the audience, purpose, background, or conducting the appropriate research. Such a project is almost certain to fail. If our initial draft reads really poorly, it will be virtually impossible to transform that document into a really-good manuscript, regardless of how much editing one does. In some cases it is probably best to simply start over entirely, but, of course, this approach does not result in high productivity or efficient writing. Although preparation is essential, it is necessary at some point to begin producing material that will go into the finished document. There is a balance to be maintained between preparation and actually writing. But, one must put "ink to paper" for if there is no true start, there can be no end.

Later in this chapter we will talk in detail about one of the important stages in the writing process, namely editing. During the editing process some items produced during the early stages of writing may be removed entirely. Other items may be modified and maintained. The important point is to produce good-quality work on an ongoing basis

or improve upon what one already has. In order to meet deadlines and finish writing projects, it is necessary to stay productive throughout the entire writing process. One must be disciplined about writing. From the beginnings with a blank "sheet of paper" to a finished manuscript, one should strive to produce quality material at every stage. At times it will be necessary to put something down on "paper," but one should always try to make that something be content that reads well.

Discipline, Scheduling, and the Laws of Writing

Suppose that one must write a 730-page book. Suppose further that one is capable of writing exactly one page of camera-ready manuscript per day. This 730-page book will require exactly two years of writing if the author *never* takes a day off. But, most people do take days off. During the course of a year, most people have an important life event interrupt the weekly routine. And, many people are out sick at least once a year. When we factor in such lost time and factor in that many people do not work on weekends, the two-year project suddenly becomes a four-year project. Four-year projects drag out though, so one's enthusiasm drops as does one's productivity. Thus the four-year project becomes a five-year project. And, in fact, most people do not finish five-year projects. We have heard that 80% of all authors who sign book contacts never actually complete their books. The reader can see why, as book projects tend to drag on and on.

The reader may not be taking on a writing project of the scope of a 730-page book, but these arguments scale down to smaller projects as well. Consider the task of writing a 50-page paper. A project that should take 50 days may end up taking far-more days, especially if one does not exercise the appropriate discipline. And, being a disciplined writer is not easy. It may take years of experience before a writer is able to perfect a method that allows one to complete assignments on schedule. The undisciplined writer will face an enormous amount of stress to meet deadlines and probably produce a less than stellar result. Some writers have a tendency to procrastinate, whether on the conscious or subconscious level. In our experience the larger the scope of the writing project is, the greater the chance is of missing a deadline and the longer overdue the project will be. In what follows we define two laws of writing based on our writing experience and that of our coauthors. These laws summarize what we have been saying in this paragraph.

Law of Large Writing

The larger the writing project is the more discipline that is required to complete the project on time. And, if the deadline on a project is missed, the length of time that the project is overdue will be proportional to the size of the project. The bigger the project is then the bigger the miss on the deadline.

Rule of Four

Writing projects will always take at least four times as long as one expects at the outset of the project.

Let us consider an example to illustrate how one can find the time to write a 100-page Java primer and to illustrate how disciplined one needs to be in order to complete a project of this magnitude. Suppose that it takes 1−3 hours to write a page of the Java book. Note that this pace is very productive. A disciplined writer could wake up at 4am each day, instead of 6am, to work on the book. In roughly three months the 100-page Java book would be finished. The Rule of Four, however, suggests that it might actually take a full year to complete the project. And, we believe that the estimate provided by the Rule of Four is far-more realistic. One should try waking up at 4am *every* day for a month in order to better appreciate how much discipline this task requires.

One will find that management of materials becomes an issue once a project gets above twenty or so pages in length. Even a single task such as going back through the manuscript to remove all commas after short introductory prepositional phrases can be time-consuming task. As a manuscript increase in length, the time spent making corrections and maintaining consistency increases rapidly. Scanning through a longer document naturally takes a longer amount of time than scanning through a shorter document, and since it is harder to remember where everything is in a lengthy manuscript more searches will be needed. We see that it is important to spend time crafting the fundamentals of a document early on in a project because making adjustments later to a manuscript that got off to a poor start can use up lots of time.

Writers generally find that having 90% of a project complete means that one still has 50% of the work remaining. What we mean by this statement is easily explained using the 100-page Java book. The time that it took one to write the first 90 pages (90% completion) is the same amount of time that it will take to write the last ten pages (50% of the work remaining). The last 10% of the project is what seems to wipe out most writers. Usually at that point, the writing is no longer fun, but rather a difficult trudge. In fact, many projects that reach a level of 90% completion are never fully completed, and the (potential) author of such a work never realizes the dream of being published. One of the best ways that we have found to stay motivated is to instill fear in oneself. One may need to scare oneself into finishing a major project. It may also help to work up a timetable, using fear a motivation. One should develop a realistic and achievable timetable. It is best to use *reverse planning* to develop such a timetable. Reverse planning means starting at the due date for one's project and then working backwards to the current date. One should, of course, keep in mind the Law of Large Writing and the Rule of Four while developing any writing schedule.

As a final point, a writer must first carefully look at other commitments and responsibilities if someone presses one to commit to a deadline. The norm is for unexpected events to happen and for unexpected interruptions to occur. One must factor such unknowns into planning, and one should again keep in mind the two laws of writing.

Notes on Notes

While in the preparation stage for writing or during the actual writing phase, some authors like to make notes. One must make sure that such note makes sense. If one cannot understand these notes at a later time, the notes are of little value. This point may seem obvious and trivial, but the author can tell the reader from personal experience that there have been times when he could not make sense of his own notes. When putting a note on a post-it or in a file, one should take the extra time to add all the necessary details. Often, it will be months before one can get back to review such notes. If one cannot decipher a note, the note may be entirely useless or one might have to waste valuable time researching the note's purpose. It is generally best just to spend a little-more time on notes and references at the time when they are first developed, as this strategy will save one lots of time in the future. This point of doing things correctly the first time around is a very important point in writing and in general. If one can follow this rule, one can become much-more efficient at many different tasks.

After one has gathered notes and source materials, there are several possible strategies that one can take to mold the accumulated information into the right form. Some authors choose to put individual notes on 3×5 cards to be sorted and organized into related topics. With cut-and-paste techniques, the same type of sorting can also be accomplished on a computer screen. A portion of one's notes may turn out to be irrelevant to the topic at hand. Nevertheless, it is probably a good idea to keep such notes around, at least until the project appears in print and maybe even longer. It is possible that a few notes may become a subsection of a larger section or perhaps the start of a new and completely separate research project. These groupings of notes can be divided into related areas and arranged in a logical sequential order. Usually, after completion of a note-taking phase one can develop an outline with sections and subsections. Whether or not the reader decides to use a note-taking phase is a personal choice. The important thing to be able to do is get to the point where one can produce a good outline for a writing project, and the next section contains remarks about outlining.

Outlining a Writing Project

It is usually a good idea to start each writing project with an outline. An outline will help to make a writing project more manageable. By breaking a large work up into chapters or sections, one can focus on developing smaller parts of the work. This divide-and-conquer strategy is a highly-useful one in writing. The nature of one's works, the number of notes taken, and the volume of preparatory research conducted will dictate how well one is able to develop an effective outline. Here we describe the basic outline of a typical technical paper. Many papers will fit this framework or a similar one. The reader can substitute in appropriate sections as needed. One often sees the following or similar sections in a paper:

1. Introduction
2. Preliminaries
3. Experimental Work
4. Our Results
5. Conclusion and Open Problems
6. References

In the next chapter on writing a technical paper we go into greater details about the parts of a technical paper. Here we simply present a brief description of each section. The introduction usually describes the goal of the work and may also summarize the results achieved. It will frequently contain a summary of research about previous approaches to the problem and also motivation for the problem. The preliminaries section usually provides any background information that a reader will need to understand the paper. This section might also include things such as conventions for notation and definitions of important terms. Sections 3 and 4 of our outline contain the core of the new work done. These sections will describe the methodologies used and the results obtained. Most technical papers finish up with a section on conclusions and open problems. Sometimes this section may be called "Summary." All technical papers end with a section citing the references used. We should point out that nearly all technical papers begin with an abstract. The abstract is a brief description of the contents and contributions of the paper. Of course, for a specific paper each section's title must be chosen to be descriptive and informative. In addition, each section will probably contain subsections. Typically, there will be five to eight sections in a technical paper. With a loose outline formed, one can begin to see if there is enough supporting material to fill in such an outline. One may end up needing to merge sections together if a division is found without enough content to support a separate section. Alternately, one may need to divide sections that contain an excessive amount of material in to subsections. We try to balance the length of sections, and also to within reason try to balance the number of subsections in each section. There are no hard-and-fast rules for such balancing. As one develops more experience, one will develop more skill at such balancing.

One can start by typing into a file an outline with sections and subsections divisions. We find that seeing the material on paper or on a screen helps us to continue to evolve the material. Viewing the material seems to enhance creativity during the outlining process. It becomes easy to merge sections, add new sections, create subsections, and so on. One can see a document taking shape, and one can then begin to fill in the pieces. It is natural to begin by writing the most-familiar parts of a manuscript first such as the previous research or results sections. As one begins to write the actual content of a document, it is important to focus on the key elements that will be read most carefully. These items will often determine whether or not the rest of the document is even read. In the next section we look at some of these key elements.

Key Elements of a Document

As with anything comprised of multiple elements, some parts will be more important than others. In the human body the appendix serves little function and is often removed. However a seriously-damaged heart or brain can cause almost-instantaneous death. In the body of a written work the reader's first impressions are crucial. For many potential readers the title will be the sole basis for deciding whether to read the work or pass over it without a second thought. The title is a vital 'organ' of any piece of work. Let us think about news for a moment. The news media lives and dies by headlines. In a matter of seconds a reader may choose which paper to buy at a newsstand, or whether or not to click on a hyperlink and follow a story. A good headline will grab a reader's attention, whereas a poorly-written headline will not. With a technical article a parallel can be drawn as researchers look for information on subjects of interest to them. Researchers comb through collections of papers and attempt to determine the material's relevancy by titles, abstracts, summaries, and introductory paragraphs. Many such searches occur online. If a researcher has hundreds of papers to scan through, there will only be time to look at those items that contain certain keywords in their titles. And, of course, search engines will only return papers that (for the most part) contain the queried keywords. If a reader takes the time to look at one's paper, the author does not want to lose the reader due to poor writing. Just as a news-article's title catches a reader's attention, so does a technical-article's title. And, just as the news article will never be read to conclusion unless it is well written, the same holds true for technical articles. Although a good title can draw in readers, one must be a capable writer in order to hold a reader's attention. Research papers will most likely never be considered for reference if they do not have good prose. In the next section we provide tips on writing effective prose.

TIPS FOR WRITING EFFECTIVE PROSE

Introduction

For some people writing good prose is simple and natural. One person may write an 'A' paper with hardly any effort while others will turn in a fifth revision and be lucky to receive a grade of 'C.' In this section we look at a few ways to make one's writing more interesting. With technical writing the goal is not to make one's writing flowery, but rather to convey information and explain difficult concepts to the reader in an interesting, unambiguous, and concise manner. The possible list of tips for writing effective prose is a long one. Here we choose to focus on the ideas of varying sentence structure, using interesting verbs, avoiding redundancy, developing good section headings, and improving one's spelling. We also include a section on editing and proofreading. In order to be able to improve one's own work one must be capable of editing it successfully. In order to be able to proofread effectively one needs to develop a critical eye. The material here complements the material presented in the remainder of this chapter. Let us first take a look at varying sentence structure.

Varying One's Sentence Structure

One of the first books that the author ever read told a story about a dog name "Spot." The book consisted of sentences such as "See Spot run," "See Spot eat," and "Hear Spot bark." The similar sentence structure used in each sentence made a lasting impression. However the book about Spot contained relatively few pages and many interesting illustrations. In a technical paper we probably will not be able to include lots of hand-drawn colorful illustrations to keep the reader's attention, but we can vary our sentence structure to make our writing more readable and more interesting.

We can think of a simple sentence as consisting of a simple subject and a simple predicate, for example, "Spot runs." This construction is so simple that it cannot convey too-much information, and it will soon make a reader bored if used to fill ten pages. We can dress the sentence up a bit by adding some adjectives and adverbs, for example, "The sleek-dog named Spot runs really fast." We can add an introductory clause to the sentence as well, for example, "When the leash is taken off of Spot's neck, Spot runs really fast." Or, we can make a compound sentence, for example, "Spot loves to swim at the beach, and Spot loves to play in the sand." We can combine two related sentences using a semicolon, for example, "Spot enjoys eating red meat; Spot enjoys eating white meat." And, we can do things such as "Spot enjoys eating red meat and white meat" making a compound object. Writers can also employ compound subjects and compound predicates. One can include a list of items such as "Spot loves the following foods the best: steak, chicken, pork, and dog bones." Clauses can follow the main thought of a sentence too. The important point to take away from this section is to be aware of the sentence structures that one is using now, to be aware of the other options available as described, and to incorporate additional variety into one's current style in order to make the writing more interesting.

Using Interesting Verbs

One way to try and inject life into one's writing is to employ more-interesting and active verbs. It is usually best to use the *active voice* rather than the *passive voice*. In the active voice the subject is performing an action, for example, "Yayah washes her hair." In this sentence Yayah is performing an action, namely, washing her hair. In the passive voice the object being acted upon is promoted to the subject position, for example, "The hair is being washed by Yayah." There may be times when the passive voice is preferred, for example, in the statement "The door was opened," we may not know who opened the door. That is, we cannot, for example, say "Jeff opened the door." As an individual reviews one's writing, one can check to see if switching some sentences to the active voice would improve the writing. One should also check to see if there are a lot of uses of verbs such as "to be" and "to have." If so, it may be possible to use more-descriptive verbs to replace them. In general, a good idea is to be descriptive in one's writing and to use a variety of different verbs.

Redundancy in Writing

It is a challenging task to ensure that we vary our vocabulary throughout our writing. One should try to avoid repeating the same words over and over again. To accomplish this goal, the most-obvious method is simply to watch for the overuse of a particular word and look to replace excess uses with a suitable synonym, perhaps found in a thesaurus (Roget's, 2011). In some cases using a word twice in one sentence will be too much. An exaggerated example of redundancy follows: "The basic premise was basically that he could not program in BASIC." The redundancy in this sentence could be removed via the following rewrite: "The initial premise was essentially that he could not program in BASIC."

There are a number of words that typically get overused in papers:

- Sometimes
- Thus
- Hence
- Also
- Therefore
- So

Individuals should review one's own writing to see if any of these words or other words is being overused. If so, one should take the time to rewrite sentences that can be improved by eliminating word-level redundancy.

There is more to avoiding redundancy than merely varying word choice. Not only does this problem occur at the word level, but it occurs at the sentence and framework level as well. We know, for example, that not every sentence should have the same length or always be a simple sentence. Structuring sentences in the same way with different words leaves the writer with framework-level redundancy. If an author has done a good job, the reader will not be distracted or bored by repetition in the writing. Writers should be conscious of word choices and structural issues. As a conclusion to this section, we should point out that there are times when redundancy can be used effectively to drive a point home. And, of course, some of the most-famous speakers of all time employed redundancy beautifully—I have a dream …, I have a dream …, I have a dream … (King, 1963).

Using Descriptive Section Headings

Readers often skim a paper and may read only the section headings. Thus it is important to use descriptive section headings. One can think of a section heading as an invitation to a reader—the more interesting the section heading is, the more likely a reader is to read the section. The section heading should convey information and should describe the information contained within the body of a given section. We should point out though that the section heading is not part of the text. One cannot begin a paragraph directly following a section heading using a pronoun to refer to the section heading itself. If one wants to talk about the section heading in the body of the section, one needs to repeat the text that is contained in the section heading. For example, in the "Example Environment" subsection contained later in this chapter, the heading is introduced in the first sentence of the section, "Many authors incorporate examples into their writing." A writer should never start the introductory paragraph with "Many authors incorporate them into their writing," where "them" refers to the section heading "Example Environment."

Spelling

Many readers will be turned off by writing that contains spelling errors. And, there is more to spelling than simply using a spell-checker program. This statement does not imply that a spell checker should not be used, but merely that spell checkers are not completely foolproof. Spell checkers may not check grammar or context. For example, standard spell checkers will not alert the writer in the situation where the contraction "you're" is used in place of the possessive "your" or the word "flour" is used in place of "flower" or among "to," "too," and "two." Consistent spelling is important when a word has more than one correct spelling. Table 1 lists a few examples of words that can be spelled two ways. For each word, only one of the spellings should be used throughout a document. If a word has multiple-correct spellings of

Table 1. Words with multiple correct spellings

First Spelling	First Spelling
analogue	analog
appendices	appendixes
colour	color
cypher	cipher
email	e-mail
ikon	icon
lollipop	lollypop

its plural form, only one-such spelling should be used throughout a given document.

The word "email" is a good example of a computer-science word morphing as it becomes part of the vernacular. Email was once spelled strictly with a hyphen. Now (maybe because it is easier to type) it is commonly spelled without the hyphen. And perhaps some people have already forgotten what the "e" stands for. It would be acceptable to use any of the spellings from Table 1, but usually it is better to choose the more-common spelling, and that spelling may depend on the particular country one's readers come from. One should not guess at the spelling of a word. If one is unsure of a word's spelling, the word should be looked up in an authoritative source such as Merriam-Webster's Dictionary (Merriam-Webster, 2011) or Oxford's English Dictionary (Oxford, 2011).

Editing and Proofreading

There are few writers who can write final manuscript the first-time around. Most writers must edit their work in order to improve it. Many forms of publications have a special team of editors who edit an author's work during a final phase of production in order to make sure that the work meets a high standard of quality. Editing is an important phase of writing. It is vital to be aware of one's own capabilities and weaknesses during the editing process. For instance some people (often younger people) can edit on a screen with as much accuracy as they can on paper. Other writers need to take a hardcopy of their work in order to perform more-accurate editing. For some writers an item might be missed on the the screen but glare out at them on the printed page; did the reader notice the intentional mistake included in this sentence? (*Hint*: look for a repeated word.)

It is folklore that in a typical production computer program roughly 30 percent of the code cannot ever be executed due to programming mistakes, that is, the program can never even get into those parts of the code. In our writing we need to do a lot better than that. When editing, it is necessary to develop a system to make sure that intended changes are not forgotten and left out of the final document. If one is working with files, a possible method is to mark places to edit with one's initials. One can then search for those initials to find the locations in the file that require more work. The point is to develop a systematic process for editing and then implement the changes. We prefer to make our final pass on paper.

Suppose that one were to do the last pass of editing on paper and then enter those changes into the computer. It is good to know what percentage of edits one typically misses or makes mistakes with during the parsing of a document. If one usually misses three percent of the corrections, it may be necessary to parse the document two or three times before all errors are caught. It is always wise to verify that all changes marked while combing through the printed document are actually made. Some authors will make a hardcopy after the changes have been entered and then go through the old hardcopy in conjunction with the new hardcopy while checking off each of the edits on the original marked-up document. It requires patience and a good eye for detail in order to avoid making mistakes. There are times when a professional *copyeditor* may make edits to a document. If the author is required to enter these edits, one must be careful in order to do so accurately.

After completing the necessary iterations of editing and not finding any further errors or improvements that can be made to the manuscript, the document is ready for a final proofreading. If the document has been sent off to a publisher and typeset, then proofreading will require looking over the document symbol by symbol to ensure that nothing has been typeset incorrectly. During this painstaking process, one should not attempt to check more symbols than one is capable of processing at a single time because otherwise errors might be missed. If the publisher is actu-

ally working from the author's electronic files, hopefully there is little chance that any text has been corrupted. The final layout and placement of floating objects, such as tables and figures, can be done once all of the editing is finished. It is during this last phase where *widows* and other spacing issues can be fixed. A widow is a line of text that carries over to the next page and stands on its own. These single lines are better placed with the paragraph that they belong to, and this placement required manual tweaking.

In the next section we look at some specific technical issues in writing.

TECHNICAL-WRITING STYLE ISSUES

Introduction

Poor research and subject matter cannot be turned in to a great technical document by the perfect use of style, but good research can be brought down quickly by poor style. Thus it is important to incorporate good style elements into one's writing and to apply that style well. In this section we cover several specific items that are often found in documents about information technology. These items when used correctly can help to facilitate a reader's understanding. We discuss using examples, symbols, statements, notation, variables, and code. Similar comments would apply to other common-style elements. Let us begin by looking at the use of examples.

Using Examples in One's Writing

Technical fields often require the use of abstract and difficult concepts. In order to help make explanations more concrete many authors incorporate examples into their writing. There needs to be a transition in the writing to the presentation of an example, and probably the best way to transition in to an example is with a lead-in. The lead-in acts as glue to connect the main text with the example. For example, "In example ABC we provide an illustration of improper tense agreement between the subject and the verb. In the example the word "continues" should be "continue.""

Example ABC

The texts, the articles, and the drafts are on the desk, forgotten by Mary, and continues to collect dust.

Notice how we referred to the example. We used the phrase "example ABC." That is, we used the word "example" and the label of the example. Notice also that the example is offset from the other text and stands on its own. We also put the example in italics. In the text there should be some description of the example as well, perhaps in addition to just a brief lead-in. Depending on the complexity of the subject being discussed and the reader's audience, it may well be appropriate to include a variety of examples in one's work.

Symbols

When dealing with symbols, certain conventions in technical writing can assist the author in conveying ideas more easily and more properly to the reader. We list a few here.

1. One should use words between symbols. For example, the statement

    If G is a clique on five vertices, G is not planar.

    will read better with the word "then" added after the comma:

    If G is a clique on five vertices, then G is not planar.

2. One should not start a sentence with a symbol. An example of this would be

    $F(x)$ is a continuous function.

    This statement is better expressed as follows:

    The function $f(x)$ is continuous.

3. When writing prose, one should not use a lot of complicated symbols and abbreviations. The statement

    $\forall j \exists k \, s.t. \, t < 9$ therefore the result holds

    would be easier to understand with the actual words used in place of the symbols $\forall$, $\exists$, and so on.

4. When using numbers, it is generally considered a good practice to spell out the natural numbers from zero to ten. However one should be aware that various publishers will have different conventions that must be followed, for example, some publishers may recommend spelling out the natural numbers from zero to forty. Obviously, such conventions do not apply to labels such as "theorem 2" or "case 1."

These items are just a few of the common issues relating to symbols, but following these rules will help one to present material that the reader can more easily follow. We do not want to write technical documents where the reader becomes lost in symbols. Such writing is not effective. During the editing phase, one should double check to make sure that these rules were followed.

Leading into Statements

With theorems and other such objects, it is important that we introduce them by properly leading in with an appropriate statement. Note that such lead-ins do not need to be complicated. Here is an example of leading in to a theorem.

We now prove an interesting result about circles.

Theorem 8.1 Let r denote the radius of a circle. The area of a circle is given by the formula $A = \pi r^2$.

One should tie mathematical functions and statements together with a verbal explanation. When explaining complicated items, one should consider expressing them in more than one way so that the reader has a second chance to grasp the concept. Notice that we presented the 'circle' theorem so that it was offset from the text. This style makes it easier for the reader to find key results in a paper more quickly. Such results are usually numbered. The numbering is usually done consecutively throughout the paper or within each main part, for example, in this book figures and tables are numbered separately and consecutively within chapters.

Notation

To keep things simple, one should use notation only when it is truly needed or helpful. As an exaggerated example, it would not be a good idea to use $\sin^2\theta + \cos^2\theta$ to represent the number one. One should use notation when it helps to make things more precise and clearer. When used properly, notation can help to present arguments in a more-compact form. With notation one must stay consistent and not represent the same item with two different symbols. Along the same lines, one should try to avoid using one symbol to represent two different things. That sounds obvious, but is easy to overlook in a long document, especially in higher mathematics. In some cases people do intentionally use the same symbol to represent two different things, and in such cases we say the symbol is *overloaded*. For example, two vertical bars, "$||$" are often used to represent the absolute value of an integer, but they are also used to represent the number of elements in a set. Some acronyms are overloaded too. For example, the letters ATM mean "Asynchronous Transfer Mode" in computer networking and "Automatic Teller Machine" in banking. If possible, one should try to avoid overloading acronyms. When it comes to superscripts and subscripts, it is a good idea to avoid using more than one level unless absolutely necessary.

Choosing Variable Names

When one is writing mathematics, one should choose variable names carefully. For example, one should try to avoid the variable name a, since it can easily be confused with the word "a" even if using italics to denote a mathematical symbol. Another variable name to avoid is the letter "l"; in many fonts it looks like the number "1." The variable "I" can also be confused with the number "1" and with the pronoun "I." One should not use the same variable to represent different things in different parts of a manuscript. Some variables have commonly used names such as i, j, and k for indices; x, y, and z for strings; f, g, and h for functions; S for sets; G and H for graphs; L for languages; M and N for machines; and so forth. When possible, one should use the customary variable names. Greek letters are sometimes used to represent certain concepts in mathematics and the sciences. Common conventions should be followed whenever possible. The key point to emphasize here is to consider carefully the choice of variable names and not simply pick any letter that pops into one's mind.

Typesetting Code

In this section we offer tips and advice for including code or *pseudo-code* in one's writing. By pseudo-code we mean computer-programming language like code, but code that does not follow the precise syntax of any particular programming language. Any time one needs to explain a complex procedure or algorithm, it may help the reader if one includes the corresponding code in a figure. Here we anchor our discussion using the sample code shown in Figure 1 which is for a well-known graph coloring algorithm (Agnarsson and Greenlaw, 2007).

The first thing to notice in Figure 1 is that the name of the algorithm is in italics and separated from the surrounding text. This style makes the name of the algorithm stand out. Then the input

Figure 1. Sample computer pseudo-code for a well-known graph coloring algorithm

```
Algorithm Delta Plus One Coloring
Input: A labeling V(G) = {u₁, ..., uₙ} of the vertices of G
and a list (N₁, ..., Nₙ) of lower-numbered neighbors.
Output: A list S = (c₁, ..., cₙ) of colors, where each cᵢ
is the color assigned to the vertex uᵢ of G.

begin
        S₁ = (1);          // initial list containing the one color 1
        for i = 2 to n do {
                cᵢ = min({1, ..., Δ+ 1} \ {cⱼ : uⱼ ∈ Nᵢ});
                Sᵢ = append cᵢ to the (i − 1)-tuple S ᵢ₋₁;
        }
        output Sₙ;
end.
```

and output for the algorithm are specified precisely. One should always explicitly state what the input and output are for an algorithm. Also, notice that key words are put in boldface and various portions of the code are indented to help the reader see the scope of the various statements. Each statement in the code should be self-explanatory to the reader, and if a statement is not easily understood, it should be explained For example, in Figure 1 it is clear that the equals sign ("=") is used to denote assignment and two forward slashes ("//") to denote a comment.

When writing code for a book or another type of document whose audience includes a wide range of knowledge and skill levels, we need to adjust accordingly. If we decided to use a high-level language such as C, we would probably leave a significant number of our readers in the dark. However if we choose to use pseudo-code, we would probably have a much-broader base of understanding. Pseudo-code is intuitive and helps us dispense with the syntactic detail necessary in actual code. For example, one line of pseudo-code can often be used to condense 5−10 lines of high-level programming-language code. This method of expression not only saves space, but as noted, it allows for a larger audience to comprehend the work.

One must not get too bogged down in typesetting code. It is much-more important to focus on getting the algorithm correct. In what follows we provide a few tips for making one's pseudo-code easier to read and more consistent:

- Decide what the keywords will be ahead of time and always display them in bold.
- Utilize tabbing for spacing in the program to obtain better readability.
- Surround multiple statements that are grouped together by a "begin" and "end" pair or a set of matching curly braces ("{ }"), for example, in a "for" loop or other type of loop construct.
- Use expressions that are easy to understand, unambiguous, and concise.
- Make sure all notation appeals to the reader's intuition.

Consistency is important as well in typesetting code. Once one implements a style such as just described, one needs to stick with those choices throughout the document. One of the most-important roles of consistency is in the code itself. For example, one should not be using English for 95% of the code and then slip in strict C code for the other 5%. Also, one needs to be consistent in the use of symbols, for example, if one is using the symbol ∅ to represent the *empty set*, then one should not switch and start using { } to represent the empty set as well. As another example, only use one of the following symbols λ, ε, or a blank space to represent the *empty string*.

As a final check after one has typeset some code, one should carefully walk through each step of the code and make sure that the code expresses an algorithm as intended. One should clarify any point where one believes the reader would have trouble understanding the pseudo-code. We have noted that it is best to display pseudo-code in a figure as we did for the Delta Plus One Coloring Algorithm in Figure 1. In the next section we discuss figures and tables in more detail. The chapter on presentations also includes material about figures and tables for inclusion in a slide show.

FIGURES AND TABLES AND CAPTIONS

Introduction

In computing, mathematical, and scientific publications authors often use tables and figures to help facilitate a reader's understanding. A figure can help make a theorem or definition more concrete. While some tables are used as a vehicle to present data, other tables may be used to focus more on relationships among concepts. Properly designed and placed figures and tables can greatly enhance a written work. Throughout a document, the style of figures and tables should be consistent. For example, if one table has headings in bold with the first letter capitalized then all tables in the document should follow similar conventions. Creating good figures and tables is a science, and we refer the reader to the *Chicago Manual of Style* for excellent discussions on how to perform both of these tasks well (Chicago,

2011). Here we include sections about rules for creating figures and tables, captions, and placement of figures and tables.

Rules for Creating Figures

In this section we describe a few rules that will help the reader know when to incorporate a figure into a manuscript. We also include a few tips about figure design. Figures should be used to enhance the quality of a document. A figure should help the reader to understand the content of the document better. A figure can be used to break up the monotony of too-much text without a break. Figures give the reader a visual break from straight text. Naturally, some ideas lend themselves more easily to visual presentation. But, if one can display an abstract concept in a figure, it may help make the concept become more concrete for the reader.

Designing visually-appealing figures can be a difficult and time-consuming task, especially for those possessing little artistic talent. It is often best to sketch out a figure by hand on paper before trying to draw an image on the screen. The many image-design and -editing programs that are available (in theory) make the task of creating figures easier. But, one must first learn the software of such a program in order to be able to use the program effectively. Since many of the image-design programs suffer from software bloat, it can be hard to zero in on just the specific features that one needs access to. We recommend choosing one such software program and trying to learn it well.

Laying out a figure takes a considerable amount of thought. For example, what thickness of lines should one use? How big should circles big? Where should the labels go? What type of arrowhead should one use on vectors? What should the positioning of objects be? One needs to consider all of these considerations carefully, make choices, and then utilize those choices consistently on all figures in a document. Some figures are best drawn with multiple small subfigures. To make a figure containing multiple subfigures more-visually appealing, one must be careful to line up the subfigures with their labels. Label choices such as (a) and (b) or (1) and (2) should be used consistently throughout the document. One must take care if drawing any lines by free hand, as it is very difficult to make an endpoint of a line stop in the exact location that one desires.

We have tried to give the reader a sense that creating good figures is challenging work. If one allocates the proper amount of time to implementing figures and makes good style choices, figures can greatly improve the appearance and readability of a manuscript. If one does include a figure, one needs to make sure to discuss the figure in the appropriate amount of detail in the text; for otherwise, the reader may not be able to understand the figure completely.

Rules for Creating Tables

In this section we describe a few rules that will help the reader know when to incorporate a table into a manuscript. We also include a few tips about table design. Tables should be used to enhance the quality of a document. A table should help the reader to understand the content of the document better. A table like a figure can be used to break up the monotony of too-much text without a break. Tables give the reader a visual break from straight text. Naturally, some ideas lend themselves more easily to a tabular presentation. But, if one can display data or express relationship among concepts via a table, it may help make the concepts become more concrete for the reader.

We describe some basic rules of thumb to follow when creating tables. A table should not have too many horizontal or vertical lines. Tables should contain enough separators to make it clear where the information in a given column or row belongs, but excessive use of lines creates a cluttered and messy look. In tables, numbers usually look better when right justified. This fact is especially true if numbers have a different numbers of digits. If a column of numbers is to be summed, they will look better if corresponding positions align, for example, the 100s position of a number should line up with the 100s position of other numbers, and not say the 10s position. Information should be listed directly underneath table headings. Such headings are commonly put in boldface and centered in their columns.

Words should be either flush right, flush left, or centered, and usually this choice of positioning should be maintained throughout a table. Although table headings can be larger than the content contained in the cells of the table, the separation in font size should be kept to a minimum. That is, in a given table one should not use a font size of say 8pt and also one of 36pt, as this spread of font sizes is too great.

As we saw in creating figures, creating a good table requires a great deal of planning and thought. One may first wish to sketch out the table before implementing it. Once various style choices have been made, similar styles for tables should be used throughout the document. One should explain tables in the text in order to make sure that the reader is getting all of the desired information from the table. In Table 2 we show a sample table with ten rows and three columns. Notice that the headings are centered in boldface, and entries within each column are centered. Also, notice that each column has the same width, which adds symmetry to the table.

For the reasons that we have already mentioned, as one is developing a manuscript, one should think about possibly including tables. One should keep in mind that it can be time consuming to implement a table properly. And, in papers with strict page limits, it may not be possible to include a table if it takes up too much space. The reader may have noticed that for figures we have placed the caption below the figure and for tables we

Table 2. A sample table illustrating words having one, two, or three vowels

One Vowel	Two Vowels	Three Vowels
What	More	Example
Not	Bike	Garage
Less	Java	Computer
Hat	Week	Bathroom
Pen	Good	Sunscreen
Car	Door	Preschool
Pet	Window	House
Disk	Lemon	Sunglasses
Chang	Food	Movie

have placed the caption above. These are (somewhat) standard conventions, and we recommend that the reader uses this style. In the next section we discuss captions.

Captions: General Principles

This section includes basic material concerning captions. Sometimes it is necessary to explain either certain items within a table or parts of a figure. A well-phrased caption can provide this explanation and enhance a reader's understanding. Over the years certain conventions for the use of captions have evolved. We list some of the generally-accepted rules for captions used in technical publications.

1. Keep captions one sentence long.
2. Decide on a format for the captions and use it consistently throughout the document. For example, always start a caption with a capital letter and end it with a period. Another consideration is whether to use 'title-style' or 'sentence-style' capitalization.
3. Place captions in a consistent location throughout one's work. There are no universal rules on caption placement. The publisher of this book prefers figure captions below and table captions above. In rare cases a caption

may be placed above or beside a figure. One must choose one of the more-accepted styles and use it consistently.

4. Use consistent caption labels. Common conventions for figures are Fig., Figure, or FIGURE followed by a label. Similar conventions are used for tables, and within a document the choices for figure and table labels should match. For example, one should use Fig. and Tab. together. Also, in some works these labels will appear in bold. One should use punctuation consistently after this label. Common conventions are ":" or "." as in Figure: 1 or Fig. 3.
5. Care and consistency should be used in referring to a figure or a table. For example, the reference Chapter 5 Figure 5.4 is redundant since the chapter is revealed by the figure number. It is always a good idea during editing and proofreading to check that the figure and table labels used in the text refer to the appropriate figure or table in the text. In this regard type-setting systems such as LATEX that provide automatic generation of labels can save the author lots of time and help ensure the accuracy of labels throughout a document.

We should note that placing captions vertically beside a figure is usually not recommended because a narrow text width may force long items to be split unnecessarily. For example, it would be awkward to have a webpage address split over three or four lines. In the next section we briefly talk about the placement of figures and tables.

Placement of Figures and Tables

Here we discuss the basic rules for positioning figures and tables within the text. Since the rules are the same for both elements, we restrict the discussion largely to figures. When possible, a figure should be placed directly after its first reference in the text. If this reference occurs near the bottom of a page, the figure may not fit on the page. In that case the figure may be moved and displayed at the top of that page or moved to the succeeding page if movement to the top of the current page is not possible. A figure should never appear on a page prior to where it is first referenced. It is a required to have a figure appear on the page that it is first referenced or a subsequent page. If a document has many fairly-large figures in succession, the figure may need to be placed several pages later. Figures are *floating objects* and some formatters will do their best to place them appropriately for the author. However an author may sometimes need to tweak the positioning of figures during the last phase of editing. That is, once all the text is finalized and all the figures and tables are finalized, one can take care of the final placement of floating objects. In some cases it may be necessary to scale a figure's dimensions in order to place it in a good location relative to the text. In general though, all figures should be scaled similarly, so one must be careful to apply scaling of figures consistently.

GRAMMATICAL TIPS

Introduction

There are many mediums in use where people exchange written correspondence. People post things on social-networking sites, send text messages, write tweets, email messages, mail letters, and so on. Many of these communications are quick and informal. Some of these forms of communication limit the number of characters that a user can send. It is common for people to violate the rules of grammar and spelling while using these communication forms. And, in fact, some people probably no longer know what is correct or incorrect usage since what they see is usually the incorrect form. We should point out that grammarians themselves do not always agree on the rules for proper English.

In this section we discuss a number of grammatical issues, but by no means try to be comprehensive. We touch on some points where the reader might get tripped up. As with many aspects of writing, one should try to use grammar consistently. In addition, one should avoiding guessing at constructs. If one is not sure of proper usage, one should look it up. There are now many websites that discuss various grammar rules and answer crowdsourced questions about the proper use of grammar. Usually, a query to a search engine will produce many hits, and it often becomes immediately clear for most simple issues what the proper way to do something is.

Let continue by including some creative examples of commonly-broken grammar rules taken from *Mathematical Writing* (Knuth et al., 1989):

- Watch out for prepositions that sentences end with.
- When dangling, consider your participles.
- About them sentence fragments.
- Make each pronoun agree with their antecedent.
- Don't use commas, which aren't necessary.
- Try to never split infinitives.

It seems that in all but the most-formal writing publishers have relaxed their standards of grammar. And, in some common usage many people are not even aware that a grammar rule has been broken. *To boldly go where no man has gone before* sounds much-more exciting than *to go boldly where no man has gone before*, but, despite the fervor of Star Trek fans everywhere, the split infinitive is still a rule not to be broken in formal writing. If one decides it is necessary to break a grammar rule, one should do so sparingly. Classic references on writing style such as the *Chicago Manual of Style* now allow for some split infinitives and the ending of sentences with prepositions (Chicago, 2011). But, it is still probably best to use these constructions in moderation, and we use these constructs sparingly in this work.

Articles

Some points on the articles "a" and "an" should be noted. One chooses which article to use based on the sound of the following word. Frequently "an" proceeds a vowel, but this is not a rule. According to the *Chicago Manual of Style*, "before a pronounced **h**, long **u** (or **en**), and a word like **are**, the independent article should be **a** as in *a* hotel, *a* historical study, or with euphonious words as in *a* one, *a* union, but *an* honor and *an* heir." One should be consistent in the use of articles. We should also note that the article "a" is usually used to refer to a nonspecific item from a group, whereas "the" refers to a specific item.

The Comma

This section discusses a variety of issues about the comma. According to *Mathematical Writing*, the word "therefore" at the beginning of a sentence should not be followed by a comma (Knuth et al., 1989). The same is true for words like "however," "thus," and "consequently." With a long sentence or an offset phrase, the comma may be included. For example, "Therefore, Theorem 9.10 can be applied to this case in conjunction with Lemmas 4.1 and 4.7 to prove the result holds in all practical situations."

Using too many commas will interfere with the flow of a sentence, whereas too few commas can make a sentence difficult to read. If a sentence contains more than three or four commas that are used other than merely to list items, one might want to consider rewriting the sentence to include fewer commas or perhaps one might break the sentence into two. Naturally there are well-written sentences that are exceptions to this guideline.

We should point out that the rules of comma style have changed over the years and are still changing. It is important to apply rules consistently within a document and to maintain readability. Commas are often needed in order to ensure that a sentence is not ambiguous. Consider the next sentence for example. These days commas are not being used after short introductory phrases of three words or less. If a comma is placed after "these days," it is clear that "these days" refer to the current-time period rather than serving as a modifier for the types of commas being talked about, that is, not these days' commas. Twenty years ago, school children would have been instructed to put a comma after "These days" in the previous sentence. And, in fact, the comma is needed to specify the meaning that most readers would garner from this sentence. When a comma makes a sentence easier to read, it may be best to use the comma as we did a couple of sentences earlier with "Twenty years ago."

When one is using commas to separate elements in a series, it is appropriate to use a comma after the penultimate item, as in the following example: the values of *a*, *b*, and *c* are equal. This comma is sometimes referred to as the *Oxford comma*. For any specific use of a comma, if one is not sure, tone should look up its proper usage in a grammar book or online.

Using Either with Or

When using the word "either" in a sentence, one should always accompany it appropriately with "or." This rule is an example of a common grammatical error. An example of proper usage is either John or Zack carried the rope off the mountain.

Using Neither with Nor

When using the word "neither" in a sentence, one should always accompany it appropriately with "nor." As with either … or, this error is also common. For example, neither Jane nor Jum is a bad cook.

Using Hyphens and Dashes

What is the difference between a hyphen, an en dash, and an em dash? The shortest dash, a hyphen, is used within a word such as scale-free or half-price. An en dash is found between numbers: pp. 50−69. It is roughly the width of an "N." Another place where an en dash may be used is with someone's date of birth such as Mick Jagger 1943−. However the en dash is no longer preferred, unless the person is dead, such as John Lennon (1940−1980). An em dash is used when one expands on a topic at the end of a sentence. It would be nice to own a house—especially the one at the end of the street. The em dash is sometimes used for parenthetical remarks too. Note that the em dash is roughly the width of "M." One should not leave space before or after an en dash or em dash.

Plural Nouns

There are many irregular plurals in English, but most plurals follow a few basic rules (Strunk and White, 2008). Usually, the plural is formed by adding "s" to the singular form.

keys, girls, cats, radios, models

If the noun ends in certain sounds such as s, sh, j, x, z, or a soft ch, the suffix "es" is added instead of "s."

boxes, churches, successes, rushes

With nouns ending in a "y," where the "y" is not preceded by a vowel, the "y" is replaced by "i" and followed with "es" in the plural.

babies, flies, pennies, tries

There are many irregular plurals. Some nouns change the vowel sound in the plural. Man becomes men and goose becomes geese. Other nouns, such as sheep or fish, do not change at all. Some loan words, like alumnus, retain the foreign plural alumni, while others, like formula, have acquired an English plural—formulas. Many of the irregular plurals can be caught with a spell checker. When unsure about a given word, one should look the word up.

When referring to variable names as plurals, one should typeset the variable name but not the "s" in italics such as xs and ys. Sometimes the reader may see an author use x's and y's. If one uses capitalized variables or acronyms, the suffix "s" should be lowercase: Ps and Qs, and URLs. For many of these special cases, there is not a hard-and-fast usage rule. We recommend referring to the *Chicago Manual of Style* for researching difficult cases (Chicago, 2011).

Pronouns

In this section we cover several issues relating to pronouns. The use of nonsexist pronouns is important in writing. Sexist language favors one sex at the expense of the other. Although sexist language can shortchange men—in most cases it shortchanges women. Dealing with the "he versus she" issue head-on is important. In this book we chose to use "one" rather than using either he or she. Some authors prefer to use the plural "they." We commonly see author's alternating between the use of feminine and masculine pronouns from sentence to sentence, but this practice can be distracting to the reader.

When writing, it is important to avoid having an ambiguous pronoun reference. This problem refers to a pronoun that follows two nouns used earlier in the same or previous sentence. We illustrate the use of an ambiguous pronoun reference in the following example. The position of the TV and the radio, so near one another, is affecting its reception. In this case we are not sure if the TV is fine or the radio is fine. When in doubt, one should repeat the original concept. The next example replaces the ambiguous pronoun and clarifies the reference. The position of the TV and the radio, so near one another, is affecting the radio's reception.

As a final note about pronouns, one should not overuse them. We sometimes see students overusing words such as "it" and "this." The word "it" is not too interesting. The word "this" can usually be followed by a noun to make a stronger construction. This fact is demonstrated in this sentence.

Roman Numerals

Roman numerals are frequently used in writing. Here we make a few general comments about them. When writing Roman numerals, placing a smaller numeral after a larger numeral indicates addition, while placing a smaller numeral in front of a larger numeral indicates subtraction. For example, four is represented by IV, and six is represented by VI. Numbers larger than 5,000 can be indicated by putting a horizontal line above the digit, which means the numeral should be multiplied by 1,000. Therefore V̄ represents 5,000. Table 3 lists the Roman numerals.

Timeless Facts

Present tense should be used when discussing timeless facts, for example, "The sun rises in the east."

Accents and Special Characters

Diacritical marks are symbols placed over, under, alongside, or attached to a letter to indicate pronunciation or stress. If one leaves out the diacritical mark, one is misspelling the word. One must be careful when using these symbols, especially when spelling people's names. Table 4 lists common diacritical marks.

Ellipses

The most-common usage of an ellipsis (…) is to indicate an omission of text. For example, one might wish to identify several members of a series without writing out the full series. In mathematics we sometimes use an ellipsis in denoting the elements of a set, for example, the set $\{1, 2, …, 10\}$ is an abbreviation for the set $\{1, 2, 3, 4, 5, 6, 7, 8, 9, 10\}$. As long as a well-established pattern is clear, one can use an ellipsis to abbreviate a series. In such uses of an ellipsis a space goes after the preceding comma, there is no space before the succeeding comma, and then a space follows the succeeding comma.

Punctuation Involving Font Change

If one encounters a situation in which a word has a punctuation mark adjacent to it, one should treat the punctuation as though it belongs with the word. This statement means that if one changes the font of the word, one should also change the

Table 3. The Roman numerals

Value	Symbol
1	I
5	V
10	X
50	L
100	C
500	D
1,000	M

Table 4. Some common accents and special characters

Name	Mark
acute accent	é
breve	ŏ
cedilla	ç
circumflex	ô
German umlaut	ö
grave accent	è
Hungarian umlaut	ő
macron	ō
tilde	õ

font of the punctuation mark. For example, notice that the semicolon in this sentence following the boldfaced-word **Theorem:** is also in bold.

Quotations

In writing it is sometimes desirable to quote someone. The writer needs to let the reader know when this happens, and we do so by using quotation marks. It is important to note that there are two types of quotes.

- Single quotes—'...'
- Double quotes—"..."

If one has a short quotation, one should use double quotes.

"To be or not to be."

In general, one should place punctuation inside the quotes.

"The chicken crossed the road to get in the car."

If one has a quote within a quote, one should use single quotes for the inner quotes.

Rita said, "He said, 'Help Me!'"

Note that one must be sure to close all quotes. This error commonly goes unnoticed by some writers. It is usually not a good idea to nest quotes more than two or three levels deep. Following this practice will make one's writing more concise and less ambiguous.

The reader may have noticed that we sometimes put a word or phrase in single quotes. We use this technique to indicate that the word is being used in some 'special way.' However, when we refer to a particular symbol and the symbol is being attributed its usual meaning, we put the symbol

in double quotes, for example, the word "yes" usually represents the symbol "1" in computing.

Summary of Grammatical Tips

In this section we have covered a wide range of grammatical tips that we hope the reader will find useful. There are many aspects of grammar that we have not covered here. The key point to remember is that if one is unsure about a grammatical construction, one should look up the structure rather than hazarding a guess. In addition, one should try to apply grammar rules consistently throughout one's work.

MISCELLANEOUS WRITING DETAILS

Introduction

One goal of this book is to teach writers to incorporate good structure throughout their writing. This section covers several rules presented in *Mathematical Writing* (Knuth et al., 1989) and some other general writing tips. These rules involve more than correct grammar. These tips cover acronyms, the Rule of Explaining Twice, double consecutive-words, double negatives, parallelism, list punctuation, reprinted illustrations, and constructions to avoid in formal writing. Let us begin with comments on acronyms.

Acronyms

When one writes any material, it is important to keep the intended audience in mind. This point is especially important when using acronyms. A person's background will define what an acronym means to them. For example, does the acronym CS mean Computer Science, Cyber Security, Credit Suisse, or Counter Strike? All are valid possibilities, but a computer scientist will likely assume the first meaning, a forensics expert the second, a banker the third, and a military officer the fourth. There are a few important rules to follow when one uses acronyms. One should define an acronym on its first use. The common style is to write the phrase and follow it with the acronym in parenthesis, for example, Hypertext Markup Language (HTML). Note that sometimes both of these expressions are put in italics when initially being defined. After defining an acronym, the writer can feel free to use the acronym throughout the rest of the document. If earlier occurrences of the acronym creep into the document, one needs to make sure to move the definition forward in the document.

In some fields such as computer networking there is a tendency to use huge numbers of acronyms. One must be mindful of one's audience. One should neither use multiple acronyms adjacent to each other nor use a large group of acronyms in a single sentence. For example, the next sentence does not flow well and is complex. HTML was displayed at CERN on a PC by TBL using TCP/IP over a CR.

The Rule of Explaining Twice

When presenting complex facts or data, the author should explain such items twice: informally and formally. The order in which the informal and formal explanations appear can vary depending on the specific material being presented. One approach is starting with an intuitive description followed by a more-formal explanation. A second approach is to present the precise details and then try to clarify them more informally. There is no hard-and-fast rule that can be applied to all cases.

Consecutive Identical Words

If one must use a word twice, one should try to separate them with a comma, if possible, or rewrite the sentence to avoid the problem entirely. There are other ways to separate words visually. For

example, utilizing a different font or capitalization may be an appropriate alternative. We provide several examples in the following:

- AND and OR and NOT
- YES and NO
- TRUE and FALSE

Double Negatives

One should avoid using words that negate in succession, as they tend to confuse the intended meaning of a sentence. Using "not" in succession with "no" or another "not" will make a potentially negative sentence into a positive one. There are times when negative expressions can read more effectively if explained in a positive way.

Parallelism

Parallelism in writing means that similar grammatical structures should be used in conjunction with one another. Items such as words, phrases, and clauses must all be parallel when they express an 'equivalent' concept and perform a similar function in a sentence. Let us consider an incorrect example. The triathlete must enjoy to swim, biking, and the running. This sentence can be rephrased using a parallel construct as follows: "The triathlete must enjoy swimming, biking, and running."

Punctuation in Lists

There are several acceptable ways to handle punctuation and capitalization of elements in a list. A simple rule is to leave items in the list in lowercase if they are not complete sentences. If each item is a complete sentence, treat it as such by capitalizing the first word and end each item with a period. What if some of the items in a list are full sentences, while others are not? One can consider rewriting the list so that all items are either complete sentences or all phrases. In any case, one should use appropriate capitalization and a period for any items that are complete sentences. The use of consistency will go a long way to producing correct, readable, and attractive lists. Here is an example of a numbered list.

1. the red house
2. the white house
3. the pink house

One should use a numbered list when the order of the items is important or when wants to refer to the items. Lists whose items are unordered can be displayed using bullets.

Reprinted Illustrations

There are times when an author wants to include illustrations from a previous work of another author. At the beginning of the relevant caption, one should acknowledge the illustration's creator in parenthesis such as (Courtesy of Mary Williams). If one wants to reprint a figure or illustration from another publication, one must obtain permission from the copyright holder, usually the publisher or the creator of the image. The publisher's website will often provide information on obtaining permission to use illustrations. A form will typically be supplied to mail to the publisher. Note that one may have to pay a fee for permission to use the image, and sometimes the fees can be quite high, for example, perhaps $500 for a single image.

Constructions to Avoid in Formal Writing

In this section we cover a few common constructions that are usually best avoided in formal writing: exclamation points, abbreviations, and contractions.

Exclamation Points

In technical writing one should generally avoid using exclamation points to express feeling or excitement, for example, "This result was quite unexpected!" Using exclamation points in technical writing is the equivalent of writing an email in all capital letters.

Abbreviations

In formal writing we recommend that one avoid the use of abbreviations. For example, rather than using the abbreviation "etc.," it is more appropriate to use "and so on." Abbreviations such as s.t. (such that), WYSIWYG (what you see is what you get), and wlog (without loss of generality) should not be used in formal writing.

Contractions

One should avoid the use of contractions in formal writing. For example, "we don't use contractions in this book" is better expressed as "we do not use contractions in this book."

Summary of Miscellaneous Writing Details

As was the case with the previous section, we covered a broad range of topics in this section. We hope that the reader will be able to utilize these techniques. The key is to become aware of acceptable and unaccepted styles. When necessary, if one cannot recall the exact details of a construct, one can look up the concept and employ it correctly in one's writing. Over time one can gradually incorporate a wider variety of styles into one's writing, and thereby become a more-versatile writer.

CONCLUSION

We have covered many practical aspects of manuscript preparation in this chapter, including how to get started and stay productive on a manuscript, prose writing tips, general technical-writing style issues, tables and figures, grammatical tips, and many miscellaneous writing details. But, by no means have we covered all the topics in this vast area. For example, we have not said much about capitalization, order of author names on a manuscript, paid writing, bibliography-entry formats, use of foreign words, citation styles, and so on. As one gains more experience, one can add additional techniques and tools to one's writing toolkit. And, we mean "tools" literally, for example, as there are online databases that are useful for locating sources and there are bibliographic software packages for helping to generate a list of references. There is really no limit to how much one can learn about writing, and there is always room for improvement. Often there is no one fixed rule for a particular issue in writing that all experts adhere to. We have stressed the idea that one tries to be consistent in one's writing. Writing is a dynamic field, and it is important that one keeps up with the latest trends. We strongly recommend that all writers obtain a copy of the classic *The Elements of Style* (Strunk and White, 2008). We devote the next chapter to covering a number of issues relating to writing a technical paper. And there, the reader will learn other important tips regarding writing.

REFERENCES

Agnarsson, G., & Greenlaw, R. (2007). *Graph theory: Modeling, applications, and algorithms.* Prentice-Hall.

Bear, J. H. (2010). *Desktop publishing job growth outlook.* Retrieved March 15, 2011, from http://desktoppub.about.com/od/professional/a/2010_outlook.htm

King, M. L. (1963). *I have a dream speech.* Retrieved March 18, 2011, from http://www.americanrhetoric.com/speeches/mlkihaveadream.htm

Knuth, D. E., Larrabee, T., & Roberts, P. M. (1989). *Mathematical writing.* The Mathematical Association of America.

Merriam-Webster's Dictionary. (2011). Retrieved on March 20, 2011 from http://www.merriam-webster.com/

Oxford's English Dictionary. (2011). Retrieved on March 20, 2011 from http://www.oed.com/

Roget's Thesaurus. (2011). Retrieved on March 29, 2011 from http://thesaurus.com/Roget-Alpha-Index.html

Strunk, W., & White, E. B. (2008). *The elements of style, 50th anniversary edition.* Longman Publishing Group.

(2011). *The Chicago Manual of Style* (16th ed.). University of Chicago Press.

Chapter 6
Structure of a Technical Paper

ABSTRACT

This chapter provides basic information about the structure of a technical paper. Some of the comments made here can be applied to non-technical papers as well. The chapter begins with a section that discusses the opening of a paper, then discusses the items that appear in the first part of a paper: in particular, the title, authors and affiliations, the abstract, and keywords are discussed. Next, the chapter discusses the role the introduction plays in a paper and the information one typically finds in the introductory section of a paper. The author includes a general section with guidelines about the content of a paper, followed by one about the closing portions of a paper. There, he talks about conclusions, acknowledgments, references, and biographies, and then he describes issues relating to paper submission and how to follow-up with a submission. He includes some other key issues that occur during the submission and acceptance phase of a paper's life cycle. The author includes a few other valuable points in the miscellaneous section, where he discusses submitting to online publications, effective collaboration among coauthors, and reusing one's own work. There is also a brief section with conclusions.

INTRODUCTION

In the scientific community in order to make a statement or claim something proven, scholars have to publish the results of their study in a *technical paper*, also commonly called a *research paper*. There are numerous conferences and journals worldwide that publish articles on a wide variety of topics—covering nearly every scientific domain. The most-prestigious information-technology conferences are usually sponsored by large corporations, such as Cisco (Cisco, 2011) or Microsoft (Microsoft, 2011), or professional organizations, such as the Institute of Electrical

DOI: 10.4018/978-1-4666-0237-3.ch006

and Electronics Engineers (IEEE, 2011) or the Association for Computing Machinery (ACM, 2011). The best journals are usually published by well-known publishing houses. Each submission typically undergoes a rigorous-review process performed by the editorial board in conjunction with volunteer reviewers. Because acceptance rates for the world's top conference proceedings and periodicals are relatively low, the number of such publications listed in one's curriculum vitæ often determines one's status within a given scientific field.

Publishing a paper is a big commitment and responsibility. First and foremost, the research that the authors intend to present has to be completed and accurately documented before the writing takes place. Second, the article should be well-organized and must demonstrate interesting ideas or conclusions to the reader. Third, since it is possible that the paper will be cited by other researchers, *no erroneous or false information* can appear in the text. In publishing a paper one is contributing to the body of human knowledge and archiving information for future generations.

OPENING OF A PAPER

Introduction

The makeup of a research paper usually depends on numerous issues. One issue is the specific requirements of the conference or journal where the paper is intended to be submitted. Another aspect is the subject matter and depth of the content. Regardless of the specific field and actual content of the paper, we can say that the opening of most papers will include some or all of the following components: a title, a list of authors' names and affiliations, an abstract, and keywords. In this section we explore each of these items in turn. We start by taking a look at the title of a paper.

Title

The title is the first thing that the reader or—perhaps, more importantly—the editor will see. When many authors compete for a publication in a prestigious periodical, all things being equal, the editor will certainly favor the paper with a more-interesting title. In certain cases, where a conference is trying to offer papers covering a broad range of topics, the initial selection may be made based largely on the title. If nothing else, the title can have an impact on which papers get read first. The paper's title is *very important*. One must make sure that the title represents the contents of the paper while at the same time is original and interesting. In order to come up with a good title one needs to spend a considerable amount of time brainstorming about a good title; good titles do not just drop out of the sky. Developing a really-good title is not an easy task. The best titles seem to express the technical aspects of the paper with easily-understandable jargon. Note that titles longer than one line can be difficult for readers to remember. The title should be written in an aesthetically-appealing way and that may mean introducing line breaks in the appropriate places. Rather than having a single word on the second line of the title in Figure 1, we introduced a line break after the word "an."

Authors and Affiliations

The title of a paper is followed by the list of authors and their affiliations. Usually, to specify the institutions that the authors represent, different super scripts, and more rarely, inline symbols are used in a footnote-like fashion. An example is shown in Figure 1. Notice that the second and third authors share the same affiliation. Notice also the technique involving curly braces that is used to provide the email addresses of these two authors. An author's affiliation should include the

Figure 1. A sample title with authors' names and affiliations

A Formal Verification of an
Airplane Chassis Control System

William Henderson[1]
Scott Greene[2], Jason Smith[2]

[1]Department of Computer Science, University of the South
P.O. Box 7912, 5660 Main Street, Savannah, GA 31420, USA
`henderson@cs`
`.south.edu`
[2]Department of Engineering Studies, Roger's Institute of Cybernetics
P.O. Box 127, 732 Park Avenue, Orlando, FL 32810, USA
`{greene,smith}@en.ric.edu`

name and the address of the author's institution along with a work- or personal-email address.

In various scientific fields, such as physics, the order in which the paper's authors are listed is very important, and the order generally corresponds to their level of contribution to the paper. This peculiarity comes into play in cases of promotion, tenure, pay raises, and so on. Sometimes more-senior authors are listed before more-junior people. In other fields, such as computer science, however, the order of the authors may not be as important. In theoretical computer science, for example, the authors' names are usually placed in alphabetical order. A student author is sometimes listed first by an advisor to help promote the student's career. In any case one needs to be aware that the ordering of authors' names can be a (very) sensitive topic in certain circles.

Abstract

In the context of this chapter an abstract is a summary of a paper; it is usually around 150–300 words. This summary should be written in the present tense, and should be clear and concise.

The abstract is extremely important because it is often used by readers to decide whether or not they will spend more time on the paper; the abstract also usually serves as an advertisement for an oral presentation of the paper. It is often easier to write the abstract after the paper itself is finished. However, one should avoid mere copying from other sections of the work because, even if the abstract is well-written, no one wants to read the exact same thing twice. Analogously, if the abstract is written first, one should avoid straightforward copying of that material into the introduction of the paper. One can look for ways to rephrase things, so that the reader does not end up reading the exact same material twice.

In Figure 2 we provide an example of an abstract from a complexity-theory paper. In the abstract one sees that the results contained in the paper are described there. In terms of the appearance of the abstract notice that the word "Abstract" is centered and appears in boldface above the abstract's text. Also, one should notice that the margins on either side of the abstract have been increased. Lastly, the abstract often is displayed using a smaller font size, as shown in Figure 2.

Figure 2. An example of an abstract for a technical paper

Abstract

Several new graph-theoretic problems, which arise naturally from existing coloring algorithms, are defined. The complementary High Degree Vertex Removal Problem and Low Degree Vertex Removal Problem are both shown to be NP-complete. The Low Degree Subgraph Problem is defined and shown to be NP-complete, whereas the 'complementary' problem for high-degree subgraphs was previously shown to be P-complete. Since the obvious sequential algorithms for computing the low-degree subgraph and high-degree subgraph are based on high-degree vertex removal and low-degree vertex removal respectively, we find this result interesting. The 'greedy' versions of the vertex-removal and subgraph problems are shown to be P-complete. In addition, a natural lexicographic version of the Low Degree Subgraph Problem is shown to be NP-complete.

Keywords

The submission guidelines for a periodical, which are often found on the inside back cover, will sometimes require an author to include a number of keywords in a paper. The keywords are a list of individual words or short phrases describing the research areas that the paper covers. Many scientific indexes that are available online can be helpful for choosing the appropriate keywords. In Figure 3 we present the keywords corresponding to the abstract shown in Figure 2. Notice that the word "Keyword" appears in boldface and is followed by a colon. The keywords are contained in a comma-separated list which ends with a period.

Keywords serve several purposes. Similarly to an abstract, they help potential readers identify the primary subjects of an article and—to a lesser extent—advertise the paper. Keywords are also used for electronic indexing and categorization of research works. As was done in Figure 3, it is common to list keywords in alphabetical order. An alternative style is to list keywords in their order of importance according to the author's judgment. It is important to select a good set of keywords for a paper, and this task can require some careful thought.

INTRODUCTION OF A PAPER

Introduction

The introduction is a key part of a paper both in terms of size and value. This section can be from one to several pages long, accounting for roughly 10−20% of an entire article. To capture the audience's attention early on and then keep them interested, the introduction is critical. It should be as polished as possible. For comparison, it is not as critical to have perfectly written sentences in the middle of an article because many readers may never even reach the middle of an article, especially if the introduction is not well written. This comment is not to say that one should get sloppy in the middle or near the end of a paper, but just

Figure 3. A list of keywords corresponding to the abstract shown in Figure 2

Keywords: complexity theory, graph theory, NP-completeness, P-completeness, subgraph problems.

that by the time a reader reaches the middle of a paper, the person is usually interested enough in the work to continue reading even if the writing is not quite up to par with the earlier sections.

The introduction of a research paper sets the general context and tone of the work. In the introductory section the author presents the subject of the study and explains why the material is relevant, whether it answers an open question, or how it extends knowledge in a specific field. One should succinctly state the main results in the introduction of a paper. Some readers will not have the time required to comb through a paper to find what they need. The introduction usually contains a brief discussion of previous results in the field. Background information can also help many non-expert readers understand what the paper presents. At the end of the introduction it is common to outline the remainder of the paper, as seen in Figure 4 for a paper that talks about a web-based simulation and training system for engineers.

When presenting the short roadmap at the end of the introduction, it is difficult to be creative. But, one should try to vary the wording a bit to avoid too-much redundancy. In a short paper this type of summary can be accomplished with well-chosen section titles and is really not necessary. In the next section we expand a bit on background and preliminaries.

Background and Preliminaries

Depending on the type and length of a paper, the introduction may contain material on background and preliminaries, or this material can follow in one or two sections based on the volume of material to be included. Usually, authors do not explain basic terminology that they use in a paper because their audience is generally familiar with standard jargon. For more-complex and specialized concepts, definitions need to be provided. However, submission guidelines may also require the authors equip the article with preliminaries—a section that defines the terms that will be used later on in the paper. For example, if a paper is written on random walks across a two-dimensional grid, the preliminaries should include definitions of the grid, the random walk, and, likely, the natural numbers.

The preliminaries should be written with a certain flow; it is not merely a vocabulary list. The order in which the terms occur should make sense. Also, one should realize that the preliminaries are subject to change, as the paper is being written. Thus if certain important terms have not been included in the preliminaries, one should not simply append those terms to the end of the section, but rather incorporate them smoothly into the text. Motivation can help to create a flow in the text of the preliminaries. For non-theoretical work, it is wise to discuss applications to real-world problems where appropriate. An author may decide to include some of the background

Figure 4. An example of the type of roadmap that is typically included at the end of the introduction of a paper

> The remainder of this paper is outlined next. In section 2 we provide essential background for understanding this study. Section 3 discusses recent work by other research and development groups in the field. We explain the main components of the proposed web-based system in section 4 with the emphasis on the interactive modules and polygonal-models acquisition process in subsections 4.2 and 4.3. Section 5 demonstrates the simulation-assessment strategies and current results. We conclude in section 6 with a discussion on the importance of online-simulation and training systems, and new technologies for the engineering field.

necessary to read the paper in the introduction, or point to the place where this background can be acquired.

Related Work

The introduction of some papers includes an extensive discussion of related work. In other papers there is a separate section devoted to presenting related work. In that case the related-work section normally follows the introduction or preliminaries. Although a discussion of related work often does not present the author's original ideas, it is a key section of a research paper. An editor and reviewers can tell a lot about the credibility of the author based on the thoroughness of the related-work section. Research as a whole rests upon the works of others, so knowing what happens in one's field of study is crucial. And providing a thorough related-work section helps to set the context for the paper and indicates that the author is knowledgeable and respectful to the efforts of other researchers.

The purpose of the related-work section is to present a brief history of the problem and different approaches utilized earlier or currently-under development. The paper might also state what advantages the author's method introduces and how it is different from the works of others. A survey, for instance, is one kind of paper that consists entirely of project descriptions, different approaches taken, and a synthesis of those results for a particular scientific area. This sort of paper could be useful for someone who wishes to become familiar with the state-of-the-art efforts of the research community in one domain.

However, if the paper is not a survey, it should not become an extensive overview of others' ideas. The authors must remember that it is their thoughts and results that the reader is after, and therefore those should be the primary focus of the paper. Related work normally accounts for a fifth or less of the length of the paper. And, if a related-work discussion is included in the introduction, it may account for about one half of the length of the introduction.

Summary of the Paper's Results

The introduction should contain a summary of the results contained in the paper. The manner in which these results are expressed is important because it can serve as an advertisement in much the same way that the abstract does. However as discussed previously, the abstract should not be repeated in the introduction. Many readers will skim the introduction to find out what results are contained in a paper and in what context the results were discovered.

In the next section we turn our attention to material that would follow an introduction, the preliminaries, and the background information, that is, the core content of the paper.

CONTENTS OF A PAPER

Introduction

In the previous sections we covered several essential opening elements of a paper. Normally, such elements will be placed in an article in a similar manner to that as we specified. This section describes other possible components of a paper. We call them study overview, methodology and implementation, and results and assessments. For each of these sections we make general comments that we hope are useful to the reader in preparing the body of a paper. Naturally, the section titles for any specific work will vary, but for a writer with little experience the information provided here may be useful for generating ideas. The more-experienced writer with several publications may decide to skim the rest of the material contained in this section.

Study Overview

At some point in an article the author needs to focus completely on the subject of the research. If the related work is placed after the introduction rather than at the end, the study overview can be the next section to follow. A study overview, as opposed to the introduction, should be an elaborate description of what the author has studied, wanted to achieve or propose, and so on. This section is a good place to explain the ideas applied to advance one's research and how others can benefit from these ideas; in case of a more-technical article, the section may contain an outline of a specific system or experiment. For instance, if the author presents a complex real-time system, the structure and role of each component as well as various topological patterns and performance considerations can be laid out; the low-level details can be provided in the methodology and implementation section described shortly. However, if the idea presented or other research product is easily comprehensible without elaborate explanations, these two sections can be combined into one.

If a paper is based largely on the team's prior research, which is not explicitly referred to in the introduction, the prior research can also be mentioned in the study-overview section. How and which previous results are employed in the current study, and what improvements and addenda are suggested may be useful pieces of information that help the reader better comprehend the context for the material that is presented. As a whole, the study overview can vary in size from a quarter to a half of the article length.

Methodology and Implementation

For subject-matter experts who are reading one's paper, the 'methodology and implementation' pieces are probably the most-important parts. Such experts might want to know in detail how some system is designed and operates; or, if the work is a theoretical, what proofs the author presents and how certain conclusions are derived. One of the primary merits of a research paper is the reproducibility of the described results. Though some experiments are quite unique and require special equipment, one still needs to explain most of the procedures thoroughly and clearly, as if assuming that any expert provided with the necessary source materials should be able to obtain similar results.

Of course, it is impossible to lay out the complete logic of, say, a complex software application in the scope of one article section. In such cases the flow or functionality of the program should be presented at a more-abstract level with special attention devoted to the peculiarities of the implementation and crucial logical blocks, advisably with pseudo-code included. When dealing with theory, this section should emphasize the methodology employed in deriving the results. The logic flow must always remain consistent, from using various theorems and premises, to deriving complicated mathematical expressions.

Results and Assessments

Most research has certain practical applications, sometimes indirectly. To demonstrate the efficacy of a new methodology or system, the authors usually include the results of their trials, experiments, or tests in the published paper. These results may include numbers or figures that illustrate various qualitative or quantitative changes after applying the proposed innovation. Normally, an author assesses the results to provide a more-descriptive interpretation of the observed change and, if it is positive, justify the study efforts. The results and assessments section may be a good indicator of the value of the research. To meet the high ethical standards of the research community, *never* publish unreliable results or unfair assessments.

Similarly to the preliminaries portion of the paper, one should write the results and assessments section to read almost as a narrative, and not simply appear as a long list of facts. The results should be grouped and ordered to illustrate how they relate to each other. The order in which the results were discovered may be completely irrelevant to the order in which they are ultimately published.

CLOSING OF A PAPER

Introduction

In this section we discuss the elements that close out a paper. This material is almost as important as the abstract and introductory material, as many readers will probably jump ahead and read the conclusions section or look to see if any open problems are discussed at the end of the paper. Here we examine the conclusions section of a paper, the acknowledgments section, and the references. A number of journals also include short biographies of authors at the end of papers. And, we provide some information about those here as well. Let us start by discussing the conclusions section of a paper.

Conclusion

The conclusion summarizes the paper and reflects back to the main goals and results. Open problems, if not given their own section, should also be briefly stated in the conclusion. If, for instance, the research for a particular subject is complete in the sense that no work is left to be done, then future papers regarding that subject would not be in high demand. Good open problems promote continued interest in a specific field of study since there is still room for ongoing research. Let us present one example of how an open problem might appear in the conclusions section. One might write the following: "We developed an algorithm that runs in $O(n \log n)$ time for solving the cybersecurity scanning problem. It would be interesting to eliminate the need for sorting in our algorithm

and thus open the door for an algorithm that runs in $O(n)$ time." Of course, the nature of the work will dictate how the open problems are actually phrased and presented.

Acknowledgments

The acknowledgments section of the paper is not always included. It should be included, however, when certain people have provided the author with significant help writing the paper, suggesting ideas, or doing research. Other types of help can be acknowledged here too, for example, if the research was funded or someone spent a substantial amount of time helping the author draw images, the person's name should probably appear in this section. Another couple of examples are assistance with a proof or an editorial revision. An acknowledgment could be based on a personal communication, which provided a portion of a result, but where the result does not merit coauthorship. A "thank you" in a research paper is quite meaningful to those being thanked. Acknowledgments usually come just prior to the list of references, which we discuss next.

References

References should list all sources that are used during the research and especially those that are incorporated in the paper. The purpose of the references section is not only to provide the information that is needed to locate an original source, but also to provide evidence that other experts, scholars, or colleagues support aspects of the research topic. Details on citing a resource usually depend on where the paper will appear. Most publishers of journals and books specify the citation style for submissions. General advice is that one should be as accurate, thorough, and as consistent as possible in organizing and listing references. If the publication offers no specific guidelines, one can adopt one of the standard styles.

It can be a long and tedious process to collect the most-complete information about a reference, for example, an author's middle name or the pages of an article in a conference proceeding. However, it is usually worth investing time into this work because an author who pays attention to such details becomes recognized in one's research community as a careful writer. Besides, authors often reuse the same references in multiple papers, so having thoroughly-prepared references might save work in the future.

Short Biographies

Scientific journals sometime publish a short biography for each author of a published article. These biographies are submitted with the paper. Biographies may include passport-like photos, so all coauthors need to have such photos ready. For every individual the full name, degree, degree-issuing institution, current work place, and research interests are usually included in the biography. Even if the status and renown among the authors are different, their biography records should be roughly even in length. To the extent possible, one should try to write such a bio in an interesting manner, so that the bio does not read merely like a list of facts. We have now covered most of the writing details for a paper. In the next section we turn our attention to submitting the paper for publication and then following up on a submission.

PAPER SUBMISSION AND FOLLOW-UP

Introduction

During the final stages of writing, an author should be considering where to submit the paper. In some cases authors will actually find conferences first and then specifically write a paper to target a given conference. In this section we discuss paper submission for both conferences and journals, correspondence with an editor, reviewer's comments, and preparing camera-ready copy. Let us first make some comments about paper submission.

Paper Submission

Introduction

In many fields it is appropriate to publish a paper as a conference paper first and then publish a more-complete or more-polished version of the 'same' paper in a journal. Usually, if presenting a paper at a conference, one will receive feedback from other conference attendees. This feedback can be used to improve the paper, for example, by pursuing a new line of work that one was not aware of or by incorporating suggestions made at the conference. For work that is not fully mature yet a conference submission is probably the way to go. For work that is completely developed a journal submission is the preferred way to go. In either case the choice of which conference or journal to submit to is an extremely-important one, and the decision of where to submit to should be taken with great care.

Conference-Paper Submission

Let us first consider a conference submission. One can find quality ratings of various conferences online. In addition, one can often find acceptance rates of paper. For example, a conference with a 50% acceptance rate means that one out of two papers is rejected. Some authors and administrators look at the acceptance rate as a measure of the quality of a conference—the lower the acceptance rate, the higher the quality of the conference. However there are some top-notch conferences with high-acceptance rates. The reason the acceptance rates are high is that authors self select. That is to say, authors will not submit to such a conference unless they have a very high-quality paper.

Of course, one of the key considerations in determining where to submit a conference paper is the subject matter. Conferences usually advertise specific topic areas of interest to the conference. One needs to make sure that one's paper falls within a category as advertised by the conference. Another key consideration is the submission deadline. One does not want to be too rushed in preparing a paper for submission. A rushed paper could mean a poorly written and somewhat-incomplete paper. We should point out that more recently conferences seem to be extending submission deadlines. Conference organizers may extend a deadline for a variety of reasons, not all of which mean that the conference did not receive the expected number of submissions.

Conferences fall into two broad categories: those where papers are selected by a program committee and those where papers are refereed. In the former case a group of about ten program-committee members will choose the papers to be published in the conference. In the latter case each paper is refereed by an anonymous reviewer, ranked, and then a program committee will make final decisions about which papers to select based largely on the reviewer ratings—high-quality conferences of both types exists. Once a paper is accepted for publication, the author will usually have at least a few weeks to prepare the final version of the paper. And in the last part of this section we provide some comments about camera-ready copy.

Journal-Paper Submission

In fields such as information technology and computer science, conference papers may be viewed as being equally important as journal papers. However in other fields journal papers carry more weight. In any case a journal paper usually represents a more-carefully prepared and more-thoroughly reviewed manuscript. Many papers that were presented in conferences can be expanded to include full details and then be submitted to a

journal. The journal-paper submission process is usually more formal than a conference-paper submission. Most journals have a page in the journal titled something like "Author Guidelines" or "Manuscript Submission Policy" that provides the author with detailed steps for article submission. Those steps include information about to whom the paper should be sent, formatting instructions, and instructions for the style of references. It is a good idea to follow those steps carefully.

As with conference-paper submissions, one must be sure to select a journal where one's research is relevant. One should not, for example, submit a paper on wireless networking to a journal about data mining. One will usually include a cover letter with a journal-paper submission. The review process for a journal paper can be a lengthy one and in some cases may take several years. The reviewers are usually unpaid volunteers. For a given journal one can usually look up how long it takes for an article to appear in print from the time of its initial submission. For reviews that seem to be taking an excessive amount of time, one may decide to send the editor a friendly note inquiring about the status of the paper. One should always make sure to receive an acknowledgement after the initial submission of the paper just to confirm that there is an assigned editor who will be handling the paper. Occasionally, a paper might fall through the cracks, so following up on a submission is important. In the next section we discuss correspondence with an editor.

Correspondence with an Editor

The first correspondence that an author will typically have with an editor is when the author submits a journal paper for publication. This initial correspondence is usually in the form of a cover letter and a manuscript. If an author is not sure if a paper is relevant to a particular journal, an author can ask the journal editor. As noted in the previous section, one should receive an acknowledgment of receipt of the submission, and if one does not receive such an acknowledgement, one should check with the editor after a reasonable period of time in order to make sure that the paper was received. Once the editor has received reviews back on the paper, the editor will usually send out a note to the designated author indicating that the paper will be accepted or rejected, or perhaps may be reconsidered after being modified. In addition to the editor's decision, one will also receive the referees' reports. In the next section we discuss such reviewers' comments. Note that the terms referee and reviewer are used synonymously.

Reviewers' Comments on a Submission

Reviewers of conference papers are often asked to respond to a set of about five questions regarding a paper, whereas reviews of journal papers tend to be more-free form. Referees will make general comments on a paper that support their decisions—either to accept or reject the paper. If a paper is accepted it might be accepted with minor or major revisions. In either case the referees' comments should be given careful consideration in revising the paper. If the paper it rejected outright, one might want to consider revising the paper and perhaps submitting it to another venue after addressing the issues that the referees raised. Sometimes a paper may be neither accepted nor rejected outright, and the editor may suggest that the paper be revised and resubmitted. If the reviewers make particularly useful suggestions, it may be appropriate to give them an acknowledgment. We spoke about acknowledgments earlier in this chapter.

Preparing a Camera-Ready Version

Once a paper has been accepted for publication, one needs to make the final edits and then prepare a *camera-ready* version. The camera-ready version is one that is ready for being printed and published. In theory, the way the manuscript appears at the time of this final submission is how it will actually appear in print. In the camera-ready version the author should take into account all formatting concerns for the given conference or journal. Most conferences and journals have their own set of specifications for how manuscripts are to be formatted. One must take into account all spacing issues in the final version as well. Since any errors that appear in the camera-ready version will actually appear in print, one should be extremely careful during these final preparations. For a more-detail discussion of the steps involved in preparing camera-ready copy, we refer the reader to the *Chicago Manual of Style* (Chicago, 2011).

MISCELLANEOUS ISSUES REGARDING PAPERS

Introduction

In this section we cover miscellaneous issues relating to papers. We briefly discuss submitting to online publications, collaborating with coauthors, and reusing one's own work. There are many other issues that would be worth discussing but are beyond the scope of this book. One point that is worth mentioning here is that in technical writing it is considered bad form to write in the first person even if there is only one author. One will rarely see the word "I" in technical writing. Instead a single author uses "we" to refer to oneself, as we have done in this book and in this sentence. Let us now turn to submitting online publications.

Submitting to Online Publications

In the 1990s there were a large number of online journals that popped up. Initially many people were skeptical about the quality of such publications; people were concerned about the quality of the peer-review process. However many top-notch researchers supported these journals by publishing their own research in these journals. This support gave the journals creditability. Now it is generally accepted that there is high-quality research published in online publications. One advantage of publishing online is that the reviewing process usually takes less time, and the time from acceptance to publication is typically much shorter than that for non-electronic publications. Throughout the past couple of decades the number of online publications has continued to grow rapidly. As the cost of publishing continues to increase, we can expect more online journals in the future. In addition, the speed at which research is being conducted continues to accelerate. It is important to publish one's results in a timely manner in order to help advance human knowledge. There are still some researchers though who prefer to publish in traditional journals, and there are still some college administrators who attribute more value to offline journals than online ones. No doubt the creditability of online journals will continue to grow, as will their numbers.

Effective Collaboration among Coauthors

Few papers are single authored in the field of Information Technology. And, a similar comment can be made for many other scientific fields too. Research is so complex and specialized these days that it often takes a team of researchers to complete a project. A tremendous amount of effort is required to prepare a paper. In many research fields it is unusual if the work on a paper is split equally among all coauthors. The distribution of labor in team work should be as fair as possible or at least 'agreed' to by all coauthors. But, the status of coauthors and their individual contributions to a paper may vary dramatically.

One division of labor is for each coauthor to be responsible for one or more individual sections of the paper. A good practice is to review each other's sections on a regular basis. And, coauthors should strive to maintain consistency of writing throughout a paper. The more iteration the paper goes through, the more structured and error free

it is likely to become. Various specialized tasks can be assigned to different coauthors. During the formatting stage, for example, one author may organize the paper according to the submission guidelines while another may be responsible for preparing illustrations. In our experience having coauthors can be a very rewarding, but it can also be demanding. One must be careful to communicate frequently with coauthors. We have found that having coauthors can help reduce one's workload, but that reduction in workload is not proportional to the number of coauthors, even when they each take on a fair share. For example, if an author has one coauthor, each author might have to do about 70% of the work that one would normally have to do for a single-authored paper. Having two coauthors might mean everyone doing about 45% of the work of a normal paper, and so on.

It may happen that some collaborators focus only on research and do not contribute to the writing process, but are acknowledged as coauthors. This situation is particularly the case when the person responsible for the writing has a better command of the language, which is typical for international collaborations. In other cases a person providing financial support or specialized equipment might be included as a coauthor for political reasons. In academia it is unethical for a professor to take advantage of students' work without giving them proper credit. If a student writes a paper based on personal research, the least a professor should do in order to qualify for coauthorship is to revise the paper and provide helpful comments. If the professor's input is negligible, the student should be the sole author. There are some professors who take advantage of students and use students essentially as slave labor. Students should be careful when they select advisors and professors with whom to collaborate.

An enormous aid to collaborative technical writing is revision tools. They allow authors to make text-specific comments and spot changes made by others—such as the "track changes" feature in WORD. Revision tools also make the integration of sections written by coauthors much simpler than without such tools. Collaborators should agree on a file-naming convention, not only for new iterations of the paper, but also for other-related resources such as images and referenced articles. We prefer to incorporate a descriptive name, date of last update, and name of person doing the last update in the file name itself, for example, introduction-RG-032811. docx. Usually, a convention such as this helps one avoid overwriting the wrong file and using the wrong version of a file. All cited sources can be managed via a shared reference library, which every member of the team can expand with new entries as needed. The use of one library of references by each coauthor improves the consistency of the paper and simplifies the collaboration process. But, the author team needs to agree to and utilize a common set of guidelines for inputting additional references.

Collaborative document systems such as *Google Docs* (Google, 2011) allow a group of authors to work together. Such systems, also called collaborative environments, allow simultaneous access to a 'document,' as well as asynchronous individual access for authorized users. These systems work particularly well for large co-authored projects, but can also be effective for smaller projects. In general, any document that needs to be updated or worked on by a group of people can benefit from the use of a collaborative document system. Such documents usually only exist in an online form and are not normally printed out. Progress reports and system specifications are often generated and maintained in such systems. When a team member makes progress on a given task, that team member can go in and update the document to make other users aware of the new progress. During meetings, a group of (possibly remote) users can view and edit such documents

Table 1. Parts of a technical paper

Element	Required	Title	Order
Title	Yes	None	Same
Authors and affiliations	Yes	None	Same
Abstract	Yes[1]	Same	Same
Keywords	No[2]	Same	Same
Introduction	Yes	Same[3]	Same
Preliminaries	No[2]	Same[3]	Same
Related work	No[2]	Same[3]	Same[4]
Study overview	Yes	Varies	Same
Methodology and implementation	No	Varies	Varies
Results and assessments	No	Varies	Varies
Conclusion	Yes[1]	Same[3]	Same
Acknowledgments	No	Same	Same
References	Yes	Same	Same
Short biographies	No[2]	Same[3]	Same[5]

[1] In certain cases these elements can be omitted.
[2] Various publications may require authors to include these elements.
[3] Authors might decide not to follow this naming convention.
[4] This section may also be placed before the conclusion.
[5] The biographical section sometimes precedes the article.

together. Users can actually see editing being done in real time.

There are many other issues that are worth discussing regarding coauthors. But, let us close with a couple of important thoughts. One should not jump into a project, even if it appears to be a golden opportunity, unless one knows the parties involved. And, communication and flexibility are the keys to successful collaborations.

Reusing One's Own Work

There are authors who are known for republishing their same work over and over again, and they are not well-respected researchers. One should not republish entire works and claim that they are new works. We noted earlier that it is traditional to publish preliminary results in a conference and then published a more-polished and complete version of such a work in a journal. This type of republishing is acceptable. If one needs to reuse a small portion of one's own work that will usually be fine. But, publishers will not want authors republishing large parts of an already published work. Sometimes with books, publishers agree to let the authors independently publish a book chapter or a survey paper that draws heavily on the material from the book. If one does use parts of one's own previously-published work, one should cite this work in a similar manner that one would cite other works.

CONCLUSION

The primary focus of this chapter has been the structure of a technical paper. We have provided many practical tips that we hope the reader can utilize immediately. In Table 1 we summarize the various parts of a technical paper. The table consists of four columns. Column one labeled element provides the name of the particular item under discussion. Column two indicates whether or not this element is truly required. The third column provides the typical name of the element, and the last column describes the order in which the element typically appears. Naturally, the names of the elements will depend on the specific field and particular results, but the names given here can serve as guidelines, especially for the inexperienced writer.

Publishing technical papers is hard work. In addition to being a good researcher, one also needs to be a good writer. Plus one needs to be familiar with the publishing process. Along the way one may receive little encouragement and research results usually come slowly. Thus one must be driven by internal motivation and not become easily discouraged. The final reward is seeing one's work in print and having the enormous satisfaction of knowing that one has helped advance human knowledge.

REFERENCES

Association for Computing Machinery. (2011). *Website*. Retrieved on March 22, 2011, from http://www.acm.org

Cisco Systems. (2011). *Website*. Retrieved on March 22, 2011, from http://www.cisco.com

Google. (2011). *Google Docs*. Retrieved on July 16, 2011, from http://docs.google.com

Institute for Electrical and Electronics Engineers. (2011). *Website*. Retrieved on March 22, 2011, from http://www.ieee.org

Microsoft Corporation. (2011). *Website*. Retrieved on March 22, 2011, from http://www.microsoft.com

(2011). *The Chicago Manual of Style* (16th ed.). University of Chicago Press.

Chapter 7
Ethical Issues in Writing

ABSTRACT

In this chapter, many ethical considerations are discussed when it comes to technical writing. One of the things that discussed is the moral and social responsibilities of scientists. That section describes the moral responsibilities of being honest in research and why it is a grave ethical violation to forge results. Regarding social responsibility, the chapter examines the issue of speaking out when one believes an ethical violation has been committed, such as when results reported are untrue or dangerous. The author included a section on the responsibility of authors to their coauthors. While working together, authors must have a way to communicate effectively and express their ideas. Once a project is agreed to and commitments are made, coauthors have a moral and ethical responsibility to follow through on such commitments.

MORAL AND SOCIAL RESPONSIBILITIES OF SCIENTISTS

Writers are conveyors of information and as such we have responsibilities to our readers. We must follow a certain code of ethics and be honest with our readers. As professionals and scientists, we must be careful to explain the assumptions underlying our work and the applications of our work. We must be careful not to misrepresent our

research or mislead our audience. An example that exemplifies what is considered unethical is when in 2005 a researcher from South Korea named Woo Suk Hwang fraudulently reported to having created human-embryonic stem cells through cloning (Cyranoski, 2009). Hwang falsified data and was convicted of embezzlement and bioethical violations. As another example, in early 2010 a foreman was ordered by his company to fake safety-inspection reports so that evacuations of a mine could be avoided even when methane levels were dangerously high in the mine (Smith,

DOI: 10.4018/978-1-4666-0237-3.ch007

2010). Clearly, this falsifying of information is extremely serious and could result in people suffering injuries and in some cases even death. Most professions have a code of ethics that needs to be followed, and we described one such code from the ACM earlier in this book. Such codes often provide steps for dealing with and reporting ethical violations. The man who was asked to fake safety inspections reportedly was so distressed that he suffered from panic attacks due to the unethical nature of the situation. Unfortunately, there are many other similar cases of ethical violations to be found in the literature.

Other topics that we cover in this chapter involve citing other work, plagiarism, copyright, permissions, and credit issues. For example, if a writer wants to include a copy of an image in a given work, permission needs to be obtained from the owner of the image, and often a fee must be paid to the owner. In referencing material that is not original, one must cite the other work, so that the original author is given proper credit and no one accidentally attributes the work to the borrowing author who is merely using the original work. We try to include practical tips throughout the chapter, so that a reader can immediately apply this material to one's own situation. Let us begin by looking at the moral and social responsibilities of scientists.

When one thinks of morality, one usually thinks of the principles involved in doing the 'right thing.' A philosophical discussion about morality is beyond the scope of this book. However, more or less by definition, the majority of people in a society know what the expression the 'right thing' means. And, most people know the difference between right and wrong even if they do not always act in a fair and just manner. As writers, scientists, professionals, and contributing members of society, we have an obligation to others to present only accurate and verifiable information. Misrepresentation or falsifying information could endanger lives. Therefore, scientists must uphold the highest standards of ethical conduct. Under

no circumstance should one intentionally mislead others or provide false information.

Let us consider the IT professional who is working on a virus-detection software product. The public relies on and to a certain extent trusts such a professional to do the right thing. If a programmer knows there are flaws in a virus-detection system, the flaws should be reported. The public should not be led to believe that a piece of software is secure if in fact the software has known problems. People count on and trust companies to produce reliable products that perform their advertised features. When that trust is broken, the reputation of an individual, a company, or even an entire discipline can be damaged. If one utilizes a program, which for example is advertised to give 100% protection against the Macro XYZ virus, one expects to be completely protected from the XYZ virus. If a programmer knows that there are cases where the XYZ virus is not defended against, the programmer should report this fact. It would be unethical not to report this fact. Users make decisions to use products based on how they are advertised. The economic cost of downtime due to infected machines could be huge. And, further, if those machines were monitoring life-support systems, the cost of downtime could be immeasurable.

Information-technology professionals and other scientists are often seen as role models in society. Thus they need to uphold the highest moral and ethical standards. Role models need to do the right thing or the moral fabric of society could start to unravel. Because of the leadership role placed on many information-technology professionals and other scientists due to their jobs and high levels of education, one must be prepared to accept the added social responsibility of acting with the highest-possible moral and ethical standards. If unable, one cannot live up to the social responsibilities of the profession. And, by acting in an immoral or unethical manner, an individual diminishes the overall trust that society has given to people working in these professions. Thus one has a tremendous obligation not only to members of society in general, but also to other members of the profession in particular. In the next section we turn to an even more-specific type of responsibility—responsibility to a coauthor.

RESPONSIBILITIES TO COAUTHORS

If two or more people agree to work on a project together, they are accepting a large commitment. Many technical-writing projects span a number of years, so such commitments are usually long-term and require follow through. Frequently, writing projects have fixed hard deadlines, one's failure to meet such deadlines is a violation of a commitment to coauthors and possible a violation of a contract. Thus before agreeing to be a coauthor, one should consider the following issues:

- Do I enjoy working with this group of authors and do I trust them?
- Are these potential coauthors good communicators?
- Are these authors working under the highest-possible ethical standards?
- Can I make a significant contribution to this work?
- Do I have the expertise needed to participate or can I develop such expertise?
- Am I comfortable with the writing style of my potential coauthors?
- Have I assessed the requirements and the true commitments needed for this project?
- Do I have the necessary time for the project?
- If money is involved, has that been discussed and clearly understood by all parties involved?
- Will author's names be in alphabetical order or by order of perceived contributions to the work, and what will that order be?
- Are my coauthors totally reliable?

- Do the benefits justify the time commitment and sacrifices that will be involved in carrying out this work?

This list captures only some of the questions that one should ask before collaborating with others on a project. If the answer to one of the questions is "no," maybe that is not a deal breaker, however, careful consideration must be given before taking on such a demanding and long-term commitment. Even with lots of experience, one will still discover new and unexpected situations. Some keys to working effectively with others are to remain flexible, to be a good communicator, and to uphold one's responsibilities and commitments. Working as a coauthor can be an extremely rewarding and educational experience, and with the complexity of projects these days, working with a team is almost a requirement.

CITATIONS AND PLAGIARISM

Introduction

Whenever an author references someone else's ideas or generates ideas based on another author's work, ethically it is the responsibility of the author to give credit to the other author whose work is used as a reference. This credit is attributed by citing the original source. Sometimes an author is not quoting exact information from another author's work but rather derived ideas from it. In this case the work should also be cited. Failure to cite the appropriate source used in a work is known as *plagiarism*. Plagiarism means stealing other's thoughts and ideas, and expressing and representing them as though they are one's own. To avoid plagiarism, it is very important to cite other work as needed. In this section we will discuss the various styles of citation and provide examples. We discuss the topic of plagiarism in detail. Let us begin with citations.

Citations

A citation is a reference to a source that is used by a borrowing author to express or explain an idea. Citations are used in introductions to inform the readers about prior work in a given field. In the process of citation the author has to cite the source of information in the text by some standard means such as by providing the source number in the reference list in square brackets, giving the author's name with the year of publication in parentheses, and so on. For example, one could write [3] or [Bailey 2012]. In this book our citation style uses parenthesis instead of square brackets. The source used by the author may be published or unpublished. Items that have appeared in print such as books, journal papers, conference papers, and so on are considered published works. On the other hand, personal conversations, emails, and class discussions are in the category of unpublished works. Sources can also be categorized into *primary* and *secondary* sources. Sometimes we read information in a paper and that information is taken from another source. The original source, which might not be available, is known as the primary source. The secondary source is the source that we read. The convention in this case is to cite both sources in the text, but in the reference section to cite only the secondary source.

Different styles of citations have been decided upon various authorities with the goals of consistency and comprehension of source information foremost in mind. Several popular styles are as follows:

- American Psychological Association (APA) (Cornell APA, 2011)
- Chicago Manual of Style (Chicago, 2010)
- Modern Language Association (MLA) (Cornell MLA, 2011)

When one is writing for a particular journal or a particular publisher, they may request that one follow a particular citation style. In general, one should pick a citation style, learn it well, and use it consistently in one's work, unless required to do otherwise. Citation styles should not be mixed within one piece of writing. The manner in which one goes about citing a work is fairly straightforward. In the references just provided one can usually look up examples of proper citations for all but the most-complicated cases. If an example cannot be found, one may need to refer to the rules governing a particular type of citation. Such rules are usually easy to apply. Let us take a look at the MLA citation style for books (Cornell MLA, 2011). References to an entire book should include the following elements:

- Author(s) or editor(s)
- The complete title
- Edition, if indicated
- Place of publication
- The shortened name of the publisher
- Date of publication
- Medium of publication

One should write down this information when one is actually reading the book. This way one can avoid having to make a return trip to a library to look up citation information. Other types of elements have similar types of required information for their citation, and again, this information should be obtained at the same time that one is actually using the reference. There is a tremendous wealth of information online about each of the citation styles mentioned in this section. And, a reader should have little trouble applying the citation styles to one's references. We should mention that it is usually a good idea to add references to a written work as one goes along. Otherwise, toward the end of a project, one may need to devote a considerable amount of time to completing the reference section. In addition, misplacing information becomes a greater concern if one delays entering reference information. If one does enter references piecemeal, one will need to make a final pass over the references to ensure their consistency. Items to look out for are consistent use of punctuation, particularly around author's initials; consistent spelling of the same author's name; consistent use of dates; and consistent capitalization of similar category titles. Now that one has a good sense of how to cite an item properly, let us turn our discussion to plagiarism.

Plagiarism

Introduction

Presenting someone else's work as one's own, or using ideas and information from another person's work to present one's ideas without citing the source is considered *plagiarism*. According to (UBC, 1999), "Plagiarism can be of two types: *complete plagiarism* and *reckless plagiarism*."

In complete plagiarism a work is copied in its entirety and claimed by someone else to be an original work. A completely plagiarized work can be copied from a book, paper, the Internet, or, for example, from another student's work. Using the same assignment for two classes without the permission of an instructor is also considered complete plagiarism. On the other hand, a work is considered to be recklessly plagiarized if it involves paraphrasing another's work without citing the source; uses the results of another's work in one's own material without referencing the source; or collects phrases, sentences, or results from different sources and puts them together into one's 'own work.' Improper citation of a source is also considered to be reckless plagiarism. Note that in reckless plagiarism one might have an honest intent; however, in complete plagiarism it is clear that one does not have an honest intent.

Plagiarism Example

In this section we present an example of a source text, followed by a plagiarized form, and an acceptable form. First we give the source text.

- **Source Text:** The beauty of Goat Rocks, especially in these stellar weather conditions, was so dramatic that I had to stop and soak it up. These special moments would never come again. Never again would I be in such a perfect setting. That day was unique, but I didn't regret its passing. I felt blessed to have experienced this setting at all. Every piece fitted together. I sat down and absorbed the situation. A gentle breeze blew on my face. I listened to the absolute silence. My mind settled in a blissful meditative state, my face in a grin. (Taken from Raymond Greenlaw's *The Fastest Hike: Quest for the Pacific Crest Trail Record*, Roxy Publishing, 2004. (Passage cited is from page 210.))

- **Borrowed Text:** During a recent hike in the White Mountains, I felt blessed to have experienced the setting. Every piece fitted together. A gentle breeze blew on my face throughout the hike. I listened to the absolute silence. My mind settled in a blissful meditative state, my face in a grin.

The *Borrowed Text* is plagiarized because it directly uses sentences from the *Source Text* without providing any citation. The order in which the sentences occur and the similarity to the original mean that one can be almost certain that the author of the *Borrowed Text* copied the original *Source Text*.

- **Acceptable Text:** During a recent hike in the White Mountains, I felt like Ray Greenlaw did on his hike of the Pacific Crest Trail "blessed to have experienced the setting. Every piece fitted together." And, throughout my hike "a gentle breeze blew on my face." Like Greenlaw, "I listened to the absolute silence" (Greenlaw, 2004; page 210).

Note that in the *Acceptable Text* the original author is given credit. The original author's name is mentioned and his book is cited, including the page number where the *Borrowed Text* is located.

Rules for Avoiding Plagiarism

There are a few basic rules that one can apply in order to avoid plagiarism. We list them next.

1. When reading other source materials, if one uses ideas or words taken directly from a source, one must provide a reference to that source and put the referenced material in quotation marks.
2. If paraphrasing someone else's work, one is required to cite that work.
3. If one is not sure whether or not a citation is required, one should err on the side of caution by citing the work. Alternatively, one can decide not to use any ideas or materials from a given source.

One should be cautious to avoid reckless plagiarism, and one should always give credit where credit is due. Obviously, wholesale copying of passages of material is never acceptable. Applying common sense and proceeding with caution are the best ways to go. But, our society has changed over the years in regard to what is right and what is wrong, for example, people widely copy software and music without purchasing it. These acts are illegal, as is improper use of another's source materials.

Comments Regarding Plagiarism with Regard to Technical Jargon

Note that in some technical fields a lot of jargon is used, and the jargon is usually written in a similar way from source to source. For example, in many books on graph theory a *path* is defined as follows: A *path* in a graph *G* is a walk with all of its vertices distinct (Agnarsson and Greenlaw,

2007). If one is literally copying the material from a source, one needs to cite the original source. However for common-knowledge items that one is describing without copying from a source or without having recently read a source, in most cases a citation is probably not needed. Again, if one is not sure, one should err on the side of caution and cite a source. For example, we just thought up and wrote down the sentence "Tim Berners-Lee invented the World Wide Web." Although one can certainly find this sentence published in other works, we did not plagiarize it. One might want to add a reference to demonstrate that the Berners-Lee fact is true, or so that a reader can obtain additional information about Berners-Lee. If one has been reading sources, it is possible to use materials subconsciously. One might need to go back and compare one's writing to the original source. If they are similar or one has paraphrased the original, one should cite the original source. And, one should keep in mind that if something 'feels wrong,' it probably is wrong.

In the previous results section of a paper, one will often make comments about the research of other authors. Even though one is not necessarily paraphrasing or quoting such works, one must make sure to cite the works. In providing a citation one avoids the possibility of a reader misplacing credit for such works. In addition, the citation allows an interested reader to obtain further information about the related works. For example, "Jones showed that the ABC hashing algorithm is not secure with keys of size less than 1,024 (Jones, 2012)" is required whereas "The ABC hashing algorithm is not secure with keys of size less than 1,024" is not acceptable. In the next section we look at a few infamous plagiarism examples.

Infamous Plagiarism Examples

In this section we present three infamous plagiarism examples involving Joe Biden, George Harrison, and Alex Haley. These are high-profile cases in which well-known people were 'found guilty' of plagiarism. We provide a reference, the result, brief description of each case, and highlight the problem.

1. *Joseph Biden*
   (Sabato, 1998)

Result: forced to withdraw from the1988 democratic presidential nomination

Joe Biden "was driven from the nomination battle after delivering, without attribution, passages from a speech by British Labor party leader Neil Kinnock. A barrage of subsidiary revelations by the press also contributed to Biden's withdrawal: a serious plagiarism incident involving Biden during his law school years" and "the discovery of other quotations in Biden's speeches pilfered from past Democratic politicians" (Sabato, 1998).

The problem in this case is that parts of the speeches were delivered as though the thoughts, language, and ideas were Biden's own; he did not give proper credit by citing the relevant sources.

2. *George Harrison*
   (Fairwagelawyers, 2011)
   George Harrison versus Bright Tunes Music Corporation

Result: paid $587,000 settlement fee

George Harrison was a member of The Beatles rock band. 'His' first solo hit was *My Sweet Lord.*

"Harrison's case waited five years to be heard, during which time George Harrison's attorneys continued to try to settle out of court" (Fairwagelawyers, 2011). "Harrison's attorneys tried to prove out the difference between the two songs, but with little success. The judge found that though he didn't believe George Harrison purposefully plagiarized the song, the two songs were essentially the same. Harrison was found guilty of 'subconscious plagiarism' " (Fairwagelawyers, 2011). Harrison paid a fee of about $600,000, and "the judgment was dismissed in 1981" (Fairwagelawyers, 2011).

The problem in this case is that the melodies of the two songs were nearly identical.

3. *Alex Haley*
   (Factoidz, 2011)

Result: paid $650,000 settlement fee

"In the early 1980s, the famous biographer and author Alex Haley was permitted to settle out-of-court for $650,000 after having admitted that he plagiarized large passages of his monumental novel, *Roots*, from *The African*, by Harold Courlander" (Factoidz, 2011).

The problems in this case are that large portions of text were copied, no citation was given, and the writing was claimed to be one's own.

There are many other cases of famous people being involved in plagiarism cases, for example, see (Onlineclasses, 2011). The interested reader can search online for additional references.

COPYRIGHT ISSUES

Introduction

We begin by discussing general issues related to *copyright*. Some of our discussion follows along similar lines to that which we presented in *Inline/Online: Fundamental of the Internet and World Wide Web* (Greenlaw & Hepp, 2001). The discussion there focused more on copyright issues relating to online materials, and the reader interested in learning more about online-copyright issues would be well served to obtain that reference new paragraph.

As one might imagine, the United States government has an extensive set of laws about copyright (Copyright, 2011). In fact, there is so much information that only an attorney specializing in copyright law is equipped to deal with the vast majority of situations. A non-specialist could easily misinterpret technical aspects of the law. "Copyright is a form of protection provided by the laws of the United States (title 17, *U. S. Code*) to the authors of 'original works of authorship,' including literary, dramatic, musical, artistic, and certain other intellectual works. This protection is available to both published and unpublished works" (Copyright, 2011). Most countries have their own laws regarding copyright, and they all have different policies about enforcing copyright violations. In many countries in Asia, for example, one can find lots of people selling bootleg DVDs, CDs, and software in highly-public areas on prominent streets. Police there take absolutely no interest in arresting such venders.

Copyrights actually originated in England and recently celebrated their 300th birthday. The *British Statute of Anne* developed in 1710 was the first copyright act (Tallmo, 2011). From its early beginnings copyright law was designed to promote creative endeavors. The idea is that people can develop innovative materials and make money from their works. For example, it might take a writer 1,000 or more hours to write a book. If that book were not protected by copyright law, anyone could copy the book and sell it. Thus the author might not make any money from the work. Many authors need to earn money from their writing in order to support themselves and their families. Without copyright protection, few people can afford to put 1,000 hours into a project from which they will derive little or no financial reward.

What Works Are Eligible for Copyright?

As we saw in the previous section, a copyright is a set of rights extended for authorship. In this section we address the topic of what works can be copyrighted in the US. "In order for a creative work to be eligible for copyright protection the work must meet three requirements:

1. The work must be original and not copied (or derived) from someone else's work.
2. The work must be in a 'tangible' form, that is, either written down, or recorded on tape, videotape, disk, CD, and so on. This explains why the spoken word is not copyrightable.
3. The work must be more than just an idea—an idea is not copyrightable, although a particular expression of the idea is" (Greenlaw & Hepp, 2001).

Note that once a work is put in a tangible form, such as being written down, it automatically gets copyrighted. This statement says that it is not required to register a copyright in order to receive copyright protection. However copyright registration is usually a good idea since a formal registration can carry some extra benefits. In the United States one can formally register a copyright with the US Copyright Office. And, as we saw in the previous section, "any forms of original authorship, including dramatic, musical, artistic, and certain other intellectual works" (Copyright, 2011) can be copyrighted. In the old days a poor man's way of 'registering' a copyright was to mail oneself a copy of a completed manuscript. The postal date on the outside of the sealed envelope served as a timestamp for when the material was completed. If ever questioned, the still-sealed envelope could be produced in a court of law to demonstrate exactly when the author developed the material.

Copyright Notices

The reader is no doubt familiar with the copyright symbol, "©". Familiar copyright notices occur in the opening pages of a book, the beginning pages of journals, and at the bottom of web pages. "In the United States a copyright notice consists of three parts:

1.   The copyright symbol © or the word 'copyright.'
2.   The year that the work was first published.
3.   The name of the owner." (Greenlaw & Hepp, 2001).

In some countries the phrase "All rights reserved" needs to be present. As an example, the copyright notice at the bottom of Yahoo!'s main web page looks as follows:

Copyright © 2011 Yahoo! Inc. All rights reserved.

Although web pages are copyrighted by default, as they are tangible objects, we advise the reader to include similar copyright notices on one's web pages. If nothing else, such notices serve as a reminder to viewers of one's web pages that the pages are indeed copyrighted.

Before the Internet, the task of copying and widely distributing material was more difficult. Now it is easy to duplicate material digitally and widely distribute the material. In the past, copyright owners sold hard copies of their works. And, that method of distribution was pretty much the only-available option to obtain a copy of a work. Because of copyright law, we know that legally one is not able to make a copy of another's work. In practice though, the copyright owner will be the one to enforce the copyright, and this enforcement can be difficult. For example, the author of this book has written many other books. Some of those books, for example, *The Fastest Hike* (Greenlaw, 2004), appears almost in its entirety on the Google Books website. "Is this copyright infringement? As a general rule, for works created after January 1, 1978, copyright protection lasts for the life of the author plus an additional 70 years, so this form of blatant copying should be illegal ..." (Greenlaw & Hepp, 2001). But, the author has been able to do little to get Google to remove the book. Note that he is part of a lawsuit against Google but that has not produced satisfactory results. The wide availability of computers, the Internet, and scanners has made copyright enforcement much-more difficult. We should point out that enforcing the copyright of electronic works is an even more-difficult problem.

Copyright Infringement

We hinted at copyright violations earlier in this section, and here we discuss them specifically. When someone uses another person's creative work without that person's authorization or without compensating the person (when compensation is due), this usage is known as *copyright infringement*. In other words, one cannot make a physical or electronic copy of a copyrighted book. Similarly, one cannot make a copy of a copyrighted music recording, movie, or software package without violating copyright law.

Copyright infringement is rampant. Many people freely 'share' copyrighted music, videos, and software. And, perhaps some people do not actually realize that they are breaking the law, or that their children are breaking the law. "A case of copyright infringement that changed the way of some 'bad habits' was *Princeton University Press against Michigan Document Services, Inc.* in 1996. This case has to do with the *Fair Use Law*, which is defined in the Copyright Act of 1976, 17 U.S.C." (Greenlaw & Hepp, 2001). Fair Use Law allows people to make use of small parts of copyrighted works. For example, one is allowed to quote a portion of text from a copyright work. Obviously, one cannot quote an entire book, but up to a paragraph or so is fine. Of course, a proper citation will be needed. "In the University of Michigan case a photocopying service was sued for copyright infringement for making 'course packs.' The course pack was bound together by a professional copy shop. In the fair use system there is a mechanism available for payment of copyright fees to publishers whose works are used in course materials. The printing-shop owner refused to pay the copyright cost. When it went to the Supreme Court, they analyzed the Fair Use Law and found that this case was not fair use, and the printing shop had to pay the copyright costs" (Bitlaw, 2011).

Let us look at a couple other examples of infamous copyright-infringement cases. In each case we provide a reference, case name, result, and a brief description. This case first involves the rocker Vanilla Ice.

1. *Under Pressure*
(Fairwagelawyers, 2011)

Case: Vanilla Ice versus Queen and David Bowie
Result: paid large settlement fee

Vanilla Ice is a rock star who has white skin. Around 1990 he sampled Queen and David Bowie's song titled "Under Pressure" without consent or license. "Ice Ice Baby hit number one on the charts in the United States and Vanilla Ice became the one 'under pressure.' Vanilla Ice altered the rhythm of the baseline thinking he would thereby avoid any question of credit, royalties, license, or even permission" (Fairwagelawyers, 2011). As with many high-profile cases, Vanilla Ice's case did not go to court. "It was clear that Vanilla Ice had stolen the sample without permission. He settled out of court with Queen and David Bowie for an undisclosed but very likely very high amount. Ice Ice Baby has been released in many different versions, since then, with all of the legal procedures followed" (Fairwagelawyers, 2011).

2. *The Betamax Case*
(Betamax, 1984)

Case: Sony Corporation of America versus Universal Studios, Inc.
Result: not liable

In the so-called Betamax case, the question was whether manufacturers of home-video recording devices could be held liable for consumers who used the equipment in such a way that they violated copyright laws. "The Supreme Court of the United States ruled that making of individual copies of complete television shows for purposes of time-shifting does not constitute copyright infringement, but is fair use. The Court also ruled that the manufacturers of home-video recording devices, such as Betamax or other VCRs, cannot be liable for infringement" (Sony, 1984).

By formulating an appropriate Internet-search query, an interested reader can locate many other cases of copyright infringement.

Copyrights, Patents, and Trademarks

Our goal in this section is to distinguish among the terms copyright, patent, and trademark. We have already seen a copyright protects intellectual property that involves creative authorship. On the other hand, a *patent* is a set of exclusive rights granted by a state to an inventor of a mechanical device, machine, and process. The key issue with patents is that they are granted for inventions. Filing for a patent is far-more expensive that formally filing for a copyright. One can also file for a *provisional patent* to protect an invention while a formal patent application is being written. Although some people are successful at filing patents or provisional patents, it may be wise to hire a patent attorney to assist in patenting an invention.

In recent years a number of companies have made a business out of patenting intellectual property and using those patents in a somewhat unethical manner. They hold patents on intellectual property, wait until another company unknowingly develops a product while violating their patent, and sue the company in violation for a large sum of many. Such predatory behavior does not seem right. This description points out the need for companies developing intellectual property to have a patent attorney on staff, or at a minimum to exercise great caution when developing new products.

Trademark law governs icons, symbols, and slogans. Trademarks are denoted using the familiar "™" symbol. Durations of trademarks and patents vary from those of copyrights and from one other. A trademark can be renewed. The trademark symbol is used by companies to protect their trademarks. It is usually up to a company itself to prosecute trademark violators. Some well-known trademarks are those used by Apple Computers, Nike, and Louis Vuitton. In certain parts of the world, it is common to see people selling fake merchandise on the streets, for example, someone might be selling a Rolex watch or a Gucci bag, but the items are imitations. These items illegally display copies of the original trademarks. At the Chiang Mai Airport in Chiang Mai, Thailand, there is sign that all traveling passengers must pass by and it reads something like "Warning: In some countries in Europe it is against the law to bring in fake goods. And, those possessing fake goods will be prosecuted." On the streets of Kuala Lumpur in Malaysia, one might repeatedly hear things such as "Rolex ten dollar." And, in any large city in China, one can purchase all sorts of 'designer' goods for a tiny fraction of the cost of originals.

Summary of Copyright Issues

The key takeaway points of this section are as follows:

1. One must be sure to protect one's own creatively authored works.
2. One must be sure not to violate the copyrights, patents, or trademarks of others.
3. One can make limited use of copyrighted materials according to the rules laid out in Fair Use Laws.
4. One should remember that copyrights, patents, and trademarks are three different items. In brief copyrights protect creative authorship; patents protect inventions; trademarks protect logos and symbols.

In the next section we discuss obtaining permission to use the tables or figures from another source. The same information we present there applies to other copyrighted items as well, for example, charts, graphics, recordings, and so on.

PERMISSIONS FOR TABLES AND FIGURES

Introduction

This section covers the proper way of requesting permission to use another person's work when the material does not fall under fair use. This process tends to take a long time and may involve substantial fees. More specifically, here we provide information on how to do the following:

- Determine if permission is needed
- Identify the owner of a copyrighted work
- Identify which rights are needed
- Contact the owner and negotiate whether payment is required
- Get a signed permission agreement

Certain exemptions may apply when it comes to whether permission is needed or not. It is always in one's best interest to follow the guidelines presented in this section and obtain permission for any work that one may want to use in one's writing.

When Is Permission Needed

This section will help a writer determine when to request permission for using another person's work. The United State's Code section 107 of chapter 1 of title 17 (Copyright 107, 2011) states the following:

"Notwithstanding the provisions of sections 106 and 106A, the fair use of a copyrighted work, including such use by reproduction in copies or phonorecords or by any other means specified by that section, for purposes such as criticism, comment, news reporting, teaching (including multiple copies for classroom use), scholarship, or research, is not an infringement of copyright. In determining whether the use made of a work in any particular case is a fair use the factors to be considered shall include—

(1)   the purpose and character of the use, including whether such use is of a commercial nature or is for nonprofit educational purposes;
(2)   the nature of the copyrighted work;
(3)   the amount and substantially of the portion used in relation to the copyrighted work as a whole; and
(4)   the effect of the use upon the potential market for or value of the copyrighted work.

The fact that a work is unpublished shall not itself bar a finding of fair use if such finding is made upon consideration of all the above factors."

Since most tables and figures are copyrighted, an author is required to get permission before using them. If an author does not request permission and uses the work, the author is required to follow fair-use laws and demonstrate compliance to the best of one's abilities.

We should point out that fees for some tables and figures may be in the $500 range per use.

Furthermore, if a figure that required a fee is included in a book and the book comes out in a second edition, one may need to pay the fee again, if the figure is to be used again. Publishers make a substantial amount of money via permission fees. Unless a figure is very specific, such as a drawing of the fields in a computer packet, an author may decide to create one's own figures rather than use an original. The 'new' figure should be created independently from the old figure. For many authors the cost of including someone else's table or illustration in a work may not be justifiable. We have been successful in the past in negotiating the fees for including figures, but this success is certainly not the norm. If one does find a figure or table which one wants to include, one will need to determine the copyright holder of the work. In the next section we provide information on how to identify the owner of a work.

Identifying the Copyright Owner

The term "owner" refers to the individual or company that currently holds the copyright for the work that one wants to use. For many works the publisher is the copyright holder. The publisher is usually found by looking at the copyright notice included in the work. Not all works contain copyright information, and copyrights can change ownership. Works where the copyright-holder information cannot be obtained are called *orphan works*. When a writer wishes to use an orphan work, the writer must make sure to research and document the thorough efforts involved in trying to determine the copyright owner. This documentation will help defend an author if any problems should arise from accidentally using a work that really was copyrighted. When researching copyright ownership, the plethora of online search tools and sites containing information about copyrighted material will prove useful. One may want to get started at a site such as the Copyright Clearance Center (Copyright Clearance, 2011).

While trying to determine the copyright holder of figures that we were interested in using in our work, we have had excellent luck tracking down leads via email. For one-particular image we found an email address associated with it. We sent out a number of emails, and all recipients were helpful in pointing us in a direction which moved us closer to the copyright holder. Eventually, we were able to 'speak' to the copyright holder, and the person was gracious enough to let us use the image for free. In such cases one needs to maintain documentation that the copyright holder granted permission. In the next section we have more to say about requesting permissions.

Requesting Permission to Include Another's Work

Introduction

Requesting permission is often the most-time consuming part of the process of obtaining permissions, since one's request might not be looked at for months on end. And, unless an acknowledgment was received, one is never quite sure if a permission request actually reached its intended recipient or if the intended recipient is really the correct person to be contacting. More or less, this pinging, re-pinging, and waiting are the nature of requesting permission and sometimes nothing much can be done about the duration of the wait. Publishers always warn authors to begin the requests for permissions process as soon as possible.

As noted earlier, obtaining the right to use another person's copyrighted material may require the payment of a fee. Not all copyright owners will request payment for using part of a work, but one should be prepared if a copyright holder does require payment. Note that for certain types of books that do a low-sales volume, the authors can easily end up spending more money obtaining permissions than they end up earning in royalties. Obviously, this model is not a sound business strategy, but some authors are writing for the love of writing and not to earn money.

Permissions Form

Many companies that hold copyrights require that a form be used to request permission for works. Sample forms can be found online for a variety of publishers. We have included the publisher of this book's form, IGI Global, in Figure 1. When reading over that form, the reader will notice that square brackets are used where one needs to fill in information. One should make sure to fill out all information completely. Usually, if one has a problem with such a form, the publisher's staff will be able to assist.

We next address the key points that are typically contained in permission forms. They are as follows:

- Name of copyright holder
- Items for which permission is being requested
- Domain of the rights being requested, for example, "non-exclusive worlds rights and permission to publish in all languages"
- Type of rights being requested, for example, "permission to publish in both print and electronic form in this publication and any subsequent publication under one or more of the IGI Global imprints"
- The citation that one will use for the work
- The date permission was granted

Most of these items are self explanatory. If the exact citation to be used is not specified in the form, it can be specified in the cover letter. For example, we plan to include a citation to your work as follows:

(Courtesy of the IEEE, 2012). Sometimes one will also offer to list such citations in the list of figures or tables, as appropriate and maybe in the acknowledgments section too.

Figure 1. The IGI Global permission-request form

701 E. Chocolate Avenue• Hershey PA 17033-1240, USA
Tel: 717/533-8845 Fax: 717/533-8661
PERMISSION FORM

[Insert name of copyright holder (or official representative thereof)] hereby indicates that [Insert name of copyright holder] is the sole copyright owner of the following images included in the chapter/article, "[Insert chapter/article title]," to be published in the book/journal, "[Insert book/journal title]": [Specify and list here the copyrighted images for which you are requesting permission]. [Insert name of copyright holder (or official representative thereof)] hereby grants IGI Global (formerly "Idea Group Inc.") permission to publish said images with the following terms:

- non-exclusive worlds rights and permission to publish in all languages
- permission to publish in both print and electronic form in this publication and any subsequent publication under one or more of the IGI Global imprints (Information Science Reference, Medical Information Science Reference, and IGI Publishing)

provided that each use of the image(s) is within the context of the chapter/article indicated above and that with each image caption, the following statement (or other statement deemed necessary by the copyright holder) is included: "© [*Insert copyright year*] [*Insert name of copyright holder*]. Used with permission."

Copyright Holder (or official representative thereof) Name (Please print):

_____

Copyright Holder (or official representative thereof) Signature:

_____

Date: _____

Accompanying Cover Letter

There are several items that should go in the cover letter accompanying the permissions-request form. It is generally a good idea to convince the copyright holder that one's inclusion of the copyrighted work is in the best interest of the copyright holder. Thus a cover letter should include one's own affiliation and title, as well as a description of where the copyrighted material will appear. For example, we are writing a book titled *Technical Writing, Presentation Skills, and Online Communication:* *Professional Tools and Insights* that will be published by IGI Global and would like to include table 2.3 from the article titled "Statistics about the Information Technology Profession" which appeared in July 2013 in the *Communications of the ACM*. We would like to include the table in our introductory material on page 10. Note that one should be polite in such requests and perhaps 'complimentary' as well. For example, we enjoyed reading your book about *Copyright Issues in the Field of Computing*. We are now writing a book for IGI Global and would like to include … By taking a friendly tone in the cover letter, one is likely to obtain better results.

If the cover letter is sent by physical mail as opposed to being emailed, one should make sure to send a self-addressed stamped envelope for the reply. One should keep a personal copy of all the correspondence that was exchanged with the copyright holder. Somewhere in this part of the process is where one will be asked to pay for the permission if a fee is required. And, one should make sure to clarify that point. It may be a good idea not to pay the fee until one is 100% certain that one's book will be published. Once a few is paid and a check is cashed, it may be difficult to get a reimbursement if for some reason one's publication never actually appears in print. We should point out that such fees are tax deductible in the sense that they can be written off against royalty income.

As a final note, in the event that one cannot obtain permission for a particular item or there is an unusually long delay in obtaining permission, one should always have a backup plan in mind. Such a backup plan will probably be replacing the desired item with a different item or simply omitting the item entirely. Such a 'deletion' may require an update of the surrounding text.

FUTURE TRENDS

As new styles of content emerge, the ethical rules for dealing with such content must evolve too. We saw this fact with the emergence of electronic forms of publications in the 1990s. New types of content may necessitate the development of new technologies to protect that content. For example, the development of documents that cannot be copied via cut and paste. Of course, one can always take a digital image of a web page or use software to image a display, but such processes are tedious and time-consuming ways to copy a book. Although in some parts of the world where labor is cheap, this copying is exactly what hap-

pens. For all the various types of media many different forms of encryption technology have been developed to protect copyrighted material. The battle of safeguarding such material is ongoing though because there will always be people who are successful at breaking such encryption mechanisms. Once an encryption mechanism is broken and the means to break it are posted on a web site, many users will illegally access, use, or copy the materials.

Readers may have noticed the proliferation of editions of some works. If the new edition is changed substantially, it can render an old edition obsolete. In this way publishers can stay one step ahead of people who are illegally copying a work, and they can also stay one step ahead of the used-book sellers. In addition to the emergence of new ethical guidelines and technologies, new laws must be created to protect copyright holders in this rapidly-changing area. These laws include new copyright laws as well as new ways of enforcing the laws, catching criminals, and bringing them to justice. We expect that international issues involving copyright will continue to plague publishers, authors, and recording artists. Discussions among governments will continue, but for many countries copyright issues, particularly regarding intellectual property originating in a different country, is not a high priority.

CONCLUSION

In this chapter we covered a wide range of topics about ethical issues relating to writing. We first discussed the moral and social responsibilities of scientists. The consequences of falsifying information are great, including the fields of science and technology losing credibility with the public, and in some cases perhaps even the loss of lives. We discussed the ethical responsibilities that one has to a coauthor. Given the consequences of broken commitments, perhaps a denial of tenure or loss of a job due to an unpublished body of work, one must take joint projects extremely seriously. One must exercise caution in selecting coauthors, especially if money will be involved. We also took a look at many issues involving citations and plagiarism. One must be careful to give credit where credit is due. If one is relying on another source, one needs to cite that source. An author must cite all sources from which material was either paraphrased or quoted. One must never intentionally attribute the work of another to oneself. We covered a wide range of issues relating to copyrights. We described the information in a practical way so that the reader now knows what can and cannot be copied and knows the ins and outs of copyright infringement and copyright notices. Finally, we covered a number of important practical issues relating to requesting permissions to include copyrighted work in one's own writing.

REFERENCES

Agnarsson, G., & Greenlaw, R. (2007). *Graph theory: Modeling, applications, and algorithms.* Prentice-Hall.

Betamax. (1984). *Sony Corporation of America v. Universal Studios, Inc.* Retrieved from http://cyber.law.harvard.edu/metaschool/fisher/integrity/Links/Cases/sony.html

Bitlaw. (2011). *Princeton University Press v. Michigan Document Services, Inc.* Welcome to Bitlaw. Retrieved from http://www.bitlaw.com/source/cases/copyright/pup.html

Copyright 107. (2011). *Limitations on exclusive rights: Fair use.* United States Copyright Office. Retrieved from http://www.copyright.gov/title17/92chap1.html#107

Copyright. (2011). *Copyright.* United States Copyright Office. Retrieved from http://www.copyright.gov/

Copyright Clearance. (2011). *Copyright Clearance Center.* Retrieved from http://www.copyright.com/

Cornell, A. P. A. (2011). *APA citation style.* Cornell University Library. Retrieved from http://www.library.cornell.edu/resrch/citmanage/apa

Cornell, M. L. A. (2011). *MLA citation style.* Cornell University Library. Retrieved from http://www.library.cornell.edu/resrch/citmanage/mla

Cyranoski, D. (2009). Woo Suk Hwang convicted but not of fraud. *Nature, 461,* 1181. Retrieved from http://www.nature.com/news/2009/091026/full/4611181a.html. doi:10.1038/4611181a

Factoidz. (2011). *Famous cases of plagiarism: More than a traditional, practically an institution.* Factoidz. Retrieved from http://factoidz.com/famous-cases-of-plagiarism-more-than-a-tradition-practically-an-institution/

Fairwagelawyers. (2011). *Famous copyright infringement cases in music. George Harrison versus Bright Tunes Music Corporation.* Retrieved from http://www.fairwagelawyers.com/most-famous-music-copyright-infringment.html

Greenlaw, R. (2004). *The fastest hike: Quest for the Pacific Crest Trail record.* Roxy Publishing.

Greenlaw, R., & Hepp, E. (2001). *Inline/online: Fundamentals of the Internet and World Wide Web.* McGraw Hill.

Onlineclasses. (2011). *Top ten plagiarism scandals of all time.* OnlineClasses.org. Retrieved from http://www.onlineclasses.org/2009/10/21/top-10-plagiarism-scandals-of-all-time/

Sabato, L. J. (1998). Joe Biden's plagarism; Michael Dukakis's 'attack video' — 1988. *The Washington Post.* Retrieved from http://www.washingtonpost.com/wp-srv/politics/special/clinton/frenzy/biden.htm

Smith, V. (2010). Mine foreman: I was ordered to fake safety data. *Williamson Daily News.* Retrieved from http://www.williamsondailynews.com/view/full_story/6593132/article-Mine-foreman--I-was-ordered-to-fake-safety-data?instance=secondary_news_left_column

Sony. (1984). *Sony Corp. of America v. University Studios, Inc.* Retrieved from http://en.wikipedia.org/wiki/Sony_Corp._of_America_v._Universal_City_Studios,_Inc

Tallmo, K.-E. (2011). *The Statue of Anne 1710 (1/6).* Retrieved from http://www.copyrighthistory.com/anne.html

(2011). *The Chicago Manual of Style* (16th ed.). University of Chicago Press.

University of British Columbia. (1999). *Plagiarism avoided.* Faculty of Arts. Retrieved from http://www.arts.ubc.ca/arts-students/plagiarism-avoided.html

Chapter 8
Professional Communication

ABSTRACT

In this chapter, the author covers a number of forms of professional communication. Although this coverage is not comprehensive, there is a discussion of a wide variety of communication mechanisms, and the techniques provided should be extensible to other forms of communication. The chapter starts by discussing four simple rules of communication. If one is able to apply these four basic rules, one will be able to become a much-more effective communicator. Following the four rules of communication, the chapter presents remarks about a wide number of types of communication mechanisms, including email, texting, and telephone calls. It also discusses communication in a group setting. This material is followed by thoughts on taking a message, memorandums, and status reports. The chapter concludes with future trends, conclusions, and references.

FOUR RULES OF COMMUNICATION

Many different communication rules have been proposed over the years, and they come in all forms and quantities (Sharma, 2011; Stennes, 2011). In this section we present four simple communications rules that we hope will help the reader to communicative more effectively.

The first rule of professional communication is that one should always be polite and professional in communications. Al Capone once said, "You can get much farther with a kind word and a gun than you can with a kind word alone" (Capone, 1940s). Although this quote may be true in various circumstances, in information technology and other fields, we should focus on being polite and professional as the means to achieve our ends. By representing oneself in the proper manner, one can build a good reputation as a professional. In addition, in most circumstances one is much more

DOI: 10.4018/978-1-4666-0237-3.ch008

likely to achieve a goal if one has not antagonized the person who may end up being able to help. As a corollary to this rule, if one does lose one's temper, an apology may go a long way toward restoring peace.

A second rule of communication is that personnel should avoid assigning tasks to people who are not direct reports. The person being assigned such a task may not be required to complete it, and the person could very well resent such an assignment. And, a person in a non-supervisory role will not have the ability to ensure that the task gets completed. One should only make formal requests of direct reports, or one should first clear the assignment of a task with the person's supervisor. When assigning tasks to supervisees, it is important that both parties have the same understanding of the task to be completed, the deliverable, the timeframe, and the consequences of missing a deadline.

A third rule of communication is to remember that not every communication which one sends will reach its target. A voicemail may be accidentally deleted and never heard, or an email may be categorized as spam so that the intended recipient never sees it. One should not assume that a recipient is deliberately ignoring a communication; instead, one should confirm that the intended communication was received. If the communication was not received, it will need to be retransmitted. If the communication was received, one should think about what the best approach is to getting the most out of the recipient. For example, one might ask "Could you please deliver that item to

me by next Friday?" Or, "Is there something else that I can do to help facilitate your work on that task?" In any case one must always keep the end goal in mind, and one must think of the best way to work toward achieving that goal.

A fourth rule of communication is to be patient, but not too patient. A person with good patience will come across as being professional. Most people do not respond well to anger or loud outbursts. If someone is late or did not deliver an item promised, the first step is to determine why while remaining patient. However, there will come a time when patience will no longer serve one well. The expression the squeaky wheel gets the oil sometimes hold true. One will have to use good judgment in determining when communications should turn from being polite and patient to a little more forceful. Achieving the desired results in such a situation can be a delicate balancing act. With practice and careful thought, good results are likely to be achieved.

Figure 1 summarizes the four rules of communication. There are many other useful rules of communication as well. However, these four seem to stand out above the rest. As we discuss the various forms of communication throughout this chapter, the reader can think of situations from one's own experience using a given communication mechanism that would have been served well by applying one of the communication rules.

Let us now turn our discussion to the first form of communication that we will consider, namely email.

Figure 1. The four rules of communication for the science and technology domains

Rule 1: One should always be polite and professional in communications.
Rule 2: Personnel should avoid assigning tasks to people who are not direct reports.
Rule 3: Not every communication that one sends will reach its target.
Rule 4: One should be patient, but not too patient.

EMAIL

Email was invented in 1971 (Tomlinson, 2011) and became a popular communication medium for the masses in the 1990s (Greenlaw and Hepp, 2002). In the year 2010 there were about 1,000,000,000 email users. In this section we discuss email for communications for professionals in fields such as IT. Email is useful because it is convenient. One can send a note quickly, including a large attachment, anywhere in the world. Email is also highly reliable. Although email is not a very secure form of communication, one can encrypt messages. In general, one should make sure that when sending an email to incorporate only things that one wants to be public knowledge. We make this statement because it is easy to forward emails, misdirect emails, break into email accounts, and in some cases intercept emails. Some employers log all employees' email as a matter of course. Therefore, in order to be on the safe side one should always treat emails as though they will be read by third parties.

Email management tools have come a long way in the past 40 years, and it is now easy to label email message, sort them, search them, filter them, and so on. When one sends emails, it is a good idea to maintain copies of those emails, and most email clients take care of this task automatically. One should recall communication rules 1 and 3 in the email domain. In sending professional correspondence one should keep it fairly formal. Usually, an email will open with a greeting such as "Dear" or "Hi." Emails should be composed similarly to a letter, spell checked, and checked for grammatical errors. The closing on a formal email should be similar to that of a letter: "Sincerely," or "Best," followed by the first and perhaps last name of the sender. It is always a good idea to read an email over just before sending it. This habit will help one catch any typos, errors of fact, missing attachments, or omissions at the last minute. Email was extremely popular among college students in the previous decade; however, new means of communication are now becoming more popular among younger generations. Thus texting is the subject of the next section.

TEXTING

Usually, if one needs to text in a professional context it is to notify someone of an event. Such as, "I arrived at the baggage claim and will meet you as I exit customs." Or, "I will pick you up for our dinner appointment at 6pm instead of 5:30pm." Even if the intended recipient has one's number, it is usually a good idea to sign the message with one's first name. When receiving a text message of this nature, it is customary to send an acknowledgment, for example, "Okay, meet you at the customs exit. Rick" or "See you at 6pm. Sally." One should keep in mind that not all phones work in all locations. If no acknowledgment comes from a text, one should probably call the person. And, in the next section we talk about telephone calls.

TELEPHONE CALLS

One should use standard phone call etiquette when engaged in professional phone calls. A person on the phone should be a good listener, give full attention to the caller, and speak loudly and clearly. If one is not able to give the required amount of the attention to the caller, one should not answer the phone. For example, if one would repeatedly need to put the phone down or say "hold on," then one is not in a position to receive a phone call. In some case one will answer the phone, give the caller full attention, and then say something like "I need to call you back in 20 minutes."

When using a telephone one should make sure that it is easy for others to get in touch. For example, if one says, I will turn on my cell phone; one is obligated to be listening for an incoming call. If one is using or is required to use a voicemail system, one must check one's outgoing voicemail message. If the recording is not spoken clearly and fluidly, one should re-record the message. Such a message should be short and straightforward. Often one will be able to make a better recording if one writes a short script, rehearses the script, and reads the script. Most systems let a user listen to a recording before accepting it. If the recording is not perfect, one should re-record the message. One must be sure to read one's number clearly. Such a message might be of the form: "You have reached Dr. Agnarsson at 710 345 1234. I cannot come to the phone right now. But, if you leave your name, number, and a brief message, I will get back to you as soon as possible." If using a voicemail system, one also has an obligation to listen to relevant voicemails.

When one is leaving a voicemail message, it is important to speak one's telephone number clearly at the beginning and at the end of the message. This approach will save a listener from having to replay the whole message in order to write down one's telephone number. If the person one is contacting has to return the call via long distance, one needs to leave the area code too. One cannot rely on people checking voicemail regularly, particularly if the person is working in the field. For example, a technician may be out working on site. Some people will not be willing or able to call back. In such cases one may want to leave a message that one will call back at a specific time or, alternatively, one can try a send an email. In the next section we discuss how to take a good phone message.

TAKING A TELEPHONE MESSAGE

When taking a (telephone) message, there are a number of important pieces of information that one needs to obtain. They are the name of the person who telephoned, the person's phone number, the time that the person called, the purpose of the call, any instructions about calling back, the name of the person taking the message, and the

phone number of the person taking the message. We visit each of these in turn. When obtaining a person's name, it is very important to read back what one has written to confirm that the name was understood and spelled correctly. The same process should be used to verify a phone number. One should jot down the time of the call. Regarding the purpose of the call, one can make a note such as "The reason that Barbara called was to provide you with parking instructions for your upcoming visit to the Columbia University. She said ..., where '...' includes a description of what she actually said." Regarding a call back, one can make a note such as "She said to call back at the number given if the instructions were not clear. Otherwise, a return call would not be necessary." The last two items are included to make sure that the recipient has a way to contact the person who took the message in case any part of the message is unclear.

MEMORANDUM

The memorandum or memo for short is a form of interoffice communication. At some worksites the form of a memo is very precise and should be followed exactly. Usually, the heading of the memo contains the information that is shown in Figure 2. Occasionally, this information may occur in a different order or use different headings. The key elements in the heading are the recipient whose name appears in the "To" field, the sender whose name appears in the "From" field, the purpose

Figure 2. Typical information that is contained in a memorandum

To:
From:
Re:
Date:
Body of the memo

of the memo which appears in the "Re" field, and the date. It is typical to sign a memo next to one's name in the "From" field. Or, sometimes people will not sign their full name, but rather just include their initials. The "Re" field is the reply, and the purpose of the memo is included there, for example, "Re: eating food in computer labs." In any case a reader should be clear about the purpose of the memo after having read the "Re" field. We should point out that the "To" field may contain a group name or several groups' names or a description of the intended recipients of the memo, for example, "To: all seniors and any student who has completed more than 90 credit hours." The body of the names contains the substance of the memo; it spells out all the necessary details to achieve the purpose of the memo.

Memos are not in use as much as they once were, as they have been replaced by more informal means of communication such as email. However, memos still serve an important purpose such as when one wants to distribute a formal policy and wants to be sure that all 'staff' members received it.

COMMUNICATING IN A GROUP SETTING

Introduction

One will sometimes be assigned to a group project with several participants. If the group can function as a team of collaborators rather than as a bunch of individuals with separates agendas, they are likely to be more productive and also enjoy working together more. When one is involved in a group project, it is important to make sure that all members of the group understand and agree on the project's goals. It is also important to establish a fair division of labor as soon as possible and to arrange a schedule so that project deadlines can be met. In group work, if one person does not meet a deadline, a chain reaction may be started

causing the whole group to be delayed. To avoid this problem, it may help to set subproject deadlines or to have some overlap in the division of labor. Usually, one person in the group will be designated as the group's leader, and this person carries a larger share of the responsibilities for the group. This person can help with management of the group, including establishing and enforcing deadlines.

Many projects in science and technology require team work due to their complexity. Getting along with others and working well as a team are skills that need to be mastered. In fact, the ABET-accreditation *Criteria* requires programs to demonstrate that their graduates are competent in teamwork (ABET, 2011). A full description of how to function well within a team framework is beyond the scope of this book. However, we can suggest to the reader that while working on group projects one should observe other members of the group who work successfully. One should make notes on what makes those individuals successful and what makes a person a leader. One can try to emulate such a person in order to improve one's own ability to work in a group. In the remainder of this section we provide some thoughts on face-to-face meetings, video conferencing, and teleconferencing.

Face-to-Face Meetings

Here we provide practical tips for face-to-face meetings. Communications rules 1, 2, and 4 should be applied in such meetings. It is also important to wait one's turn for speaking out; it is important not to interrupt anyone who is speaking. Body language, tone and volume of voice, and eye contact play keys roles in face-to-face meetings. During a group meeting, one will want to be able to take notes, refer to one's own notes, and not be interrupted by any device such as a cell phone or beeper, if possible. The manner in which one speaks, what one says, and how one says something will depend heavily on the status and the personalities of the other members in the room. Before saying anything one should be very careful to think through one's point. And, as a general rule, it is important to be a good listener. Someone who listens to other people's points of view is usually well respected. One should never insult another person; one should demonstrate respect for colleagues. As with most things, it is extremely important that one be well organized and properly prepared for any meetings.

When one has a face-to-face meeting, one can later assess how well the meeting went. This assessment and the taking of corrective actions will help one to succeed in future meetings. Several questions follow that would be worthwhile answering after each such a meeting:

- Was the meeting successful?
- What should I have done differently?
- Was I a good listener?
- Did I express myself clearly?
- How were my remarks received?
- Was I properly prepared for the meeting?
- Was my timing right?

For face-to-face meetings one needs to wear appropriate attire. Hygiene is also important. Generally, one should not bring anything to such meetings except things such as a laptop, notepad, pens, and so on. That is to say, one should not bring items such as food or drinks, unless one knows in advance that this is acceptable. If food and drinks are provided, one should follow the lead of others regarding consumption. And, as a final point, one should arrive on time for meetings. It is better to arrive early rather than late. If one does arrive late, it may be worth politely apologizing to the group. The circumstances will dictate what is appropriate. In the next section we discuss video conferencing.

Video-Conference and Teleconference Meetings

The rules of communication for video conferencing and teleconferencing are somewhat different from those for face-to-face meetings. But, many of the comments made in the previous section do apply. In a video conference or teleconference one must be careful to select the venue from which one will conference in from, at least to the extent possible. For example, it is important to be in a quiet setting and one with a high-speed connection or a good phone connection. For a video conference the camera's background should not be distracting. Even if one is not intending to appear on camera, it is probably a good idea to dress appropriately just in case one must appear on camera. During a video conference, participants may be staring at one's image even more than in a face-to-face meeting, so it is important not to fidget or do anything distracting. Gesturing does not work as well during a video conference.

As with a face-to-face meeting, preparation is crucial for a video conference or a teleconference. There are many different software packages available for video conferencing and teleconferencing. (Adobe, 2011) and (Wimba, 2011) are two popular systems. One must make sure that the appropriate software has been loaded and tested. And, one must be sure about how to use the software effectively. For example, some video-conferencing software asks a user to 'raise a hand' before speaking. Other software lets a user type and send a message to the entire group or an individual. At the beginning of a video conference one needs to make sure that others can view one's camera. At the beginning of a video conference or teleconference one needs to confirm that others can hear one's voice. So, one must be able to make adjustments to these systems in real time.

When joining a meeting online or via a phone call, it is usually appropriate to indicate that one has joined the meeting, for example, one might say something such as "Hi. This is Ray Green-law from the United States Naval Academy." Similarly, at the end of the meeting it is usually appropriate to say something such as "Thank you. Goodbye, everybody." During a video conference or teleconference, one must avoid distractions and should give full attention to the meeting, even if it proceeds slowly at times. Thus it would be a bad idea to be typing or surfing the web during a meeting. And, if one must type during such a meeting, one should be careful that others do not hear or see the typing. One can have notes spread around a table during such meetings, and when referring to such notes, one should be careful not to make a lot of noise shuffling papers. Lastly, if a video connection is too slow, it is better to turn off one's camera.

STATUS REPORTS

Status reports are updates about the state of work on a given project. Status reports are also called *progress reports*, and here we use these terms synonymously. When one is working on a joint project or a project for a supervisor, it is important to keep colleagues or one's supervisor up-to-date, especially if the project is delayed or experiencing other issues. When one first notices that it will be impossible to meet a deadline, one should contact one's colleagues or supervisor to let them know that there will be a delay. In this case there are several different things that one might do:

- Send a status report, letting one's col-leagues or supervisor know the current de-gree of completion and that the project is running past the schedule, or
- Send one's colleagues or supervisor the part of the project that one has completed, if it is a project that is useful in sections, or
- Send a status report along with part of the project, or

- If it appears that the project cannot be com-pleted as planned, one should consult with one's colleagues or supervisor about the project's feasibility.

Most often, the best approach is to send a status report with a revised completion date for the project and an explanation of the delay. The longer a given project is delayed, the more important it becomes to send frequent status reports—of course, one does not want to spend more time sending status reports than actually working on the project. Projects do often get off schedule, however, col-laborators or employees who keep other parties informed about problems and project delays are much-better respected than those who simply try to ignore a problem that will not go away.

In Figure 3 we show a template for a status report. This template can be modified to suit the needs of any given project. The initial part of the template includes "To," "From," and "Date" fields. The "To" field is important so that all par-ties involved can see who actually received this status report. The "Date" field is also important, as one might be sending out numerous reports. If the reports are not dated, recipients will not be sure if they have the latest status report. The next part of the template shows the originally planned completion date and the new expected comple-tion date, plus the number of days delayed. When estimating new completion dates, one should be conservative. People who are constantly missing deadlines can lose credibility. It is usually better to push a completion date out much further and meet it rather than having to push the date out many times and keep missing the new target. In the rare case when a project will be completed ahead of schedule, one may also want to send out a status report. When the schedule of other projects is based on the completion date of one's project, status reports become even more important.

The remainder of the items in the template explain the reason for the delay, offer a general update, give plans on how the remaining work

Figure 3. A template for a status report

Status Report
Project's Name

To: list of people receiving the status report
From: sender
Date: date the report is being sent

Originally planned completion date:
Expected completion date:
Number of days delay:

Reason for delay:

General update:

Plans to get the project back on track:

Any actions items:

Any plans for meetings:

Summary:

---

will be completed, provide actions items, include a meeting schedule, and summarize any remaining issues. This information will be useful to supervisors and colleagues. The list of action items is important because it documents which people are responsible for a given task. Table 1 shows a portion of an action-item table. Action items are tasks that need to be performed, and they usually have personnel assigned to them along with due dates. This table can be modified to suit one's own situation.

Table 1 has four columns with headings No., Description, Assignee, and Due. The No. heading gives the action item a number so that the item can easily be referred to and tracked. In this case the number indicates the month, the day of the month, and the number of the action item for that month. So, for example, in the third row of the table, this action item was created on April 17 of the year in question, and it is the second item that came up in April of that year. The description should provide a clear and concise explanation of the item. The assignee column lists the indi-

Table 1. A small portion of an action item table

No.	Description	Assignee	Due
Jan10-01	Determine the number of engineers required to implement the nutrition game and communicate that information to Anthony and Lou.	Ray & Jim	3/11/2011 **CLOSED**
Apr17-02	Identify and notify two developers to test the game's user interface and to review the web instructions.	Stan	ASAP **OPEN**

vidual or individuals responsible for the action item. When possible, it is a good item to have two persons responsible for each action item. By having two people responsible for a given task, one builds in some redundancy. If one person drops the ball, the other person can hopefully get the job done. Also, some tasks require the effort of more than one person. The last column contains the due date. Notice the use of the words "CLOSED" and "OPEN" to indicate the status of an action item. The person managing the list of action items should be someone who is well organized. That person must keep the table up-to-date and send reminders and updates to those responsible for completing the action items, as well as any other parties who need to be kept informed about the ongoing work.

Other items that could be included in a status report are a timetable and a schedule of important milestones. Regular status reports or more-informal updates are excellent mechanisms to keep teammates, co-workers, colleagues, or supervisors up-to-date on a current project. One should send such notifications out as needed to keep everyone in the loop. A final point is that one should not pin the blame on anyone for delaying a project. If blame must be attributed to someone, it should be done in a factual manner rather than involving emotions or derogatory comments. A person's supervisor should be responsible for monitoring the person's performance.

FUTURE TRENDS

The mechanism by which we will perform the majority of our communications in the future cannot be predicted at this time. As the email, tweeting, texting, and social-networking revolutions have shown, new forms of communication will emerge on an ongoing and sometimes unexpected basis. The theme that will remain constant is the need to provide accurate, timely, and complete infor-mation in whatever form of communication is involved. And, when collaborating with others, one must be sure to keep them informed about the status of a given project, particularly if the original schedule cannot be met.

CONCLUSION

The stereotype of an IT professional or scientist is not one a good communicator. These intelligent people typically enjoy working with computers, solving problems, and conducting research. However, as we have seen in this chapter, being a good communicator is of paramount importance in these disciplines. The problems which we are now faced with are so complex that they can rarely be solved by one person. When working with a team, in order to work efficiently and productively, all team members must be kept up-to-date on the status of a project. So it is critically important for IT professionals and scientists to develop excellent communication skills. With practice and a periodic assessment of one's own skills, one can improve one's communication abilities and eventually become a good communicator.

REFERENCES

ABET. (2011). ABET *Criteria*. Retrieved April 1, 2011, from http://www.abet.org

Adobe. (2011). *Adobe Connect 8*. Retrieved April 1, 2011, from http://www.adobe.com/products/adobeconnect.html

Capone, A. (1940s). *Brainy quote*. Retrieved on February 21, 2011, from http://www.brainyquote.com/quotes/authors/a/al_capone.html

Greenlaw, R., & Hepp, E. (2001). *Inline/online: Fundamentals of the Internet and World Wide Web*. McGraw Hill.

Sharma, V. P. (2011). *Ten golden rules of communication*. Mind Publications. Retrieved on April 3, 2011, from http://www.mindpub.com/art196.htm

Stennes, B. (2011). *Six rules of effective communication*. Retrieved on April 2, 2011, from http://www.scribd.com/doc/2096451/The-Six-Rules-of-Effective-Communication

Tomlinson, R. (2011). *The first network email*. Retrieved March 25, 2011, from http://openmap.bbn.com/~tomlinso/ray/firstemailframe.html

Wimba. (2011). *Wimba*. Retrieved April 1, 2011, from http://www.wimba.com

Chapter 9
Documenting an Event, and Reports

ABSTRACT

In this chapter the author describes a number of key issues in documenting an event. He covers issues related to details, accuracy, timing, note taking, and audience. He also describes the types of events that typically need documenting. The chapter includes detailed discussions about three types of events that IT professionals are commonly required to document: a computer-bug report, a trip report, and a lab experiment. In each of the corresponding sections, the author describes the specifics of these events. The information provided for these specific events can be generalized and applied to other common events. In this way, the author hopes to prepare readers to be competent to document any type of event that may be required. The chapter ends with conclusions.

INTRODUCTION

There are many times in our lives when we need to document a specific event. We may need information about that event for a particular purpose later. More often, we want to give information to people who will use it for some specific purpose. In these instances we should do everything possible to give the information accurately, comprehen-

DOI: 10.4018/978-1-4666-0237-3.ch009

sively, clearly, and in a timely manner. There are a number of skills that a writer needs to develop in order to document an event effectively, and we cover those skills in this chapter.

First, attention to detail is important in documenting an event. Every event is described by a number of details that are important to a reader. Each event is different and through experience one needs to develop a sense for what information is important and needs to be documented versus what information is peripheral. It is usually better to over document rather than to under document. Even if a person is going to be the sole user of the documentation, one may forget a great deal about an event over time, so it is important to describe an event thoroughly. One must be careful to describe an event accurately and make sure not to embellish or exaggerate descriptions. One should be careful to record facts and real details rather than opinions. And, of course, for certain types of events one must be sure to record the chronology of events accurately.

Second, when one is documenting an event, one must always remember who the audience is. If one is writing for oneself, this task is easy. However, as noted, most event documentation is for the benefit of others, and they will have specific likes and dislikes in a report. Experience with the audience is the best way to find out what they want. Obtaining audience feedback and incorporating it in the next iteration is a good way to improve documentation. A detailed approach will still prove useful. Missing details are hard to fill in, but it is easy to delete excess information. And, one should maintain one's notes for an appropriate amount of time, especially if not all the information was incorporated into one's formal description of the event. Let us begin by looking at some key issues relating to documenting an event.

KEY ISSUES

Introduction

In everyday life we encounter events of all kinds. These events are usually interesting to us, but they may also be interesting to someone else, and we want to document the event to communicate it clearly. For instance a computer bug may impede our ability to use an application. In this case we want to communicate the bug to an application programmer so that the bug can be fixed. One can think of documenting an event as akin to giving someone directions. If at any step along the way the information is inaccurate, the user will not be able to arrive at the desired destination, or in the case of an event the user will not have the required information to draw the desired conclusions. In order to prepare proper documentation one must have an eye for details, and we discuss the importance of paying attention to details in the next section.

Importance of Attention to Detail

One of the most-difficult parts of communication in general is detail. A speaker will often take certain facts for granted when communicating with an audience. However, audience members may not be aware of these facts, and may not be able to reach the speaker's desired conclusion. This fact is especially true of a document, where the readership may not be able to get the information from the author, if it is not immediately available.

In preparing technical reports, writers must carefully document everything that they have done, and why they have done it. Writers, especially those experienced in a field but new to technical writing, may be tempted to assume that the audience is already aware of certain facts, which seem obvious. An author may omit some details in order to provide a more-concise account of the event or perhaps save time in the write-up. This approach can backfire though and in the long run probably will not save any time.

With a technical report a good rule of thumb is for an audience member to have immediate access to any information that is not known to anyone with a college-level education. Writers should carefully evaluate their statements and question their assumptions to ensure that they are communicating what they actually wish to communicate. That is, once a report is complete, one needs to be able to go back through the report and critically evaluate whether a general reader can get all the necessary information from the report. This type of critical reading is difficult, and it will take time to develop this skill.

Let us consider the process of writing down the steps of a sequential procedure. We must clearly list each step in order, and we must fully describe each step, so that a reader can interpret each step accurately and unambiguously. If a reader faithfully carries out the steps in the procedure, the desired end result should be reached. For example, if someone writes down a recipe, a cook who follows the recipe precisely should end up with a dish of food tasting as intended. If someone follows the documentation to repair a computer glitch, the glitch should end up being resolved. And, it is usually helpful to include recovery steps as one does when giving directions, for example, "if you see the billboard on the right displaying a great white shark, you have gone too far. Turn around and take a right when you see the sign for Sam's Diving School". Any slipup in accuracy can call an author's credibility into question and lose one's readership. In the next section we add general comments about accuracy of documentation.

Accuracy

All types of documentation must be accurate in order to be useful. Each individual has a different capacity for handling details and for remembering them. One must be aware of one's own abilities in this regard. A person who is not gifted in this area must spend more time and be more careful in preparing documentation. One should try to learn one's weaknesses and work hard to improve them. For example, a person who routinely mixes up the order of events can focus more energy on getting the order of events correct. Sometimes an IT professional may be called to testify in a court case. If the person does not provide accurate information, the person's testimony will be dismissed. One needs to be able to get the details right, and through practice, one can become more skilled in working with details.

Timeliness

When documenting an event, it is important to record the facts as soon after the event as possible. By following this recommendation one can ensure that details which need to be recalled are fresh in one's mind. As a simple exercise, one can take a quick glance at the items on a nearby surface and immediately try to write up a description of the objects, including their sizes, number, shapes, colors, and locations. One can try the same exercise again. This time glance at a nearby surface and later the next day try to write up a similar piece of documentation. It is pretty obvious that the former documentation will be more accurate and more complete than the latter documentation. One can develop better situational awareness through practice. And, one can learn to record what one saw more accurately through practice. If one does not have the time required to document an event fully at the moment, one can jot down some notes, and later try and reconstruct the event. This leads us into the next section on note taking.

Note Taking

Notes can serve many purposes and in the context of documenting an event one of their most-important purposes is to jar our memories so that we can write down complete descriptions of what we witnessed or heard. If one is jotting down hand-written notes, it is important that the notes not be so rushed that they become illegible. If one is typing notes, it is important to be complete enough so that the original event can be reconstructed at a later time—usually, the sooner the better. Notes are most useful when one does not have the time required to record full details. When making notes, one should be sure to record major points and points that one will be able to expand upon at a later date. It is also helpful to include sketches in some forms of documentation, for example, while documenting the scene of a car accident, one might draw the location and number of lanes on the road, locations of signs, locations of vehicles, locations of pedestrians, and so on.

Remembering the Audience

Audiences are as variable as events. If a document is produced for a specific audience, it may be acceptable to omit certain details that are known to that audience. General audiences, however, should be assumed to have far-less internal information. Direct experience with the audience is the best way to handle this determination. If direct knowledge of the audience cannot be obtained, one should simply produce documentation in the same way that one would for a general audience. As one is recording notes to document an event, one can think of the audience and record salient facts that are pertinent to them.

Types of Events that Need Documentation

There are many types of events that require documentation. In the next three sections we consider bug reports, trip reports, and experiments in that order. The materials that we present for those situations can be modified and used in other situations. Other types of events that need documentation are as follows: report about an employee's behavior, computer-crime scene investigation, steps required to perform a given computer action, procedure for using a coffee maker, method for shutting down a computer system, steps required to use a smart classroom's equipment, method for recording data in an experiment, and so on. If one follows the ideas outlined in this section, one will be well on the way to producing useful documentation. Let us now turn our discussion to bug reports.

COMPUTER-BUG REPORTS

Introduction

Filing a bug report can be a difficult task. In general, well-managed projects (especially open-source ones) tend to have bug trackers that invite a user to fill in specific information about a problem that one has encountered. However, sometimes no clues are given, and the user must figure out what information is useful. Typically, programmers want more information, not less—but assisting the search for clues can make their lives easier, and get the problem fixed more quickly. The right approach can make this task easy. The keys are to be informative and accurate.

Bug trackers are specifically designed to handle a spectrum of projects, so they must request a wide variety of information that is common to all bug reports—type of system, version of the software used, and description of what the user was doing when the bug appeared. In Figure 1 we show a sample bug report. Some projects will have custom fields that request information unique to that project; one must pay special attention to those fields. Also, if possible, it may be helpful to browse other bug reports to see what programmers tend to look for and what other users often forget to mention.

When providing a description of a bug, clarity is important. The user must consider how a bug report is to be used by a programmer. In general, programmers will want to reproduce the bug, if possible. If the user can reproduce the bug, providing precise information on how this was done will be extremely helpful. One should list in clear enumerated steps the process that was taken to produce the bug. One should note as many details as possible. The user, if unable to reproduce the bug, should try to remember as much as possible about what happened before the bug resulted. If details are too sparse, it may not even be worthwhile to file a computer-bug report.

Figure 1. A sample computer-bug report that has been filled in

Computer-Bug Report Form
Your email: roger.smith@softwareconcepts.com
Date: July 30, 2013
Summary: The opening of the IE browser on my Windows 8 System causes the operating system to crash.
Computer: Dell Adamo, Model 13, 2010
Product: Internet Explorer Version, 10.3
Description: When I open IE Version 10.3 from the Windows 8 operating system, the system does a reboot. I have closed all other programs. Double-clicking on the IE icon forces a reboot of the system. The browser opens and flashes on the screen for just a brief moment before the reboot happens.

Steps to Reproduce:
    1. Boot the Windows 8 operating system.
    2. Double click on the IE Version 10.3 icon.

Expected results: Browser opens and is ready for web surfing.
Actual result: The operating system reboots and one needs to login again.
Attachments: Screenshot of version information for the Windows 8 operating system, including the patches installed. Screenshot of the version information for the IE browser.

Required Information

Most bug reports will begin with the email address of the person reporting the bug, the time, and a summary of the problem. This data is followed by information about the computer being used. If a user is unsure about how to obtain the required details about the computer, the type and version of the operating system should be included so that a programmer can instruct the user on how to get the needed computer information. When discussing how to reproduce the bug, one must remember that every action is important, even if nothing actually seemed to occur—something may have been changed behind the scenes. As we pointed out earlier in this chapter, one's attention to detail is extremely important in writing reports of this nature.

Thinking Similarly to One's Audience

In a bug report the audience is one of the project's programmers. The most-important aspect about this programmer is that the person wants to fix the bug—a truth that is often not accounted for by a user. When there is no clear method for reporting a bug, to the extent that a user is able to, it can be helpful to think about how programmers approach bugs. Writing with the audience in mind, as before, will make for clear and more-useful writing. And, this statement holds particularly true for any type of report writing.

A programmer will first look for signs of current or alleged bugs. If the project has a bug tracker, the user can browse recent bugs that sound like the current problem and see if the problem has already been found or if the assumed problem is actually a bug at all. If there is no bug tracker, a manual or FAQ may also be tried. Few things frustrate a programmer more than having to answer a bug report that is actually not a bug, but something described in a FAQ or manual. Thus a user needs to do the required homework before reporting a bug.

If the bug turns out to be novel, the next step is to reproduce the bug. A programmer will utilize the system information provided in order to reproduce the bug. With this information the programmer will know certain limitations of the given environment and how that will affect the application. Once the system is in place, the programmer will proceed with a step-by-step generation of the bug. And, we can see why the steps must be clearly and precisely documented in the bug report—a small misstep by the programmer may cause the bug to go undetected and unfixed. Many types of reports require the same level of detail and precise writing as bug reports, so the comments made in this section can be applied to other situations as well.

Sample Computer-Bug Report

In Figure 1 we provided a sample computer-bug report. Each part of the report provides specific information. The descriptions contained in the report are brief and concise. The information should be a superset of what a programmer actually needs to fix the bug. That is, we need to be sure to provide the programmer enough information. If we provide too-little information, the programmer might not be able to fix the bug. If some of the information goes unused, however, that would be okay. When writing such a report, the author should carefully review the completed report to make sure that it contains all the required information. And, to perform that final proofreading effectively, one should try to stand in the shoes of an audience member.

TRIP REPORTS

Introduction

Businesses will often allow their employees to take trips to expand the employees' knowledge, present information about the company, or increase the company's visibility. For example, an employee may be asked to attend a conference on behalf of the company. Since not all company members can travel, the person who is actually taking the trip often prepares a report for other members of the company. In order to prepare a good report, the encounters during the trip, facts learned while visiting display booths, the information presented in talks, and the hallway conversations must be well-documented. In addition, if the company will reimburse one's expenses then accurate records of trip details must be kept, as well as receipts for purchases. Quality trip reports depend on attention to detail and an understanding of what the company hopes to achieve with the trip. In this section we will present thoughts about what information to collect during a trip, trip reporting, how to produce an executive summary, and expense reporting.

What to Record during a Trip

An accurate trip report depends on detailed recording during the trip itself. However, energy should be concentrated on the trip in order to get the most out of it. One can divide the trip into events and interludes. During an event, one may only be able to keep sparse notes. During the next interlude, one can go back and fill in more details. One should record times and dates of events if this information is not listed on a program. While on a trip, one should keep more notes than needed. This habit ensures that nothing important is missed. It is much easier to start with too-much information and condense it, rather than to have too-little and to try to reconstruct what was forgotten. One should spend plenty of energy on documenting anything that was learned during the trip.

Two useful items to bring on a trip are a notebook and a camera. The notebook can be a paper notebook or a computer. There are times when a paper notebook can be used, when a computer could not be. Regarding the camera, even if pictures are not to be added to the trip report, they can still be a valuable tool for remembering important events. Pictures can provide an overview of what happened at an event. In other words the type of pictures that one wants to take should be self-explanatory. For example, if allowed, one could take a picture of the title slides of several different presentations. One should take notes on the most-useful and interesting events, as defined in relation to the company. If the trip report is to include a recommendation, information from the relevant events will need to be collected in order to support the recommendation.

We find that a lot of work can be accomplished while waiting for taxis, sitting in airports, or while flying. Once the event is over, one can organize notes and condense them into an easily-readable and clear format—the people who will read the report will usually not have a lot of free time. If pictures are allowed, they can be used to help bring the report to life. In the report one should talk about how what was learned and observed can be used to benefit the company. We always try to finish writing such reports before returning to the office. Once one comes back to the office, there is usually a backlog of work waiting, so it is difficult to find the time to write-up unfinished reports. In the next section we get into more-specific details about writing a trip report.

Trip Report

Assuming that one has maintained good notes during the trip, the actual write-up of the trip report should not be too time consuming or difficult. Events should be listed chronologically and their important details should be described. Figure 2 shows a sample description of an event. For each event the description should try to answer the six questions:-who, what, where, when, how, and why. A description should start with the date (the when), the location if the events are not all in the same place (the where), and the title (the what). One should note the names of the individuals involved, if any (the who). From there, one should explain what happened at the event (the how) and why it was useful and interesting (the why). The latter item might sometimes be called the impact, as it is in Figure 2.

Figure 2. A description of an event that would be part of a trip report

Date: March 30, 2011
Where: Baltimore, Maryland
What: CyberWatch Meeting
Who: Robert Spear

How: Robert Spear presented an overview of the CyberWatch organization. There are 25 community colleges and 35 universities involved. The headquarters is located at Prince George's Community College. The URL for CyberWatch is www.cyberwatchcenter.org. The schedule of upcoming events is listed at the CyberWatch website.

Impact: This organization is leading activities in the cyber-security domain on the east coast. We recommend that our university join this organization. The benefits are increased visibility, immediate contacts establish among the other 60 institutions, and access to their large repository of cyber-security materials.

As noted earlier, one's employer is mostly looking for what the company gained from the event, not the direct benefits to the employee. After collecting together and organizing the event descriptions, one can produce the recommendations section. This section will contain any recommendations that arose from the trip. For example, "I recommend that we assign two of our engineers the task of researching the literature on computer forensics. And, I recommend they develop a report about the types of computer evidence." Following the recommendations section, one can add a section on action items. Action items were discussed in the previous chapter in the section covering status reports. Once action items are assigned to individuals, those employees have the responsibility of carrying out the action and at a later date reporting their results. Figure 3 shows what the overall structure of a report would look like. Of course, the nature of any given trip and its goals will dictate the sections included in any particular report.

A final part of the report may concentrate on whether the employee would recommend the trip for others. This section is important because it summarizes the value of the experience in a paragraph. If the trip was useful, one should describe the most-valuable parts, particularly ones that may interest other employees and motivate them to participate. If the trip was a bust, it may be interesting to document what went wrong, and the recommendations sections can include cor-rective measures or notes about why none of the company's employees need to participate in the event in the future. The reader may have noticed the second item shown in Figure 3 is an executive summary. This piece of a report is one of the most-important parts, so we discuss it in more detail in the next section.

Executive Summary

An *executive summary* provides an overview of a longer report; the executive summary focuses on the big picture and omits unimportant details. This short report allows an 'executive' to learn about the contents of the larger report quickly. Rather than reading a 100-page report, an executive can read a 1-page summary. On an as needed bases, the longer report can be used as a reference. The executive summary should present essential facts, recommendations, and action items. A well-designed table or figure could be shown in the executive summary if a great deal of information can be compressed into it. The executive summary should be written so that in conjunction with the table of contents a reader can quickly jump to interesting parts of the larger report. One should devote the appropriate amount of time to producing the executive summary because this section of the report will be the one that is most-frequently read, and in many cases the executive summary may be the only part of the report that is read. This statement is not to say that other

Figure 3. The structure of a trip report

Title Page—includes name, date, and event
Executive Summary—short overview of the entire report
Table of Contents—descriptive section headings with their locations
Introduction—background and basic details
Events—descriptions of the events that one attended and important encounters
Recommendations—descriptions of recommendations plus their justifications
Action Items—what needs to be accomplished, by whom, and by when
Conclusions—whether the trip was worthwhile and its benefits or problems
References

parts of the report should be neglected, rather we want to stress that the executive summary is the most-important part of a report.

Expense Report

When one travels for work, it will be necessary to file an expense report in order to obtain reimbursement for usual-and-customary travel expenses. The key to performing expense reporting in an efficient manner is to be organized and thorough. One must also know the company's rules pertaining to expenses. We generally keep a 'folder' of materials relating to a given trip. In this folder we put receipts for all expenses that can be reimbursed. At the time we put the receipts in the folder, we do things such as date them as needed, sign them, and perform currency conversions as required. We maintain the receipts in chronological order. If traveling on a per diem, one will not need to collect receipts for meals. Figure 4 shows some of the common types of receipts that one will need to collect.

We will not delve into all the details of expense reporting here, but let us mention a few items that will help a reader the most. If one will be driving a personal auto, one needs to remember to jot

Figure 4. Common business-trip expenses

Accommodations
Airfares
Insurance
Meals
Miscellaneous
Parking receipts
Personal-auto mileage
Registration fees
Rental cars
Social or entertainment expenses
Taxis, trains, buses, subways, tuk tuks
Tips
Tolls
Travel-agent service fees

down the starting and ending odometer readings. If one is going to be traveling to a foreign country and exchanging money, one will need to document the exchange rate. This documentation can be from a bank receipt or a money-exchange house receipt, or perhaps it may be acceptable to print out the daily exchange rate from an online site. Although one probably will not be riding in a tuk tuk, we included that item to illustrate that it is sometimes not possible to obtain receipts. For one thing, a traveler may not speak the local language, and for a second thing, no receipts are involved with certain types of expenses. Tips would be another example of an item for which a receipt is unlikely.

Some companies require employees to send in an estimate of trip expenses prior to departure. One should be aware that some entities will not reimburse the employee for an amount greater than this estimate. Thus it is worthwhile to include a large miscellaneous item in the preliminary estimate just in case expenses are larger than anticipated. Regarding social and entertainment expenses, one must make sure of the company's policy before claiming such expenses, for example, some businesses will not reimbursement for purchases of alcohol. Depending on one's own personal financial situation, we should point out that some businesses may be able to pay for certain-travel costs up front. These items would usually include such items as airfare, accommodation, and event-registration fees.

Once one has collected all the expenses and the trip is complete, one should file the expense report in a timely manner. Most companies have special forms for reporting expenses. One should be sure to take these forms along on the trip, and it is a good idea to read them in advance of traveling. Such forms can be in paper format or digital format. We always try to complete our expense reports as fully as possible before returning from the trip. When filing a trip report, one should always keep a backup copy of the report, as well as copies of the receipts. Although this latter task can be onerous for an extended trip, it has saved many a traveler lots of money. After the report has been filed, one must be sure to follow up on the reimbursement if the repayment does not arrive as expected. When funds will be deposited electronically, one must remember to verify that the appropriate account was actually credited with the appropriate amount. As a final note, when problems with reimbursements arise, there is usually at least one company representative, who can assist, and it is a good idea to stay on that person's good side.

REPORTS FOR EXPERIMENTS

Introduction

Scientists must conduct experiments to test hypotheses. Experiments must be well-documented in order to be useful. Every tool, every measurement, and even accidents should be described and later assessed. With the notes recorded during the experiment a scientist can write a report about the experiment. Once a hypothesis is either proven or disproven, a scientist can either publish the findings, use the information to formulate a new experiment, or discard the results entirely.

In this book we assume that the reader has some experience with performing an experiment and writing up a lab report. When documenting an experiment, a scientist must be clear about the procedure utilized in the experiment, so that the information can be used later. This information is needed not only by the scientist conducting the experiment, but also by future scientists who may wish to reproduce the experiment and use its results, or use it for the basis of their own experiments.

Various write-ups should be performed before, during, and after an experiment. Before the experiment, one should take notes of the apparatus and surroundings. During the experiment, one should document the results and anything out of

the ordinary—history is full of examples of new discoveries resulting from mistakes; for example, consider the invention of super glue (Coover, 2004). After an experiment is finished, one should prepare the results and convert them into a useful form. Writing the final report generally involves a certain structure. If the results are to be sent to a major conference or journal, the publication may require a specific format. Otherwise, a simple format describing the experiment and results should suffice. When writing such a report, remembering the audience is the most-important part.

Taking Notes during the Experiment

As the earlier, the write-up should begin even before the experiment. In general, a scientist should begin with the hypothesis, since this point is the start of every experiment. The experimental design follows the hypothesis, and the design is usually based on similar works in the literature, available equipment, cost, and other practical considerations. The details of the experimental design must be carefully and clearly documented. In a chemistry experiment, for instance, one should indicate which chemical is added to which, their quantities, their temperatures, the order of mixing, method of mixing, and so on. In addition to jotting down thorough notes during an experiment, one can also record an experiment in its entirety, or perhaps a video recorder can be used. Note that some labs are full of sensors that automatically record all activities which take place in the lab.

With the experimental design in hand, one should acquire the various tools, things to be experimented with (that is, chemicals, apparatus, and other items) and subjects, if any. Next one performs the experiment as indicated in the design. One should take note of anything unusual such as an unexpected phenomenon. If any errors occur, one must note them. If possible, one should try to fix errors and restart the trial, if possible. One must be careful to record any needed data. Throughout the experiment, one should be recording environmental conditions, times, and so forth. Once the experiment has been conducted and all the data recorded, one can make another pass to fill in any items that need to be expanded upon. If the experiment was filmed or recorded, one can make notes from this media as well. With suitable documentation in hand, one is ready to begin preparing a report, and we discuss this topic in the next section.

Preparing a Report for an Experiment

If a scientist is not required to use a specific format for a report, a simple structure will be needed. A sample format is shown in Figure 5. For any particular report the actual sections will vary. It is a good idea to use descriptive section headings. If the report is to be published, perhaps the most-important item is its title. Without an interesting title the report may not be read, and if the report is not read, it will have little value. A good title should capture the hypothesis in a clear and concise way. After the title the abstract is the second most-important part. Assuming that the title is sufficient to pique a reader's interest, the abstract must then sell the report to the reader. The abstract should focus on the hypothesis and

Figure 5. A sample structure for a report for an experiment

1. Title
2. Abstract
3. Introduction
4. Hypothesis
5. Apparatus
6. Experimental Design
7. Experiment
8. Data Collected
9. Analysis
10. Results
11. Conclusion

conclusion, as well as a quick discussion of the real-world value or importance of the results.

The rest of the report is based on the documentation. If one closely follows the recommendations that we presented in the previous section, one should have a clear and structured set of notes that can be cleanly translated into a report. As a result, a scientist should be focused on *communicating* the results to the reader—ensuring that the reader can quickly absorb what the results are. In general, a writer must carefully assess how much knowledge a reader is likely to possess. For specialized research the reader and the writer are likely to be in similar fields, so certain assumptions can be made about the knowledge of the reader, which can help make the report more concise. Reports that contain many abstract ideas, complex equations, or difficult proofs can quickly become confusing for readers. Thus an author must be careful to treat the subject matter appropriately according to its level of difficulty and its intended audience.

Proofreading an Experiment's Report

Once a report is 'finished,' one must verify that the report is completely accurate. One should maintain a checklist and go over each section in the report. If at all possible, one should try to carry out the experiment again and duplicate its results by following the description in the report. If steps are missing or inaccurate, one needs to correct them. This process is important because a faulty report can both damage a researcher's reputation and lead to other scientists basing their work on incorrect information.

CONCLUSION

Documenting an event can be a fairly-complex process. In some instances it may be easy if the audience simply specifies what it wants; but oftentimes, a certain amount of thought and innovation will be necessary. There is no substitute for experience—after a few attempts at documenting a certain event; one will become clear about what is expected from a specific audience. However, events and audiences come in many different forms, so it is useful to have a few general skills. We have discussed several key items in this chapter, including attention to details, thorough note taking, initial preparation, and timeliness. Example reports are helpful—if a good example is found, it can be modified to suit one's needs. Failing that, the user must think about the audience's goals and motives in order to assess the best way to communicate the event to the audience. We have included the basic structures in this chapter for computer-bug reports, trip reports, reports of an experiment, expense reports, and executive summaries. These items should serve a reader well in preparing successful reports. And recall that in chapter 9 we discussed status reports, also known as progress reports. For other types of reports, such as book reports, business reports, or research reports, one can apply the ideas described here as well, albeit modified slightly. There are also hundreds of thousands of references online that one can find to assist with report writing, as well as thousands of books. Report writing has been around for hundreds of years, and it will continue to be important in the foreseeable future.

REFERENCES

Coover, H. (2004). *Harry Coover, inventor of the week archive*. Massachusetts Institute of Technology. Retrieved March 30, 2011, from http://web.mit.edu/invent/iow/coover.html

Chapter 10
Fundamentals of Presentation

ABSTRACT

In this chapter, the author considers general topics relating to presentations. The idea is to provide the reader with knowledge that can be put into practical use. It is impossible to cover all the important aspects of presentations in this book, but it is hoped that the reader will find useful items in this chapter. The next chapter covers delivering the presentation and the basic use of PowerPoint. Before launching into the material contained here, here is a roadmap. First discussed are key points relating to topic selection. This section is followed by one on the setting of the presentation. Next discussed are tips for preparing for a presentation, including comments about multimedia. Given the variety of equipment that one might find at a given setting, included are notes about equipment. Many speakers provide handouts to audience members, so a discussion about these items is included too. Of course, if a presentation is not properly advertised, the audience maybe smaller than anticipated. Therefore there is a section on talk advertising. The chapter wraps up with conclusions and references.

SELECTING A PRESENTATION TOPIC

Introduction

So far, this book has been mostly about writing, but we now shift our focus to speaking. Unlike working with manuscripts, oral presentations allow for direct and real-time interaction with the audience. When presentations are properly prepared and delivered, they are engaging and informative. An effective presentation can help land a job or seal a deal with a potential client while a poorly-executed presentation can damage a reputation or lose a sale. A good writer is not necessarily a good presenter, and vice versa. These two skills are fairly independent, and both need to be practiced and developed.

DOI: 10.4018/978-1-4666-0237-3.ch010

The general steps for giving a successful presentation are as follows:

1. Analyze the audience in advance
2. Research and gather information
3. Organize the content
4. Develop the slides
5. Practice delivery
6. Prepare for any unexpected circumstances

There is much more to presentations than just following these steps. Every day many people are exposed to presentations covering all sorts of topics. Television-news teams present stories on crime and car crashes; college math teachers prove the Fundamental Theorem of Calculus; corporate-sales teams demonstrate new products and services offered by their companies. A person can learn from all such presentations—make note of techniques that work well and others that do not. The *topic* of a presentation is the discussion's central theme or focal point, and as a presenter, an individual must be knowledgeable about that topic. Sometimes a person may not be able to choose the topic for a presentation. For example, a boss may ask an employee to research a software application and present the findings to a committee. Even if an individual does choose the topic, every presentation requires research. The reader should consider the following items when choosing and researching a topic:

- Area of personal expertise
- The audience
- The desired outcome
- Time constraints
- Available resources

In what follows we make comments on each of these general considerations.

Area of Expertise

It is not wise for anyone to address an audience about a topic that one does not have personal confidence in one's own knowledge of the subject. In addition to perhaps bumbling things up and failing to be able to answer even routine questions, a person's case of nerves will be much worse. As noted, a boss may select a topic for an employee. Sometimes an individual needs to deliver a presentation on a subject where personal knowledge is weak. In such a situation the individual must do the best possible to channel the fear about delivering the presentation into energy for expanding knowledge of the topic. When the author of this book was preparing to give an address at his high-school graduation, he asked his dad for advice. His dad, who had won many speaking awards in toastmaster competitions (Toastmaster, 2011) told his son to talk about what his son knew the best. And, when the author got up in front of about 3,000 people at the age of 17, he was (very) glad that he had followed his dad's advice. The author has spoken at about 15 graduations since that time, and those audiences are the largest that the author has ever faced. The author has always followed his dad's advice, and the author has always been happy that he did.

Although it is not always possible, as a general rule of thumb, a speaker should try to be more of an expert on the topic which the individual is speaking about than anyone in the audience. And, by all means, if someone there knows more than the speaker does, than the speaker should simply admit that fact. For example, if an individual does not know the answer to a question, but someone in the audience does, it might be appropriate to let that person answer the question. An individual must never step over the bounds of personal knowledge during a talk, and must never guess at answers to questions without prefacing such a guess by something like "If I were to hazard a guess, I might ..." One should be careful not to let an audience member (try to) take over the floor during a talk. The more expert that an individual is on a particular subject, the more difficult it would be for an audience member to attempt this takeover. We will have more to say about handling questions in the next chapter.

Audience

Conducting an analysis of an audience prior to a talk is a good way to gauge the appropriate level of the talk, and this knowledge is helpful in knowing how to keep the audience's attention during the talk. A speaker should try to find out as much as possible about the audience's knowledge on the given topic before giving the presentation. Who will be in the audience? Are they undergraduates, graduate students, professors, technical specialists, and so on? How much do they already know about the topic? Are they novices or do they all have PhDs in the subject area? This analysis will help to determine the appropriate level of jargon to employ, to identify the items that need to be defined in the talk itself, and to make clear the background concepts to cover. A presenter must avoid speaking over an audience's head. At the same time, one should not insult an audience by oversimplifying details. A speaker must be aware of the time of the day, the temperature of the room, and any other details that may affect the audience's comfort level. For example, if an individual is speaking late in the day, the person should realize that the audience might be tired. As appropriate and feasible, an individual should tailor a talk to meet the audience's needs. This adjustment may mean shortening the talk or adding a personal anecdote to recapture their attention near the end of the presentation. One should always dress appropriately for the expected, audience, and one should never wear distracting clothing or jewelry.

Desired Outcome

Presentations are used to inform or to persuade, or both. To inform or educate an audience, a speaker should provide the facts with illustrative examples. A political candidate interested in expanding the military should explain how to pay for the expansion without raising taxes. A car salesperson should be able to detail the results of a government crash test in which the vehicle in question outperforms the competition. We suggest writing down the goal of the presentation. While an individual rehearses, the person can ask if the goal is truly being met. The talk may need to be refined repeatedly until the presenter is sure that the talk achieves its desired outcome.

Time Constraints

The time allotted for a presentation is usually known well in advance. If not, a person should evaluate the situation to determine a reasonable amount of time to use and remember to allow time for questions. If time is short, a speaker might request that the audience hold all questions until the end. At many conferences speakers are only allotted about 15 to 20 minutes for their presentations. An individual should choose a topic that can be appropriately presented in the allotted time, and the person should use enough time to warrant the audience members' attendance. However speakers should not over step time limits. Going beyond the scheduled time is inconsiderate to the audience and in some circumstances to other presenters. One should keep in mind that nearly everyone has a short attention span. If a speaker has fifty minutes to present and five minutes are allotted for questions, the speaker should consider stopping the actual presentation at forty-five minutes. Often, people who do not ask questions during the 'official' question period will come up to discuss something with the speaker once the talk is completed. Such interactions are often more valuable than the official question-and-answer period.

During a timed conference presentation, the session chair may give the speaker a 10-minute, a 5-minute, and a 1-minute notification. Speakers must not get distracted or intimidated by such warnings. We recommend that the speaker occasionally glance at the person who is timing the presentation in order to keep track of the elapsed time. The speaker can then adjust the rate at which information is being presented, and complete the presentation on time. Speakers should have a time piece. Many presentations leave the most-important points for the end as a 'grand finale.' If time runs short, the temptation is to rush through all the remaining material, including critical items and items that may have been carefully prepared. But obvious rushing will turn an audience off, so one should not feel obligated to give the entire presentation as rehearsed. A speaker should plan to spend plenty of time on the most-important parts of the presentation. Speakers can incorporate the techniques of summarizing and cutting materials into rehearsals to ensure important points receive appropriate coverage. And one should remember that just because hours were spent creating the perfect slide does not mean that one actually has to use the slide.

Available Resources

The next section covering the setting of a presentation delves into the available resources, as does the section on equipment. The reader is referred to those sections for detailed information about available resources.

SETTING FOR A PRESENTATION

Introduction

When a speaker chooses a topic, the person should pick one that lends itself well to the available resources. For example, speaking from a podium without visual aids will work with a topic that can be explained with statements and facts. A political speech or a talk about the history of the Internet is a good example. Detail-oriented topics that involve proofs and graphics, such as random walks or tips on webpage design, require visual aids such as a projector or a whiteboard. Although a speaker cannot always know what resources will be available in advance, it is a good idea to try and find out. One can simply ask the host or the conference organizers what materials will be available in the presentation room. Many conference organizers ask presenters to fill in a form that describes the resources required to give the presentation.

Room Size

Room size will dictate a number of things. The larger the room, the more nervous a speaker is likely to be. Also, an individual may need to speak more loudly in a larger room, especially if no audio system is available. In a large room a person may be separated from the audience, creating a different atmosphere than in a small room. Acoustics could be a factor in a large room, for example, there might be a distracting echo produced by the speaker's voice. In a large room that contains desks in the seating area audience members may feel comfortable taking out and using their laptops rather than listening to the presenter. In some countries it is not uncommon to have people talking on cell phones during a presentation. Needless to say, the latter two situations are distracting to a speaker. In a small room people are usually not able to work on their laptops or speak on cell phones during a presentation. If an individually really needs to work on a laptop or speak on a cell phone during a presentation, the person should just skip the presentation.

One should think about where to be positioned if the presentation room is large. If a person is off to one side, half the audience may not be able to see the person very well. In particularly-large rooms audience members may need a microphone to ask questions, or the speaker may need to repeat their questions so that all audience members can hear the questions. Or, the presenter may need to walk down toward the audience and let them share the microphone in order to ask questions, so that the questions can be heard by all audience members. Sometimes it is helpful for the speaker to enlist an audience member to assist in determining who had the next question. When the speaker first enters the presentation room, the person should think about the issues that we have mentioned, including whether the audience will be able to hear the talk and see the presentation.

Stage

A stage may be used in a large venue. One should be careful getting up on and coming off of the stage. It is easy to trip on a cable, especially if the lights are already dimmed. The stage may separate the presenter from the audience, requiring the person to project one's voice more loudly or to adjust the volume on the audio system. An individual should feel free to move around on the stage, but one should not feel a need to cover the entire stage during a talk. An individual may be 'tied' to a laptop if the person needs to advance one's own slides. If awaiting a lengthy introduction before taking the stage, it is wise for the speaker to take a few depth breaths to in order to remain calm.

Podium

In some venues a person might be required to use a podium. The advantage of a podium is that one has a place to rest notes. One should not use the podium as an arm rest. Many podiums have adjustable height microphones. One should adjust the height of the microphone at the beginning of a talk. We will have more to say about microphone shortly. Some speakers detest the use of a podium. They want to be out where they can mingle with the audience; they do not want to hide behind a podium. If a person is speaking from behind a

podium, from time-to-time the person may want to step out from behind the podium. Moving out from behind podium allows there to more of a connection between the speaker and the audience. Whether or not the speaker can become more visible to the audience will greatly depend on the particular setting. A podium does introduce a more-formal atmosphere for a talk. If a person is not the first speaker to talk at the podium, it may be necessary to first clear it from another person's things. We recommend that such items be cleared off the podium before beginning a talk.

Lighting

Usually a host or the conference organizers will adjust the lighting in the room. However, if they have done their jobs poorly and a speaker can improve the lighting, then by all means, at the beginning of the talk a speaker should adjust the lighting. A presenter can solicit input from the audience while performing this action. Is this better? How about now? One should not depend on good lighting for reading handheld notes. Sometimes a room is simply too dark to read notes written on paper. If a person requires reading glasses, it may be awkward to be reading notes in a dark room. Many venues have blinds or curtains on the windows. A speaker can solicit the help of an audience member or two to open or close these as needed.

Microphone

There are at least three ways of speaking from a microphone, and the most-common ways are reviewed next.

- *Lapel*: Lapel microphones are small ones that typically attach to a shirt collar, pocket, or a pinch of clothing. A host will usually assist in pinning the microphone on the individual giving the talk. Before the presentation, a speaker should learn how to turn the microphone on and off; this statement applies to all types of microphones. There may be times during the talk when a speaker needs to turn the microphone off, for example, if a presenter is getting feedback from another microphone in the room where an audience member is asking a question from. Once the microphone is on, a speaker should test it. One should adjust the microphone to the best position—ideally where one is still able to turn one's head, speak, and have the audience hear. It is uncomfortable to have to give an entire presentation with speak, one's neck bent over in a particular direction. The lapel microphone is convenient because it is small, comfortable, often has a good sound, is wireless, and keeps one's hands free to gesture.

- *Handheld:* Handheld microphone require skill to use properly. It is important to keep the microphone the proper distance from one's mouth while speaking. Holding a microphone up to one's mouth for an hour can become tiring. If the microphone is not wireless, a speaker must be careful not to trip over the cord. When using the microphone, an individual should try not to breathe into it directly, as this action can make a loud and distracting sound. For those who have little experience using microphones, one should be aware that sometimes microphones can produce an echo-like effect that is distracting to the speaker. Having the microphone in one's hand makes it more difficult to gesture or to point to objects on slides.
- *Stand:* Before one begins to a presentation, one should adjust the height of the microphone stand to suit one's needs. It is very awkward to be leaning over or straining upward to a microphone for an hour.

One should try to adjust the microphone so that one is comfortable behind it, and one's mouth is located the proper distance away from it. Note that in some countries it is traditional to stand before a microphone while in others it is traditional to sit. In either case, similar adjustments will need to be made. While using the stand, one's hands will be free to gesture. Some people tend to fidget while sitting, so when an individual is using a microphone stand and sitting down, the person may want to fold one's hands in front while not gesturing.

In each of the three cases just described, at the beginning of a talk, an individual should make sure that the microphone volume is appropriately adjusted. If at all possible, one should try to practice using each of these types of microphones. Even better, an individual should try to arrive at the presentation venue in advance to test the microphone. Of course, in many circumstances this practice run will not be feasible. One should be aware that some venues have echoes and possibly feedback with their sound systems. This noise can be a distraction, and a speaker may not be able to remedy the situation. One should not let such issues become real distractions, but rather use them to concentrate even harder on the material at hand.

As noted earlier, the organizers at large venues often provide the audience members with a couple of microphones for asking questions. These microphones can interfere with the one used by the speaker. So, when questioned are being asked, it may be a good idea for a speaker to switch off the primary microphone temporarily.

Some speakers are simply not comfortable using any type of microphone. If someone is giving a talk in a small venue, the person may be able to politely refuse the use of a microphone. One should project one's voice loudly and ask the audience if they are able to hear clearly. If the audience responds 'yes' to this test, then the speaker can safely dispense with the microphone. As the talk goes on and one becomes fatigued, one should make sure to continue projecting one's voice.

Summary of the Setting for a Presentation

As we have seen in this section, there are many different aspects to the setting of a presentation. An individual must be prepared to handle different situations and to adjust on the fly. One should always try to make the best use of the setting, and if possible, one should make all the necessary adjustments to things such as sound, lighting, positioning of the microphone, and so on at the beginning of a talk. When necessary, an individual can ask the host, the conference session chair, or any available technical support for assistance.

PREPARING FOR A PRESENTATION

Introduction

In this section we provide additional tips about preparing for a presentation. Once an individual has selected a topic, one should begin preparing the presentation by clearly defining objectives. One should continually evaluate and tweak the presentation based on these objectives. One should avoid procrastination as much as possible, especially when research is necessary. We recommend that everyone create a timeline for the development of a talk. As with most projects, one frequently needs to budget a great deal more time than one had anticipated.

Specifically, in this section we present ideas about rehearsing a talk; notes corresponding to a talk; many aspects of multimedia, including figures and tables, hypertext, audio, videos, and demos; and conclusions.

Rehearsal

To perfect a presentation, one must rehearse frequently. One should rehearse alone, perhaps in front of a mirror, as well as in the presence of others. The trial audience should match the profile of the real audience, and they should be encouraged to provide honest feedback. During a rehearsal, one needs to carefully note and correct flaws, as they are discovered. One should not delay in making corrections because if one forgets about these changes, they may accidentally appear in the live show.

As an individual rehearses, one should pay special attention to transitions between visual aids. One should also time the rehearsals. One needs to be aware that the actual presentation may be delivered faster because of the adrenaline rush involved. On the other hand, questions might slow a speaker down considerably. For optimal results it is wise to rehearse in the presentation room and with the equipment that will actually be used during the live show. One should be prepared to extend a talk if one would finish too early, or cut some material out if one is running out of time. It is almost always preferable to finish early rather than late.

The one caution to rehearsing a talk is that it is possible to over rehearse. When a person actually delivers a talk, the person should not appear as a robot who has simply memorized the talk. Nor should the speaker appear bored with the material in the talk. A good talk usually involves some ad libbing. An individual wants to be prepared, but one needs to keep the content fresh. One's enthusiasm for the material will go a long way toward keeping up the audience's energy level.

Notes

One should prepare notes regardless of how confident the person feels about an upcoming presentation. These notes will come in handy if the speaker gets stuck. A large audience can rattle most speakers. The notes should be an outline comprised of keywords and short phrases. Notes can be recorded on index cards, sheets of paper, using a mechanism from the slide-formatting tool, or in a variety of the other ways. A speaker should not rely on the notes as a script. Reading directly from note cards is boring and may be impossible in poor lighting. One should always use a large font when preparing notes. We recommend that a speaker rehearse enough not to need notes, except for requiring them in emergency situations when drawing a total blank. Presenters are generally more nervous when they start a presentation, so have more-comprehensive notes for the beginning of the talk. Once a speaker's talk is flowing well, the notes can be used to monitor where the person is in the presentation. Then, if a speaker gets off track, the person can quickly regain position without the audience realizing the lapse. Once a talk is finished, speakers should be sure to gather up any notes and take them for the next time that the presentation is given.

MULTIMEDIA

Introduction

In this section we provide tips about using multimedia in a presentation. Multimedia can be used to spruce up a presentation. However, designing good-quality visuals, audio, video, demos, and the like can require enormous amounts of time. This time can sometimes be spent more effectively on improving the text on the slides, augmenting the list of references, or rehearsing the presentation. When employed effectively, multimedia can be used to capture the audience's attention and get a point across. But, in many presentations where there is a glitch, the glitch is due to a problem with the technology involving the multimedia in the presentation. If a person does decide to use multimedia in a presentation, the person needs to

make the materials as robust as possible. Also, individuals need to make sure that the venue provides the capability to utilize or play the materials at presentation time. There is little point spending long hours developing materials that have no chance of being seen.

In this section we briefly discuss the use of figures and tables, hypertext, audio, video, and demos. Similar comments would apply to other forms of multimedia.

Figures and Tables

The type of content that a presentation contains will determine how well the presentation can benefit from the inclusion of figures and tables. Introductory figures are a nice way to explain concepts to an audience, and many people find images more appealing than reading a bunch of text on a slide. Tables can be used to express relationships among a set of variables or concepts. A well-designed table can usually convey a great deal of information clearly and in a small amount of space. A thoughtful sprinkling of figures and tables throughout a presentation can often make the presentation more accessible and interesting to audience members.

Hypertext

In the previous section we talked about including figures and tables in a presentation. The comments given in that section apply to static webpages. For example, a speaker might want to display a figure of rendered hypertext. Or, a person might decide to display a set of webpages that reside locally on a personal machine. These situations usually present few problems. However, sometimes a presenter might want to go live to the web and display hypertext, and possibly follow live hyperlinks. Obviously, inclusion of such hyperlinks during a talk requires a good and reliable Internet connection, and the ability to select such links in real-time. If at all possible, in advance of the talk, it would be good to load the webpages to be used on the system where the talk will actually be given. In this way, if the material is cached, it will reduce the load time during the actual presentation. In going live to a site there is always a chance that the site will be down or perhaps even blocked by a firewall. Thus one cannot rely too heavily on surfing the web during a presentation. Many speakers have become flustered and wasted several minutes of time trying to load webpages during a presentation.

Audio

Selective use of audio clips can be a great way to enhance a presentation. However, an individual must be sure that the resources in the room are appropriate to broadcast the sound loudly enough so that all audience members can hear the audio well. In a large auditorium, holding a microphone up to the laptop's speaker may not produce the desired sound quality. There are certainly cases where audio inclusion is an absolute must, but in most cases, it may be just another nice touch. Thus a presenter must exercise careful judgment in using audio.

Video

A well-prepared video can add a great deal to a presentation and really capture an audience's interest. However producing a high-quality video takes a tremendous amount of time. For those planning to include a video presentation, we strongly recommend testing the video on the actual system where the presentation will be held before giving the talk. There are a host of different reasons why videos can fail, and they do fail often and trip up speakers. It is not a good idea to use a video during a presentation unless the video is stored on the local machine and truly adds value to the presentation.

Demos

In this section when we refer to a *demo* we mean a digital demonstration and not a physical demonstration. Just as in the case of videos, demos can add a great deal to a presentation. However an effective demo usually takes a lot of time to prepare. In addition, even well-rehearsed demos seem to fail and at the worst-possible times (Jobs, 2011). If someone has the time and energy to produce a high-quality demo, the demo could greatly enhance a talk. However the audience usually gets restless while waiting for a presenter who is struggling to get a demo working. So, for those who decide to include a demo, it is also necessary to prepare a backup plan in case for some unforeseen reason the demo fails.

Multimedia Summary

Adding multimedia to a presentation can enhance it both in facilitating the audience's understanding of a concept and by adding a dynamic aspect to the presentation that appeals to the senses of the audience members. However preparing high-quality multimedia often requires lots of time. In addition, the multimedia involved in a presentation is usually more prone to failure than straightforward PowerPoint material. Multimedia requires the use of more-complex software and equipment than a standard presentation would. Thus, when developing a presentation, one should use careful judgment about whether or not to include multimedia in a presentation and about which types of multimedia to include.

Summary of Preparing for a Presentation

In this section we began by discussing the process of rehearsing a talk. The key points were to make sure that one is thoroughly prepared to deliver the talk, but yet not over prepared to the point where one is bored with the content or appears to be an automaton delivering something with no feeling and from rote memory. We next described the utilization of notes. For those who have given just a handful of presentations, notes can be a tool that can boost one's confidence enough to get the person up in front of an audience. On the other hand, an individual should not rely on notes too heavily, and no one should be consistently reading from notes during a technical presentation. Following this material, we included a lengthy discussion about multimedia. It seems that about 50% of all talks that include multimedia suffer from a glitch. However, given that properly-prepared and -executed multimedia can add so-much value to a talk, it is sometimes worth the risk and investment of time to develop high-quality multimedia, including videos or demos. Generally, figures and tables should be included in talks to help make the presentation more-visually appealing and to facilitate the audience's understandings of hard-to-grasp concepts. In the next section we turn our focus to equipment.

PRESENTATION EQUIPMENT

Introduction

This section provides a number of useful tips regarding the equipment that will be used during a presentation. Although we have not intended this material to be comprehensive, the reader will find that it covers many different items. We discuss projection systems, laptops, memory sticks, CDs, VGA cables, email, Internet connectivity, fonts, caching, displays, blackboards, whiteboards, easel pads, laser pointers, remote controls, overhead projectors, and smart rooms. Let us begin by providing comments about projection systems.

Projection Systems

The more a person knows about the basic setup of projection systems, the better off the person will be. And, with the current mobile projection systems, some presenters prefer to bring one's own pocket portable projector. If one is carrying around a light-weight projector at all times, one can give ad hoc presentations, for example, while traveling. Although convenient to carry around, one does give up a degree of brightness and contrast with the smaller systems. For a review of mobile projection systems, we refer the reader to TopTenReviews (Mini Projectors, 2011). One should be ready to setup one's presentation, hook together the various cables, switch on the projector, and adjust the projector's settings. Many venues will not have a technical-support person available to assist, and (surprisingly, or not) sometimes the host will not be capable of setting things up properly either. Thus it is best to be able to handle the basics individually. If is a person is not sure about the way to connect computers, projectors, and cables, that person may want to get a lesson about this process before taking a show on the road. Some systems are finicky about the order in which various items are switched on, and they may only work properly when the 'correct' order is followed. If at all possible, one should arrive at the venue where one will give a talk about ten minutes in advance in order to try to set things up. Even better is the situation where the host can have someone set the presentation up in advance of the speaker's arrival, and then when the speaker arrives ten minutes early, the speaker can check to make sure that everything is working and being displayed properly. Ten minutes prior the talk is when one can learn the operation of the remote control, microphone-volume setting, and so on. There may be times when one needs to make adjustments to the screen as well. Some presenters seem to enjoy using two projectors and screens in parallel, but this technique is rarely used effectively. So we recommend using one screen only rather than bouncing back and forth.

Laptops and Tablets

Many presenters prefer to deliver a presentation from a personal laptop or tablet. In this section one should read laptop, as "laptop or tablet." This situation is understandable, especially if the person plans to make use of many different files on the laptop. In addition, a personal laptop will have all the correct fonts loaded; the person will be familiar with its mouse; and so on. However, for security reasons there are venues, for example, the United States Naval Academy, where a speaker would not be allowed to connect a laptop to the network. Thus it is always a good idea to check in advance and see if one can use a personal laptop, or if one will need to get the materials sent over to a different system somehow. And, of course, the question is how to get the materials to that system in advance of a talk. When a group of people are presenting their work in succession, it is sometimes not practical to have every presenter use a personal laptop. Switching out laptops can take a considerable amount of time. In this case a speaker may need to email the presentation to the person whose laptop is going to be used to deliver all of the presentations. This machine could be one that the speaker is not familiar with, or it may be running an operating system that the speaker is not comfortable using. It is worthwhile trying to get basic familiarity with as many types of computers as possible and also with the main operating systems in use. Finally, one should be cognizant of the amount of battery life remaining on a machine. We usually just plug in to the nearest power source in order to have one-less thing to be concerned about.

Memory Sticks

If an individual plans to arrive with a talk loaded on a memory stick, it would be a good idea to check with the host in advance if one can actually use thumb drives at that venue. For example, at the United States Naval Academy, no one is allowed to use flash drives due to the security risks associated with them (USB, 2011). As noted in the previous section, one laptop may be 'chosen' to be the laptop that all presentations are given from during, for example, a conference session. Individuals should consider the security risks to personal laptops when having other presentations loaded onto personal machines, particularly if the presentations are to be loaded from a thumb drive. When an individual is delivering a presentation from a thumb drive, it is usually a good idea to copy the presentation to the local machine. After a talk, if one is intending to delete a talk from the local machine, one should make a note to do that since one will usually be busy answering questions and be distracted at the end of a talk.

CDs

If a person plans to arrive with a CD with multimedia or a presentation loaded on it, the same comments made about memory sticks apply. In addition, one will need to make sure that the venue provides a place where a CD can be read, unless, of course, the individual will be able to use a personal laptop. It is a good idea to copy the material from the CD onto the local machine, and then at the end of a talk to clean up the local machine as appropriate.

VGA Cables

It is usually a good idea to carry one's own VGA cable to a talk since they seem to disappear like frosted cupcakes at a gathering of young children.

Email

If possible, an individual should email the host the presentation and other materials in advance of one's arrival. It is also a good idea to email the presentation to oneself. Sometimes it is also worth putting the presentation on the web, either in a 'secret location' where one can grab it or simply put it out there for the general public where it can be accessed, for example, via a hyperlink.

Internet Connectivity

If an individual plans to use the Internet, one should check with the venue in advance and let them know that one requires Internet connectivity. Once an individual arrives at the venue, one should test out the Internet from the presentation room. If one is downloading any material from the Internet, it is a good idea to download all materials in advance of a talk. This strategy should reduce download times during a talk.

Fonts

If one is using any nonstandard fonts in a presentation, it will be important to make sure that the machine one will be using for the presentation (in this case not a personal machine) contains those fonts. We have seen many presentations involving mathematics where the formulas were completely unreadable due to font issues. Again, if possible, one should conduct a trial run of the talk on the actual system where one will deliver the talk to help detect any font issues in advance.

Caching

We mentioned in the previous section that, if at all possible, when using the web during a presentation to preload all the pages and materials that will be viewed over the course of the presentation. This step should reduce the load time for these materials during the actual presentation since they will be retrieved from cache on the local machine rather than over the Internet.

Displays

When speaking, an individual should be able to view the personal display while facing the audience. If one needs to rely on the main screen to see materials, one may find that one often has to turn one's back to the audience. An individual may need to use a certain function-key combination to get the display from the laptop to show up on an external projector. For example, one might need to press the FN + F4 keys in combination. On some systems repeatedly pressing these keys will allow one to display on the laptop only, the projector only, or a combination of both, respectively, and the latter is usually what works the best. It is a good idea to do all required password entries, manipulations, and last-minute tweaking before projecting the material on the main screen. If the display cannot be located near the presenter, the person may be forced to use the audience's screen to see the slides, for example, in this case someone may be advancing the slides for the speaker or a speaker may be using a remote control to advance the slides personally. In the case of distant display as in others, one should try to face the audience as much as possible.

Blackboards, Whiteboards, and Easel Pads

When using blackboards, whiteboards, or easel pads, an individual will need appropriately colored markers or chalk, and an eraser. One should write with a large legible block-style font, and use only the areas of the board or pad that are visible to the entire audience. Writing in this manner may require practice. A speaker should give a courtesy query to the audience such as "Can everyone read this material?" If the presenter will be referring to written text repeatedly, such as an outline, then that information should be recorded in a special place such as the far-left edge of the board. After writing points of interest on the board, an individual should move to a location that does not obstruct the view of audience members. As much as is practical, one should always face the audience when one talks about the information on the board.

If writing in a restricted space, the presenter will need to erase material. One should practice erasing in a systematic way. Before erasing something one should make sure that the audience has had the appropriate amount of time to view the material, and perhaps jot the material down. After one has confirmed this fact, the person should quickly erase the material so that no time is wasted. If using chalk, one should not touch one's clothes or bang the eraser on the board. When erasing a board, one should try to erase the writing completely. When using markers, one should keep them ink-side down. This way ink will be near the tip of the marker when one needs to write. One should not assume that any markers which one finds in the room will still contain ink; markers need to be checked before one begins. It is a good idea to keep in mind that black ink and blue ink are much easier for the audience to see than red ink and green ink. One should not fidget with markers, for example, one should not click their caps. With both chalk and markers, one should take care not to touch one's face for that might leave distracting smears.

Generally, an individual will use blackboards, whiteboards, and easel pads in more-intimate settings. Such tools are probably not appropriate for large audiences unless one has excellent lighting or can project what one is writing onto a larger screen. The advantages of these tools are that they are somewhat interactive and dynamic, plus one can erase, delete, edit, and so on. That is, these media are free form. The disadvantage is that it takes considerable time to write things down and erase them, and there is quite a bit of skill involved in writing neatly and in an organized fashion in a small space. Of course, while writing on a board, one will pretty much have to turn one's back to the audience. Another option is writing on an overhead-projector-like screen where one's output will be displayed by a projector. In this case the individual will be facing in the direction of the audience, but the person's head will be facing down while writing.

Laser Pointers

Laser pointers are a good tool for pointing to specific items on the screen, particularly if one needs to be positioned far from the screen. However laser pointers can be abused. People who point to every bullet on every slide are overusing the laser pointer. Nervous speakers often have shaky hands. While using a laser pointer, this shaking causes the laser light to rock back and forth; this flashing is distracting to the audience rather than helpful. If an individual does not have a steady hand, the person should refrain from using a laser pointer. Note that laser-pointer batteries do occasionally die during talks. One should change a laser-pointer's batteries periodically and perhaps bring a back-up pointer as well. Individuals should be careful not to shine the laser in the eyes of audience members.

Remote Controls

If is an individual is positioned far from the computer and cannot advance slides without a long walk, it might be helpful to use a remote control. It is a good idea to learn to use the buttons on the remote control before beginning a talk. This lesson will prevent one from going backward with the slides when one meant to go forward, and vice versa. If the battery in the remote control dies, one may need to ask an audience member to assist one in advancing the slides. The requests that one will give in this case are "next slide please" or "next," and "back." At the end of the talk, a question might necessitate one giving a request such as "please go to slide 17." For this reason and others, it is worth numbering the slides.

Overhead Projectors

Overhead projector use has fallen off dramatically since the year 2000. If an individual decides to use an overhead project with transparencies, the person should first confirm that one is actually available at the presentation venue. One needs to practice placing slides efficiently and accurately on the projector, and it can be helpful to practice rotating or flipping slides over that have gotten switched around. One should be careful to place the slides so that the edges are parallel to the edges of the projector. This technique will prevent audience members from having to tip their heads to view the slides. Inserting spacers between plastic slides is a good idea in order to prevent them from sticking together, and for the speaker to be able to separate them quickly. One should not abuse the technique of overlaying slides because frequently having to put up a series of slides and align them can be time consuming and also distracting to the audience. If an individual is writing on an overhead-projector screen, the person needs to write in straight lines across the screen, neatly, and large enough that audience members can read what one is writing.

Smart Rooms

The venue of a presentation may be a *smart room*. These rooms usually provide various types of multimedia equipment and projection systems. Most smart rooms have a set of instructions taped to the top of one of the nearby desks that describes how to use the equipment. However they do not typically have a password displayed in public view. Hopefully, the host can provide a speaker with the password required to logon to the system. If

the host has never used the smart room before, a speaker may need to read the instructions in order to be able to setup the presentation. If one has access to a smart room, it is worth going there to practice learning how to use the equipment. The operation of the equipment in many smart rooms is similar. Many of these rooms have cables taped to the floor in places that would be natural for a presenter to walk. One should avoid stepping on cables or accidentally unplugging a cable by a kick, as this action could cause a reboot of a computer and that could delay a talk by five minutes. In such rooms one needs to be careful not to trip on cables to prevent injury and embarrassment.

Summary

In this section we covered a wide range of issues relating to equipment. If an individual gives a lot of presentations, the person is bound to come up against many of the issues mentioned here and perhaps others. If a host or no technical-staff members are available to assist an individual, the person will need to take charge. Thus it is important to have a basic working knowledge of presentation equipment. Equipment does fail occasionally, so it is always worth having a backup plan. That plan may sometimes mean delivering a talk with no visual aids. For this reason we always bring a hardcopy of our entire presentation to deal with a worst-case scenario.

SUPPLEMENTAL MATERIALS

Introduction

This section covers a number of important topics relating to supplemental materials. Even though a person has designed a great talk, there may be other items that could enhance one's efforts and help the audience gain a better understanding of the presentation. We cover issues such as glossaries, copies of slides, forms and questionnaires, and exercises and problems in this section. Of course, if one is giving a talk to a large audience, individual handouts are impractical. This section pertains to smaller audiences where handing out individual materials is reasonable. Most technical talks do not include props, but if appropriate, props can often be used effectively at a talk. Grace Hopper was known for bringing a nanosecond with her.

Glossaries

Suppose that one is giving a highly-technical talk. In such a case it may be worthwhile distributing a one-page glossary to members of the audience so that they can refer to it to jog their memories about terms that were presented earlier in the talk. Distributing such a glossary could help a speaker retain members of the audience who otherwise would be lost due to having had a key definition slip their minds. Of course, if a talk involves only a few relatively unknown terms, it does not make sense to go to the effort of putting out a glossary.

Copies of Slides

There are people who distribute copies of their slides to all audience members. Usually, the slides are printed six per page and duplexed to save paper. Sometimes the slides are handed out well in advance of the actual presentation so that audience members will have a chance to review the contents of the talk, and have an opportunity to do some homework in preparation for the talk. Distributing a hardcopy of the slides also means that audience members have something to take with them to remember the presentation. In addition, during the presentation, audience members can jot down notes on the actual slides. If audience members are attending a handful of talks on a given day, they may prefer to have a hardcopy of an individual's slides since it may not be possible for an audience member to absorb the material contained in all of the talks in real time. At some events presenters are requested to bring a predetermined number of copies of their slides for distribution. This number may not be enough to hand out copies of the slides to everyone in the room, but those most interested can pick up a copy of the slides either on the way into the talk or the way out, if copies remain.

Forms and Questionnaires

There are times when an individual needs to or wants to obtain feedback from audience members about a talk or the research presented in a talk. In this case one might decide to distribute a form or questionnaire to the audience members. If the material requires completion with a number-two pencil, one will want to bring pencils to the presentation. Usually such forms and questionnaires will consist of a single page, as one does not want to burden audience members with work for attending the talk. Note that at some conferences organizers distribute talk-evaluation sheets in order to solicit audience feedback on the quality of a talk.

Exercises and Problems

Occasionally a speaker may distribute a page of exercises or problems to the audience. These items are usually to engage the audience further. Such materials can enhance the audience's understanding of the presentation. They can also be designed for active learning, and they add a dynamic component to the talk. If an individual decides to distribute materials to the audience for completion during a presentation, one will need to be careful with time management. It can be difficult to have the audience regroup after they have been working on individual or team exercises. However it is worth noting that such dynamic exercises seem to engage the audience in ways that a more-standard presentation cannot.

Summary

In this section we have covered a number of issues relating to supplemental materials to be distributed at a talk. The comments in this section pertain to relatively small audiences say in the range of 10 to 30 people. One should carefully evaluate the advantages and disadvantages to handing out supplemental materials. If used properly, supplemental materials can enrich an audience's engagement and understanding of a presentation. It is wise to include contact information and a link to a website in any materials that one distributes. We usually include the date on such materials as well.

TALK ADVERTISEMENTS

Introduction

This section deals with the standard ways of advertising a talk. It is usually up to the speaker to provide advertising materials. Advertising a talk properly can mean the difference between having a respectable-size audience and having essentially no audience at all. Here we discuss the abstract for the presentation, fliers, and email notifications.

Presentation Abstract

It is common practice to provide an abstract for a host, and this abstract usually serves as the primary advertisement for a talk. The abstract describes a talk in summary format. At a bare minimum one will need to provide a descriptive title of a talk. But, the abstract should also make the talk sound interesting and relevant in order to encourage people to attend. Even if the talk is technical, it is not wise to make it sound out of reach to potential audience members.

There are several important issues involved in developing an abstract for a talk. In all likelihood a speaker probably has an abstract prepared for a paper on the subject of the talk. Even if this abstract is nicely formatted in a particular typesetting system such as LATEX (see the chapter covering LATEX), it cannot be used for the talk abstract 'as is.' Even if the content were proper for advertising a talk, which is quite unlikely, the formatting of the document will need to change. For example, when a LATEX file gets opened at its destination, it will have $'s and other special symbols that are not formatted correctly. Once the abstract is sent via email, the receiver is likely to forward the email directly to the intended audience. Therefore an abstract should be sent in plaintext to avoid formatting problems, unless other arrangements are agreed upon.

Figure 1 shows a sample plaintext abstract. Note that with plaintext, the absence of formatting may be noticed by the reader. In our example, the umlaut is missing in 'Prüfer,' and the variables are not italicized. However these variances will be much less distracting than the code needed to apply them.

It is fine to work with the abstract from a paper, but it should be reviewed and tweaked for the talk. Edit out-of-place terms such as 'paper' to make the abstract relevant for the presentation. If the abstract begins "This paper proves" then change it to read "This talk delves into" or some other appropriate phrase. Sometimes a poster for a talk will be created and displayed on bulletin boards. As in Figure 1, an individual will want to center titles and names (by adding white space to the plaintext) to suggest an appropriate display format.

Another consideration is the audience of a talk. The talk needs to be tailored to the audience, and the abstract should describe the talk as one intends to deliver it. If the audience is highly knowledgeable on the subject, then one should present the talk differently than if one is presenting to a group for whom the subject is entirely new. The abstract that one provides should reflect such differences. A presentation on node rankings can be quite different if the audience is a group of general

Figure 1. Sample abstract for advertising a talk

Sequential and Parallel Algorithms
for Some Problems on Trees

by Raymond Greenlaw
United States Naval Academy

A node (edge) ranking of a tree is a labeling of the nodes (respectively, edges) using natural numbers such that on the path between any two nodes (respectively, edges) with the same label there is an intermediate node (respectively, edge) with a higher label. A node (edge) ranking is optimal if the highest label used is as small as possible. These problems have applications in scheduling the manufacture of complex multi-part products. A Prufer code of a labeled free tree with n nodes is a sequence of length n-2 constructed by the following sequential process: for i ranging from 1 to n-2 insert the label of the neighbor of the smallest remaining leaf into the i-th position of the sequence, and then delete the leaf. Prufer codes provide an alternative to the usual representation of trees. We'll discuss algorithms for these problems from both sequential and parallel perspectives. The talk only assumes a basic knowledge of graph theory and should be accessible to computer-science undergraduate majors. This research is joint work with Pilar de la Torre, Magnus Halldorsson, Rossella Petreschi, Teresa Przytycka, and Alex Schaffer.

---

students versus a group of graph theorists. It may be possible to restructure the presentation on the spot to account for audience variance, but if the abstract is written at an inappropriate level for the target audience, potential audience members may not show up. It is important to remember that the title and the abstract are key advertisements for most talks.

Frequently, one will give the same talk at multiple venues. It is a good idea to tailor each talk and abstract for the different audiences. We recommend maintaining a directory containing all versions of the talk with the accompanying abstracts. By keeping a copy of all abstracts, one can quickly choose an existing abstract which will require a minimum of tweaking for a repeat presentation. We usually name the abstracts based on where the talk was given. For example, here are labels for three versions of an abstract provided to the University of Washington (uw-030410.txt), the University of Central Florida (ucf-022208.txt), and the Georgia Institute of Technology (gatech-050108.txt). If one decides to recycle an abstract, one should make certain to use the name of the current institution in the advertisement.

While preparing a talk abstract, if the subject is in a discipline that few people are familiar with include language such as "this introductory talk covers ..." or "no prior knowledge about ... is assumed." Hopefully, potential audience members will attend the talk for the opportunity to explore a new subject. If they feel the talk is too in-depth, over their heads, or too far from their field, people will not attend. One should not promise things that one cannot deliver, but by the same token one should try to make the abstract appealing.

If co-authors are involved with the work, they should be acknowledged at the end of the abstract (see Figure 1). It may be appropriate to send a biographical sketch, also in plaintext, along with the abstract. The biographical sketch may also need to be adjusted for the given venue.

Individual should try to be prompt when submitting abstracts and biographical sketches. An efficient means of turning off a host is to make them have to track down a speaker for information. One should keep in mind that hosts are busy. One should do everything in one's power not to overburden a host regarding a visit. An individual should send the abstract and biographical sketch (if included) in a timely manner in plaintext with the title prominently displayed. This habit will make it more likely that the speaker will be invited back.

Flier

If a person is giving a talk at one's home site, one may be individually responsible for producing an advertisement for the talk. The basic contents of the flier should be similar to the talk abstract. One may decide to include a graphic to catch a passerby's eye, but usually one does not want to make the flier for a technical talk too flashy, of course, the style of the flier is a matter of taste. One needs to make sure to specify the title, location, date, and time for the talk. It is often wise to include contact information as well. An email address along with a phrase such as "Please send inquiries to ABC" allows potential audience members to inquire about the presentation. If an individual is preparing a flier for a speaker who is being hosted, it is nice to provide the speaker with a couple of copies of the flier for personal records.

Email Notification

Presentations are frequently advertised by email. Such messages should include key information in the subject line. The body of the message should contain similar timing and venue information as would be contained in a flier. The email message should be clear about where to seek additional information about the talk. It is traditional to include a biographical sketch of the speaker in such email talk announcements as well. Email notifications about talks can be sent out more than once. Generally speaking, such an announcement should be sent out two or three times—the last time usually on the day before the talk is given. This last-minute reminder can often help bring in a few more audience members.

CONCLUSION

In this chapter we have covered a broad range of topics about presentations: from topic selection to the setting to presentation tips to equipment to handouts to advertising a talk. We hope that the reader will find a number of the suggestions here useful in personal presentations. Undoubtedly, other issues will come up, but the key is to remain flexible and calm. Each time a person gives a presentation one should try to learn something new either about the audience, how to field questions, or how to explain a concept better. As travel costs continue to grow, it may be common to have more talks given online or in a webinar format. For such remote talks the preparation of appropriate materials is even more important, as a speaker will not be able to rely as much on interaction with the audience. In the next chapter we focus on the actual delivery of a presentation, as well on a few issues related to developing materials for a talk.

REFERENCES

Jobs, S. (2011). *Steve Jobs unveiling iPhone 4G: Embarrassing moment for Apple's CEO.* Retrieved March 4, 2011 from http://www.youtube.com/watch?v=oITln1SZe9U

Mini Projectors. (2011). *TopTenReviews: Mini projector reviews.* Retrieved July 14, 2011 from http://mini-projector-review.toptenreviews.com

Toastmasters. (2011). *Toastmasters international: Become the speaker and leader you want to be.* Retrieved March 3, 2011, from http://www.toastmasters.org/

USBs. (2011). *National cyber security alert: Cyber security tip ST08-001, using caution with USB drives.* Retrieved March 4, 2011 from http://www.us-cert.gov/cas/tips/ST08-001.html

Chapter 11
Delivering a Presentation and More

ABSTRACT

In the last chapter, the author described many of the fundamentals of presentations, including items such as the setting of the presentation, multimedia, topic selection, advertising, and equipment. This chapter continues the discussion of presentations with a focus on the delivery, beginning with a section on presentation style, discussing things such as inclusion of audio, animations, pictures, tables, and so on. This material is followed by a section on presentation genres. Next, the chapter talks about articles, surveys, and interview talks. PowerPoint is the topic of the next section, and the chapter provides helpful hints about this presentation software. A section on key slides that appear in most presentations, as well as how to craft them, follows. Then the chapter provides a section on how to cope with common trouble spots. The main content of the chapter wraps up with a section on miscellaneous tips, where a number of useful practical tips are provided regarding presentations. Conclusions and references close out the chapter.

PRESENTATION STYLE

Introduction

Everybody has their own style when it comes to presentations and by no means do we want to stifle anyone's creativity. However some thought should go into developing one's style. And, there are a few basic rules that most of us can agree on to that end. A speaker always needs to be professional and to follow appropriate etiquette. For example, it is not acceptable to be eating a meal or talking to a friend on a cell phone while giving a formal presentation. It is also usually in poor taste to be too flashy, for example, having one's computer play the theme to "Rocky" as one ap-

DOI: 10.4018/978-1-4666-0237-3.ch011

proaches the podium is probably not a good idea. Also, one should not criticize audience members. One should remember The Golden Rule: "Do unto others as you would have others do onto you" (Golden Rule, 2011). Many aspects of a presentation involve common sense and courtesy. Now let us look at a few style issues that address specific topics.

Style Issues Involving PowerPoint

Most people are now using PowerPoint presentation software to create their slides for a presentation. And, we include a full section on PowerPoint later in this chapter. Given that this book is written for a technical audience, there is no need to explain how to use the majority of features of PowerPoint, but rather we will talk about general issues. Note that there are so many features in PowerPoint, the software is bloated. There are features that allow a user to include various animations and sound effects. For example, a user can have text spiral in and when it stops sound a 'bomb' that will startle everyone. This trick might be amusing, but certainly not professional. One should not overdo special effects. Just because there are fifteen-different visual effects available when transitioning from one slide to the next, this fact does not mean that a user should use any of them. If a feature enhances a presentation for most of the audience members, the feature is probably worth using. If the feature only demonstrates to the audience that the presenter is a PowerPoint guru, then the feature should be left out. In any case the features that are used should to a certain degree reflect the style and personality of the presenter.

Most often the content for one's talk will determine how garish the slides should be. If flashy presentations fit an individual's personality, then the person can include animations and sound effects, but their use should not be overdone. One well-placed animation or sound effect will be impressive, but ten will probably be annoying. In general, there are four primary special elements that can be included in a presentation—sound, animation, pictures, and tables. We examine sound and animation in the next section, and pictures and tables after that. Note that PowerPoint has easy ways for us to include these features in presentations.

Sound and Animation

First we will consider sound and then animation. Sound usage should be limited and used only in rare instances. One would not use a typewriter effect that sounds after every letter of every word. An abundance of different sound effects will be distracting. Breaking glass and whistling effects add little to professional presentations. Digital applause as one's talk concludes is in bad taste. Even though friends in the audience may find the clapping amusing, one should not include it. Sound seems to be most effective when someone is playing a recording. For example, in a presentation about Amelia Earhart which the author attended in 2010, the presenter included simulated recordings of Amelia's last transmissions. These recordings were very effective, as one could hear the desperation in her voice escalate as the search for Howland Island was failing—creating a harrowing effect.

Animation is occasionally useful, but it should be used with caution. Animation does not have to be cute little creatures. Some animated transitions might enhance a presentation, as a speaker goes from slide-to-slide. Ideally, animation should be 'invisible.' For example, if a person wants to compare the graphs of several functions together, having them appear one-by-one on the screen in different colors could be an effective way of explaining the issues involved without detracting from the talk. One should not annoy an audience with an excessive amount of animation. The author once attended a talk where each slide looked liked the Ginza District of Tokyo, and although he remembers the appearance of the slides, he remembers nothing of the content. One should not script a talk to parallel an animation. If one gets interrupted or gets out of sync, the plan will backfire unpleasantly.

Pictures on Slides to Simplify Explanations

By including the appropriate pictures on slides one can often help the audience to better grasp a concept that is included in a talk. One can show an image or a chart, and then explain its meaning. In most cases one will not include any text or very limited text with the picture, but instead will simply talk about the graphic. One does not want to make the audience feel that they are viewing a subtitled movie. Many people are visual learners, so understanding a concept via a picture is often easier for them than reading text. And, truth be told, it requires less energy to look at most pictures than it does to read a lot of text.

Figure 1 provides a picture of a circuit as a way of introducing the Boolean-circuit model. Using this graphic, an expert can easily explain the concepts of the model. We would like the reader to contrast the simplicity of this picture with definition 1 that defines a Boolean circuit. (Note that some of the notation used in the definition would also need to be defined.)

Definition 1. *A* **Boolean circuit** *is a labeled finite oriented directed acyclic graph. Each vertex v has a type $\tau(v) \in \{I\} \cup B_0 \cup B_1 \cup B_2$. A vertex v with $\tau(v) = I$ has indegree 0 and is called an* **input**. *The inputs of α are given by a tuple $x_1, ..., x_n$ of distinct vertices. A vertex v with outdegree 0 is called an* **output**. *The outputs of α are given by a tuple $y_1, ..., y_m$ of distinct vertices. A vertex v with $\tau(v) \in B_i$ must have indegree i and is called a* **gate**.

Although the definition gives a precise description of Boolean circuits, inputs, outputs, and gates, the definition would be cumbersome to present on a slide during a talk. Usually, one uses a large font size on slides and with a large font size this material would fill an entire slide, and may even run over. Many audience members would find it difficult to scan and understand such a definition in real time. One needs to balance technical details with the limitations of what the audience can handle in a brief amount of time.

Tables in Slides for Concise Presentation

Data presented in a tabular format can help to make slides concise and simple. Tables can convey lots of information in a small amount of space. As with pictures, one should not include elaborate descrip-

Figure 1. An example of a Boolean circuit

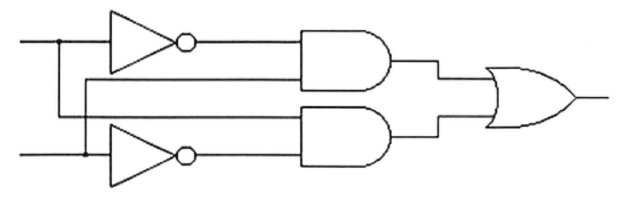

tions with tables—simply explain the meaning of a table verbally. There is no need for a drawn out caption. Table 1 shows a portion of a hiking schedule. Notice how items are positioned within the columns, the spacing between columns, and the (limited) spacing between rows. The material is laid out consistently and aligned precisely. The table conveys a great deal of information in an easy-to-understand and compact format. When including tables in a presentation, one should be careful not to use fonts that are too small for the audience to read. Table 1 contains 10 rows which are probably about the maximum number of rows that one could display effectively on a slide. Note that Table 1 would fill an entire slide when displayed a bit larger.

Slides containing long paragraphs reduce the accessibility of a presentation, so if possible, one should avoid such constructions when developing slides. Presenters should try to be concise and consistent in the development of slides. For example, one should not use the word 'Definition' one time and the phrase 'Term Defined' another if the presenter means the same thing. Generally speaking, one should strive for consistency in slides. However, there are times when one might, for example, take the time to include a formal statement for one problem and then state the suc-

ceeding problems informally in the interest of saving time. One should not make slides too complicated, and one should not include excessive information on a given slide. Leaving an appropriate amount of 'whitespace' contributes to the readability of each slide. There are times when reading aloud the exact content of the slide can be effective, but one should not simply read the content of every-single slide to the audience. This style would get very boring.

It is considered a bad practice to show a busy slide and then tell the audience that one does not have time to talk about it. For example, Table 2 (Greenlaw, Hoover, and Ruzzo, 1995) contains a great deal of information, but if flashed on the screen, even experts in complexity theory would not understand it. A speaker will not impress anybody by showing a crowded and complicated slide. If one is running out-of-time, it is better to skip a slide and not talk about it. One should always be prepared to omit information if there is not enough time to explain it properly. Speakers should avoid the tendency to show a slide simply because it took a long time to prepare. The audience cares little about how much time the speaker put into something. They are interested in seeing an effective and enlightening presentation.

Table 1. A portion of a hiking schedule to illustrate the use of a table in a presentation

Date	Day	Resupply	Location in Evening	Today	Avg.	Total
12	1		Boulder Oaks	26.1	26.1	26.1
13	2	G	Pioneer Mail Trailhead	26.9	26.5	53.0
14	3		Highway 78	25.1	26.0	78.1
15	4		Barrel Springs	23.8	25.5	101.9
16	5	M	Chihuahua Valley Road	26.4	25.7	128.3
17	6	M	Pines-to-Palms Highway	25.4	25.6	153.7
18	7	G, M, L	Idyllwild	26.5	25.7	180.2
19	8		Falls Creek Road	28.2	26.1	208.4
20	9		Mission Creek	25.9	26.0	234.3
21	10		Arrastre Trail	23.0	25.7	257.3

Table 2. A complex table and caption that requires a great deal of explanation. Let be the class of languages accepted by machines of any type in the first column, with Resource 1 polynomially bounded, and some simultaneous bound on Resource 2. 'Max R2' gives the maximum consumption of Resource 2 for which $\mathcal{C} \subseteq NC$ is known. 'Min R2' gives the minimum consumption of Resource 2 for which $\mathcal{C} \supseteq P$ is known. In all cases shown, $\mathcal{C} \subseteq P$, independent of Resource 2, so $\mathcal{C} \supseteq P$ implies $\mathcal{C} = P$. In all cases except the first row, with Resource 2 usage $(\log n)^{O(l)}$, $\mathcal{C} = NC$

Model	Resource 1	Resource 2	Max R2 $\mathcal{C} \subseteq NC$	Min R2 $\mathcal{C} \supseteq P$
DTM	Time $= n^{O(1)}$	Space	$\log n$	$n^{O(1)}$
DTM	Time $= n^{O(1)}$	Reversals	$(\log n)^{O(1)}$	$n^{O(1)}$
D- or NauxPDA	$2^{space} = n^{O(1)}$	log(Time)	$(\log n)^{O(1)}$	$n^{O(1)}$
Alternating TM	$2^{space} = n^{O(1)}$	log(Treesize)	$(\log n)^{O(1)}$	$n^{O(1)}$
Uniform Circuit	Size $= n^{O(1)}$	Depth	$(\log n)^{O(1)}$	$n^{O(1)}$
PRAM	Procs $= n^{O(1)}$	Time	$(\log n)^{O(1)}$	$n^{O(1)}$

A Legacy Technique from the Day of Transparencies

When using transparencies in the days of yore, many presenters preferred to cover up the lower part of the slide and gradually reveal each portion of a slide by sliding down the blocking sheet of paper, as each succeeding point was discussed. The technique worked pretty well if there was a small 'jump in content' between each pair of elements on the slide. In PowerPoint, for example, one can use animation to have these portions appear one-by-one down a page. Another simple way to accomplish this effect is to have a series of slides in which each successive slide contains an additional portion of the page. Creating this effect is easy. One can just take the finished slide, duplicate it several times, and erase the portions in increasing amounts. Then one needs to reorder the slides from the least-to-most material. In this manner one can generate a fully-numbered set of slides displaying the desired effect. And to display them, one simply has to advance the slides by any of the usual methods. This technique works most effectively when the presenter knows what is coming in the next item and does not have to 'backtrack.'

PRESENTATION GENRES

Introduction

Once a topic has been chosen, selecting the content for the presentation depends on the type of talk and the audience. Selecting content for a ten-minute talk at a national conference may involve picking the most-significant theorems and any-supporting definitions. Since the research for such a conference paper has already been done, one can jump right into preparing slides. Developing a fifteen-minute survey talk on vitamins for a nutrition class will require that one factors in students' backgrounds, current research, and future trends. Preparing a thirty-minute talk on the required topic of sorting algorithms for a college-teaching position will require considerable thought up front. How can one make the talk understandable for students? How can one impress the search committee who will see five talks on the same subject? Besides additional audience considerations, in this section we also discuss time constraints, preparation for answering questions, and additional topics on presentation style. We start with issues for a talk based on an article.

Presenting an Article

Article presentations are usually given at conferences. To make the most out of one's limited amount of time, one should select to present only the most-important elements of the paper. Obviously one cannot cover the contents of an entire paper in a short period of time, especially for an audience that may not be expert in the area. One needs to realize that the proof details of one's favorite theorem cannot be appreciated in a ten-minute talk. Complex theorems often require an extensive mathematical background, so merely presenting the preliminaries may take fifteen minutes. If a particular theorem is the most-important result in the work, then it may be worth the extra time. If the theorem is not critical, then simply motivate the theorem, state it, and move on to other considerations. One can state that the paper contains more details, and interested audience members can read the proof of the theorem on their own.

One needs to be realistic about the time slotted for the presentation. Conference-paper talks are usually between ten and forty minutes, with twenty minutes being the norm. Deep results that require extensive proof can be discussed, but only briefly. In mathematical talks of twenty minutes or less, proofs are almost always excluded, unless they are extremely short and easy-to-grasp. It is usually preferable to explain why a result is important rather than to go through its proof in a rushed fashion.

Typically one will begin a talk by providing background for the research. This introduction may include a discussion of the problem's origin. For example, does the work solve a long-standing open problem? How does the work relate to previous research? One must to be sure to credit and cite other people's work if one's results are an expansion of theirs. It is important to discuss the motivation behind one's work before one jumping into specific results. Why are the results interesting and important? As one introduces a topic, one should show illustrative examples so that the audience can quickly grasp definitions. One should avoid long technical definitions, if possible, and to the extent that is possible, one should try to use jargon and notation that is familiar to the audience.

After the including the required preliminary information, one should discuss the results that are described in the paper. One can briefly state the results without going into elaborate explanations. If there is still time left, one can go into the details of one of the more-important results. One should not choose the most-difficult result or rush through an explanation. Placing an explanation directly after a result should help with the flow of the talk. One must check during rehearsal that one has enough time to complete the talk. One should always try to develop the context for one's work, and when appropriate, one should include a section on related research.

It is a good idea to finish a talk by giving some unsolved problems. Researchers are always looking for new problems to study. Posing interesting open questions is an important and an expected contribution of a talk. Figure 2 shows a sample slide with four open problems from a talk on parallel computation. One should explain the questions and their significance. Usually, it is appropriate to include three-to-five problems.

In advance, a speaker should find out whether questions will be allowed during a session or only afterward. If one is running late, the speaker can decide to ask the audience to hold their questions until the end. One may also need to defer a question for later discussion. Methods for handling questions are discussed in the section titled "Trouble Spots" that occurs later in this chapter.

One may decide to bring copies of the full paper to distribute after the talk. The hardcopies become quite useful when one cannot remember all of the details from the paper. For example, if a person asks a question about one of the theorems, a speaker could respond "Good question. The proof details of that theorem are contained

Figure 2. An example of an open-questions slide

Open Questions
• Can an optimal parallel algorithm be developed for building a tree given its Prüfer code?
• Can the Element Distinctness Problem be solved on a CREW-PRAM in $O(\log n)$ time using $n/\log n$ processors?
• Is the edge ranking problem on trees P-complete?
• Can all n-node trees be labeled with the values 1 through n such that neighbors receive pairwise relatively prime labels?

in the paper. I can give you a copy after the talk." As of late, it would be more customary to simply provide an online reference for the paper, from where interested audience members could download the paper.

One must remember to be very selective in what one presents. The success of a presentation depends heavily on the content that one decides to deliver. Too-little content will result in a weak and short presentation, whereas too-much content may frustrate the audience if one does not cover the material effectively. If one plans to give a repeat performance of a presentation at a later date, it is a good idea to make adjustments to the talk shortly after one gives it. In this way desired improvements will be fresh in one's mind. It is very easy to delay making an edit to a presentation and then to completely forget to make the edit at all. Let us build on what we have been discussing in this section but now turn our attention to giving a survey talk.

Giving a Survey Talk

If one is applying for a teaching job, one may be asked to give a survey talk regarding a particular topic or one's current work. Usually these talks are forty-five or fifty minutes long. However a survey talk at a conference might be between ten and thirty minutes long. It is important to provide a good list of references at the end of a survey talk since one will not be able to touch on all aspects of a given topic. Audience members will find the list of references useful.

The content that one selects for a survey talk depends on the audience. One will have to do a lot of research and possess a great familiarity with the topic in order to answer questions related to the subject. The material that one researches must be current. As one delivers the talk, it will be obvious to the audience if one is under-prepared. One should avoid presenting something that one barely understands; if one is not comfortable explaining the topic, it is probably best to present a topic that one is comfortable with.

Collectively, the audience may be very knowledgeable about a topic. And, despite our earlier comments about one trying to be the most expert on a topic in the room, it is possible that some member of the audience will know more about the subject than the speaker. In the best-case scenario this person may be able to add value to the talk, and in the worst-case scenario the person could try to take over the floor or question the speaker's credibility.

When preparing a survey talk, it is okay to omit things in order to save time or to narrow the focus of the talk. If somebody asks a question regarding a topic that one has omitted and is not familiar with, one should feel comfortable saying, "I don't know." If one has some knowledge about the question and some idea of how to respond, but one is not sure how to answer the question directly, one can also say something like "Glad you asked that. This is a technical question that we can discuss after the talk." This postpones the answer until later, so buys the speaker a little-more time to think about the answer, and such a reply may also create a one-on-one discussion opportunity where the solution to the question emerges naturally in a collaborative effort.

A good way to start a survey talk or, for that matter, any talk is with an outline. This road-map tells the audience what to expect from the presentation. At a conference with many talks running simultaneously, an outline allows an audience member to quickly discern if the talk is worth one's time. An outline will also allow a speaker to defer some questions by saying that "Your question is out of the scope of this presentation. I will provide a couple of references after the talk." One should not spend too much time talking about the outline, especially for short talks under fifteen minutes. It will be crucial to spend time explaining the results contained in the presentation.

If possible, in a survey talk one should do more than merely present facts. One should try and synthesize information, group related materials, compare and contrast various items, and organize things in ways that non-obvious relationships among items emerge from the presentation. If possible, the audience should be engaged to contribute, as a survey covers a lot of ground. Surely there will be audience members who can add value to the presentation. And, their contribution may be best added via a short discussion at the end of the talk, just prior to finishing up with references. We like to display references at the end of the talk, and then switch to a slide containing a link to our website. During the closing discussion, we leave that slide displayed so that audience members can jot down OK website's URL. We noted at the beginning of this section that sometimes when requested to give an interview talk one is asked to present a survey. In the next section we focus specifically on general interview talks.

Interview Talk

A topic for an interview talk may be assigned to an individual. This assignment does not necessarily mean that one has to accept any subject. One can ask to present only a specific part of the originally-requested topic. One can also ask to present material for a similar problem, if it is more familiar. In other words, there may be a small amount of room for negotiating a presentation topic for an interview talk. One needs to exercise common sense and a bit of caution in attempting such a negotiation.

In some interview talks one will need to present more than one topic. For example, a teaching position at an undergraduate institution may require an individual to give a 'teaching presentation' on an assigned topic followed by a description of one's research. In such cases it is important to have a good outline, and when necessary, to spend extra time on major transitions. A speaker should not jump from one subject to another without transitioning. Having smooth transitions is one of the key parts of an interview talk. This skill demonstrates that one can effectively switch gears and process a number of different trains of thoughts at once.

For teaching positions at undergraduate institutions, a common request for applicants is that they prepare a talk on their research at a level suitable for upper-class students. The diligent applicant does so and gets a surprise when entering the presentation room and finds there are no students, only faculty! This situation does not mean a disaster. The faculty wants to discern if the applicant can communicate complicated ideas at a level that an undergraduate can understand. The downfall comes when the faculty members get the incorrect impression that the applicant's research is too basic. To avoid this problem, an applicant might want to keep some additional slides handy to raise the level of the presentation for the last ten-to-fifteen percent of the time. If the majority of the talk is easy-to-follow, interesting, and presented well, then losing the audience in the last few minutes with more-complex ideas may work in an applicant's favor, especially at an institution where research is expected. If the position is strictly teaching or the research component is downplayed, then losing the audience is obviously a bad idea. Again, the key idea to grasp is to be prepared and to be flexible.

When preparing for an interview talk, one needs to find out who will be in the audience. One should think about what qualities the interviewers will base their judgment on. Does one need to communicate complex ideas in a clear manner to students? Does one need to convince other researchers that the person is a competent and enthusiastic researcher with whom they would enjoy collaborating? And so on. These days many people have personal webpages displaying résumés and descriptions of one's research interests and accomplishments. In advance of giving a presentation one should look up this information of potential audience members in order to determine who may be knowledgeable about one's research area. One should look at the number and types of publications listed on the résumés of the individuals at the institution where one will interview. This information is a good indication of the research expectation. This can also help one determine how deeply one should discuss one's own research at the interview.

During an interview talk, questions may arise about a topic that one knows little about. One should always be honest, but one can try to put a positive spin on a response such as: "I am interested in learning more about that area, but have not had a chance to explore it yet." One should not get flustered by questions that one cannot answer, but perhaps instead one, can explain how one would go about researching the answer to the given question. One can also use questions as lead-ins to provide more information about one's particular strengths.

Presumably, an interview audience will see presentations from several candidates. One's presentation needs to stand out, especially if all of the candidates are presenting on the same topic. Many of the following ideas are tailored towards teaching positions in undergraduate institutions. One should choose something from the list that fits one's personal style. Or, one can use this list of items to generate additional ideas for how to proceed.

- If one's talk contains a long list of definitions, one can make a handout of them listed in alphabetical order for lists of size ten or less, and listed as they appear in the talk for longer lists. One might decide to use colored paper, but one should be careful to make sure the list is easily readable.
- If students are in the audience, one might incorporate some questions for them into the talk. One can offer a small prize such as a novelty pen or a coin for the correct answer.
- If the talk is on teaching a specific topic, one can design and handout an interesting project or worksheet based on that topic—going beyond the usual textbook problems.
- Also for teaching a topic, one should find out what textbook the institution uses. One should strive to present the material in a more-effective way than the book does. One can ask professors at one's graduate institution for input.
- One should spend some time investigating the topic online and offline. One can look for applications, new developments, figures, or cartoons that could liven up the presentation.
- If using PowerPoint, one might decide to include some limited sound or animation effects. The reader should remember earlier comments presented about these items and not go overboard. Such effects need to be carefully integrated into the presentation.

- One can close the talk with a joke or funny personal anecdote if it relates directly to the material. In any case the talk should end on a positive memorable note, and during the talk, one should attempt to convey one's personality to the extent that is feasible.

More than for any other type of talk, for the interview talk conscientious preparation and practice are vital. This talk is one's best opportunity to secure a position. While one is interviewing, one may not have a chance to meet all the people who influence the hiring choice. The talk may be the only factor these people have as a basis on hiring an individual or not. Even if one does connect with a few people during one-on-one conversations, a poorly-executed talk will likely eliminate one from the competition. It may be a good idea to ask the person in charge of the interview for fifteen minutes down time before the talk. This time can be used to catch one's breath, to perform any last-minute review, to verify that equipment is functioning properly, to go through the slides one-final time, and to check one's appearance during a restroom break. An interview talk can have a huge impact on one's life. One should make sure to deliver such a talk to the best of one's abilities.

POWERPOINT

Introduction

PowerPoint is a software package for developing presentations; it is included in the Microsoft Office Suite. One should not be intimidated by its seemingly infinite number of features. One does not need to know about all these features to make a good presentation with informative and attractive slides. In fact, as we noted earlier, the 'extra' features, such as the animation of objects or sound effects, should be used sparingly. This section considers details such as contrast, repetition, alignment, and proximity of the text to other

content. We also handle issues on font size, tables, and typesetting mathematics. Lastly, we discuss using the software during a presentation. Although this section does not contain a comprehensive treatment of PowerPoint, the material presented here is enough to get one on the way to preparing a good presentation. Readers who already have experience with PowerPoint may decide to skim this section.

PowerPoint-File Formats

There are two types of common PowerPoint files: the *presentation file* (*ppt-file*) and the *show file* (*pps-file*). The ppt-file is used while developing the presentation. When a pps-file is opened, it automatically starts a full-screen slide show. Many people do not realize that the only difference between the two files is the file extension. One can easily convert between these two types by simply switching the file extension. The software handles the files differently based on their file extensions.

Backward Compatibility

Before presenting a talk, one should find out which version of PowerPoint is on the host's computer and which platform the slide show will run on. Every new version of PowerPoint introduces additional features, and a slide show designed in PowerPoint 2010 might not display correctly on PowerPoint 2007. One should test the slides on an equivalent system prior to the actual talk. One needs to verify that the slides will display correctly on that system. There is no universal fix for issues of backward compatibility. If one must use an older version of PowerPoint, one may need to consult the Web to locate a fix to a specific problem. However, the best approach may simply be to upgrade to the latest version.

In order to avoid basic-compatibility problems, we recommend that one uses simple PowerPoint features that comply with all versions. Note that any add-ins—special files imported into the slide show and special fonts—will have to be transferred to the live computer before the presentation begins. One should always make sure to load the presentation onto the computer's hard drive for efficiency purposes. One should not run a presentation from a diskette, CD, or other mobile-storage device. After one finishes the presentation, one may want to delete the materials from the host's computer. It is a good idea to use the most-recent version of PowerPoint, but sometimes one can end up being one version ahead of everyone else. One should at least be aware of potential compatibility problems among the different versions of the software; it is not hard to lookup what the actual issues are between any two specific versions.

PowerPoint Basics

In this section we will discuss some of the commonly-used features of PowerPoint. For anyone who uses Microsoft Word, many of the options, menus, and buttons will look familiar. For people working in the field of information technology, it is probably easiest to simply explore the PowerPoint software on one's own. As one pokes around, one will find that nearly everything is self evidence. For example, there are tools to help with the slide layout. The layouts include several options for including lists, tables, and graphics. Note that most of these selections include a text box at the top for a slide title. Once a user selects a layout that choice will appear each time one inserts a new slide into the presentation. If one prefers to layout one's own slides, one should select the blank layout. One can modify the layout selection at any time.

After one enters a title into a slide, one may wish to manipulate its size or position. However one should keep in mind that the titles in a series of slides generally look best if kept consistent in size. It is often best to simply stick to defaults, unless one is really an expert with the software. When inserting items such as definitions, theorems, equations, and so forth, it is a good idea to use separate

text boxes for each. This style will give the most flexibility for rearranging items. So, whenever one is tempted to hit "Return" while composing, one should consider bringing in another text box instead. If one needs to move the information in a text box to another slide, one should use cut-and-paste. However one must highlight the text one wishes to move because clicking inside a text box and attempting to cut-and-paste will not work, unless some text is highlighted. Inserting new slides and adding material is generally straightforward. One can explore the various options available by checking out all of the pull-down menus.

Before investing too much time into slide development, it is important to save the presentation in a folder. Saving the file is straightforward. One should choose a descriptive name, and we prefer to include the author's initials and date in the name as well, for example, lecture2Week14CyberAttacks-RG-022111.pptx. We prefer to save presentations in their own folders along with any supplemental materials and notes. We should note that PowerPoint has a number of different views—"standard," "formatting," and "slide manipulation." When using the slide-manipulation view, the titles of slides can help one locate a slide quickly from a long list of slides. This view is helpful not only during slide construction, but during the actual slide show, and question-and-answer period. PowerPoint also allows one to associate notes with a given slide.

During the presentation development, one may wish to devote more of the screen to PowerPoint's slide-composition window.

Using Math Type in PowerPoint

For simple mathematical expressions such as variables, one may simply decide to put those in italics. For example, let x denote a natural number greater than five. However, for more-complex mathematical objects, such as formulas, using italics alone may not be enough. Instead of using just italics, we can use the equation editor. On our system this process involves choosing "Object" under the "Insert" pull-down menu, and from there choosing "Microsoft Equation 3.0." After one creates a formula, equation, or variable, one needs to close the dialog box. The object will appear in its own text box in the PowerPoint composition window. One can enlarge this box and move it into any existing text box. We should point out that getting a formula to match the font size of the existing text and aligning the formula with existing text takes some care. By bringing in this object from the equation editor, one has essentially added a graphic to the slide. One will not be able to highlight the formula or variable and make adjustments to the font size, as one can with regular text. One must change the size of the text box containing the object from the equation editor. To help fine tune an object's placement, click inside the text box and use the four directional arrow keys. Sometimes one might not be satisfied with the appearance of mathematical objects as created by the equation editor and displayed in PowerPoint. In that case one might need to create a separate graphic using a different program, and then insert that graphic into PowerPoint. This process can be rather time consuming. Note that there exist freeware programs for both PC and Macintosh machines that allow the user to incorporate LATEX (see chapter on LATEX) into a PowerPoint slide.

Miscellaneous Useful Features in PowerPoint

Introduction

In this section we mention a few additional useful features of PowerPoint. Our goal is not to provide a tutorial on these features but rather to let the reader know what some of the other available PowerPoint options are. The reader will undoubtedly discover other useful features as well.

Lists

PowerPoint contains a feature that allows one to insert lists of all types. The feature is simple to use. Occasionally, one may find PowerPoint doing something strange and displaying one bullet in a size different from the rest. It may not be easy to figure out why, and at times, it is actually easier just to start a new list from scratch.

Tables

PowerPoint provides a convenient feature for inserting tables. We recommend that one designs the table fully before actually implementing it in PowerPoint. Once one knows the table's dimensions, headings, positions of items in each column, and so forth, PowerPoint's table feature will be easy-to-use to enter the table.

PowerPoint Macros

PowerPoint provides a way for a user to create macros. Suppose one has a certain list of steps that one performs over-and-over again during the creation of a presentation. Using PowerPoint's macro feature, it is possible to customize a button that can perform this list of tasks. It will not be difficult for those working in information technology to learn to use PowerPoint macros.

Designing PowerPoint Slides

Introduction

When designing PowerPoint slides, it is important to consider many different elements. Unlike other mediums, a slide offers only a limited space for ideas. Therefore the challenge is to convey roughly the same information in one slide as contained in three or more paragraphs in a paper. Ignoring this space issue may lead to a poor presentation.

It takes a considerable amount of time and effort to create an eye-catching and informative slide show, as well as patience, ingenuity, skill, and a little bit of luck. However one can make an effective slide show by taking into account the four design principles that we discuss next: contrast, repetition, alignment, and proximity.

Contrast

When creating PowerPoint slides, visual *contrasts* will emphasize similarities or differences. Choices must be made on type size and face, color, and spacing. As one creates each slide, one may find it appropriate to group some items. In slide design, regarding contrast, one should keep the following two principles in mind:

- Related items should appear similar to each other from slide-to-slide.
- Unrelated items should appear differently.

Contrast is often one of the first things noticed on a slide.

Repetition

Closely related to the idea of contrast is the design element called *repetition*. By repeating elements, themes, orientations, and other visual structures, a slide show gains coherence. This consistency means we take into account the same elements that were considered for contrast. Again, the choice of type size and face, color, and spacing will create a coherent look. The goal of repetition is to establish consistency and coherence throughout the slide show.

Alignment

As one creates a slide, information should be positioned strategically. Nothing should be placed on a whim or without prior thought. One should use *alignment* to control where the viewer's eyes travel and what catches the eye in what order. The elements of contrast and repetition give the slide uniformity, and alignment links the uniform blocks of information together to create a clean polished appearance.

Proximity

Tying in with the concept of creating blocks of related information is *proximity*. Proximity is the actual physical distance items are placed from each other on the slide. Similar to contrast, items that are related to each other should be grouped together and items that are different should be separated.

FAQ about Slide Design

This section addresses some frequently-asked questions about designing a slide or slide show.

How Much Information Should Go on Each Slide?

There is no precise answer to the question, "How much information should go on each slide?" Obviously, one does not want to overcrowd a slide with too-much information. Each slide should generally get a few points across. Each slide needs to be clear and visible to the audience. One should leave plenty of space between objects to give the slide a more-professional look. Objects include not only text, but tables and figures as well. One can easily change the size of objects to prevent either an overcrowded slide or an excessive amount of empty space. When composing slides, one should plan to leave extra space at the top for a slide title. Also, one should leave an appropriate amount of whitespace on both margins and at the bottom of a slide.

When in doubt, one should put less material on a slide instead of more. Audience members generally have short-attention spans and are exposed everyday to media with images that change every few seconds. So one should keep the slide show moving. One should not spend more than a couple of minutes on a single slide, and most slides will take far-less time to present. It is important to remember that during the presentation one should generally not read the slides verbatim. The slides are merely a visual aid to support one's comments. One should make sure to discuss all the material on a slide. And, one should not expect an audience to read everything on a slide, unless one guides the audience through it. Ideally, the audience is listening to the speaker. The slides help the audience to keep definitions, algorithms, or other concepts in mind, as they hear about these concepts. If one wants to define a term verbally that is also presented on a slide, one can use a slightly different phrasing.

Due to space limitations on a slide, one should not use complete sentences or lots of punctuation, unless really necessary. Abbreviations and keywords take up little space, while keeping the audience informed and the speaker on track. Not only do abbreviations prevent the speaker from reading a slide, they also ensure that each element is pertinent and potent. Acronyms can and should be expanded on verbally. If one has several related items of information that belong on the same slide, they can be put together into a bulleted list for a neat orderly appearance. A bulleted list along with the appropriate commentary can be used to present a lengthy result on just one slide.

Is Changing the Default Font Size a Mistake?

As with many design issues, adjusting font size is a judgment call on the part of the designer. As a general rule, one will use the four design principles described early in the decision-making process, but sometimes one may have to adjust the font size to fit several ideas onto one slide. A font size of 18 point or smaller may be *too* small for the audience to view. It is best to stay at 24 point or higher. One should be as consistent as possible with font size throughout the presentation, especially for similar elements. Note that instead of trying to squeeze more information onto one slide by adjusting the font, one can simply use a series of slides to present the information. This technique will maintain structure and balance between the slides. The opposite problem of having too-little content on a slide can also occur. To within certain limits one can try increasing the font size or adding a figure to help eliminate some of the whitespace.

When Should Tables be Used?

Tables help organize and express relationships among a group of items. Tables can sometimes help consolidate information. One should be careful to make a table visually appealing by applying the four design principles. There should be a discernible contrast between the header and body. All related information within a column should be aligned the same whether right justified, left justified, or centered. A consistent use of type face for equivalent items will create a polished look.

Should Default PowerPoint Templates be Used?

PowerPoint comes with a number of predefined templates. These are convenient to use, and one may find them visually appealing. Whether to use these templates or not depends partly on one's own design abilities. A disadvantage is that the canned slides may look a little less than professional. Since PowerPoint is used worldwide, another concern is that audience members who are familiar with a common template, such as the one labeled "Blends," may find one's presentation stale in its appearance. One advantage to using a template is saving time. Default templates can be lifesavers, especially for a novice. They can also add coherence to the presentation by giving a uniform look to the slide set.

Tips and Common Problems

This section provides a list of hints, and also provides a list of items that are useful for trouble-shooting common problems.

Hints for Composing Slides

The following general items will help one compose consistent and informative slides:

- Use a maximum of five main bullets per slide.
- Use the same conventions throughout the presentation.
- Number the slides.
- Include a footer.
- When there are hyphenated words in titles capitalize both words. For example, write "Self-Loop'" not "Self-loop."
- Punctuation should be in the same style as the text that it follows. For example, a colon following an underlined word should also be underlined.

As a reminder, one should not show a slide to the audience if the slide will not be discussed properly.

When Things go Wrong

Good preparation minimizes the amount of things that are likely to go poorly. Nevertheless, some situations are unavoidable and miscommunications can occur. If something misfires, one should not panic. The following are some tips to help one handle problems and remain flexible:

- Always bring a hardcopy of slides when giving a presentation. In the worst-case scenario a host can make photocopies of key slides and distributed them to the audience.

- Bring a CD and/or pen drive containing the slides. As noted earlier, some settings may not allow one to make use of such items due to security reasons. Also, note that few installations are able to read CDs now.
- Make sure that when the technical-support staff is fixing a problem during a live talk, one has enough room. If one is speaking and the situation permits, one should move away from support personnel who are troubleshooting a problem. If someone else must be at the podium, one should give that person enough room to work. For major problems one may need to delay the presentation until the problem is fixed.
- Prior to beginning a presentation, one can ask for pagers and cell phones to be turned off or placed in silent mode, if the event-directors do not make this request. When cell phones or pagers go off, it is distracting to both the audience and the presenter. And, of course, one needs to make sure to turn silence one's own communication device.
- After the presentation, one should remember to collect all items that one has brought to the talk. People tend to forget laser pointers, purses, briefcases, diskettes, CDs, and pen drives.

Delivering the Slide Show

To start a PowerPoint presentation, one can select "View Show" on the pull-down menu under "Slide Show." There is also a button to start the show on the lower-left hand corner menu bar under the slide-list window. During a slide show, several shortcuts are available to navigate between slides. The following options may be available depending on the system being used. Any of following keys move to the next slide: left mouse button, enter, right-arrow, down-arrow, page-down, and the "N" key. In a similar fashion these keys move to the previous slide: right mouse button, backspace, left-arrow, up-arrow, page-up, and the "P" key.

To go to a specific slide, one can type the slide number followed by the enter-key. Depressing the right mouse button (PC) or moving the cursor around (Macintosh) yields a pop-up menu. Selecting "go" from this pop-up, followed by either "Slide Navigation" or "By Title" gives one a numbered list of the slides plus their titles. One can mouse down in order to select and display a particular item. One can press the ESC-key to finish. Also, at the end of the show, the navigation keys will not 'wrap around' to slide one again. If one hits the right-arrow key after the last slide, the show will end. Similarly, hitting the left-arrow key while on the first slide will not bring one to the last slide.

A complete list of shortcut keys can be found in the online help for PowerPoint. A user may develop a preference of keys for navigating, but one should be aware of alternative keys that perform the same function. It is wise to learn to use mouse pads, 'eraser-like' mice, and hand-held attached mice, too.

KEY SLIDES IN A PRESENTATION

Introduction

Preparing a presentation takes a considerable amount of work. Here we discuss preparing several types of key slides that would normally go in most presentations, including those for an article, a survey talk, and an interview talk. Naturally, an individual will develop one's own style, but the comments given here should be helpful for those with less experience. One can adopt the points covered here that are appropriate to one's own style.

Title Slide

Every presentation should begin with a title slide. This slide includes the title of the talk, the author or authors' names, and acknowledgments for any co-authors and contributors. Many times author affiliations will be included. If the work was supported by a grant, this information can be placed on the title page. One should make sure that the name of the talk is well balanced on the slide. Figure 3 shows an unbalanced title, while Figure 4 shows how to balance the title for a better look. Another version showing additional information appears in Figure 5. Notice that we capitalized the "a" in the words "and" and "at" to make the title more-visually appealing.

Typically, an individual will present one's own work, and the name will appear below the title of the talk. When presenting somebody else's work, include the phrase 'presented by' below the title (see Figure 6).

Figure 3. An example of an unbalanced title

Giving Effective and Colorful Presentations at Any Venue

Figure 4. The title slide originally shown in Figure 3, but balanced

Giving Effective and Colorful Presentations at Any Venue

Figure 5. A sample title slide containing additional information

> Giving Effective And Colorful
> Presentations At Any Venue
>
> by
> Liy Chang
> Chiang Mai University
>
> Joint work with: Karen Gomey (Mountain Front, Inc.)
> John Badham (PCT Brothers & Sons)

Figure 6. An example of a title slide when presenting another's work

> A Trip to the South Pacific:
> Fiji and the Cook Islands
>
> presented by
> Louise Travolta
>
> Work of David Jones and Rachel Green

It is important to distinguish one's original contribution in a talk from the work of others. One must make a special effort to inform the audience of transitions between one's own work and the work of other's. While it is very important to acknowledge other people's contributions, one does not usually identify the specific parts of co-authored papers that an individual contributed to. For example, one would not say that I wrote sections 1, 3, and 7, and Barbara wrote the remainder of the paper.

Overview Slide

An outline or an overview slide usually follows the title slide. Typically, an outline will include five or six bullets. If one has many more than that, it may be a good idea to combine or even omit some sections. As the presentation is being given, one should indicate to the how audience which section of the talk one is presenting. This courtesy will establish a better sense of the presentation's overall structure. One can indicate transitions between sections by displaying another outline slide with the next section to be presented highlighted. Color can be used to accomplish this result.

Following the slide containing the outline of the talk, one will generally start each new section of the talk with a section-opening slide. A series of slides will follow until the desired material in a given section has been covered. In the next section we discuss the 'final' slide.

Concluding Slide

A concluding slide ends the talk. This 'final' slide can be used to wrap up a presentation with a clear ending. If one omits the concluding slide, an audience may have the impression that a speaker left things out, did not finish the talk, or stopped because time ran out. The last slide often contains a summary, references, or a URL where additional information can be found. These days many presentations are available online, and a URL can be given to the presentation itself. Figure 7 provides a sample concluding slide.

References Slide

If there are a lot of references and they are not displayed on the concluding slide, it may be worthwhile to include a separate references slide. One should keep in mind that in order for the references to be readable to the audience, one needs to use a large font. Thus it may not be appropriate to merely copy a bibliography to the back of a talk without making some edits. One may also include a slide at the very end that lists a personal URL. It is worth repeating that when answering questions, one can leave this final slide displayed so that audience members have a chance to write it down.

TROUBLE SPOTS

Introduction

As we have mentioned, trouble spots can come from various sources. And, no doubt preparation is one's best defense against any problems. In this section we provide information about how to avoid and deal with common issues. We cover key things to remember, more on how to handle questions, how to avoid disasters, and how to cope with nervousness. Once one has mastered this material, one can be confident in a fall-back plan in case things do not go as smoothly as hoped. This added confidence will help one deliver a better presentation, and perhaps allow one to think more clearly on one's feet.

Key Things to Remember

Here we summarize important things to remember when one is performing any type of presentation.

- Always have a backup plan for equipment malfunctions.
- Find out how strict the time limit is for one's slot. Be prepared to trim parts of a presentation. Find out if one's time allotment includes a question-and-answer pe-

Figure 7. An example of a concluding slide for a presentation

---

Summary

- Cyber-crime is growing at a rate of 50% per year

- USNA needs a cyber-security center

- Funding is available for such a center

- See `www.usna.cybersecurity` to obtain a copy of this presentation

---

riod, and whether or not the room will be needed immediately afterward.

- Everyone gets flustered at some time—have a way to keep from amplifying the situation if it occurs. Have a plan to move on with minimal pauses. Keep notes handy. The unexpected will happen; the key is to recover from it.

- Respect the audience, and hopefully they will do the same. If they do not, one may have to rectify the situation by politely asking offending members to cease what they are doing. For example, "I think that foot tapping is distracting to other audience members. Thank you."

- If one runs out of material before the allotted time is up, one can solicit questions. Be prepared to answer them.

- If giving a presentation via an electronic medium, be sure one has everything needed. Bring any special fonts or packages used in the presentation. Remember that not everyone uses the same operating system or programs. In advance of one's talk ask what facilities will be available, and try one's best to practice with the same type of equipment. Learn more than one way to navigate through one's slides in case the mouse or other equipment is unfamiliar.

It is usually favorable to keep presentation mechanics and design simple. This approach prevents many of the problems mentioned already, as well as others, from distracting one's audience.

Handling Questions

Practice plays an important role in answering questions effectively. One of the most helpful preparation exercises is to present in front of a friendly audience and let them ask questions. As one answer their questions, one can write down the queries that are likely to come up again. One can then prepare answers for those specific questions. One should also think about other natural questions. Perhaps the best way to prepare for a question-and-answer session is to develop the answers in advance. While this technique may sound trivial or obvious, we know of few speakers who employee it.

Another important tip is to avoid getting flustered. If an audience member pursues an annoying line of questioning during the presentation, one should not lose patience. In fact, if the line of questioning is putting the presentation off schedule, it is acceptable to ask for all further questions to be held until the end. If an audience member becomes an extreme nuisance then one can politely suggest meeting after the presentation.

When asked a question, there are a few common scenarios that may occur. If one knows the answer, then simply present the correct response. One should make sure to answer the question posed, and one should try not digress in the response. If one does not know the correct answer, there are a wide variety of techniques to employ. Perhaps one simply cannot recall the answer at the moment, but perhaps one thinks the answer can be recovered. If so, one may elect to take a few other questions and come back to the original question. If the answer is provided in a particular reference, refer to that reference. One should not be afraid to admit that one does not know the answer to a question, but approach such a response with tact. For example, one might say that one has not run across the information necessary to respond, or that this direction would be an interesting avenue to pursue. Or simply, "Good question. I never thought about that before. I'll look in to it further."

Sometimes another audience member may chime in with a response. Thank the person. One should also try to make sure the conversation does not digress too much. One does not want to get into a situation where audience members are conversing among themselves, unless one has a small audience or is speaking in an informal setting. One should monitor audience participation. One must watch out for an individual who tries to take the floor or garner attention. One can politely say "Does anyone else have a question?" When the questions are finished, simply say "Thank you" or "Thanks for your attention."

If an audience member asks a multi-part question, it can be difficult to recall all the parts as one proceeds to answer. One can jot down brief notes as the question is being posed. Alternatively, one can answer the parts that can be recalled, and then ask for the other parts to be repeated. Another technique is to ask the person making the query to repeat it, immediately. Hearing the question twice could help cement it in one's mind. Alternatively, one can repeat the question, "Did you just ask…?"

This technique is also useful to make sure that all audience members heard the question clearly.

Beware of a 'ruthless' audience member. Some people enjoy trying to discount the intelligence of the speaker or the relevance of the presentation. In such rare situations like this, one must maintain composure. The easiest way to handle difficult people is to defer all contact with them until after the presentation. This approach may deflect unnecessary distractions. In most circumstances the majority of the audience will be friendly, especially if it is obvious that a speaker is properly prepared.

One should try to remain relaxed and confident. As noted previously, most people find it easier to think on their feet if they are not nervous. Preparation is an important confidence builder.

Avoiding Disasters

As the saying goes: "What can go wrong will go wrong, and at the worst-possible moment." So a general rule-of-thumb for presentations is to expect the unexpected. However, with careful planning most disasters can be prevented. Imagine one has a beautifully-prepared slide show that needs a laptop and a projector to play. Suppose the laptop provided cannot read one's disk or the projector breaks down. What can one do? One backup strategy would be to make transparencies of one's slides. Many venues still have old-fashioned projectors. In the worst-case scenario one may have to speak without any visual aids. Giving such a presentation will be challenging, especially for a technical talk. And, this is why we have recommended on several occasions that one always brings a hardcopy of the talk along.

The more prepared one is, the easier it will be to recover from a mishap. Avoid last-minute surprises by finding out ahead of time what one needs to bring and what will be available. If one is not sure, simply ask one's host. One can use the checklist in Table 3 to verify that one has everything one's choice of medium requires. In any case one should not get discouraged or upset if something goes wrong. One can try to

Table 3. Checklists for various media to ensure that no important items are forgotten

Medium	Items to Check
Notebook with Projector	CD or diskette containing backup Mouse VGA cable Power cord Notebook battery for laptop (charged) Network cable for Internet connection Speakers Laser pen and backup battery Spare bulb for projector Remote-control batteries
Transparencies	Unused transparency sheets Transparency cleaner Felt-tip markers Paper printouts of slides Electronic version of slides Spare light bulb for projector
Blackboard/ Whiteboard	Cleaning supplies Markers/chalk Eraser
Easel pad	Markers Blank pages Easel stand Pre-written sheets Clear tape

troubleshoot the problem with the assistance of one's host. Eventually, one is bound to have an unexpected problem that is beyond one's control. Part of one's preparation should be anticipating these problems so that one can successfully present even under difficult circumstances.

Once all the research and preparation are done, the time to give one's presentation finally arrives. A major concern for many individuals who do not enjoy public speaking is how to cope with one's nerves. In the next section we provide some thoughts on this topic.

Coping with Nerves

Presenters of every caliber experience some level of nervousness before a performance. Common fears include forgetting everything, doing something embarrassing, or not being able to sustain the audience's attention. As long as one has rehearsed, one will normally be fine. One should not worry, but if one does, that nervous energy should be used to do additional preparation. If fear or nervousness does set in, remember the following:

- You are much more aware of your nervousness than anyone else.
- After a few minutes of talking, the nervousness will pass, and you will settle down.
- The audience is not there to judge you. They want to hear what you have to say.
- You are prepared; you know the topic well.

If possible, try to use one's nervousness to generate energy and enthusiasm about the topic. Without this energy, one's presentation might seem dull. While most technical presentations require an air of seriousness, one should make sure to smile and appear that giving the presentation is something one enjoys, even if one cannot wait until it is over. The audience can sense if one is overly tense and does not want to be there. This demeanor will make the presentation awkward and painful for both the speaker and the audience. One should not feel as though one has to entertain the audience with clever jokes, but do convey the attitude that one is really interested in sharing the topic with them. One should make eye contact with audience members throughout the talk. Even if one is using a computer or other media, one should try to move around a bit. Staying glued to a podium or sitting by a projector will make the presentation static. Unless one has difficulty standing, we believe that one should not be seated for a presentation. If it feels natural, one can use hand gestures to capture the audience's attention. However one should not gesture so frequently that one distracts the audience.

The manner in which one opens a presentation is extremely crucial. The start of one's delivery is the last chance for making final adjustments, and sets the pace for the rest of the presentation. One should make a conscious effort to start slowly, and take the extra time to ensure that everything is in place. For example, one can focus and adjust the projector so that all members of the audience can see well. If a microphone is being used, set the volume to an appropriate level. One should keep notes readily available and have water nearby in case one's mouth goes dry. Before starting, one should ask the audience members if they can see and hear well. Throughout the presentation, project the same type of confidence that one would during a job interview. One should speak clearly and with conviction. It may help to imagine that one is merely rehearsing. One can take a few deep breaths and then begin.

MISCELLANEOUS PRESENTATION HINTS

There are many common-sense considerations when giving a talk, and we have already addressed many of these, such as avoiding tripping on a power cord. Here we cover a final few tips. It is a good idea to visit and to assess the room where one's presentation will take place. If possible, visit during the same time of the day as one's scheduled presentation. Note details such as how window placements and lighting combinations create glares and hinder reading at the podium. Notice the noise level of air units, and items on the floor near where one will be standing. One can sit in various sections of the room and identify areas where the view of the talk may be obstructed. One should try and resolve any problems discovered during this setting assessment before the presentation is scheduled to start.

One needs to consider attire ahead of time. One should dress appropriately. Some settings require formal dress, and it is probably better to dress up more formally than necessary rather than to under dress. It is often a good idea to bring a sweater or jacket to combat an over-active air-conditioner. However, if the room is likely to be warm, for example presenting in Thailand, one should wear lightweight clothing. One should wear shoes that are comfortable. It is best to avoid noisy bulky hand-jewelry that might hinder one's ability to manage slides or use a keyboard. Flashy jewelry and loud clothing are also discouraged since these items may distract audience members. It is not a good idea to wear a hat. One should avoid wearing clothing that may need adjusting. If one's talk is to be given right after a meal, one should be careful about the type and quantity of food consumed. For example, one should not drink carbonated beverages if they cause burping. It is a good idea to use restroom facilities prior to long talks. Obviously, it is preferable not to take a break to leave in the middle of a presentation.

Many public speakers would agree that it is important to know one's own abilities when presenting. This knowledge allows an individual to emphasize one's strengths and to work on one's weaknesses. Projecting confidence is an important trait. Some other important tips to remember are as follows:

- Speak loudly and clearly so that all the audience members can hear. For a group of retirees, for example, one may need to talk louder than usual.
- Do not speed up a talk when presenting. Define target times beforehand and stick to them. Hitting target times can be difficult if one is nervous.
- Perform all equipment adjustments before beginning a talk. Try to arrive early to ensure that mechanical devices are functioning properly.
- If using a projector, check the image at various times during the talk to make sure that it stays focused.
- Keep a bottle of water handy to avoid cottonmouth.
- Have a routine that will allow one to get back on track if one gets distracted or flustered. Having a few seconds of quiet time is preferable to rushing forward and botching the talk.
- Wear a watch and subtly monitor the time.

When speaking at a conference, especially one that is not proceeding according to the schedule, one should communicate with the session chair about time limits, signals, and other relevant issues. One needs to be ready to make cuts in order to shorten a presentation. As note previously, one should make sure to develop eye contact with all areas of the audience. This goal can be achieved by practicing with groups of people. A final tip when practicing a talk is to ask one's trial audience for criticism and constructive comments.

CONCLUSION

It seems that there are few people who truly enjoy public speaking, and, in fact, most people seem to actively dislike it. This chapter has provided the reader with many tips and techniques in order to present a good-quality presentation. Although we have focused on PowerPoint, the same hints hold for any presentation software. Such software includes Apple's *Keynote* (Keynote, 2011), OpenOffice's *Impress* (Impress, 2011), and *Prezi* (Prezi, 2011), but as of this writing, they are in far less use than PowerPoint. Becoming a good public speaker will pay many dividends in one's career, so it is important to develop this skill. And, it seems the best way to develop this skill is to actually get out there and give talks. We believe that if one follows the material presented in this chapter, as well as material from the previous chapter, one can become a highly-capable public speaker.

REFERENCES

Golden Rule. (2011). *The golden rule*. Retrieved March 8, 2011, from http://en.wikipedia.org/wiki/The_Golden_Rule

Greenlaw, R., Hoover, H. J., & Ruzzo, W. L. (1995). *Limits to parallel computation: P-completeness theory*. Oxford University Press.

Impress. (2011). *Impress: More power to your presentations*. Retrieved July 13, 2011, from http://www.openoffice.org/product/impress.html

Keynote. (2011). *Apple's keynote*. Retrieved July 13, 2011, from http://www.apple.com/iwork/keynote

Prezi. (2011). *Prezi: Zooming presentations*. Retrieved July 13, 2011, from http://prezi.com

Chapter 12
Writing a Résumé

ABSTRACT

The book now turns its attention to writing a résumé and the equivalent document in academic fields, the curriculum vitæ (CV). These documents represent essentially all that an individual has done in a professional career. In the absence of a face-to-face meeting, these documents represent a person and are used to evaluate a person. Another document called the biographical sketch (or bio sketch for short), used for example with the submission of a talk abstract, is usually much less formal than the résumé or CV. If someone has a résumé, it should be fairly easy to draft a bio sketch, but going in the other direction will require the person to fill in a considerable number of details. Nearly all job openings require the applicant to submit a résumé before the applicant will be considered for the position. A well-formatted résumé could dramatically improve an individual's chances of successfully obtaining a desirable job. Thus the subject of this chapter bears serious consideration.

HISTORY AND PURPOSE OF THE RÉSUMÉ

In the first few sections of this chapter we examine the essential, common, and miscellaneous parts of a résumé. We then examine the common parts of a CV. We include a section titled Final Checklist which will help a person to ensure that no important items were missed. Then we offer suggestions on résumé and CV submission and how to follow up on such a submission. The chapter ends with a section containing conclusions.

In this section we explore the history and purpose of the résumé, make general comments about résumés and CVs, address integrity, and conclude the section with a discussion of style issues. Let us now turn our focus to the history and purpose of the résumé.

DOI: 10.4018/978-1-4666-0237-3.ch012

The résumé has a relatively short history. Executives and upper-level managers began creating lists of their work experience and accomplishments in the late 1950s and early 1960s; these lists were used as notes during interviews. Frequently, the applicant gave a copy of these notes to the interviewer to remind the person of the candidate's qualifications when the hiring decision was actually being made. During the 1970s, résumés became more common for professional positions at all levels as a supplement to the standard employment application. By the early 1980s virtually all applications for skilled or specialized positions were expected to include a résumé. The résumé highlights a potential candidate's education and experience as qualifications for the position.

As the popularity of the Internet increased in the late 1990s and from 2000 onward, it became popular to maintain a résumé online. In fact, many employers require that potential employees submit their résumés online. There are many job sites on the Internet where job candidates can submit their résumés to a résumé database and search for available jobs (Indeed, 2011; JobCentral, 2011; Monster, 2011). Some employers may search these databases for job candidates. In this chapter we focus on the fundamentals of résumé writing, so that a person can develop either an online or printed version of a résumé. There are a number of books available that contain additional information about résumé writing, and we provide a few references in the following list: (Curtis and Simons, 2004), (Moreira, 2007), and (Rosenberg, 2008).

From this short history we see that the main purpose of a résumé is to demonstrate to a potential employer an individual's qualifications for the job being sought. One of the best ways of thinking about a résumé is as an advertising or marketing tool for selling oneself as the most-qualified candidate. A well-written résumé should differentiate a candidate from the rest of the pack of applicants—as both a worker and an individual.

Sometimes the words *résumé* and *curriculum vitæ* are written with the special characters as shown here, but the most-recent trend is to use the more-easily typed equivalents with standard English letters, *resume* and *curriculum vitae*, or simply *vita* or *CV*. Either form is acceptable, but pick one and use it consistently. Likewise, avoid switching back and forth between the words résumé and curriculum vitæ. Lastly, there are two other alternative spellings of résumé—*resumé* and *résume*. Again, if someone has a favorite, it should be used consistently.

Résumé or Curriculum Vitæ

While a résumé and curriculum vitæ are roughly equivalent documents, there are important differences in usage and content. In the United States, a one-to-two page résumé (three-to-five pages for executive levels) is typically used in business, whereas CVs are typically used for teaching and research positions in academia and for physician positions in medicine. A CV for a professional with considerable experience may be as long as 20 pages or even more. In Europe and many other parts of the world, CVs are commonly used in business as well. In content, CVs typically include more sections and details than résumés, as indicated in Table 1.

Integrity

Under no circumstances should a résumé or a CV purposely contain false or inaccurate information. Of course, blatantly-false information is unethical and dishonest. Keep in mind that even seemingly-innocuous embellishments and exaggerations of education, work history, skills, or other information are deceitful as well. A résumé is likely a first introduction to a potential employer and nothing will sour that introduction faster than having one's integrity questioned. Even if a potential employer does not discover dishonest representation, once hired, a lack of skills or experience that one purported to possess will, at best, create an adversarial relationship between an employee and an employer and, at worst, could lead to immediate dismissal, embarrassment, and/or a lawsuit. Always remember that a résumé is an advertisement, and the last thing one wants is to advertise oneself as dishonest.

The more prestigious the position, the greater the likelihood of a thorough résumé and background check. Under no circumstances should inaccurate information be intentionally included in a résumé. A former Georgia Tech football coach lost his job because he listed a Masters that he had never received. This example illustrates the consequences for upgrading a résumé with false information.

Table 1. A comparison of sections in a résumé and a curriculum vitæ

Section	Résumé	Curriculum Vitæ
Name	Required	Required
Contact Information	Required	Required
Objective	Required	Rare
Skills	Common	Less Common
Employment	Required	Required
Education	Required	Required
Honors and Awards	Common	Common
Courses Taught	Rare	Required
Grants and Scholarships	Less Common	Common
Publications	Rare	Required
Talks and Conferences	Rare	Required
Manuscripts	Rare	Common
Committees	Rare	Common
References	Less Common	Less Common
Projects	Less Common	Less Common
Volunteer Work	Less Common	Less Common
Hobbies	Less Common	Less Common
Photos	Rare	Rare

Style and Keywords

Although a résumé, as mentioned earlier, is similar to an advertisement, it differs in that a résumé's presentation and language should not be colorful or flashy—literally or linguistically—as in a typical printed advertisement. Instead, a résumé should be professional and succinct. The goal is to provide an aesthetically pleasing and easy-to-read document that effectively conveys one's qualifications. Though much of a résumé is composed of names and dates that offer little opportunity for language-style choices, one should put considerable thought into wordsmithing the text that does, such as the *objective* and one's accomplishments. Both of these parts of a résumé are discussed in subsequent sections of this chapter.

A person's style of writing has as much subjective influence as their body language does in a face-to-face meeting. The writing style should always present the most-positive traits of the applicant's personality. For example, the use of colloquialisms or a cutesy phrase may portray one as informal and not serious. Avoid the use of words with a negative connotation which may portray one as bitter or difficult to work with. Consider the choice of the word *forced* in the following accomplishment: *Forced executive management to retain our top talent during the economic downturn of 2008.* Simply substituting the word *convinced* for *forced* softens the tone and sounds more flexible and less combative, yet the strength of the statement remains. One final note on style is to be consistent. While it is acceptable to express accomplishments as complete sentences or as phrases/sentence fragments, do not mix the two styles.

Due to the rise in the popularity of Internet job and résumé posting sites and the ease with which one can electronically apply for posted positions, it is not uncommon for employers to receive hundreds of résumés for a posted position.

In addition, employers and employment recruiters are more frequently taking a proactive approach to filling an open position by searching Internet job sites for qualified candidates. For these two reasons it has become common for employers to use software that searches and sorts résumés based on *keywords*. Typically, keywords are industry specific terms, job titles, or terms for a particular technology, although just about any word that has a specific meaning in relation to the open position may be used. Therefore, to improve the chance of having a résumé reviewed by a person, it is necessary to include important industry and technology terms. This suggestion should not be taken to mean that a résumé should be peppered with the latest industry buzz-words, yet the résumé needs to include words that may be used as keywords in the applicant's field. Include such keywords purposely and elegantly.

Résumés and CVs should be kept up-to-date. We do not mean to suggest that one is in the market for a new job all the time, but it is easier to add things one at a time to a résumé than to have three years worth of personal history to enter overnight. In academic positions it is common to be asked to submit an updated CV annually. Such CVs are used, for example, to quantify the amount of research done in a particular department, as well as for individual promotion and tenure decisions. Also, when moving to a new address, a résumé should be updated at the same time as changes of address forms are being completed. This edit will be one-less thing for an applicant to think about when submitting the résumé again.

In the next section we turn our attention to a more-detailed look at résumés and their essential parts.

ESSENTIAL PARTS OF A RÉSUMÉ

Although a résumé can have many sections, some required and others optional, we have broken them into two major groups to facilitate our discussion.

First, we consider the elements in the top or *title* section; next, we consider the various options for the *body* section. To illustrate the topics in this discussion, we have included a sample résumé in Figure 1.

Header

The title section is the introduction to the reader and always includes the applicant's name and contact information. Of course, a résumé or CV is absolutely useless if the reader cannot concisely determine the person's name and how to contact the person for an interview. For a business résumé it is no longer common to title the document with the word résumé. More commonly, the title section of a résumé contains only the applicant's name, complete contact information, and possibly the date of submission. For academics the convention continues to be to title the document with the words Curriculum Vitæ in the header either before or, more commonly, directly after the name. A carefully-chosen combination of fonts and sizes adds variety and improves readability, but use good judgment. Too many different fonts in a résumé will make it appear cluttered.

Name

Since one's name is the most-important part of the title, the name should be set in a large font and emphasized. If the body of the résumé will be in a 12-point font, a 16-point bold-face font would be appropriate for the name at the top, but a 30-point font would probably be too much. In our example in Figure 1, we did not use all capital letters for the name, but that is certainly an option. Be aware that it is easier to read words using lower-case letters since they have more variation in their appearance than upper-case letters. While the readability of the name may not be an issue since the font size is large, avoid using all upper-case letters elsewhere in the résumé or use the small-caps font (as we do in Figure 1).

The name should be emphasized enough to be noticeable, but try not to make it stand out so much that it appears flamboyant—unless that is a desirable character trait in the particular field of job search.

Statistically, the average résumé is looked at for about twelve seconds. If there is something really strange at the top of a résumé, the document may go straight into the trash (maybe that is part of the reason why the average is so low).

Contact Information

The résumé should include several means by which one may be contacted. At a minimum the résumé should include one's home address and home-phone number. Additionally, it has become common to include one's email address and cellular-phone number. Though less typical, a current work address may also be included.

The most-common format is to place the contact information immediately after one's name and in the same general style. Figure 1 illustrates how this information should look.

Email addresses that are silly, cute, or indicate some aspect of one's personality are best avoided when used as contact email addresses on résumés, CVs, and other professional documents. It is much better to simply use one's name or some abbreviated version of one's name (such as first initial and last name) than to use an email address like *ilovecats@catlovers.com* or *darthvader12@hotmail.com*. If necessary, in order to follow this suggestion, one should create a new email address or an alias for a current email account. Also, one should not use a current work email address on résumés being submitted for employment opportunities. Pursuing employment is a personal endeavor and, as such, is not an appropriate use of a current employer's resources.

Figure 1. The upper portion of a well-formatted résumé

Thomas Meredith
January 30, 2013

123 Elmwood Avenue
Savannah, GA 10001
home: 912-897-0000 cell: 912-655-0000
tom.meredith@gmail.com

OBJECTIVE:
To obtain a position as a research assistant in a science-related field at a medium-sized university, where I can apply my current skills, adapt to new situations, and learn more laboratory techniques.

EDUCATION:
- ➢ BS   Valdosta State University   2010
- ➢ MS   Armstrong Atlantic State University   2012

PREVIOUS EXPERIENCE:
- ➢ Research Assistant   The Oceanography Institute   July, 2010–present
  Assisted three professors in conducting lab experiments. Ordered, purchased, and inventoried chemicals.

Date

It is helpful to have a date on one's résumé. A date works a little like a software version number. Suppose that some information suddenly changes or requires updating. One should immediately add the new information to one's résumé and update the date. By getting in the habit of checking the date and only sending out the current version, one is far less likely to omit something important. In addition, it is a good idea to update the date each time a résumé is submitted; this update helps indicate to the reader that the résumé received is current. We recommend that the name of the electronic file also include the date of the last update, for example, *resume-TM-03022013.tex*.

Objective

An objective, although not required, is usually included in résumés. The objective should be a one- or two-sentence statement about one's employment goals and should also say something about one's willingness to adapt and learn. One needs to be realistic in setting goals. Note that the curriculum vitæ typically does not list an objective.

Skills

It is common to list specific technical skills such as programming languages, operating systems, laboratory techniques, and so forth on one's résumé. Many times these skills are also excellent keywords, which will be caught by résumé software processing tools, as mentioned previously. Acronyms are acceptable when listing skills if they are both well known in the particular job field and easy-to-read for those familiar with them. But, one does need to be somewhat cautious when listing skills. A person should not list trivial skills that one would be expected to know or that are not relevant to the position being sought. The goal is not to make the longest list possible, but to demonstrate that one possesses the mastery of skills needed to be successful in the desired position. An individual should not list skills unless one is truly adept at them.

Body

The body section of the résumé consists of several independent subsections that describe various aspects of one's career. Referring back to Table 1, the reader can see that some sections are required on all résumés and CVs. Generally, a productive person with greater experience will have more and longer subsections than someone just starting a career. Although some guides recommend that a résumé be limited to one or two pages, this limit does not apply in the academic world. Since the custom for academic résumés is to include *everything* related to an academic career, these documents often grow to be 20 pages or longer for senior people. A curriculum vitæ (as it is more commonly called in academia) of five-to-ten pages is common, and we have seen CVs over 100 pages long.

If one's résumé has only a small amount of content, one may decide to use wider margins to give the document more visual impact. The length of a résumé is not something to worry too much about though. The key is to include all of the information that is relevant to the position and follow the conventions for the field in which one is applying. It is the quality of the information presented that is most important. One should also be mindful of the overall look of the résumé. It is far better to let the content determine the length of the résumé rather than an artificial constraint on the number of pages.

The headings for each of the subsections of the résumés body can be set in small caps or a boldface sans-serif font, but limit the number of different typefaces to two or three. In our example résumé in Figure 1, we used the same font size of 12pt and a style of small capitals for the headings. The content of the résumé shown there was also typeset in a 12pt font. The convention for headings is to set a heading apart from the text, but allow for a neat and uniform overall appearance. Try to maintain consistent style choices from one section to the next. For example, if using arrow-shaped bullets in one section, do not use round bullets in another. Consistency in typesetting will help improve the overall appearance of a résumé.

Employment (Previous Experience)

One's previous employment and experience is typically the longest section of a business résumé for an experienced professional. Typically, the previous-experience section is also the most important. Obviously, for someone just starting a career this section is much smaller and, in that case, the education section will likely be the most-important section. Twenty years into one's career, one will not necessarily include details on every single job worked, but one should include such positions if they relate to the field in which one is applying. As one gains more experience, it is important to include those positions that show continuity of employment and have a significant connection to career goals. In the academic world it is customary to include everything one has done related to the areas of teaching, research, and service.

On a résumé it is most common to list previous-employment experience in reverse-chronological order. For a CV the convention is to list previous-employment experience in chronological order (van Leunen, 1992). For each position held one should list the title, the organization, and the employment period. Figure 2 illustrates a typical format for this section. One should be consistent in listing previous-employment positions.

Besides being a list of past positions held, the previous-employment section should enumerate one's accomplishments and achievements, where appropriate and possible. Each entry should include several statements that demonstrate what one did to add value to the organization. (Note

that in Figure 2 forward pointers are given so that this material can be expanded on later in the CV.) These statements may be in the form of complete sentences or may be written as sentence fragments or phrases. As previously mentioned, once a style is chosen, one should remain consistent throughout. Each statement should convey something unique and important new paragraph.

Previous-employment statements should be worded to highlight successes and achievements and not simply list activities and responsibilities. For example, a software-development manager might be tempted to say the following: *Managed a team of six software engineers that coded the web interface for the billing system.* Though this statement describes what this person did, it does not tell us anything about how well the job was done. Consider a statement like the following instead: *Assumed leadership of a previously under-performing development team and delivered a quality web interface on-time and on-budget for the billing system; this work resulted in a 10-percent yearly cost savings to our clients for its ease-of-use.* Notice how much-more appealing the person's previous experience becomes in the second statement. This technique should also be used in the education section, especially by those with less employment experience. Note that some positions may speak for themselves and do not need a great deal of elaboration, for example, *President of Harvard University* requires no further details.

While consistency with bullets is important, do not use a bullet in a section containing just one item. A single item should be aligned so that the left margin lines up with the bullets in the other sections, not the first letter of the bulleted items.

Education

Both résumés and CVs should always include a section listing one's educational history. As with employment experience, résumés typically list education in reverse-chronological order and CVs in chronological order. This material should be a complete list of all degrees, educational certifications, and professional-development courses. Each entry should list the degree (or certification or course); the institution from which it was obtained, possibly the location of the institute, and the year the item was earned. For degrees one should also include the major field of study and, optionally, the minor field of study. If there is not enough room on a single line, these might be listed on additional lines just below each degree.

High schools are generally not listed on a résumé, unless one was a valedictorian, salutatorian, or achieved some other important distinction, or attended a noteworthy high school. If one attended high school abroad, noting it may be useful when applying for a job in the United States since overseas experience is atypical.

Use bullets to itemize educational history and a consistent format to keep the history neat. In Figure 3 we used extra spacing to align the information in each line. Try to balance the tab settings so there is approximately the same amount of space between each set of columns. For those that have exceptional grades, they may want to list their GPA along with their degree. If one provides a GPA for one degree, one should probably provide GPAs for all degrees to be consistent. If one's high school GPA is outstanding, but one's undergraduate record was not exemplary, it is probably best to leave both out.

COMMON PARTS OF A RÉSUMÉ

Introduction

In this section we describe common parts of a résumé. Later in the chapter we include a section that covers the typical parts of a curriculum vitæ. In the next section we present additional parts of these documents. Note that the specific sections to include in a résumé or CV depend on each individual; there is not a single format that works best for all, and there is no hard and fast rule about what is right and what is wrong.

Honors and Awards

It is an excellent idea to list awards and honors that are relevant to the position for which one is applying, as these items demonstrate achievement and success. If one has no honors or awards to list, this section should be omitted. Sometimes in a biographical sketch the sections required are supplied, but in a résumé or CV, one should only include a given section if it contains applicable items. Honors may consist of being recognized by management for outstanding work, being on the Dean's List, or receiving special recognition for an outstanding contribution to a particular area of research. Place items in this section in chronological order with the more-recent ones at the bottom. Use a bulleting and tabbing scheme that stays consistent with the other sections in the body.

If one was inducted into a legitimate honor society, one should place that in the *Honors and Awards* section. However, beware of lists such as "Who's Who in . . .," where anyone can get on these lists simply by ordering the publication in which the list of honorees appears. Do not degrade the value of one's education by including a trivial purchased "honor."

Personal References

References can either be included as part of the résumé or provided on a separate page. Three or four references are usually sufficient, unless a person is applying for a position such as a president or a CEO. Attempting to put references in order of preference is not likely to be useful, since they will not necessarily be called in that order. List the references in alphabetical order and supply titles so that the interviewer will know in what

Figure 2. An example of previous-employment experience from a CV

EMPLOYMENT		
➤ University of New Hampshire (Durham, New Hampshire)		
– Assistant Professor of Computer Science		1989–94
– Associate Professor of Computer Science (early tenure)		1994–98
See page 36 for administrative experience.		
➤ Armstrong Atlantic State University (Savannah, Georgia)		
– Professor of Computer Science (tenured)		1998–10
– Department Head		1998–02
Founding Head for Department of Computer Science		
See page 36 for administrative experience.		
– Founding Dean, School of Computing		2002–07
See page 37 for administrative experience.		
➤ University System of Georgia (Savannah, Georgia)		
– Regional Coordinator of Yamacraw Project		2000–04
Coordinate the southeastern region of Georgia on the		
$100,000,000 strategic-economic-development Yamacraw		
Project designed to make the state of Georgia a world		
leader in the design of broadband-infrastructure systems,		
devices, and chips. Serve as regional spokesperson.		
See page 39 for further details.		
➤ Management and Science University (Kuala Lumpur, Malaysia)		
– Visiting Professor		2003–
➤ Chiang Mai University (Chiang Mai, Thailand)		
– Distinguished Professor of Computer Science		2006–
– Member of Graduate Faculty		2007–
➤ Elbrys Networks, Inc. (Portsmouth, New Hampshire)		
– Research Scientist		2009–
– Consultant on regulatory matters and issues relating to health		
and wellness technologies.		
➤ United States Naval Academy (Annapolis, Maryland)		
– Leighton Endowed Distinguished Visiting		2010–
Professor of Information Technology		
– Institutional Representative for Cyberwatch		2011–

Figure 3. An example of a bulleted educational section of a résumé

EDUCATION				
•	BA	Pomona College (Mathematics) cum laude	(10.9/12.0)	1983
		Harvey Mudd College (3 courses senior year)	(11.3/12.0)	1982–83
•	MS	University of Washington (Computer Science)	(3.61/4.00)	1986
•	PhD	University of Washington (Computer Science)	(4.00/4.00)	1988

capacity each reference is related to the applicant. Ask references for permission to use their names. A candidate should let references know when the candidate is entering the job market, so that the references have a chance to refresh their memories and not be caught off guard by an unexpected phone call or email. References should be kept up-to-date as much as possible; recent contacts can usually provide a better picture of one's current career. It may be necessary to send references a copy of one's latest résumé. A current résumé will help to keep an individual's personal references up-to-date on recent activities, as well as help them to recall useful information.

Some people prefer to furnish references upon request, but taking this approach could cause a candidate to miss opportunities, especially if the search pool is large. If the interviewer has to contact a candidate to get references, but other similarly qualified candidates provided their references, one résumé may be set aside in favor of the other which has easier access to information.

MISCELLANEOUS PARTS OF A RÉSUMÉ

The types of items that we have covered in the previous sections appear most frequently on résumés and curriculum vitæ, but they do not always tell the whole story. In this section we look at other types of items that may be useful to include. Most people will not include all (or perhaps any) of these categories. The nature of the position that one is applying for will dictate which items to include.

Projects

When applying for positions in industry, it is helpful to describe a few projects that one has worked on: a simulation, an expert system, or a game, for example. For each project provide a paragraph that expresses the level of sophistication. Projects from classes can go in résumés early in one's career, but use experience that is appropriate. Be selective—above all, a résumé should show that a candidate will be a good employee and exercise good judgment. The more depth a project has, and the greater one's involvement, the better.

Activities

For positions in industry it may be useful in certain circumstances to list activities such as sports, club memberships, student-government participation, and so on, though in the academic environment, these entries are not particularly valuable. Such items may need to be customized for a given job application.

Volunteer Work

For those who have participated in community volunteer work such as Scouts, Learning for Life, or the United Way, one should definitely consider finding a place to include this information if applying for a position in industry. Corporate people like to see community involvement. For most job applications it is probably a good idea *not* to list volunteer work with political- or religious-activist groups. The most-appropriate volunteer work to list is work that is related most closely to one's field.

Hobbies

Hobbies are more typically included in applications for positions in industry. Golf is a popular hobby to include on résumés because many corporate executives participate in the sport. The decision to include a hobby should be taken with care and will depend on the position being applied for.

Photos

In some industries, like marketing or journalism, it may be appropriate to include a photo; this practice is also more common in Europe and on other continents. However, providing a picture is almost unheard of in business résumés and academic CVs in the United States. Some scholarships may occasionally ask one for a photo which is used for creating an identification card, though this request is more typically part of the hiring procedure. If a picture is requested, then it is probably best to send one or the application may be considered incomplete. In any case, learn about the field and what is expected. In engineering, science, and technology a photo is rarely included. Although photos are not usually part of an academic résumé, IEEE journals often include a thumbnail photo and a biographical sketch of authors at the end of each article—a nice touch.

COMMON PARTS OF A CURRICULUM VITÆ

In this section we cover many of the common parts of a CV that we have not yet addressed.

Courses Taught

When applying for a teaching position, the "List of Courses Taught" section of a CV is almost as important as the previous-employment experience is for a business résumé. The courses should be listed in some reasonable and consistent order and include the name of the institution where they were taught, the name of the course, and the years taught. Note that sometimes the name of the institution may not need to be supplied explicitly because if dates are given for when the courses are taught, it will likely be easy to infer where the courses were taught. For experienced teachers it is customary to provide a summary of teaching-evaluation data. Courses can sometimes be partitioned, for example, grouping undergraduate courses in one area and graduate courses in another. Figure 4 shows a portion of the teaching sections of a CV. Note that in this case there is also a section on courses developed.

Grants, Scholarships, and Contracts

Those pursuing an academic career should seek external funding where appropriate. People in academia will want to know that one is willing and able to obtain external funding. One should list all grants, scholarships, and contracts for which one was awarded money. Include the amount of the award for each item. Including the amount is essential for grants and contracts, but one should also do this for scholarships. Even small scholarships sometimes carry a reasonable amount of prestige, especially if they are competitive. It is important to list the names of collaborators that were involved in grant and contract work. Do not list proposals that were submitted but not funded. Figure 5 shows a portion of a grants and scholarship section of a CV. In this example the items are numbered, but bullets may be appropriate for listing just a few items. Notice that awards that were won but not accepted can also be included, especially if they come from a prestigious source.

One should not make the mistake of assigning a monetary value to gifts of equipment or software from businesses. It may be impressive that one received 1,000 copies of Microsoft Windows valued at $100 each, however, this value is not equivalent to a $100,000 grant from Microsoft.

Publications

A publications section should be included for those who have *any* published work related to the field in which one is applying. This fact is particularly true in the academic environment where custom dictates that every publication be included on a CV. As with the other sections of listed items, these works should be listed chronologically with

Figure 4. A portion of the teaching section of a CV

COURSES DEVELOPED INCLUDING ACCOMPANYING MATERIALS
Undergraduate
  ➢ CS 403, On-Line Network Exploration†
  ➢ CS 659, Introduction to the Theory of Computation†
  ➢ CSCI 1150, Introduction to the Internet and World Wide Web†
  ➢ CSCI 1210, Understanding Practical Unix†
  ➢ Armstrong Atlantic's Bachelor of Information Technology
    I developed the curriculum for this entire program including eleven new courses.

Graduate
  ➢ CS 942, Parallel Computers and Computations†
  ➢ CS 959, Theory of Computation†
  ➢ CSCI 6100, Technical Writing†
  ➢ Armstrong Atlantic's Master of Computer Science
    I developed the curriculum for this entire program including thirteen new courses.

†Denotes I wrote a text for the course.

COURSES TAUGHT
Undergraduate
  ➢ Introduction to the Internet and World Wide Web, CSCI 1150
    (Fall 2000–01, Fall 2001–02, Fall 2007–08, Spring 2007–08, Fall 2008–09, Spring 2008–09,
    Fall 2009–10, Spring 2009–10)

  ➢ Introduction to Computer Ethics and Cyber Security, CSCI 2070
    (Fall 2009–2010)

  ➢ Discrete Mathematics and Probability, SM 242
    (Fall 2010–11)

---

the most-recent one appearing last. It is important that one's first publication be a good one since it will always appear first on the CV.

Use bullets or other formatting to itemize the publications and use a style that is consistent with the formatting of items in other sections. Information to include for each publication is similar to what one would include in a bibliographic entry. For five or more publications it is better to number them in order of the publication date using Arabic numerals. Figure 6 provides an example with five publications. Notice the technique used to include co-authors. Of course, it is assumed that the person to whom the CV belongs is an author

on all of these publications, so there is no need to list the CV-owner's name separately.

When a person publishes a first work, it is important to think about how the name should appear. For example, if a person's name is Jeffery Thomas Smith, but everyone knows the individual as Jeff, should Jeff use his real name or the name that all of his colleagues know him by. We suggest always using the full given name. In any case it is important that an author use the same name on all works. For example, do not use Jeff Smith, Jeffery T. Smith, and Jeffery Thomas Smith, but rather stick to a single option such as Jeffery Thomas Smith. There is a great deal of software

Figure 5. A portion of the grants and scholarship section of a CV

GRANTS/FELLOWSHIPS/CONTRACTS
1. ...
2. The Complexity of Parallel Computations. Research Initiation Award, National Science Foundation, 1992–96. $58,000.
3. Research in Parallel Approximation Algorithms. Fulbright Scholarship, Senior Research Award, 1995. $15,000.
4. Investigations in Parallel Computing. Humboldt Fellowship, Research Award, 1995–96. $30,000. I declined this award to accept a Senior Fulbright Scholarship.
5–12. ...
13. Yamacraw Project. Awarded to Armstrong Atlantic State University. I wrote the proposal for this project. State of Georgia, 2000–04. $2,723,000.
14–20.
21. (with Chris McCarthy and Suzy Carpenter) Empowering Financially Disadvantaged Students with Talents in Biology, Chemistry, Computer Science, Information Technology, Mathematics, and Physics. National Science Foundation, 2007–2012. $483,760.
22. (with Sanpawat Kantabutra) Royal Golden Jubilee Scholarship for Pattama Longani. Collaborator, 2009–2011. $47,000.
...

on the Internet that automatically trawls the web and generates lists of an individual's publications; hopefully, by using consistent naming on all works, all of an individual's publications will be collected together and attributed to the person. Similarly, the CV owner should list all author names in a reference list consistently when the CV owner is certain that the author is one and the same. For example, in the actual second publication of Figure 6 perhaps the author name was listed as M. Douglas, however, the CV owner being a co-author knows the name is really M. C. Douglas—the same person as in items 4 and 5. The CV owner can take the liberty of listing the names consistently. Note that some conferences may require authors to use just initials instead of a full name, and similarly, some publications may ask that the reference list to contain initials rather than full names.

Over time, as one continues publishing more work, one may gather a large collection of a particular type of publication—conference papers, for example. When it makes sense to do so, divide up the list of publications using some sensible division like Refereed and Un-refereed. If one did not get back referee reports for a particular conference submission, it is considered un-refereed and specified in the CV that the papers were selected by a program committee. Some of the best conferences select papers using a program committee, so this listing is not necessarily a negative thing.

If a complete listing has a substantial collection of works in several categories, it is recommended to have a section for each. These sections can be organized in order of importance: books, journal papers, book chapters, conference papers, and collections (online publications will probably fall into this last category). If there is no work in a particular category, do not include that division. The order of importance may be open to discussion. For example, some people may feel a 50-page book chapter is more important than a 5-page conference paper. In any case make sure to use consistent formats throughout the various categories. Note that in some fields it is traditional to publish research in a conference, obtain feed-

Figure 6. Sample publications section of a CV

PUBLICATIONS

1. "Tom's First Conference Paper," *Proceedings of the 1st Annual Anything Goes Conference*, **1**(3–6), 2011.

2. (with M. C. Douglas) "A Method for Calculating Something to Do with Sediment," *The Journal of Oceanography*, **114**(338–361), 2011.

3. *Salt Water Computing: A Wet-Lands Survival Guide*, The Publishing Company, New York, 2012.

4. (with M. C. Douglas and H. Kessler) "A Random Walk Method for Characterizing the Dispersion of Toxins in Tidal Marshes," *31st Annual Southeast Conference on Oceanography*, **31**(21–27), March 2013.

5. (with M. C. Douglas and J. Petrovich) "Muck-rakers, Bottom-feeders, and Other Slime of the Coastal Marshes," *The Coastal Gazette Online*, August 21, 2014.

---

back on that research, revise the paper, and then publish the more-mature work in a journal paper. When such publications are related or similar to each other, it is worth including a note indicating this fact, or a pointer to the other publication, for example, "A preliminary version of this work appeared in [10]." One does not want to give the impression of trying to pad a CV.

All publications should be listed in a curriculum vitæ. Once a work is in print, the publication belongs on the CV, even if it is not a strong one. Some people will put "Selected Publications," but this approach is not really wise if one is asked to provide a complete CV. Suppose one listed only ten publications in a selection from several hundred. Most people will assume that the person chose their best work, but perhaps those viewing the CV would have chosen a different set of ten than CV owner chose. It is better to list everything: the good and the bad. Unless someone is a recognizable novelist, or the like, they will generally only include publications related to the field in which they are applying for a position. The publications to list are those that are geared towards academic interests.

Invited Talks and Conference Presentations

Some people have a section for talks in their résumé where they include conference talks, invited talks, distinguished-speaker engagements, panels served on, and so on. If one has a lot of talks, they can be numbered like the same way as publications or be divided into sections. One should but keep punctuation to a minimum if it does not add anything. If a particular talk is related to a conference paper, one can reference the paper in the "Publications" section from the "Talks" section. Be careful to include only significant and worthy talks. For example, do not include a "talk" that is given in a regular-class meeting.

Manuscripts

The manuscripts section is where one should list unpublished works, technical reports, important web pages, or perhaps other online publications, and any additional relevant items that do not fit into the standard categories. Only include such items if they are significant to the position for which one is applying. And, of course, the CV owner should only include sections for which the person has items.

Committees

If one has been involved in a lot of professional service, it may be useful to list the committees served on. This list says to the reader that one is willing to do service work and also suggests that the individual has some expertise in the areas of committee work. A typical list of academic committees may include search, planning, promotion, tenure, and curriculum committees. Committees should be listed in alphabetical order along with the years served. It is a good idea to note any committees that were chaired. A consistent style should be used for dates served. Again, it is important to list only those committees that were significant and to which a contribution was made. Figure 7 provides an example. Notice that the committees are numbered and special roles, such as chair, are noted. Also, one can infer the institution where these committees were served on from the earlier section of the CV listing employment experience.

Other Considerations

As one's career advances, the style and categories on the CV will evolve. One should include key points, and be complete and consistent. From time-to-time one should review the entire CV for overall style. It is a good idea to update one's CV on a regular basis rather than having to add many pages to it all at once. This way it is less likely that some items are accidentally omitted.

FINAL CHECKLIST

This section contains a list of items to check before submitting a résumé or CV. The list is meant to be helpful to catch minor problems at the last minute, but not a comprehensive checklist.

- Make sure that contact information is up-to-date.
- Include the current date.
- Add any recent experience and accomplishments.
- Check for spelling errors.
- Verify the consistency of recently added material with that of already exiting items.
- Scan the document as a whole for bad page breaks or poor spacing issues.
- Verify that no important item is omitted.

In the next section we describe the process of submitting a résumé.

Figure 7. Example of a listing of committees served on

> ...
> 28. Center for Armstrong Atlantic Research in the Sciences (1998–99)
> 29. Certificate Program in Computer Science (1998–99)
> 30. College Computing (1997–98)
> 31. Computer Engineering (1998–99)
> 32. Cybersecurity (2002–07, Chair 2004)
> 33. Dean's Council (2002–07)
> 34. Electronic Campus (Chair 1998)
> 35. Executive Committee Division of Continuing Education (1994–95, 1996–98)
> 36. Faculty Senator to University Senate (1996–98)
> ...

SUBMITTING A RÉSUMÉ OR CURRICULUM VITÆ

Computers appear in almost all facets of life from personal, to professional, to academic, and the rise of email and the Internet have rendered the question of how and on what type of paper to print a résumé virtually irrelevant. Résumés are most likely to be submitted via email in some other electronic form. Printed versions are mostly only used to provide additional copies at an interview and even that use is becoming more and more unnecessary. The days of mailing résumés on specialized résumé paper are gone. Printed copies, if needed, should be printed on plain white stock with a reasonable quality printer. Electronic submission should be done per the instructions of the employer—typically in MS Word or PDF format, as an attachment. The email to which the résumé is attached can read like a cover letter. A person should make sure to attach the résumé before sending the email. Email programs such as Gmail will ask users whether or not they want to continue sending an email that contains the word "attach" but does not actually have an attachment. After a week or two, if no acknowledgement of receipt of an email was given, an individual may need to follow up. One should not automatically assume that lack of news means not a desirable candidate.

CONCLUSION

A résumé is a representation of an individual's professional experience and accomplishments. The care with which a person prepares a résumé and the quality of a résumé will be used by potential employers to judge an individual and to make hiring decisions. As such, it is important to prepare a résumé well and keep it up-to-date. If possible, an individual should ask someone with experience to review a draft résumé and to make suggestions. In some cases it may be worth hiring a professional service to assist in the preparation of a résumé. In this chapter we have included many suggestions that we hope the reader finds useful in preparing a high-quality résumé, but one should keep in mind that résumé styles change over time and that a résumé is a personal document.

REFERENCES

Curtis, R., & Simons, W. (2004). *The resume. com guide to writing unbeatable resumes.* McGraw Hill.

Indeed. (2011). *One search. All jobs.* Retrieved January 27, 2011, from http://www.indeed.com

JOBcentral. (2011). *National labor exchange.* Retrieved January 27, 2011, from http://www. jobcentral.com

Monster. (2011). *Your calling is calling.* Retrieved January 27, 2011, from http://www.monster.com

Moreira, P. (2007). *Ace the IT resume.* McGraw Hill.

Rosenberg, A. D. (2008). *The resume handbook: How to write outstanding resumes and cover letters for every situation.* Adams Media.

Van Leunen, M. (1992). *A handbook for scholars (Revised edition).* Oxford University Press.

Chapter 13
Introduction to LATEX

ABSTRACT

Professionals and students in scientific fields need to write technical manuscripts such as white papers, technical reports, journal articles, conference papers, dissertations, and theses. LATEX (pronounced "lay-tech," "lay-TEX," or "lah-tech") is a state-of-the-art typesetting system that is ideal for preparing such documents (Lamport, 1994). Note that LATEX is usually typeset with special positioning of the letters "A" and "E," but throughout this work we write it as LATEX because in the fonts used in this book writing all capital letters looks better than trying to write LATEX the way that it is supposed to be written, and similarly, for TEX which is usually written with a special positioning of the letter "E."

INTRODUCTION

LATEX is based on the TEX-typesetting system developed by Donald Knuth (Knuth, 1984). The output from LATEX's *math* and *display math* modes is superior to other formatters for mathematical expressions, equations, and formulas. LATEX includes resources for properly producing mathematical statements such as equations and theorems. This complete typesetting system affords the user superb output and total control of the appearance of the output. LATEX has many advantages such as

- Produces excellent quality output
- Is ideal for typesetting all forms of mathematics
- Is a publishing industry standard
- Allows for maximum flexibility and user control
- Was designed with quality in mind
- Is easy-to-use and customize
- Has many extensions to provide typesetting for nearly all situations (Goossens, 1999)

DOI: 10.4018/978-1-4666-0237-3.ch013

LATEX is also available on nearly all computing systems. The reader may need to consult with a "local guru" to learn the mechanics of using a specific system.

Becoming an expert with LATEX takes time because of the wealth of features this typesetting system supports. But, it is more satisfying for the novice to see some output quickly rather than to spend too much time studying the numerous features. In the next few sections we show the user how to get started in producing LATEX documents. We include several common features to familiarize the user with LATEX code. Later sections will handle specific items such as the following:

- LATEX environments
- Style files
- Labeling items, and
- Referencing

Typesetting other items such as figures and tables will be presented later. For a good general reference we recommend Lamport's *LATEX: A Document Preparation System* (Lamport, 1994). To learn about the many extensions to LATEX, the reader is referred to *The LATEX Companion* (Goossens, 1999). This chapter contains a basic introduction to LATEX, but the reader may find these references helpful, as they are quite comprehensive.

ESSENTIAL CONCEPTS

Command-Syntax Overview

Commands in LATEX are case sensitive and begin with the backslash character, \. The commands usually have descriptive names. Because the backslash is a special LATEX character, a LATEX command is required in order to display backslash properly in the output. Be careful, the escape character in LATEX is not the backslash. Using two successive backslash characters, \\, forces a newline. To produce the backslash character in the output one uses the command

```
\textbackslash
```

or in *math mode* one uses the

```
\backslash
```

command. We discuss math mode in the section on environments.

Some commands require parameters, which must be specified inside of curly braces, { }. Many commands allow for optional parameters, which are enclosed in square brackets, [ ], and follow the command name. The documentclass command is an example of a command that has optional parameters, for example, the general syntax for this command is as follows:

```
\documentclass[options]{style}
```

Options for commands are comma separated. Here style refers to a specific document style, and this concept is discussed in more depth in the section titled Basic-Document Structure.

LATEX Input File

Using a favorite text editor, for example, *emacs* or *vi*, a user will create a file with an extension of .TEX. Into this file the user will insert text and various LATEX-typesetting commands. The file should contain only plaintext. LATEX needs to be compiled in order to view its output. That is, the system is not WYSIWYG (what you see is what you get). In the next main section we describe how to process a file, but first we present a handful of other important concepts.

Whitespace

Whitespace characters in the input file, such as a space or tab, are treated the same way by LATEX. Multiple whitespace characters are treated as a single space, although multiple spaces can be forced by prefixing each space with the backslash character. Using the tab key has no effect on the output; LATEX will automatically indent new paragraphs. Automatic indentation can be suppressed by using the

```
\noindent
```

command. Conversely, to insert a tab use the

```
\indent
```

command. For example, the input text

```
Inserting multiple spaces    does not
affect the output.
```

produces the following:

Inserting multiple spaces does not affect the output.

LATEX has predefined commands for producing various amounts of whitespace; these commands are listed in Table 1.

Special Characters

LATEX reserves the following set of symbols:

Table 1. Producing whitespace in LATEX

Command	Size
\thinspace textit or \, \enspace \quad \qquad	1/12 em 1/2 em 1 em 2 em

These symbols have special meanings. Inserting them into an input file will cause unintended results for the uninformed user. Except for the backslash, one can use these symbols in documents by prefixing them with a backslash. For a complete listing of special characters refer to Table 2.

Comments

The percent sign (%) is the LATEX comment symbol. When the LATEX interpreter scans an input file and encounters %, LATEX ignores the succeeding characters until the end of the line is reached. The characters following % will not show up in the final document. Comments are a useful way of leaving notes in the file without altering the appearance of the output.

Processing a LATEX Source File

A LATEX file contains LATEX commands and text. In order to see the results of the LATEX commands, the user must compile the LATEX code with the appropriate software. Compiling the

Table 2. LATEX's special characters. Shown are the symbol in column one and the code to produce the symbol in column two. Column three describes what the symbol is used for.

Symbol	LATEX Code	Meaning
\	\textbackslash	Command character
$	\$	Math mode delimiter
%	\%	Comment character
^	\^{}	Mathmode superscript character
&	\&	Tabular column separator
_	_	Mathmode subscript character
~	\~{}	Non-breaking space
#	\#	Macro parameter symbol
{	\{	Argument start delimiter
}	\}	Argument end delimiter

source code means processing the file. Processing the file foo.TEX can easily be accomplished by the following command:

```
latex foo
```

or in some cases by selecting the appropriate item from a pull-down menu. In the case of a mistake in the LATEX source file, the system will return an error message, giving the user information on the type of bug that was found along with its location. Once all such errors have been corrected, the file will compile to completion.

LATEX generates a number of files when the initial .TEX file is processed. For example, files with extensions dvi, aux, and log are produced. The dvi file can be previewed on many systems using the xdvi command. On other systems, the dvi file can be converted into a postscript file, using the dvips command, and then previewed or printed. There is also a converter called pdfLATEX that converts LATEX into the popular PDF format. Sometimes it may be necessary to consult with a local LATEX guru or to search online to determine how to process a LATEX file on a particular system.

BASIC-DOCUMENT STRUCTURE

Introduction

To get started users have to specify the type of document that they want to prepare. This specification can be done by using the

```
\documentclass[options]{style}
```

command. In the square braces the user can specify comma-separated optional arguments such as the font size for the document. In the curly braces the user can specify the document style; some options are as follows:

- article
- book
- letter
- report, and
- slides

The next section contains more information on using document styles. To start inputting text into a new document, the user should enter the

```
\begin{document}
```

command. This command specifies that any following text and commands are part of the particular document currently under construction. Each "begin" statement has to have a corresponding "end" statement. Therefore the

```
\end{document}
```

is required at the end of the source code for the LATEX file.

Packages

LATEX allows for increased functionality through the use of add-on features called *packages*. Many packages are pre-installed and available for immediate use. Additional packages are available on the Comprehensive TEX Archive Network (CTAN, 2011). For an abbreviated listing of useful packages refer to Table 3.

To include packages in a LATEX document, the following command must be used:

```
\usepackage[options]{name}
```

where options is a list of package specific user-controllable variables provided by the user, and name is the package name.

Table 3. Some useful LATEX packages

Package	Description
amsmath	Advanced mathematical
color	Provides support for color in a document's output
setspace	Provides support for setting the spacing between lines in a document
hyperref	Used to produce hypertext links in the document
pstricks	Set of commands that allow for the creation of drawings directly inside LATEX code

Document Styles

Document styles determine how the document will be displayed; factors such as default font and margin sizes are determined by the style file. Refer to Table 4 for a brief description of a few popular document styles included with LA-TEX. *Style files* set values for parameters used by LATEX-source files. While LATEX-source files have the extension TEX, style files have the extension sty. Some experienced users create their own style files. Developers of LATEX-produced style files generally adhere to known conventions for the type of document being produced. For example, the *letter* style puts the return address in the customary place for a letter. Therefore it is best to use the default LATEX style files, unless there is a good reason not to.

LATEX Hello World

Using what we have learned about LATEX so far, we can compile a basic document using the following code:

```
\documentclass{article}

\begin{document}
    Hello World
\end{document}
```

This document simply displays the phrase "Hello World" at the top of a page. In subsequent sections we discuss other commands that help us enhance our LATEX document.

LATEX COMMANDS

Introduction

By now the reader should have been able to produce a LATEX file successfully with text showing some of the features described earlier in this chapter. To someone with minimal computing background, LATEX may seem intimidating at first, but with patience and practice LATEX is easy to learn and use. The commands used in LATEX are similar to the tags used in HyperText Markup Language

Table 4. LATEX document classes

Class	Explanation
article	For conference papers and short reports that do not require chapters
book	For books such as this one
letter	For written correspondences
report	For documents that are not quite a full book but more than an article. Documents such as PhD dissertations and Masters theses
slides	For presentations using a projector

(HTML) for creating web pages. LATEX also has some other useful features. For example, a LATEX file can incorporate another file with the usepackage command or using the include command.

Now that we have covered a number of basics, we will present more-sophisticated features and additional LATEX commands, including covering the following topics:

- Styling text
- Fonts
- LATEX environments
- Labels and references

A number of commonly used LATEX commands are presented in this section. A beginner should experiment with these commands to get a feel for how LATEX works. Once a user grasps the basics, the remainder of LATEX is easy to learn. Note that the web is also an excellent source for learning more about LATEX. In the spring of 2009 a query to the search engine Google of "LATEX documentation" turned up 3,760,000 hits. Many of the hits are in fact for pages describing features of LATEX.

Justifying Text

In order to center text horizontally on the page, one can use the following:

```
\begin{center} . . . \end{center}
```

command sequence. The text entered between the two commands will be centered horizontally on the page. For example, the code

```
\begin{center} in the middle \
end{center}
```

Produces the output
in the middle

To create right-justified text, use the following:

```
\begin{flushright} . . . \
end{flushright}
```

command sequence. The text entered between those two commands will be right justified. The code segment

```
\begin{flushright} To the right \
end{flushright}
```

Produces
To the right

The flushleft command works analogously.

Styling Text

To underline text or portions of the text, one can use the

```
\underline{phrase}
```

command. The "phrase" entered in the curly braces will be underlined in the final document. For example, the code

```
\underline{green grass}
```

will produce <u>green grass</u>. Notice that in WORD the line goes through the tail of the two g's, but in LATEX the underline command is "smart enough" to not draw through characters.

To create boldfaced text, one can use the

```
\textbf{bold}
```

command. All the text entered between the curly braces will appear bold. This code generates **bold**. Alternatively, one can use the

```
\begin{bf} dark text \end{bf}
```

command sequence that produces **dark text**. As a third option, one can choose the

```
{\bf black}
```

command, which will produce **black**. If one wants to create *italicized* text, this result can be achieved simply by exchanging bf with it in the preceding examples. Additionally, *italic* text can be created with the \emph{. . .} command.

Fonts in LATEX

A wide range of fonts may be used in LATEX. In fact, there is an entire font-project page devoted to LATEX fonts (Tug, 2011). At the TUG site, the LATEX Font Catalogue website, most of the fonts that are available for LATEX may be found. And, there are perhaps a dozen different font families available. There are several ways to change font face and font size, and here we just give a brief introduction. In Table 5 we provide examples of three font faces and how to code those in LATEX. For example, to typeset text in a Sans-serif font, one uses the following command:

```
\textsf{Text}
```

The resulting output is

Text

The *article* style used for writing papers uses a default font family of Times Roman. If a different font family is desired, say avant-garde, a specification for that font can be given at the beginning of the document. Such a specification is done as follows:

```
\documentclass[12pt]
{article,avantgarde}
```

In this case the document will be typeset in an avant-garde font whose base size is 12 point. The LATEX fonts are of superior quality to those of many other typesetting systems.

Text Size

When creating a document using a style file, LATEX uses the font and font size specified in that style file. This predefined font size can be overridden for the whole document using the options field in the documentclass command that we discussed previously. To adjust the font size to 12pt in an article, the following documentclass command is used:

```
\documentclass[12pt]{article}
```

Font sizes can also be changed temporarily. Unlike the previous example where font point size is specified, special predefined commands are used to temporarily override the default font size of the document. For a complete listing of these commands and their respective point sizes, refer to Table 6. The application of these commands is rather trivial, for instance the following would adjust the font size to small:

Table 5. LATEX font-face commands

Command	Declaration	Effect
\textrm{text}	{\rm text}	Roman family
\textsf{text}	{\sf text}	Sans serif family
\texttt{TEX}	{\tt text}	Typewriter family

```
{\small This is how small text would
look.}
```

and would produce the following output:

This is how small text would look.

STYLE FILES

Just as source files in object-oriented programming languages use libraries and class files, style files are "imported" by LATEX-source files via the following syntax:

```
\usepackage{packagename}
```

The style file, preamble.sty, is one of approximately twenty such files used by a LATEX version of this book's main source file, main. TEX. An excerpt from main.TEX is displayed in Figure 1. Notice how main.TEX incorporates psfig, preamble, and amssymbol with the usepackage command.

ENVIRONMENTS

Introduction

Environments are sections of a LATEX-source file delimited by

```
\begin{environment}. . .\
end{environment}
```

While in an environment, an author can freely type text without having to worry about formatting the document. This is because LATEX formats the document according to the environment's specifications. Such specifications can be created by the author and are kept in a separate file. Therefore, decisions on the style of the environment can be changed as often as the author would like, and

Figure 1. Excerpt from main.TEX *illustrating the* usepackage *command*

```
.
.
.
\usepackage{psfig}
\usepackage{preamble}
\usepackage{amssymbol}
.
.
.
```

these changes need only be coded in one place. While working in the environment, an author can focus on the content.

Later in this section we will see how the newtheorem command is used to create new theorem-like environments. However the

```
\newenvironment{name}
```

command is used to create other types of environments. LATEX contains a set of built-in environments, and many of the common ones are listed in Table 7. We discuss a variety of these environments in the remainder of this section.

Verbatim

The *verbatim* environment is used to produce text that is identical to the text inserted into the LATEX-source file. The LATEX interpreter ignores all text and commands inside the verbatim environment. The following code:

```
\begin{verbatim}
$ \lim_{x \to \infty} \exp(x) = 0 $
\end{verbatim}
```

produces the following output:

```
$ \lim_{x \to \infty} \exp(x) = 0 $
```

Table 6. LATEX font-size commands and point sizes

Command	Size	Command	Size
\tiny	5pt	\large	12pt
\scriptsize	7pt	\Large	14pt
\footnotesize	8pt	\LARGE	18pt
\small	9pt	\huge	20pt
\normalsize	10pt	\HUGE	24pt

Table 7. An alphabetical listing of LATEX environments

abstract	enumerate	large	tabular
appendix	eqnarray	longtable	thebibliography
array	equation	picture	theorem
axiom	figure	quotation	verbatim
center	flushleft	quote	verse
corollary	flushright	smallmatrix	
description	gather	tabbing	
document	itemize	table	

When interpreted by LATEX, this code would normally produce a limit with a subscript of *x* going to infinity and the limit equaling zero. Because we have used the verbatim environment, the code is not interpreted. The verbatim environment is sometimes useful for displaying code or writing things such as poetry.

List Building

LATEX provides three different environments for building lists:

- *Itemize* for bulleted lists
- *Enumerate* for numbered lists
- *Description* for labeled lists

A bulleted list is produced using the following code:

```
\begin{itemize}
  \item First item
```

```
  \item Second item
\end{itemize}
```

where each item in the list is prefixed with the \ item command which generates the item label. This LATEX code generates the following output:

- First item
- Second item

Lists can be nested up to four levels deep to produce outline-styled lists, for example, the following code shows two levels of nesting:

```
\begin{itemize}
  \item First item
  \item Second item
      \begin{itemize}
          \item First nested item
          \item Second nested item
      \end{itemize}
\end{itemize}
```

produces the following output:

- First item
- Second item
  - First nested item
  - Second nested item

At this point we should note that this display of output does not really look like the actual LA-TEX output. However this output is roughly the equivalent looking output in WORD. In LATEX the spacing is much nicer, as the items actually appear closer to the bullets. Altering the previous example to use the enumerate environment produces the following output:

1. First item
2. Second item
   a. First nested item
   b. Second nested item

When using the itemize environment, the bullet character can be altered for each level of the list by using the following commands:

Level 1: `\renewcommand{\labelitemi}{$\bullet$}`
Level 2: `\renewcommand{\labelitemii}{$\bullet$}`
Level 3: `\renewcommand{\labelitemiii}{$\bullet$}`
Level 4: `\renewcommand{\labelitemiv}{$\bullet$}`

where `\bullet` is the bullet symbol desired.

Tabular

The *tabular* environment can be used to create nicely arranged tables in LATEX. Arguments are required after the begin-environment declaration; they specify the alignments of each column. For example, the following LATEX code:

```
\begin{tabular}{|l|l|}
\hline
\multicolumn{2}{|c|}{State Abbrevia-
tions} \\
\hline
FL & Florida \\
GA & Georgia \\
NC & North Carolina \\
\hline
\end{tabular}
```

produces the following table:

State Abbreviations	
FL	Florida
GA	Georgia
NC	North Carolina

In this example the format specification `{|l|l|}` after the command

```
\begin{tabular}
```

specifies that the table should consist of two columns of left-justified text with vertical lines to the left and right of the table and between columns. For a listing of possible format-specification arguments, refer to Table 8. Of course, nearly all other LATEX commands can be used to format items inside the tabular environment.

Table 8. Arguments for the tabular environment

Argument	Description
`l`	Column with left-justified text
`c`	Column with centered text
`r`	Column with right-justified text
`p{width}`	Column with left-justified text of a specified width
`|`	A vertical line between columns
`@{text}`	Inserts the given text between columns

If a writer wants to display a table, as we have been doing with tables throughout this chapter, one can make use of the *table* environment. This environment can be wrapped around the tabular environment. The table environment is called a floating environment, and LATEX will place the table where it believes is the best location for the table. It will not display the table in a preceding page. Of course, larger tables are harder to place well. To display the automatically-generated table label and the caption, one uses the

```
\caption{. . .}
```

command. By default tables are numbered in consecutive order within chapters when using the book style. We discuss how to refer to labels in the next main section.

Figures and Captions

LATEX includes a *figure* environment for displaying figures. This environment behaves similarly to the table environment, and like the table environment, the figure environment is a floating environment. The *picture* environment is sometimes nested inside the figure environment. A complete description of positioning of tables and figures in LATEX is outside the scope of this brief introduction, but the basics involve an optional argument such as [htb]which follows the opening command for the environment:

```
\begin{figure}[htb]
```

The 'h' means *here*, the 't' means *top*, and the 'b' means *bottom*. LATEX will try to position the figure in those three positions on the page where it would fall in the order in which the positions are specified.

Mathematics

LATEX has a special *math mode* for typesetting mathematics. To enter LATEX's math mode, the user simply enters the following:

```
$desired command(s)$
```

The dollar signs instruct the system to enter math mode. The math-mode environment enables the user to enter math equations, special characters, other symbols, and statements of a mathematical nature. One example of a command used in math mode is `$\ldots$`. This command adds three dots to text at the bottom of the line. For example,

```
$a, b, \ldots, z$
```

yields $a, b, ..., z$. Note that in the LATEX output the three dots are spaced evenly and a bit more than would be just three periods typed in WORD. Also, noticed that symbols in math mode appear in an italics-looking font.

To enter a certain numerical value or a special symbol, the user enters math mode as well. For example, `$\pi$` produces π as output. Other mathematical symbols are also easy to specify in LATEX. Table 9 provides a number of common symbols and their LATEX equivalents.

When creating a mathematical document, LATEX allows the writer to control exactly how one wants to present theorems in the text. This is done in such a way that the writer only types in the code to configure a theorem's style once. But, first we need to create what is called a special environment. For example, an environment for a theorem might create text where the word "Theorem" is in boldface and the text of the theorem is in italics. Before we get into those details, we first need to specify that we want an environment to write a theorem, how we are going to number our theorems, and what identifier is used to reference that theorem anywhere in the text. These tasks are completed using the `newtheorem`

Table 9. A collection of common symbols and how to express them in LATEX. All symbols must be used in math mode

Symbol	LATEX	Symbol	LATEX
<	<	□	\Box
>	>	♣	\clubsuit
≠	\neq	←	\leftarrow
≤	\leq	~	\sim
÷	\div	⊥	\perp

command. Figure 2 contains an excerpt from a file called `preamble.sty`. This file uses variations of the `newtheorem` command. The line

```
\newtheorem{theorem}{Theorem}[chapter]
```

defines the parameters for a Theorem. "Theorem" is a reserved keyword while "theorem" is the name of an environment. The parameter in the square brackets indicates the scope of the numbering scheme. In this case, all theorems are sequentially numbered within each "chapter." For example, using the `\begin{theorem}` and `\end{theorem}` pair with the theorem's text in between produces the following output:

Other theorem-like environments such as lemmas, corollaries, and definitions are defined in the preamble.sty file as well. The lemma environment is defined by the following command:

```
\newtheorem{lemma}[theorem]{Lemma}
```

Here "lemma" is the name of an environment, and "Lemma" is the keyword. Similarly, "corollary" is an environment and "Corollary" is the keyword. By placing the word "theorem" in the square brackets for the lemma and corollary environments, we have chosen these three items to be numbered in increasing increments. In other words, a document might have Lemma 4.1, Theorem 4.2, Corollary 4.3, Theorem 4.4, and Lemma 4.5 as its sole objects.

LABELS AND REFERENCES

Introduction

Nearly all authors of technical documents cite sources that they used during their document preparation. Books, papers, and research reports are typical examples of referenced documents. In LATEX by default a reference is represented in the text by a number included in square brackets, for example, [5]. Such a reference might be incorporated as follows: "In [5] Jones and Smith show..." Some authors reject this technique because they do not promote the use of references as a noun. One possible solution to this conflict is to turn the statement into an action. For example, Jones and Smith show ... [5]. The placement of a citation depends on the sentence structure. We discuss

Figure 2. Excerpt from preamble.sty illustrating the use of the newtheorem command

```
.
.
.
\theoremstyle{break}
\newtheorem{theorem}{Theorem}[chapter]
\newtheorem{lemma}[theorem]{Lemma}
\newtheorem{corollary}[theorem]{Corollary}
.
.
.
```

here how to use LATEX to reference many kinds of items, not just bibliography entries.

Many different types of numbered items will often need to be referenced in a document. LATEX allows the author to do referencing efficiently. The commands `\label` and `\ref` are used for labeling and referencing all numbered objects such as theorems, figures, and tables. How does this work? Quite simply, the author can label every theorem, section, picture, and so on, and then use the keyword along with this unique label when typing the actual reference. Here are the details.

First a name must be associated with the object. The `label` command is embedded within an environment and requires the following syntax:

```
\label{labelname}
```

where the user-defined `labelname` is the unique name to be referenced with the `ref` command in other parts of the document. It is wise to be consistent with the choice of labels throughout a document. For example, the labeling convention used in many of my books is

```
\labelname = abc:name
```

where `abc` corresponds to the first three letters of the environment type and name is a unique name for the specific instance of that environment. For example, the following lines demonstrate how to label a theorem:

```
\begin{theorem}
\label{the:mainresult}
Theorem statement goes here.
\end{theorem}
```

Notice in this case we put the label on its own line for the purposes of readability. The command

```
~\ref{labelname}
```

references the environment with the matching label name. So, to reference our "theorem," we type

```
See Theorem~\ref{the:mainresult}.
```

In this case LATEX would output something like the following:

```
See Theorem 5.3.
```

The reader may be wondering why we included a tilde, ~. The tilde prevents a label from being separated from its name. This technique prevents bad breaks at the end of a line.

That is, the word Theorem and the number (5.3 in this case) will not be split even at the end of a line.

Notice that the instructions for referencing an item do not require the author to know the item's number in the document, only the unique label. A *counter* is used for enumerating each labeled environment and is based on the environment's pre-established numbering scheme. So, in LATEX, the author can move all items around as many times as needed without worrying about renumbering any reference. Recompiling a LATEX document produces updated labels. Thus the labeling and referencing process frees the author from the details of the numbering scheme altogether. We should note that a file may need to be processed by LATEX twice in a row to ensure that all the values of the labels are correct. When producing large documents and where some items may need to be moved around, it is extremely useful to have an automatic general labeling and referencing system.

Referring to Specific Things

The capitalization of the first letter in words like lemma and theorem should be consistent throughout the document. For example, referring to both lemma 2.1 and Theorem 3.2 within one document

Figure 3. The LATEX-source code for a portion of a CV

```
\begin{center}
{\large\bf Raymond Greenlaw}\\[.15in]
Curriculum Vit\ae\\
\today\\
\end{center}

\begin{tabbing}
Department of Computer Science \hspace*{.7in}
    \= P.O.~Box 60786 \\
Armstrong Atlantic State University  \> Savannah,
    Georgia 31420 \\
11935 Abercorn Street \> (912) 777-3333 \\
Savannah, Georgia 31419-1997 \\
(912) 344-2988 \\
{\tt rgreenlaw@armstrong.edu}\\
{\tt www.raymondgreenlaw.com}
\end{tabbing}

\vspace*{-.2in}

\noindent
\begin{tabbing}
\hspace*{.3in}\=ARCSK d\=Scholar
(Achievement Reward for College Scient\=ists) DDMMM\=\kill

\head{Education}                       \\[4pt]
  \> $\rhd$ BA
\> Pomona College (Mathematics) cum laude \>1983\\

  \>\> Harvey Mudd College
(3 courses senior year) \>1982--83\\

  \> $\rhd$ MS
\> University of Washington (Computer Science) \>1986\\

  \> $\rhd$ PhD
\> University of Washington (Computer Science) \>1988\\[20pt]

\head{Awards and Honors}          \\[4pt]

  \> $\rhd$ {\em Rensselaer Mathematics Medal\/}
\>\> 1979\\[8pt]
  \> $\rhd$ {\em Bausch \& Lomb Science Medal\/}
\>\> 1979\\[8pt]

\end{tabbing}
```

would be inconsistent. These types of references can be coded in LATEX as follows:

```
Lemma~\ref{lem:coloring}
```

Again, the tilde symbol prevents bad line breaks, so that Lemma and its reference number stay on the same line. Notice the label `lem:coloring` indicates the type of object being referred to, namely a lemma.

Figures and tables should be positioned in the LATEX file immediately after they are first referenced. Since these are floating objects, their placement in the text is not necessarily sequential. Figures and tables should not appear before they have been referenced, so do not introduce a figure or table itself until it has been referenced.

Page References and Citations

Page numbers and *citations* are frequently referenced in a technical paper. The page number can be referenced via the following command:

```
\pageref{labelname}
```

where `labelname` corresponds to any label that can be referenced with the `ref` command. Citations are referenced via the following command:

```
\cite{labelname}
```

where `labelname` corresponds to the label used in the bibliography. A convention for labeling bibliography entries should be established because the list of entries may get large. One convention might be to use a concatenation of the first two letters of each author's last name, and then an appropriate tie-breaking convention.

Gather citation information during the research phase. Do not wait until after completing the document. This method will save time and prevent the tedious task of locating and entering this information throughout the document at a later time.

INSTALLING LATEX

Up until this point we have described how to perform basic functions in LATEX. In this section we briefly discuss how to install TEX Live, and in the next section we present a sample document.

Figure 4. Output produced by the sample LATEX code displayed in Figure 3

Department of Computer Science	P.O. Box 60786
Armstrong Atlantic State University	Savannah, Georgia 31420
11935 Abercorn Street	(912) 777-3333
Savannah, Georgia 31419-1997	
(912) 344-2988	
`rgreenlaw@armstrong.edu`	
`www.raymondgreenlaw.com`	

Education
   ▷   BA   Pomona College (Mathematics) cum laude   1983
             Harvey Mudd College (3 courses senior year)   1982—83
   ▷   MS   University of Washington (Computer Science)   1986
   ▷   PhD   University of Washington (Computer Science)   1988

Awards and Honors
   ▷   *Rensselaer Mathematics Medal*   1979
   ▷   *Bausch & Lomb Science Medal*   1979

There are many good references for LATEX, and these should be consulted for additional information. In addition to the references already cited, there are many useful online references, and a query of "latex tutorial" to most search engines will generate many hits.

`TEX Live` is the currently supported TEX distribution; this version replaces the no-longer supported `teTEX`. `TEX Live` is designed to be cross-platform; running on Unix, Windows, and Mac OS X; but it lacks platform-specific features that other distributions offer. For this reason we will discuss two re-distributions of `TEX Live` available for Windows and Macintosh systems.

- For Unix `TEX Live` is a good choice for producing LATEX documents and is frequently bundled or available for most-major distributions including Linux (TL, 2011).
- For Windows `MiKTEX` is most frequently used (MIKTEX, 2011).
- For OS X `MacTEX` is a good choice (MACTEX, 2011).

For more information including installation instructions on the previously mentioned distributions of TEX Live visit their respective websites: (TL, 2011), (MIKTEX, 2011), and (MacTEX, 2011).

SAMPLE DOCUMENT

We provide the LATEX code for a partial Curriculum Vitæ in Figure 3. The rendering of the code by LATEX is shown in Figure 4. By now the reader will have little trouble matching (most of) the LATEX commands to the output that they produce.

CONCLUSION

The LATEX-typesetting system is an ideal typesetting system for IT professionals. The system provides extremely high-quality output and is very useful for typesetting mathematics. The many extensions that have been created by the LATEX community make the system the one of choice for those with a bit of programming experience. The system continues to evolve and improve, and will likely have a loyal following for many years to come. Thus the system is well worth learning for those with an interest in excellent looking output.

REFERENCES

CTAN. (2011). *The comprehensive TEX archive network*. Retrieved February 14, 2011, from http://www.ctan.org/

Goossens, M. (1999). *The LATEX companion* (2nd ed.). Addison-Wesley.

Knuth, D. E. (1984). *The TEXBook*. Addison-Wesley.

Lamport, L. (1994). *LATEX: A document preparation system* (2nd ed.). Addison-Wesley.

MacTEX. (2011). *The MacTEX-2010 distribution*. Retrieved February 14, 2011 from http://www.tug.org/mactex/

MIKTEX. (2011). *MIKTEX ... Typesetting beautiful documents*. Retrieved February 14, 2011, from http://miktex.org/

TL. (2011). *Welcome to the TEX users group website*. Retrieved February 14, 2011, from http://www.tug.org/texlive

TUG. (2011). *The LATEX font catalogue*. Retrieved February 14, 2011, from http://www.tug.dk/FontCatalogue/

Compilation of References

(2011). *The Chicago Manual of Style* (16th ed.). University of Chicago Press.

ABET. (2011). ABET *Criteria*. Retrieved April 1, 2011, from http://www.abet.org

ACM. (1992). *ACM code of ethics and professional conduct*. Retrieved December 1, 2010, from http://www.acm.org/constitution/code

Adobe. (2011). *Adobe Connect 8*. Retrieved April 1, 2011, from http://www.adobe.com/products/adobeconnect.html

Agnarsson, G., & Greenlaw, R. (2007). *Graph theory: Modeling, applications, and algorithms*. Prentice-Hall.

Arlinghaus, S. L., & Zander, R. H. (1993). Electronic journals: Observations based on actual trials, 1987–present. *Solstice, 19*(2). Retrieved April 4, 2011, from http://www-personal.umich.edu/~copyrght/image/monog17/fulltext.pdf

Arlinghaus, S. L., & Zander, R. H. (2008). Electronic journals: Then and now... A fifteen year retrospective. *Solstice, 19*(2). Retrieved April 4, 2011, from http://www.mobot.org/plantscience/resbot/Repr/Arling-Zand-ElecJour-Solstice08c31.pdf

Association for Computing Machinery. (2011). *Website*. Retrieved on March 22, 2011, from http://www.acm.org

Baase, S. (2008). *A gift of fire: Social, legal, and ethical issues for computing and the Internet* (3rd ed.). Prentice Hall.

Barger, J. (2011). *Jorn Barger*. Retrieved from http://en.wikipedia.org/wiki/Jorn_Barger

BBC. (2007). *Blog death threats spark debate*. BBC News. Retrieved from http://news.bbc.co.uk/2/hi/technology/6499095.stm

BBC. (2008). *Burma blogger jailed for 20 years*. BBC News. Retrieved from http://news.bbc.co.uk/2/hi/asia-pacific/7721271.stm

Bear, J. H. (2010). *Desktop publishing job growth outlook*. Retrieved March 15, 2011, from http://desktoppub.about.com/od/professional/a/2010_outlook.htm

Betamax. (1984). *Sony Corporation of America v. Universal Studios, Inc*. Retrieved from http://cyber.law.harvard.edu/metaschool/fisher/integrity/Links/Cases/sony.html

Bitlaw. (2011). *Princeton University Press v. Michigan Document Services, Inc*. Welcome to Bitlaw. Retrieved from http://www.bitlaw.com/source/cases/copyright/pup.html

Blog. (2011). *Blog*. Retrieved from http://en.wikipedia.org/wiki/Blog

Blogger. (2011). *Blogger: Create a blog, it's free*. Google, Inc. Retrieved from http://www.blogger.com

BlogPluse Live. (2011). *BlogPulse Live*. The Nielsen Company. Retrieved from http://www.blogpulse.com/bplive_full.html

BlogPluse. (2011). *BlogPulse*. The Nielsen Company. Retrieved from http://www.blogpulse.com/

Capone, A. (1940s). *Brainy quote*. Retrieved on February 21, 2011, from http://www.brainyquote.com/quotes/authors/a/al_capone.html

Christakis, N. A., & Fowler, J. H. (2009). *Connected: The surprising power of our social networks and how they shape our lives*. Little, Brown and Company.

Cisco Systems. (2011). *Website*. Retrieved on March 22, 2011, from http://www.cisco.com

Coover, H. (2004). *Harry Coover, inventor of the week archive*. Massachusetts Institute of Technology. Retrieved March 30, 2011, from http://web.mit.edu/invent/iow/coover.html

Copyright 107. (2011). *Limitations on exclusive rights: Fair use*. United States Copyright Office. Retrieved from http://www.copyright.gov/title17/92chap1.html#107

Copyright Clearance. (2011). *Copyright Clearance Center*. Retrieved from http://www.copyright.com/

Copyright. (2011). *Copyright*. United States Copyright Office. Retrieved from http://www.copyright.gov/

Cornell, A. P. A. (2011). *APA citation style*. Cornell University Library. Retrieved from http://www.library.cornell.edu/resrch/citmanage/apa

Cornell, M. L. A. (2011). *MLA citation style*. Cornell University Library. Retrieved from http://www.library.cornell.edu/resrch/citmanage/mla

CTAN. (2011). *The comprehensive TEX archive network*. Retrieved February 14, 2011, from http://www.ctan.org/

Curtis, R., & Simons, W. (2004). *The resume.com guide to writing unbeatable resumes*. McGraw Hill.

Cyranoski, D. (2009). Woo Suk Hwang convicted but not of fraud. *Nature, 461*, 1181. Retrieved from http://www.nature.com/news/2009/091026/full/4611181a.html. doi:10.1038/4611181a

Digg. (2010). *Social news site*. Retrieved December 5, 2010, from http://www.digg.com

DownloadSquad. (2011). *DownloadSquad: The latest app news*. AOL, Inc. Retrieved from http://downloadsquad.switched.com/

ECCC. (2011). *Electronic colloquium on computational complexity*. Retrieved April 4, 2011, from http://www.eccc.uni-trier.de/

Elbrys. (2011). *Secure personal sensor platform*. Elbrys Networks, Inc. Retrieved April 5, 2011, from http://elbrys.com

Engadget. (2011). *Engadget*. AOL, Inc. Retrieved from http://www.engadget.com/

Facebook Stats. (2011). *Facebook statistics*. Retrieved April 5, 2011, from http://www.facebook.com/press/info.php?statistics

Facebook. (2011). *Facebook*. Retrieved April 5, 2011, from http://www.facebook.com

Factoidz. (2011). *Famous cases of plagiarism: More than a traditional, practically an institution*. Factoidz. Retrieved from http://factoidz.com/famous-cases-of-plagiarism-more-than-a-tradition-practically-an-institution/

Fairwagelawyers. (2011). *Famous copyright infringement cases in music. George Harrison versus Bright Tunes Music Corporation*. Retrieved from http://www.fairwagelawyers.com/most-famous-music-copyright-infringment.html

Flickr. (2010). *Share your photos. Watch the world*. Retrieved December 5, 2010, from http://www.flickr.com

Flier, A. C. M. (2011). *ACM code of ethics and professional conduct flier*. Retrieved on April 5, 2011, from http://plone.acm.org/membership/COE_Flyer.pdf

Galido. (2011). *Information Technology blog—Galido. net: Computer tips, tricks, solutions, links and relevant information to IT related topics*. Galido Networks. Reference retrieved on 4/8/2011 from http://galido.net/blog/index.php/ITOnlyBlog/

Golden Rule. (2011). *The golden rule*. Retrieved March 8, 2011, from http://en.wikipedia.org/wiki/The_Golden_Rule

Google. (2011). *20 year Usenet timeline*. Google Groups. Retrieved April 4, 2011, from http://www.google.com/googlegroups/archive_announce_20.html

Google. (2011). *Google Docs*. Retrieved on July 16, 2011, from http://docs.google.com

Goossens, M. (1999). *The LATEX companion* (2nd ed.). Addison-Wesley.

Greenlaw, R. (2004). *The fastest hike: Quest for the Pacific Crest Trail record.* Roxy Publishing.

Greenlaw, R., & Hepp, E. (2001). *Inline/online: Fundamentals of the Internet and World Wide Web.* McGraw Hill.

Greenlaw, R., Hoover, H. J., & Ruzzo, W. L. (1995). *Limits to parallel computation: P-completeness theory.* Oxford University Press.

Howe, J. (2009). *Crowdsourcing: Why the power of the crowd is driving the future of business.* Three Rivers Press. iPad. (2011). *iPad 2.* Apple. Retrieved April 3, 2011, from http://www.apple.com/ipad/

Impress. (2011). *Impress: More power to your presentations.* Retrieved July 13, 2011, from http://www.openoffice.org/product/impress.html

Indeed. (2011). *One search. All jobs.* Retrieved January 27, 2011, from http://www.indeed.com

Institute for Electrical and Electronics Engineers. (2011). *Website.* Retrieved on March 22, 2011, from http://www.ieee.org

JIITO. (2011). *Journal of Information, Information Technology, and Organizations.* Retrieved April 12, 2011, from http://jiito.org/

JIT. (2011). *Journal of Information Technology.* Palgrave Macmillan. Retrieved April 4, 2011, from http://www.palgrave-journals.com/jit/index.html

JITR. (2011). *Journal of Information Technology Research.* Hershey, PA: IGI Global. Retrieved April 4, 2011, from http://www.igi-global.com/bookstore/titledetails.aspx?TitleId=1100

JOBcentral. (2011). *National labor exchange.* Retrieved January 27, 2011, from http://www.jobcentral.com

Jobs, S. (2011). *Steve Jobs unveiling iPhone 4G: Embarrassing moment for Apple's CEO.* Retrieved March 4, 2011 from http://www.youtube.com/watch?v=oITln1SZe9U

Keynote. (2011). *Apple's keynote.* Retrieved July 13, 2011, from http://www.apple.com/iwork/keynote

Kindle. (2011). *Kindle wireless reading device, Wi-Fi, Graphite, 6" display with new e ink pearl technology.* Amazon. Retrieved from http://www.amazon.com/dp/B002Y27P3M/?tag=gocous-20&hvadid=5729884517&ref=pd_sl_992dhxljd6_b

King, M. L. (1963). *I have a dream speech.* Retrieved March 18, 2011, from http://www.americanrhetoric.com/speeches/mlkihaveadream.htm

Knuth, D. E. (1996). *Selected papers on computer science.* Center for the Study of Language and Information. Co-published with Cambridge University Press.

Knuth, D. E. (1984). *The TEXBook.* Addison-Wesley.

Knuth, D. E., Larrabee, T., & Roberts, P. M. (1989). *Mathematical writing.* The Mathematical Association of America.

Lamport, L. (1994). *LATEX: A document preparation system* (2nd ed.). Addison-Wesley.

L-Soft. (2011). *CataList: The official list of LISTSERV lists.* Retrieved April 4, 2011, from http://www.lsoft.com/lists/listref.html

MacTEX. (2011). *The MacTEX-2010 distribution.* Retrieved February 14, 2011 from http://www.tug.org/mactex/

Merriam-Webster's Dictionary. (2011). Retrieved on March 20, 2011, from http://www.merriam-webster.com/

Microsoft Corporation. (2011). *Website.* Retrieved on March 22, 2011, from http://www.microsoft.com

MIKTEX. (2011). *MIKTEX ... Typesetting beautiful documents.* Retrieved February 14, 2011, from http://miktex.org/

Mini Projectors. (2011). *TopTenReviews: Mini projector reviews.* Retrieved July 14, 2011 from http://mini-projector-review.toptenreviews.com

Monster. (2011). *Your calling is calling.* Retrieved January 27, 2011, from http://www.monster.com

Moreira, P. (2007). *Ace the IT resume.* McGraw Hill.

Nook. (2011). *Nook e-reader.* Barnes & Noble. Reference retrieved on April 3, 2011, from http://www.barnesandnoble.com/nook/index.asp

O'Reilly, T. (2007). *Code of conduct: Lessons learned so far*. O'Reilly Radar. Retrieved from http://radar.oreilly.com/archives/2007/04/code-of-conduct.html

O'Reilly, T. (2007). *Draft blogger's code of conduct*. O'Reilly Radar. Retrieved from http://radar.oreilly.com/archives/2007/04/draft-bloggers-1.html

Onlineclasses. (2011). *Top ten plagiarism scandals of all time*. OnlineClasses.org. Retrieved from http://www.onlineclasses.org/2009/10/21/top-10-plagiarism-scandals-of-all-time/

Oxford's English Dictionary. (2011). Retrieved on March 20, 2011, from http://www.oed.com/

Prezi. (2011). *Prezi: Zooming presentations*. Retrieved July 13, 2011, from http://prezi.com

Quinn, M. J. (2006). Case-based analysis: A practical tool for teaching computer ethics. *Proceedings of the Special Interest Group on Computer Science Education*, (pp. 520–524).

Quinn, M. J. (2011). *Ethics for the information age* (4th ed.). Addison-Wesley.

Roget's Thesaurus. (2011). Retrieved on March 29, 2011, from http://thesaurus.com/Roget-Alpha-Index.html

Rosenberg, A. D. (2008). *The resume handbook: How to write outstanding resumes and cover letters for every situation*. Adams Media.

Sabato, L. J. (1998). Joe Biden's plagiarism; Michael Dukakis's 'attack video' — 1988. *The Washington Post*. Retrieved from http://www.washingtonpost.com/wp-srv/politics/special/clinton/frenzy/biden.htm

Schneier, B. (2011). *Schneier on security*. Retrieved from http://www.schneier.com/

Sharma, V. P. (2011). *Ten golden rules of communication*. Mind Publications. Retrieved on April 3, 2011, from http://www.mindpub.com/art196.htm

Smith, V. (2010). Mine foreman: I was ordered to fake safety data. *Williamson Daily News*. Retrieved from http://www.williamsondailynews.com/view/full_story/6593132/article-Mine-foreman--I-was-ordered-to-fake-safety-data?instance=secondary_news_left_column

Solstice. (2011). *Solstice: An Electronic Journal of Geography and Mathematics*. Retrieved April 4, 2011, from http://www-personal.umich.edu/~copyrght/image/solstice.html

Sony. (1984). *Sony Corp. of America v. University Studios, Inc*. Retrieved from http://en.wikipedia.org/wiki/Sony_Corp._of_America_v._Universal_City_Studios,_Inc

Spinello, R. (2002). *Case studies in Information Technology ethics* (2nd ed.). Prentice Hall.

Stennes, B. (2011). *Six rules of effective communication*. Retrieved on April 2, 2011, from http://www.scribd.com/doc/2096451/The-Six-Rules-of-Effective-Communication

Strunk, W., & White, E. B. (2008). *The elements of style, 50th anniversary edition*. Longman Publishing Group.

Tallmo, K.-E. (2011). *The Statue of Anne 1710* (1/6). Retrieved from http://www.copyrighthistory.com/anne.html

TL. (2011). *Welcome to the TEX users group website*. Retrieved February 14, 2011, from http://www.tug.org/texlive

Toastmasters. (2011). *Toastmasters international: Become the speaker and leader you want to be*. Retrieved March 3, 2011, from http://www.toastmasters.org/

Tomlinson, R. (2011). *The first network email*. Retrieved March 25, 2011, from http://openmap.bbn.com/~tomlinso/ray/firstemailframe.html

TUG. (2011). *The LATEX font catalogue*. Retrieved February 14, 2011, from http://www.tug.dk/FontCatalogue/

University of British Columbia. (1999). *Plagiarism avoided*. Faculty of Arts. Retrieved from http://www.arts.ubc.ca/arts-students/plagiarism-avoided.html

USBs. (2011). *National cyber security alert: Cyber security tip ST08-001, using caution with USB drives*. Retrieved March 4, 2011 from http://www.us-cert.gov/cas/tips/ST08-001.html

Ushahidi. (2010). Open source crowdsourcing tools. Retrieved on December 4, 2010, from http://www.ushahidi.com

Van Leunen, M. (1992). *A handbook for scholars (Revised edition)*. Oxford University Press.

Wall Street. (2011). *The Wall Street Journal Asia*. Dow Jones & Company, Inc. Retrieved from http://asia.wsj.com/home-page

Whitehouse. (2011). *The Whitehouse blog*. Retrieved from http://www.whitehouse.gov/blog/

Wikipedia. (2010). *The free encyclopedia*. Retrieved December 4, 2010, from http://www.wikipedia.org

Wikipedia. (2011). *Muhammad ibn Mūsā al-Khwārizmī*. Retrieved on July 14, 2011, from http://en.wikipedia.org/wiki/Al-Khw%C4%81rizm%C4%AB

Wikipedia. (2011). *Technical writing*. Retrieved on July 15, 2011, from http://en.wikipedia.org/wiki/Technical_writing

Wimba. (2011). *Wimba*. Retrieved April 1, 2011, from http://www.wimba.com

WordPress. (2011). *WordPress: Free blogging software*. Retrieved from http://wordpress.com/

Related References

To continue our tradition of advancing information science and technology research, we have compiled a list of recommended IGI Global readings. These references will provide additional information and guidance to further enrich your knowledge and assist you with your own research and future publications.

Abdolmohammadi, M. (2007). Measuring Ethical Reasoning of IT Professionals and Students. In M. Quigley (Ed.), *Encyclopedia of Information Ethics and Security* (pp. 440-444). doi:10.4018/978-1-59140-987-8.ch065

Aguado, M., Toledo, N., Berbineau, M., & Jacob, E. (2012). Communication Architectures and Services for Intelligent Transport Systems. In R. Aquino-Santos, A. Edwards, & V. Rangel-Licea (Eds.), *Wireless Technologies in Vehicular Ad Hoc Networks: Present and Future Challenges* (pp. 205-225). doi:10.4018/978-1-4666-0209-0.ch010

Aikens Wolfe, C., North-Coleman, C., Wallis Williams, S., Amos, D., Bradshaw, G., & Emert, T. (2009). Stepping into the Role of Professional Writer. In J. Salmons, & L. Wilson (Eds.), *Handbook of Research on Electronic Collaboration and Organizational Synergy* (pp. 250-260). doi:10.4018/978-1-60566-106-3.ch017

Akoumianakis, D. (2009). New Media, Communities, and Social Practice: An Introductory Tutorial. In D. Akoumianakis (Ed.), *Virtual Community Practices and Social Interactive Media: Technology Lifecycle and Workflow Analysis* (pp. 1-16). doi:10.4018/978-1-60566-340-1.ch001

Al-Hakim, L., & Xu, H. (2005). Data Quality and Work Alignment: Do IT Professionals Think Differently? In A. Sarmento (Ed.), *Issues of Human Computer Interaction* (pp. 291-320). doi:10.4018/978-1-59140-191-9.ch015

Alshawi, M., & Salleh, H. (2012). IT/IS Readiness Maturity Model. In M. Alshawi, & M. Arif (Eds.), *Cases on E-Readiness and Information Systems Management in Organizations: Tools for Maximizing Strategic Alignment* (pp. 1-14). doi:10.4018/978-1-61350-311-9.ch001

Ampuero, M. A., Baldoquín de la Peña, M. G., & Castillo, S. T. (2010). Identification of Patterns for the Formation of Software Development Projects Teams. [IJHCITP]. *International Journal of Human Capital and Information Technology Professionals*, 1(3), 69–80. doi:10.4018/jhcitp.2010070105

Anderson, J. E., Barrett, K., & Schwager, P. H. (2005). An Exploration of the Value of Information Systems Certification: The Perspective of the Human Resource Professional. In M. Nakayama, & N. Sutcliffe (Eds.), *Managing IT Skills Portfolios: Planning, Acquisition and Performance Evaluation* (pp. 210-231). doi:10.4018/978-1-59140-515-3.ch009

Andò, R. (2012). The Challenge of Audience Research on Web 2.0: The Possibilities, Problems and Perspectives of Sentiment Analysis. In F. Comunello (Ed.), *Networked Sociability and Individualism: Technology for Personal and Professional Relationships* (pp. 63-77). doi:10.4018/978-1-61350-338-6.ch004

Andriole, S. J. (2010). Templates for the Development of Business Technology Strategies. [JITR]. *Journal of Information Technology Research*, 3(3), 1–10. doi:10.4018/jitr.2010070101

Ansari, J., Zhang, X., & Mähönen, P. (2010). Practical Experiences and Design Considerations on Medium Access Control Protocols for Wireless Sensor Networks. In H. Jin, & W. Jiang (Eds.), *Handbook of Research on Developments and Trends in Wireless Sensor Networks: From Principle to Practice* (pp. 128-158). doi:10.4018/978-1-61520-701-5.ch007

Armstrong, D. J., Nelson, H. J., Nelson, K. M., & Narayanan, V. K. (2010). Building the IT Workforce of the Future: The Demand for More Complex, Abstract, and Strategic Knowledge. In M. Khosrow-Pour (Ed.), *Global, Social, and Organizational Implications of Emerging Information Resources Management: Concepts and Applications* (pp. 323-340). doi:10.4018/978-1-60566-962-5.ch017

Arndt, T., Chang, S. K., Guerico, A., & Maresca, P. (2007). An XML-Based Approach to Multimedia Engineering for Distance Learning. In T. Shih, & J. Hung (Eds.), *Future Directions in Distance Learning and Communication Technologies* (pp. 108-137). doi:10.4018/978-1-59904-376-0.ch006

Ash, R. A., Rosenbloom, J. L., Coder, L., & Dupont, B. (2006). Personality Characteristics of Established IT Professionals II: Occupational Personality Characteristics. In E. Trauth (Ed.), *Encyclopedia of Gender and Information Technology* (pp. 990-998). doi:10.4018/978-1-59140-815-4.ch156

Asprey, L., Green, R., & Middleton, M. (2009). Integrative Information Systems Architecture: Document & Content Management. In V. Ferraggine, J. Doorn, & L. Rivero (Eds.), *Handbook of Research on Innovations in Database Technologies and Applications: Current and Future Trends* (pp. 682-692). doi:10.4018/978-1-60566-242-8.ch073

Bamberg, J., & Lehtonen, P. (2012). Facilitating Knowledge Sharing in E-Governance: Online Spatial Displays as Translating Devices. In A. Manoharan, & M. Holzer (Eds.), *E-Governance and Civic Engagement: Factors and Determinants of E-Democracy* (pp. 149-172). doi:10.4018/978-1-61350-083-5.ch008

Banks, W. P., & Van Sickle, T. (2011). Digital Partnerships for Professional Development: Rethinking University–Public School Collaborations. In M. Bowdon, & R. Carpenter (Eds.), *Higher Education, Emerging Technologies, and Community Partnerships: Concepts, Models and Practices* (pp. 153-163). doi:10.4018/978-1-60960-623-7.ch014

Barrett, W., Lau, M. S., & Dew, P. M. (2000). Facilitating Knowledge Transfer in an R&D Environment: A Case Study. In D. Schwartz, T. Brasethvik, & M. Divitini (Eds.), *Internet-Based Organizational Memory and Knowledge Management* (pp. 147-169). doi:10.4018/978-1-878289-82-7.ch008

Barroso, A. C., Ricciardi, R. I., & Junior, J. A. (2012). Web 2.0 and Project Management: Reviewing the Change Path and Discussing a Few Cases. In I. Boughzala, & A. Dudezert (Eds.), *Knowledge Management 2.0: Organizational Models and Enterprise Strategies* (pp. 164-189). doi:10.4018/978-1-61350-195-5.ch009

Baumeister, A., & Ilg, M. (2010). Activity Driven Budgeting of Software Projects. [IJHCITP]. *International Journal of Human Capital and Information Technology Professionals*, *1*(4), 14–30. doi:10.4018/jhcitp.2010100102

Bechchi, M., Raschia, G., & Mouaddib, N. (2011). Practical Approaches to the Many-Answer Problem. In L. Yan, & Z. Ma (Eds.), *Advanced Database Query Systems: Techniques, Applications and Technologies* (pp. 28-84). doi:10.4018/978-1-60960-475-2.ch002

Beckerman, C. (2010). Transforming and Computerizing Professional Artifacts: An Underestimated Opportunity for Learning. [IJHDRI]. *International Journal of Healthcare Delivery Reform Initiatives*, *2*(3), 1–10. doi:10.4018/jhdri.2010070101

Beise, C. M., Niederman, F., & Mattord, H. (2006). IT Project Managers' Perceptions and Use of Virtual Team Technologies. In M. Khosrow-Pour (Ed.), *Advanced Topics in Information Resources Management, Volume 5* (pp. 25-43). doi:10.4018/978-1-59140-929-8.ch002

Blanchard, A., Askay, D. A., & Frear, K. A. (2010). Sense of Community in Professional Virtual Communities. In S. Long (Ed.), *Communication, Relationships and Practices in Virtual Work* (pp. 161-176). doi:10.4018/978-1-61520-979-8.ch009

Boehm, D., & Aniola-Jedrzejek, L. (2009). Seven Principles of Good Practice for Virtual International Collaboration. In M. Chang, & C. Kuo (Eds.), *Learning Culture and Language through ICTs: Methods for Enhanced Instruction* (pp. 298-317). doi:10.4018/978-1-60566-166-7.ch018

Boot, E., Nelson, J., & De Faveri, D. (2008). Lost In Translation: Improving The Transition Between Design And Production Of Instructional Software. In L. Botturi, & T. Stubbs (Eds.), *Handbook of Visual Languages for Instructional Design: Theories and Practices* (pp. 366-379). doi:10.4018/978-1-59904-729-4.ch018

Bowdon, M. (2005). Virtual Networks: Mapping Community-Based Collaboration and Professional Writing. In K. St.Amant, & P. Zemliansky (Eds.), *Internet-Based Workplace Communications: Industry and Academic Applications* (pp. 107-129). doi:10.4018/978-1-59140-521-4.ch006

Brabston, M., & Dahl, J. (2005). Limitations of Having Diversity in Codes of Information Ethics: A Professional and Corporate Perspective. In L. Freeman, & A. Peace (Eds.), *Information Ethics: Privacy and Intellectual Property* (pp. 239-256). doi:10.4018/978-1-59140-491-0.ch014

Brady, A. (2009). Speaking of Software: Case Studies in Software Communication. In H. Ellis, S. Demurjian, & J. Naveda (Eds.), *Software Engineering: Effective Teaching and Learning Approaches and Practices* (pp. 75-97). doi:10.4018/978-1-60566-102-5.ch005

Brescia, W., & Cline, T. (2006). Online Calculator Training in Mathematics and Technology. [JCIT]. *Journal of Cases on Information Technology*, 8(2), 1–29. doi:10.4018/jcit.2006040101

Brewer, E. W. (2010). The History of Career and Technical Education. In V. Wang (Ed.), *Definitive Readings in the History, Philosophy, Theories and Practice of Career and Technical Education* (pp. 1-14). doi:10.4018/978-1-61520-747-3.ch001

Brewer, P. (2007). Researching Online Intercultural Dialog in Business: Using Established Methods to Create New Tools. In K. St.Amant (Ed.), *Linguistic and Cultural Online Communication Issues in the Global Age* (pp. 121-122). doi:10.4018/978-1-59904-213-8.ch008

Brook, C., & Lock, G. (2010). Reflective Practice, Professional Learning, and Educational Partnerships: Effecting Change in Classroom Settings. In E. Ng (Ed.), *Comparative Blended Learning Practices and Environments* (pp. 188-203). doi:10.4018/978-1-60566-852-9.ch010

Brown, E. (2006). Technical Research for Improving Web-Based Instructional Artifacts. In B. Mann (Ed.), *Selected Styles in Web-Based Educational Research* (pp. 202-219). doi:10.4018/978-1-59140-732-4.ch014

Buitenhuis, J. M. (2011). In the Pipeline: The New Generations of IT Professionals. In J. Luftman (Ed.), *Managing IT Human Resources: Considerations for Organizations and Personnel* (pp. 150-177). doi:10.4018/978-1-60960-535-3.ch011

Bullen, C. V., & Abraham, T. (2011). Patterns of Skills and Careers in the Information Technology Workforce. In J. Luftman (Ed.), *Managing IT Human Resources: Considerations for Organizations and Personnel* (pp. 1-9). doi:10.4018/978-1-60960-535-3.ch001

Bullen, C. V., Abraham, T., Gallagher, K., Kaiser, K. M., & Simon, J. C. (2009). Changing IT Skills: The Impact of Sourcing Strategies on In-House Capability Requirements. In M. Khosrow-Pour (Ed.), *Consumer Behavior, Organizational Development, and Electronic Commerce: Emerging Issues for Advancing Modern Socioeconomies* (pp. 148-170). doi:10.4018/978-1-60566-126-1.ch009

Burgess, S., Carmine Sellitto, C., & Karanasios, S. (2009). Web Presence Promotion. In S. Burgess, C. Sellitto, & S. Karanasios (Eds.), *Effective Web Presence Solutions for Small Businesses: Strategies for Successful Implementation* (pp. 197-222). doi:10.4018/978-1-60566-224-4.ch008

Burlea, A. S. (2010). Ethics of Information in Distributed Business Environment. In M. Pankowska (Ed.), *Infonomics for Distributed Business and Decision-Making Environments: Creating Information System Ecology* (pp. 301-315). doi:10.4018/978-1-60566-890-1.ch018

Bygstad, B. (2006). Managing Socio-Technical Integration in Iterative Information System Development Projects. [IJTHI]. *International Journal of Technology and Human Interaction*, 2(4), 1–16. doi:10.4018/jthi.2006100101

Casado-Lumbreras, C., Colomo-Palacios, R., Hernández-López, A., & Soto-Acosta, P. (2011). Personnel Performance Appraisal Coverage in ITIL, COBIT and CMMi: A Study from the Perspective of People-CMM. [IJKSR]. *International Journal of Knowledge Society Research*, *2*(2), 59–70. doi:10.4018/jksr.2011040106

Castelfranchi, C., Pezzulo, G., & Tummolini, L. (2010). Behavioral Implicit Communication (BIC): Communicating with Smart Environments. [IJACI]. *International Journal of Ambient Computing and Intelligence*, *2*(1), 1–12. doi:10.4018/jaci.2010010101

Cata, T. (2009). Understanding Outsourcing of Web-Based Applications in Organizations: The Case of E-Insurance. In M. Khosrow-Pour (Ed.), *Consumer Behavior, Organizational Development, and Electronic Commerce: Emerging Issues for Advancing Modern Socioeconomies* (pp. 171-187). doi:10.4018/978-1-60566-126-1.ch010

Cawthon, S., & Harris, A. (2008). Developing a Community of Practice in an Online Research Lab. In K. Orvis, & A. Lassiter (Eds.), *Computer-Supported Collaborative Learning: Best Practices and Principles for Instructors* (pp. 41-65). doi:10.4018/978-1-59904-753-9.ch003

Cecez-Kecmanovic, D., & Nagm, F. (2011). Have You Taken Your Guys on the Journey?: An ANT Account of IS Project Evaluation. In A. Tatnall (Ed.), *Actor-Network Theory and Technology Innovation: Advancements and New Concepts* (pp. 1-19). doi:10.4018/978-1-60960-197-3.ch001

Chakrabarty, S. (2007). The Journey to New Lands: Utilizing the Global IT Workforce Through Offshore-Insourcing. In P. Yoong, & S. Huff (Eds.), *Managing IT Professionals in the Internet Age* (pp. 277-318). doi:10.4018/978-1-59140-917-5.ch012

Chao, L. (2008). Introduction to Online Teaching of Technology-Based Courses. In L. Chao (Ed.), *Strategies and Technologies for Developing Online Computer Labs for Technology-Based Courses* (pp. 1-31). doi:10.4018/978-1-59904-507-8.ch001

Chen, A. Y., & McLeod, D. (2006). Collaborative Filtering for Information Recommendation Systems. In M. Khosrow-Pour (Ed.), *Encyclopedia of E-Commerce, E-Government, and Mobile Commerce* (pp. 118-123). doi:10.4018/978-1-59140-799-7.ch020

Cleary, Y. (2010). Online Support for Students' Writing Skills Development in a Technical Communication Introductory Module. In R. Donnelly, J. Harvey, & K. O'Rourke (Eds.), *Critical Design and Effective Tools for E-Learning in Higher Education: Theory into Practice* (pp. 280-293). doi:10.4018/978-1-61520-879-1.ch017

Codone, S. (2009). Decision Point: IT Infrastructure Mismatch. [JCIT]. *Journal of Cases on Information Technology*, *11*(3), 18–30. doi:10.4018/jcit.2009070102

Colomo-Palacios, R. (2009). Semantic Competence Pull: A Semantics-Based Architecture for Filling Competency Gaps in Organizations. In R. Garcia (Ed.), *Semantic Web for Business: Cases and Applications* (pp. 321-335). doi:10.4018/978-1-60566-066-0.ch015

Colomo-Palacios, R., Ruano-Mayoral, M., Soto-Acosta, P., & García-Crespo, Á. (2010). The War for Talent: Identifying Competences in IT Professionals through Semantics. [IJSKD]. *International Journal of Socio-technology and Knowledge Development*, *2*(3), 26–36. doi:10.4018/jskd.2010070103

Colomo-Palacios, R., Tovar-Caro, E., García-Crespo, Á., & Gómez-Berbís, J. M. (2010). Identifying Technical Competences of IT Professionals: The Case of Software Engineers. [IJHCITP]. *International Journal of Human Capital and Information Technology Professionals*, *1*(1), 31–43. doi:10.4018/jhcitp.2010091103

Conlin, M. (2011). E-Novation Collaboration. In H. Pattinson, & D. Low (Eds.), *E-Novation for Competitive Advantage in Collaborative Globalization: Technologies for Emerging E-Business Strategies* (pp. 92-121). doi:10.4018/978-1-60566-394-4.ch007

Correia, A. M., & Sarmento, A. (2005). The European Challenge of KM and Innovation: A Skills and Competence Portfolio for the Knowledge Worker in SME's. In B. Montano (Ed.), *Innovations of Knowledge Management* (pp. 252-284). doi:10.4018/978-1-59140-281-7.ch012

Cottrill, B. (2010). Complicating Communication in Computer Mediate Environments: A Textual Analysis of Blogs in the First-Year Writing Classroom. In J. Park, & E. Abels (Eds.), *Interpersonal Relations and Social Patterns in Communication Technologies: Discourse Norms, Language Structures and Cultural Variables* (pp. 202-219). doi:10.4018/978-1-61520-827-2.ch011

Cuel, R., & Ferrario, R. (2009). The Impact of Technology in Organizational Communication. In B. Staudinger, V. Höß, & H. Ostermann (Eds.), *Nursing and Clinical Informatics: Socio-Technical Approaches* (pp. 198-217). doi:10.4018/978-1-60566-234-3.ch013

Cuganesan, S., & Petty, R. (2010). Intellectual Capital Measurements and Reporting: Issues and Challenges for Multinational Organizations. In K. O'Sullivan (Ed.), *Strategic Intellectual Capital Management in Multinational Organizations: Sustainability and Successful Implications* (pp. 75-94). doi:10.4018/978-1-60566-679-2.ch005

D'Angelo, B., & Maid, B. (2009). Assessing Outcomes in a Technical Communication Capstone. In C. Schreiner (Ed.), *Handbook of Research on Assessment Technologies, Methods, and Applications in Higher Education* (pp. 152-166). doi:10.4018/978-1-60566-667-9.ch009

Daniele, M., Martellotto, P., & Baum, G. (2007). Generic Model of the Business Model and Its Formalization in Object-Z. In A. Dasso, & A. Funes (Eds.), *Verification, Validation and Testing in Software Engineering* (pp. 358-384). doi:10.4018/978-1-59140-851-2.ch012

Darisipudi, A., & Sharma, S. K. (2008). Blogs: A Computer Mediated Communication Tool for Virtual Team Collaboration. In S. Kelsey, & K. St.Amant (Eds.), *Handbook of Research on Computer Mediated Communication* (pp. 720-730). doi:10.4018/978-1-59904-863-5.ch051

Datta, A. (2011). Information Technology Capability, Knowledge Assets and Firm Innovation: A Theoretical Framework for Conceptualizing the Role of Information Technology in Firm Innovation. [IJSITA]. *International Journal of Strategic Information Technology and Applications*, 2(3), 9–26. doi:10.4018/jsita.2011070102

Davis, B. H., Smith, M. K., & Tsai, S. (2010). When the Online Conversation is Prompted. In R. Taiwo (Ed.), *Handbook of Research on Discourse Behavior and Digital Communication: Language Structures and Social Interaction* (pp. 579-591). doi:10.4018/978-1-61520-773-2.ch037

Davis, J., Harding, L., & Mascle, D. (2010). Digital Connections and Learning Styles. In W. Ritke-Jones (Ed.), *Virtual Environments for Corporate Education: Employee Learning and Solutions* (pp. 302-320). doi:10.4018/978-1-61520-619-3.ch017

Dietz, P., van den Berg, A., Marth, K., Weigert, T., & Weil, F. (2007). Practical Considerations in Automatic Code Generation. In D. Zhang, & J. Tsai (Eds.), *Advances in Machine Learning Applications in Software Engineering* (pp. 346-408). doi:10.4018/978-1-59140-941-1.ch014

Downey, J. P., & Smith, L. A. (2011). The Role of Computer Attitudes in Enhancing Computer Competence in Training. [JOEUC]. *Journal of Organizational and End User Computing*, 23(3), 81–100. doi:10.4018/joeuc.2011070105

Downing, K. F., & Holtz, J. K. (2008). Online Science: Contemporary Approaches to Practical Work. In K. Downing, & J. Holtz (Eds.), *Online Science Learning: Best Practices and Technologies* (pp. 121-158). doi:10.4018/978-1-59904-986-1.ch007

Downing, K. F., & Holtz, J. K. (2008). The Role of Practical Work in Online Science. In K. Downing, & J. Holtz (Eds.), *Online Science Learning: Best Practices and Technologies* (pp. 73-97). doi:10.4018/978-1-59904-986-1.ch005

Eardley, A., & Uden, L. (2011). The Use of 'Web 2.0' and Social Software in Support of Professional Learning Communities. In A. Eardley, & L. Uden (Eds.), *Innovative Knowledge Management: Concepts for Organizational Creativity and Collaborative Design* (pp. 204-214). doi:10.4018/978-1-60566-701-0.ch012

Ebner, N. (2008). Trust Building in E-Negotiation. In L. Brennan, & V. Johnson (Eds.), *Computer-Mediated Relationships and Trust: Managerial and Organizational Effects* (pp. 139-157). doi:10.4018/978-1-59904-495-8.ch010

Edwards, K., Yates, S., Dujardin, A., & Green, G. (2008). Writing Research into Professional E-Mail Communication. In P. Zemliansky, & K. St.Amant (Eds.), *Handbook of Research on Virtual Workplaces and the New Nature of Business Practices* (pp. 364-381). doi:10.4018/978-1-59904-893-2.ch026

Fägersten, K. B., Holmsten, E., & Cunningham, U. (2010). Multimodal Communication and Meta-Modal Discourse. In R. Taiwo (Ed.), *Handbook of Research on Discourse Behavior and Digital Communication: Language Structures and Social Interaction* (pp. 145-163). doi:10.4018/978-1-61520-773-2.ch009

Fairchild, J., Cassidy, S., Cushenbery, L., & Hunter, S. T. (2011). Integrating Technology with the Creative Design Process. In A. Mesquita (Ed.), *Technology for Creativity and Innovation: Tools, Techniques and Applications* (pp. 26-51). doi:10.4018/978-1-60960-519-3.ch002

Farmer, L. (2010). Designing Culturally-Sensitive Career and Technical Career Curriculum. In V. Wang (Ed.), *Definitive Readings in the History, Philosophy, Theories and Practice of Career and Technical Education* (pp. 43-61). doi:10.4018/978-1-61520-747-3.ch004

Fauzi, S. S., Ramli, N., & Noor, M. K. (2012). Implementing Internal Software Process Assessment: An Experience at a Mid-Size IT Company. In S. Fauzi, M. Nasir, N. Ramli, & S. Sahibuddin (Eds.), *Software Process Improvement and Management: Approaches and Tools for Practical Development* (pp. 78-99). doi:10.4018/978-1-61350-141-2.ch005

Federici, T., & Braccini, A. M. (2012). The Interplay between Practitioners and Technological Experts in the Design Process of an Archaeology Information System. [JCIT]. *Journal of Cases on Information Technology*, *14*(1), 26–45. doi:10.4018/jcit.2012010103

Fernandes del Maschi, V., Souza, L. S., de Mesquita Spínola, M., Vendramel, W., Costa, I., Pirola, J., & de Lima Esteves, A. (2008). Practical Experience in Customization for a Software Development Process for Small Companies Based on RUP Process and MSF. In H. Oktaba, & M. Piattini (Eds.), *Software Process Improvement for Small and Medium Enterprises: Techniques and Case Studies* (pp. 71-93). doi:10.4018/978-1-59904-906-9.ch003

Ferris, T. L. (2012). Engineering Design as Research. In M. Mora, O. Gelman, A. Steenkamp, & M. Raisinghani (Eds.), *Research Methodologies, Innovations and Philosophies in Software Systems Engineering and Information Systems* (pp. 389-402). doi:10.4018/978-1-4666-0179-6.ch020

Finkelman, J., & Kelly, L. (2012). Management Ethics: The Psychology of Positive vs. Destructive Rule Breaking. In C. Wankel, & A. Stachowicz-Stanusch (Eds.), *Handbook of Research on Teaching Ethics in Business and Management Education* (pp. 164-180). doi:10.4018/978-1-61350-510-6.ch010

Fioravanti, F. (2006). Training. In F. Fioravanti (Ed.), *Skills for Managing Rapidly Changing IT Projects* (pp. 36-43). doi:10.4018/978-1-59140-757-7.ch003

Fok, A. W., & Ip, H. H. (2009). An Agent-Based Framework for Personalized Learning in Continuous Professional Development. In M. Syed (Ed.), *Strategic Applications of Distance Learning Technologies* (pp. 96-110). doi:10.4018/978-1-59904-480-4.ch007

Forte, M. C. (2006). Web Site Development in Action Research. In S. Marshall, W. Taylor, & X. Yu (Eds.), *Encyclopedia of Developing Regional Communities with Information and Communication Technology* (pp. 729-734). doi:10.4018/978-1-59140-575-7.ch130

Franz, T., & Sizov, S. (2008). Communication Systems for Semantic Work Environments. In J. Rech, B. Decker, & E. Ras (Eds.), *Emerging Technologies for Semantic Work Environments: Techniques, Methods, and Applications* (pp. 16-32). doi:10.4018/978-1-59904-877-2.ch002

Freiermuth, M. R. (2005). A Bridge to the Workplace: Using an Internet-Based Simulation in the Writing Classroom. In K. St.Amant, & P. Zemliansky (Eds.), *Internet-Based Workplace Communications: Industry and Academic Applications* (pp. 180-210). doi:10.4018/978-1-59140-521-4.ch009

Frey, B. A., Fuller, R., & Kuhne, G. (2010). Designing Skills Based Classes. In R. Fuller, G. Kuhne, & B. Frey (Eds.), *Distinctive Distance Education Design: Models for Differentiated Instruction* (pp. 169-187). doi:10.4018/978-1-61520-865-4.ch013

Fry, S. W. (2010). The Professional Handbook: Developing Professionalism and Reflective Skills while Connecting Theory and Practice through Technology. In J. Yamamoto, J. Kush, R. Lombard, & C. Hertzog (Eds.), *Technology Implementation and Teacher Education: Reflective Models* (pp. 347-364). doi:10.4018/978-1-61520-897-5.ch020

Gabarre, C., & Gabarre, S. (2012). Designing, Developing and Evaluating Professional Language and Intercultural Competencies with Phone Simulations. In N. Alias, & S. Hashim (Eds.), *Instructional Technology Research, Design and Development: Lessons from the Field* (pp. 319-334). doi:10.4018/978-1-61350-198-6.ch020

Ghosh, S. (2010). Adhering to Open Technology Standards. In S. Ghosh (Ed.), *Net Centricity and Technological Interoperability in Organizations: Perspectives and Strategies* (pp. 142-154). doi:10.4018/978-1-60566-854-3.ch010

González, D. P., & González, P. S. (2012). Interactions and Effects of CRM 2.0 in Public Administration: Issues of Interest to IT Professionals. [IJHCITP]. *International Journal of Human Capital and Information Technology Professionals, 3*(1), 26–41. doi:10.4018/IJHCITP.2012010103

Gould, H., Hughes, M., Maharg, P., & Nicol, E. (2009). The Narrative Event Diagram: A Tool for Designing Professional Simulations. In D. Gibson, & Y. Baek (Eds.), *Digital Simulations for Improving Education: Learning Through Artificial Teaching Environments* (pp. 101-118). doi:10.4018/978-1-60566-322-7.ch006

Greil, M. J., & Millam, E. (2011). Building IT Capacity for Leadership in a New Age. In J. Luftman (Ed.), *Managing IT Human Resources: Considerations for Organizations and Personnel* (pp. 255-270). doi:10.4018/978-1-60960-535-3.ch016

Habil, H. (2010). Functions and Strategies of Email Communication at the Workplace. In R. Taiwo (Ed.), *Handbook of Research on Discourse Behavior and Digital Communication: Language Structures and Social Interaction* (pp. 479-489). doi:10.4018/978-1-61520-773-2.ch030

Hawk, S., & Witt, T. (2006). Telecommunications Courses in Information Systems Programs. [IJICTE]. *International Journal of Information and Communication Technology Education, 2*(1), 79–92. doi:10.4018/jicte.2006010107

Hawk, S., & Zheng, W. (2006). Interaction Standards in E-Business. In M. Khosrow-Pour (Ed.), *Encyclopedia of E-Commerce, E-Government, and Mobile Commerce* (pp. 648-652). doi:10.4018/978-1-59140-799-7.ch104

Hawkey, K., & Kellar, M. (2009). Recommendations for Reporting Web Usage Studies. In B. Jansen, A. Spink, & I. Taksa (Eds.), *Handbook of Research on Web Log Analysis* (pp. 181-204). doi:10.4018/978-1-59904-974-8.ch010

Hegarty, R., Lunney, T., Curran, K., & Mulvenna, M. (2009). Ambient Communication Experience (ACE). [IJACI]. *International Journal of Ambient Computing and Intelligence, 1*(2), 53–58. doi:10.4018/jaci.2009040107

Hegarty, R., Lunney, T., Curran, K., & Mulvenna, M. (2011). Ambient Communication Experience (ACE), Information Interaction in Design Space. In K. Curran (Ed.), *Ubiquitous Developments in Ambient Computing and Intelligence: Human-Centered Applications* (pp. 139-146). doi:10.4018/978-1-60960-549-0.ch014

Hegazy, M., & Hamdy, R. (2010). The Role of Computer-Mediated Communication Modes in Enhancing Audit Quality: An Empirical Study. In V. Godara (Ed.), *Pervasive Computing for Business: Trends and Applications* (pp. 77-93). doi:10.4018/978-1-60566-996-0.ch006

Hemphill, L. S., & McCaw, D. S. (2009). Moodling Professional Development Training that Worked. In L. Tan Wee Hin, & R. Subramaniam (Eds.), *Handbook of Research on New Media Literacy at the K-12 Level: Issues and Challenges* (pp. 808-822). doi:10.4018/978-1-60566-120-9.ch050

Henry, J. (2011). Hybridizing F2F and Virtual Collaboration between a Government Agency and Service-Learning Technical Writing Students. In M. Bowdon, & R. Carpenter (Eds.), *Higher Education, Emerging Technologies, and Community Partnerships: Concepts, Models and Practices* (pp. 58-67). doi:10.4018/978-1-60960-623-7.ch006

Hermeking, M. (2012). Culture, Online Technology and Computer-Mediated Technical Documentation: Contributions from the field of Intercultural Communication. In K. St.Amant, & S. Kelsey (Eds.), *Computer-Mediated Communication across Cultures: International Interactions in Online Environments* (pp. 77-90). doi:10.4018/978-1-60960-833-0.ch006

Hernández-López, A., Colomo-Palacios, R., García-Crespo, Á., & Cabezas-Isla, F. (2011). Present, Past and Future of IT Careers, a Review: From the Local Pyramid to the "Flat World". In J. Luftman (Ed.), *Managing IT Human Resources: Considerations for Organizations and Personnel* (pp. 218-243). doi:10.4018/978-1-60960-535-3.ch014

Hernández-López, A., Colomo-Palacios, R., García-Crespo, Á., & Cabezas-Isla, F. (2011). Software Engineering Productivity: Concepts, Issues and Challenges. [IJITPM]. *International Journal of Information Technology Project Management, 2*(1), 37–47. doi:10.4018/jitpm.2011010103

Hewett, B. L., Remley, D., Zemliansky, P., & DiPardo, A. (2010). Frameworks for Talking about Virtual Collaborative Writing. In B. Hewett, & C. Robidoux (Eds.), *Virtual Collaborative Writing in the Workplace: Computer-Mediated Communication Technologies and Processes* (pp. 28-52). doi:10.4018/978-1-60566-994-6.ch002

Hoffman, G. M. (2004). Ethical Challenges for Information Systems Professionals. In L. Brennan, & V. Johnson (Eds.), *Social, Ethical and Policy Implications of Information Technology* (pp. 118-129). doi:10.4018/978-1-59140-168-1.ch007

Hou Vat, K. (2010). Virtual Organizing Professional Learning Communities through a Servant-Leader Model of Appreciative Coaching. In Y. Inoue (Ed.), *Cases on Online and Blended Learning Technologies in Higher Education: Concepts and Practices* (pp. 183-206). doi:10.4018/978-1-60566-880-2.ch011

Hsu, J., Hamilton, K., & Wang, J. (2010). Educating IT Professionals Using Effective Online, Pedagogical, and Scheduling Techniques. [IJHCITP]. *International Journal of Human Capital and Information Technology Professionals, 1*(3), 15–31. doi:10.4018/jhcitp.2010070102

Huang, L. K. (2010). Innovation Managed and IT Infrastructure Capability. [IJSITA]. *International Journal of Strategic Information Technology and Applications, 1*(4), 19–41. doi:10.4018/jsita.2010100102

Huggins, R., & Weir, M. (2012). Managing Intellectual Assets in Small Knowledge-Intensive Organizations. In I. Management Association, USA (Ed.), *Organizational Learning and Knowledge: Concepts, Methodologies, Tools and Applications* (pp. 2158-2180). doi:10.4018/978-1-60960-783-8.ch608

Hunsinger, D. S., Land, J., & Chen, C. C. (2010). Enhancing Students' Loyalty to the Information Systems Major. [IJICTE]. *International Journal of Information and Communication Technology Education, 6*(1), 81–95. doi:10.4018/jicte.2010091107

Hunter, M. G., Tan, F. B., & Tan, B. C. (2010). Voluntary Turnover of Information Systems Professionals: A Cross-Cultural Investigation. In M. Hunter, & F. Tan (Eds.), *Technological Advancement in Developed and Developing Countries: Discoveries in Global Information Management* (pp. 1-22). doi:10.4018/978-1-60566-920-5.ch001

Hussain, K. (2009). A Practical Approach to Computerized System Validation. In A. Lazakidou, & K. Siassiakos (Eds.), *Handbook of Research on Distributed Medical Informatics and E-Health* (pp. 456-469). doi:10.4018/978-1-60566-002-8.ch032

Hynes, B. (2007). Creating an Entrepreneurial Mindset: Getting the Process Right for Information and Communication Technology Students. In G. Lowry, & R. Turner (Eds.), *Information Systems and Technology Education: From the University to the Workplace* (pp. 105-127). doi:10.4018/978-1-59904-114-8.ch006

Igberaese, D. E., & Obinyan, G. A. (2010). Duties and Ethics of Information Scientists. In E. Adomi (Ed.), *Handbook of Research on Information Communication Technology Policy: Trends, Issues and Advancements* (pp. 106-120). doi:10.4018/978-1-61520-847-0.ch008

Isenmann, R. (2010). Progression in Corporate Sustainability Reporting: XBRL Taxonomy for Sustainability Reports. In F. Teuteberg, & J. Marx Gomez (Eds.), *Corporate Environmental Management Information Systems: Advancements and Trends* (pp. 289-317). doi:10.4018/978-1-61520-981-1.ch018

Jacob, M. E. (2006). Skills of Women Technologists. In E. Trauth (Ed.), *Encyclopedia of Gender and Information Technology* (pp. 1099-1104). doi:10.4018/978-1-59140-815-4.ch173

Jahn, K., & Nielsen, P. A. (2011). A Vertical Approach to Knowledge Management: Codification and Personalization in Software Processes. [IJHCITP]. *International Journal of Human Capital and Information Technology Professionals, 2*(2), 26–36. doi:10.4018/jhcitp.2011040103

Jahnke, J., Bychkov, Y., Dahlem, D., & Kawasme, L. (2006). Semantic Composition of Web Portal Components. [JOEUC]. *Journal of Organizational and End User Computing, 18*(4), 66–87. doi:10.4018/joeuc.2006100104

Jeuniaux, P., Olney, A., & D'Mello, S. (2012). Practical Programming for NLP. In P. McCarthy, & C. Boonthum-Denecke (Eds.), *Applied Natural Language Processing: Identification, Investigation and Resolution* (pp. 122-156). doi:10.4018/978-1-60960-741-8.ch008

Johnson, A. M., & Lederer, A. L. (2009). CEO/CIO Communication and the Strategic Grid Dimensions. In A. Tan, & P. Theodorou (Eds.), *Strategic Information Technology and Portfolio Management* (pp. 206-229). doi:10.4018/978-1-59904-687-7.ch011

Joseph, D., Tan, M. L., & Ang, S. (2011). Is Updating Play or Work?: The Mediating Role of Updating Orientation in Linking Threat of Professional Obsolescence to Turnover/Turnaway Intentions. [IJSODIT]. *International Journal of Social and Organizational Dynamics in IT, 1*(4), 37–47. doi:10.4018/ijsodit.2011100103

Kacirek, K., Beck, J. K., & Grover, K. (2010). Career and Technical Education: Myths, Metrics, and Metamorphosis. In V. Wang (Ed.), *Definitive Readings in the History, Philosophy, Theories and Practice of Career and Technical Education* (pp. 27-42). doi:10.4018/978-1-61520-747-3.ch003

Kafai, Y. B., Fields, D. A., & Burke, W. Q. (2010). Entering the Clubhouse: Case Studies of Young Programmers Joining the Online Scratch Communities. [JOEUC]. *Journal of Organizational and End User Computing, 22*(2), 21–35. doi:10.4018/joeuc.2010101906

Kaluzniacky, E. (2005). Towards an Emotionally Intelligent IT Organization. In M. Khosrow-Pour (Ed.), *Advanced Topics in Information Resources Management, Volume 4* (pp. 173-214). doi:10.4018/978-1-59140-465-1.ch008

Kamal, M., Qureshil, S., & Wolcott, P. (2011). Promoting Competitive Advantage in Micro-Enterprises through Information Technology Interventions. In I. Lee (Ed.), *E-Business Applications for Product Development and Competitive Growth: Emerging Technologies* (pp. 117-142). doi:10.4018/978-1-60960-132-4.ch006

Kampf, C. (2009). Extending Sociotechnical Design to Project Conception: Knowledge Communication Processes for Situating Technology. [IJSKD]. *International Journal of Sociotechnology and Knowledge Development, 1*(2), 47–61. doi:10.4018/jskd.2009040105

Kania-Gosche, B. (2011). Using Principles of Andragogy to Teach Writing to Graduate Students Online. In V. Wang (Ed.), *Encyclopedia of Information Communication Technologies and Adult Education Integration* (pp. 1113-1150). doi:10.4018/978-1-61692-906-0.ch068

Kaufman, E. (2010). The Argentine IT Professionals Forum: Building the Basis for the Back Office through Communities of Practice. In N. Karacapilidis (Ed.), *Web-Based Learning Solutions for Communities of Practice: Developing Virtual Environments for Social and Pedagogical Advancement* (pp. 285-305). doi:10.4018/978-1-60566-711-9.ch019

Khandelwal, V. K., & Gottschalk, P. (2003). Information Technology Support for Interorganizational Knowledge Transfer: An Empirical Study of Law Firms in Norway and Australia. [IRMJ]. *Information Resources Management Journal, 16*(1), 14–23. doi:10.4018/irmj.2003010102

Khazanchi, D., & Owens, D. M. (2011). Retaining Global IT Talent. In J. Luftman (Ed.), *Managing IT Human Resources: Considerations for Organizations and Personnel* (pp. 178-193). doi:10.4018/978-1-60960-535-3.ch012

Kirk, M. (2009). Partnership Language and Media: Creating a New IT Culture. In M. Kirk (Ed.), *Gender and Information Technology: Moving Beyond Access to Co-Create Global Partnership* (pp. 193-211). doi:10.4018/978-1-59904-786-7.ch008

Kirkgöz, Y. (2010). Analyzing the Discourse of E-mail Communication. In R. Taiwo (Ed.), *Handbook of Research on Discourse Behavior and Digital Communication: Language Structures and Social Interaction* (pp. 335-348). doi:10.4018/978-1-61520-773-2.ch021

Klein, M. J. (2008). Reconsidering the Lay-Expert Audience Divide. In P. Zemliansky, & K. St.Amant (Eds.), *Handbook of Research on Virtual Workplaces and the New Nature of Business Practices* (pp. 692-701). doi:10.4018/978-1-59904-893-2.ch050

Klein, S., Poulymenakou, A., Riemer, K., Papakiriakopoulos, D., Gogolin, M., & Nikas, A. (2005). IOIS and Interfirm Networks - Interdependents and Managerial Challenges. In S. Eom (Ed.), *Inter-Organizational Information Systems in the Internet Age* (pp. 170-213). doi:10.4018/978-1-59140-318-0.ch007

Kluzniacky, E. (2007). Increasing the Effectiveness of IT Management through Psychological Awareness. In P. Yoong, & S. Huff (Eds.), *Managing IT Professionals in the Internet Age* (pp. 191-232). doi:10.4018/978-1-59140-917-5.ch009

Kock, N., & Garza, V. (2008). The Ape that Used E-Mail: An Evolutionary Perspective on E-Communication Behavior. In N. Kock (Ed.), *E-Collaboration in Modern Organizations: Initiating and Managing Distributed Projects* (pp. 1-13). doi:10.4018/978-1-59904-825-3.ch001

Koh, S., Lee, S., Yen, D. C., & Havelka, D. (2004). The Relationship Between Information Technology Professionals' Skill Requirements and Career Stage in the E-Commerce Era: An Empirical Study. [JGIM]. *Journal of Global Information Management, 12*(1), 68–82. doi:10.4018/jgim.2004010105

Koh, S., Lee, S., Yen, D. C., & Havelka, D. (2005). Information Technology Professional Career Development: A Progression of Skills. In M. Hunter, & F. Tan (Eds.), *Advanced Topics in Global Information Management, Volume 4* (pp. 142-157). doi:10.4018/978-1-59140-468-2.ch009

Koh, S. L., & Maguire, S. (2009). System Development and Project Management. In S. Koh, & S. Maguire (Eds.), *Information and Communication Technologies Management in Turbulent Business Environments* (pp. 132-147). doi:10.4018/978-1-60566-424-8.ch008

Kollmann, T., & Häsel, M. (2009). Competence of Information Technology Professionals in Internet-Based Ventures. In A. Cater-Steel (Ed.), *Information Technology Governance and Service Management: Frameworks and Adaptations* (pp. 239-253). doi:10.4018/978-1-60566-008-0.ch013

Krechmer, K. (2007). Teaching Standards to Engineers. [IJITSR]. *International Journal of IT Standards and Standardization Research, 5*(2), 17–26. doi:10.4018/jitsr.2007070102

Kuivalainen, O. (2009). Complementary Role of Website in Business Model Development. In I. Lee (Ed.), *Emergent Strategies for E-Business Processes, Services and Implications: Advancing Corporate Frameworks* (pp. 136-154). doi:10.4018/978-1-60566-154-4.ch010

Kumar, V., Chang, M., & Leacock, T. L. (2012). Mobile Computing and Mixed-Initiative Support for Writing Competence. In S. Graf, F. Lin, Kinshuk, & R. McGreal (Eds.), *Intelligent and Adaptive Learning Systems: Technology Enhanced Support for Learners and Teachers* (pp. 327-341). doi:10.4018/978-1-60960-842-2.ch021

Lagraña, F. A. (2010). Ethical Issues Arising from the Usage of Electronic Communications in the Workplace. In D. Palmer (Ed.), *Ethical Issues in E-Business: Models and Frameworks* (pp. 200-219). doi:10.4018/978-1-61520-615-5.ch014

Lane, J. A., Petkov, D., & Mora, M. (2008). Software Engineering and the Systems Approach: A Conversation with Barry Boehm. [IJITSA]. *International Journal of Information Technologies and Systems Approach, 1*(2), 99–103. doi:10.4018/jitsa.2008070107

Lansiquot, R. D. (2011). Making the Virtual Real: Using Virtual Learning Communities for Research in Technical Writing. In B. Daniel (Ed.), *Handbook of Research on Methods and Techniques for Studying Virtual Communities: Paradigms and Phenomena* (pp. 224-232). doi:10.4018/978-1-60960-040-2.ch012

Lee, J., & Lee, C. (2009). IT Governance-Based IT Strategy and Management: Literature Review and Future Research Directions. In A. Cater-Steel (Ed.), *Information Technology Governance and Service Management: Frameworks and Adaptations* (pp. 44-62). doi:10.4018/978-1-60566-008-0.ch002

Lee, S., & Fang, X. (2010). Perception Gaps about Skills Requirement for Entry-Level IS Professionals between Recruiters and Students: An Exploratory Study. In M. Khosrow-Pour (Ed.), *Global, Social, and Organizational Implications of Emerging Information Resources Management: Concepts and Applications* (pp. 341-367). doi:10.4018/978-1-60566-962-5.ch018

Liao, L. (2009). Securing E-Mail Communication with XML Technology. In J. Gupta, & S. Sharma (Eds.), *Handbook of Research on Information Security and Assurance* (pp. 202-217). doi:10.4018/978-1-59904-855-0.ch017

Logan, J. (2005). Managing and Practicing OD in an IT Environment: A Structured Approach to Developing IT Project Teams. In T. Torres-Coronas, & M. Arias-Oliva (Eds.), *e-Human Resources Management: Managing Knowledge People* (pp. 236-268). doi:10.4018/978-1-59140-435-4.ch010

Logan, K. A., & Crump, B. (2007). Managing New Zealand Women in IT. In P. Yoong, & S. Huff (Eds.), *Managing IT Professionals in the Internet Age* (pp. 1-17). doi:10.4018/978-1-59140-917-5.ch001

Logie, J. (2005). Cut and Paste: Remixing Composition Pedagogy for Online Workspaces. In K. St.Amant, & P. Zemliansky (Eds.), *Internet-Based Workplace Communications: Industry and Academic Applications* (pp. 299-316). doi:10.4018/978-1-59140-521-4.ch014

Loucky, J. P. (2009). Improving Online Readability in a Web 2.0 Context. In M. Thomas (Ed.), *Handbook of Research on Web 2.0 and Second Language Learning* (pp. 385-410). doi:10.4018/978-1-60566-190-2.ch021

Lounsbury, J. W., Studham, R. S., Steel, R. P., Gibson, L. W., & Drost, A. W. (2009). Holland's Vocational Theory and Personality Traits of Information Technology Professionals. In Y. Dwivedi, B. Lal, M. Williams, S. Schneberger, & M. Wade (Eds.), *Handbook of Research on Contemporary Theoretical Models in Information Systems* (pp. 529-543). doi:10.4018/978-1-60566-659-4.ch030

Luor, T., Lu, H., Johanson, R. E., & Yu, H. (2012). Minding the Gap Between First and Continued Usage of a Corporate E-Learning English-language Program. [IJTHI]. *International Journal of Technology and Human Interaction, 8*(1), 55–74. doi:10.4018/jthi.2012010104

Luppicini, R. (2010). Educational and Professional Technoethics. In R. Luppicini (Ed.), *Technoethics and the Evolving Knowledge Society: Ethical Issues in Technological Design, Research, Development, and Innovation* (pp. 163-180). doi:10.4018/978-1-60566-952-6.ch009

Luppicini, R. (2010). Technological Consciousness and Moral Agency. In R. Luppicini (Ed.), *Technoethics and the Evolving Knowledge Society: Ethical Issues in Technological Design, Research, Development, and Innovation* (pp. 47-66). doi:10.4018/978-1-60566-952-6.ch003

Lynch, D., Thomas, C., Green, W., Gottfried, M., & Varga, M. (2012). Rethinking the Measurement of Training and Development in the Professions: A Conceptual Model. In V. Wang (Ed.), *Vocational Education Technologies and Advances in Adult Learning: New Concepts* (pp. 24-36). doi:10.4018/978-1-4666-0252-6.ch003

Lynch, K., & Fisher, J. (2007). Tomorrow's Workforce Today: What is Required by Information Systems Graduates to Work in a Collaborative Information Systems Workplace? In G. Lowry, & R. Turner (Eds.), *Information Systems and Technology Education: From the University to the Workplace* (pp. 311-326). doi:10.4018/978-1-59904-114-8.ch015

Mackiewicz, J. (2005). The State of Online Writing Labs: Have They Fulfilled Their Potential? In K. St.Amant, & P. Zemliansky (Eds.), *Internet-Based Workplace Communications: Industry and Academic Applications* (pp. 211-230). doi:10.4018/978-1-59140-521-4.ch010

Madlberger, M. (2009). What Drives Firms to Engage in Interorganizational Information Sharing in Supply Chain Management? [IJeC]. *International Journal of e-Collaboration, 5*(2), 18–42. doi:10.4018/jec.2009040102

Magnusson, J. (2010). Professional Analysts and the Ongoing Construction of IT Governance. [IJITBAG]. *International Journal on IT/Business Alignment and Governance, 1*(2), 1–12. doi:.doi:10.4018/jitbag.2010040101

Mahatanankoon, P. (2012). The Impact of Personal Electronic Communications on Work-Life Balance and Cognitive Absorption. In S. Chhabra (Ed.), *ICTs for Advancing Rural Communities and Human Development: Addressing the Digital Divide* (pp. 1-14). doi:10.4018/978-1-4666-0047-8.ch001

Mandal, A. K., Mandal, C., & Reade, C. (2009). Interface and Features for an Automatic 'C' Program Evaluation System. In N. Karacapilidis (Ed.), *Solutions and Innovations in Web-Based Technologies for Augmented Learning: Improved Platforms, Tools, and Applications* (pp. 168-185). doi:10.4018/978-1-60566-238-1.ch010

Mara, A., & Mara, M. (2012). Irish Identification as Exigence: A Self-Service Case Study for Producing User Documentation in Online Contexts. In K. St.Amant, & S. Kelsey (Eds.), *Computer-Mediated Communication across Cultures: International Interactions in Online Environments* (pp. 173-186). doi:10.4018/978-1-60960-833-0.ch012

Marquez, A. C., & Gupta, J. N. (2004). Modern Maintenance Management for Enhancing Organizational Efficiency. In J. Gupta, & S. Sharma (Eds.), *Intelligent Enterprises of the 21st Century* (pp. 321-332). doi:10.4018/978-1-59140-160-5.ch019

Matsuo, T., & Fujimoto, T. (2010). Analogical Thinking Based Instruction Method in IT Professional Education. [IJHCITP]. *International Journal of Human Capital and Information Technology Professionals, 1*(3), 1–14. doi:10.4018/jhcitp.2010070101

McDonnell, L. R., & Salazar, S. G. (2010). Information System for Management of Organisation and Its Activity. In M. Cruz-Cunha, A. Tavares, & R. Simoes (Eds.), *Handbook of Research on Developments in E-Health and Telemedicine: Technological and Social Perspectives* (pp. 511-532). doi:10.4018/978-1-61520-670-4.ch024

McPherson, M., Baptista Nunes, M., Sandars, J., & Kell, C. (2008). Technology and Continuing Professional Education: The Reality Beyond the Hype. In T. Kidd, & I. Chen (Eds.), *Social Information Technology: Connecting Society and Cultural Issues* (pp. 296-312). doi:10.4018/978-1-59904-774-4.ch019

Meng, Z., Fahong, Z., & Lei, L. (2008). Information Technology and Environment. In Y. Kurihara, S. Takaya, H. Harui, & H. Kamae (Eds.), *Information Technology and Economic Development* (pp. 201-212). doi:10.4018/978-1-59904-579-5.ch014

Mescan, S. (2010). Putting Their Heads Together Virtually: Case Studies on Collaboration using Content Management Technology. In B. Hewett, & C. Robidoux (Eds.), *Virtual Collaborative Writing in the Workplace: Computer-Mediated Communication Technologies and Processes* (pp. 158-173). doi:10.4018/978-1-60566-994-6.ch009

Miranda, S. M., & Carter, P. E. (2007). Innovation Diffusion and E-Collaboration: The Effects of Social Proximity on Social Information Processing. In N. Kock (Ed.), *Emerging e-Collaboration Concepts and Applications* (pp. 136-165). doi:10.4018/978-1-59904-393-7.ch008

Mousten, B., Humbley, J., Maylath, B., & Vandepitte, S. (2012). Communicating Pragmatics About Content and Culture in Virtually Mediated Educational Environments. In K. St.Amant, & S. Kelsey (Eds.), *Computer-Mediated Communication across Cultures: International Interactions in Online Environments* (pp. 312-327). doi:10.4018/978-1-60960-833-0.ch020

Munk-Madsen, A., & Nielsen, P. A. (2011). Success Factors and Motivators in SPI. [IJHCITP]. *International Journal of Human Capital and Information Technology Professionals, 2*(4), 49–60. doi:10.4018/jhcitp.2011100105

Murphy, M., & Matas, C. P. (2009). Politeness in Intercultural E-Mail Communication. In R. de Cássia Veiga Marriott, & P. Lupion Torres (Eds.), *Handbook of Research on E-Learning Methodologies for Language Acquisition* (pp. 253-270). doi:10.4018/978-1-59904-994-6.ch016

Murphy, M. G., & Calway, P. B. (2011). Continuing Professional Development: Work and Learning Integration for Professionals. In P. Keleher, A. Patil, & R. Harreveld (Eds.), *Work-Integrated Learning in Engineering, Built Environment and Technology: Diversity of Practice in Practice* (pp. 25-51). doi:10.4018/978-1-60960-547-6.ch002

Nel, J. (2007). Information Technology Investment Evaluation and Measurement Methodology: A Case Study and Action Research of the Dimensions and Measures of IT-Business-Value in Financial Institutions. In S. Lubbe (Ed.), *Managing Information Communication Technology Investments in Successful Enterprises* (pp. 147-168). doi:10.4018/978-1-59140-802-4.ch009

Nelson, M. R., & Katz, H. (2010). Digital Metrics: Getting to the Other 50 Percent. In M. Eastin, T. Daugherty, & N. Burns (Eds.), *Handbook of Research on Digital Media and Advertising: User Generated Content Consumption* (pp. 314-334). doi:10.4018/978-1-60566-792-8.ch017

Németh, G. Á. (2011). Protocol Operation. In K. Tarnay, G. Adamis, & T. Dulai (Eds.), *Advanced Communication Protocol Technologies: Solutions, Methods, and Applications* (pp. 20-37). doi:10.4018/978-1-60960-732-6.ch002

Newton, Sandra K., J. Ellis Blanton and Richard Will. "Innovative Work and Citizenship Behaviors from Information Technology Professionals: Effects of Their Psychological Contract," *Information Resources Management Journal (IRMJ)* 21 (2008): 4, accessed (February 06, 2012), doi:10.4018/irmj.2008100102

Niederman, F., & Sumner, M. (2012, Feb.). "Effect of Tasks, Salaries, and Shocks on Job Satisfaction Among MIS Professionals." *Advanced Topics in Information Resources Management, Volume 5.* IGI Global, 2006. 184-210. *Web.*, 7. doi:.doi:10.4018/978-1-59140-929-8.ch009

Nilsson, L., Eklöf, A., & Ottoson, T. (2008). Unstructured Information as a Socio-Technical Dilemma. In T. Hansson (Ed.), *Handbook of Research on Digital Information Technologies: Innovations, Methods, and Ethical Issues* (pp. 482-505). doi:10.4018/978-1-59904-970-0.ch031

Nuninger, W., & Châtelet, J. M. (2011). Work-Integrated Learning for Engineers in Coordination with Industries. In P. Keleher, A. Patil, & R. Harreveld (Eds.), *Work-Integrated Learning in Engineering, Built Environment and Technology: Diversity of Practice in Practice* (pp. 85-109). doi:10.4018/978-1-60960-547-6.ch005

Olaniran, B. A., Rodriguez, N., & Williams, I. M. (2012). Social Information Processing Theory (SIPT): A Cultural Perspective for International Online Communication Environments. In K. St.Amant, & S. Kelsey (Eds.), *Computer-Mediated Communication across Cultures: International Interactions in Online Environments* (pp. 45-65). doi:10.4018/978-1-60960-833-0.ch004

Orgeron, C. P. (2008). A Model for Reengineering IT Job Classes in State Government. In G. Garson, & M. Khosrow-Pour (Eds.), *Handbook of Research on Public Information Technology* (pp. 735-746). doi:10.4018/978-1-59904-857-4.ch066

Otto, B. (2011). Quality Management of Corporate Data Assets. In C. Praeg, & D. Spath (Eds.), *Quality Management for IT Services: Perspectives on Business and Process Performance* (pp. 193-209). doi:10.4018/978-1-61692-889-6.ch010

Papazafeiropoulou, A., & Gandecha, R. (2007). Interpretive Flexibility Along the Innovation Decision Process of the UK NHS Care Records Service (NCRS): Insights from a Local Implementation Case Study. [IJTHI]. *International Journal of Technology and Human Interaction, 3*(2), 1–12. doi:10.4018/jthi.2007040101

Paraponaris, C. (2008). Managing Knowledge Diversity in Distributed Organizational Structures. In K. O'Sullivan (Ed.), *Strategic Knowledge Management in Multinational Organizations* (pp. 275-298). doi:10.4018/978-1-59904-630-3.ch018

Parkinson, C. M., & Olphert, C. W. (2010). Website Accessibility and the Role of Accessibility Statements. In T. Spiliotopoulos, P. Papadopoulou, D. Martakos, & G. Kouroupetroglou (Eds.), *Integrating Usability Engineering for Designing the Web Experience: Methodologies and Principles* (pp. 166-190). doi:10.4018/978-1-60566-896-3.ch009

Parry, D. (2009). Coding and Messaging Systems for Women's Health Informatics. In D. Parry, & E. Parry (Eds.), *Medical Informatics in Obstetrics and Gynecology* (pp. 38-52). doi:10.4018/978-1-60566-078-3.ch003

Patel, N. V. (2009). The Theory of Deferred Action: Informing the Design of Information Systems for Complexity. In Y. Dwivedi, B. Lal, M. Williams, S. Schneberger, & M. Wade (Eds.), *Handbook of Research on Contemporary Theoretical Models in Information Systems* (pp. 164-191). doi:10.4018/978-1-60566-659-4.ch010

Patke, A., & Hooper, T. (2007). Professional Skills Acquisitions in the Internet Age: Exploring the Perceptions of Undergraduates and Recent Graduates. In P. Yoong, & S. Huff (Eds.), *Managing IT Professionals in the Internet Age* (pp. 140-158). doi:10.4018/978-1-59140-917-5.ch007

Pena-Sanchez, R., & Hicks, R. C. (2008). Faculty Preferences for Communications Channels. In N. Kock (Ed.), *Encyclopedia of E-Collaboration* (pp. 292-300). doi:10.4018/978-1-59904-000-4.ch045

Peslak, A. R., & Boyle, T. A. (2010). An Exploratory Study of the Key Skills for Entry-Level ERP Employees. [IJEIS]. *International Journal of Enterprise Information Systems, 6*(2), 1–14. doi:10.4018/jeis.2010040101

Petrina, S. (2007). Organizing Knowledge for Instruction. In S. Petrina (Ed.), *Advanced Teaching Methods for the Technology Classroom* (pp. 26-57). doi:10.4018/978-1-59904-337-1.ch002

Petty, G. C. (2010). Teaching Philosophies of Career and Technical Education. In V. Wang (Ed.), *Definitive Readings in the History, Philosophy, Theories and Practice of Career and Technical Education* (pp. 62-83). doi:10.4018/978-1-61520-747-3.ch005

Pilkington, R. (2010). Building Practitioner Skills in Personalised eLearning: Messages for Professional Development. In J. O'Donoghue (Ed.), *Technology-Supported Environments for Personalized Learning: Methods and Case Studies* (pp. 167-184). doi:10.4018/978-1-60566-884-0.ch010

Piñeiro, E., & Case, P. (2008). Outsourcing in High-Tech Corporations: Voices of Dissent, Resistance, and Complicity in a Computer Programming Community. In D. Jemielniak, & J. Kociatkiewicz (Eds.), *Management Practices in High-Tech Environments* (pp. 209-227). doi:10.4018/978-1-59904-564-1.ch012

Pipoli, G., & Fuchs, R. M. (2011). Retaining IT Professionals. In J. Luftman (Ed.), *Managing IT Human Resources: Considerations for Organizations and Personnel* (pp. 130-149). doi:10.4018/978-1-60960-535-3.ch010

Popescu, G. V. (2010). Distributed Indexing Networks for Efficient Large-Scale Group Communication. In N. Antonopoulos, G. Exarchakos, M. Li, & A. Liotta (Eds.), *Handbook of Research on P2P and Grid Systems for Service-Oriented Computing: Models, Methodologies and Applications* (pp. 360-381). doi:10.4018/978-1-61520-686-5.ch015

Postula, A. (2008). Professional Dimension of IT Specialists' Social Role. In D. Jemielniak, & J. Kociatkiewicz (Eds.), *Management Practices in High-Tech Environments* (pp. 94-109). doi:10.4018/978-1-59904-564-1.ch006

Postula, A. (2009). Creativitiy and Control in IT Professionals' Communities. In D. Jemielniak, & J. Kociatkiewicz (Eds.), *Handbook of Research on Knowledge-Intensive Organizations* (pp. 295-309). doi:10.4018/978-1-60566-176-6.ch018

Pourezzat, A. A., & Taheri Attar, G. (2009). Professional Adhocracy, an Appropriate Design for Knowledge Economy in the Light of Mintzberg's Perspective. [JECO]. *Journal of Electronic Commerce in Organizations*, 7(4), 1–20. doi:10.4018/jeco.2009100101

Qayyum, M. A. (2008). Using Annotations for Information Sharing in a Networked Community. In G. Putnik, & M. Cruz-Cunha (Eds.), *Encyclopedia of Networked and Virtual Organizations* (pp. 1722-1729). doi:10.4018/978-1-59904-885-7.ch227

Quan, J. J., Dattero, R., Galup, S. D., & Dhariwal, K. (2011). The Determinants of Information Technology Wages. [IJHCITP]. *International Journal of Human Capital and Information Technology Professionals*, 2(1), 48–65. doi:10.4018/jhcitp.2011010104

Rada, R. (2008). Information Networks. In R. Rada (Ed.), *Information Systems and Healthcare Enterprises* (pp. 170-186). doi:10.4018/978-1-59904-651-8.ch007

Raghavan, V. V., Sakaguchi, T., & Mahaney, R. C. (2010). An Empirical Investigation of Stress Factors in Information Technology Professionals. In M. Khosrow-Pour (Ed.), *Global, Social, and Organizational Implications of Emerging Information Resources Management: Concepts and Applications* (pp. 421-445). doi:10.4018/978-1-60566-962-5.ch022

Robbins, J. (2012). Defining Integrity for Individuals and Organizations: A Cognitive-Linguistic Modeling Approach. In C. Wankel, & A. Stachowicz-Stanusch (Eds.), *Handbook of Research on Teaching Ethics in Business and Management Education* (pp. 124-143). doi:10.4018/978-1-61350-510-6.ch008

Rochet, S. (2007). An Evolutionary Algorithm for Decisional Assistance to Project Management. In J. Rennard (Ed.), *Handbook of Research on Nature-Inspired Computing for Economics and Management* (pp. 444-464). doi:10.4018/978-1-59140-984-7.ch030

Rodrigues, L. C. (2012). Technical Competitive Intelligence System: An Innovation and Technology Management Tool. In N. Delener (Ed.), *Service Science Research, Strategy and Innovation: Dynamic Knowledge Management Methods* (pp. 202-226). doi:10.4018/978-1-4666-0077-5.ch013

Romance, N. T., Whitesell, M. V., Smith, C. L., & Louden, A. M. (2006). Career ePortfolios in the IT Associates at DePauw University. In A. Jafari, & C. Kaufman (Eds.), *Handbook of Research on ePortfolios* (pp. 532-538). doi:10.4018/978-1-59140-890-1.ch047

Russell, M. G. (2010). Evolving Media Metrics from Assumed Attention to Earned Engagement. In M. Eastin, T. Daugherty, & N. Burns (Eds.), *Handbook of Research on Digital Media and Advertising: User Generated Content Consumption* (pp. 125-145). doi:10.4018/978-1-60566-792-8.ch006

Ruzic, F. (2007). Information-Communications Systems Convergence Paradigm: Invisible E-Culture and E-Technologies. In W. Law (Ed.), *Information Resources Management: Global Challenges* (pp. 54-74). doi:10.4018/978-1-59904-102-5.ch003

Ruzic, F. (2009). New Ethics for E-Business Offshore Outsourcing. In R. Luppicini, & R. Adell (Eds.), *Handbook of Research on Technoethics* (pp. 843-870). doi:10.4018/978-1-60566-022-6.ch054

Sammon, D. (2008). Understanding Sense-Making. In F. Adam, & P. Humphreys (Eds.), *Encyclopedia of Decision Making and Decision Support Technologies* (pp. 916-921). doi:10.4018/978-1-59904-843-7.ch103

Sampson, D., & Manouselis, N. (2005). A Flexible Evaluation Framework for Web Portals Based on Multi-Criteria Analysis. In A. Tatnall (Ed.), *Web Portals: The New Gateways to Internet Information and Services* (pp. 185-211). doi:10.4018/978-1-59140-438-5.ch009

Sanders-Reio, J., & Reio, T. G. (2012). Writing: The Neglected "R" in the Workplace. In V. Wang (Ed.), *Encyclopedia of E-Leadership, Counseling and Training* (pp. 479-490). doi:10.4018/978-1-61350-068-2.ch035

Schneidermeyer, P. (2011). IT Human Resources: Experts at Talent Management & Critical Partners to the CIO. In J. Luftman (Ed.), *Managing IT Human Resources: Considerations for Organizations and Personnel* (pp. 38-45). doi:10.4018/978-1-60960-535-3.ch004

Scholarios, D., van der Schoot, E., & van der Heijden, B. (2006). Employability Management of ICT Professionals. In S. Marshall, W. Taylor, & X. Yu (Eds.), *Encyclopedia of Developing Regional Communities with Information and Communication Technology* (pp. 282-288). doi:10.4018/978-1-59140-575-7.ch049

Schultz, R. A. (2006). Professional Duties. In R. Schultz (Ed.), *Contemporary Issues in Ethics and Information Technology* (pp. 44-59). doi:10.4018/978-1-59140-779-9.ch004

Schwind, M., Stockheim, T., & Weiss, K. (2008). A Diffusion Model for Communication Standards in Supply Networks. In K. Jakobs (Ed.), *Standardization Research in Information Technology: New Perspectives* (pp. 105-121). doi:10.4018/978-1-59904-561-0.ch007

Scott, D. J., Coursaris, C. K., Kato, Y., & Kato, S. (2009). The Exchange of Emotional Content in Business Communications: A Comparison of PC and Mobile E-Mail Users. In M. Head, & E. Li (Eds.), *Mobile and Ubiquitous Commerce: Advanced E-Business Methods* (pp. 201-219). doi:10.4018/978-1-60566-366-1.ch011

Seidman, S. B. (2009). An International Perspective on Professional Software Engineering Credentials. In H. Ellis, S. Demurjian, & J. Naveda (Eds.), *Software Engineering: Effective Teaching and Learning Approaches and Practices* (pp. 351-361). doi:10.4018/978-1-60566-102-5.ch018

Settles, A. (2005). What Skills are Needed in an E-World: E-Government Skills and Training Programs for the Public Sector. In M. Khosrow-Pour (Ed.), *Practicing E-Government: A Global Perspective* (pp. 383-414). doi:10.4018/978-1-59140-637-2.ch017

Shah, J. R. (2009). Privacy Protection Overseas as Perceived by USA-Based IT Professionals. In M. Hunter, & F. Tan (Eds.), *Handbook of Research on Information Management and the Global Landscape* (pp. 44-58). doi:10.4018/978-1-60566-138-4.ch003

Sharkey, J., & Brandt, D. S. (2008). Integrating Technology Literacy and Information Literacy. In P. Rivoltella (Ed.), *Digital Literacy: Tools and Methodologies for Information Society* (pp. 85-97). doi:10.4018/978-1-59904-798-0.ch005

Siakas, K. V., Gevorgyan, R., & Georgiadou, E. (2011). IT Methods and Techniques Applied to Educational Quality Enhancement. [IJHCITP]. *International Journal of Human Capital and Information Technology Professionals, 2*(3), 79–90. doi:10.4018/jhcitp.2011070106

Simoff, S., & Sudweeks, F. (2007). The Language of Leaders: Identifying Emergent Leaders in Global Virtual Teams. In K. St.Amant (Ed.), *Linguistic and Cultural Online Communication Issues in the Global Age* (pp. 93-111). doi:10.4018/978-1-59904-213-8.ch007

Sitthisak, O., & Gilbert, L. (2011). Interoperable Assessment Based on Competency Modelling. In F. Lazarinis, S. Green, & E. Pearson (Eds.), *Handbook of Research on E-Learning Standards and Interoperability: Frameworks and Issues* (pp. 21-40). doi:10.4018/978-1-61692-789-9.ch002

Skinner, L. B., Witte, M. M., & Witte, J. E. (2010). Challenges and Opportunities in Career and Technical Education. In V. Wang (Ed.), *Definitive Readings in the History, Philosophy, Theories and Practice of Career and Technical Education* (pp. 197-215). doi:10.4018/978-1-61520-747-3.ch012

Skulmoski, G. J., & Hartman, F. T. (2009). The Progression Towards Project Management Competence. In T. Kidd (Ed.), *Handbook of Research on Technology Project Management, Planning, and Operations* (pp. 37-57). doi:10.4018/978-1-60566-400-2.ch003

Solomon, P., & Baptiste, S. (2010). Fundamentals of Interprofessional Communication: A Case Study of an Online Facilitated Learning Experience. In A. Bromage, L. Clouder, J. Thistlethwaite, & F. Gordon (Eds.), *Interprofessional E-Learning and Collaborative Work: Practices and Technologies* (pp. 90-103). doi:10.4018/978-1-61520-889-0.ch008

Springer, S. (2008). Achieving a Working Balance Between Technology and Personal Contact Within a Classroom Environment. In S. Negash, M. Whitman, A. Woszczynski, K. Hoganson, & H. Mattord (Eds.), *Handbook of Distance Learning for Real-Time and Asynchronous Information Technology Education* (pp. 212-226). doi:10.4018/978-1-59904-964-9.ch011

Stahl, B. C., & Wood, C. (2007). Forming IT Professionals in the Internet Age: A Critical Case Study. In P. Yoong, & S. Huff (Eds.), *Managing IT Professionals in the Internet Age* (pp. 120-139). doi:10.4018/978-1-59140-917-5.ch006

Stowell, F. (2008). Do We Mean Information Systems or Systems of Information? [IJITSA]. *International Journal of Information Technologies and Systems Approach, 1*(1), 25–36. doi:10.4018/jitsa.2008010102

Strøm, G. (2007). Information and Function Chunks as Building Blocks in the Control Room of Life. In S. Heilesen, & S. Jensen (Eds.), *Designing for Networked Communications: Strategies and Development* (pp. 97-117). doi:10.4018/978-1-59904-069-1.ch005

Switzer, J. S. (2008). Successful Communication in Virtual Teams and the Role of the Virtual Team Leader. In P. Zemliansky, & K. St.Amant (Eds.), *Handbook of Research on Virtual Workplaces and the New Nature of Business Practices* (pp. 39-52). doi:10.4018/978-1-59904-893-2.ch004

Taghavi, M., Patel, A., & Taghavi, H. (2011). Design of an Integrated Project Management Information System for Large Scale Public Projects: Iranian Case Study. [JITR]. *Journal of Information Technology Research, 4*(3), 14–28. doi:10.4018/jitr.2011070102

Thion, R. (2008). Network-Based Passive Information Gathering. In L. Janczewski, & A. Colarik (Eds.), *Cyber Warfare and Cyber Terrorism* (pp. 120-128). doi:10.4018/978-1-59140-991-5.ch016

Thompson, J. B. (2009). Ensuring Students Engage with Ethical and Professional Practice Concepts. In H. Ellis, S. Demurjian, & J. Naveda (Eds.), *Software Engineering: Effective Teaching and Learning Approaches and Practices* (pp. 327-350). doi:10.4018/978-1-60566-102-5.ch017

Thornton, J. B. (2010). The Career Development Compass: Roadmap to Building a Diversified Portfolio of Professional Capabilities for Information Professionals. In E. Pankl, D. Theiss-White, & M. Bushing (Eds.), *Recruitment, Development, and Retention of Information Professionals: Trends in Human Resources and Knowledge Management* (pp. 191-205). doi:10.4018/978-1-61520-601-8.ch011

Toleman, M., Darroch, F., & Ally, M. (2007). The Impact of Agile Methods on Managing IT Professionals. In P. Yoong, & S. Huff (Eds.), *Managing IT Professionals in the Internet Age* (pp. 233-253). doi:10.4018/978-1-59140-917-5.ch010

Toroi, T., & Eerola, A. (2007). Requirements for the Testable Specification and Test Case Derivation in Conformance Testing. In A. Dasso, & A. Funes (Eds.), *Verification, Validation and Testing in Software Engineering* (pp. 136-156). doi:10.4018/978-1-59140-851-2.ch006

Tran, Q. N., Henderson-Sellers, B., & Hawryszkiewycz, I. (2009). Agile Method Fragments and Construction Validation. In M. Syed, & S. Syed (Eds.), *Handbook of Research on Modern Systems Analysis and Design Technologies and Applications* (pp. 243-270). doi:10.4018/978-1-59904-887-1.ch017

Trigo, A., Varajão, J., Soto-Acosta, P., Barroso, J., Molina-Castillo, F. J., & Gonzalvez-Gallego, N. (2010). IT Professionals: An Iberian Snapshot. [IJHCITP]. *International Journal of Human Capital and Information Technology Professionals*, *1*(1), 61–75. doi:10.4018/jhcitp.2010091105

Turner, M. W., Benfield, M. P., Utley, D. R., & McPherson, C. A. (2011). Integrated Product Teams at The University of Alabama in Huntsville. In M. Bowdon, & R. Carpenter (Eds.), *Higher Education, Emerging Technologies, and Community Partnerships: Concepts, Models and Practices* (pp. 68-76). doi:10.4018/978-1-60960-623-7.ch007

Unhelkar, B., Ghanbary, A., & Younessi, H. (2010). Emerging Technologies for Business Collaboration. In B. Unhelkar, A. Ghanbary, & H. Younessi (Eds.), *Collaborative Business Process Engineering and Global Organizations: Frameworks for Service Integration* (pp. 37-64). doi:10.4018/978-1-60566-689-1.ch002

van der Aalst, W. M., & Nikolov, A. (2010). Mining E-Mail Messages: Uncovering Interaction Patterns and Processes Using E-Mail Logs. In V. Sugumaran (Ed.), *Methodological Advancements in Intelligent Information Technologies: Evolutionary Trends* (pp. 212-234). doi:10.4018/978-1-60566-970-0.ch011

Venis, L. (2010). E-Mentoring the Individual Writer within a Global Creative Community. In G. Berg (Ed.), *Cases on Online Tutoring, Mentoring, and Educational Services: Practices and Applications* (pp. 98-116). doi:10.4018/978-1-60566-876-5.ch008

Verville, J., Bernadas, C., & Halingten, A. (2005). A Three-Dimensional Approach in Evaluating ERP Software Within the Acquisition Process. [IJEIS]. *International Journal of Enterprise Information Systems*, *1*(3), 1–16. doi:10.4018/jeis.2005070101

Wallace, J. (2007). Computer-Mediated Communication Research. In R. Reynolds, R. Woods, & J. Baker (Eds.), *Handbook of Research on Electronic Surveys and Measurements* (pp. 207-223). doi:10.4018/978-1-59140-792-8.ch022

Wang, H. (2009). Survivability Evaluation Modeling Techniques and Measures. In J. Gupta, & S. Sharma (Eds.), *Handbook of Research on Information Security and Assurance* (pp. 504-517). doi:10.4018/978-1-59904-855-0.ch045

Wang, J. (2012). Human Resource Development and Technology Integration. In V. Wang (Ed.), *Encyclopedia of E-Leadership, Counseling and Training* (pp. 391-407). doi:10.4018/978-1-61350-068-2.ch029

Wang, V. C. (2010). Principles of Scientific Management and Occupational Analysis. In V. Wang (Ed.), *Definitive Readings in the History, Philosophy, Theories and Practice of Career and Technical Education* (pp. 15-26). doi:10.4018/978-1-61520-747-3.ch002

Westlund, S. (2011). Leading Techies: Assessing Project Leadership Styles Most Significantly Related to Software Developer Job Satisfaction. [IJHCITP]. *International Journal of Human Capital and Information Technology Professionals*, *2*(2), 1–15. doi:10.4018/jhcitp.2011040101

Weston, J. L., Crossley, S. A., & McNamara, D. S. (2012). Computationally Assessing Expert Judgments of Freewriting Quality. In P. McCarthy, & C. Boonthum-Denecke (Eds.), *Applied Natural Language Processing: Identification, Investigation and Resolution* (pp. 365-382). doi:10.4018/978-1-60960-741-8.ch021

Wilkinson, K., & Crews, T. B. (2011). Business Report Writing Students' Perceptions of Their Ability to Succeed in an Online Environment vs. Students' Performance in an Online Course. In L. Tomei (Ed.), *Online Courses and ICT in Education: Emerging Practices and Applications* (pp. 290-299). doi:10.4018/978-1-60960-150-8.ch022

Williams, S. D. (2010). Forming Trust in Virtual Writing Teams: Perspectives and Applications. In B. Hewett, & C. Robidoux (Eds.), *Virtual Collaborative Writing in the Workplace: Computer-Mediated Communication Technologies and Processes* (pp. 88-111). doi:10.4018/978-1-60566-994-6.ch005

Wilsey, B. B., & Keengwe, J. (2012). Technology Integration Curriculum Framework for Effective Program Evaluation. [IJICTE]. *International Journal of Information and Communication Technology Education, 8*(1), 15–25. doi:10.4018/jicte.2012010102

Witman, P. D. (2009). A Guide to Non-Disclosure Agreements for Researchers Using Public and Private Sector Sources. In A. Cater-Steel, & L. Al-Hakim (Eds.), *Information Systems Research Methods, Epistemology, and Applications* (pp. 104-119). doi:10.4018/978-1-60566-040-0.ch006

Witte, M. M., Witte, J. E., & Skinner, L. B. (2010). Workforce Competencies and Career and Technical Education. In V. Wang (Ed.), *Definitive Readings in the History, Philosophy, Theories and Practice of Career and Technical Education* (pp. 103-121). doi:10.4018/978-1-61520-747-3.ch007

Witten, I. H., Paynter, G. W., Frank, E., Gutwin, C., & Nevill-Manning, C. G. (2005). KEA: Practical Automated Keyphrase Extraction. In Y. Theng, & S. Foo (Eds.), *Design and Usability of Digital Libraries: Case Studies in the Asia Pacific* (pp. 129-152). doi:10.4018/978-1-59140-441-5.ch008

Woodfield, R. (2006). Women and Recruitment to the IT Profession in the UK. In E. Trauth (Ed.), *Encyclopedia of Gender and Information Technology* (pp. 1238-1244). doi:10.4018/978-1-59140-815-4.ch195

Yokomizo, C. A., & Nakata, L. E. (2011). Attracting and Retaining ICT Professionals in Brazilian Companies: Expectancies, Learning, and Gender in the Workplace. In J. Luftman (Ed.), *Managing IT Human Resources: Considerations for Organizations and Personnel* (pp. 194-217). doi:10.4018/978-1-60960-535-3.ch013

Young, A., Gurzick, D., & Quan-Haase, A. (2011). Online Multi-Contextual Analysis: (Re)Connecting Social Network Site Users with Their Profile. In B. Daniel (Ed.), *Handbook of Research on Methods and Techniques for Studying Virtual Communities: Paradigms and Phenomena* (pp. 542-554). doi:10.4018/978-1-60960-040-2.ch032

Zemliansky, P. (2010). Preparing Writers for Virtual Environments. In B. Hewett, & C. Robidoux (Eds.), *Virtual Collaborative Writing in the Workplace: Computer-Mediated Communication Technologies and Processes* (pp. 335-349). doi:10.4018/978-1-60566-994-6.ch018

Zemliansky, P. (2010). Workplace Use of Web 2.0 Communication Tools and its Implications for Training of Future Communication Professionals. In W. Ritke-Jones (Ed.), *Virtual Environments for Corporate Education: Employee Learning and Solutions* (pp. 50-68). doi:10.4018/978-1-61520-619-3.ch004

Zhang, M., Sarker, S., & McCullough, J. (2010). Development of a Scale to Measure Information Technology Capability of Export-Focused SMEs in China. In M. Hunter, & F. Tan (Eds.), *Technological Advancement in Developed and Developing Countries: Discoveries in Global Information Management* (pp. 222-247). doi:10.4018/978-1-60566-920-5.ch011

Zirkle, C., & Fletcher, E. C., Jr. (2009). Utilization of Distance Education in Career and Technical Education (CTE) Teacher Education. In V. Wang (Ed.), *Handbook of Research on E-Learning Applications for Career and Technical Education: Technologies for Vocational Training* (pp. 1-13). doi:10.4018/978-1-60566-739-3.ch001

Zirkle, C., Fletcher, E. C., Sander, K. L., & Briggs, J. (2010). Certification and Licensure Requirements for Career and Technical Educators. In V. Wang (Ed.), *Definitive Readings in the History, Philosophy, Theories and Practice of Career and Technical Education* (pp. 122-139). doi:10.4018/978-1-61520-747-3.ch008

About the Author

Raymond Greenlaw received a BA in Mathematics from Pomona College in 1983, and an MS and a PhD in Computer Science from the University of Washington in 1986 and 1988, respectively. He is a Research Scientist at Elbrys Networks, Inc. Ray is also the Leighton Endowed Distinguished Professor of Information Technology at the United States Naval Academy in Annapolis, Maryland. He is also the Distinguished Professor of Computer Science at Chiang Mai University in Thailand. Ray holds a visiting professorship at the University of Management and Science in Kuala Lumpur, Malaysia. He was the Founder and Dean of the School of Computing and Professor of Computer Science at Armstrong Atlantic State University in Savannah, Georgia. Ray also served as the Regional Coordinator for the State of Georgia's $100,000,000 Yamacraw Project, which was designed to make the state of Georgia a leader in the telecommunications field. Ray has won three Senior Fulbright Fellowships (Spain, Iceland, and Thailand), a Humboldt Fellowship (Germany), a Sasakawa Fellowship, and fellowships from Italy, Japan, and Spain. He has published over 20 books in the areas of complexity theory, graph theory, the Internet, parallel computation, networking, operating systems, technical communications, theoretical computer science, the Web, and wireless. He is one of the world's leading experts on P-completeness theory. His books have been used in over 140 Computer Science and Information Technology programs in the United States, as well as internationally, and have been translated into several languages. Ray has lectured throughout the world presenting over 210 invited talks. He served on the Executive Committee for the Computing Accreditation Commission of ABET and was Chair of the Training Committee. His research papers have appeared in over 85 journals and conference proceedings. As a PI or co-PI, Ray has been awarded over $6,500,000 in grants and contracts, and his research has been supported by the governments of Germany, Hong Kong, Iceland, Italy, Japan, Malaysia, Spain, Taiwan, Thailand, and the United States. Ray is an avid outdoorsman. In 2003 Ray broke the world record for the fastest thru-hike of the Pacific Crest Trail by completing the 2,659-mile trail in 83 days. His book titled "The Fastest Hike" describes that epic journey. In 2011 Ray bicycled 3,477 miles across the USA from east to west in 36 days. Ray has run over 125 races, including the big four 100-mile runs, and completed many Ironman triathlons. He has climbed 6 of the world's 7 summits. He is a NAUI Dive Master. Ray has been to 49 of the United States, 69 of 77 provinces in Thailand, half of the provinces in China, 102 countries, 7 continents, and many islands, including Aruba, Bali, Boracay, Bermuda, Cooks, Cozumel, Fiji, Galapagos, Guam, Half-Moon Bay Cay, Heimaey, Isla del Sol, Koh Nang Yuan, Livingstone, Magdelena, Palau, Peleliu, Reunion, Similian, Tahiti, Tobago, and US Virgin Islands, among others. He has traveled about 2,000,000 miles.

Index

CPSIA information can be obtained at www.ICGtesting.com
Printed in the USA
BVOW020459090513

320253BV00008B/212/P

9 781466 602373